OXFORD STUDIES IN EUROPEAN LAW

Series Editors

PAUL CRAIG

Professor of English Law at St John's College, Oxford

GRÁINNE DE BÚRCA

Professor of Law at New York University School of Law

The Criminalization of European Cartel Enforcement

OXFORD STUDIES IN EUROPEAN LAW

Series Editors

Paul Craig, Professor of English Law at St John's College, Oxford and
Gráinne de Búrca, Professor of Law at New York University School of Law

The aim of this series is to publish important and original research on EU law. The focus is on scholarly monographs, with a particular emphasis on those which are interdisciplinary in nature. Edited collections of essays will also be included where they are appropriate. The series is wide in scope and aims to cover studies of particular areas of substantive and of institutional law, historical works, theoretical studies, and analyses of current debates, as well as questions of perennial interest such as the relationship between national and EU law and the novel forms of governance emerging in and beyond Europe. The fact that many of the works are interdisciplinary will make the series of interest to all those concerned with the governance and operation of the EU.

OTHER TITLES IN THIS SERIES

Fundamental Rights in Europe
Challenges and Transformations in Comparative Perspective
Federico Fabbrini

The Principle of Loyalty in EU Law
Markus Klamert

Constitutional Pluralism in the EU
Klemen Jaklic

EU Consumer Law and Human Rights
Iris Benöhr

The Principle of Mutual Recognition in EU Law
Christine Janssens

The Coherence of EU Free Movement Law
Constitutional Responsibility and the Court of Justice
Niamh Nic Shuibhne

European Law and New Health Technologies
Edited by Mark L Flear, Anne-Maree Farrell, Tamara K Hervey, and Thérèse Murphy

The Legal Effect of EU Agreements
Mario Mendez

The Enforcement of EU Law
The Role of the European Commission
Stine Andersen

European Agencies
Law and Practice of Accountability
Madalina Busuioc

The Foundations of European Union Competition Law
The Objective and Principles of Article 102
Renato Nazzini

The Emergence of EU Contract Law
Exploring Europeanization
Lucinda Miller

Participation in EU Rule-making
A Rights-Based Approach
Joana Mendes

Regulating Cartels in Europe
Second Edition
Christopher Harding, Julian Joshua

Religion and the Public Order of the European Union
Ronan McCrea

Governing Social Inclusion
Europeanization through Policy Coordination
Kenneth A. Armstrong

Judicial Control in the European Union
Reforming Jurisdiction in the Intergovernmental Pillars
Alicia Hinarejos

EU Counter-Terrorist Policies and Fundamental Rights
The Case of Individual Sanctions
Christina Eckes

From Dual to Cooperative Federalism
The Changing Structure of European Law
Robert Schütze

Conflicts of Rights in the European Union
A Theory of Supranational Adjudication
Aida Torres Pérez

Judicial Deliberations
A Comparative Analysis of Transparency and Legitimacy
Mitchel de S-O-l'E Lasser

Racism and Equality in the European Union
Mark Bell

The Criminalization of European Cartel Enforcement

Theoretical, Legal, and Practical Challenges

DR PETER WHELAN

LLB (Ling Fran), LLM, PG Cert, PhD (Cantab)
Attorney-at-Law (New York)

OXFORD
UNIVERSITY PRESS

OXFORD
UNIVERSITY PRESS

Great Clarendon Street, Oxford, OX2 6DP,
United Kingdom

Oxford University Press is a department of the University of Oxford.
It furthers the University's objective of excellence in research, scholarship,
and education by publishing worldwide. Oxford is a registered trade mark of
Oxford University Press in the UK and in certain other countries

First Edition published in 2014

Published in the United States of America by Oxford University Press
198 Madison Avenue, New York, NY 10016, United States of America

British Library Cataloguing in Publication Data
Data available

Library of Congress Control Number: 2014933419

ISBN 978–0–19–967006–2

Dedicated to Pınar and Erin

Series Editors' Preface

Competition law has been shaped almost as much by the remedial regime that is applied for breach of the relevant substantive rules as it has been by the content of those rules. Nor is this surprising. The parties involved in such disputes, more especially those concerned with horizontal cartelization, are often numerous and wealthy. This raises the ever present dilemma as to how to frame legal rules that will really bite on such parties, as opposed to being seen as part of the possible cost of engaging in certain types of transaction, where any fine is discounted against the likelihood of being caught and the relative probability of the judgment going against those who transgress the rules. It is against this background that the debate concerning competition or antitrust remedies has been conducted, with vibrant discourse as to the relative efficacy of civil and criminal sanctions in this regard.

Peter Whelan's book is therefore a timely and valuable contribution to this debate, which will be read with interest not only by those who have an interest in this particular area of the law, but also by all those concerned by the more general relationship between substantive law and its attendant remedial regime. The book contains a rigorous analysis of the relevant issues as to the application of the criminal law to remedy violation of competition law, and does so from three distinct, albeit related perspectives.

Thus after the initial introductory chapter that lays out the aims and structure of the book, Part I addresses the theoretical issues concerning the possible justification for criminalization of EU antitrust. This includes detailed analysis of the challenges of applying deterrence theory and retribution theory respectively to this area of the law. This is followed in Part II by the legal challenges flowing from criminalization, which includes the possible need to strengthen the rights of the accused so as to ensure due process, the legal complexities entailed by application of criminal sanctions alongside civil sanctions and issues relating to legal certainty, such as the meaning of dishonesty in this context. The focus in Part III shifts to the practical challenges attendant on criminalization of European antitrust. There is discussion of the problems surrounding definition of the criminal cartel offence, issues concerning leniency/immunity and the design of enforcement strategies. The concluding chapter brings together the themes from the book, with the emphasis being on the connections between the issues addressed in Parts I-III.

Paul Craig and Gráinne de Búrca

Acknowledgements

This book is the final result of years of researching, contemplating, and writing about the concept of imposing custodial sentences upon individuals convicted of cartel activity. The seeds of my enthusiasm for this topic were planted at an excellent lecture (delivered by Terry Calvani) that I attended at King's College London almost ten years ago and developed further throughout my doctoral studies at St John's College, University of Cambridge. During the course of my research for this book, I have read many enlightening publications which not only have fostered my passion for the topic, but have also influenced my thinking enormously; there are too many authors to mention by name, but I am grateful to all of them.

Quite a number of people have provided support (and/or encouragement) in one form or another over the years covered by the research conducted for this book. They include: Dr Albertina Albors-Llorens; Dr Oles Andriychuk; Dr Louise Aspinwall; Professor Caron Beaton-Wells; Professor John Bell; Professor Ariel Ezrachi; Dr Jonathan Galloway; Sven Gallasch; Angus Johnston; Professor Bill Kovacic; Angus MacCulloch; Dr Philip Marsden; Ruairi Molloy; Dr Oke Odudu; Tom O'Sullivan; Nicola Padfield; David Reader; Professor Andreas Reindl; Professor Andrew Simester; Professor Andreas Stephan; Scott Summers; Professor Floris Vogelaar; and Dr Wouter Wils.

The vast majority of this book was written while I was based at UEA Law School, University of East Anglia, where I was a Senior Lecturer in Law and a Faculty Member of the ESRC Centre for Competition Policy ('CCP'). While at UEA, I benefited from a fully funded, six-month research 'buy out' at the CCP, which helped enormously in bringing this book to fruition. I would like to thank the Economic and Social Research Council for the vote of confidence, as well as the Director of the CCP, Professor Morten Hviid, and my Head of School, Professor Alastair Mullis. During the final stages of writing this book, I took up my current position of Associate Professor in Law at the School of Law, University of Leeds. I would like to express my gratitude to Professor Jeremy Higham and to Professor Ian Cram at the University of Leeds for their support.

My gratitude also extends to Alex Flach, Natasha Flemming, and Clare Kennedy at Oxford University Press for maintaining the highest standards of professionalism throughout the process involved in bringing this book from proposal to finished product. I would also like to express my thanks to the editors of this series (Professor Paul Craig and Professor Gráinne de Búrca) for believing in me.

Finally, a word of thanks should go to my family. My siblings, Nicola and Michael, may never have fully investigated the specifics of my chosen academic subject, but what they may lack in enthusiasm for EU competition law, they more than make up for in their wholehearted support for all my endeavours, academic or otherwise. For this, I am extremely grateful. My mother, Ann, and her husband, Martin, have also been unwavering in their support, as have my remarkable in-laws, Yücel and Nihal Akman. My beautiful wife, Pınar, deserves an equal measure of praise. She was (and is) a constant source of emotional and intellectual support. Her astute and incisive comments always improve my academic writing. She continues to inspire me. I hope this book will make her as proud of me as I am of her. *Ona herşey için teşekkür ederim*. One person I know who would certainly have been proud is my late father, Peter. Unfortunately, he never got to see me qualify as a lawyer, complete a PhD, or publish my first book. Without his love, support, and understanding, I would never have achieved any of these things. We all miss him deeply. The latest addition to my family, my daughter Erin, gets the final word. Erin makes me laugh every day, and for this alone I adore her. This book is dedicated to her and to her brilliant mother.

Dr Peter Whelan
School of Law
University of Leeds

Table of Contents

List of Abbreviations

AAI	American Antitrust Institute
ABA	American Bar Association
AC	Appeal Cases (UK)
ACCC	Australian Competition and Consumer Commission
AG	Advocate General
BAILII	British and Irish Legal Information Institute
BIICL	British Institute of International and Comparative Law
BIS	Department for Business, Innovation and Skills (UK)
CA	Competition Act 1998 (UK)
CAT	Competition Appeal Tribunal (UK)
CCP	Centre for Competition Policy (UK)
CDO	Competition Disqualification Order
CFI	Court of First Instance
CFR	Charter of Fundamental Rights of the European Union
CLR	Commonwealth Law Reports (Australia)
Cox CC	Cox's Criminal Cases (UK)
Crim App R	Criminal Appeal Reports (UK)
Crim LR	Criminal Law Reports (UK)
DG Comp	Directorate General for Competition
DGFT	Director General for Fair Trading (UK)
DoJ	Department of Justice (US)
DPP	Director of Public Prosecutions (UK)
DR	Decisions and Reports of the European Commission on Human Rights
DTI	Department of Trade and Industry (UK)
EA	Enterprise Act 2002 (UK)
EC	European Community
ECHR	European Convention on Human Rights
ECN	European Competition Network
ECR	European Court Reports
ECtHR	European Court of Human Rights
ECU	European Currency Unit
EEA	European Economic Area
EEC	European Economic Community
EHRR	European Human Rights Reports
ERRA	Enterprise and Regulatory Reform Act 2013 (UK)
EU	European Union
EWCA Crim	England and Wales Court of Appeal Criminal Division (Neutral Citation)
EWHC	England and Wales High Court (Neutral Citation)
FBI	Federal Bureau of Investigation (US Government)
FCR	Federal Court Reports (Australia)
GC	General Court
ICN	International Competition Network
ICPAC	International Competition Policy Advisory Committee (US)
IEHC	Irish High Court (Neutral Citation)
IR	Irish Reports (Ireland)
KB	King's Bench (Reports) (UK)
LJ	Lord Justice
MLAT	Mutual Legal Assistance Treaty

NCAs	National Competition Authorities
OECD	Organisation for Economic Cooperation and Development
OFT	Office of Fair Trading (UK)
OJ	Official Journal
OWiG	*Ordnungswidrigkeitsgesetz* (Administrative Offences Act (Germany))
PED	Price elasticity of demand
PIPA	Program on International Policy Attitudes
QB	Queen's Bench (Reports) (UK)
RSC	Revised Statutes of Canada
SFO	Serious Fraud Office (UK)
SI	Statutory Instrument
SSRN	Social Science Research Network
StGB	*Strafgesetzbuch* (Criminal Code (Germany))
StPO	*Strafprozeßordnung* (Criminal Procedure Code (Germany))
TEC	Treaty Establishing the European Community
TEEC	Treaty Establishing the European Economic Community
TEU	Treaty on European Union
TFEU	Treaty on the Functioning of the European Union
TPARC	Trade Practices Act Review Committee (Australia)
UK	United Kingdom
UKHL	United Kingdom House of Lords (Neutral Citation) (UK)
US	United States Reports (US)

Table of Cases

A. AUSTRALIA

B. CANADA

C. EU LEVEL

(a) European Commission

(b) General Court

(c) **Court of Justice**

D. EUROPEAN CONVENTION ON HUMAN RIGHTS

(a) European Commission on Human Rights

(b) European Court of Human Rights

E. IRELAND

F. UNITED KINGDOM

G. UNITED STATES

Table of Instruments

D. LEGISLATION

Note to the Reader

I have attempted to state the relevant law as at 1 January 2014, when the text for this book was completed. On that particular date, the Office of Fair Trading ('OFT') was still the UK public body that enforced competition law: its (competition enforcement) powers had yet to be ceded to the newly created Competition and Markets Authority ('CMA'). For this reason, references in the book to the OFT (rather than to the CMA) have been retained. By contrast, references to the EU Courts employ their current respective names even if at the relevant times their names were indeed different. A similar principle applies to the use of the Treaty articles: their current (rather than past) numbering is employed, unless the context dictates otherwise.

INTRODUCTION

1

An Introduction to European Antitrust Criminalization and Its Theoretical, Legal, and Practical Challenges

A. Background and Context to the Book: 'The European Antitrust Criminalization Debate'

Article 101 of the Treaty on the Functioning of the European Union ('TFEU')[1] contains, inter alia, the EU's prohibition on cartel activity. That prohibition is enforced by the European Commission ('the Commission') and the national competition authorities ('NCAs') and courts of the EU Member States.[2] In its cartel law enforcement role, the Commission can impose only administrative fines on undertakings;[3] it does not have the power to inflict criminal punishment on individuals.[4] Traditionally, within Europe, cartel law enforcement at national level has tended to avoid the employment of personal criminal punishment: such enforcement 'has been of a predominantly administrative character, and when penalties have been imposed these have, in legal terms, commonly been of an administrative or civil nature'.[5] This tradition notwithstanding, over the last decade or so there has been increasing debate within Europe concerning the imposition of the sanction of imprisonment on individuals who have engaged in cartel activity contrary to Article 101 TFEU.

This particular debate has been fostered and advanced at different stages by the activities of various European and non-European entities. The Competition Committee of the Organisation for Economic Cooperation and Development ('OECD') can be easily identified as one of these entities. While the OECD has not adopted a formal position on the issue of whether its members should impose individual criminal punishment for cartel activity, its work (viz., recommendations, reports and best practice roundtables) evidently recognizes that such punishment can be useful in the fight against such

[1] This particular provision of European law has appeared in three other guises since 1957: Article 85 TEEC (from 1957 to 1993); Article 85 TEC (from 1993 to 1999); and Article 81 TEC (from 1999 to 2009). However, its content has essentially remained the same: Article 101 TFEU merely changed the words 'common market' to 'internal market'. For the full text of Article 101 TFEU, see Annex I. For consistency, throughout this book the provision in question will be referred to as Article 101 TFEU.

[2] See Council of the European Union (2003) ('Regulation 1/2003'). Private enforcement of Article 101 TFEU, i.e. the use of private entities to enforce that particular provision in a civil action (for damages, for example), is also a feature of EU law; see: Case C-453/99, *Courage v. Crehan* [2001] ECR I-6297, [26]–[36]; and Joined Cases C-295–8/04, *Vincenzo Manfredi and others v. Lloyd Adriatico Assicurazioni SpA and others* [2006] ECR I-6619.

[3] On the concept of 'undertaking', see, e.g.: Odudu (2006), Chapter 3; Odudu (2005); Townley (2007); and Wils (2002), Chapter 7.

[4] Regulation 1/2003, Article 23(5). It has been argued, however, that the EU-level competition regime 'has criminal characteristics in that it is intended to impose a high level of moral condemnation and disapproval, to inflict severe punishment, to deter future wrongdoing by others, and to unravel unlawful conspiracies': Forrester (2011), 200.

[5] Harding (2006), 181, relying on Gerber (2001).

anticompetitive conduct.[6] In particular, its 'Second Cartel Report' advised its Member States (the majority of which are within the EU) to consider: (i) introducing and imposing antitrust sanctions against natural persons; and (ii) introducing criminal sanctions in cartel cases in jurisdictions where it would be consistent with social and legal norms.[7] Given these efforts, it should be no real surprise then that 'countries in virtually every region of the world' have criminalized cartel activity.[8] The Antitrust Division of the US Department of Justice ('DoJ') is also responsible for bringing the issue to the European arena,[9] particularly as a result of the publication of its policy statements.[10] In fact, its officials have publicly espoused a consistent message concerning its role of enforcing Section 1 of the Sherman Act 1890;[11] for them, 'the most effective deterrent for hard-core cartel activity, such as price fixing, bid rigging, and allocation agreements, is stiff prison sentences'.[12] Academics have also responded to these claims and have analysed the issue of personal criminal antitrust sanctions in considerable detail. Conferences and panel discussions dedicated to the topic have been held across Europe, including in the cities of Florence (in 2001[13] and 2006[14]), Amsterdam (in 2005[15]), Oxford (in 2009[16]), Luxembourg (in 2012[17]), and Rome (in 2013[18]). Along with antitrust officials, academics represent the majority of the contributors to what can be termed 'the European antitrust criminalization debate'. None of this is to say, however, that the European debate is merely an academic exercise: national legislators have also offered their contributions. Indeed, the legislatures of some European jurisdictions have attempted to analyse the issue of personal criminal antitrust sanctions and some—such as the United Kingdom[19]—have changed their laws as a result of their analyses. While the relevant official outputs of these jurisdictions (viz., governmental reports and parliamentary debates) are relatively limited in number, they nonetheless represent an important contribution to the criminalization debate.

The European antitrust criminalization debate itself is a lively one; it has raised a number of controversial and difficult issues.[20] Both the necessity and the appropriateness of personal criminal antitrust sanctions have been examined,[21] as have the origins

[6] Reindl (2006), 111. See also Jenny (2011). [7] OECD (2003a), 46.
[8] Shaffer and Nesbitt (2011). See also Lipsky (2009), 967.
[9] Joshua et al. (2008–09), 359.
[10] See generally <http://www.justice.gov/atr/public/speeches/speech_criminal.htm>.
[11] 15 USC §§ 1–7 (2000 & Supp IV, 2004). [12] Barnett (2009), 2.
[13] Panel IV of 'Effective Private Enforcement of EC Antitrust Law', 6th Annual EU Competition Law and Policy Workshop, European University Institute, Florence, 1–2 June 2001.
[14] Panel III of 'Enforcement of Prohibition of Cartels', 11th Annual EU Competition Law and Policy Workshop, European University Institute, Florence, 2–3 June 2006.
[15] 'Remedies and Sanctions in Competition Policy: Economic and Legal Implications of the Tendency to Criminalize Antitrust Enforcement in the EU Member States', Amsterdam Center for Law and Economics, Amsterdam, 17–18 February 2005.
[16] 'Criminalising Cartels: A Critical Interdisciplinary Workshop on an International Regulatory Movement', Centre for Competition Law and Policy, Oxford, 12 November 2009.
[17] 'Per Se Cartel Offences—Legitimacy and Utility of Criminal Sanctions?', University of Luxembourg, Luxembourg, 23–4 March 2012.
[18] 'Panel IV: Criminal Enforcement', Antitrust Marathon V: Public and Private Enforcement of Competition Law, Italian Competition Authority, Rome, 18 March 2013. For the transcript of this panel, see Marsden et al. (2013).
[19] See Section 188 of the Enterprise Act 2002 ('EA') ('The UK Cartel Offence').
[20] For a flavour of these issues, see: Furse (2012); Beaton-Wells and Ezrachi (2011a); and Cseres et al. (2006a).
[21] See, e.g.: Aylward (2007); Baker (2001); Beaton-Wells (2007); Buccirossi and Spagnolo (2005); Calkins (2007); Calvani (2004a); Calvani (2004b); Capel (2007); Clarke (2005); Clarke and Bagaric (2003); Farmer (2013); Gray (2008); King (2010); MacCulloch (2010a); Rosochowicz (2004); Stephan

of the current manifestation of this particular debate in Europe.[22] The potential for differences in attitude concerning the criminality of cartel activity has also been investigated.[23] Scholarship has been dedicated to the analysis of some of the practical difficulties that the implementation of individual criminal antitrust sanctions allegedly engenders.[24] Some commentators have attempted to analyse the specific requirements of a criminal antitrust regime,[25] including those relating to human rights,[26] political and public support,[27] and publicity.[28] A limited number of articles also consider the competence of the EU institutions to mandate the use of individual criminal sanctions;[29] others, by contrast, have focused on international aspects of antitrust criminalization, such as the concepts of cooperation between states and extradition,[30] as well as the potential for the development of an international consensus on the criminality of cartel activity.[31] Commentators have even offered their opinions on the specific outcomes of actual criminal antitrust cases whenever they have arisen in the EU Member States,[32] as on occasion have the relevant enforcers.[33] A number of scholars have responded to (European and non-European[34]) government consultations on current and proposed cartel offences—the most important of which for present purposes is arguably the 2011–12 consultation on the (unsuccessful) operation of the UK Cartel Offence[35]—highlighting in the process some problematic aspects of design and implementation which are relevant to the European antitrust criminalization debate.[36] In addition, there are a number of studies either describing the specifics of the criminal antitrust regime in a given (European) jurisdiction[37] or detailing how and why a particular criminalized jurisdiction has failed to deliver on its objectives.[38] There are other country-specific reports which detail how future criminal enforcement can be improved, offering in the process some useful insights for other jurisdictions across Europe which are contemplating criminalizing cartel activity.[39] Some scholarship also exists which compares different approaches to cartel criminalization which have been adopted across the EU.[40] It is

(2008c); Wardhaugh (2014); Werden (2009); Werden and Simon (1987); Whelan (2009a); Whelan (2007); Wils (2006b); and Wils (2005b).

22 See, e.g., Harding (2006).

23 See, e.g.: Baker (2009); Harding (2010); Harding (2002); Stephan (2011c); Stephan (2010b); and Stephan (2008e).

24 See, e.g.: Frese (2006); Joshua (2011); and Massey (2006). For useful Australian literature on this topic, see: Senate Standing Committee on Economics (2009); Beaton-Wells and Fisse (2008a); Fisse (2008); Fisse (2007a); and Fisse (2007b).

25 See, e.g., Morgan (2010).

26 See, e.g.: Parkinson (2004); Whelan (2010); and Whelan (2011a).

27 See, e.g., Beaton-Wells (2008a).

28 See, e.g.: Stephan (2011c); and Wagner-von Papp (2011).

29 See, e.g.: Hakopian (2010); Simonsson (2011); Whelan (2008); Wils (2006b); Wils (2005b); and Zuleeg (2002).

30 See, e.g.: Furse (2006); Joshua (2008c); Joshua (2006a); Joshua (2005); O'Kane (2009b); and O'Kane (2008).

31 Ezrachi and Kindl (2011).

32 See, e.g.: Curtis and McNally (2007); Joshua (2008a); Osepciu (2009); Stephan (2008b); Tassopoulou (2009); and Whelan (2009b).

33 See OFT (2010d).

34 Literature from Australia and New Zealand has been particularly instructive in the European antitrust criminalization debate; see, e.g.: Beaton-Wells (2007); and King (2010). See also the output of the 'Cartel Project' at the University of Melbourne: <http://www.cartel.law.unimelb.edu.au>.

35 See: BIS (2011), Chapter 6; BIS (2012), Chapter 7; and the Enterprise and Regulatory Reform Act 2013, Section 47.

36 See, e.g.: MacCulloch (2012); Summers (2012); Wardhaugh (2012a); and Whelan (2012b).

37 See 'Part III: Country Experiences with Law Sanctions' in Cseres et al. (2006a).

38 See, e.g., Furse (2011).

39 See, e.g., Calvani and Carl (2013).

40 See, e.g., Whelan (2012c).

clear, then, that a variety of issues informs the relevant literature and contributes to this particular criminalization debate.

It is submitted that the issues noted above are as pressing now as they were when the relevant literature was first published. Three points can be advanced in support of this assertion. First, as will become apparent below, currently a consensus is lacking on some of the central issues in the debate. In particular, important stakeholders in the process of antitrust criminalization (such as legislators, antitrust officials, and academics) have failed to reach agreement concerning the necessity and appropriateness of personal criminal antitrust sanctions.[41] In the absence of such agreement, continued discussion is likely (not to mention necessary), particularly given the seriousness of the potential consequences facing those cartelists operating within the jurisdiction of any given criminalized antitrust regime. In short, while there is 'general consensus in the US that jail sentences are warranted and effective',[42] the debate in the EU remains 'heated',[43] a fact which underlines the accuracy of Fingleton's contention as far back as 2002 that the criminalization debate then germinating in Europe was likely to be a 'long-term debate'.[44] Second, some EU Member States have already introduced personal criminal sanctions for cartel activity. If the authorities in these jurisdictions are intent on pursuing criminal antitrust cases, it is imperative that they are capable of: (i) justifying the employment of personal criminal punishment; (ii) demonstrating that in imposing such punishment they are respecting the rule of law; and (iii) putting in place the correct practical measures that will ensure that the employment of criminal antitrust punishment actually achieves its aims while maintaining its legitimacy. Whether—and indeed how—these requirements can be fulfilled remains to be conclusively decided; hence continued debate is necessary. Third, as examined directly below, there are a number of deficiencies in the literature which need to be addressed if the relevant authorities are to make informed decisions as to whether to introduce (or to continue to maintain) personal criminal sanctions for cartel activity. Consequently, continued, focused scholarship in this area is required, a fact that helps to underline the value of the contribution represented by this book.

B. Aim of the Book

It was noted above that the European antitrust criminalization debate is still important as, inter alia, there are gaps to be filled in the literature. In order to comprehend fully the aim of this book, it is necessary to articulate the specifics of these gaps. There are at least three categories of deficiencies in the current literature on the employment within the EU of personal criminal sanctions for cartel activity. The first category contains those deficiencies related to the analysis of the application of justificatory criminal punishment theories to cartel activity. The second category encompasses those deficiencies related to the analysis of the legal restraints facing those who wish to introduce individual criminal antitrust sanctions. The third category corresponds to those deficiencies related to the examination of the practical aspects of a successful policy of European antitrust criminalization.

[41] See Joshua (2011), 132. This lack of consensus has been acknowledged for a long time; see: Bloom (2005), 62; and Lowe (2007), 102.

[42] Klawiter and Driscoll (2009), 77. Admittedly, some US critics have argued that criminal antitrust sanctions may be 'unduly harsh': Cavanagh (2005), 162–3.

[43] Hüschelrath (2010), 528.

[44] Fingleton (2003), 310.

The following two points can be made regarding the first category. First, although deterrence theory has been used to construct[45] (and to deconstruct[46]) arguments in favour of European antitrust criminalization, little scholarship has been devoted to the systematic critical analysis of the problematic aspects of employing the theory of deterrence to justify antitrust criminalization. As a result, a number of potential limitations of the application of deterrence theory in this context have not received adequate attention. Examples include the rationality or otherwise of cartelists, the assumption of risk neutrality, and the difficulties associated with securing *efficient* deterrence through personal criminal antitrust sanctions. Second, the relevance and the strength of any plausible alternative arguments in favour of criminalization (i.e. those not built upon deterrence theory) have yet adequately to be tested in the literature. It is sometimes claimed, for example, that cartel activity should be criminalized because it is 'wrong';[47] but more often than not, such statements are not followed by rigorous analysis of the application of criminal punishment theory to the specific case of cartel activity.[48] In order to rectify both of these deficiencies in the literature, one must analyse what can be termed 'the theoretical challenges of antitrust criminalization'.

The following three points can be made regarding the second category of deficiencies. First, a thorough and comprehensive examination of the restraining influence of due process on a project of European antitrust criminalization has yet to be undertaken. Second, this due process-related deficiency in the literature relates to the validity and impact of two contentions, both of which need to be examined if a comprehensive understanding of the restraining influence of due process is to be achieved: (i) that the creation of a criminal antitrust offence necessarily leads to a 'strengthening of rights' in favour of the accused in comparison to the accused's position under an administrative regime; and (ii) that the introduction of criminal antitrust sanctions does not preclude the concurrent imposition of administrative antitrust sanctions for a given cartel. Third, there is little detailed scholarship which specifically focuses on the restraining influence of legal certainty on a project of European antitrust criminalization. In order to rectify the specific deficiencies in this category, one must analyse what can be termed 'the legal challenges of antitrust criminalization'.

The following points can be made about the third category of deficiencies. Real-world examples of failures in the design of the various cartel offences across the EU reflect the relative scarcity of debate concerning the essential practical elements of a European criminal antitrust regime. The UK Cartel Offence was badly drafted in 2002 and a public consultation on the future definition of this offence was recently conducted in an attempt to deal with this issue.[49] Greece recently criminalized cartel activity, but did so without paying close attention to practical implementing measures, and the resultant criminal antitrust regime is considered by antitrust scholars to be less than optimal.[50] By failing to publicize the workings of its criminal antitrust regime, Germany has failed to consolidate public support for its criminal (bid-rigging) offence.[51] Other examples of such failures exist. All of these failures demonstrate that achieving a workable criminal antitrust regime in practice is a far from easy task. Unfortunately, the literature currently

45 See, e.g.: Wils (2006b); and Wils (2005b).

46 See, e.g., Spagnolo (2006).

47 See, e.g., Vickers (2003), 4. For Werden, for example, cartel activity is 'properly viewed as a property crime, like burglary or larceny, although cartel activity inflicts far greater economic harm': Werden (2009), 23.

48 See, e.g., King (2010).

49 See: BIS (2011), Chapter 6; and BIS (2012), Chapter 7. The final outcome of this process was, inter alia, the adoption of Section 47 of the Enterprise and Regulatory Reform Act 2013.

50 See, e.g., Brisimi and Ioannidou (2011).

51 See, e.g., Wagner-von Papp (2011).

provides little in the way of guidance concerning a number of practical issues that need to be considered and resolved by a jurisdiction that wishes to criminalize cartel activity effectively. A number of deficiencies can be detected. First, the potential (negative) impact of Regulation 1/2003 on the actual design and operation of a national criminal cartel offence (and what can be done to reduce the scope for such impact in this context) remains to be articulated in detail. Second, in a process of antitrust criminalization, how one can ensure through legislative drafting that 'acceptable' (i.e. legitimate and/or efficiency-enhancing) cartel activity is not subjected to criminal sanctions is also far from clear. Third, a detailed, systematic analysis that focuses on the practical challenges of leniency/immunity for European antitrust criminalization is also absent from the current literature. In particular, the specifics of the challenge of ensuring peaceful co-existence of both administrative leniency/immunity and criminal cartel sanctions remain to be articulated. Finally, the current literature, while informative to a degree, can nonetheless be criticized for failing to provide a systematic, detailed analysis of the important enforcement strategies that help to ensure that the criminal cartel regime is effective in practice. In order to rectify the specific deficiencies in this category, one must analyse what can be termed 'the practical challenges of antitrust criminalization'.

This book aims to inform the debate at issue by rectifying the identified deficiencies in the current literature. It does so by analysing the theoretical, legal, and practical challenges of European antitrust criminalization. There is a clear need for analysis of these challenges.[52] An examination of the theoretical challenges is advisable in order to determine the obstacles facing those who seek to justify criminal antitrust sanctions in a rational, objective manner as a method of achieving stated predetermined objectives. In other words, it helps to inform the process of justification which should face conscientious, principled legislators. An examination of the legal challenges helps to avoid the creation of a criminal antitrust regime that violates fundamental legal norms. Such an examination helps to prevent the 'short-circuiting' of a given project of antitrust criminalization: it facilitates the introduction and maintenance of a criminal antitrust regime which is legally sound from the outset. An examination of the practical challenges is warranted as such challenges—if unmet—can undermine the effectiveness in practice of a given jurisdiction's efforts to achieve the theoretical objectives of antitrust criminalization, even if legalities have been respected. It is not enough to demonstrate the case for criminal cartel sanctions and to explain how criminal punishment can be legally sound; to create a criminal antitrust regime that works in reality, one may need to put in place particular practical measures and make concrete decisions on the content of the criminal cartel offence and on the specifics of the criminal antitrust regime. An understanding of these practical challenges is therefore very important.

In order to understand fully the challenges relevant to European antitrust criminalization, it is not sufficient to consider the above three categories of challenges in isolation. Some of the responses to a given challenge, say the challenge of respecting legalities, may have a potential negative impact on efforts to overcome a different type of challenge, say a theoretical or practical challenge. Accordingly, to present a fuller picture of the complexities of European antitrust criminalization, not only must one understand the specifics of the theoretical, legal, and practical challenges, but one must also determine how choices concerning one challenge may impact upon the specifics of another, separate challenge. To date, the available literature has failed to provide a detailed analysis of this dynamic interaction, a fact which may explain some of the recent failures in criminal enforcement

[52] See, e.g., Harding (2012), 139.

of cartel activity in Europe. In short, then, the interrelationships between the theoretical, legal, and practical challenges are not fully understood. In examining all three types of challenges for antitrust criminalization, as well as their dynamic interaction, this book contributes to the current literature on European antitrust criminalization.

C. Scope of the Book

As noted above, this book is centred on the theoretical, legal, and practical challenges for European antitrust criminalization. In order to understand fully the scope of this book, however, one should also appreciate both: (a) the definitions of the important terms in this book; and (b) the specific limitations imposed upon that scope.

(a) Definitions employed

A number of important terms are used throughout this book: 'punishment'; 'sanction'; 'criminal punishment'; 'criminal sanctions'; 'personal criminal sanctions'; 'personal criminal punishment'; 'individual criminal sanctions'; 'individual criminal punishment'; 'corporate criminal sanctions'; 'corporate criminal punishment'; 'antitrust'; and 'cartel activity'. In order to avoid ambiguity, these terms should be expressly defined at the outset.

'Punishment' has traditionally been defined as a disposition: (i) involving pain or some other consequences normally considered unpleasant; (ii) for an offence against the legal rules; (iii) imposed on an actual or supposed offender for his offence; (iv) intentionally administered by human beings other than the offender; and (v) imposed by an authority constituted by a legal system against which the offence is committed.[53] This definition is employed in this book. For the purposes of this book, the term 'sanction' is used interchangeably with the term 'punishment'.

The term 'criminal punishment' refers to punishment for an act capable of being followed by criminal proceedings having a criminal outcome.[54] Wils identifies six characteristics of the criminal law which set it apart from other areas of law: (i) the existence of criminal penalties (including imprisonment); (ii) the requirement of criminal intent; (iii) the existence of moral condemnation; (iv) the fact that there is a less strict relationship between penalty and harm; (v) the existence of criminal powers of investigation; and (vi) the existence of criminal rights of defence.[55] The term 'criminal punishment' is used interchangeably with the term 'criminal sanction'.

The term 'personal criminal sanctions' refers to criminal sanctions which are imposed only on natural persons (i.e. individuals), as opposed to corporate entities. For the purposes of this book, it is used interchangeably with the terms 'personal criminal punishment', 'individual criminal sanctions', and 'individual criminal punishment'. The term 'corporate criminal sanctions' refers to criminal sanctions which are imposed only on corporate entities (e.g., firms, undertakings, corporations), as opposed to natural persons; it is used interchangeably with the term 'corporate criminal punishment'.

The term 'antitrust' generally refers to the law and policy developed by a jurisdiction to deal with anticompetitive market behaviour. It encapsulates a number of different

[53] See: Benn (1958); Feinberg (1970), 95; and Hart (1959–60), 4.
[54] Williams (1955). See also Fitzgerald (1960), 259.
[55] Wils (2006b), 61–3. See also Lamond (2007).

branches of enforcement activity, such as those relating to cartel activity, horizontal agreements, vertical distribution agreements, and unilateral conduct. However, when the terms 'antitrust criminalization' and 'criminal antitrust sanctions' are employed in this book—unless another meaning is obvious or specified—they should be taken as referring specifically to one particular branch of antitrust law and policy (viz., that relating to cartel activity) and not any of its other branches.

As noted by Harding, despite its wide usage, the word 'cartel' still 'lacks precise definition' and—depending on the context—can be used to encapsulate: '(a) an agreement; (b) a practice which is the subject-matter of agreement; and (c) a form of organisation to give effect to such an agreement'.[56] That said, the OECD has provided a useful working definition of 'cartel activity' in its 1998 Recommendation; accordingly, one can conceptualize 'cartel activity' as making or implementing:

> an anticompetitive agreement, anticompetitive concerted practice, or anticompetitive arrangement by competitors to fix prices, make rigged bids (collusive tenders), establish output restrictions or quotas, or share or divide markets by allocating customers, suppliers, territories, or lines of commerce.[57]

The OECD's definition of 'cartel activity' has a number of important merits: 'clarity and simplicity, while covering what are agreed to be the principal categories of anti-competitive strategy, but also linking the agreement of anti-competitive purpose with its material realisation'.[58] It also limits the definition of 'cartel activity' to agreements, concerted practices, or arrangements that are horizontal in nature, thereby ensuring that their vertical counterparts (which often display efficiency-enhancing properties) are excluded. Such a definition of 'cartel activity' is therefore adopted in this book.[59] Article 101(1) TFEU prohibits

> all agreements between undertakings, decisions by associations of undertakings and concerted practices which may affect trade between Member States and which have as their object or effect the prevention, restriction or distortion of competition within the internal market.

The prohibition in Article 101(1) TFEU, then, while necessarily more inclusive, nonetheless captures the concept of 'cartel activity' as defined by the OECD.[60]

(b) Limitations imposed upon the scope

The scope of this book is limited in six distinct ways. First, it focuses on the employment of *personal* criminal sanctions for cartel activity and leaves it for others to examine the specific issues raised by the imposition of *corporate* punishment (whether criminal or administrative) for cartel activity. Second, in the analyses conducted, it is assumed that criminal antitrust punishment necessarily includes the potential imposition of custodial sanctions on individuals. This book, then, does not consider the use of criminal antitrust sanctions where imprisonment is not a potential outcome. Third, its findings are (often) EU-specific, particularly as regards the legalities which must be respected in criminalizing cartel activity. That said, while the focus of this book is indeed on national

[56] Harding (2004), 278. [57] OECD (1998), [2(a)].
[58] Harding (2004), 279. Cf. ICN (2005), 11–12.
[59] To be clear, the terms 'cartel activity' and 'hard-core cartel activity' are used interchangeably in this book, unless the context clearly dictates otherwise. On the use of the term 'hard-core cartel', see: Harding (2011b), 44; and Massey (2012), 153.
[60] For a general overview of the substantive content of EU cartel law, see Whish and Bailey (2012), Chapter 13.

enforcement of EU competition law (specifically the cartel prohibition in Article 101(1) TFEU), its analyses and conclusions may well be of interest to entities in non-European jurisdictions which have recently introduced criminal cartel sanctions, which are in the process of so doing, or which may consider such an approach in the future. Fourth, this book only examines the theoretical, legal, and practical challenges concerning the criminalization of *cartel activity*. Other aspects of antitrust law (such as unilateral behaviour) are not considered. Fifth, this book does not attempt to provide a framework according to which one can determine the actual level (i.e. the severity) of personal criminal punishment which should be imposed in any given (criminal) case involving cartel activity. Finally, this book does not attempt to propose a 'model' criminal antitrust offence (i.e. a statutory offence that can be employed by any EU jurisdiction contemplating the criminalization of cartel activity). The author has left that particular task to the legislators. It is hoped, however, that such legislators will find the analyses contained in this book to be of use.

D. Methodology Employed in the Book

This book employs the analytical method of research. In order to fully comprehend how this method is utilized in this book, one should understand: (i) the pertinent aspects of the analytical approach adopted concerning the examination of the theoretical, legal, and practical challenges for antitrust criminalization; and (ii) the specific sources which were relied upon in attempting to achieve such an examination.

(a) Critical analysis of the theoretical, legal, and practical challenges

There are seven important aspects to the analytical approach employed in this book concerning the examination of the theoretical, legal, and practical challenges of antitrust criminalization. First, this book identifies and critically analyses each category of challenges (namely, the theoretical, legal, and practical) separately. Second, the theoretical challenges are considered before the other categories of challenges. Third, the legal challenges are considered before the practical challenges. Fourth, some of the specifics of the approach taken to the theoretical challenges are not relevant to the approaches adopted concerning the legal and practical challenges. Fifth, some of the specifics of the approach taken to the legal challenges are not relevant to the approaches adopted concerning the theoretical and practical challenges. Sixth, some of the specifics of the approach taken to the practical challenges are not relevant to the approaches adopted concerning the theoretical and legal challenges. Finally, any links between the theoretical, legal, and practical challenges analysed are eventually identified in this book.

(i) Each category of challenges is analysed separately

The first point to note in relation to the approach adopted concerning the identification and analysis of the challenges of antitrust criminalization is that this book considers each category of challenges separately. There are three reasons for this. For a start, there is a conceptual distinction between each of the three categories of challenges under examination: the analysis of the theoretical challenges focuses on the existence or otherwise of a sound *justification* for antitrust criminalization; the analysis of the legal challenges focuses on the *legalities* restraining the implementation of a project of antitrust criminalization which relies upon such a justification; and the analysis of the practical challenges focuses on the most important *practicalities* which need to be considered and implemented in order to ensure a successful, workable project of antitrust criminalization. Second, as a result of the conceptual differences noted, the research question pertaining to each category of challenges is inevitably unique. Third, the theoretical, legal, and practical challenges raise important yet complicated issues that deserve considerable (and comparable) space in order to be understood and investigated fully. For reasons of clarity and comprehension, then, it is preferable to separate the categories of challenges and devote sufficient space to the consideration of all three types of challenges. This is not to say, however, that the links between the theoretical, legal, and practical challenges will not be investigated where appropriate, as explained below. So, while the theoretical, legal, and practical analyses are separated in this book, they are not necessarily isolated from one another.

(ii) Theoretical challenges analysed before legal and practical challenges

For a number of reasons, the theoretical challenges should be considered first in a book analysing the inherent difficulties associated with the process of antitrust criminalization. For a start, one must first know *why* one is doing something (i.e. introducing criminal antitrust sanctions) before deciding *how* to do it effectively (i.e. introducing criminal antitrust sanctions in a manner that respects legal norms *while nonetheless achieving its objectives*). It is possible that in adhering to the rule of law—without anything more—one undermines to a degree the objectives of the criminal antitrust offence. If this is so, in order to achieve the objectives of the criminal antitrust law one must put certain (practical) measures in place to offset the negative impact. However, without first understanding these objectives, one cannot design such practical measures. Put differently: one cannot come to a conclusion as to whether adhering to the relevant legalities will negative a given project of antitrust criminalization without first understanding what the purpose of such a project could or should be. Furthermore, there may be a number of ways of respecting a given legality (e.g., drafting a criminal antitrust offence in a manner that respects legal certainty); and in such a case a decision will have to be made concerning the approach to be taken concerning this legality. If the approach decided upon is to be consistent with the aim(s) of antitrust criminalization, it is imperative that one first comprehends the actual objectives of the given criminalization project. Considering the actual theoretical justifications for antitrust criminalization before the legal and practical requirements affecting the implementation of those theories is therefore sensible.

(iii) Legal challenges analysed before practical challenges

Following the theoretical challenges, the next challenges to be analysed are the legal challenges. The legal challenges are analysed prior to the practical challenges for two reasons. The first is that any practical measures designed to give effect to the theoretical justifications for antitrust criminalization are inevitably restricted in their application due to the mandatory nature of respecting any identified legalities. In short, the practical measures chosen cannot involve measures which run counter to what is required in order to respect the relevant legalities: the legal challenges may place restrictions on the choices concerning the practical measures that ensure effective criminal cartel enforcement.

Understanding and articulating the relevant legalities prior to determining the practical measures is therefore warranted: it avoids a potential waste of time and resources on creating practical measures that run counter to the specific mandatory legal dictates that are relevant to the process of European antitrust criminalization. Second, analysis of the legal challenges may highlight additional problematic issues regarding the achievement of the underlying objectives of criminal antitrust enforcement. If so, the articulation of the practical measures that can help a jurisdiction to achieve these underlying objectives should consider the extent of any legal challenges. Given this fact, it makes good sense to analyse the legal challenges prior to the practical challenges.

(iv) Unique aspects of the approach to theoretical challenges

Two points are specific to the approach taken in this book concerning the identification and analysis of the theoretical challenges for antitrust criminalization: first, a fundamental assumption is made, namely, that finding a workable justification for European antitrust criminalization is not required in order to proceed to the analysis of legalities and then practicalities; and, second, two distinct processes ('filtration and application') are involved regarding the relevant identification and analysis.

1. A fundamental assumption: finding a workable theoretical justification is not required to proceed to legalities or practicalities

It should be noted here that, irrespective of the points raised directly above, the following argument is rejected in this book: that there is little point in spending time and resources analysing whether and how legalities can be respected and what practical measures need to be employed if it is difficult to place cartel activity within a given criminal justificatory theory. The reason for this should be clear. One can still offer advice concerning legalities and practicalities to those European jurisdictions that wish to criminalize cartel activity for a given reason (e.g., deterrence or retribution), even if there are limitations to their deterrence- or retribution-based argument. At the very least, such advice—if taken—would ensure that their approach to legalities and practicalities does not undermine the objectives they seek to achieve; in other words, their efforts may be less disappointing than would otherwise have been the case. As a result of this attitude, one does not need actually to discover a workable justification for the criminalization of antitrust behaviour in order to proceed to the analyses of legalities and practicalities conducted in this book. Consequently, the part of this book dealing with theoretical challenges does not necessarily set out to argue in favour of antitrust criminalization. Rather, it seeks to identify and analyse the theoretical challenges for antitrust criminalization. The assumption that finding a workable theoretical justification for antitrust criminalization is not required in order to proceed to the analyses of the legal and practical challenges, then, has an observable impact upon the analysis of the theoretical challenges conducted in this book: it ensures that any (problematic) limitations of the application of a given justificatory theory to cartel activity are acknowledged and analysed in detail.

2. Two relevant processes: filtration and application

There are two processes to the identification and analysis of the theoretical challenges for antitrust criminalization: filtration and application. First, the justificatory theories of criminal punishment that are potentially relevant for antitrust criminalization are identified ('filtration'). Second, the potentially relevant criminal punishment theories are applied to the concept of 'cartel activity' ('application'). By ensuring that irrelevant punishment theories do not form part of the detailed analyses of the process of application, the two-step approach adopted has obvious benefits in terms of efficiency and spatial considerations.

The process of filtration: In determining whether a given justificatory theory of criminal punishment is of potential relevance for antitrust criminalization, one can consider at least three factors: (i) whether the objective(s) underlying that justificatory theory is/are consistent with current antitrust enforcement practice; (ii) whether there is consensus in the current academic literature on its potential relevance for antitrust criminalization; and (iii) whether there are a priori reasons to dismiss the theory as an unsuitable justification for the creation of an antitrust regime that imposes the criminal sanction of imprisonment. These factors will be considered when the process of filtration is conducted in this book. As will be demonstrated below, the process of filtration produces two potentially relevant justificatory theories: deterrence and retribution.

The process of application: This process is conducted separately for both deterrence and retribution. The approach to deterrence differs somewhat from the approach taken with retribution. With deterrence theory, three steps are taken in the process. The first, preliminary step helps to inform the two steps which follow it: it involves the demonstration that current EU antitrust enforcement efforts aimed at deterring cartel activity are deficient. With the second step, (economic) deterrence theory is employed to present as strong an argument as possible concerning the use of personal criminal antitrust punishment. With the third and final step, the criminalization argument advanced is then critically examined for its (problematic) limitations. The specific problematic limitations identified are deemed collectively to comprise the 'challenge' of deterrence theory for European antitrust criminalization. With retribution theory, two steps are taken in the process. The first, preliminary step again helps to inform the step which follows it: it involves the articulation of a framework which can be used to determine the moral content of cartel activity. The second step, by contrast, employs the framework and examines in the process: (i) the extent to which such activity displays sufficient (negative) moral content to be put forward as a suitable candidate for criminalization if retribution theory is employed as a rationale; and (ii) the limitations and weaknesses of a retribution-based antitrust criminalization argument and, hence, the theoretical challenge of retribution in the context of European antitrust criminalization.

(v) Unique aspects of the approach to legal challenges

Three points are specific to the approach taken concerning the identification and analysis of the legal challenges of antitrust criminalization: first, a preliminary acknowledgement is advanced, namely, that legalities need to be adhered to by any European antitrust criminalization project; second, two particular types of legal challenge represent the substance of the analysis; and, third, for analytical purposes a choice needs to be taken concerning the identity of the 'controlling' legal documents.

1. A preliminary acknowledgement: legalities must be respected

Two justificatory theories of criminal punishment are analysed in this book: deterrence and retribution. As examined below, both of these theories of punishment have specific underlying principles that come into effect once a given justificatory theory is chosen: efficiency in relation to (economic) deterrence, and responsibility and proportionality in relation to retribution. Choosing one of these theoretical foundations for antitrust criminalization over the other, then, arguably allows one to place a stronger emphasis upon the chosen theory's principle(s) than the principle(s) of the remaining theory. This is not to say, however, that the principle(s) underlying the chosen theoretical justification should in fact be allowed to 'trump' all other relevant principles, values, or concerns: one should not assume that, simply by choosing the theoretical justification for antitrust criminalization, one ipso facto elevates its principle(s) to an unassailable position on the hierarchy of societal values. Indeed, other values will also need to be respected; the punishment theories cannot be applied in a vacuum. This is the case, as it is unquestionable that there are more ideals that are important to us as citizens than simply the prevention of crime or the seeking of retribution. Society is founded upon a plurality of values and principles, including those enshrined in human rights documents. Any proposed criminalization project should take account of this fact. As Packer states in relation to deterrence theory in particular, theories of criminalization have 'to be qualified by other social purposes, prominent among which are the enhancement of freedom and the doing of justice'.[61] To this, one can add two additional purposes: respect for human rights and respect for the rule of law. This book takes account of this reality and therefore analyses the legal challenges that one faces when attempting to create a criminal antitrust regime within the EU.

2. Focus of the analysis: two particular types of legal challenge

Two types of legal challenge are deemed to be of central importance and are critically analysed in detail in this book. The first ('due process') concerns the restraining influence on European antitrust criminalization of the minimum level of procedural rights protections which is required across the EU. The second ('legal certainty') relates to the restraining influence of the principle of legal certainty on the concept, substance, and existence (or otherwise) of European antitrust criminalization. While both of the challenges identified are human rights-related, they differ in terms of their focus: one challenge is procedural in perspective (due process), the other is substantive (legal certainty).

A thorough understanding of these two particular legal challenges is important for three reasons. First, the legal requirement to protect the human rights of the accused applies to all of the Member States of the EU due, inter alia, to their respective national constitutions, and international and regional human rights law. In fact, the protection of the human rights of the accused is now widely considered to be an essential element in the judicial system of a democratic regime.[62] Such is the importance currently attributed to human rights that one commentator has even argued (perhaps with a degree of hindsight) that the idea of '[d]emocracy was founded on the primacy of the law and the exercise of human rights'.[63] In any case, a project of European antitrust criminalization that does not respect such rights will certainly violate an essential element of democratic regimes, in the process losing its legitimacy as well as its ability to adhere to the rule of law.

Second, in certain circumstances, the dictates of EU law itself mandate that due process and legal certainty be respected. Specifically, as a result of the EU Charter[64] as well as EU jurisprudence,[65] when Member States are acting within the scope of EU law

[61] Packer (1968), 16. See also Hart (1968), 21–4 and 177–85.

[62] See, e.g., the comments of the Office of the United Nations High Commissioner for Human Rights: <http://www2.ohchr.org/english/issues/rule_of_law/democracy.htm>.

[63] Ramcharan (2008), 80.

[64] Charter of Fundamental Rights of the European Union [2000] OJ C364/1 ('EU Charter' or 'CFR').

[65] Fundamental rights are respected as general principles of EU law. See: Case 29/69, *Stauder v. City of Ulm* [1969] ECR 419, [7]; and Case 11/70, *Internationale Handelsgesellschaft v. Einfuhr- und Vorratstelle für Getreide und Futtermittel* [1970] ECR 1125, [3]–[4]. On this, see: Craig and de Búrca (2011), Chapter 11; and Scheuner (1975).

they are under the obligation to comply with EU requirements concerning the protection of fundamental rights,[66] which includes rights concerning due process and legal certainty.[67] According to the Court of Justice, Member States act within the scope of EU law where they apply Treaty provisions,[68] i.e. any provisions of the Treaty on European Union ('TEU') or of the TFEU. It is important to remember here that for the Member States of the EU, adherence to the dictates of EU law is not optional; they cannot choose whether or not to comply with EU law. In legal terms, EU law is 'supreme' in the constitutional order of each Member State.[69] Accordingly,

> every national court must, in a case within its jurisdiction, apply Community law in its entirety and protect rights which the latter confers on individuals and must accordingly set aside any provision of national law which may conflict with it, whether prior or subsequent to the Community rule.[70]

This doctrine of supremacy therefore also ensures that human rights (including rights concerning due process and legal certainty) must be respected by any EU Member State that attempts to enforce Article 101 TFEU with criminal sanctions.[71]

Finally, respecting due process and legal certainty helps to ensure that a given European jurisdiction is perceived to be legitimate not only by its citizens, but also by other Member States of the Union. This perception of legitimacy is particularly important when cooperation is required between Member States in order to ensure the effective enforcement of criminal antitrust laws. Respecting due process and legal certainty, then, is not only necessary in principle, but also helps to develop effective enforcement in practice.

3. Source of the analysis: the 'controlling' legal documents

Acknowledging the fact that legalities must be respected inevitably leads one to consider the specifics of those legalities. In order to determine these specifics, one must first identify their actual source (i.e. the relevant 'controlling' legal documents). As noted directly above, two particular types of legal challenge are examined in this book: (i) the challenge of due process; and (ii) the challenge of legal certainty. The 'controlling' documents to be identified should address both of these types of challenges.

For both of the legal challenges, the 'controlling' document for present purposes is the European Convention on Human Rights,[72] as interpreted by the jurisprudence of the European Court of Human Rights ('ECtHR').[73] This document has been chosen over other (EU/national) sources of human rights, such as the EU Charter or national constitutional provisions, for a number of reasons. First, the aim here is to articulate the impact upon antitrust criminalization provided by the *minimum level* of human rights

[66] See: Article 51(1) CFR; and Case 222/84, *Johnston v. Chief Constable of the Royal Ulster Constabulary* [1986] ECR 1651, [18].

[67] See, e.g., EU Charter, Chapter VI.

[68] See, e.g., Case 222/86, *Union Nationale des Entraîneurs et Cadres Techniques Professionnels du Football (UNECTEF) v. Heylens* [1987] ECR 4097, [14]–[16] (Article 45 TFEU).

[69] See generally: Case 6/64, *Falminio Costa v. ENEL* [1964] ECR 585; Case 11/70, *Internationale Handelsgesellschaft v. Einfuhr- und Vorratstelle für Getreide und Futtermittel* [1970] ECR 1125; and Case 106/77, *Amministrazione delle Finanze dello Stato v. Simmenthal SpA* [1978] ECR 629.

[70] Case 106/77, *Amministrazione delle Finanze dello Stato v. Simmenthal SpA* [1978] ECR 629, [21].

[71] Likewise, any action by the EU institutions must also respect the dictates of EU law; see Article 263 TFEU.

[72] *Convention for the Protection of Human Rights and Fundamental Freedoms as amended by Protocols No. 11 and No. 14*, Rome, 4.XI.1950 (hereinafter 'the European Convention' or 'the ECHR').

[73] On this, see generally: Mowbray (2012); and Ovey and White (2010).

protections required across the EU. Consequently, the specific requirements of national human rights law—which may or may not be stricter than the minimum European standard[74]—are not considered. Second, EU-level jurisprudence is itself directly inspired to a very large degree by the jurisprudence of the ECtHR.[75] Indeed, the Court of Justice 'has always indicated its willingness to follow the case-law of the ECtHR'.[76] Third, the jurisprudence of the ECtHR is arguably more extensive at present than that offered by the EU Courts, and therefore offers more substance upon which an analysis can be conducted. It should be remembered here that the EU Charter, for example, only achieved full legal effect in December 2009. Fourth, the rulings of the General Court ('GC')[77] and the Court of Justice in relation to antitrust procedures and the protection of human rights in particular concern the operation of a regime which imposes administrative sanctions of a corporate, as opposed to a personal, nature, and are therefore of limited relevance in the context of the imposition of personal criminal sanctions.[78] That said, such EU-level jurisprudence is examined when necessary: for example, to highlight how current (lawful) procedures at EU level would need to be modified if criminal sanctions were to be imposed at that particular level. Finally, the jurisprudence of the ECtHR has become even more relevant lately with the entry into force of the Lisbon Treaty, as at that point a legal obligation for formal EU accession to the European Convention was created.[79]

(vi) Unique aspects of the approach to practical challenges

This book acknowledges that the theoretical and legal challenges cannot be fully appreciated without considering some of the most important practicalities involved in criminalizing cartel activity: a number of practical measures can help one to respond to the theoretical and legal challenges; without analysing these, one cannot come to a firm conclusion on the level of difficulty associated with each of the other types of challenges. Therefore, in conducting its critical analyses, this book not only determines the main problematic issues with European antitrust criminalization presented by the theoretical and legal challenges, but also identifies the chief practical measures which can be used to overcome some of these issues. In doing so, this book demonstrates how the responses to the theoretical and legal challenges identified can have an impact upon the actual specifics of the measures required to ensure that the enforcement regime is effective in practice. The practical challenges, then, are unique, in that they result from the need to respond to the theoretical and legal challenges identified.

Three types of practical challenge are analysed. The first practical challenge is the challenge of defining the criminal cartel offence itself. In this context, it is important to understand the potential (negative) impact of Regulation 1/2003 on the design and operation of a national criminal cartel offence and what can be done to reduce the scope

[74] For a general (albeit not completely up-to-date) overview of the differences in human rights protections across the Member States, see, e.g.: Kortmann et al. (2006); and Prakke and Kortmann (2004).

[75] See, e.g.: Case C-260/89, *Elliniki Radiophonia Tileorassi AE v. Dimotiki Etairia Pliroforissis and Sotirios Kouvelas* [1991] ECR I-2925, [41]; *Opinion 2/94* [1996] ECR I-1759, [33]; and Case C-299/95, *Kremzow v. Austria* [1997] ECR I-2629, [14].

[76] Slater et al. (2008), 3.

[77] Formerly known as the Court of First Instance ('CFI').

[78] On human rights and (administrative) antitrust enforcement, see generally: Ameye (2004); Andreangeli (2008); Andreangeli (2006); Benjamin (2006); and Roth (2006).

[79] See Article 6(2) TEU. See also: Article 59(2) of the ECHR (as amended by Protocol 14, which entered into force on 1 June 2010); and <http://hub.coe.int/what-we-do/human-rights/eu-accession-to-the-convention>.

for such an impact. In addition, it is also clear that some types of cartel that fit within the OECD definition may in fact be deemed to be 'acceptable' cartels under EU competition law and therefore not subject to a prohibition under Article 101 TFEU. In designing a criminal cartel offence, one should respond to the challenge of dealing effectively with such 'acceptable' cartel activity. Both of these issues for the first practical challenge are considered in this book. The second practical challenge involves articulating and overcoming the unique challenges of criminal immunity for cartelists and responding to the challenge of ensuring peaceful co-existence of both administrative leniency/immunity and criminal cartel sanctions. The final practical challenge involves the identification of important enforcement strategies that help to ensure the criminal cartel regime is effective in practice in achieving its underlying objectives. In responding to each of these unique types of practical challenge, one can draw upon the experiences of other (non-European) jurisdictions which have used criminal sanctions to enforce their cartel laws, chief among which is the US.

(vii) The critical analyses are used to identify potential links between the respective challenges

It was noted above that this book critically examines each category of challenges for antitrust criminalization separately. These separate examinations form the vast bulk of the substantive analysis presented in this book. However, this book also acknowledges that all three types of challenges may be interrelated. Therefore, after analysing all three types of challenges in detail, this book proceeds to identify any links between all of the challenges analysed. In particular, this book examines: whether the theoretical challenges display any common traits; the extent to which adherence to legalities may create tensions with the theoretical justifications of antitrust criminalization and what (if anything) can be done to reduce such tensions; and the extent to which the theoretical and legal challenges dictate the adoption of certain practical measures (thereby creating additional, *practical* challenges) and whether responding to those practical challenges impacts further upon the theoretical and/or legal challenges. Given that employing antitrust criminalization in order to achieve retribution or deterrence is inherently costly (and, if unsuccessful, brings with it reputational risks for the competition enforcers), the identification of any links between the theoretical, legal, and practical challenges is of considerable importance and should be included in this book.

(b) Specific sources relied upon in the book

This book relies upon a wide range of sources in order to identify and analyse the theoretical, legal, and practical challenges of antitrust criminalization. These sources include case law, legislation, treaties, explanatory memoranda, peer-reviewed articles, government reports, parliamentary debates, speeches, theses, books, chapters, conference papers, presentations, conference discussions, essays, editorials, survey data, newspapers, and even video posts on YouTube. Almost all of these sources are in the English language; a limited number of French articles represent the exceptions. The majority of the sources were found by searching through, inter alia, the Social Science Research Network ('SSRN'), Westlaw UK, JustCite, HeinOnline, Lexis Library, Lawtel, Practical Law Company, British and Irish Legal Information Institute ('BAILII'), and Google Scholar. The websites of the many different antitrust authorities and antitrust organizations and think tanks were also useful for research purposes.

However, not all of the sources are antitrust-specific. In fact, some of the originality of this book consists in applying general criminal scholarship to the specific case of cartel activity. Likewise, not all of the sources are Europe-specific. Indeed, while EU Member States like the UK and Ireland provide excellent case studies concerning the employment of criminal cartel sanctions, other non-European states, such as the US, Australia, and New Zealand, also provide a growing source of scholarship in this area. Furthermore, not all of the sources are 'legal' sources. Actually, a number of different disciplines help to inform the analyses undertaken, including economics, criminology, and statistics. These sources, then, help to provide a degree of interdisciplinarity to the research.

Empirical and non-empirical sources were consulted. The empirical sources were particularly helpful in analysing the size (and impracticality) of an optimal cartel fine, as well the degree of social harm due to cartels—measurements which are of considerable relevance to the theoretical challenges of deterrence and retribution. The author himself did not conduct empirical research, surveys, or interviews. However, a number of informal conversations with leading antitrust scholars, practitioners, and officials helped to focus and refine the research. This is not to concede that further empirical evidence would not have facilitated a deeper understanding of the (theoretical) challenges for antitrust criminalization. In fact, as noted in some of the chapters below, robust empirical evidence is currently lacking concerning important issues in the European antitrust criminalization debate.

E. Structure and Layout of the Book

This book is divided into three substantive parts. Part I deals with the theoretical challenges of European antitrust criminalization; Part II deals with the legal challenges; and Part III deals with the practical challenges. Each part comprises three chapters. Part I includes Chapters 2, 3, and 4. Part II contains Chapters 5, 6, and 7. Part III is composed of Chapters 8, 9, and 10. A final, concluding chapter (Chapter 11) 'links' the findings in Parts I, II, and III.

(a) Part I: theoretical challenges

Chapter 2 concerns itself with the process of 'filtration' noted above in the section on methodology. This chapter presents two different *criminal punishment theories* which are potentially relevant to the European antitrust criminalization debate: deterrence and retribution. It details the inherent (general) limitations of these theories and provides an insight into the extent to which their objectives are already pursued by EU antitrust enforcement policy. By doing so, it provides sufficient context to enable one to appreciate the arguments raised in the two remaining chapters of Part I.

Chapter 3 represents the first treatment of the process of 'application' noted above. This chapter focuses on the criminal punishment theory of *deterrence*. It considers the extent to which deterrence theory can be used to justify the imposition of personal criminal antitrust sanctions, as well as the specific limitations (and thereby the main theoretical challenge) of any deterrence-based antitrust criminalization argument.

Chapter 4 represents the second (and final) treatment of the process of 'application' noted above. This chapter focuses on the criminal punishment theory of *retribution*. It considers the extent to which retribution theory can be used to justify the imposition of personal criminal antitrust sanctions, as well as the specific limitations (and thereby the main theoretical challenge) of a retribution-based antitrust criminalization argument.

(b) Part II: legal challenges

Chapters 5 and 6 both examine the first type of human rights-based legal challenge noted above in the section on methodology: protecting the due process rights of the accused in the context of European antitrust criminalization. In considering this *procedural aspect* of the human rights-related legal challenge to European antitrust criminalization, Chapters 5 and 6 consider respectively the validity and impact of the following two contentions in the European antitrust criminalization debate: (i) that the introduction of criminal antitrust sanctions, including imprisonment, results in a 'strengthening of rights' in favour of the accused; and (ii) that the introduction of criminal antitrust sanctions in a particular jurisdiction does not preclude the imposition of civil/administrative sanctions alongside criminal sanctions for a given cartel. In doing so, these two chapters present analyses concerning a number of different procedural issues that are of relevance to the European antitrust criminalization debate, such as: the standard of proof; the right to silence; the division of functions; the exchange of information; double jeopardy; and concurrent proceedings.

By contrast, in considering the *substantive aspect* of the human rights-related legal challenge to European antitrust criminalization, Chapter 7 focuses on the impact in this context of the principle of legal certainty. In doing so, this chapter presents analyses concerning: legal certainty and the concept of a criminal antitrust offence; legal certainty and the definition of a criminal antitrust offence; and legal certainty and the existence of a criminal antitrust offence (i.e. the awakening of so-called 'sleeping giants' in the laws of the Member States).

(c) Part III: practical challenges

Chapter 8 analyses what is deemed in this book to be the 'first (practical) challenge of design' for European antitrust criminalization: defining the criminal cartel offence itself. In particular, it focuses on two issues: (i) the potential (negative) impact of Regulation 1/2003 on the design and operation of a national criminal cartel offence and what can be done to reduce the scope for such impact in this context; and (ii) how the issue of 'acceptable' cartel activity can be dealt with in the context of European antitrust criminalization.

Chapter 9, by contrast, focuses on what is deemed in this book to be the 'second challenge of design' for European antitrust criminalization: articulating and overcoming the unique challenges of criminal immunity for cartelists and responding to the challenge of ensuring peaceful co-existence of both administrative leniency/immunity and criminal cartel sanctions. In particular, it considers the potential for the existence of criminal cartel sanctions to have a negative impact upon administrative leniency/immunity policies and whether any mechanisms (such as a criminal immunity policy) can be put in place to counteract any negative effects. In addition, it considers the challenges that are specific to the use of a criminal immunity policy to secure successful cartel prosecutions.

Chapter 10, for its part, examines what is here termed the 'third (practical) challenge of design' for European antitrust criminalization: the identification of important enforcement strategies that help to ensure that the criminal cartel regime is effective in practice. In doing so, it: (i) explains the importance of creating and fostering political and public support for the criminal cartel regime; (ii) analyses the strategic issue of ensuring sufficient support in practice from important stakeholders (the general public, potential jury members, and the judiciary) in the cartel criminalization project; (iii) critiques the strategic issue of which entity/entities should exercise the investigative and/or prosecutorial functions in a criminal cartel regime; and (iv) considers the importance of international cooperation for those criminalized regimes that are serious about tackling the most harmful cartels, the difficulties engendered in this context by criminal antitrust enforcement, as well as strategies that can be adopted in order to overcome these difficulties.

(d) The concluding chapter: linking the theoretical, legal, and practical challenges

The concluding chapter of this book, Chapter 11, provides final remarks on the theoretical, legal, and practical challenges of European antitrust criminalization. In doing so, it highlights the difficulties presented by all three types of challenges. Importantly, however, it also: (i) emphasizes the potential 'points of contact' between the two theoretical challenges identified; (ii) underlines the extent to which the legal challenges further complicate the theoretical challenges under examination; and (iii) articulates any additional links between the theoretical and legal challenges and the practical challenges. It clarifies, in other words, the extent to which the theoretical, legal, and practical challenges are interrelated. It demonstrates that the theoretical, legal, and practical challenges of European antitrust criminalization cannot be analysed in isolation and that a dynamic relationship exists between all three types of challenges. Suggestions for future research in this area are also advanced in that final chapter.

PART I

THEORETICAL CHALLENGES

2

Potential Theoretical Justifications for European Antitrust Criminalization

A. Introduction

One cannot examine effectively the challenge of applying a given justificatory theory of criminal punishment to the concept of 'cartel activity' without first understanding the substance of that theory. Indeed, ignorance of the essentials of a chosen criminal punishment theory risks inconsistent argumentation and illogical conclusions on the challenge it presents in this specific context. Therefore, before analysing the theoretical challenges of criminalizing cartel activity, one must first identify and elucidate the specifics of any relevant theory of criminal punishment. The word 'relevant' is significant here. Not all justificatory criminal punishment theories will be useful in the European antitrust criminalization debate; in fact, some theories will have no valid connection with the concept of cartel activity. Consequently, there is no real need to consider the specific challenges presented by such irrelevant theories. In recognition of this fact, and as noted in Chapter 1, a two-step approach is adopted concerning the analysis of the theoretical challenges for antitrust criminalization: first, one identifies and elucidates the specifics of the actual theories of criminal punishment that have potential relevance for cartel activity; and second, one analyses in detail the difficulties of applying the identified theories to the concept of cartel activity. The present chapter concerns itself with step one—the 'filtration' process—while the remaining chapters of Part I (Chapters 3 and 4) are devoted to step two—the 'application' process.

In fulfilling its role of 'filtration', this chapter identifies and clarifies the potential theoretical justifications for antitrust criminalization; it also notes the current status of these theories in European antitrust enforcement, allowing one further to understand the potential relevance of these theories and to comprehend more fully the theoretical challenges analysed in later chapters. It is divided into three sections. Section B focuses on two distinct justificatory theories which are relevant for antitrust criminalization: deterrence and retribution. After explaining why deterrence and retribution are potentially relevant for antitrust criminalization and why other theories of criminalization are of limited use in the European antitrust criminalization debate, that particular section provides a concise overview of the essentials of both of the relevant justificatory theories. Section C proceeds upon the basis that, while both deterrence and retribution represent justificatory theories with their own merits, neither of these theories is challenge-free: both theories impose inherent limitations upon those who seek to employ them. These (general) limitations are detailed in order for this book to provide a fuller understanding of the challenge which one faces when applying either of the theories to the specific case of antitrust enforcement. Finally, Section D provides an insight into the extent to which deterrence and retribution are already pursued by current European antitrust enforcement policy. This section underlines the potential relevance of these theories of punishment in the European antitrust criminalization debate; but it also informs the analyses undertaken in the remainder of Part I. To be clear, however: it should be understood that, by containing sections on the criminal punishment theories of deterrence and retribution as well as a section on the status of deterrence and retribution in European antitrust enforcement, this chapter does not attempt to argue (even implicitly) that, because deterrence and retribution are already established aims of European antitrust law enforcement, one should ipso facto introduce personal criminal sanctions if they pursue such objectives. Rather, this chapter merely aims to provide sufficient context to enable one to appreciate fully the theoretical challenges for antitrust criminalization considered in Chapters 3 and 4.

B. Two Relevant Theories of Antitrust Criminalization

This section focuses on two distinct justificatory theories which are relevant for antitrust criminalization: deterrence and retribution. A firm understanding of these theories is essential for a thorough comprehension of this book. Consequently, after explaining why other theories of criminalization are of limited use in the European antitrust criminalization debate, this section provides a concise overview of the essentials of both of these theories.

(a) Focusing on deterrence and retribution

There are at least four different theoretical justifications for the imposition of individual criminal sanctions, namely: deterrence; retribution ('just deserts'); rehabilitation; and incapacitation.[1] Each one of these justifications is conceptually distinct and pursues a specific aim. Deterrence seeks to prevent future activity, either in a general (public-focused) or specific (individual-focused) sense.[2] Retribution posits that individuals should face a criminal charge due to the fact that they have committed a moral wrong.[3] Rehabilitation attempts to treat an individual engaging in unlawful behaviour in order to prevent habitual reoffending.[4] Incapacitation refers to the prevention of activity through the direct deprivation of the ability or capacity to engage in such activity.[5] For the purpose of this book, however, only the punishment theories of deterrence and retribution will be examined as potential rationales for antitrust criminalization.

There are a number of reasons for this approach. First, and as examined further below, both deterrence and retribution are already relevant for European antitrust enforcement; indeed, according to the EU Courts, 'both the deterrent effect and the punitive effect of the fine are reasons why the Commission should be able to impose a fine'.[6] Therefore, at the very least, considering either of these theories for the purposes of antitrust enforcement would not be inconsistent with current practice.

Second, such an approach would also be consistent with the literature on antitrust criminalization.[7] Indeed, both of these theories have been considered to varying degrees by commentators both in support of and against criminal cartel sanctions.[8] Most of those legal commentators who advocate the imposition of personal criminal sanctions

[1] See, e.g.: Ashworth (2004), 65 et seq.; Banks (2004), Chapter 5; and Yeung (2004), 62–3.
[2] Walker (1980), 26. [3] Galligan (1981), 144. [4] Packer (1968), 48.
[5] Morris (1994), 238.
[6] Case T-329/01, *Archer Daniels Midland v. Commission* [2006] ECR II-3255, [141].
[7] It would also be in line with the argument of Fisse, who posits that the imposition of criminal sanctions in the corporate context should only be for the purposes of retribution or deterrence: Fisse (1983).
[8] As is apparent from Chapters 3 and 4 of this book.

on individuals for engaging in cartel activity find inspiration for their arguments in the theory of deterrence. In a nutshell, those who advocate criminalization highlight its necessity for the achievement of optimal deterrence,[9] while those opposed to it argue the contrary.[10] While less room is reserved in this debate for consideration of the concept of retribution, it is nonetheless possible to find statements in the literature on the (negative) moral character of cartel activity.[11] Admittedly, however, these are more often than not given in addition to, and in order to bolster, a (positive) argument concerning deterrence.[12] Moreover, those who depend upon deterrence theory to oppose criminalization may sometimes emphasize the (relatively) neutral moral character of cartel activity in order to underline further the inappropriateness of criminal antitrust punishment.[13] Consequently, retribution, like deterrence, has influenced the debate on antitrust criminalization, a fact which ensures its potential relevance for the theoretical analyses to be conducted in this book.

Finally, for reasons which follow, the theories of rehabilitation and incapacitation should be discarded: a priori, they represent unsuitable justifications for the creation of an antitrust regime that imposes the criminal sanction of imprisonment. The point of this book is to examine, inter alia, the theoretical challenges of antitrust criminalization. As noted in Chapter 1, the focus of the analysis is the employment of the criminal sanction of *imprisonment*. Therefore, when the theories of criminal punishment are employed in this book, they are employed for the purpose of analysing whether a European jurisdiction would be justified in imposing custodial sanctions on individuals for cartel activity; they are not employed for the purpose of analysing whether that jurisdiction would be justified in imposing any other type of sanction on individuals for cartel activity (e.g., administrative sanctions or criminal sanctions not amounting to custodial sanctions). So, when rehabilitation and incarceration are at issue in this book, it is as justifications for the imprisonment of individuals, and not merely as justifications for punishment per se. Here, it is more accurate to use the terms 'rehabilitation through incarceration' and 'incapacitation through incarceration', rather than simply 'rehabilitation' or 'incarceration'.

It is submitted that both rehabilitation through incarceration and incapacitation through incarceration are inappropriate in the antitrust context.[14] The literature appears to support this view: generally speaking, deterrence and retribution are perceived as representing the more appropriate objectives of the imposition of criminal sanctions on business enterprise.[15] The concept of 'rehabilitation through incarceration'—with its focus on those recividivist individuals who, after being punished, are, by their very nature, still incapable of adhering to the law—is of limited relevance when one is considering the punishment of rational and educated corporate decision-makers who are capable, one assumes, of learning from their mistakes.[16] Unlike other types of crime—drugs-related crime, for example—the actions of such educated decision-makers cannot be easily perceived as being symptomatic of a wider social disease that needs to be treated.[17] For its part, 'incapacitation through incarceration' is inappropriate as we

9 See, e.g., Wils (2006b).
10 See, e.g., Buccirossi and Spagnolo (2005).
11 See, e.g., Vickers (2003), 4.
12 Clarke (2005); Clarke and Bagaric (2003); and Fels (2002). Even the US antitrust authorities (who consider cartel activity to be 'morally wrong') feel obliged to construct a (positive) deterrence-based argument for criminal antitrust sanctions; see OECD (2003b), 99.
13 See, e.g., the comments of Switzerland in OECD (2003b), 106.
14 See: Werden (2009); and Renfrew (1977), 592–3.
15 See Fisse (1983).
16 See Baker and Reeves (1977), 619.
17 On this function of rehabilitation, see Bean (1981), 54.

do not wish to put cartelists (who, their cartel activity notwithstanding, are usually productive, law-abiding members of society) behind bars *merely* to prevent them from being physically able to cartelize again in the future. If one wished physically to prevent a given individual from engaging in cartel activity, one could use other, far less severe/costly methods, such as court orders preventing an individual from being involved in the management of a business. It is true that these types of orders—more accurately, director disqualification orders—are criticized in a later chapter of this book and that it is argued that imprisonment appears to offer advantages over such orders;[18] but such criticism concerns the ability of director disqualification orders to achieve *(general) deterrence* rather than incapacitation. Indeed, it is not argued that such orders are ineffective at ensuring that the (detected) individual concerned does not engage in cartel activity in future.

None of the above is to say that rehabilitation and incapacitation are both irrelevant to antitrust enforcement. In fact, the objective of incapacitation is pursued by some European jurisdictions. The UK authorities, for example, have the power under the UK Enterprise Act 2002[19] to secure a Competition Disqualification Order ('CDO') against a company director if his company breaches the competition law rules and a court finds that his behaviour renders him unfit to be concerned in the management of a company.[20] Pursuing rehabilitation (i.e. the 'forced' changing of attitudes) through, for example, the imposition of mandatory attendance at competition compliance seminars may also have its merits, particularly for those employees who have worked for a company where adherence to the antitrust laws has not been high on the agenda. The point here is that such incapacitation and/or rehabilitation in the antitrust context does not—and for reasons given above, should not—involve imprisonment; hence their irrelevance for the analyses undertaken in this book.

(b) The concept of deterrence

Deterrence theory finds its roots in the classic utilitarian argument that suffering is a pain that should be avoided and that, as a result, punishment, itself a form of suffering, could not be justified unless a specific social benefit or utility can be derived from its imposition.[21] At its most basic, this theory holds that punishment can only be justified if it leads to the prevention or reduction of future crime.[22] Deterrence is thus consequentialist; 'it looks to the preventive consequences of sentences'.[23] Unlike retribution, deterrence does not concern itself with punishment for punishment's sake. Rather, it sees punishment as a method of maximizing utility, to be employed only when the disutility of its imposition is less than the utility to society secured by its deterrent effect.

There are two variants of deterrence: special and general. Special deterrence relates to the act of preventing the offender himself from reoffending, while general deterrence refers to the preventive effect of punishment on the wider public.[24] This distinction is important, as (empirical) criticism of deterrence theory often rests on the special variant.[25] Special deterrence is rarely used as the primary rationale of sentencing

[18] See Chapter 3, Section D(c)(ii) of this book.

[19] Section 204 the UK Enterprise Act 2002 (amending the Company Directors Disqualification Act 1986).

[20] On this, see: OFT (2010b); and Rayment (2004).

[21] See: Beccaria (1767), 31; Bentham (1789), footnote 158; Bentham (1838), 165–6; and Easton and Piper (2005), 104.

[22] Walker (1980), 26.

[23] Ashworth (2005), 75.

[24] Andenaes (1974).

[25] Packer (1968), 39.

policy; general deterrence is therefore more significant.[26] It is acknowledged that, in the context of cartel law, the specific deterrence of convicted cartelists is secondary to the general deterrence of potential cartelists.[27] The main reason for this is that, with cartel activity, (individual) recidivism following incarceration is considered to be 'virtually non-existent',[28] even if recidivism by the corporate body is acknowledged by EU antitrust enforcement policy and practice.[29] Nevertheless, special deterrence may also be achieved along with general deterrence.[30]

(i) An economic variant

A relatively recent development in the debate on deterrence concerns the introduction of economics as a method of analysing the deterrent effect of a given law. The chief proponent of this approach was Becker, who placed the maximization of wealth, as opposed to the more nebulous concept of 'happiness' advocated by the classic utilitarians, at the centre of any evaluation of deterrent effects.[31] Posner, in particular, highlights this difference between economic analysis of law and utilitarianism; for him, 'wealth' is defined as the 'value in dollars or dollar equivalents... of everything in society'.[32] Two central concepts in this theory concern 'rationality' and 'economic efficiency'.

Rationality: Economic deterrence theory is based upon the fundamental assumption that individuals/undertakings are rational economic actors who act in their own interest in order to maximize their own welfare.[33] Accordingly, a rational actor can be deterred from engaging in a given conduct if the cost to him of such conduct is greater than its benefit. By ensuring that the 'price paid' by the offender is greater than he is willing to pay, one can disincentivize the potential offender and thereby reduce the incidence of unwanted behaviour.

Efficiency: Economic deterrence theory attempts to achieve economic efficiency in order to maximize the total welfare of society. Conduct is seen as efficient, and therefore should be encouraged, if its welfare benefits to society are greater than its costs (including the cost of law enforcement); by contrast, inefficient conduct, where costs outweigh benefits, should be prohibited. Economists will usually look to the margins in order to determine the efficient amount of crime enforcement.[34] Efficiency is obtained, and welfare maximized, where the marginal benefit of punishment is equal to its marginal cost.[35]

[26] Ashworth (2005), 75; and Wechsler (1952), 1105. [27] Werden (2009), 24.

[28] Calvani and Calvani (2009), 127. Admittedly, Connor argues that recidivism is a significant factor in international cartel enforcement; but his focus (on 389 recidivists in international cartels over 20 years) is on the corporate body, as opposed to merely the individual: Connor (2010). For a (rather convincing) counter-argument concerning the existence of (corporate) recidivism, see Werden et al. (2011).

[29] Indeed, according to one source, the Commission has taken recidivism into consideration (as an aggravating factor) when determining the relevant fine in more than 40 per cent of the cartel decisions that it has adopted between 2006 and 2011: Barennes and Wolf (2011). On recidivism and EU anti-cartel enforcement policy, see generally Wils (2012).

[30] Baker and Reeves (1977), 619. [31] Becker (1968).

[32] Posner (1979b), 129. See also Posner (1980a), 247.

[33] See: Becker (1978), 14; Cooter and Ulen (2004), 455 et seq.; and Gerla (1988), 893. On this, see also Veljanovski (2006a), 49 et seq. Rationality, at least in its modern form, is a concept that is devoid of moral normativism; see: Alvey (1999); and Stucke (2007), 520.

[34] See: Block and Sidak (1980), 1131; Breit and Elzinga (1976), 7–16; and Posner (1976), 221–2.

[35] On this, see Cooter and Ulen (2004), 25 et seq.

(ii) Harm versus gain

Unlawful conduct may involve both benefits and costs for society, especially in the regulatory context; the economic models are cognizant of this fact. The model of *unlawful gain* applies to behaviour that is never beneficial to society, or for which the costs always outweigh the benefits.[36] It holds that for a given punishment to have (efficient) deterrent effect, it must be set at a level at least equal to the gain of the offender. If this were not so, the offender would not be deterred and inefficiency would result. This model does not foresee any problem with over-deterrence, as no potential benefits are lost through the elimination of the relevant behaviour. By contrast, the *harm to others* model applies to conduct which, while harmful and not costless, nonetheless exhibits potential benefits for society.[37] Under this model, only inefficient conduct should be deterred; efficient (albeit unlawful) conduct that provides net gains to society should not, as it is welfare-enhancing. Punishment is set at a level that equals the societal harm caused by the conduct in question, and not the gain of the offender, effectively internalizing the external cost and ensuring that the entity engaging in the behaviour suffers its detriment and not society. By so doing, the model avoids over-deterring, and thus penalizing, efficient behaviour.

This book, when calculating an optimal cartel sanction, will focus on the gain to the offender and not on the harm to others.[38] This approach is generally consistent with the academic literature on antitrust criminalization.[39] There are three merits to this approach. First, the harm to others variant relies upon the assumption that cartels are capable of being efficient, something that is extremely unlikely to be the case.[40] Second, calculation of the relevant variables should be easier, as the 'deadweight loss' is not considered.[41] Finally, the condemnation effect of criminal sanctions is likely to arouse less hostility when applied to conduct that is perceived as having no redeemable (i.e. efficient) features. It is conceded that this choice reflects a personal interpretation of the purpose of the cartel law rules, namely, the achievement of maximum consumer, as opposed to producer or indeed total, welfare.[42] Nonetheless, it is submitted that such a choice, while arguably consistent with current European practice,[43] does not materially affect the argument presented that financial cartel sanctions alone are ineffective.[44]

(iii) Necessary adjustments

The following assumptions have been made in relation to the above two economic models of deterrence:[45] that the cost of detection and prosecution is zero; that the probability

36 See Yeung (1999), 448–9.

37 See Yeung (1999), 447–8.

38 Cf. Connor and Lande (2005), 516; and Landes (1983).

39 See, e.g.: Calvani (2004a); Werden (2009); and Wils (2006b). See also Lande and Davis (2010), 5, footnote 15. Cf. Connor and Lande (2012), 432.

40 On efficiency, see Landes (1983), 653 et seq. Cf. Werden and Simon (1987), 932 ('efficient hard-core price-fixing is no more likely than efficient child molestation').

41 See Breit and Elzinga (1986), 11–12. On the concept of 'deadweight loss', as well as its measurement, see, e.g., Leslie (2006a). See also Annex III to this book.

42 On this, see, e.g., Wils (2006a), 191–3. On the choice between consumer, producer, and total welfare, see: Farrell and Katz (2006); Foer (2006); Harker (2011); Kerber (2008); Lande (1999); Motta (2004); and Pittman (2007). See also the discussion in relation to 'stealing' in Chapter 4, Section C(c) (i) of this book.

43 See, e.g., OECD (2007a). See also European Commission (2006a).

44 That is, fines calculated under either of the models are of such a quantum to justify the analysis presented in Chapter 3, Section B(b) of this book.

45 The assumption that all actors act rationally has already been noted.

of detection and prosecution is one; that all rational actors are risk neutral; and that no legal errors occur. Since these assumptions are not entirely realistic, a number of adjustments should be made when employing deterrence theory.

Costs: Enforcement costs will be treated differently depending upon which deterrence model is adopted.[46] With the 'harm to others' variant, costs are considered as part of the harm caused to society and are therefore internalized. With the 'unlawful gain' model, enforcement costs will be used to determine whether or not intervention is warranted.

Probability of detection and prosecution: Since not all offences will be detected, the expected cost of any future unlawful action will always be lower than the actual penalty imposed on apprehended offenders; it will be determined by multiplying the actual penalty by the probability of getting caught.[47] In order to deter effectively under both models, the actual penalty should be raised by dividing it by the probability of getting caught. The severity of an effective penalty and the rate of detection, therefore, have an inverse relationship.[48]

Risk neutrality: Risk-averse offenders will be deterred by a lower penalty than the one contemplated under either economic model.[49] Risk-seekers, conversely, will only be deterred by higher penalties.[50] The penalty should be adjusted accordingly if either of these situations is the case.

Legal error: Errors that allow guilty people to go free are simply reductions in the level of detection; they thus ensure a higher penalty.[51] Random erroneous convictions affect the deterrent penalty as follows: it falls if one is swayed by considerations of fairness, but rises if deterrence is the sole aim.[52] Non-random erroneous convictions chill (beneficial) behaviour at the borderline of criminality and thus should lead to a lower penalty.[53]

(c) The concept of retribution

At their most basic, theories of retribution hold that punishment ought to be justified not by reference to its ability to prevent future crime, but rather because human beings are responsible for their actions and must thus receive what they deserve when they have made what society deems are wrong choices.[54] Such theories employ an approach to punishment that is backward-looking to the offence, rather than forward-looking to the offender or to the consequential effects of punishment on the rest of society; they are centred on the concept of retribution for offences against the moral code.[55] Unlike theories based around the idea of deterrence, just deserts theories view punishment as a justification in itself for a wrong that has been committed; they argue for the imposition of punishment irrespective of its impact upon future crime levels.[56] For retributionists, it is the nature of the prohibited act, and not the consequences of punishment, that matters.[57]

[46] Yeung (2004), 67. [47] Cooter and Ulen (2004), 456–7.
[48] Block and Sidak (1980), 1132. [49] Cooter and Ulen (2004), 50–1.
[50] Cooter and Ulen (2004), 52. [51] Werden and Simon (1987), 921.
[52] Werden and Simon (1987), 921.
[53] Werden and Simon (1987), 921. See also Posner (1985), 1206.
[54] Packer (1968), 37. The conventional wisdom is therefore that retribution dictates individual rather than corporate responsibility, although this has been questioned in the literature. It has been argued, for example, that 'retribution is not inherently tied to the requital of individual desert; the notion of desert may be corporate or individual': Fisse and Braithwaite (1993), 44. As noted in Chapter 1, Section C(b) of this book, the focus of this book is individual punishment, not corporate punishment; therefore, there is no need to analyse Fisse and Braithwaite's interesting contention in this book.
[55] Galligan (1981), 144. [56] Boonin (2008), 85.
[57] See Duff and Garland (1994), 4.

(i) 'Unfair advantage' and 'communicative function' variants

Most modern retribution theorists generally attempt to distance themselves from the 'strong form' retributive arguments which claim that just deserts theories not only offer society a justification for the imposition of punishment, but also impose an obligation concerning its use.[58] These theorists attempt to move beyond the intuitive assertion that 'those who have done wrong should be punished' and incorporate social justifications into the use of their retribution models.[59] Two variants of the modern approach to just deserts are particularly noteworthy:[60] one relates to the concept of 'unfair advantage',[61] the other to the 'communicative function' of the criminal law.[62] Both are detailed in turn.

For some, punishment neutralizes an unfair advantage secured by a non-compliant citizen in his breach of the law, and in the process restores the social balance.[63] By exercising his own freedom of choice and consequently acting against the defined common interest, an offender effectively gains an unfair advantage over those who restrain themselves;[64] punishment seeks to restore the 'distributively just balance' of advantages between the offender and the law-abiding members of society so that no one in society should have been disadvantaged.[65] As Galligan explains, this unfair advantage may reflect itself in gains in goods, welfare, or position.[66] But these gains are not what is significant; what matters is the gain inherent in 'indulging one's will, exercising one's freedoms beyond the restrictions imposed by law'.[67] There are two elements which need to be established with this theory: (i) a voluntary breach of the law that gives the offender an illicit advantage; and (ii) the fact that justice requires that the resultant wrong to the rest of the community be remedied.[68]

A variant of retribution theory which appeals more to the intuitive feelings towards punishment is developed in the arguments of those who espouse a communicative function of punishment. This variant can be based upon the argument that the acquisition of an unfair advantage per se is not what should be condemned, and thus punished, by the law; rather, it is the illegal act, in and of itself, which is morally repugnant and thus liable to punishment.[69] Von Hirsch, for example, argues that punishment has a communicative element, in that it conveys to society the inherent wrongness of an act and the appropriateness of a resultant legal sanction; treating an offender as a wrongdoer, and by consequence conveying blame, is central to the idea of punishment.[70] A neutral sanction, i.e. one not involving censure, 'would treat offenders and potential offenders much as beasts in a circus—as beings which must be restrained, intimidated, or conditioned into submission because they are incapable of understanding that predatory conduct is wrong'.[71] Such a sanction would thus deny a person's status as a moral being. For him,

[58] See Yeung (2004), 72–3. There are, however, 'modern' retributionists who still hold steadfast to the idea of there being an obligation in this context. Moore, for example, states: 'for a retributionist, the moral culpability of an offender also gives society the *duty* to punish. Retributivism, in other words, is truly a theory of justice such that, if it is true, we have an obligation to set up institutions so that retribution is achieved': Moore (1987), 150.

[59] Galligan (1981), 153–4.

[60] Lippke (2006), 15.

[61] See: Sadurski (1985); and Sher (1987), 69–90.

[62] See: Hampton (1991), 377–414; and Anderson (1999).

[63] In general, see: Finnis (1980), 262–4; and Finnis (1972). See also von Hirsch (1993), 7 et seq.

[64] Finnis (1980), 263. In the words of Morris, 'a person who violates the rules has something others have—the benefits of the system—but by renouncing what others have assumed, the burdens of self-restraint, [he] has acquired an unfair advantage': Morris (1995), 63.

[65] Finnis (1980).

[66] Galligan (1981), 155.

[67] Finnis (1980), 265.

[68] Galligan (1981), 155.

[69] See Yeung (2004), 73.

[70] Von Hirsch (1993), 9.

[71] Von Hirsch (2000), 170.

the use of punishment as a form of communication has the advantage of comprehensibility, in that blaming is something we engage in every day, and is easier to link to the principle of proportionality than the unfair advantage theory.[72]

(ii) The principles of proportionality and responsibility

According to retribution theory, punishment has as its sole purpose *deserved* suffering; it follows that punishment should only be imposed to the extent that the offender is actually responsible for his behaviour.[73] The principles of responsibility and proportionality are therefore of central concern to this theory. The concept of 'just deserts' acts not only as a justification for punishment, but, through the operation of the proportionality principle, it also dictates the severity of any punishment imposed; both punishment per se and the extent of such punishment must be justified according to what one deserves. Punishment, however, is not only dictated by the degree of culpability of a person: both the gravity of the harm and the degree of culpability affect the seriousness of an offence, and thus the severity of punishment.[74]

Two types of proportionality can be distinguished.[75] Ordinal (or relative) proportionality, a concept rooted in comparative punishment, dictates that persons convicted of offences of like gravity should receive punishments of a like severity. Cardinal proportionality, on the other hand, refers to the relationship between the gravity of the offence and the severity of punishment. Although the existence of the proportionality principle in just deserts theory in general is not disputed, there are a number of conceptual disagreements between various retributionists regarding its implementation. For example, some commentators see the principle as a defining, central concept in the determination of the severity of punishment,[76] while others see it simply as a limiting principle which should be used as a guide to ensure that punishment is neither too lenient nor too severe.[77] Indeed, even its ability to act as a precise guideline in any given situation has been questioned.[78]

C. The Relative Merits and Demerits of the Two Theories

While both deterrence and retribution represent justificatory theories with their own merits, neither of these theories is free from challenges. In fact, both theories impose

[72] Von Hirsch (2000). For some, however, the communicative theory fails to account for the fact that: '[t]here are many situations in which we condemn a person's actions yet feel no obligation to tell them so': Walker (1992b), 532.

[73] See Packer (1968), 140. On the concept of responsibility, see generally Cane (2002).

[74] See Galligan (1981), 164 ('the proportion must be between the seriousness of the offence on one side, which includes not just the harm caused but also the culpability of the offender, and on the other side the severity of the punishment').

[75] See: Easton and Piper (2005), 63–5; von Hirsch (1993), 18–19; and von Hirsch (1990).

[76] Von Hirsch argues, for example, that as the purpose of punishment is censure, and thus the highlighting of moral blameworthiness, any punishment imposed conveys the extent to which one is held to be responsible for a given action; consequently, punitive sanctions should be arranged according to the degree of blameworthiness, i.e. the seriousness, of the action: von Hirsch (1993), 15.

[77] See Morris (2000), 181–3. For him, a retributionist of sorts, just deserts can be applied in a parsimonious way so that sentencing aims can be met with a lower anchoring point. Proportionality should prevail at higher levels of severity, but parsimony is allowed at lower levels of severity. See Easton and Piper (2005), 64.

[78] See: Ashworth (1989), 344 (there is 'no clear notion of how to set the overall level of penalties so as to achieve cardinal proportionality'); and Finnis (1980), 264.

inherent limitations upon those who seek to employ them. These (general) limitations must be acknowledged if one is to have a full understanding of the challenge one faces when applying either of theories to the specific case of antitrust enforcement.

(a) Principal strength of each rationale

Deterrence theories find their primary advantage in their ability to set a specific quantum for an effective penalty. Such theories, it can be argued, employ a non-arbitrary, principled approach based upon theoretically quantifiable variables and thus represent a more 'scientific' method of resolving questions related to the criminalization of a given behaviour.[79]

The principal strength of theories of just deserts is the fact that individuals are treated as moral agents responsible for their own choices. Holding at their centre the acknowledgment of the moral worth of the individual, these theories, unlike their deterrence-based counterparts, cannot be criticized as falling foul of the Kantian admonition that individuals should be treated as an end in themselves, not as a means towards an end.[80]

(b) Moral considerations

The failure of deterrence-based theories to account for why excessive punishment, or indeed the punishment of the innocent, should not be allowed remains one of their principal weaknesses. According to these theories, punishment of the innocent, for example, would be an acceptable state action if it were to lead to an increase in societal utility; they allow for the sacrifice of an individual for the benefit of all and, therefore, potentially violate the warnings of Kant. Indeed, on their face such theories are capable of rendering invalid the liberal prescription that punishment be limited to those morally responsible for their actions, and only to the extent of such moral responsibility; they have difficulty in finding a satisfactory explanation for the constraints imposed by the responsibility principle.[81] That said, certain 'costly constraints', such as the requirement of mens rea, are often placed on the use of deterrence theories by those who advocate them; such constraints usually attempt to achieve one of two different aims.[82] Either they are used to achieve the general purpose of crime prevention, an aim that is fulfilled, inter alia, through ensuring that respect for the law exists;[83] or, alternatively, one places the deterrence model within a system of independent values, each of which, while not justifying punishment, nonetheless acts as a limiting influence upon its imposition.[84] The latter approach is advantageous in that it can regard justice (and thus the responsibility principle) as a value in itself that must be respected even if its effect on utility is negative; the former approach, while accepting that constraints

[79] Cf. Beyleveld (2000), 76.

[80] See Kant (1785), 429.

[81] Von Hirsch (1993), 152.

[82] Von Hirsch (1993), 147. Another aim could be efficiency in law enforcement: one could argue that as a matter of practicality it would be extremely difficult to design an efficient punishment regime without limiting the imposition of criminal sanctions to those responsible: Rawls (1967), 144 et seq.

[83] Respect for the law would be undermined by putting innocent people in prison; this reduces the value reinforcement effect of the law, and may ultimately increase crime levels. It should thus be avoided; hence the use of restraints. See Packer (1968), 65.

[84] See Packer (1968), 65–6.

may be necessary in some circumstances in order to maximize utility, ultimately fails to explain adequately why the responsibility principle should be adhered to if its imposition leads to net utility losses.[85]

Retributionists can claim that they, at least, do not violate the liberal requirement of respect for individual autonomy and the separateness of persons; they hold that humans are moral agents responsible for their actions and should only be punished to the extent that they are morally responsible for their behaviour. Such theories are not immune, however, from criticism in relation to their approach to moral reprobation. The main criticism relates to their inability to justify *criminal* sanctions for unwanted behaviour, in contrast to simple condemnation or social avoidance: while just deserts theories may well justify moral reprobation for a given behaviour, they alone do not explain exactly why such reprobation should translate into penal hard treatment. This objection is so compelling that it has led some retributionists to acknowledge the (secondary) role of forward-looking punishment in their theories.[86] For von Hirsch, for example, moral censure in and of itself is not sufficient to justify penal hard treatment; it should be 'supplemented' by a 'prudential disincentive'.[87] People are assumed to be moral agents capable of understanding the reprobative function of the law, but as they are human, and thus weak, they may fall foul of temptation and break the law. The penal sanction therefore acts as a supplementary preventative measure to reinforce the moral censure it embodies.[88]

(c) Practical implementation

While modern deterrence theories are *theoretically* capable of producing an exact quantum of punishment required for deterrence to occur, they can nonetheless be criticized on the basis of the practicalities encountered in their implementation. Three criticisms can be advanced.

First, the theoretically quantifiable variables themselves may not be so easy to calculate in practice. Therefore, while economic theory can indeed be used to set the quantum of punishment, its application in a real world scenario, where the variables may not be determined accurately, can prove difficult, if not impossible. Such problems, however, may be less restrictive when economic crimes are concerned. With price fixing, for example, economists have indeed made concerted efforts to determine an average mark-up, time period, and probability of detection.[89]

Second, strict adherence to the dictates of economic deterrence theory would lead, in certain circumstances, to the generation of counter-intuitive outcomes which on their face appear to violate (popular) community values of fairness or morality. Three scenarios are conceivable: (i) imposing extremely high penalties and low levels of enforcement for minor offences (so that overall costs will be reduced) in order to reach a given level of deterrence; (ii) the imposition of

[85] The latter approach is not without its problems, however; see Galligan (1981). It may be tempting to use a 'definitional stop' here and argue that if hard treatment is imposed upon an innocent person, then it is not actually 'punishment'; see Benn (1958), 332. According to Hart, however, no account of punishment can afford to dismiss this issue with a definition: Hart (1968), 6.

[86] Both Duff's and Finnis's accounts of retribution theory, for example, hold that it may be necessary to employ forward-looking concerns. See: Duff (1999), 52; Finnis (1980), 262–4; and Yeung (2004), 75–6. For criticism of the inability of retribution theories to 'substantiate the link between crime and punishment without relying on consequentialist considerations', see Bagaric and Amarasekara (2000).

[87] Von Hirsch (1993), 13. [88] Von Hirsch (1993), 13.

[89] See Chapter 3, Section D(b)(i) of this book.

increasingly lower penalties on those who continually break the law (as recidivism increases the rate of detection for those offenders); and (iii) ignoring the effects of an offence when setting the quantum of punishment according to the gain of the offender.[90] The above scenarios can be avoided, however, if one takes an instrumentalist view of the law, and calculates its deterrent effect by reference to (inter alia) the level of respect that it generates.[91] Nevertheless, such an approach would not prevent these scenarios from taking place if, following their occurrence, overall utility would be higher.

Third, by relying upon the assumption that potential offenders act rationally when deciding to break the law, deterrence theories are open to the criticism that they do not adequately reflect reality. Detractors could argue that rationality is not a dominant feature of the human condition, that many factors influence how people order their behaviour, and that, as a result, one cannot adequately predict how people will act in given situations.[92] Even so, the strength of this argument may vary depending upon the type of behaviour in question: some types of behaviour may be more 'rational' than others. The extent to which this argument is valid for cartel behaviour is therefore an important issue that needs to be considered.[93]

Unlike economic deterrence, just deserts models are not theoretically capable of providing an exact penalty for a given offence.[94] While the proportionality principle can act as a limiting or defining element in the determination of punishment, it cannot produce scientifically verifiable answers to the question of its severity. Indeed, not only are there disagreements about whether the principle should act as a guide or as a central concept in such an evaluation,[95] the severity of punishment to be imposed once a particular approach is agreed upon is also disputed. This is due to two reasons: (i) the difficulty in comparing unlike crimes in order to set the scale of ordinal proportionality;[96] and (ii) the difficulty in setting an anchor of punishment, i.e. cardinal proportionality, for any given crime, in particular because the perceived gravity of an offence is often a social construct.[97] Any attempt to use just deserts theory and its concepts of ordinal and cardinal proportionality[98] to set an adequate severity of punishment is therefore likely to be a relatively subjective exercise, and one prone to controversy.[99]

[90] This would be a particularly sensitive issue when the gain to the offender is significantly lower than the injury to the victim. This particular concern may not be very pressing for antitrust law, where victims often find themselves among thousands of others and where the gain to the offender is usually higher than the loss experienced by each individual victim.

[91] See Packer (1968), 65; his deterrence-based argument against the imposition of punishment on the morally innocent can be extended without difficulty to include the imposition of extremely harsh penalties on those who have committed relatively minor transgressions of the law.

[92] See, e.g., Bromberg (1965) and Zilboorg (1954), who both argue that man is governed by unconscious impulses and does not have systematic regard to the rational principle of maximizing one's welfare.

[93] On this, see Chapter 3, Section D(b)(ii) of this book.

[94] See Walker (1992a), 156–7. Cf. von Hirsch and Jareborg (1991).

[95] See Section B(c)(ii) of this chapter.

[96] See Hart (1968), 162–3.

[97] This is acknowledged by von Hirsch (1993), 19.

[98] Von Hirsch accepts, however, that the amount of punishment dictated by cardinal proportionality itself is limited and that as a result trivial crimes should not result in severe punishment such as imprisonment: von Hirsch (1993), 19.

[99] See Zedner (1994), 231.

D. The Current Relevance of Both Theories for EU Antitrust Enforcement

This section provides an insight into the extent to which deterrence and retribution are already pursued by current European anti-cartel enforcement policy.[100] By doing so, this section underlines the potential relevance of these theories of punishment in the European antitrust criminalization debate; but it also informs the analyses undertaken in the remainder of Part I of this book.

(a) The existing enforcement framework

Regulation 1/2003[101] is the specific piece of EU legislation which implements the competition rules laid down in, inter alia, Article 101 TFEU. As a result of this Regulation, the European Commission is empowered to impose administrative fines on undertakings which negligently or intentionally violate the European cartel rules.[102] Subject to certain limits, the Commission enjoys a wide discretion when imposing these fines,[103] in particular, 'as regards the choice of factors to be taken into account for the purposes of determining the amount of the fines'.[104] Regard must be had, however, to the gravity and duration of the violation.[105] Furthermore, the Commission cannot impose a fine exceeding 10 per cent of the undertaking's total turnover in the preceding business year.[106] In addition, the Commission is 'bound to comply with general principles of law, in particular the principles of equal treatment and proportionality' as developed by the jurisprudence of the EU Courts.[107] Neither Regulation 1/2003 nor its predecessor Regulation 17/62[108] explicitly states that antitrust enforcement must pursue the objective(s) of deterrence and/or retribution; in fact, both Regulations are silent as to the exact aims of EU antitrust enforcement. The objectives of such enforcement have, however, been articulated by the European Courts.

The jurisprudence of the Courts clearly establishes that deterrence is an essential element of the function of antitrust fines: when fixing the amount of a fine, the Commission must ensure that 'its action has *the necessary deterrent effect*, especially as regards those types of infringements which are particularly harmful to the attainment of the objectives of the Community'.[109] Indeed, for the Courts, the supervisory role of the Commission

[100] On EU anti-cartel policy generally, see McGowan (2010).

[101] Council of the European Union (2003) ('Regulation 1/2003'). On this Regulation, see generally Wils (2013).

[102] Council of the European Union (2003), Chapter VI, especially Article 23(2)(a).

[103] See Joined Cases C-189, 202, 205–8 and 213/02 P, *Dansk Rørindustri A/S and others v. Commission* [2005] ECR I-5425, [172]. This discretion is not contrary to the principle of legality: Case T-43/02, *Yungbunzlauer v. Commission* [2006] ECR II-3435, [69] et seq. For discussion of the (extremely wide) discretion of the European Commission in this regard, see: Hviid and Stephan (2009); and Stephan (2006).

[104] Case C-289/04 P, *Showa Denko v. Commission* [2006] ECR I-5859, [36]; and Case C-3/06 P, *Danone v. Commission* [2007] ECR I-1331, [37].

[105] Council of the European Union (2003), Article 23(3).

[106] Council of the European Union (2003), Article 23(2). With an association of undertakings, the upper limit is equal to 10 per cent of the sum of the total turnover of each member active on the affected market: Article 23(2).

[107] Case T-279/02, *Degussa v. Commission* [2006] ECR II-897, [77].

[108] Council of the European Economic Community (1962). Regulation 17/62 was the Regulation that implemented the EU competition provisions prior to the entry into force of Regulation 1/2003.

[109] Joined Cases 100–3/80, *Musique Diffusion Française and others v. Commission* [1983] ECR 1825, [106] (emphasis added).

in the context of antitrust law includes 'in particular, suppressing illegal activities and preventing their reoccurrence',[110] and any penalties imposed in connection with EU competition law should be 'effective, proportionate and persuasive'.[111]

Interestingly, the European Courts have stated that the function of (public) antitrust enforcement includes not only deterrence, but also 'punishment';[112] and the European Commission has acknowledged this dualist objective.[113] As stated by the GC, 'both the deterrent effect and the punitive effect of the fine are reasons why the Commission should be able to impose a fine'.[114] While the objectives of EU competition law are still being debated,[115] 'those of punishment are clear';[116] accordingly, in determining cartel fines, 'the considerations are the punishment of past, and deterrence of future infringements'.[117] In addition to deterring, then, the fines imposed are 'designed to punish the unlawful acts of the undertakings concerned'.[118] This punitive aspect of its sanctioning power enables the Commission to increase its fine beyond the profit expected by the undertaking in question.[119] Furthermore, the Courts have held that, as well as being persuasive, these fines must also be 'proportionate';[120] the Courts have thus emphasized the importance of a principle that is particularly relevant to retribution theory. It is no surprise, then, that retributivist considerations are not completely absent from the Commission's enforcement policies.

As noted above, it was the EU Courts—not EU legislators—which have articulated the aims of European (public) antitrust enforcement.[121] Regrettably, like their legislative counterparts, the EU judiciary has not actually determined the exact relationship between the objectives of deterrence and retribution in the context of cartel fines; indeed, this relationship remains unclear at present.[122] Over the years, the Commission has also failed to establish an explicit hierarchy between these two functions. At different times, the Commission's fining policy has relied to a lesser or greater extent upon aspects of both of these theories of punishment.[123] In the late 1990s, for example, it is arguable that 'punishment' was a noticeable feature of the Commission's fining policy. Nonetheless, it

[110] Case C-76/06 P, *Britannia Alloys v. Commission* [2007] ECR I-4405, [22].

[111] See Case 68/88, *Commission v. Greece* [1989] ECR 2965, [24].

[112] See, e.g.: Case 41/69, *ACF Chemiefarma v. Commission* [1970] ECR 661, [173]; Case T-329/01, *Archer Daniels Midland v. Commission* [2006] ECR II-3255, [141]; and Case C-289/04 P, *Showa Denko v. Commission* [2006] ECR I-5859, [16].

[113] See, e.g., European Commission (1983), [62].

[114] Case T-329/01, *Archer Daniels Midland v. Commission* [2006] ECR II-3255, [141].

[115] On this, see Geradin et al. (2012), [1.61] et seq.

[116] Torre (2013), 313.

[117] Torre (2013), 313.

[118] See: Joined Cases 100–3/80, *Musique Diffusion Française and others v. Commission* [1983] ECR 1825, [105] and [106]; and Case C-289/04 P, *Showa Denko v. Commission* [2006] ECR I-5859, [16].

[119] Case T-329/01, *Archer Daniels Midland v. Commission* [2006] ECR II-3255, [141].

[120] See, e.g., Case 68/88, *Commission v. Greece* [1989] ECR 2965, [24].

[121] Some academics have also been keen to articulate the correct objectives of public antitrust enforcement in the EU; see, e.g., Wils (2009) (arguing that deterrence and punishment (retribution) are the correct aims of public enforcement, and that the aim of compensation should be left to private enforcement).

[122] Mazák AG has, however, explained that a de facto hierarchy exists between public anti-cartel enforcement (with the objectives of deterrence and punishment) and private anti-cartel enforcement (with the objective of compensation): 'I consider that Regulation 1/2003 and the case-law of the Court have not established any *de jure* hierarchy or order of priority between public enforcement of EU competition law and private actions for damages. While no *de jure* hierarchy has been established, at present the role of the Commission and national competition authorities is, in my view, of far greater importance than private actions for damages in ensuring compliance with Articles 101 and 102 TFEU': Case C-360/09, *Pfleiderer AG v. Bundeskartellamt* [2011] ECR I-05161 (Mazák AG, [40] (footnotes omitted)).

[123] See Sections D(b) and D(c) of this chapter.

can also be argued that the current dominant objective of EU antitrust enforcement[124] is indeed the prevention of harm to competition in the common market (i.e. deterrence), and not the punishment of cartelists for so-called 'immoral' behaviour.[125]

(b) Deterrence theory and EU antitrust enforcement

It is very difficult in practice to divorce current European anti-cartel enforcement policy from the concept of deterrence; indeed, according to some commentators, deterrence is the 'most important element of competition enforcement'[126] and 'the central aim of cartel enforcement'.[127] In fact, it is hard to deny that according to EU competition enforcers '[e]ffectiveness in the field of the fight against cartels is ultimately about deterrence'.[128] Policy statements from the Directorate General for Competition ('DG Comp') often underline the need for effective deterrence of anticompetitive conduct, particularly cartel activity. One of DG Comp's major current external policy messages is 'effective deterrence'.[129] Indeed, in its 2013 'Management Plan', DG Comp expressly stated that 'cartels are clearly very harmful restrictions of competition and therefore high priority continues to be given to the effective detection and prosecution and thereby deterrence of cartels'.[130] These statements are not mere rhetoric either, as evidenced by the substantial fines imposed by the Commission in recent years.[131] Even the economic downturn post 2008 did not impact upon the Commission's desire to ensure deterrence by pursuing with vigour those firms that collude: no special approach was adopted to deal with 'crisis' cartels and Article 101 TFEU continued to be strictly applied to cartels.[132] Importantly, over the last number of years a number of soft law instruments have been adopted by the Commission which implement the policy message that cartels need to be deterred. The current (2006) Fining Guidelines,[133] for example, place deterrence theory at the centre of EU antitrust enforcement.[134]

According to those particular Guidelines, the Commission will use a two-step procedure when calculating its fines: (i) it sets a basic amount for each undertaking; and (ii) it adjusts this amount upwards/downwards depending upon the particular circumstances of the case.[135] In setting the basic amount, the Commission considers the pre-tax

[124] Of course, the objective(s) of enforcement (deterrence and/or retribution) should be considered to be conceptually different from the ultimate objectives of EU competition law (protection of the institution of competition, market integration, the maximization of consumer welfare, etc.). On the objectives of EU competition law—as opposed to the enforcement of that law—see generally Jones and Sufrin (2011), 38–54.

[125] See: Frese (2005), 5; and Joshua and Camesasca (2004), 5. This approach would be consistent with the thinking of the OECD: OECD (2002a).

[126] See Rosochowicz (2004), 757. According to Werden, 'deterrence is the only significant function of sanctions for cartel activity': Werden (2009), 24.

[127] Stephan (2008a), 25. See also: ICN (2005), 52–3; and OECD (1998). There is in fact a growing (international) literature on cartel deterrence; see generally Toby (2011).

[128] Guersent (2004), 44.

[129] See, e.g., European Commission (2010a), 37.

[130] European Commission (2013c), 7.

[131] See generally: de la Serre and Lagathu (2013); and de la Serre and Winckler (2012).

[132] See McGowan and Morgan (2012).

[133] European Commission (2006a). On these, see generally: de Broca (2006); Killick (2006); and Wils (2007b). For detailed criticism of these Guidelines, see Riley (2011).

[134] The leniency policy operated by the Commission (representing as it does a method of detecting cartelists) also highlights the importance of deterrence; see: European Commission (2006b), 3; and European Commission (2004a), [37]. Indeed, it has been posited that the 'very existence of leniency programmes suggests that competition enforcement recognises efficiency objectives and prioritises these over moral condemnation': Furse (2012), 46.

[135] European Commission (2006a), [9]–[11].

value of the undertaking's sales of goods/services to which the infringement directly or indirectly relates in the relevant geographic area within the EEA.[136] As a general rule, the proportion of the value of sales taken into account will not exceed 30 per cent.[137] The relevant proportion is then multiplied by the number of years of participation in the violation.[138] To this figure is added an 'entry fee' of 15 to 20 per cent of the value of sales.[139] This final figure represents the basic amount of the fine. Aggravating and mitigating circumstances can then be used to increase or reduce the fine respectively.[140] In the interests of deterrence, the Commission may impose higher fines on those undertakings which have a particularly high turnover beyond the relevant value of sales;[141] the Commission may also increase the fine in order to exceed the unlawful gains where it is possible to estimate them.[142] Importantly, too, in the interests of deterrence, the methodology in the Guidelines may be departed from in a particular case.[143]

At least four features of the current Fining Guidelines are clearly intended to ensure that deterrence actually occurs. The first feature concerns the proxy of up to 30 per cent of the value of sales, which is used to help the Commission to calculate the appropriate fine. This can be interpreted as an attempt to represent the unlawful gains obtained due to the cartel, and therefore reflects a preoccupation with the specifics of deterrence theory. The second feature concerns the ability of the Commission to impose higher fines on those undertakings that have a particularly high turnover beyond the relevant value of sales. This feature is clearly intended to ensure that deterrence is achieved: its rationale is that a fine imposed on large multi-product undertakings should not be too low compared to the overall ability to pay of the undertaking as a whole.[144] In fact, it helps to ensure that the fine imposed fulfils 'its objective of disciplining the infringing undertaking having taken into account its overall size'.[145] The third feature concerns the ability of the Commission to increase the fine in order to exceed the unlawful gains where it is possible to estimate them. This feature helps to avoid the situation where, in following the methodology of the Guidelines, the Commission would knowingly set the fine at a level which is 'obviously under-deterrent'.[146] The final feature is the ability of the Commission to depart from the methodology in the Guidelines in a particular case: the achievement of the objective of deterrence is held in higher regard than the mere observance of the above-noted methodology. It is clear, then, that in practice deterrence is a very influential theory for EU antitrust enforcement. Indeed, according to a recent empirical study, EU corporate cartel fines generally follow the precepts of optimal deterrence theory.[147] This finding is in accordance with the literature that holds that the 2006

[136] European Commission (2006a), [13] and [17].

[137] European Commission (2006a), [21]. [138] European Commission (2006a), [24].

[139] European Commission (2006a), [25].

[140] European Commission (2006a), [28]–[29].

[141] European Commission (2006a), [30]. The Court of Justice itself has held that 'the size of the undertaking concerned is one of the factors which may be taken into account for the purpose of calculating the fine and, therefore, setting the "deterrence multiplier"': Case C-289/04 P, *Showa Denko v. Commission* [2006] ECR I-5859, [29].

[142] European Commission (2006a), [31]. [143] European Commission (2006a), [37].

[144] De Broca (2006), 5.

[145] *Professional Video Tapes* (Case COMP/38.432), Commission Decision, 20 November 2007, [2008] OJ C57/10, [245]. For a national judgment with a similar viewpoint, see, e.g., *Napp Pharmaceutical Holdings Ltd v. DGFT* [2002] CAT 1, [502].

[146] De Broca (2006), 5. Indeed, 'a fine below the illicit gains could certainly never deter, not even under the unrealistic assumption that all infringements are detected and penalised': Wils (2007b).

[147] Connor and Miller (2013). This is not to say, however, that optimal deterrence has been achieved by the Commission, or indeed that optimal deterrence is capable of being achieved by the Commission with its current enforcement tools. On this, see Chapter 3, Section B(b) of this book.

Guidelines have a significant 'basis' in optimal fining,[148] even if they can be criticized for failing to articulate the exact (optimally deterrent) fines that the Commission should actually impose in practice.[149]

(c) Retribution and EU antitrust enforcement

As noted above, at different times the Commission's fining policy has relied to a varying extent on aspects of both deterrence and retribution. Elements of retribution theory are evident in the (repealed) Fining Guidelines from 1998.[150] This is arguably the case irrespective of the fact that those particular Guidelines apparently attempted to implement a policy of deterrence.[151] Notably, they display a lack of a firm economics-based methodology throughout, leaving 'undertakings unable to ascertain where their behaviour falls within the 1998 Guidelines'.[152] Indeed, despite their intention,[153] the 1998 Guidelines have generally been criticized as being obscure and linguistically vague.[154] Particular types of violations were allotted fine ranges, irrespective of their actual effects in practice and with no apparent link to the size of an optimal fine. The Guidelines essentially established a tariff-based system by reference to the 'seriousness' of the violation. Importantly, there was no explicit link between the gravity of a violation and a quantitative measure of its effect—'in fact a qualitative criterion was claimed to be the most important element'.[155] The 'nature' of the infringement was highlighted as being a crucial element in the analysis; no reference was made to the economic value of the market concerned.[156] In the context of cartels, then, it was the *nature of the agreement* concluded by an undertaking which was taken into account. Horizontal cartels were deemed to be 'very serious infringements' attracting likely fines of above ECU 20 million.[157] However, the essential calculations necessary for optimal deterrence theory to be implemented were not made. Fines were not based upon the turnover of the undertaking,[158] for example, and while fines were increased to take account of the duration of the violation, this was done without considering the actual harm or gain caused by a cartel in a given year.[159] For one commentator at least, this approach can reasonably be interpreted as an attempt to 'accomplish the punitive aim of the sanction, on the basis of a retributive setting'.[160]

The latest (2006) Guidelines on fines attempted to introduce an additional level of transparency and predictability to Commission fining policy.[161] These came at a time in the history of EU competition enforcement that was characterized by relatively high

[148] See Wehmhörner (2006). [149] Heimler and Mehta (2012), 104.

[150] European Commission (1998) ('1998 Fining Guidelines').

[151] Wils (2002), 71. Cf. Killick (2005), 13: the Commission's approach under the 1998 Fining Guidelines displays a 'fundamental absence of a theoretical underpinning'.

[152] Geradin and Henry (2005), 413.

[153] According to its Preamble, 'the principles outlined here should ensure the transparency and impartiality of the Commission's decisions in the eyes of the undertakings and of the Court of Justice alike': European Commission (1998).

[154] See: Geradin and Henry (2005); Joshua and Camesasca (2004); Killick (2005); Korah (1998); Richardson (1999); and van Bael (1995). For an overview of the use of the 1998 Guidelines in practice, see Veljanovski (2009).

[155] Camilli (2006), 592–3. [156] See European Commission (1998), [1.A].

[157] See European Commission (1998), [1.A].

[158] See Joined Cases C-189, 202, 205–8 and 213/02 P, *Dansk Rørindustri and others v. Commission* [2005] ECR I-5425, [225]. Some commentators have argued that in practice the value of the market was indeed taken into account by the Commission; see, e.g., Arbault (2003).

[159] See European Commission (1998), [1.B]. [160] Camilli (2006), 592–3.

[161] Wils (2007b).

fines[162] and a determination on behalf of the (then) Commissioner for Competition (Ms Neelie Kroes) to eradicate what her predecessor had termed the 'cancer' of cartel activity.[163] They can squarely be placed within a deterrence-based policy, as explained above. That said, a number of retributive features are also arguably present. The concepts of cardinal and ordinal proportionality were explained above and can be loosely transposed to the methodology in the 2006 Guidelines: the basic amount of a fine is set according to the gravity of the violation (itself determined by a percentage of the volume of sales in the affected market);[164] aggravating and mitigating circumstances may increase or decrease the fine respectively.[165] As a result of Regulation 1/2003, the Commission cannot impose a fine exceeding 10 per cent of the undertaking's total turnover in the preceding business year.[166] This limitation is acknowledged in the Guidelines.[167] By capping the maximum fine at 10 per cent of total annual global turnover, the EU institutions have attempted to ensure that fines are not 'disproportionate in relation to the size of the undertaking'.[168] If the size of the undertaking is interpreted as a proxy for the harm it can cause, the 10 per cent limit can be interpreted in turn as a crude implementation of one element of the proportionality principle of retribution theory (viz., proportionality between harm—as opposed to the degree of culpability for immoral behaviour—and the severity of the sanction). Furthermore, for those who believe optimal cartel fines (at 150 per cent of annual turnover in the cartelized market, according to Wils)[169] are disproportionate, it may operate in effect as a restraint on undue (optimal) punishment of the undertaking. Two other elements may also operate as retributive features: the entry fee of 15 to 25 per cent of the volume of sales (which, it must be noted, is imposed 'irrespective of the duration of the undertaking's participation in the infringement');[170] and the mark-ups for recividivists, uncooperative undertakings, ringleaders, and instigators.[171] These measurements are not related to the harm or illegal gain attributable to cartel activity (discounted for the probability of detection and prosecution) and should not usually figure in the calculation of an optimal fine.[172] It is true, however, that if the fine that is calculated according to the Guidelines (without implementing these features) is sub-optimal, these apparently retributive features may be interpreted merely as additional steps towards the achievement of an optimal fine.[173] Nonetheless, for the reasons given above, one can still argue that retribution is not a completely alien concept in EU antitrust law, hence its potential relevance in the European antitrust criminalization debate.

[162] See Veljanovski (2007).

[163] See, e.g., Kroes (2005a). For use of the anatomical phraseology under former Commissioner Mario Monti, see: Monti (2000), 1; and European Commission (2001a), 4.

[164] European Commission (2006a), [21].

[165] European Commission (2006a), [28]–[29].

[166] Council of the European Union (2003), Article 23(2).

[167] European Commission (2006a), [32]–[33]. A similar limitation under Article 15(2) of Regulation 17/62 was also acknowledged in the 1998 Guidelines: European Commission (1998), [5(a)].

[168] Joined Cases 100–3/80, *Musique Diffusion Française and others v. Commission* [1983] ECR 1825, [109].

[169] See Chapter 3, Section B(b) of this book.

[170] European Commission (2006a), [25].

[171] European Commission (2006a), [28].

[172] If the optimal fine is determined according to the unlawful gain model, these apparent retributive aspects can, however, be included within the calculation of an optimal fine. The optimal fine in this case will be *at least equal to* the gain: it can be higher and still be termed an optimal sanction.

[173] This is not to concede, however, that the optimal fine will actually be reached by these measures. On the problems with the 2006 Guidelines and fine optimality, see Chapter 3, Section B(b) of this book.

E. Conclusion

This chapter proceeded on the basis that one cannot examine effectively the challenge of applying a given justificatory theory of criminal punishment to the concept of 'cartel activity' without first understanding the substance of that theory. By first identifying and elucidating the relevant justificatory theories of criminal punishment, this chapter therefore facilitated more internally consistent, logical analyses of the theoretical challenges facing the process of antitrust criminalization—analyses which are conducted in later chapters.

Two potentially relevant justificatory theories of criminal punishment were identified: deterrence and retribution. These theories were deemed to be of potential relevance for antitrust criminalization because: (i) the current literature on criminal cartel sanctions focuses to varying degrees on both of these theories; and (ii) the objectives of deterrence and retribution are currently pursued—again to varying degrees—by the EU antitrust enforcers. Other theories of criminal punishment—rehabilitation and incapacitation—were found to be of less relevance than deterrence and retribution and so did not survive the filtration process conducted by this chapter.

The potentially relevant theories of deterrence and retribution present inherent limitations for those who wish to use them to justify the criminalization of a given behaviour. These general limitations were noted in this chapter. While this book does not attempt to create a general theory of criminalization that deals with these limitations, it does aim to analyse the theoretical challenges of criminalization in a specific context, namely that of antitrust enforcement. To understand these specific challenges fully, one should also be aware of the general limitations presented by the use of the relevant theories: some of the general limitations of a given theory may not be as pronounced in the context of antitrust criminalization as they are in other contexts, and vice versa. The extent to which this is true is examined below when necessary; this chapter merely provided the requisite detail for those particular examinations.

Finally, this chapter provided an overview of the current status of the enforcement theories of deterrence and retribution in EU antitrust law. This overview achieved two aims: (i) it underlined the potential relevance of these theories of punishment in the European antitrust criminalization debate; and (ii) it provided information which is crucial to the appreciation of the theoretical analyses undertaken in the remainder of Part I of this book.

An important caveat should now be advanced regarding this overview: its inclusion in a chapter containing sections on the justificatory theories of criminal punishment does not—and should not be taken to—imply that, since deterrence and retribution are already established aims of European antitrust law enforcement, one should ipso facto introduce personal criminal sanctions if they pursue such objectives. In fact, the analyses in this book are far more robust than that. They acknowledge that, even if a particular punishment theory is deemed to be of potential relevance to antitrust criminalization, this fact alone does not ensure that antitrust criminalization will inevitably be justified: potential relevance does not necessarily lead to theoretical robustness; hence the need for the second step in the approach adopted ('the process of application'). With this caveat established, one can now turn to the first treatment of the process of application: that concerning the criminal punishment justificatory theory of deterrence.

3

European Antitrust Criminalization and the Challenge of Deterrence Theory

A. Introduction

As noted in the preceding chapter, most legal commentators who advocate the imposition of personal criminal sanctions on individuals for engaging in cartel activity find inspiration for their arguments in the theory of deterrence. These commentators believe, in short, that criminal punishment represents an effective method of preventing the occurrence of such activity in a given economy.[1] They link, in other words, a criminal punishment theory with one of the objectives of European antitrust enforcement: the deterrence of anticompetitive behaviour. The key to an effective antitrust enforcement policy that ensures deterrence, so they argue, is the existence of the non-indemnifiable individual sanction of imprisonment. As observed by the OECD, '[a]s agents of corporations commit violations of competition law, it makes sense to prevent them from engaging in unlawful conduct by threatening them directly with sanctions and to impose such sanctions if they violate the law':[2] hence the rationale for a personal sanction. To avoid indemnification by the corporation, however, the personal sanction is coupled with the use of the criminal law—thereby introducing the (non-indemnifiable) threat of imprisonment—and accordingly becomes 'the most meaningful deterrent to antitrust violations'[3] and a forceful method of sending 'a message to other business executives about the risks and penalties for this kind of behaviour'.[4]

Such claims are bolstered by the (anecdotal) experience not only of officials,[5] but also of practitioners.[6] Unsurprisingly, they find expression in various governmental reports emanating from those countries which have introduced personal criminal antitrust sanctions. The report prepared for the UK Office of Fair Trading ('OFT') by Sir Anthony Hammond and Roy Penrose, for example, maintains that for potential cartelists 'the threat of custodial sentences should act as a significant deterrent',[7] while the (then) Department of Trade and Industry ('DTI') claimed that 83 per cent of the competition experts it interviewed believed that criminal penalties would improve the effectiveness of the UK regime, by increasing its deterrent effect.[8] Likewise, and among others, the Trade Practices Act Review Committee ('TPARC') in Australia was 'persuaded, in the light of the submissions made to it and growing overseas experience, that criminal sanctions deter serious cartel behaviour and should be introduced'.[9]

These types of statement expressly approve of the application of the justificatory criminal punishment theory of deterrence to the concept of cartel activity. It is

[1] See, e.g.: Baker (2001); Calkins (2007); Calvani (2004a); Ginsburg and Wright (2010); Stephan (2008a); Vogelaar (2008); Werden and Simon (1987); and Wils (2006b).

[2] OECD (2003b), 2. [3] Liman (1977), 630–1. [4] Bauer (2004), 307.

[5] See, e.g.: Baker (2001); and Hammond (2004), 8–9.

[6] See, e.g.: Calvani (2004b); and Ehlermann and Atanasiu (2003), 404 (Antoine Winckler: 'My experience as a legal practitioner is that criminal sanctions are an extremely effective deterrent').

[7] OFT (2001), [6.3]. [8] DTI (2001a), 25. [9] TPARC (2003), 163.

submitted that, given the significant resources required for the creation of a criminal antitrust regime, not to mention the potentially very serious consequences which face an individual cartelist subjected to a criminal process (i.e. imprisonment), one should not simply take these statements at face value. A robust analysis should be undertaken concerning the application of deterrence theory to cartel activity before deciding whether to introduce criminal sanctions (including imprisonment) as punishment for such activity. This chapter aims to undertake such a robust analysis: it represents the first treatment of the process of 'application' noted above in the methodology section of Chapter 1. Specifically, it examines the challenge of deterrence theory for antitrust criminalization and therefore whether deterrence theory can actually be relied upon as a solid foundation for such criminalization. By doing so, it also determines the extent to which deterrence theory should be relevant to the discussions concerning legalities and practicalities that occur respectively in Parts II and III of this book.

A three-step approach is adopted in this chapter in order to analyse the theoretical challenge of deterrence in the context of the criminalization of cartel activity. The first step identifies how the current European approach to cartel activity is deficient regarding deterrence. It relies to a large degree upon the overview of the current status of deterrence in EU antitrust enforcement provided in Chapter 2; it identifies the problems of deterrence that the introduction of criminal sanctions attempts to resolve. The second step applies the criminal punishment theory of deterrence to cartel activity. It employs the current literature in order to demonstrate how criminal sanctions (in particular imprisonment) can arguably be employed to rectify the deficiencies of the current approach to deterrence under EU antitrust law. In so doing, it attempts to construct a robust deterrence-based argument in favour of European antitrust criminalization. It is, however, imperative to remember here that this chapter does not aim to argue in favour of criminalizing cartel activity for the purposes of deterrence; rather, it sets out to analyse the challenge of justifying criminal cartel sanctions by reference to the theory of deterrence—hence the need for the third step. This particular step analyses the limitations of the 'robust' deterrence-based argument in favour of antitrust criminalization and consequently the theoretical challenge of deterrence. The final step is arguably the most important: it has the potential to negative the deterrence-based argument presented in favour of antitrust criminalization.

In following the above-mentioned methodology, this chapter is divided into three substantive sections. Section B outlines the deficiencies of the current approach to deterrence in EU antitrust enforcement. Section C uses the current literature to present a robust deterrence-based argument in favour of antitrust criminalization, an argument that attempts to address the identified deficiencies of the current approach to deterrence. Section D analyses the limitations of this deterrence-based argument and, hence, the theoretical challenge of deterrence in the context of antitrust criminalization. Some concluding observations are then offered.

B. Step 1: Identifying the Deficiencies of the Current Approach to Deterrence

It can be argued that the current European approach to deterring cartel activity is deficient in at least three respects: (i) its lack of individual sanctions; (ii) its imposition of inadequate fines; and (iii) its failure to subject cartel behaviour to adequate condemnation (for the instrumental purpose of deterrence).[10]

[10] See: Whelan (2008); and Whelan (2007).

(a) Lack of individual sanctions

As explained in Chapter 1, the Commission only imposes sanctions on undertakings, not their constituent individuals. Some have argued that this approach is sufficient in that the undertaking involved usually possesses effective means to prevent its employees from acting against its interests.[11] More recently, other scholars have disagreed.[12] It is argued that the ability of a firm to discipline its employees is limited to the impact of dismissal (itself undermined by the existence of alternative employment prospects) as well as the value of the personal assets of the employee in question.[13] This is especially so when the alternative to an (uncertain) dismissal for engaging in price-fixing is poor performance at work and certain adverse consequences, including dismissal.[14] In addition, there is a clear agent-principal issue when individual cartelists are not punished by law, as

> [t]he benefits of cartel membership are common to shareholders and managers alike: any increase in revenue to a company results in an increase in share value. Managers also gain from an increase in a firm's value; the extent of gain is determined by the remuneration scheme in place. In terms of costs, the picture is different. In the absence of individual sanctions, detection leads in most jurisdictions to administrative and/or monetary fines, borne by the firm as a whole. Shareholders bear all the prejudice, while managers may avoid direct personal punishment for their actions completely.[15]

It may also be the case that the employee is aware that he will have left the firm by the time the infraction is discovered.[16] (One should also understand here that a 'belated corporate punishment will harm individuals who did nothing wrong'.[17]) The firm could also be management controlled and fines may only represent a minor financial burden for each of the individual shareholders.[18] Furthermore, firms may have incentives not to take disciplinary actions against their employees: 'a disciplinary programme may be disruptive, embarrassing for those exercising managerial control, encouraging for whistleblowers, or hazardous in civil litigation against the corporation or its officers'.[19] These (persuasive) points may ensure that employees are not sufficiently deterred from behaving according to their own interests when they are in conflict with those of their employer. In addition, there is the problem that some firms may simply 'forgive or even reward their price-fixing employees—either directly or indirectly, legally or not—after they "take a bullet for the team" by going to prison'.[20] In any case, by not holding an individual *legally* responsible for his unlawful actions, one reduces somewhat the moral force of the cartel law rules, thereby undermining deterrence efforts. Finally, overuse of corporate, as opposed to individual, sanctions may result in lower internal corporate enforcement efforts, as undertakings become more anxious about unfavourable cartel investigations resulting from the possible publicity derived from the punishment of their staff.[21] Current EU enforcement efforts that only focus on undertakings therefore need serious reconsideration, particularly if deterrence is to be achieved in practice.

[11] See Posner (1976), 226.
[12] See, e.g.: Beaton-Wells and Fisse (2011a), 295–307; and Polinsky and Shavell (1993).
[13] Polinsky and Shavell (1993). [14] Polinsky and Shavell (1993); and Wils (2002), 208.
[15] Thépot (2011), 227.
[16] See Calkins (1997), 142. On this, see also Abrantes-Metz and Sokol (2013), 3.
[17] Calkins (1997), 142. [18] See Blair (1985).
[19] Beaton-Wells and Fisse (2011a), 299.
[20] Connor and Lande (2012), 440 relying upon, inter alia, Levine (2010) and Denvil (2010). Cf. Rosenboom (2012) (who demonstrates that Dutch managers involved in a cartel faced negative career effects (compared to a control group of Dutch non-cartel managers) after the prosecution of the cartel).
[21] See Arlen (1994).

(b) Inadequate fines

The theory of economic deterrence can be used to evaluate the size of fines that deter effectively.[22] As noted in Chapter 2, the optimal cartel fine should be set at least equal to the unlawful gain secured by the cartelist. There are a number of academic papers that aim to calculate this optimal cartel fine.[23] Wils in particular has analysed this concept in detail. In 2002, Wils argued that the fine required to ensure effective deterrence is, at its absolute minimum, equal to at least 150 per cent of the firm's annual turnover in the product market affected by the violation.[24] In 2005, he re-examined this figure, and although he varied the data involved in his calculation,[25] the size of the optimal fine did not change.[26] Calvani agrees with the estimation offered by Wils,[27] as do others.[28] Werden goes even further, however; he argues that the optimal cartel fine should be in the region of 200 per cent of annual turnover.[29] A figure of 150 per cent is obviously conservative compared to 200 per cent; if 150 per cent is accepted as an accurate measurement of the optimal cartel fine,[30] it provides a sufficient foundation upon which to construct the deterrence-based criminalization argument: to go even further and establish an optimal fine of 200 per cent will not be necessary. Consequently, this book will employ (and later examine) the figure of 150 per cent of annual turnover as the absolute minimum of an optimal cartel fine.

In Wils's original (2002) calculation, the size of the gain (at half the mark-up) was set at 5 per cent, the average cartel length at five years, and the probability of detection at one-sixth. All of these figures were determined using the then available empirical economic evidence. The size of the mark-up was estimated at 10 per cent by relying upon the road-building cartel cases of the 1980s and the subsequent use of this figure in the US Sentencing Guidelines.[31] Since this only represented the gain if price elasticity of demand ('PED') was zero,[32] adjustments were required to be made;[33] the gain was thus set at a significantly lower level of 5 per cent.[34] The literature available at that time suggested an average cartel lifespan of over six years.[35] Finally, the rate of detection took its inspiration from the only comprehensive study on the issue by Bryant and Eckard, involving a statistical birth and death model on a sample of 184 price-fixing cases for the period 1961 to 1988 to establish the rate at between 13 and 17 per cent.[36] Wils's (2005) recalculation, however, acknowledged that the original rate of detection and prosecution had presumably increased since 1988, due to the operation of leniency policies; this rate was therefore increased from one-sixth to one-third.[37] As a result of studies by the OECD[38] and Connor,[39] Wils also increased the figure taken for the cartel overcharge from 10 to 20 per cent.[40] By multiplying the mark-up (discounted to

[22] On this, see generally: Heimler and Mehta (2012); Manzini (2008); and Wils (2006a).

[23] See, e.g.: Calvani (2004a); Calvani (2004b); Werden (2009); Wils (2005b); and Wils (2002), Chapter 8.

[24] Wils (2002), 199 et seq.

[25] A higher rate of detection and a higher cartel mark-up were employed in order to take account of more recent literature on these concepts: Wils (2005b), 138 et seq.

[26] Wils (2005b), 138 et seq.

[27] See: Calvani (2004a); and Calvani (2004b).

[28] Including: Clarke and Bagaric (2003); and Vogelaar (2008).

[29] Werden (2009), 29.

[30] For criticism of this figure, see Section D(b)(i) of this chapter.

[31] US Sentencing Commission (1999), §2R1.1, 231. See also: Froeb et al. (1993); and Gallo et al. (1994), 58.

[32] The PED is a measurement of the responsiveness of the quantity of a product or service demanded to changes in its price; see generally Mankiw (2008), 90 et seq.

[33] On this, see Motta (2008), 219.

[34] See Wils (2002), 200.

[35] See: Connor (2003); Evenett et al. (2001), 1226; and Werden and Simon (1987), 925. Wils decided to be conservative and employ the figure of five years.

[36] Bryant and Eckhard (1991).

[37] Wils (2005b), 139–40.

[38] OECD (2002b).

[39] Connor (2004).

[40] Wils (2005b), 139.

take account of price elasticity) by the duration[41] and dividing it by the probability of being caught and prosecuted, one arrives (once more) at an optimal fine of 150 per cent of annual turnover. This is a crucial calculation and has a number of implications for EU anti-cartel enforcement. Most importantly for present purposes, it is used in the literature to construct a pro-criminalization argument, as demonstrated in Section C of this chapter. Before getting to that argument, a number of salient points need to be made concerning the figure of 150 per cent of annual turnover.

First, if one restates Wils's effective fine as 30 per cent of annual turnover in the affected product for each year of the violation, one can see that, leaving aside Regulation 1/2003[42] and other concerns, the 2006 Commission Guidelines on fines[43] are theoretically capable of imposing a fine reaching this figure: the highest starting point for cartel fines is 30 per cent of affected sales. However, fines would not always reach such a quantum despite the Commission's insistence that hard-core cartel fines will be imposed at the higher end of the spectrum: such fines presumably represent an extreme weapon in the antitrust enforcement armoury. This presumption can be supported by the wording of the Guidelines. First, the fine will only 'generally' be imposed at the higher end of the scale; it does not automatically occur and can in fact be anywhere between 15 and 30 per cent of affected sales. Second, the actual words employed, 'the higher end of the scale', do not state categorically that the 30 per cent figure will be used; indeed, 25 per cent could be seen as falling within this category. The point is this: anything less than 30 per cent for each year of the violation risks being considered an acceptable 'licence fee' that can be more than recouped by breaking the law.[44] The presumption that cartel fines would not always have a starting point of 30 per cent of value of sales is also supportable on the basis of the available empirical evidence. Connor, for example, has provided robust empirical evidence which demonstrates that, although under the 2006 Guidelines fines are certainly higher in practice than those imposed under the previous (1998) Guidelines, there has been significant reluctance on the part of the Commission to set a starting point at the higher end of the spectrum.[45] Of the first 22 cartel decisions of the Commission adopted following the publication of the 2006 Guidelines, all but three 'hovered near the bottom of the fining range'.[46] The three exceptions were 25, 21, and 20 per cent, with the remaining 19 cases establishing an average starting point of 17 per cent, which is, of course, a considerable distance from 30 per cent.[47]

Second, the figures used are conservative estimates.[48] For example, a detailed study by Connor and Lande, involving analysis of over 600 cases of cartel activity, argues that in Europe average overcharges were in the 28 to 54 per cent range;[49] only 20 per cent is assumed by Wils in his most recent calculation. Further, Connor and Lande also estimate the average lifespan of cartels to be seven to eight years,[50] whereas Wils decided to use the figure of five years. In fact, another study, this time focusing on 56 recent international cartels, found the average duration of an international cartel to be 6.6 years; and the median mark-up was estimated at 27 per cent.[51] In 2011, Combe

[41] The duration in Wils's 2005 calculation remained the same as that used in 2002, namely, five years.

[42] Council of the European Union (2003).

[43] European Commission (2006a).

[44] It is conceded, however, that: (i) the value of sales for each year of the violation is not the only determinant of the fine; (ii) the 'entry fee' will increase the fine; and (iii) aggravating and mitigating circumstances can be used to increase or reduce the fine respectively; see European Commission (2006a).

[45] Connor (2013). See also de la Torre (2010).

[46] Connor (2013).

[47] Connor (2013).

[48] See generally the Appendix to Connor and Lande (2012).

[49] Connor and Lande (2005). See also Connor (2007b).

[50] Connor and Lande (2005).

[51] Bolotova and Connor (2008).

and Monnier published their study which analysed 64 cartel decisions adopted by the Commission between 1975 and 2009.[52] The average duration of cartels in their sample was seven years, with a median of 5.6 years.[53] Most recently, Smuda, using a sample of 191 overcharge estimates and several parametric and semiparametric estimation procedures, found that the mean and median overcharge rates are 20.7 and 18.37 per cent of the selling price and that the average cartel duration is 8.35 years.[54] As regards the rate of detection, a 2008 study estimated a detection rate of 12.9 to 13.3 per cent in any given year in the EU during the period 1969 to 2007,[55] which is a rate considerably lower than the 33 per cent chosen by Wils. If any of these studies are representative,[56] fines far in excess of 150 per cent of annual turnover would be required to ensure effective deterrence; current Commission fining practice would, accordingly, be even more deficient.

Third, fines are often paid years after the gain from the cartel has been obtained; a reasonable rate of interest should consequently be assumed if one does not wish to underestimate the required fine.[57] It is axiomatic, then, that the minimum effective fine will be even higher than 150 per cent of annual turnover when such interest payments are taken into account.[58]

Fourth, it should be noted that if one were to use the 'harm to others' model—and not the 'unlawful gain' variant—to set the level of the fine, the percentage of annual turnover would be even higher, as the fine should include not only the wealth transfer, but also the 'deadweight loss' (i.e. the allocative inefficiency). In the literature, the 'deadweight loss' has been assumed to be in the region of 50 per cent of the overcharge[59] and has been estimated by Connor and Lande at somewhere between 3 and 20 per cent.[60] However, although an optimal fine based on 'harm to others' would indeed be higher, the fine would not be a minimum requirement; rather, it would represent the exact payment necessary in order to ensure optimal deterrence.[61]

Fifth, a significant (albeit ultimately removable) obstacle to the imposition of effective fines remains the legal limitation contained in Regulation 1/2003. By capping the maximum fine at 10 per cent of total annual global turnover, the EU institutions have attempted to ensure that fines are not 'disproportionate in relation to the size of the undertaking'.[62] Presumably, the authorities are concerned with the size of the undertaking because, inter alia, they do not wish to impose a fine that cannot be paid. They have placed, in any case, a considerable restraint on their ability to impose fines of the quantum dictated by the theory of economic deterrence.[63] As pointed out by Wils himself, fines of that size are very likely to exceed regularly the 10 per cent ceiling; they will exceed it in all cases except those where the violation concerns less than one-fifteenth of the products sold by the undertaking.[64] EU cartel fines, then, will more often than not fall below their optimal level.

[52] Combe and Monnier (2011).
[53] Combe and Monnier (2011), 240.
[54] Smuda (2014).
[55] Combe et al. (2008).
[56] On the problems with using empirical evidence to construct an optimal fine, see Section D(b)(i) of this chapter.
[57] See: Connor and Lande (2005), 518; and Lande (1993), 130–4.
[58] Werden includes a measure for interest rates in his estimation of the optimal fine: Werden (2009), 28.
[59] Easterbrook (1985), 455.
[60] Connor and Lande (2012), 457–61.
[61] This is so as the 'harm to others' model permits efficiency arguments, and is in reality a mechanism that forces the potential cartelist to compare his cost saving (from the cartel) with the 'deadweight loss' triangle: Breit and Elzinga (1986), 11; and Landes (1983), 656.
[62] Joined Cases 100–3/80, *Musique Diffusion Française and others v. Commission* [1983] ECR 1825, [109].
[63] Stephan (2008a), 177.
[64] Wils (2002), 202–3.

By relying upon the above points, one may well agree with Stephan's assertion that it is no surprise that the considerable fines imposed by the European Commission 'have been shown to fall well short of the illegal profits earned by the international cartels they ostensibly punish'.[65] This assertion is consistent with the views long held by the OECD Competition Committee[66] and is supported by the available empirical evidence.[67] Connor,[68] Connor and Miller,[69] Geradin and Henry,[70] and Veljanovsky,[71] for example, have all researched cartel fines and have come to the conclusion that fines are usually suboptimal and below the gains obtained by the cartel. More recently, Combe and Monnier have demonstrated that the 'risk of overenforcement is a myth' as 'fines regularly fall below the minimum illegal profit realized by the cartel'.[72] For them, fines imposed by the Commission from 1975 to 2009 would remain suboptimal even with a rate of detection of 100 per cent.[73] Smuda's detailed study is equally critical: 'a comparison between cartel overcharges and the existing fine level according to the current [2006] EU Guidelines shows that collusion has been a lucrative business for most firms from an ex-post perspective'.[74]

(c) Lack of adequate condemnation

It can be argued that fines fail to reflect an adequate level of condemnation of cartel activity as an instrumental factor in ensuring deterrence. At least three points can be advanced in support of this assertion. First, only the undertaking is subject to an administrative fine; its employees, i.e. those ultimately responsible for the active implementation of the cartel scheme, are not held accountable before the authorities. Actual condemnation, then, occurs at one level removed from the natural persons involved in the cartel. It is believed that the undertaking will discipline its own employees; a form of official condemnation by proxy is therefore assumed to exist. However, as explained above, the ability of the undertaking to discipline its agents is not without serious drawbacks. Even with this ability, it is not guaranteed that firms will actually discipline those involved, especially considering that the employees' actions may have been motivated by the interests of their firm, and that the expected gain from the unlawful activity for the undertaking may well have been in excess of the actual fine imposed. This argument is consistent with a survey of legal opinion conducted in the mid-1980s which revealed that one of the significant reasons for cartel activity included the fact that subordinates did not believe that company management actually wanted to respect the law.[75] Second, as seen above, current fines imposed by the Commission are in the vast majority of cases merely a 'licence fee' that must be paid in order to access the (more extensive) gains acquired from cartel activity. Pricing of the unlawful activity at such a low level undermines the expression of any resultant condemnation. By taxing instead of prohibiting[76] cartel activity, one sends out a signal that society does not disapprove of such behaviour as strongly as it does (or would

[65] Stephan (2010b), 347.

[66] See OECD (2005), 26: 'It is widely believed that corporate sanctions in the form of fines are almost never sufficiently high to be an optimal deterrent'. Cf. Motta (2008).

[67] For a survey of the fines actually imposed by the EU authorities in recent years, see, e.g., Connor (2013).

[68] Connor (2006).

[69] Connor and Miller (2010).

[70] Geradin and Henry (2005).

[71] Veljanovski (2007). See, however, Veljanovski (2011).

[72] Combe and Monnier (2011), 267.

[73] Combe and Monnier (2011), 267.

[74] Smuda (2014).

[75] Feinberg (1985), 380.

[76] See: Coffee (1992), 1876–7 and 1882–7; Cooter (1984), 1523; and Shavell (1987), 590.

if sufficient understanding of the concept of a cartel existed). Third, by refusing to use criminal sanctions for cartel activity, the authorities invite the criticism that they do not seek the same level of condemnation for cartel activity as they do for other (comparably harmful or, indeed, less harmful) white-collar crimes, such as conspiracy to defraud.[77]

C. Step 2: A 'Robust' Criminalization Argument: Employing Criminal Punishment to Rectify the (Deterrence-Related) Deficiencies Identified

This section applies the criminal punishment theory of deterrence to cartel activity.[78] It relies upon the current literature to argue how personal criminal sanctions (in particular imprisonment) can be employed to rectify the above-mentioned deficiencies of the current approach to deterrence under EU antitrust law. In doing so, it attempts to construct a robust deterrence-based argument in favour of European antitrust criminalization. This section aids the (later) identification of the limitations of the deterrence-based antitrust criminalization argument, an identification that facilitates the analysis of the theoretical challenge of deterrence.

(a) Individual punishment

It was detailed above how one can argue that current EU anti-cartel enforcement is not an effective deterrent as it is concerned solely with undertakings and not individuals. Problems included the inability of firms to discipline employees effectively, the existence of perverse incentives directly occasioned by excessive use of corporate sanctions, and a deficiency in individual condemnation. One could argue that the use of personal criminal punishment avoids these problems: the state can discipline cartelists through coercive measures, including imprisonment; perverse incentives are avoided[79] as those actually responsible for cartels will be held accountable;[80] and criminal sanctions, by definition, involve a significant degree of moral condemnation.[81] Further, individuals may be compelled by a normative (moral) commitment to obey the law that is not felt by undertakings.[82] Finally, individual sanctions may well strengthen a (natural) person's 'moral imperative' to overcome any blind commitment to an ingrained common mindset in a given organization concerning the acceptability of cartel activity.[83] None of this should suggest, however, that corporate sanctions are not required;[84] in fact, such sanctions may also be necessary under deterrence theory.[85] One could argue that if this were not so, firms would have the incentive to encourage cartel activity among their employees, to reduce or eliminate any monitoring activities, and/or to deal lightly

[77] See generally Clarke (2005), 152–4. Cf. Boberg (2010), 96–7.

[78] For earlier treatments of this topic, see: Whelan (2008); and Whelan (2007).

[79] Individual punishment is in fact widely understood to be a very useful method of rectifying the agent-principal issue noted above; see, e.g., Leslie (2008).

[80] Cf. Beaton-Wells and Fisse (2011a) (who question whether the DoJ's approach to criminal cartel enforcement actually achieves individual accountability (rather than general deterrence) in practice).

[81] See Lynch (1997), 39–40.

[82] Stone (1991), 389. [83] Khan (2012), 78–82. [84] See Morgan (2010), 79–80.

[85] It was noted in Chapter 1, Section C(b) that the issue of 'corporate' as opposed to 'individual' punishment is outside of the scope of this book; hence this book does not attempt to analyse the arguments noted in relation to corporate punishment.

with any employee transgressions.[86] As Baker notes, corporate fines 'are necessary to give the enterprise a serious stake in educating, supervising, and monitoring employee performance'.[87] Such fines, then, help to motivate competition compliance programmes within firms and in doing so can help competition authorities to achieve the objective of deterrence.[88] Other reasons for including corporate sanctions could include economies in enforcement costs[89] and the increased potential for plea bargaining.[90]

(b) Threat of custodial sentences

One can argue, as noted above, that EU anti-cartel enforcement practice is deficient in that fines are usually lower than their effective level due, amongst other things, to the legal limitations of Regulation 1/2003. It is tempting to reply that fines should be increased and that the 10 per cent cap should be removed.[91] Indeed, according to the literature, increasing a fine to achieve optimal deterrence would cost less (i.e. would be more efficient) than imposing a non-monetary sanction such as a prison sentence.[92] But those who support European antitrust criminalization would argue that this approach would not solve the fundamental problems associated with antitrust fines. Indeed, for them, one of the main reasons why individual *criminal*, as opposed to *administrative*, sanctions should be imposed for cartel activity is that imprisonment—a reserve of the criminal process—helps, inter alia, to overcome the significant problems associated with optimally deterrent fines, in particular inability to pay, difficulties with individual (financial) responsibility, and proportional justice. Such punishment may also negate the criticism that current anti-cartel enforcement lacks adequate condemnation of offenders (as an instrumental factor in ensuring deterrence).

(i) Inability to pay

An optimal fine of the magnitude discussed above (i.e. 150 per cent of annual turnover) would in most cases exceed the undertaking's ability to pay. First, the fine imposed is significantly higher than the gain derived from cartel activity as one must take account of the fact that rates of detection are never 100 per cent. The firm, then, will not actually have received payment from the cartel of the magnitude of the optimal fine. Second, as there is an appreciable time lapse between the occurrence of the cartel and the imposition of the fine, it is highly likely that any profits gained would already have been paid out in taxes, dividends, salaries, and/or wages.[93] Indeed, according to Werden and Simon, there is empirical evidence to demonstrate that unions capture most of the monopoly profits earned by US manufacturing firms.[94] It is no surprise, then, that the literature has offered an estimate of 18 per cent as the percentage of firms convicted of price fixing that would have had sufficient resources to pay an optimal fine.[95] This figure would have been

[86] See Baker (2001), 699. [87] Baker (2012), 2.

[88] Rodger (2005), 358. Criminalization can also impact on compliance programmes; see, e.g.: Furse and Nash (2004a), Chapter 7; and Stephan (2009c).

[89] Coffee (1981), 387, footnote 6. [90] See Wils (2002), 217–18.

[91] On the removal of the 10 per cent cap, see Frese (2005), 14–15.

[92] See: Becker (1968); Elzinga and Breit (1973); and Posner (1980b).

[93] Werden and Simon (1987), 928.

[94] Werden and Simon (1987), 928, citing Karier (1985) and Salinger (1984).

[95] Craycraft et al. (1997), whose study was based on a sample of 386 convicted firms between 1955 and 1993.

even lower had the study not omitted all defendants for which financial data could not be found.[96] Bankruptcy itself is not an acceptable by-product of the pursuit of optimal fines. Liquidating a firm's assets will rarely generate enough funds to pay an optimal fine; only large, diversified corporations with extremely high assets to sales ratios would have the ability to pay.[97] Further, the effects of bankruptcy go beyond those required for optimal deterrence; undesirable social costs are imposed on those with interests in the firm who are innocent of cartel activity, such as employees, creditors, customers, suppliers, and the taxpayer.[98] Calvani notes in this context that forcing a company into liquidation would not be a politically acceptable move; for him it is 'very doubtful whether any parliament would have the stomach for what is the equivalent of corporate capital punishment for price-fixers'.[99] Bankruptcy would also result in further concentration of the market.[100] This is something to be avoided:

> It is generally recognized as undesirable for an enforcement action to result in the removal of a competitor, for then the benefits of restored competition will be lost or, at least, reduced.[101]

Inability to pay will therefore be used by the authorities to reduce the fine imposed on an undertaking,[102] resulting in a suboptimal level of deterrence. According to those in favour of criminalization, this (deterrence-related) deficiency can be rectified effectively through the use of imprisonment (which would be imposed upon the responsible individual cartelists within the undertaking), a non-financial penalty without such direct adverse effects upon other stakeholders in the convicted company.[103] This line of argument is also consistent with Posner's contention that imprisonment should only be imposed as a last resort when the company (and the individual) is unable to pay an optimal fine.[104]

(ii) Individual (financial) responsibility

Although fines imposed on individuals help to achieve deterrence, it is arguable that sole reliance upon such measures should be avoided. For one, evaluating the exact size of an optimal fine for individuals, as opposed to firms, would involve a level of analysis for which courts may be ill-equipped.[105] The courts may also display a hesitancy to engage in the process of determining an optimal fine, as appears to have occurred in the leading Irish criminal cartel case of *Duffy*,[106] where all of the relevant benchmarks used to determine an optimal fine were open to the Court, but none was employed.[107] More importantly, however, the difficulty of preventing firms from indemnifying their employees for any cartel fines[108] helps to ensure that the corporate cost/benefit analysis described above (and the resultant 150 per cent of annual turnover as the minimum

[96] Werden (2009), 30, footnote 67. [97] Werden and Simon (1987), 929.

[98] Kraakman (1984), 882. However, even fines below the level of inability to pay may involve undesirable side-effects, e.g. increased prices. See: Coffee (1981), 401–2; and Wils (2002), 205.

[99] Calvani (2006), 271. [100] Calvani (2004b), 9; and Schoneveld (2003), 448–9.

[101] Jacobs (2007), 34. Cf. Schoneveld (2003), 449 ('there are likely to be few situations where one company's failure would be a real danger to competition').

[102] See European Commission (2006a), [35]. [103] See Wils (2005b), 141.

[104] See Posner (1979–80).

[105] See Calvani (2004b), 10. It is also true that the individual may be unable to pay the optimal fine: Calvani (2004b), 10.

[106] *DPP v. Duffy and Duffy Motors (Newbridge) Ltd* [2009] IEHC 208.

[107] Gorecki and Maxwell (2013b), 246.

[108] On this see: ICN (2005), 65; and OECD (2007b), 19–20. According to one authority, 'there is a significant, virtually unavoidable risk that corporations will pay individuals' fines': King (2010), 17.

fine) is still applicable, even when it is the firm's employees who are facing the formal financial sanction. Employees act as proxies for their company and, in the absence of non-financial punishment (or an optimal fine that, in all likelihood, results in the firm's liquidation), will be incentivized (by their employer) to enter into cartels on their employer's behalf.[109] The threat of imprisonment overcomes both of these shortcomings: since cartelists are unlikely to accept payment to go to prison for their firm,[110] a specific 'cost price' cannot be put into the equation of cost versus benefit in their evaluation of the expected net gain of their activities. As stated by Chemtob, 'criminal enforcement has the potential to improve deterrence markedly by introducing non-monetary costs into the equation'.[111] This increase in deterrent effect may be particularly noticeable among the professional classes or those who have 'invested' a great deal in their reputation.[112] This argument is supported to a degree by empirical evidence: according to the available data (which, admittedly, is only relevant up until 2003), never has an individual accused of cartel activity in the US offered to go to jail in lieu of paying a fine.[113] Given this context, it is not really surprising that some jurisdictions believe that the deterrent effect of imprisonment is a major factor that contributes to the success of their leniency/immunity programmes.[114]

(iii) Proportional justice

It is also arguable that the imposition of optimally deterrent fines, unlike imprisonment, risks conflicting with the concept of proportional justice.[115] This is due to the fact that detection rates are relatively low and that consequently deterrent fines are multiple (i.e. at least six) times the size of the unlawful gain obtained.[116] Such concerns may not be significant when criminal punishment is contemplated:

> The penalty for cartel behaviour should fit the crime. Penalties should reflect the fact that cartels inflict enormous consumer harm with no likelihood of corresponding efficiency gains. Penalties should also take into account the facts that cartelists' motivation is strictly financial and that cartelists are quite capable of making a cost/benefit decision that factors in an occasional discovery and fine as a cost of doing their illegal business. Therefore, cartel penalties not only should be large enough to remove financial incentives, but also should look at past financial incentives to affect cartelists directly: cartel penalties should include substantial jail time for responsible individuals.[117]

In New Zealand, Section 80A-B of the Commerce Act 1986 expressly prohibits indemnification of a cartel fine; but this 'prohibition is not infallible and could potentially be circumvented by individual bonuses that circumspectly include a risk premium': Boberg (2010), 91. On indemnification, see also Bucy (1991).

109 It is interesting to note here that according to the US DoJ at least, it 'has rarely, if ever, seen a case where an employee who committed an antitrust violation was acting solely for [his] own benefit and not the company's': Kolasky (2002), 14. See also Parker and Nielsen (2008), 583 (the 'history of antitrust prosecutions is rife with examples of ministerial employees who participated in the crime even though they personally would not profit').

110 On this, see: Barnett (2009); and Liman (1977), 630–3. Cf. Coffee (1980), 423–4.

111 Chemtob (2000), 19. Cf. Australian Industry Group (2002), 61.

112 See Katyal (1997), 2416.

113 OECD (2003b), 100.

114 See OECD (2003b), 49 (Canada), 68 (Israel), 79 (Norway), and 100 (the US).

115 Sunstein et al. (2000); and Wils (2002), 206–7.

116 Cf. Parker (1989), 563–6, who argues that by choosing an offence with a lower probability of detection, one deserves a higher penalty.

117 Barnett (2006b), 4.

According to (the US antitrust official) Barnett, then, proportional justice concerns are easily overcome, particularly given the harm caused by cartels, as well as the risk-reward analysis that is undertaken by the cartelist.

(iv) Deterrence through condemnation

Finally, it is often argued that criminal punishment, in particular imprisonment, establishes a noteworthy degree of condemnation for what is significantly harmful and unjustifiable behaviour.[118] By actually imposing custodial sanctions for cartel activity, the authorities express how seriously they consider such behaviour and in so doing—it is argued—deter potential cartelists.[119] As Posner indicates, criminal sanctions 'are not really prices designed to ration the activity; the purpose so far as possible is to extirpate it',[120] hence their condemnatory nature. For corporate individuals, with their particular sensitivity to public censure and deprivation of liberty, the threat of imprisonment would not go unnoticed.[121] One should understand here that the 'average white collar criminal fears the shame of a prison term more than a fine, which is not so shameful'.[122] He also presumably fears the stigma associated with a criminal conviction (whether it concerns a fine or custodial sentence) more than any embarrassment caused by an adverse decision of a civil court.[123] Furthermore, prison sentences carry a stronger message than fines as they are more newsworthy and are more noted by other business people; they therefore arguably reduce ignorance about the law and, according to some, enhance deterrence.[124] This particular argument was one of the expressed rationales for introducing the UK Cartel Offence.[125]

D. Step 3: Identifying and Analysing the Limitations of the Criminalization Argument Advanced (and Therefore the Challenge of Deterrence Theory)

This section uses the deterrence-based criminalization argument advanced above to identify and analyse the limitations of the theory of deterrence in the context of antitrust criminalization. It was noted in Chapter 2 that, to understand fully the specific theoretical challenges of antitrust criminalization, one should also be aware of the general limitations presented by the relevant theories: some of the general limitations of a given theory may not be as pronounced in the context of antitrust criminalization as they are in other contexts, and vice versa. In identifying and analysing the relevant limitations of the deterrence-based criminalization argument, this section takes account of this fact: when necessary, it considers the general limitations of deterrence theory in the specific context of antitrust criminalization. It is submitted that the challenge of

118 See, e.g., Clarke (2005), 152–4.

119 Baker and Reeves (1977), 625.

120 Posner (1985), 1215.

121 Furse and Nash (2004b), 140.

122 Posner (2000), 89. See also: Posner (2000), 108–10; and Kahan (1997).

123 See Comino (2006), 438.

124 Liman (1977), 631–2; Lynch (1997), 47; and Werden and Simon (1987), 943.

125 See the comments of Patricia Hewitt MP in Hansard, House of Commons Debates, 10 April 2002, Column 47: 'We regard forming cartels as very serious offences, and the threat of imprisonment is important to deterring them. The new criminal offence will send out a strong message to the perpetrators, their colleagues in business, the general public, and the courts'.

overcoming the identified limitations of the deterrence-based criminalization argument represents the main theoretical challenge of deterrence in the context of antitrust criminalization: a deterrence-based criminalization argument can be constructed, as demonstrated above; importantly, however, its actual strength is determined by the extent to which the limitations identified are problematic.

(a) The 'appropriateness' of criminal antitrust sanctions in the absence of (negative) moral content

Debate surrounding the use of criminal sanctions for what is considered to be 'morally neutral' or 'morally ambiguous' conduct has been going on for almost three-quarters of a century. While there are of course morally neutral/ambiguous offences,[126] it does not necessarily follow that morality is no longer a concern for those who advocate criminalizing a given behaviour, including cartel activity.[127] Of continuing importance is the question of whether the criminal law should extend beyond its traditional conception of criminality and concern itself with conduct which does not attract the unequivocal moral opprobrium of the community. The answer to that question not only has repercussions for current criminal laws, but may also influence the success or failure of a proposed antitrust criminalization plan. For some,

> [w]ithout general community consensus that egregious anti-competitive conduct is criminal and ought to be punished rather than deterred, it may be appropriate that such commercial contraventions continue to be penalised civilly... rather than introduce a regime of criminal sanctions.[128]

Indeed, if the use of deterrence theory to justify criminal antitrust sanctions results in the creation of a morally neutral criminal offence, a number of negative consequences may be engendered.[129]

According to some legal commentators, applying the criminal law to morally neutral/ambiguous conduct is not only unjust, but is also counterproductive, in that by unfairly labelling offenders as criminals, the moral authority of the law is undermined, resulting as a consequence in a weakening of the deterrent value of criminal sanctions.[130] As Sayre noted many years ago:

> When the law begins to permit convictions for serious offences of men who are morally innocent and free from fault, who may even be respected and useful members of the community, its restraining power becomes undermined. Once it becomes respectable to be convicted, the vitality of the criminal law has been sapped.[131]

The criminal law, then, 'is not merely a device for promoting particular economic and social ends', but is 'directed to the moral standards of society'.[132] For the Law Commission, 'criminal law should only be employed to deal with wrongdoers who deserve the stigma associated with criminal conviction because they have engaged in seriously reprehensible conduct'.[133] Ashworth argues a similar point when he posits that the 'central function' of the criminal law involves: '(a) the declaration of forms of wrongdoing that are (b) serious enough to justify (c) the public censure inherent in conviction and (d) punishment'.[134] Some even contend that applying the criminal sanction to morally neutral conduct in fact 'decriminalizes' the criminal law, and taken to its extreme

[126] See, e.g., Green (2004).
[127] See Parker and Nielsen (2008), 601.
[128] Castle and Writer (2002), 23–4.
[129] See Whelan (2009a).
[130] Green (1997), 1536.
[131] Sayre (1933), 79–80.
[132] Burns (1958), 112.
[133] Law Commission (2010), [1.28].
[134] Ashworth (2008), 408–9.

either results in nullification or, more subtly, a changing of people's attitudes towards the meaning of criminality.[135] For them, the criminal law should be concerned solely with conduct which unequivocally attracts the moral opprobrium of society; it should in other words concentrate on 'traditional' crimes and not morally neutral conduct.[136] They argue that, in the absence of such a restraint, the criminal law may begin to lose its legitimacy.[137]

Such arguments, however, do not entertain the possibility that by criminalizing cartel activity one may influence others as to how they perceive the nature of that behaviour.[138] In other words, such arguments ignore the educative function of the criminal law. More specifically, they do not allow for the criminal law actually to *create*, and not just *reflect*, a moral opprobrium for what is, at least according to those who legislate, undesirable behaviour, albeit behaviour failing somewhat short of 'immoral' according to a significant percentage of the population. It is difficult to deny that there is some reciprocal relationship between the content of the criminal law and society's perception of the morality of the conduct it regulates.[139] According to Coffee, the line between malum in se and malum prohibitum has been crossed many times and has largely been discredited—particularly in the field of white-collar crime—and in fact the public learns a significant deal of its morality from what is punished by the criminal law.[140]

Even if one accepts that the criminal law has an educative function, it does not necessarily follow that it should be unrestrained in its attempts to develop a morality. First, there is the so-called problem of 'sticky norms'.[141] This problem of resistance to change can occur when there is a wide disparity between the views of the criminal law and those of society in general as regards the moral character of a given conduct. To avoid such a situation, one may need to apply 'gentle nudges' as opposed to 'hard shoves'. Such nudges, with their relatively mild degrees of condemnation, can help to initiate 'a self-reinforcing wave of condemnation', thereby allowing legislators to increase the severity of the law at a later date without facing resistance from decision-makers such as prosecutors, judges, and juries.[142] Second, given the arguments above, one must be conscious of the fact that overusing the criminal law will ultimately reduce its moral stigma and therefore undermine the aim of educating citizens as to the immoral character of the conduct. So, while an educative function is accepted, it cannot be unrestrained, lest the distinctive stigma of the criminal law be lost and the attempts to change attitudes fail. The problem here, then, is to decide where to draw the line. One method of filtering suitable from unsuitable candidates for criminalization would involve gauging the morality of the conduct not by the standards of society at large, but by those of a particular (relevant) well-developed industry or profession.[143] Another, perhaps more useful, method would focus on the temporal relationship between the civil and the criminal law.[144] Using this method, one would first use the civil law to harden attitudes towards a given conduct before moving at a later time (i.e. when the norm has become internalized) to the criminal law so as to prohibit rather than to price this conduct.[145] So, when assessing whether to create a moral norm with the educative function of the criminal law,

135 Packer (1968), 359.
136 Richardson et al. (1982), 14–15.
137 See: Allen (1981), 738; Galligan (2007), 228; Kadish (1963), 425–6; Packer (1968), 359; and Robinson (1996).
138 See Stucke (2006), 537.
139 Coffee (1991), 200. See also Ball and Friedman (1964), 217.
140 Coffee (1991), 200. See also: Soper (1985), 85; Tyler and Darley (2000), 714–24; and Williams (2011), 295–8.
141 Green (2004), 507–8.
142 Kahan (2000).
143 Coffee (1991), 201.
144 Coffee (1991), 201.
145 Coffee (1991), 201.

one would first ensure that the conduct underlying that prospective norm has already been nurtured by virtue of the processes of the civil law. This process has arguably already begun in Europe concerning cartel activity: such conduct is prohibited by Article 101 TFEU and results in the imposition of large corporate fines. Such 'norm nurturing' may explain to a degree why 60 per cent of British citizens surveyed in 2007 believe that cartel activity is a dishonest practice.[146]

Although not all criminal offences involve intrinsic moral wrongs, the more negative that conduct is in terms of its moral qualities, the likelier it will be appreciated as undesirable conduct requiring criminal sanctions,[147] and the easier it would be to employ the educative function of the criminal law, particularly if attitudes have been hardened by an already-existing civil enforcement regime. Even further, a number of important advantages can be achieved if a proposed criminal antitrust offence relates to conduct which is morally questionable, advantages which may be lost if morality is overlooked, such as a reduction in enforcement costs due to an internalization of the moral norm.[148] Indeed, '[s]ocial norms opposing cartels have the potential . . . to complement sanctions and encourage desistence'.[149] Criminalization of so-called 'acceptable' cartel behaviour may increase the probability of a negative outcome, such as nullification or a change of attitudes towards the nature and fairness of the criminal law:

> Legal enforcement mechanisms cannot function unless they are based on a broad consensus about the normative legitimacy of the rules—in other words, unless they are backed by social norms.[150]

In fact, some believe that the success of a project of antitrust criminalization 'depends on the emergence of a genuine sense of "hard core" delinquency, without which effective regulation by means of criminal law is unlikely to be achieved'.[151] In order to avoid undesirable outcomes with antitrust criminalization, one could create an antitrust law which has a sufficient degree of moral content. Chapter 4 below considers in detail the extent to which cartel activity can be conceptualized as 'immoral'. The point here, however, is that the deterrence-based criminalization argument may be weakened somewhat if cartel activity does not have a sufficient degree of moral content.[152]

(b) The difficulty of applying *economic* deterrence theory to justify criminalizing cartel activity

In conformity with the current literature,[153] the deterrence-based argument advanced above is founded upon the *economic* variant of the criminal punishment theory of deterrence. As noted in Chapter 2, there are a number of inherent limitations involved in the employment of this particular variant of deterrence theory to justify the criminalization of any given behaviour. The extent to which these limitations are problematic in the specific context of cartel activity—and therefore the extent to which they contribute to the theoretical challenge of deterrence—is considered below.

146 See Stephan (2008e). 147 See, e.g., Packer (1968), 262.
148 For a more detailed overview of the advantages of a finding of immorality in the context of antitrust criminal sanctions, see Stucke (2006), 505–24.
149 Stephan (2010b), 355. See also MacCulloch (2009), 260.
150 Fehr and Fischbacher (2004), 185. 151 Harding (2006), 183.
152 On this, see also Quaid (2012), 169. 153 See, e.g., Furse (2012), Chapter 2.

(i) The use of empirical data to construct an optimal fine

The employment of an economics-based theory of criminalization in practice calls for the existence of robust empirical data. An argument employing such theory is, therefore, by definition, limited: current empirical evidence in support of different elements of an argument may eventually be called into question, if not completely undermined, by later (more robust) empirical evidence. When empirical evidence does not exist, (non-empirical) reasoning may take its place; but such reasoning is merely a substitute for empiricism and may be trumped by relevant evidence if and when it becomes available.

This caveat should be understood by those who seek to comprehend the limitations of the deterrence-based argument concerning antitrust criminalization. Indeed, central to this argument is the concept of an optimal fine. As explained above, Wils argues that this fine would need to be at least 150 per cent of the annual turnover earned by the cartelist from the cartelized market,[154] that the imposition of such a fine would, for various reasons, be practically impossible, and that the non-indemnifiable individual sanction of imprisonment can be employed to make up for the shortfalls of a suboptimal fine. This optimal fine of 150 per cent is constructed using the available empirical evidence, hence the applicability of the (general) caveat. In addition, however, one can identify a number of specific problematic issues with this figure and consequently a potential limitation of the deterrence-based criminalization argument.

1. Estimating the gains from a cartel

According to the economic deterrence model of 'unlawful gain', the cartel fine should be set at least equal to the unlawful gain secured by the cartelist (discounted to reflect the probability of detection and prosecution).[155] If one wishes to construct a single optimal fine to be used as a general deterrent, one will inevitably attempt to use an average measure of the gain in question. As noted, above, the optimal fine of 150 per cent of annual turnover is constructed using this model and the average 'gain' from a cartel was deemed to be 10 per cent of the annual turnover in the cartelized market. The limitation that should be noted here relates to the fact that the figure used is not exactly an average measure of the actual gains attributable to cartel activity (i.e. the average profit one can expect to make by engaging in such activity), but rather an average measure of a *proxy* for such gains. The proxy used is half of the cartel mark-up, i.e. half of the difference between the cartelized price and the competitive price. There may be good reasons for this approach, chief among which is the fact that it is very difficult to determine the value of the average profit attributable to cartel activity: as noted by one astute commentator, 'cartel profitability is not an entirely straightforward concept'.[156] Furthermore, it is logical to assume that the actual gains from a given cartel—if they in fact exist—find their source in the cartel overcharge and that the extent of the gains is dependent upon the size of the overcharge: a likely aim of a cartel, after all, is to make profits through the construction of a non-competitive price. The chosen proxy thus has potential to reflect the gain due to a cartel. But, as a proxy, by definition it can only be a rough approximation of the actual gain.

Indeed, the cartel overcharge does not necessarily equal the actual profits for any given cartelist. For a start, as noted above, (US) empirical evidence demonstrates that

[154] For the sake of economy, the analysis which follows focuses on Wils's calculation. To be sure, it is of equal validity to the calculations conducted by both Werden and Calvani.

[155] See Chapter 2, Section B(b)(ii) of this book. [156] Simonsson (2009), 115.

unions may capture a significant portion of the economic rent earned by US manufacturing firms.[157] This may also be true for European firms. Moreover, according to the 'law of demand' in micro-economic theory, by increasing the price of a product, one reduces the demand for such a product.[158] An increase in the price of a cartelized product may thus actually result in lower demand for such a product. Wils acknowledges this point when constructing the optimal fine: he reduces the cartel overcharge by 50 per cent to account for the fall in demand.[159] The point here, however, is that a reduction of 50 per cent is based upon a mere estimation of the average price elasticity of demand ('PED'). This estimation may not be accurate for quite a number of different product markets. Indeed, the exact size of the PED varies between products and depends upon a number of different factors, including market definition, the nature of the product itself, the availability of substitutes, etc.[160] In other words, a 'one size fits all' approach may be questionable here. Additionally, and more importantly, as it is based solely upon the overcharge (discounted to take into account the 'law of demand'), the proxy does not take into account the costs of organizing and monitoring the cartel,[161] costs that will need to be covered by any increase in revenue occasioned as a result of the overcharge if the cartelist is to receive a gain for engaging in cartel activity.

In any case, there are difficulties associated with the calculation of the cartel overcharge itself, difficulties which may affect the reliability of the sources used to construct the average overcharge for the purposes of the optimal fine. In particular, the actual method used to calculate the overcharge for a given cartel is not standardized. There are a number of relevant methods of calculation, including the before-and-after approach, the yardstick approach, and the cost-based approach, as well as econometric models; each possesses various merits and demerits. As noted in the 'Ashurst Report':

> assessing damages for overcharging cases (e.g. cartels) may be far from straightforward, with the analysis ranging from the relatively simple (i.e. before and after, and yardstick approaches) to the complex (i.e. theoretical simulation models and econometric modelling to predict but for prices). This will inevitably lead to some judgment being required as to which presumptions are the most plausible given the data available.[162]

The words 'data available' are important: the quality of any analysis here will inevitably be affected by the quality of the input data which is available for each cartel overcharge.[163] Furthermore, some of the available methods of calculation lead to higher estimates of the overcharge than others.[164] These two issues, then, raise the question of reliability concerning any given set of figures on cartel overcharges: some estimates of cartel overcharges may be inaccurate. The extensive study by Connor and Lande,[165] focusing as it does on hundreds of cases of cartel activity (including those from as far back as 1780), inevitably contains such estimates. Some economists, however, while acknowledging the methodological limitations of some of the relevant figures, nonetheless believe that they reflect a relatively accurate picture of the size of the average overcharge. According

[157] Werden and Simon (1987), 928, citing Karier (1985) and Salinger (1984).

[158] Hall and Lieberman (2007), 58.

[159] Wils (2005b), 138. See also Werden (2009), 28, footnote 60.

[160] Mankiw (2008), 90–1.

[161] Indeed, regular meetings are a common feature of international cartels in particular; see, e.g., Levenstein and Suslow (2006), 42. These types of costs can be understood as the 'social costs' of monopoly profits; on this, see Posner (2001), 13–18.

[162] Ashurst (2004), [3.37].

[163] Alfter and Young (2005), 553.

[164] See Connor and Lande (2005), 550–1.

[165] Connor and Lande (2005).

to an eminent economist, for example, although it exhibits methodological problems, the 2005 study by Connor and Lande is still useful:

No quality screening was done in compiling these estimates, and many surely were not produced using reliable measurement techniques... The most interesting estimates are the relatively few made by applying the tools of modern economics to data relating to cartel activity prosecuted in the United States under the felony statute enacted in 1974. Considering just these estimates vastly reduces the amount of evidence but does not greatly change the picture. Cartel activity risking serious sanctions has been consistently found to have inflicted substantial harm.[166]

Even so, Simonsson notes two further problematic issues with the empirical literature on cartel overcharges:[167] (i) *historical* data on cartel overcharges may be of limited use for understanding the workings of cartels in the twenty-first century (cartel overcharges may be lower these days due to greater antitrust enforcement efforts, for example);[168] and (ii) there is a sample selection bias, as only *detected* cartels form the subject matter of the studies on cartel overcharges.[169] As the data used to construct optimal cartel fines in the literature depends to a degree on historic data and solely upon data derived merely from detected cartels, one can question at least whether such optimal fines are as robust as one would have wished.[170]

2. The probability of detecting and prosecuting a cartel

There are two problems concerning the calculation of the probability of detection and prosecution of cartels. These problems affect the accuracy of any measurement of the optimal fine which should be levied to ensure deterrence; they also therefore affect the strength of the deterrence-based criminalization argument. The first problem concerns the determination of the actual number of cartels that have been discovered by a given jurisdiction. As noted by one cartel expert:

There are no official figures on the number of detected cartels. Estimations can be found in academic writing and occasionally from other sources. There is a scarcity of aggregated data since estimations of how many cartels that have been detected [sic.] proves to be a task for academic research. And the academic findings in the field are difficult to compare since there is no unitary standard, either for the basis of the estimations or how to present them.[171]

[166] Werden (2009), 27. In coming to this conclusion, Werden relied upon, inter alia, the following studies: Brannman and Klein (1992) (bid-rigging in highway construction raised prices by 18 per cent in one state and 6.5 per cent in another); Connor (2001), 157–8, 264, 336 (price-fixing increased lysine prices by 17 per cent, citric acid prices by 11–24 per cent, and prices of various other vitamins by 25–8 per cent); Froeb et al. (1993) (bid-rigging on frozen fish raised prices by between 23 and 30 per cent); Lanzillotti (1996), Lee (1999), Pesendorfer (2000), Porter and Zona (1999) (bid-rigging in the procurement of milk by schools raised prices by 6.5 per cent in one state and by at least 14 per cent in two others): Werden (2009), 27–8. (On these studies, see also Werden (2003).) For a less supportive view of Connor's work in particular, see Rosati and Ehmer (2009).

[167] Simonsson (2009), 120–2.

[168] This point is conceded by Connor and Lande (2005), 541: 'The influence of the spread of effective anticartel enforcement is perhaps the most obvious explanation [for the downward trend in (international) cartel overcharges since 1990]'.

[169] See Harding (2011b). [170] See King (2010), 8.

[171] Simonsson (2009), 109. One is subsequently invited by Simonsson (2009) to compare the following (often contradictory) literature related to cartel statistics: Connor and Helmers (2007); Evenett et al. (2001); Geradin and Henry (2005); Guersent (2004); ICN (2005), 56; Jephcott (2005); Lowe (2003); Sakkers and Ysewyn (2008); Schinkel (2007); and Veljanovski (2006b).

This problem is relatively easy to overcome for a given jurisdiction: an official register of all publicly recorded cartel decisions could be established.[172] The jurisdiction would of course be required to articulate what it means by a 'cartel decision', as, otherwise, unreliable results may be obtained. However, the second problem is far more difficult. Such is its significance that it has been termed the 'one hitch' in the apparent US success at cartel prosecution.[173] It concerns the inability actually to know the percentage of cartels that are detected and proven.[174] This is due to the secret nature of cartels: one only knows about the existence of a cartel once it has been discovered by the antitrust authorities. It is almost certain that cartels exist which have not yet been discovered;[175] the problem is that one cannot be sure of their exact number. It is no surprise, then, that '[t]here is little evidence on the probability with which cartel activity is detected'.[176] Indeed, as a result of cartel secrecy, any alleged estimation of the probability of detection and prosecution will be open to discussion.[177]

Irrespective of these problems, the optimal fine of 150 per cent of annual turnover constructed by Wils includes a measurement of the probability of detection and prosecution. A figure of one-third is employed.[178] This figure finds at least some of its inspiration in a study conducted by Bryant and Eckhard in 1991.[179] That particular study focused on a sample of 184 cartels, determined that the average duration of a cartel was between five and seven years, and, by using a statistical birth and death model, concluded that the probability of getting caught in a given year was between 13 and 17 per cent. However, there are a number of problems with this study. For a start, the methodology employed 'does not seem to have gained any widespread use in the legal or economic communities',[180] a fact that calls into question its usefulness. Second, there are issues with the sample selection. The authors used the duration of each of the 184 (detected) cartels in the sample to calculate the duration of non-detected cartels, and hence the probability of detection. As pointed out by Simonsson,[181] one cannot be sure that the authorities exposed the full duration of the detected cartels; consequently, any calculation based upon their duration may not be as accurate as one would have wished. Indeed, there are a number of methodological issues specific to the calculation of cartel duration,[182] a fact that further limits the potential accuracy of the approach adopted by Bryant and Eckhard. In addition, the method adopted in the study does not take account of changes in enforcement policy: it fails to acknowledge that 'increased enforcement activities can be expected to generate a higher probability of detection'.[183] Finally, one

[172] In the US, there is an obligation on the chief judge of each District Court 'to submit, for every [cartel] conviction, the judgment and commitment order, the written statement of reasons, any plea agreement, the indictment or other charging document, and the presentence report': Markham (2012), 119, referencing 28 USC §994(w)(1). Thus, 'there is a body of data that might be of use in evaluating whether criminal prosecutions have had any discernible deterrent effect': Markham (2012), 119.

[173] Fox (2006), 239.

[174] See Connor and Lande (2005), 519.

[175] See Stephan (2008a), 25.

[176] Werden (2009), 29.

[177] According to the economist who argues that an optimal cartel fine would be 200 per cent of annual turnover in the market affected, his argument 'is built on many assumptions, only one of which lacks empirical support. There is little evidence on the probability with which cartel activity is detected. However, the fact that major international cartels continue to be uncovered despite the significant fines imposed by multiple jurisdictions, and prison sentences imposed in the United States, indicates that cartel participants reckoned the probability of detection to be rather low, quite plausibly less than the assumed 25 percent': Werden (2009), 29. Cf. Reindl (2006), 116.

[178] Werden uses the figure of one-quarter in his calculation: Werden (2009), 29.

[179] Bryant and Eckhard (1991). See Wils (2005b), 139–40. Wils's original calculation (16 per cent) relied more closely on the findings of Bryant and Eckhard; see Wils (2002), Chapter 8.

[180] Simonsson (2009), 114.

[181] Simonsson (2009), 114.

[182] See Levenstein and Suslow (2004), 14.

[183] Simonsson (2009), 114.

could argue that all that really matters in this context is the actual *perceptions* of potential cartelists (or their legal advisers) concerning the rate of discovery and successful prosecution of cartels. If so, (reliable) survey evidence concerning such perceptions could be of more use in the criminalization debate than the type of study conducted by Bryant and Eckhard.[184] For these reasons, then, the figures advanced by Bryant and Eckhard may be unreliable,[185] and any criminalization argument finding inspiration in these figures may also be questioned. To be fair, however, Wils only uses the figures to construct a very 'conservative' estimate of the probability of detection and prosecution:[186] 33 per cent is not exactly 17 per cent.[187] By including such a conservative estimate (in comparison to that of Bryant and Eckhard), Wils effectively avoids the criticism which he would otherwise have faced concerning his reliance upon this study—a criticism that would almost certainly have been applicable to his original (2002) estimate. In fact, intuitively a rate of 33 per cent appears reasonable: cartels are after all secret and often the 'victim' is not even aware of the loss he has suffered.[188] Even so, the caveat above would still apply: due to the secretive nature of cartels, Wils's—like anybody's—estimate of the probability of detection and prosecution cannot be conclusively verified.

3. Risk neutrality and cartel activity

The optimal fine of 150 per cent of annual turnover appears to be based upon the assumption that the corporate entity facing the potential fine is risk neutral. As noted in Chapter 2,[189] risk-averse offenders will be deterred by a lower penalty than the one otherwise constructed using optimal deterrence theory and risk-seekers will only be deterred by a higher penalty.[190] The optimal fine should be adjusted accordingly if either of these situations is the case. If the corporate entity facing the cartel fine is a risk-seeker, there will be no problem here for the deterrence-based criminalization argument. According to this argument, criminal sanctions should be introduced to overcome the practical problems of imposing a fine which is 150 per cent of annual turnover. The problems with imposing a fine *in excess of* 150 per cent of annual turnover (e.g., the possibility of liquidation and the consequent social costs) would be *even more* pronounced than those evident when a fine of 150 per cent is at issue. In fact, if the corporate entity facing the cartel fine is a risk-seeker, there would be an even stronger case for criminal sanctions in the context of a deterrence-based criminalization argument. If, however, the corporate entity facing the cartel fine is risk averse, the figure of 150 per cent of annual turnover may represent an overestimation of the optimal fine. If this overestimation can be established, the deterrence-based criminalization argument will be somewhat weakened: the practical problems with imposing the optimal fine will be less pronounced. In other words, the possibility of corporate entities being risk averse is a potential limitation of the deterrence-based argument.[191]

[184] For an early example of such a survey, see Beckenstein and Landis-Gabel (1982). For a more recent survey of this type, see Beaton-Wells and Parker (2013).

[185] Cf. Connor and Bush (2008), 55: 'there is little reason to believe that the true probability of detection is outside this range'.

[186] See Wils (2005b), 140.

[187] To be fair to Werden, neither is 25 per cent.

[188] For the sake of comparison: the arrest rates for the most common property-related felonies—felonies that are not necessarily committed in secret or that do not necessarily have 'unaware' victims—in the US are estimated at between 13 and 17 per cent: Polinsky and Shavell (2000), 71, footnote 77.

[189] Chapter 2, Section B(b)(iii) of this book.

[190] Cooter and Ulen (2004), 52.

[191] There appears to be a significant (and surprising) lack of research on the extent to which corporations—as opposed to individuals—are (or are not) risk averse. More experimental work in this area would therefore be appreciated. It should be noted, however, that it has been suggested that public corporations are in fact risk neutral: Posner (1976), 269.

(ii) The assumption of rationality

By relying upon the assumption that potential offenders act rationally when deciding to break the law, the deterrence-based criminalization argument advanced above may be open to the criticism that it does not adequately reflect reality.[192] Detractors could argue that rationality is not a dominant feature of the human condition, that many factors influence how people order their behaviour and that, consequently, one cannot adequately predict how people will act in given situations.[193] One could argue, for example, that the assumption of rationality does not take sufficient notice of a citizen's normative commitment of obedience to the law, or that it fails to acknowledge that individuals do not always respond as predicted to financial incentives.[194] For Prentice, 'the rational man model, with no room for cognitive limitations, emotion, or altruism, describes neither how man does act nor how man should act'.[195] Other objections may relate to the existence of bounded rationality, bounded will power, and bounded self-interest.[196] In the corporate context, it ignores the potential influence of the work environment, as well as other internal and situational factors.[197] Indeed, such a model ignores the criminological literature concerning compliance and the law. Such literature argues, for example, that, irrespective of the potential punishment for violation of the law, individuals will often adhere to the law if they perceive it to be legitimate.[198] For some, the existence of business ethics goes a long way to deterring 'economic crime':

> ethical orientations are of greater importance [than sanctions]. They filter out considerations based on pure calculation. That crimes are committed depends less on pure cost-benefit calculations—like mild sanctions and relevant opportunities—than, above all, on a lack of moral and legal restraint... Most people do not commit crimes simply because they consider it to be wrong and unacceptable. They generally do not even think about criminal options, and, as a result, they never come to balance opportunities against risks.[199]

Furthermore, there is some evidence to suggest that informal social and economic sanctions in fact may also have a significant influence upon calculative thinking and behaviour.[200] Such informal economic and social sanctions—which may include social embarrassment[201]—influence compliance by appealing to people's conscience as well as to their own perceptions of their moral obligations towards law compliance.[202] In short, the available empirical evidence tends to suggest that self-interested calculation is not the only factor determining whether an individual adheres to the law.[203]

192 See the discussion in Harding (2011a), 357–60.

193 See, e.g., Bromberg (1965) and Zilboorg (1954), who both argue that man is governed by unconscious impulses and does not have systematic regard to the rational principle of maximizing one's welfare. See also Zimbardo (2008), who argues that there are at least ten situational factors which can cause ordinary people to 'turn evil'.

194 See Gneezy and Rustichini (2004).

195 Prentice (2003), 1672.

196 See: Jolls et al. (1998); and Stucke (2007), 527.

197 See: Baucus and Near (1991), 12; Daboub et al. (1995); and Stucke (2006), 486. For illustration as to how such situational factors may influence the existence of antitrust offending, see Conley and O'Barr (1997), 13.

198 See Tyler (2006).

199 See Bussmann (2003), 4.

200 Parker and Nielsen (2008), 563.

201 On such informal sanctions, see generally: Grasmick and Bursik (1990); Simpson (2002), 43; and Thornton et al. (2005), 264.

202 See: Braithwaite (1989), 71–5; and Grasmick and Bursik (1990), 841.

203 Parker and Nielsen (2008), 556, relying on: Ayres and Braithwaite (1992), 19–53; DiMento (1989); Suchman (1997); Sutinen and Kuperan (1999); and Winter and May (2001).

For some commentators, the failure of rational choice theory to predict outcomes in certain scenarios renders it 'dead', 'sick', or 'peaked out'.[204] That said, modern economists have regularly put forward evidence in support of the view that we live in 'a world in which people can generally be expected to make rational decisions, and where those rational decisions suggest some astonishing explanations for many of life's mysteries'.[205] Studies have even suggested a certain degree of rationality concerning a diverse range of decisions including those relating to sexual practices,[206] sexuality,[207] drug addiction,[208] divorce,[209] and the effects of architecture upon crime,[210] to take a few interesting examples. This is not to say that one should necessarily believe that human beings always act in a rational manner.[211] In fact, rational choice theory—like any economic analysis—merely 'relies on simplifying assumptions that sacrifice realism for tractability';[212] the 'rationality assumption plays so prominently in literature because it is tractable... and yields some quite accurate predictions'.[213]

In the current literature there is a lack of rigorous empirical studies of the existence or otherwise of rationality in the context of cartel activity.[214] A number of studies, however, provide some useful data concerning the motivations of cartelists, as well as the effects of legal prohibitions and enforcement on cartel activity.[215] While not without their flaws, these studies nonetheless provide some constructive input into the discussion at hand; in particular, they can be used to underline the fact that antitrust law compliance in practice is not as simplistic as that assumed by the model of economic deterrence. The findings of four different studies are sufficient to establish this point.

The first study concerns the heavy electrical equipment cartel that was active in the 1950s in the US.[216] According to its findings, a number of different factors led the individuals concerned to get involved in the cartel. Importantly for present purposes, the intention to obtain personal gains was indeed among these factors:

> [the cartelists in question] had to perceive that there would be gains accruing from their behaviour. Such gains might be personal and professional, in terms of corporate advancement toward prestige and power; they might be vocational, in terms of a more expedient and secure method of carrying out assigned tasks.[217]

The cartelists in this study, then, apparently displayed a degree of self-interest. However, this does not necessarily mean that they systematically conducted cost/benefit analyses prior to their engagement in cartel activity; it does not mean that they were 'rational' in the economic sense of the term. Indeed, it appears that the cartelists also needed to be able to rationalize their conduct in a manner which was consistent with their highly regarded positions in society.[218] To the extent that that is so, one could argue that social

[204] Stucke (2007), 513, referencing: Bernstein (2005), 303–4; Korobkin and Ulen (2000), 1053; and Ormerod (2006), 17.

[205] Harford (2008), xii. Cf. Posner (1992), 224 (a better test of the theory than the realism of its assumptions is its predictive power; and the available empirical evidence vindicates the effectiveness of the predictive power of the economic approach to the criminal law). See also: New Zealand Ministry of Commerce (1998), 12; Packer (1968), 41; and Pyle (1983), Chapters 3–4 (summarizing the literature on empirical evidence).

[206] Klick and Stratmann (2008).

[207] Francis (2008).

[208] Becker et al. (1991); and Becker and Murphy (1988).

[209] Stevenson and Wolfers (2007).

[210] Glaeser and Sacerdote (2000).

[211] Reeves (2010), 1–2.

[212] Salinger (2010), 67.

[213] Salinger (2010), 67.

[214] Cf. Stucke (2007), 515; and Foer (2003), 33. This scarcity of empirical evidence has long been noted; see, e.g., Posner (1979a), 931, footnote 13.

[215] For an overview and criticism of these studies, see Parker (2011).

[216] Geis (1995).

[217] Geis (1995), 163.

[218] See Geis (1995), 155–6 and 163.

pressure also has an impact upon whether the cartelist decides to collude: if cartel activity cannot be perceived as being consistent with one's social duty as a respectable employee/citizen, such activity is less likely to occur.

The second study that should be noted focused on the impact of the enforcement activity of the Australian Competition and Consumer Commission ('ACCC') in cartel cases.[219] Again, as with the previous study, the cartelists tended to rationalize their behaviour in a manner that was consistent with their image of themselves as respectable, law-abiding citizens. As summarized by MacCulloch,

> the various rationalisations in these studies can be generalised as arguing the acts: were only to defend the company in difficult times, did not cause any harm, or were someone else's responsibility.[220]

Both of these studies, then, if representative, question to a degree the reliability of the assumption of rationality: the fact that cartelists feel the need to rationalize their behaviour as 'acceptable' suggests that other factors than mere potential for gain (such as public or personal perceptions) also have an impact upon the decision whether or not to collude.

The third study to be noted, an in-depth analysis of Australian views on antitrust compliance,[221] further underlines this point. Having requested 999 of Australia's largest businesses across all industries to fill in a detailed questionnaire and having achieved a response rate of 43 per cent,[222] Parker and Nielsen found that Australian businesses, while concerned about the formal legal sanctions for non-compliance, also worry about informal economic and social losses when contemplating cartel activity.[223] Furthermore, a range of factors affect the extent to which businesses fear non-compliance, including an organization's size and resources.[224] The findings of this study in particular lend support to the argument that 'the rhetoric of the cartel criminalization proponents focuses too simplistically on calculated self-interest as the motivation for compliance and non-compliance, while ignoring the complex normative and social contexts in which cartel behaviour and enforcement occur'.[225]

The final study that should be mentioned relates to 'The Cartel Project' carried out at the University of Melbourne between 2009 and 2011.[226] This project involved, inter alia, a survey of a representative cross-section (567 people in total) of the business community.[227] The academics involved in this survey have argued that their findings expose 'significant weaknesses' in the traditional foundations for antitrust criminalization, including the assumption of rationality.[228] The authors present a strong case for their conclusions and it is likely that they are of wider application beyond Australia. In particular, the authors highlight that a number of factors influence knowledge and perceptions of detection, prosecution, and sanction, such as gender and normative appraisal of the law, undermining the assumption of the rationally calculating self-interested actor.[229] As noted by the authors:

> The rhetoric supporting criminalization would assume that it should not matter what age or gender a business person is, or what their level of education, job position or workplace size is—they should still fear criminal enforcement and be deterred from engaging in cartel conduct if it is at

219 Parker et al. (2004).
220 See MacCulloch (2007), 362.
221 Parker and Nielsen (2008). See also Parker and Nielsen (2011).
222 Parker and Nielsen (2008), 568–9.
223 Parker and Nielsen (2008), 596.
224 Parker and Nielsen (2008), 597.
225 Parker (2011).
226 See <http://www.cartel.law.unimelb.edu.au>.
227 See Beaton-Wells and Parker (2013).
228 Beaton-Wells and Parker (2013), 200.
229 Beaton-Wells and Parker (2013), 208–10.

all relevant to their work. Nor should it matter what their prior awareness of the law or opinions about what the law should be [sic.]. These should all be irrelevant once they know what the law is—they should simply fear jail and comply.[230]

In addition, the authors found that one in ten surveyed would seriously consider engaging in cartel activity even when they know the risk of a jail term,[231] a finding that further calls into question the realism of the assumption that cartelists act rationally.

All of the above notwithstanding, one must mention here that there is (limited) anecdotal evidence which suggests that (crude) cost/benefit analyses are often undertaken by potential cartelists prior to their engagement in cartel activity.[232] Admittedly, these anecdotes are usually provided by antitrust officials[233] and/or national judges.[234] Importantly, however, this anecdotal evidence is predicted by (non-empirical) reasoning.[235] In this regard, it should not be forgotten that the corporate context presents a more unusual set of circumstances than those usually constructed in the social laboratory: firms and their directors are required under law to maximize the interests of the shareholders.[236] Profit maximization, then, can become not only an objective, but also an obligation. Such profit maximization is best served through the employment of rational cost/benefit analyses prior to making a decision. Furthermore, if this obligation is on the firm and its directors, it is not inconceivable that the firm, in the first instance through its directors, would incentivize employees to achieve as much profit as possible. If efficient law-breaking is possible, it would arguably be in the interests of the firm to seek to indemnify those employees who have transgressed the law in the name of profit maximization.[237] Such indemnification would in turn further incentivize other employees to engage in future (efficient, profit-maximizing) law-breaking. The existence of a financial crisis or recession may also have a part to play here, and may ensure that rational (i.e. profit-maximizing) behaviour trumps the ethical concerns of employees. As suggested by Stephan:

When faced with the prospect of losing one's job or becoming insolvent, the range of options or strategies for increasing a firm's performance may become wider. Individuals who would normally consider price fixing to be objectionable (and thus not consider it as an option) might in desperate times put any ethical objections aside.[238]

This is not to admit, however, that by assuming rationality in the context of cartel activity one does not overlook important situational factors which may influence the decision to cartelize a given market.[239]

In any case, an economic approach to sanctions in the antitrust context is more attractive than in others as the firm and its executives are more likely to undertake a

230 Beaton-Wells and Parker (2013), 209.

231 Beaton-Wells and Parker (2013), 211.

232 See, e.g.: Baker (2001), 705; and Baker (1981), 531. Cf. Stucke (2011): 'Executives often engage in cost-benefit analyses, but it is unknown how many, before fixing prices, actually calculate their likely fine and sentence'.

233 See Bennett (2009), 1.

234 See *DPP v. Duffy and Duffy Motors (Newbridge) Ltd* [2009] IEHC 208, [47]: 'A person seeking to successfully implement a price-fixing agreement... typically will be well educated, businessly astute, either owns the business or has risen to senior management, and *almost certainly will have done a value benefit/detection appraisal*' (emphasis added).

235 According to some, it 'is certainly plausible to assume that calculated self-interested thinking does play an important part in motivating business' compliance and non-compliance': Parker and Nielsen (2008), 556. The following literature is offered in support of this assertion: Braithwaite and Makkai (1991), 10; and Vaughan (1998), 27–8.

236 Greenfield (2002), 605.

237 Cf. Peel (2008).

238 Stephan (2009a), 5.

239 On these situational factors, see Stucke (2011).

cost/benefit analysis of their (market) behaviour than, say, the ordinary citizen unconnected in a direct way with the dynamics of business.[240] As noted by Massey:

> Unlike many violent crimes, participation in a cartel is not the result of a moment's passion or transient rage. Unlike many criminal actions undertaken in the heat of the moment, those contemplating participating in a cartel are far more likely to weigh the benefits from such participation against the consequences of getting caught and, therefore, take the threat of imprisonment into account.[241]

So, although rationality may not be an accurate assumption for traditional crimes—which may be committed in response to situational factors—'it is legitimate for white-collar crimes, as executives have the time and resources to consider logically their decision to offend'.[242] Some have argued that the more competitive the environment, the more likely it is that actors act rationally: non-rational (i.e. non-profit-maximizing) firms (and their employees) will eventually be driven out of the market.[243] At least in a business context, then, where the environment can generally be considered to be competitive,[244] the concern with rationality may therefore be subject to overstatement. So even if one concedes that the criticism of unreality may have value when analysing, for example, the existence of crimes of passion or impulse, it loses its potency somewhat when applied to economic offences which are committed after long periods of deliberation by educated, intelligent, and otherwise morally functional persons.[245]

It is conceded, nonetheless, that more empirical work is indeed required on this issue in the particular area of antitrust.[246] Such research should be interdisciplinary and should encompass analysis of

> social psychology and organizational behavior, in order to fully understand how decisions are made (including the extent to which such decisions are influenced by risk taking or conformity) in different corporate settings.[247]

In particular, it should consider the extent to which dispositional and situational factors encourage cartelists to engage in collusion.[248] One way of conducting this research would involve the US DoJ and/or other antitrust authorities (if necessary in conjunction with social scientists) interviewing under conditions of anonymity and confidentiality convicted price-fixers in order to determine, inter alia, how the cartels in question were formed and enforced, what specific factors enabled collusion, and, most importantly, whether the cartelists acted as predicted by rational choice theory.[249] While such interviews may produce self-serving statements and may represent a biased sample (e.g., only *detected* cartelists would be interviewed), they may nonetheless produce more revealing

[240] See: Paternoster and Simpson (1996), 550–1; and Vaughan (1998), 27–8. Cf. Thornton et al. (2005), 279: commercial firms 'have not been particularly attentive to penalty information, nor have they made special efforts to obtain timely and accurate information'.

[241] Massey (2004), 31. See also: Clarke (2005), 149; and Hoel (2008), 109.

[242] Boberg (2010), 88. See also Clarke and Bagaric (2003), 204–5.

[243] Nelson and Winter (1982). See also: Jolls et al. (1998), 1487; and Stucke (2007), 515. Cf. Korobkin and Ulen (2000), 1070–1.

[244] It should be remembered that even if the product market is not competitive, the job market for managers can be expected to be fairly competitive so that rational, profit-maximizing managers are selected: New Zealand Ministry of Commerce (1998), 12.

[245] See: Baker and Reeves (1977), 620; Lynch (1997), 45; and Renfrew (1977), 593–4.

[246] See: Coase (1992), 714 and 718; and Parker (2011).

[247] Stucke (2007), 536. See also: the comments of Lyons in Cseres et al. (2006a), 325; and Whelan (2006), 170.

[248] Stucke (2011).

[249] Stucke (2011). See also the comments of Schroeder in Cseres et al. (2006a), 327.

data than other empirical studies.[250] Until (more of)[251] this type of research is forthcoming, however, one will have to continue to rely to some degree upon (non-empirical) reasoning to determine whether rationality is an accurate assumption in the context of cartel activity. To the extent that it is not, the deterrence-based criminalization argument is undermined.

(iii) Securing efficient *deterrence of anticompetitive behaviour*

The deterrence-based criminalization argument advanced above employed the 'unlawful gain' model of economic deterrence. Accordingly: (i) the expected value of punishment should be at least equal to the cartelist's unlawful gain; and (ii) optimal enforcement strategy is determined by the resultant benefits and costs of maintaining such a value. The deterrence-based argument holds that fines are incapable of reaching the minimum required and that criminal law—with its threat of custodial sanctions for the responsible individual cartelists—is a plausible alternative capable of negativing the unlawful gain and thereby achieving deterrence. Even if one accepts that custodial sanctions are capable of negativing the unlawful gain, it does not necessarily follow that such sanctions secure *efficient* deterrence of anticompetitive behaviour: by satisfying condition (i) one does not necessarily satisfy condition (ii). Indeed, the use of criminal sanctions involves social costs which must be considered if accurate pronouncements on the efficiency of this alleged deterrent are to be made.[252] More specifically, in order to establish a strong deterrence-based criminalization argument, one must be able to demonstrate that the introduction and maintenance of criminal sanctions generates more benefits than costs.[253] This is not an easy task; in fact, it is one of the most difficult challenges facing those who advocate the imposition of criminal punishment to deter cartel activity.

The problem is that one does not have accurate measurements of the exact costs and benefits of criminal antitrust sanctions. According to the OECD:

> Anecdotal evidence exists that criminal sanctions against individuals can have deterrent effects. There is, however, no systematic empirical evidence available to prove such effects, and to assess whether the marginal benefit of introducing sanctions against individuals (in the form of less harm from cartel activity) exceeds the additional costs that in particular a system of criminal sanctions entails (including the costs of prosecution as well as of administering a prison system). There appears to be agreement that it would be virtually impossible to generate the relevant data.[254]

For Harding, a 'politically and socially responsible impact assessment' would also necessarily 'have to consider the relative cost of different options of legal control'.[255] Unfortunately, this 'may not be an easy exercise if carried out rigorously'.[256] Nonetheless, there are arguments supporting the assertion that criminal sanctions are at least *capable* of generating more benefits than costs. First, the imposition of administrative fines also involves costs; any reduction in the use of an administrative regime in favour of increased

[250] Parker (2011).

[251] Some empirical studies involving interviews with cartel participants have already been conducted; see, e.g.: Parker (2013); Parker (2012); Parker et al. (2011); Parker et al. (2004); Sonnenfeld (1981); and Sonnenfeld and Lawrence (1978).

[252] See Reindl (2006).

[253] Or, more accurately, if they can be imposed where their marginal cost is equal to their marginal benefit; see Cooter and Ulen (2004), 25 et seq. See also Block and Sidak (1980).

[254] OECD (2003b), 7. See also the discussion in Harding (2011b).

[255] Harding (2012), 145.

[256] Harding (2012), 145.

criminal punishment results in saved expenditure which should be added to the calculation of the benefits of criminal sanctions. Although fewer (administrative) fines would thereby be recovered, nothing is preventing the criminal regime from also employing this particular sanction; in fact, fines should continue to be imposed, as they have some deterrent abilities and stigmatizing effects, and are relatively cheap to administer. Subject to considerations of inability to pay and proportional justice, such fines could even be increased to cover some of the costs of the criminal regime.

Second, the benefits of criminal sanctions in terms of reductions in cartel activity could well be substantial. According to some commentators, imprisonment is a very effective measure that delivers a considerable degree of deterrence.[257] The US is often put forward as the example in chief,[258] with its enormous success in deterring cartelists through criminal sanctions, as evidenced by, inter alia, reductions in domestic cartel activity, the reluctance of global cartelists to embrace the US market, and the success of its criminal immunity programme.[259] Any increased powers of investigation due to criminalization also presumably improve the rate of discovery of (secret) cartels[260] and thus help to add to the beneficial effect.[261] As cartel activity involves significant harm to society estimated at billions of dollars annually,[262] even the prevention/termination of only a few major (potential/actual) cartels would be likely to 'save' exorbitant amounts of societal wealth.[263]

Third, useful methods of increasing the benefits and reducing the costs of criminal enforcement exist; they relate to severity, prosecution levels, cooperation, and the imposition of costs upon the convicted cartelist.

Severity: Since the severity of an effective penalty and the rate of detection have an inverse relationship, to reduce costs and maintain the same expected value of punishment one could raise the severity and reduce enforcement efforts.[264] It may be tempting, therefore, to impose an exorbitant custodial sentence in only a number of cases; but for reasons of proportional justice, this should not occur. Nevertheless, one could attempt to reduce costs by actually lowering the penalty. The desire of cartelists to avoid the unpleasantness of prison is often reported.[265] They, like other white-collar criminals, may well be 'unprepared for the emotional and physical trauma of prison'.[266] If true, relatively short sentences may be sufficient for optimal deterrence and incarceration costs can be kept to a minimum, as can the cost of keeping usually productive business people out of the economy.

257 See: Bauer (2004), 307; or Liman (1977), 630–1. Some commentators have questioned the deterrent effect of imprisonment for cartel activity on the grounds that it had been rarely imposed; see, e.g., Posner (2001), 270–1. The statistics, however, do not appear to support such arguments; see Werden (2009), 22. Others have questioned the empirical support, positing that deterrence-based pro-criminalization arguments are 'based mostly on intuition, hearsay, anecdotes and personal perceptions': Reindl (2006), 116.

258 Cf. Connor (2011).

259 See: Bloom (2005); and Kolasky (2004), 11–12. See also: Wils (2006b), 83; and Calvani and Calvani (2011), 193.

260 See Markham (2012), 124: 'Enchanced criminal enforcement efforts have resulted in the detection of a large number of cartels'.

261 Such powers have helped secure current US enforcement successes; see Baker (2001).

262 See: Connor (2007a), especially Chapters 2 and 17; and OECD (2002a), 90.

263 With the 'Lysine Cartel' alone, for example, prices rose by 70 per cent in a market worth $500 million annually: Klein (1999a), 2.

264 The cost of legal error will still be active: Block and Sidak (1980).

265 See, e.g., Liman (1977), 630–1. See also: O'Kane (2011b); Packer (2011); and Szockyj (1998–99), 490.

266 Szockyj (1998–99), 490.

Prosecution levels: If only the most serious cartels are prosecuted, the deterrent message can be sent to the most destructive elements in the economy without incurring unnecessary and frivolous costs.[267] Further, since the penalty of imprisonment is presumably already relatively more severe in the eyes of cartelists than administrative fines,[268] detection rates may not need to be as high as those under administrative regimes in order to deter effectively.[269]

Cooperation: The successful use of plea-bargaining, corporate leniency/immunity programmes, individual criminal immunity programmes, and bounties has some potential to reduce significantly the costs of investigation, prosecution, and incarceration. Plea-bargaining leads to guilty pleas and, inter alia, reductions in the costs of both the resultant trials and incarcerations.[270] Leniency/immunity, in particular, increases the difficulty of creating and maintaining cartels, improves collection of intelligence and evidence at low expense, and reduces considerably the costs of adjudication.[271] Likewise, the use of bounties—that is, the payment of sums of money for information that leads to a sustainable cartel conviction—may be an attractive method of detecting cartels which does not involve the use of significant (scarce) resources of the authority.[272]

Imposition of costs: Another relevant technique would be the imposition of cost orders upon the convicted cartelist. This particular technique has been introduced in Ireland in order to reduce the public costs of criminal cartel enforcement.[273] Section 2(h) of the Competition (Amendment) Act 2012 provides that when a person is convicted of a (criminal) offence under the Competition Act 2002, the court shall order the offender to pay to the relevant authority the costs incurred concerning the investigation, detection, and prosecution of the offence, 'unless the court is satisfied that there are special and substantial reasons for not so doing'. An example of a special and substantial reason for not imposing such orders in a given case could be the desire to ensure that the punishment meted out to the convicted cartelist is not disproportionate to his actions.

There are, however, limitations to a number of these arguments. First, any measurement of the benefits of any form of anti-cartel enforcement is likely to be speculative due to the absence of certainty concerning the number of cartels that are in existence at any given time.[274] This fact alone undermines one of the alleged advantages of using economic deterrence theory: the exactitude it provides in determining an optimal enforcement strategy. Second, the use of one of the identified methods to facilitate more efficient antitrust enforcement—namely, plea-bargaining—is not without its own problems.[275] For a start, although it can be understood as 'a prompt, efficient and simple manner' of disposing of criminal cases,[276] the use of plea-bargaining may be a relatively alien concept to a given jurisdiction. In many EU Member States (particularly the civil jurisdictions), there is no formal system of plea-bargaining, unlike the US,

[267] See Bloom (2002a), 9.

[268] Cf. Parker and Nielsen (2008), 600: 'Our data does not support the proposition that business people see imprisonment as substantially more serious than the [administrative] penalties already available [for cartel activity under Australian law], although this may reflect the way we asked the questions rather than how business people in fact respond to criminalization and jail penalties for cartel conduct'.

[269] But *some level* of enforcement is required to ensure that citizens do not forget about the offence: Werden and Simon (1987), 934–5.

[270] See: Easterbrook (1983); and Victor (2004), 88–9. Cf. Garoupa and Stephen (2006).

[271] See Wils (2007a).

[272] See generally Kovacic (2007).

[273] See Whelan (2013d).

[274] Some commentators believe that the deterrence-based argument for cartel criminalization may therefore be based on 'wishful thinking': Harding and Joshua (2010), 354.

[275] For the literature on this, see Stephan (2008a), 39–40.

[276] Kathuria (2007), 60.

where plea-bargaining is seen as 'virtually indispensable' within its justice system.[277] While US successes in criminal antitrust enforcement may be due in part to the ability of US enforcers to rely upon the system of plea-bargaining,[278] that does not necessarily mean such a system should be created in the European regimes that wish to criminalize cartel activity: it would be naïve in the extreme to assume that (apparent) US successes in anti-cartel enforcement can be achieved in Europe by the mere transposition of their enforcement mechanisms and techniques.[279] Plea-bargaining also introduces the risk of undermining the procedural guarantees for the defendant, not to mention the risk of placing pressure on innocent people to plead guilty.[280] As noted by Wils, if the 'reward' for pleading guilty were

> so large that a 'flagrant disproportion' would exist been the two alternatives facing the defendant, it might be argued that the pressure to [accept the plea-bargain] would be compelling.[281]

Such pressure would clearly be inconsistent with European human rights law.[282] In addition, the existence of plea-bargaining can undermine efforts to underline the criminality of cartel activity and create support for the existence of criminal sanctions, as a 'full, well-publicised adversarial proceeding with undiscounted penalties (including a prison term) may help to bring into sharper focus the inherent criminality and egregious nature of cartel conduct'.[283] In any case, for plea-bargaining to work effectively, it is vitally important that the antitrust enforcement regime be transparent with regard to the severity of the sanctions facing those who violate the cartel prohibition: in the absence of transparency, potential plea-bargainers will be deterred from making guilty pleas.[284] By contrast, if plea-bargaining is combined with other features of the legal regime that are to the detriment of the accused (e.g., 'deliberately unbalanced procedural devices, psychological zealotry of enforcement officials and disproportionate penalties'[285]), it may result in 'far more negotiated pleas than would be warranted on the merits'.[286]

Third, the use of short custodial sentences to keep enforcement costs low is not without its own problems. Importantly, some jurisdictions (even where they have introduced criminal sanctions primarily for reasons of deterrence) may feel that long prison sentences would more adequately reflect society's condemnation of cartel activity than relatively short ones.[287] This is likely to be the case where significant numbers of stakeholders in the criminal antitrust regime view cartel activity as inherently morally wrong.[288] The extent to which cartel activity can be viewed as morally wrong is examined in Chapter 4.

[277] Vamos (2009), 621. It appears that over 90 per cent of criminal cases are resolved in the US through the use of plea-bargains; see, e.g., Gazal-Ayal (2006), 2311.

[278] See generally: Furse (2012), 98–105; and Stephan (2009d). On the advantages of the US system of plea-bargaining for antitrust enforcement, see Hammond (2006), 18–21.

[279] See, e.g., Beaton-Wells and Ezrachi (2011b), 20.

[280] Lawrence et al. (2008), 26. See also Darbyshire (2000), 902.

[281] Wils (2008b), 20.

[282] See, e.g., *Deweer v. Belgium* (1979–80) 2 EHRR 439. See also: OECD (2008), 39; and Ashworth and Redmayne (2010), 312–16.

[283] Gamble (2011), 452.

[284] Riley (2007), 3.

[285] Jacobs (2007), 50.

[286] Jacobs (2007), 45.

[287] See OECD (2007b), 7 and 12: 'having longer statutory sentences expresses a society's condemnation of hard-core cartels. This might be important also with respect to prosecutors and courts, who may sometimes fail to recognise that cartels are serious offences. With shorter statutory sentences, prosecutors might be less likely to pursue a case, and courts might be more inclined to let defendants off the hook and impose alternative sentences instead. Longer sentences can send a signal to them that cartels should be considered a serious criminal violation'.

[288] The US DoJ, for example, has been criticized in the past for seeking rather low sentences for antitrust offences; see, e.g., Smith (2005), 7–10.

Fourth, the arguments advanced do not take account of the fact that it will probably be more difficult (and therefore more costly) to secure a criminal conviction than it will be to impose an administrative fine. This is due to the fact that the human rights protections of the accused may have to be more robust if criminal sanctions are to be introduced.[289] The extent to which this is true in Europe is examined in detail in Chapter 5.

Fifth, some of the methods of increasing the benefits and reducing the costs of enforcement are already employed in administrative European antitrust proceedings. (Leniency is a case in point. This is also true, but to a lesser extent, for bounties.) In order for these methods to facilitate more efficient antitrust enforcement when *criminal* sanctions are employed, they must display *additional* benefits (or fewer costs) in this context. The extent to which this is true for leniency and bounties is also examined in Chapter 5.

Finally, there may be reluctance on behalf of the judiciary concerning the imposition of custodial sentences for economic crimes committed by 'respectable' members of society, an issue that is examined in Chapter 10 as one of the practical challenges of antitrust criminalization.

All of the six points noted directly above, then, demonstrate how difficult (efficient) deterrence is as a challenge for antitrust criminalization. Four of the points also bring into play additional categories of challenges for antitrust criminalization. Point three noted directly above highlights that the challenge of identifying the immorality of cartel activity (an additional *theoretical* challenge) can be relevant even when deterrence theory is employed to argue in favour of cartel crimination. Points four, five, and six also highlight the relevance of both *legal* and *practical* challenges for the application of the justificatory theory of deterrence. Specifically, the issue of human rights can impact upon the specifics of the challenge of deterrence theory. Furthermore, the achievement of (efficient) deterrence through criminalization of cartel activity also depends to an extent on the workability in practice of a number of enforcement mechanisms and strategies, such as the use of leniency/immunity or the encouragement (by, e.g., the legislature) of the judiciary to impose custodial sentences upon convicted cartelists. These particular points are central to the thesis of this book: that there is a dynamic relationship between the theoretical, legal, and practical challenges of European antitrust criminalization and that an effective antitrust criminalization policy is one which recognizes and respects this complex interaction.

It should be further noted here that the benefits of introducing and maintaining personal criminal sanctions for cartel activity may only be visible in the long term, that is, a considerable time after the outlay of the additional costs involved in setting up such a regime. Accordingly, one should be aware that 'introducing a criminal enforcement regime should be seen as a long-term, front-end loaded investment'[290] which may require a wide range of criminal prosecutions to 'give birth to a new culture'.[291] In the US—a jurisdiction with a very strong political commitment to criminal antitrust punishment—the creation of a norm accepting criminal antitrust sanctions took many years and required, inter alia, '[r]epeated well-publicized prosecutions' which 'served to persuade courts, legislators, business leaders, and the public generally that cartel activity warranted severe sanctions'.[292] It is important in this regard, then, that at the outset law-makers in particular are cognizant of the time lapse between cost and benefit. In the absence of such an understanding, antitrust enforcers could 'find that the patience of law-makers might be tested if the greater powers and resources they were willing to confer on a

289 See: Simonsson (2011); Spagnolo (2006), 135; and Stucke (2006), 532–3.
290 See Reindl (2006), 115. 291 Fingleton et al. (2007), 23.
292 Kovacic (2003–04), 422.

competition authority showed no immediate result'.[293] Patience and understanding, then, are both required if personal criminal sanctions are to lead to increased levels of deterrence of cartel activity. Such patience and understanding may be particularly difficult to maintain if there are 'teething problems' with the first number of criminal cartel trials.[294]

(c) The lack of an effective alternative

In order to justify the imposition of criminal antitrust sanctions for the purpose of deterring cartel activity, one would have to demonstrate, inter alia, that there is no other effective alternative: the criminal law must be the 'last resort'.[295] This is so for at least two reasons. First, the creation of a criminal antitrust regime requires a significant expenditure of resources. Second, potentially very serious consequences face an individual cartelist subjected to a criminal process. If one can achieve the objective of deterrence but nonetheless avoid these negative outcomes, such an approach should be adopted.

Economic deterrence theory is used below to argue that there are no equally effective alternatives to the introduction and maintenance of the threat of imprisonment so as to deter cartel activity:[296] private enforcement, director disqualifications, and negative publicity orders suffer from critical defects which undermine their efforts to rectify the identified enforcement deficiencies—defects which are not present with the non-indemnifiable individual sanction of imprisonment. Consequently, by employing this theory, the requirement of no effective alternative can be met and the deterrence-based argument advanced above would not be limited in this regard.

A caveat needs to be advanced here, however: the arguments detailed below would only be valid if economic deterrence theory can actually be applied to cartel activity in the first place. This was an inquiry that was conducted directly above.[297] So even if the arguments which follow are accepted, they are still subject to the specific limitations identified above regarding the employment of economic deterrence theory to justify the criminalization of cartel activity.

(i) Private enforcement

It was argued above using economic deterrence theory that the imposition of an optimal fine would be likely to lead to the liquidation of the infringing company, that this is to be avoided, and that any sanction which depends solely upon *financial impact* for its effectiveness will not ensure optimal deterrence, as the corresponding optimal financial penalty cannot be imposed in practice. According to this argument, penalties which deter solely through their financial impact are not, therefore, effective alternatives to imprisonment.[298] Unfortunately, private enforcement, as a mechanism of imposing financial liability through damages awards, is such a penalty.[299] Consequently, 'the deterrent effect of private actions is limited by the same factors that apply to high fines imposed as a result of public enforcement actions'.[300] Following this line of argument, private enforcement is not an effective alternative to imprisonment. This argument has

[293] See Reindl (2006), 115.

[294] The first (unsuccessful) UK criminal antitrust case that went to trial comes to mind here: *R v. Burns and others*, Unreported Judgment, Southwark Crown Court, 10 May 2010; see, e.g.: OFT (2010c); and OFT (2010d).

[295] See generally: Ashworth (2000); and Husak (2004).

[296] On this, see OFT (2007b).

[297] See Section D(b) of this chapter.

[298] Cf. Lande and Davis (2011).

[299] See Wils (2006b), 87.

[300] OECD (2011), 15.

been advanced most forcefully by Werden et al.,[301] who have posited in the process that the (claimed) success of private antitrust enforcement in the US 'depends on the work of the Antitrust Division' in that '[a]voiding criminal fines is a powerful inducement to apply for leniency, and leniency applications are the most important means of cartel detection, which in turn makes them critical in cartel deterrence'.[302]

This is not to say, however, that private enforcement, even with its evident difficulties,[303] should not be used as a *complement* to other enforcement efforts,[304] in particular given that it may help to fulfil secondary objectives of antitrust enforcement, such as compensating victims and reducing the regulatory burden of the antitrust authorities. The European Commission has acknowledged the role that private enforcement can play in this context and has been consistent in its efforts to encourage the development of this form of competition law enforcement in Europe,[305] above all in order to ensure that the victims of competition law violations exercise their Treaty rights to compensation.[306] An investigation of the advisability of encouraging private enforcement in order to fulfil any secondary objectives of antitrust enforcement is outside of the scope of this book.[307]

(ii) Director disqualification

In general terms, director disqualification orders are court orders which make it a criminal offence for an affected individual to act as a director of a company for a defined period of time. They exist in a number of EU Member States, such as Estonia, Sweden, and the United Kingdom. The relevant UK legislation provides an illustrative example of how this type of enforcement technique can be designed.[308] Section 204 of the UK Enterprise Act 2002 amends the Company Directors Disqualification Act 1986 and allows the OFT to secure a Competition Disqualification Order ('CDO') against a company director if his company breaches the competition law rules and a court finds that his behaviour renders him unfit to be concerned in the management of a company. During the time period of the CDO (which can be up to 15 years), it is a criminal offence for the affected individual to act as a director of a company, to act as receiver of a company's property, or, in any way, whether directly or indirectly, to be concerned or take part in the promotion, formation, or management of a company, or to act as an insolvency partner.[309]

It has been argued that director disqualification is a more appropriate method of ensuring deterrence of cartel activity than the introduction and maintenance of criminal cartel sanctions: they are less costly to implement; they do not necessitate an intensive reform of the enforcement landscape; and they do not require the enforcer to meet criminal standards of proof.[310] It is submitted here, however, that although useful to some degree in deterring cartel activity[311]—in that they force directors of companies to think twice

301 Werden et al. (2011).
302 Werden et al. (2011), 233–4.
303 Relating to issues such as, inter alia, passing-on, direct and indirect purchasers, causation, incentivizing claimants, and calculation of damage; see, e.g.: <http://ec.europa.eu/competition/antitrust/actionsdamages/white_paper_comments.html>; and Baker (2004).
304 See Lowe (2007), 101. Cf. Wils (2003c).
305 See generally <http://ec.europa.eu/competition/antitrust/actionsdamages/index.html>.
306 See European Commission (2008b), [14].
307 On private enforcement generally, see Foer and Cuneo (2010).
308 On the UK approach, see generally Hughes (2008), 642 et seq.
309 Sections 1 and 13 of the Company Directors Disqualification Act 1986.
310 See Khan (2012). Cf. Morgan (2010), 82; and Harding and Joshua (2010), 356.
311 See OFT (2010a), 7–9.

about the (financial and non-financial) consequences of their actions and/or to encourage their firm to comply with competition law[312]—director disqualification orders do not rectify the identified enforcement failures as effectively as imprisonment.[313] First, serious drawbacks concerning their implementation exist: they cannot be used against non-directors (actively) involved in cartel activity; their deterrent effect depends to a large degree upon how close the director is to retirement; and suitable indemnification by the company may still be possible.[314] Second, they are unlikely to be very effective in jurisdictions where relatively small companies, in particular family-owned businesses, are the norm (such as, for example, Ireland, Malta, or Cyprus). A disqualified director in such a jurisdiction 'might still exercise control through having a family member act in their stead, thus limiting the deterrent effect of such measures'.[315] Third, in principle, they are less condemnatory of an individual's behaviour than imprisonment; therefore, the deterrent effect of the moral consequences of unlawful activity will not be as strong as is possible.[316] This line of argument is consistent with recent developments in *Marine Hoses*,[317] a criminal case that resulted in the imposition of terms of imprisonment and of CDOs on three UK nationals.[318] As noted by MacCulloch, the appeal in that case indicated a clear desire on the part of the appellants to minimize the pain of jail, but did not include an attempt to reduce the length of the director disqualifications; for him, '[t]hat choice suggests that CDOs constitute a much less effective deterrent; perhaps because imprisonment would effectively end a career, or it may be that CDOs are not, in reality, a significant hindrance to future earnings'.[319] Nonetheless, since with disqualification, punishment is more condemnatory and indemnification less straightforward than is the case with fines, it is submitted that these orders should exist as a complementary mechanism for achieving deterrence.[320]

(iii) Negative publicity orders

Adverse publicity orders generally involve a court, in addition to any other sentence imposed, ordering that a notice be placed in an appropriate publication (including a company's annual report) within a specified period acknowledging a wrongful act by a corporate body.[321] Such orders find their rationale in 'the notion of shaming: their purpose is to damage the offender's reputation'.[322] One can argue that the potential for financial loss occasioned by damage to a company's reputation has the potential to secure a deterrent effect. Unfavourable publicity occasioned by discovery of a competition law infringement can lead to an adverse effect on a company's reputation.[323] This in turn can lead to financial losses for a company. Presumably, the possibility of

312 See Morgan (2010), 80.

313 See generally Stephan (2011a). See also Ellison (2011).

314 Wils (2006b), 86.

315 Massey (2012), 163.

316 Wils (2006b), 86.

317 *R v. Whittle and others* [2008] EWCA Crim 2560.

318 To be clear, the three individuals who were imprisoned in this case received CDOs under a separate provision contained within Section 2 of the Company Directors Disqualification Act 1986, which allows the disqualification of directors who have committed a criminal offence.

319 MacCulloch (2010a), 291.

320 Wils also holds this view: Wils (2006b), 87. Interestingly, some authors do not even consider the usefulness of disqualification in their criminalization arguments; see, e.g., Calvani (2004b).

321 See Macrory (2006), 92 et seq.

322 See Law Reform Commission of New South Wales (2003), [11.2].

323 There is in fact some evidence in the literature that a finding of a violation of competition law has a negative reputational effect; see van den Broek et al. (2012).

suffering such publicity stimulates deterrence as it may reduce a firm's profit-maximizing potential.[324] Research, however, suggests that adverse publicity orders deter through their non-financial impacts; executives, apparently, are concerned with 'corporate prestige'.[325] Reputation and self-esteem seem to be particularly important for firms and their senior executives, as evidenced by a number of case studies and empirical observation.[326] For this reason, negative publicity may be a useful sanction. Advocates of such punishment argue that 'public humiliation of the offender will, in some circumstances, deter criminal behaviour in a highly cost-effective way'.[327] The French and Brazilian competition authorities have powers to order competition law infringers to publicize their infringements and may thus be able to benefit from the deterrent effects of such humiliation.[328] It is submitted, however, that, according to economic deterrence theory, such orders, while valuable, are inferior to criminal sanctions and are not an effective alternative (as opposed to complement). First, although concerned with corporate prestige, executives and the companies for which they work also value profit.[329] The research referred to does not establish that the ability of unlawful activity to create profit will by necessity always be trumped by possible effects on reputation, but, rather, that possible negative reputation per se has an ability to deter. But cartel activity, as we know, stimulates profits.[330] The expected cost of apprehension associated with adverse publicity orders—uncertain loss of reputation (with minimal financial effect)—therefore should be balanced against the benefits of cartel activity. It is submitted that the substantial benefits from cartel activity, the low chances of getting caught, the link between corporate prestige and profit, the pressures felt by executives to secure shareholder returns, not to mention the minimal financial impact of negative publicity orders, are sufficient factors to tip the balance in favour of cartel activity. Second, publicity orders, like director disqualification orders, are less effective at deterring through condemnation, as they involve a far less severe form of denunciation than imprisonment,[331] and one focused more on the company than its constituent individuals. Third, by favouring the use of such a mechanism over criminal sanctions, the authorities are still open to the criticism that they do not seek the same level of condemnation for cartel activity as they do for other (comparably harmful) white-collar crimes, such as conspiracy to defraud.[332] Fourth, by employing such measures, even if they secure optimal deterrence, one sends out a signal that society does not disapprove of such behaviour as strongly as it does (or

[324] For an interesting empirical article which argues that cartel offenders are disciplined largely through market-induced reputational penalties rather than legal penalties, see van den Broek et al. (2012).

[325] Fisse and Braithwaite (1983). The effects of such orders on profitability seem to be minimal: Fisse and Braithwaite (1983). Cf. Ministry of Economic Development (2010), [54].

[326] Yeung (2006), 549, relying upon studies such as: Cowan (1992); Curcio (1996); Kahan and Posner (1999); and Skeel (2001).

[327] Posner (2000), 88.

[328] See Lusty (2010), 345–6.

[329] Corporate prestige, in any case, is not wholly independent of profit. For one, a firm cannot dedicate sufficient resources to maintaining/improving its reputation without first satisfying shareholders with adequate investment returns; if profit is secured through cartel activity more resources will be available to devote to improving a firm's reputation. Also, the mere fact that a firm secures exorbitant profit in itself may generate a desirable reputation.

[330] It may also lead to direct financial gain for the cartelists; see Joyce (1989), 34. See also: Ministry of Economic Development (2010), [48]; and Furse (2012), 35: 'Executives who engage in cartel activity may do so in order to secure enhanced profits for their employer *and* rewards for themselves. Typically these might be higher salaries reflecting increased profitability, promotion, or simply the ability to bask in the warm glow of a superior's approval'.

[331] Cf. Beaton-Wells (2008b), 226.

[332] On the moral content of cartel activity, see Chapter 4 of this book.

would if sufficient understanding of the concept of a cartel existed); this is avoided with optimal criminal sanctions. Finally, some potential benefits of criminalization (e.g., a criminal immunity programme and increased investigatory powers) would no longer be available; this could be particularly damaging to the fight against cartels, where evidence of unlawful behaviour is often difficult to uncover.[333]

E. Conclusion

This chapter identified and examined the theoretical challenge of deterrence for European antitrust criminalization. In doing so, it demonstrated that a strong deterrence-based criminalization argument can be constructed concerning cartel activity: imprisonment helps, inter alia, to overcome the significant problems associated with optimally deterrent cartel fines, in particular: inability to pay; difficulties with individual (financial) responsibility; and proportional justice. It would also ensure that European anti-cartel enforcement would no longer lack adequate condemnation of offenders (as an instrumental factor in ensuring deterrence). Arguably, then, deterrence theory can be relied upon as a foundation for antitrust criminalization, and this justificatory theory is therefore relevant to the discussions which are later conducted in this book concerning the legalities to be adhered to in criminalizing cartel activity.

However, the deterrence-based criminalization argument is not as robust as some legal commentators would have one believe; in fact, it suffers from a number of potential limitations. Specifically, the case in favour of the employment of criminal antitrust sanctions to deter cartel activity is vulnerable to the extent that one can demonstrate that: (i) cartel activity is morally neutral conduct; (ii) undertakings are risk averse; (iii) undertakings/individuals do not act rationally; and (iv) personal criminal sanctions are incapable of generating more benefits than costs. It is submitted that these specific limitations together form the main theoretical challenge of deterrence as the basis for European antitrust criminalization and that, given the extent of the (above-examined) difficulties associated with each of the identified limitations, this challenge will continue to confront those who argue in favour of antitrust criminalization for reasons of deterrence.

It was illustrated in this chapter that the (deterrence-focused) challenge of demonstrating that personal criminal sanctions are capable of generating more benefits than costs involves consideration of legal challenges (i.e. respecting human rights) as well as practical challenges (i.e. designing effective mechanisms of detection and strategies to reduce enforcement costs and ensure the judiciary impose custodial sentences). These issues will be considered respectively in Parts II and III of this book.

As was also demonstrated in this chapter, the challenge of deterrence is not altogether removed from the other theoretical challenge under investigation: the challenge of retribution. Indeed, one of the specific limitations of the deterrence-based antitrust criminalization argument is the potential for cartel activity to be criminalized even if its content is 'morally neutral': in the absence of (negative) moral content, the criminalization of cartel activity may result in unfair labelling of offenders as criminals, a process which may undermine the moral authority of the law, change people's attitudes towards the

[333] An administrative leniency programme could still be established, however, although the authorities would still have less to bargain with (i.e. they could not threaten individuals with imprisonment) and probably fewer investigatory powers. On leniency, see Chapter 5, Section D(b)(ii) and Chapter 9 in this book.

meaning of criminality, and/or cause the criminal law to lose some of its legitimacy. If cartel activity can be conceptualized as a moral wrong, these negative outcomes can be avoided and the deterrence-based argument in support of antitrust criminalization will be strengthened. Yet such a conceptualization also introduces the possibility of reliance upon retribution as a justificatory theory for criminal antitrust punishment. It is true, however, that with retribution theory the moral content of cartel activity is of more importance than with the theory of deterrence: the former theory, after all, actually *requires* the existence of immoral behaviour. The chapter which follows (Chapter 4)—focusing as it does on the challenge of retribution for antitrust criminalization—therefore examines in detail the moral quality of cartel activity. While that chapter does not consider directly the challenge of deterrence theory for antitrust criminalization, it is clear nonetheless that its findings are also of crucial importance for a comprehensive understanding of the complexity of that particular challenge.

4

European Antitrust Criminalization and the Challenge of Retribution Theory

A. Introduction

As explained in Chapters 2 and 3, the European antitrust criminalization debate has focused for the most part on the deterrent effect of personal criminal sanctions for cartel activity. This reflects the fact that deterrence 'is the generally accepted rationale for public antitrust sanctions'.[1] In a nutshell, those who advocate antitrust criminalization highlight its necessity for the achievement of optimal deterrence,[2] while those opposed to it argue the contrary.[3] Relatively little room is reserved in this debate for consideration of the justificatory punishment theory of retribution. Indeed, there 'has been only a limited amount of work analysing the relationship between morality and competition law specifically'.[4] That said, it is true that those who depend upon deterrence theory to oppose antitrust criminalization sometimes emphasize the neutral moral character of cartel activity in order to underline further the inappropriateness of criminal punishment.[5] Others have argued that 'moral ambiguity' surrounds cartel activity.[6] Some commentators also highlight that a criminal cartel offence, if it is to exist, should be constructed on the basis of definitional elements relevant to retribution.[7] Furthermore, it is possible to find some pro-criminalization arguments centred on the (negative) moral character of cartel activity.[8] Admittedly, however, these are more often than not supplied in addition to, and in order to bolster, a (positive) argument concerning deterrence.[9] In fact, the issue of the morality of cartel activity is far from settled. Even in the US, where political and popular support for severe criminal sanctions for hard-core cartels exists, the moralistic aim of the Sherman Act 1890 has been questioned. For Hovenkamp, for example, antitrust law is 'an economic, not a moral, enterprise'.[10] Others, by contrast, have likened cartel activity to 'economic racketeering'[11] or accepted that 'antitrust has always had a strong moral dimension less apparent in the rest of the world'.[12] For the Bureau of

[1] Calvani and Calvani (2011), 186. [2] See, e.g., Wils (2006b).

[3] See, e.g., Buccirossi and Spagnolo (2005). [4] Furse (2012), 14.

[5] See, e.g., the comments of Switzerland in OECD (2003b), 106. Some commentators who are actually in favour of antitrust criminalization for reasons of deterrence believe that the moral quality of cartel activity is not sufficient to support by itself the existence of criminal sanctions; see, e.g., Simonsson (2009), 126.

[6] Beaton-Wells and Haines (2009).

[7] See Braum (2012), 113 (a cartel offence 'must be based on guilt and must be a proportionate reaction to deviant behaviour').

[8] See, e.g.: Hoel (2008); and King (2010).

[9] See, e.g.: Clarke (2005); Clarke and Bagaric (2003); Fels (2002); and King (2010). Even the US antitrust authorities (who consider cartel activity to be 'morally wrong') feel obliged to construct a (positive) deterrence-based argument for criminal antitrust sanctions; see OECD (2003b), 99.

[10] Hovenkamp (2005a), 10, 54. See also Crane (2007), 1196. Interestingly, this view appears to exist in the jurisprudence of Australia, a country that recently introduced criminal antitrust sanctions; see: *Queensland Wire Industries Pty Ltd v. Broken Hill Pty Co. Ltd* (1989) 167 CLR 177; and Brunt (1990), 88–9.

[11] See the comments of Attorney General Robert Kennedy in Spivack (1963), 45.

[12] Baker (2011), 32.

Immigration and Customs Enforcement, criminal violations of the US Sherman Act are 'crimes involving moral turpitude, which may subject an alien to exclusion or deportation from the United States',[13] a claim that has been subjected to academic criticism.[14]

For some commentators, cartel activity is a sophisticated form of theft involving the deceitful acquisition of wealth that rightly belongs to the consumer;[15] accordingly, such activity 'robs consumers and other market participants of the tangible blessings of competition'[16] or ensures that 'customers or suppliers are deceived into believing that their suppliers or customers are competing with each other'.[17] These sorts of arguments were accepted by the Australian Competition and Consumer Commission ('ACCC') and the Australian Government in the context of the criminalization of cartel activity in Australia,[18] even though cartel activity was not perceived by the public as unambiguously criminal.[19] Interestingly, the US Supreme Court, for its part, views cartels as 'the supreme evil of antitrust',[20] a phrase that is not without its own measure of moralistic overtones. The US antitrust official, Klein, offers the most memorable phrase, however; for him, cartel activity is nothing more than 'theft by well-dressed thieves'.[21] While such moralistic claims have been questioned somewhat by antitrust academics,[22] the relevant literature presents comparatively few thorough analyses of the morality of cartel activity[23] or of the desirability of introducing criminal antitrust sanctions for retributive reasons.[24] In short, a comprehensive retribution-based argument in favour of (or indeed against) antitrust criminalization has not been established: the theoretical challenge of retribution in the context of antitrust criminalization has yet to be examined in any great detail.

The challenge of the theory of retribution requires attention in the European antitrust criminalization debate.[25] Chapter 3 demonstrated, inter alia, that there is a strong argument for the imposition of criminal punishment on individuals in order to deter future cartel activity. That is not to concede, however, that an equally valid argument is incapable of being constructed in this context concerning the use of criminal punishment for retributive reasons: a robust deterrence-based antitrust criminalization argument does not preclude a strong retribution-based argument. In fact, if both deterrence theory and retribution theory could be relied upon to justify criminal antitrust sanctions, the case in favour of such sanctions would be even more compelling than would be the case if only deterrence theory could be employed. (The opposite is also true of course: if neither deterrence theory nor retribution theory offers convincing justifications for

[13] DoJ and INS (1996), 1.

[14] See Grannon and Kownacki (2012).

[15] See, e.g.: Beaton-Wells and Fisse (2008b), 186; Bloom (2002a); Pate (2003), 2; and Whish (2009), 498.

[16] Werden (2009), 23. See also Stelzer (2001), 38.

[17] Warren-Boulton (1990), 346.

[18] See: Beaton-Wells and Parker (2013), 199; Beaton-Wells (2008b), 210–13; and Beaton-Wells and Haines (2010).

[19] See: Beaton-Wells and Haines (2009); and Haines and Beaton-Wells (2012).

[20] *Verizon Communications v. Law Offices of Curtis V. Trinko* (2004) 540 US 398, 408. See also Barnett (2007). The OECD argues that hard-core cartels are 'the most egregious violations of competition law': OECD (1998), Part A2(a).

[21] Klein (1999a), 1; and Klein (1999b), 3.

[22] See Furse and Nash (2004a), ix and 27, footnote 77.

[23] The notable exceptions are: Beaton-Wells (2007); Stucke (2006); Harding (2010); Harding (2006); Harding (2004); Harding (2002); Gray (2008); and MacCulloch (2012).

[24] Stephan has even argued that morality should be excluded from the debate: Stephan (2012). Clarke has argued that immorality should not be a basis for criminalization, but 'may help to garner public support for criminalization': Clarke (2012), 83.

[25] For an earlier treatment by the author, see Whelan (2013a).

antitrust criminalization, the case in favour of criminal antitrust sanctions would be untenable. It should be remembered here that theories of criminalization other than deterrence and retribution are of limited use in the antitrust context.[26]) Retribution theory, then, remains relevant, irrespective of the findings in Chapter 3. Indeed, given the existence of the specific limitations noted in the previous chapter concerning the use of deterrence theory, conscientious legislators may wish to examine the viability of an alternative justification for the introduction of personal criminal antitrust sanctions. To legislators, retribution theory—with its focus on the morality of a given conduct—may actually appear more attractive than deterrence as a justification for criminal antitrust sanctions, especially given the traditional link between the criminal law and immoral behaviour.[27] One should not forget either that forceful rhetoric about punishing 'theft by well-dressed thieves'[28] may also be particularly appreciated by (voting) consumers.[29] In actual fact, the mere existence of such comments in the literature is sufficient to warrant an examination of the moral content of cartel activity: to date, such comments remain for the most part uninvestigated; in the absence of clarification and verification, they engender the risk of introducing emotive sentiment into what should be a critical and objective criminalization debate. In short, these comments should not be taken at face value: the application of retribution theory to cartel activity would need to be robust if it is to be taken seriously by conscientious law-makers, not to mention legal commentators and scholars. In addition, it has been argued that there is considerable merit in using retribution theory to analyse the criminality of cartel activity: it offers a 'compelling' explanation for 'a new emphasis on cartels as truly criminal' as it 'links the special attributes that set cartels apart from other anticompetitive conduct with a general rationale for criminal enforcement'.[30] However, as noted in Chapter 2, it is clear that retribution theory itself suffers from a number of general limitations. For some, these limitations may ensure its undesirability as a justificatory theory for criminalization. Even so, an analysis of the challenge of the theory of retribution for antitrust criminalization would still be welcome: such an analysis explores the moral content of cartel activity. As mentioned in the conclusion to Chapter 3, the degree to which cartel activity displays moral content is also relevant for the *deterrence*-based antitrust criminalization argument: it determines the extent to which that particular argument suffers from an inherent limitation, namely, whether it would lead to the imposition of criminal punishment for morally neutral behaviour. For all of these reasons, then, the application of the criminal punishment theory of retribution to cartel activity requires attention from legal academics; consequently, it is considered in this chapter.

This chapter, then, aims to analyse the challenge of retribution theory for antitrust criminalization and therefore whether retribution theory can actually be relied upon as a solid foundation for such criminalization: it represents the second (and final) treatment of the process of 'application' noted above in the methodology section of Chapter 1.[31] By doing so, it also determines the extent to which retribution theory should be relevant to the discussions concerning legalities and practicalities that occur in Parts II and III of this book. A two-step approach is taken in this chapter: the first step involves the establishment of a framework to determine the 'moral content' of a given behaviour; the second step applies that framework to cartel activity and in the process examines: (i) the extent

[26] See Chapter 2, Section B(a) of this book.
[27] On the (un)tenability of this 'traditional' link, see Smith (2002), 17 et seq.
[28] Klein (1999a), 1; and Klein (1999b), 3.
[29] See, e.g., O'Dea (1998). See also Massey (2012), 166.
[30] Quaid (2012), 154.
[31] See Chapter 1, Section D(a)(iv)(2) of this book.

to which such activity displays sufficient (negative) moral content to be put forward as a suitable candidate for criminalization if retribution theory is employed as a rationale; and (ii) the limitations and weaknesses of a retribution-based antitrust criminalization argument and, hence, the theoretical challenge of retribution in the context of European antitrust criminalization. This chapter is divided into two substantive sections, each of which reflects the two-step approach adopted herein: Section B presents the first step and Section C deals with the second step. Some concluding observations are also offered.

B. Step 1: Establishing a Framework to Determine 'Moral Content'

Employment of the theory of retribution in the European antitrust criminalization debate forces one to analyse the moral quality of cartel activity. To do so, one requires a general framework which can be used to determine the moral content of a given behaviour. The American legal theorist Green presents a useful tripartite framework for such purposes.[32] It is employed in this book. According to this framework, moral content can be analysed by examining three interrelated concepts: culpability; social harmfulness; and moral wrongfulness.

(a) The tripartite framework

The first element in determining the moral content of a given activity, 'culpability', relates to the moral value of the state of mind of a given defendant at the time when he commits an offence; it reflects the degree to which one is blameworthy or responsible.[33] Traditionally under the criminal law, there have been two necessary components of a crime: the actus reus (i.e. a wrongful act) and the mens rea (i.e. a guilty mind).[34] The former component concerns itself with the actions of the defendant and their consequences, while the latter focuses on the actor himself and, more specifically, on the intent behind his actions. In terms of morality, a defendant without a guilty mind is usually deemed to be less culpable, and therefore less deserving of punishment, than a defendant who intends his actions or has no excuse for his conduct. In terms of law, however, it is true that 'strict liability' crimes have become increasingly common, reducing somewhat the moral content of the criminal law. That said, these offences are often viewed as being inconsistent with the moral role of criminal punishment.[35]

The second element in determining the moral content of a given activity is the concept of 'social harmfulness'. Unlike culpability, this element focuses on the consequences of the conduct of a defendant and not on particular aspects of the defendant himelf; rather, it reflects the degree of harm caused, or which risks being caused, by the defendant.[36] Mill argued as far back as the 1850s that the criminal law should only be concerned with behaviour that harms others.[37] If society values individual liberty, the criminal law should serve a minimalist role and not be concerned with all morally

[32] See: Green (2006); and Green (1997). For criticism of the framework, see: Berman (2007); Henning (2008); Milligan (2007); and Steel (2006).

[33] See Green (1997), 1547–8. See also Loewy (1988), 285–7.

[34] See, e.g.: Loewy (1988), 283; and Padfield (2006).

[35] On this debate, see generally: Brickey (1982); Diamond (1996); Hart (1958), 422; and Wasserstrom (1960). See also Simester (2005).

[36] See Green (1997), 1549.

[37] Mill (1859).

wrongful behaviour; it should attempt to identify and regulate only the wrongful conduct which causes or risks causing significant social harm.[38] As others have put it, the criminal law should be the 'last resort' concerning regulation of behaviour.[39] According to Feinberg, state interference with a given citizen's behaviour can be justified on moral grounds when it is 'reasonably necessary' to prevent harm (or the unreasonable risk of harm) to third parties.[40] Social harm in this context can be defined generally as the 'negation, endangering, or destruction of an individual, group or state interest which was deemed socially valuable',[41] where an interest refers to something in which one has a stake.[42]

The final element in determining the moral content of a given activity is the concept of 'moral wrongfulness'. Conduct constitutes a moral wrong if the conduct in question is in violation of a moral norm,[43] such as that prohibiting stealing, deceiving, or cheating.[44] In contrast to culpability, moral wrongfulness is concerned with the nature of the conduct in question, and not with the state of mind of the defendant. That said, the nature of certain acts may be so intrinsically linked to the mental state of an actor that his culpability should be taken into account in determining whether that act is morally wrong.[45] Unlike social harmfulness, it does not reflect the consequences of the conduct, but rather the inherent moral value of that conduct. So although socially harmful conduct, such as murder, may also constitute a moral wrong, it does not necessarily follow that a moral wrong will always occasion a social harm. It is axiomatic that those crimes which are justified solely by reference to retribution theory will display a strong degree of moral wrongfulness, as retribution theory by definition dictates the (deserved) punishment of those who have engaged in what society deems to be morally objectionable conduct.[46]

(b) The merits of the framework

Both Stucke and Beaton-Wells have acknowledged the value of Green's framework and have employed it in their analyses of the morality of antitrust. The former believes that the framework is 'helpful' in evaluating the moral content of the antitrust conduct that has been criminalized by the Sherman Act 1890,[47] while the latter contends that it is 'of substantial assistance in tackling the moral debate surrounding the criminalization of cartels and, in particular, in identifying the source(s) of moral wrongfulness in such activity'.[48] Neither of these legal commentators used the framework to establish a retribution-based argument in favour of criminalization; by contrast, they used it to analyse the moral

[38] Dressler (2001), 2. [39] See Husak (2004). See also Ashworth (2009), 31–4.

[40] Feinberg (1984), 11. [41] Dressler (2001), § 9.10[B].

[42] Green (1997), 1549, referring to Feinberg (1984), 33–4.

[43] A 'norm' can be understood 'as a rule that distinguishes desirable and undesirable behavior and gives a third party the authority to punish a person who engages in the undesirable behavior. Thus, a norm constrains attempts by people to satisfy their preferences. In these ways, a norm is like a law, except that a private person sanctions the violator of a norm, whereas a state actor sanctions the violator of a law': Posner (1996), 1699. An alternative conceptualization of a norm is as a 'standard of behaviour' that is 'based on widely shared beliefs how individual group members ought to behave in a given situation': Fehr and Fischbacher (2004), 185. On norms generally, see Mitchell (1999).

[44] See Green (1997), 1551 et seq.

[45] Green (1997), 1552. Some scholars have used this fact to criticize the tripartite division of culpability, social harmfulness, and moral wrongfulness; see, e.g., Berman (2007), 314: 'it would seem that *mens rea* is built into moral wrongfulness and therefore should not be an independent requirement'.

[46] See Chapter 2, Section B(c) of this book. [47] Stucke (2006), 491.

[48] Beaton-Wells (2007), 679.

content of a given law or a specific proposal.[49] It should be noted that Green himself conceded that he did not argue that the elements of the framework constitute a set of necessary or sufficient conditions for criminalization.[50] In fact, he did not claim to be a retributionist at all. Rather, he sought to use the framework as an analytical structure 'for describing white-collar crime's moral complexity'.[51] That said, Green nonetheless submitted that a lack of one or more of the elements in the framework should call into question the desirability of criminalization.[52] This concern with what can be termed 'over-criminalization' was considered in detail in Chapter 3 and represents the primary rationale for constructing a retribution-based criminalization argument: avoiding moral neutrality.

The framework is useful for present purposes. First, as detailed in Chapter 2, there are two important principles inherent in the use of a retribution-based theory: responsibility and proportionality. The framework is capable of capturing and respecting these two principles and, therefore, if employed, would help to provide a solid foundation for locating cartel activity within a retribution-based argument. 'Culpability', as noted above, reflects the degree to which one is *responsible* for one's action; in other words, it implements the responsibility principle, whereby punishment is imposed only if one is accountable for the underlying conduct. As also explained above, both the gravity of the harm (i.e. 'social harmfulness') and the degree of blameworthiness (i.e. 'culpability') affect the seriousness of an offence and thus, following the proportionality principle of retribution theory, the severity of punishment.[53] The framework focuses on and develops both of the concepts of culpability and social harmfulness—essential components of retribution theory. In order to respect the proportionality principle, however, they must also be *commensurate* with the severity of punishment. The framework acknowledges this relationship.[54] 'Moral wrongfulness' for its part represents quite clearly the underlying concern of retribution theory: punishment for offences against the moral code.[55] The framework thus takes account of the essential concerns of retribution theory. Second, if one uses the framework advocated by Green, one must acknowledge (inter alia) that moral wrongfulness is a norm-based concept, not a rights-based one.[56] This approach is less abstract than its 'traditional' counterpart, and therefore has the advantage of comprehensibility: 'Even people who have never had occasion to read a single page of moral philosophy are capable of making finely grained distinctions about, say, what properly constitutes cheating or stealing'.[57] Indeed, it is Green's treatment of moral wrongfulness that is particularly useful for present purposes, i.e. determining the moral quality of a particular type of conduct which may at first glance seem innocuous or morally neutral. The framework, then, fills the 'critical gap in the literature... by supplying a new tool kit for understanding why everyday conduct, from speaking to investors to making campaign contributions to politicians, can be a crime worthy of society's moral condemnation';[58] to this list can be added the concept of cartel activity. Finally, the framework, by concentrating on morality, provides a means of ensuring that a distinction is made between the criminalized conduct and conduct which is subject to only civil or administrative sanctions.[59] According to Beaton-Wells, it 'is crucial to the integrity

[49] Beaton-Wells used the framework to analyse a proposal to introduce criminal sanctions for cartel activity in Australia: Beaton-Wells (2007), 679.

[50] Green (2006), 30. [51] Green (2006), 30. [52] Green (2006), 30.

[53] See Galligan (1981), 164.

[54] Explicitly with respect to culpability: Green (2006), 31; and implicitly with respect to social harmfulness: Green (2006), 34–9.

[55] See Galligan (1981), 144. [56] Steel (2006), 350. Cf. Feinberg (1984).

[57] Green (2006), 44. [58] Henning (2008), 354.

[59] Beaton-Wells (2007), footnote 23.

and effectiveness of the criminal [antitrust] regime (if not competition policy and doctrine more generally) that these differences are both evident and justifiable'.[60]

C. Step 2: Employing the Framework to Examine the Moral Content of Cartel Activity (and Hence the Challenge of a Retribution-Based Criminalization Argument)

This section applies the tripartite framework set out directly above to the concept of 'cartel activity'. In doing so, it examines the extent to which cartel activity displays sufficient (negative) moral content to be put forward as a suitable candidate for criminalization if retribution theory is employed as a rationale. Furthermore, in examining the moral qualities of cartel activity, this section also identifies the limitations and weaknesses of a retribution-based antitrust criminalization argument and, hence, the theoretical challenge of retribution in the context of European antitrust criminalization.

Before proceeding, one should recall that the definition of 'cartel activity' which is employed below is the definition offered by the 1998 OECD Recommendation.[61] This definition is implemented in practice within the EU by virtue of Article 101 TFEU. At EU level, sanctions are only imposed on undertakings, not on individuals. Even so, while the argument presented below concerns the introduction of *individual* criminal sanctions, current EU-level cartel law enforcement (i.e. a system imposing *corporate* sanctions) is nonetheless used where necessary to demonstrate a number of important points.

(a) Culpability

Under current EU law, undertakings that have engaged in cartel activity are only subject to fines when they have 'intentionally or negligently' infringed Article 101 TFEU.[62] Actual knowledge of Article 101 TFEU is not required for an intentional infringement to be found.[63] For the European Courts, it is sufficient that the undertaking engaging in cartel activity 'could not have been unaware that its conduct was aimed at restricting competition'.[64] 'Intention' in this context refers to the intention to prevent, restrict, or distort competition; it does not refer to an intention actually to violate the European cartel rules themselves.[65] Intention will usually be found without much difficulty if an undertaking has previously been held to be in violation of the EU antitrust rules for the same practices.[66] Negligence, for its part, is determined according to an objective standard which is focused on the consequences of the undertaking's conduct. It occurs where 'the author of the infringement, although acting without any intention to perform an unlawful act, has not foreseen the consequences of [his] action in circumstances where

[60] Beaton-Wells (2007), footnote 23.

[61] OECD (1998). See Chapter 1, Section C(a) of this book.

[62] Council of the European Union (2003), Article 23(2).

[63] Case 19/77, *Miller v. Commission* [1978] ECR 131, [18]. See also: Case T-29/92, *SPO v. Commission* [1995] ECR II-289, [356]–[358]; Case T-61/89, *Dansk Pelsdyravlerforing v. Commission* [1992] ECR II-1931, [157]; and Case C-279/87, *Tipp-Ex v. Commission* [1990] ECR I-261.

[64] Case T-143/89, *Ferriere Nord v. Commission* [1995] ECR II-917, [41].

[65] Joined Cases T-305–7, 313–16, 318, 328–9, and 335/94, *Limburgse Vinyl Maatschappij and others v. Commission* [1995] ECR II-00931, [1111].

[66] See *Michelin* (Case COMP/E-2/36.041/PO), Commission Decision, 20 June 2001, [2002] OJ L143/1, [352].

a person who is normally informed and sufficiently attentive could not have failed to foresee them'.[67] A negligent infringement is treated less severely than an intentional one: under the 2006 Guidelines, for example, the basic amount of the fine may be reduced where the undertaking provides evidence that the infringement has been committed as a result of negligence.[68] Both intention and negligence are manifestations of the concept of culpability, as defined above. Current enforcement of EU cartel law, then, is required to take into account the culpability of the cartelist—at least when a fine is being imposed.

This is not to say, however, that if a case could be made out for the imposition of a fine under the current law that ipso facto one establishes sufficient culpability for the imposition of a *criminal* sanction. Indeed, one could argue that the current approach does not necessarily establish a sufficient degree of culpability to warrant the imposition of a criminal sanction: it imposes sanctions for negligent behaviour.[69] For Wils, 'the commission of a criminal offence usually requires that the prohibited act be committed with a guilty state of mind (criminal intent), and not by mere negligence'.[70] The US courts take a similar approach to that suggested by Wils. While, surprisingly, the exact mens rea for criminal hard-core cartel activity is unresolved in the US,[71] it is clear that proof of a defendant's guilty state of mind is indeed an essential element of a criminal antitrust offence.[72] According to the US Supreme Court, an antitrust offence based around verification of pricing information (admittedly not a hard-core activity) at least requires: (i) an intention to cause a clearly illegal result; or (ii) knowledge that illegal, actual results were 'probable'.[73] Due to the 'silence' of the US Supreme Court on the requisite mens rea for a per se antitrust offence under the Sherman Act 1890, where a court determines that the alleged conduct falls within a per se violation, it is assumed that the prosecutor merely needs to prove the existence of a (cartel) conspiracy into which the defendant *knowingly* entered.[74] It is accepted by US courts, then, that negligence is an insufficient mental state for the commission of a criminal cartel offence.[75] In the context of a retribution-based rationale for punishment, negligence, as the lowest level of culpability,[76] may well represent a degree of blameworthiness which does not fulfil the proportionality principle if used in the context of criminal sanctions.[77] This is a qualitative inquiry, and one which is difficult to judge in a scientific manner. In order to avoid controversy—or, more specifically, a potential disproportionate use of the criminal sanction—it may well be advisable to require a higher standard of culpability

[67] Case C-26/75, *General Motors v. Commission* [1975] ECR 1367, 1389 (Opinion of AG Mayras).

[68] European Commission (2006a), [29].

[69] Matikkala has noted, however, that negligent ('accidental') cartel activity is likely to be rare as 'such activity is by nature conscious and purposeful': Matikkala (2009), 285. See also Whalley (1988), 569 (price-fixing 'cannot be inadvertently committed').

[70] Wils (2006b), 62.

[71] Cf. Cass and Hylton (2000–01).

[72] *United States v. US Gypsum Co.* (1978) 438 US 422, 435.

[73] *United States v. US Gypsum Co.* (1978) 438 US 422, 444–6. See Stucke (2006), 491 et seq. See also Loughlin (1979–80).

[74] Cooper and Dedjinou (2005), 190. See also: *United States v. Gillen* (1979) 599 F.2d 541 (3rd Circuit); and Stucke (2012).

[75] In practice, only 'clear, intentional violations, mostly cases of explicit price-fixing or bid-rigging' result in criminal proceedings: Jones and Sufrin (2011), 1167, relying upon Hovenkamp (2005b), [15.1a].

[76] The highest level of culpability is 'intention', while 'recklessness' occupies an intermediate level; see Smith (2002), 70–85. Strict liability crimes, by contrast, do not involve a culpability standard: Smith (2002), 115.

[77] It is noted that negligence is only used in 'exceptional circumstances' as a mens rea in a criminal offence, such as when a death has been caused; see Robinson (2002), 1001.

when imposing criminal sanctions on individuals for retributive reasons, such as recklessness or intention. Admittedly, recklessness has also been criticized as an insufficient mental state for the commission of a criminal cartel offence.[78] For example, Rogers, commenting in February 2009 on Australian proposals to criminalize cartel activity, informed the Australian Senate Standing Committee on Economics that recklessness was 'quite low' as a degree of culpability for a criminal cartel offence and that it 'is not enough' for parties to be simply reckless regarding cartel activity if a jail term is to be imposed: what is required 'is a deliberate knowledge or belief of the parties involved'.[79] For Steel, the choice concerning the appropriate mens rea is also obvious: 'to ensure that only serious or "hard core" cartels fall within the criminal offence, there should be proof of a clear intention to act in an anti-competitive manner'.[80]

It is clear, then, that a decision is required concerning the 'level' of culpability (i.e. *how* the culpable state of mind is defined) that should actually be employed in a criminal cartel offence. This decision may involve the creation of different levels of culpability between the civil and the criminal antitrust offences, and may thus help to distinguish between these types of offences.[81] The distinction between civil and the criminal antitrust offences may also be further underlined by requiring sufficient culpability in order to find a *violation* of the criminal prohibition. Indeed, at present under EU law, culpability is only relevant to the *imposition of an administrative fine*, not the finding of a violation of Article 101 TFEU. It should also be understood that a decision regarding the 'target' of the culpable state of mind (i.e. *what* the culpable state of mind refers to) is also required. For the sake of convenience, the above discussion proceeded on the basis that the target of the culpable state of mind would be engaging in 'cartel activity' (based on the OECD definition[82]). However, given that legislators may wish to create a stand-alone cartel offence which does not contain a definitional link requiring the violation of Article 101 TFEU, legislators are presented with a significant number of choices when determining the 'target', as different formulations that capture the culpability of cartel activity (and thus help to substantiate a retribution-based criminalization argument) are possible. For example, and assuming that intention is chosen as the level of culpability, the criminal cartel offence could require: (i) proof of an intention to engage in cartel activity; (ii) proof of an intention to make a cartel agreement or arrangement; (iii) proof of an intention to implement a cartel agreement or arrangement; and/or (iv) proof of an intention to prevent, restrict, or distort competition through cartel activity. In the recent consultation process on the workings of the UK competition regime conducted by BIS, one prominent commentator argued that the UK Cartel Offence—a stand-alone criminal offence not linked to a violation of Article 101 TFEU—should be amended to include a definitional element requiring proof that the defendant intended to 'subvert the competitive process'.[83] Others have

[78] Interestingly, an amendment (Amendment No. 179A to the Enterprise Bill) to allow the UK Cartel Offence to encompass cartel activity committed recklessly (as opposed to dishonestly) was proposed during the legislative debates on what was to become the Enterprise Act 2002 (see the comments of Lord Hunt of Wirral in Hansard, House of Lords Debates, 18 July 2002, Column 1537), but this amendment failed to be adopted into law. The amendment was 'resisted by the Government on the grounds that that would have significantly *extended* the scope of the offence': Marco Colino (2011), 240 (emphasis in the original).

[79] Senate Standing Committee on Economics (2009), [3.16], citing the comments of Rogers, Proof Committee Hansard (Australia), 16 February 2009, 6. Use of the mens rea of 'recklessness' in the context of antitrust criminalization has also been criticized by other Australian legal commentators; see Beaton-Wells and Fisse (2008a), Section 2.1.2. The US Supreme Court is also sceptical of 'recklessness' in this context; see *United States v. US Gypsum Co.* (1978) 438 US 422, 444.

[80] Steel (2010), 225. [81] See Steel (2010), 225–6. [82] OECD (1998), [2(a)].

[83] MacCulloch (2012).

displayed a similar view of the matter.[84] According to The City of London Law Society's Competition Law Committee, such an amendment 'would sufficiently limit the scope of the offence in order to capture individuals who truly deserve criminal punishment, focusing on the mental state of the individual at the time of entering into the agreement that bears a real relation to the mischief that is sought to be avoided'.[85] There is merit to this claim. The point to be made here, however, is that even if, for example, the relevant target of the mental state in the cartel offence must be committed intentionally, it would not put cartel activity in general (as opposed to a specific cartel) outside the scope of the criminal law in a de facto sense: some cartelists are capable of displaying the required culpability. This is evidenced by, for example, the cases (with 'intentional' cartels) decided by the European Commission[86] as well as by statements from national judges who have appraised the culpable aspects of the behaviour of cartelists which have appeared before them.[87]

One could, however, approach this issue from a different angle and take notice of Green's admission that the nature of certain acts may be so intrinsically linked to the mental state of an actor that his culpability should be taken into account in determining whether that act is morally wrong.[88] In other words, one could examine the issue of culpability when determining whether the cartelist's actions are morally wrong. As will become apparent below, each of the moral norms examined when moral wrongfulness is analysed displays a culpable state of mind. In each case, intention is required, but the 'target' of that intention differs. One cannot, therefore, make a final judgment on the issue of culpability without analysing the issue of moral wrongfulness: the relevant moral norms under examination may in fact be violated by cartelists, and, if so, cartel activity per se may display sufficient culpability for criminalization purposes when the justificatory theory of retribution is active. If this is the case, there may not be a need to include express provision for the proof of such culpability in the criminal cartel offence itself.

(b) Social harmfulness

This sub-section employs Green's conceptualization of 'social harmfulness' to identify the 'social harm' caused by cartel activity. A retribution-based criminalization argument could be bolstered if (in addition to culpability) cartel activity involved 'social harmfulness'. However, there may be limitations imposed upon a retribution-based criminalization argument if the type of social harm identified is not perceived to be significant by the general population. Consequently, once the social harm of cartel activity is established, this sub-section articulates the problematic issues with the type of social harm at issue when presenting a retribution-based argument for cartel criminalization.

[84] During the passage of the Enterprise and Regulatory Reform Bill through the House of Commons, Chi Onwurah MP tabled an (unsuccessful) amendment which would have amended the UK Cartel Offence so that it requires proof that the defendant had an 'intention of substantially reducing competition': Hansard, House of Commons Debates, 10 July 2012, Column 551.

[85] The City of London Law Society's Competition Law Committee (2012).

[86] See, e.g., *Organic Peroxides* (Case COMP/E-2/37.857), Commission Decision, 30 April 2005, [2005] OJ L110/44.

[87] See, e.g., *DPP v. Duffy and Duffy Motors (Newbridge) Ltd* [2009] IEHC 208, [47] ('Whatever his public persona, which I have no doubt was a positive one, he was, in private, deliberately engaging in wanton criminal conspiracy against the greater public with the intention of defrauding them for financial gain').

[88] Green (1997), 1552.

(i) Identifying the social harmfulness of cartel activity

It has been posited that the 'central purpose' of competition law is the protection and promotion of a competitive, market-driven economy in which efficient firms prosper and inefficient firms fail.[89] According to neo-classical economic theory, this 'unrestrained interaction of competitive forces' yields 'the best allocation of our economic resources, the lowest prices, the highest quality and the greatest material progress'.[90] Cartel formation aims to cripple this interaction; and as such is an activity that has a number of destructive effects for customers, consumers, the competitive process, and ultimately the economy.[91] These destructive effects are very unlikely to be offset by efficiencies due to the cartel.[92] As noted by the International Competition Network ('the ICN'), there is a 'consensus that such conduct is devoid of pro-competitive benefits'.[93] In short, cartels reduce competition on a given market and have the potential to reduce or eliminate the gains which such competition secures.[94] From a welfare perspective, a successful cartel (particularly if it involves all market participants) 'leads to the same market outcome as a monopoly and therefore causes similar types and degrees of allocative, productive, and dynamic inefficiencies'.[95] According to a former Commissioner for competition, cartel activity strikes 'a killer blow at the heart of healthy economic activity'.[96] In other words, cartel activity has a negative impact upon a socially valuable interest, viz., the successful operation of a free market. For some, this fact alone warrants the complete prohibition of such activity.[97] It is no surprise, then, that internationally there has been an apparent growing consensus among antitrust enforcers that cartel activity is harmful and should be detected and prosecuted;[98] indeed, competition officials, legislators, and governments regularly remind us of their destructive effects, particularly at EU level.[99]

Specifically, cartels engender the following harmful consequences.[100] First, they involve a transfer of wealth from the consumer to the producer, effectively reducing the consumer surplus;[101] this transfer manifests itself in increased prices and a reduction in output.[102] In actual fact, the average price increase due to cartel activity in Europe has

[89] Bailey (2009), 100–24.

[90] *Northern Pacific Railway Co. v. United States* (1958) 356 US 1, 4. See also *United States v. Syufy Enterprises* (1990) 903 F.2d 659 (9th Circuit), 662 (it is the 'nature of free enterprise that fierce, no holds barred competition will drive out the least effective participants in the market, providing the most efficient allocation of productive resources').

[91] See Connor (2007a), especially Chapters 2 and 17.

[92] See OECD (1995), 8. See also: Audretsch (1989); and Morgan (2010), 68. Cf.: Skilbeck (2002); and Skilbeck (2003).

[93] ICN (2005), 14.

[94] See: OECD (2003a); OECD (2002a); and OECD (1998). See also Breit and Elzinga (1989), 12 ('economic analysis shows that cartels are inefficient and lessen consumer welfare').

[95] Hüschelrath (2010), 523.

[96] Kroes (2006). Cartel activity has not always been taken so seriously by the Commission; see, e.g., Joshua (2000b), 3.

[97] See, e.g., Cairns Committee (1955), [246].

[98] See: Shaffer and Nesbitt (2011); ICN (2005); OECD (1998); and OECD (2003b). See also: ICPAC (2000), 164; and Kovacic (2007), 689.

[99] See, e.g., Kroes (2009), 4–5.

[100] See generally: Carlton and Perloff (2005), Chapter 4; and Scherer and Ross (1990), Chapter 18. For a diagrammatical representation of the social harm due to cartel activity, see Annex III to this book.

[101] The 'consumer surplus' is defined as the 'aggregate measure' of the surplus of all individual consumers, where the surplus of a given consumer is equal to 'the difference between the consumer's valuation for the good considered . . . and the price which she has to pay for it': Motta (2004), 18.

[102] See Landes (1983). See also Diaz et al. (1999), 337: 'Price competition is an essential form of competition, and it follows that price fixing constitutes the most obvious infringement to competition law'.

been estimated to be between 28 and 54 per cent.[103] Most recently, Smuda found that the mean and median overcharge rates are 20.7 and 18.37 per cent of the selling price.[104] Although some have argued that cartels are inherently unstable, and therefore that the market will 'correct' these arrangements,[105] the average lifespan of cartels has been estimated to be about seven to eight years.[106] In 2011, Combe and Monnier published their study which analysed 64 cartel decisions adopted by the Commission between 1975 and 2009.[107] The average duration of cartels in their sample was seven years, with a median of 5.6 years.[108] In a later study by Smuda, the average cartel duration was in fact found to be 8.35 years.[109] Second, allocative inefficiency occurs,[110] as evidenced by the presence of the 'deadweight loss' welfare triangle;[111] scarce economic resources are therefore not being employed to their potential.[112] This inefficiency is not trivial either: as noted in Chapter 3, the 'deadweight loss' has been assumed to be in the region of 50 per cent of the overcharge[113] and has been estimated by Connor and Lande at somewhere between 3 and 20 per cent.[114] Third, higher prices may be charged by non-violating cartel members due to the higher cartel prices.[115] Fourth, non-price effects on quality, choice, and innovation may arise from the reduction in competition.[116] According to the OECD, although accurate quantification of the exact harm from cartels is not currently possible,[117] there is no doubt that it is very large, amounting to the equivalent of many billions of US dollars annually.[118] Savage believes that, for this reason alone, the 'biggest global financial fraud above other financial crimes' is due to international cartels.[119] For Furse, the 'evidence that cartels are not rare, that they are very harmful, and that they are organised in knowing defiance of legal prohibition is overwhelming'.[120]

Some scholars view the harm from cartels as so reprehensible that it provides a sufficient normative ground for criminalization. Wardhaugh, for example, argues that criminalization of cartel activity can be rationalized as an acceptable response to the fact that its harm strikes at a valuable institution which provides an individual with the ability to secure his own welfare in a liberal society.[121] Likewise, Clarke and Bagaric, on the assumption that criminal sanctions can be justified as a method of preventing serious

[103] Connor and Lande (2005). See also Connor (2007b). [104] Smuda (2014).
[105] See Hylton (2003), 68 et seq. [106] Connor and Lande (2005).
[107] Combe and Monnier (2011). [108] Combe and Monnier (2011), 240.
[109] Smuda (2014).
[110] 'Allocative efficiency' relates to the difference between the cost of producing the marginal product and the valuation of that product by consumers: Bishop and Walker (2010), 25. 'Allocative inefficiency' therefore occurs if the cost of producing one more unit is different from the amount that consumers are willing to pay for that extra unit.
[111] The presence of 'deadweight loss' in a given market ensures that some consumers who would have paid the competitive price for a product are deprived of that product and will spend their income on other products: Jones and Sufrin (2011), 9. 'Deadwieght loss', then, is the cost to society of a market not operating efficiently: Bishop and Walker (2010), 27–8.
[112] See Katz and Rosen (1998), 114. [113] Easterbrook (1985), 455.
[114] Connor and Lande (2012), 457–61. [115] Connor and Lande (2005), 518.
[116] Connor and Lande (2005), 518.
[117] There are, however, a number of studies that attempt to quantify both the cartel overcharge as well as the average duration of cartels; see Chapter 3, Section D(b)(i) of this book.
[118] OECD (2002a), 90. Having conducted a detailed review of the current empirical evidence on cartel duration and overcharges, King believes that 'it is difficult to disagree with' this conclusion of the OECD: King (2010), 10. This is not to concede, however, that cartels are the *most damaging* form of anticompetitive conduct: analyses comparing the damage due to cartels with the damage due to other anticompetitive behaviour do not appear to have been presented in the literature. On this, see: Skilbeck (2002); and Skilbeck (2003). Cf. DTI (2001b), [7.2].
[119] Ramage (2008), 5. [120] Furse (2012), viii. Cf. Spagnolo (2006), 133–4.
[121] See: Wardhaugh (2014), Chapter 1; and Wardhaugh (2012b). Others are critical of rationalizing criminal cartel sanctions on the basis of the mere existence of harm; see, e.g., Quaid (2012), 175–9.

harm to others, point out that 'a relatively firm foundation' can be found for the criminalization of cartel conduct in the impact such conduct has on living standards: 'higher prices for consumers interferes with their capacity to fully enjoy the material amenities of life'.[122] Their conclusion is expressly based upon an innovative framework created by von Hirsch and Jareborg which rates the seriousness of a criminal offence by considering its impact upon interests relevant to a person's living standard.[123] Important interests in this context are: physical integrity; material support and amenity; freedom from humiliation; and privacy/autonomy.[124] The argument is that, as cartel activity impacts significantly upon a person's amenity interest, it can be classed as a seriously harmful activity.[125] Given the above, then, one can argue that the existence of harm to a social value in the context of cartel activity is not really an issue:[126] to borrow the words of Dressler, cartel activity causes or risks causing the 'negation, endangering, or destruction of an individual, group or state interest which [is] deemed socially valuable'.[127]

(ii) Problematic issues with the type of social harm identified

There are two potential limitations with the particular type of social harm due to cartels identified directly above. The first concerns the requirement that the operation of a free market should be considered as a socially valuable interest, while the second raises the issue of the nature of the negative impact of cartel activity on the free market.

1. Acceptance of the value of the free market

The identification of all of the various social harms associated with cartel activity relies upon the existence of a particular counterfactual. This counterfactual is the situation where competition exists between competitors in the context of a free market. It is by comparing this counterfactual with the situation arising when cartel activity occurs that one can locate the social harm. For cartel activity to have a *negative* impact, one must demonstrate a *positive* feature of the counterfactual: one must demonstrate that a free market is valued by society. If a free market is not valued by society, then the 'harm' identified will not fulfil the 'social harmfulness' criteria of Green's framework. If this is so, a retribution-based criminalization argument will suffer from an inherent weakness. The strength of a retribution-based criminalization argument therefore depends upon the acceptance by society of the value of the free market; it depends, in other words, upon a particular economic and political ideology.

It is submitted here that while a retribution-based criminalization argument is indeed limited in this regard, it is not necessarily weakened. The reason for this is that a strong argument can be put forward that European citizens—as opposed to, say, citizens of the Democratic People's Republic of Korea[128]—do indeed value the free market. In fact, since the end of the Cold War, one has witnessed an increase in the number of jurisdictions whose economies are founded upon the principles of the free market, jurisdictions which include those from Europe. Furthermore, there are relatively rigorous surveys which suggest that, while individuals find unbridled capitalism objectionable, they nonetheless support the concept of the free market. A case in point is the 20-country poll which was conducted in 2005 by the international polling firm GlobeScan in conjunction with

122 Clarke and Bagaric (2003).
123 Von Hirsch and Jareborg (1991).
124 Von Hirsch and Jareborg (1991), 19–21.
125 Clarke and Bagaric (2003).
126 See Whelan (2007), 28–9.
127 Dressler (2001), § 9.10[B].
128 See, e.g., <http://www.korea-dpr.com>.

the Program on International Policy Attitudes ('PIPA') of the University of Maryland. According to its findings, in all bar one country polled, either a majority or a plurality agreed with the statement that 'the free enterprise system and free market economy is the best system on which to base the future of the world'.[129] In fact, on average, 61 per cent agreed with this statement, while only 28 per cent disagreed.[130] While a more recent (2008) study detected a fall in support for the free market system, it also found that majorities in most countries continue to support the free market system.[131] These findings are also consistent with those of the 'Pew Global Attitudes Project', a project which presents a series of worldwide public-opinion surveys on various important issues. In its 2003 survey, it was found that majorities in 33 of 44 countries surveyed believed that people are better off if they live in a jurisdiction with a free-market economy.[132] Countries with a relatively high majority included Italy (71 per cent), Germany (69 per cent), and the United Kingdom (66 per cent).[133] Some of these figures have not changed much in the last ten years.[134] In a 2012 survey, for example, Germany still registered 69 per cent (and even registered 73 per cent in 2010) and the UK's percentage stood at 61 per cent (down from a high of 72 per cent in 2007).[135] Admittedly, Italy's percentage has moved down considerably in the last number of years and in 2012 stood at 50 per cent,[136] but it is submitted that the figure is still a high one. If these types of surveys are to be believed, there should be little concern over whether European citizens actually value the free market;[137] there should be little concern, in other words, for one of the identified limitations of a retribution-based criminalization argument.

2. The challenging nature of the harm due to cartels

The nature of the particular harm engendered by cartel activity (viz., rises in prices, allocative inefficiency, and reductions in quality and innovation) is challenging in three respects.[138] First, it is often the case that the harm is 'diluted' across many different victims.[139] Each victim (say, the consumer who pays extra for a cartelized litre of milk) will be harmed, but the harm he has suffered may well be almost negligible. If the price of a litre of milk was increased by 5 per cent due to a cartel, for example, a consumer may only lose in the region of 10 to 20 pence per week. Even if the cartel lasted for a year, such a consumer's loss would still be relatively low, i.e. 5 to 10 pounds. So, while such harm may well be extensive in *aggregate* terms, its actual impact upon a given *individual* entity (i.e. a particular consumer) may be minimal. Consequently, cartel activity may be perceived as a 'victimless crime'.[140] Looking at it from another perspective, one can posit that criminal antitrust enforcement is different from the enforcement of 'traditional' crimes (e.g., murder, robbery, rape, etc.) where the existence of an obvious victim is unquestionable: criminal antitrust enforcement 'begins with an alleged perpetrator and

129 See <http://www.globescan.com/news_archives/pipa_market.html#media>.

130 See <http://www.globescan.com/news_archives/pipa_market.html#media>.

131 See PIPA (2008).

132 Pew Global Attitudes Project (2003), 103.

133 Pew Global Attitudes Project (2003), 103.

134 See <http://www.pewglobal.org/database/indicator/18/survey/all/>.

135 See <http://www.pewglobal.org/database/indicator/18/survey/all/>.

136 See <http://www.pewglobal.org/database/indicator/18/survey/all/>.

137 It is worth noting that the value of the concept of a market economy has been expressly acknowledged in the TEU. According to Article 3(3) TEU, the EU 'shall work for the sustainable development of Europe based on balanced economic growth and price stability, [and, *inter alia*] a highly competitive social market economy'.

138 Cf. Competition and Mergers Review Group (2000), [4.5.4].

139 Evans and Lundman (1983), 538.

140 See Massey (2004), 32.

various dubious persons eager to claim victim status, often with no obvious injuries, and a search for a crime'.[141] Second, as the individual loss may be minimal, the victims themselves (i.e. those who buy the cartelized product) may not be aware that they are in fact victims: they may not detect the price increase. Due to the inherently secret nature of cartels, they are unlikely to know that any price increase detected is due to collusion.[142] In short, 'the victims are not always aware of the existence of the competition law infringement, often secret or difficult to appreciate, or of the extent of the losses suffered due to this infringement'.[143] Third, as allocative inefficiency is a potential harm due to cartel activity, one may not be able in practice to identify the victims even when a cartel is discovered: it is difficult to determine who exactly would have bought the cartelized product at the competitive price, but was priced out of the market by the price rise due to collusion. In fact, it is probably for such evidential reasons that civil damages actions for cartel activity are not initiated by individuals who have not actually purchased (whether directly or indirectly) a cartelized product/service.[144] Some may argue, then, that the *nature* of the harm engendered by cartel activity introduces a limitation in a retribution-based criminalization argument: for them, the 'harm' identified would be irrelevant, given the fact that at an individual level it is likely to be undetected, undetectable, and/or relatively minimal.

It is submitted, however, that the fact that this harm may be spread out over many individuals—who, indeed, may even be unaware that they are victims of cartel activity—is of no concern in the analysis of social harmfulness.[145] Social harmfulness, according to Green's framework, refers to 'the sort of harm that somehow properly concerns the community as a whole, rather than just individual citizens within such community'.[146] Such an approach recognizes, in effect, that while economic activities may often involve minor harms to a large number of (potentially unaware) victims, these can become significant in their aggregate effects.[147] Such is the case with cartel activity. Indeed, as noted above, according to the OECD, although accurate quantification of the exact harm from cartels is not currently possible, there is no doubt that it is very large, amounting to the equivalent of many billions of US dollars annually.[148] In principle, then, a retribution-based criminalization argument is not limited due to the type of harm engendered by cartel activity. Irrespective of the fact that its harm is diluted across many 'victims', cartel activity nonetheless displays significant aggregate social harmfulness to support a retribution-based criminalization argument. To be sure, however, such dilution may still be problematic in practice, even if the 'social harmfulness' requirement is fulfilled.

[141] Jacobs (2007), 25.

[142] Ministry of Economic Development (2010), [2]. For some, this lack of awareness actually strengthens rather than undermines arguments about the immoral quality of cartel activity; for Lipsky, e.g., '[p]rice fixing and the like are similar to theft—the perpetrators obtain money from victims by stealth—but they can be far more pernicious because they often occur without the victims' awareness': Lipsky (1992), 567.

[143] European Commission (2008b), [39].

[144] On this, see Wils (2003c), 481.

[145] Others have also argued that dilution of harm across victims is irrelevant for the existence of moral wrongfulness (as opposed to social harmfulness); see Gray (2008), 374. In addition, some have argued that the fact that victims of cartel activity may be unaware of their losses is also irrelevant when considering the morality of the activity; for Massey, for example, cartel activity can be compared to ATM skimming 'where it may be difficult to estimate the full extent of the harm caused, while individuals who do not check their bank statements closely may not realise that money has been stolen from their bank accounts': Massey (2012), 164. Whalley goes even further and argues that cartel activity is 'theft that is even more egregious because people don't even know that they've been robbed': Whalley (1988), 572.

[146] Green (2006), 34. See also Green (1997), 1549–50. See generally: Duff (2001); and Schonsheck (1994).

[147] Green (2006), 36. See also Feinberg (1984), 187–217.

[148] OECD (2002a), 90.

For example, it may affect people's perception of the importance of dedicating adequate resources to criminal anti-cartel enforcement; likewise, educative efforts concerning the morality of cartel activity may be more challenging than would have otherwise been the case. Such practical limitations are considered in more detail in Chapter 10.

(c) Moral wrongfulness

It was argued directly above that cartel activity involves socially harmful behaviour and that in order to 'capture' the immorality of such behaviour one should, inter alia, ensure that a sufficient degree of culpability is included within the (criminal) definition of cartel activity (which may be as strict as 'intention' to distort competition). The question which needs to be answered here, then, is whether the concept of cartel activity (as defined by the OECD) actually encompasses, to use the words of Green, 'some intrinsic violation of a freestanding moral rule or duty':[149] that is, whether the notion of cartel activity can be conceptualized as a moral wrong per se. If cartel activity can be seen as 'morally wrong' (in addition to displaying sufficient culpability and engendering social harmfulness), a solid retribution-based criminalization argument could be advanced. In addition to this, if cartel activity is indeed perceived as 'morally wrong', then one of the identified inherent challenges of deterrence theory can also be met.[150] It should be no surprise, then, that the issue of 'moral wrongfulness' is 'of paramount importance in advancing meaningful reform' of antitrust enforcement through criminalization.[151]

Identifying moral wrongfulness is where the real difficulty lies. It may be the case that cartel activity does indeed violate a moral norm, in that it entails one or more of stealing, deception, or cheating.[152] If so, the third element in Green's framework can also be realized and a solid retribution-based criminalization argument could be constructed. If not, a retribution-based criminalization argument would be considerably weakened.

To investigate this issue, one must first provide a definition of the relevant moral norms. Stealing—an activity with 'an independent moral significance, which is neither wholly derivative of law nor wholly reducible to other moral norms'[153]—is defined by Green as an intentional and fundamental violation of another's rights of ownership in something that is capable of being bought or sold.[154] Deception occurs where: (i) a message is communicated, with (ii) an intent to cause a person to believe something that is untrue, and (iii) a person is thereby caused to believe something that is not true.[155] While deception may include express lies, it does not require them: misleading communication is sufficient.[156] Finally, cheating occurs where a natural or legal person has: (i) violated a fair, legitimate, and fairly enforced rule, with (ii) the intent to 'obtain an advantage over a party with whom she is in a cooperative, rule-bound relationship'.[157] The 'rule' in question must also be general, prescriptive, mandatory, conduct-based, and represent a standard.[158] It is noted that 'cheating' so defined is a manifestation of the unfair advantage variant of retribution theory discussed in Chapter 2.[159]

149 Green (2006), 39.
150 See Chapter 3, Section D(a) of this book.
151 Ezrachi and Kindl (2011), 432.
152 See Beaton-Wells (2007), 694–701 and 703–4.
153 Green (2006), 88. Cf. Gert (1988), 135–6.
154 Green (2006), 89–91.
155 See: Adler (1997), 437; and Green (2006), 76.
156 On this distinction, see Green (2006), 77–81.
157 Green (2006), 57.
158 Green (2006), 58–62. Green notes that cheating can involve both constitutive and regulative rules, although it will generally involve the latter: Green (2006), 61.
159 See Chapter 2, Section B(c)(i) of this book. The difference here, however, is that the concept of cheating is not put forward as a rationale for all types of criminal punishment; rather it is posited as merely one of a number of different constructs that help explain the moral wrongfulness of different white-collar crimes.

(i) Cartel activity as stealing

As noted in the introduction, it is not difficult to find statements in the literature comparing cartel activity to the concept of stealing.[160] The well-known example is Klein's comment that collusion is the equivalent of 'theft by well-dressed thieves'.[161] Likewise, Whish, a considerable UK authority on competition law, believes that there 'is not a great deal of difference between price-fixing and theft'.[162] For Werden, cartel activity is 'properly viewed as a property crime, like burglary or larceny, although cartel activity inflicts far greater economic harm'.[163] To compare cartel activity to stealing or theft, then, is not something new.[164] But is such an assertion theoretically sound? Can cartel activity be interpreted as a sophisticated form of stealing?

As noted above, stealing can be conceptualized as an intentional and fundamental violation of another's rights of ownership in something that is capable of being bought or sold. There are four elements present in this definition. The first to be determined should be the existence of something that is capable of being bought or sold. This element can be fulfilled in the context of cartel activity. Successful cartels lead to a higher price for the cartelized product/service. For the sake of simplicity, one can restate this situation as follows: with a successful cartel, a given amount of money would purchase fewer goods/services following cartel activity than it would have done in the absence of such activity. The goods/services represented by this reduction are capable, by definition, of being bought or sold.

The second condition is that the victim of the cartel (i.e. he who bears the burden of the overcharge) actually has a right of ownership over the property represented by the overcharge. This is where the real potential for disagreement lies concerning a potential violation of the moral norm against stealing. In contrast to the contention of Gert,[165] Green argues that the right of ownership in question does not necessarily owe its existence to the law; rather, such rights can have a non-legal character: the concept of stealing is 'in some fundamental way pre-legal'.[166] One could argue that, irrespective of their legal rights, consumers are nonetheless entitled to a competitive price for the goods/services on the market; that, for example, due to the endorsement of free market economics by the majority of European citizens, consumers have a right to a competitive market.[167] It is difficult, however, to pinpoint exactly how and when such a right is created, hence the room for disagreement. It might be best in these circumstances to consider the role of the law. Indeed, with cartel law one can create such a right of ownership. One could criminalize the wealth transfer from the consumer to the purchaser, for example. Indeed, according to Calvani, this is what occurred in Ireland: criminalization resolved the issue of ownership of the consumer surplus.[168] It would of course be circular to argue here that criminalization provides the basis for moral wrongfulness and therefore for criminalization. But this is not a problem that is difficult to overcome: the *civil* law also can

160 See, e.g., Samuel (2009).

161 Klein (1999a), 1; and Klein (1999b), 3.

162 Whish (2009), 498. See also: Bloom (2002a); Clarke (2005); Clarke and Bagaric (2003); Fels (2002); and Vickers (2003), 4. Cf. Furse and Nash (2004a), ix and 27, footnote 77.

163 Werden (2009), 23.

164 See Connor et al. (2010). See also Lewisch (2006), 301–2.

165 Gert (1988), 135–6.

166 Green (2006), 89.

167 In support, one could even argue that the wording of Article 101(3) TFEU *impliedly recognizes* the right of consumers to a competitive market: if an agreement, a decision of an association of undertakings, or a concerted practice is anticompetitive and violates Article 101(1) TFEU, the undertaking(s) in question must demonstrate, inter alia, that consumers are compensated in order to ensure that Article 101(1) TFEU is declared inapplicable: consumers must receive a fair share of any efficiencies secured due to the anticompetitive agreement, decision, or concerted practice.

168 Calvani (2004b), 3.

be used to create such rights prior to criminalization. There is a strong case that this has already occurred under EU law.[169] Indeed, in recent years an increasing importance has been given to the place of the consumer in antitrust law,[170] and consumers have been encouraged by the European (and some national) institutions to sue for damages caused by cartel activity,[171] as is evidenced by recent moves towards the adoption of an EU Directive on damages actions.[172] Most importantly, at some point a consumer welfare standard was apparently adopted in EU competition law, at least in relation to Article 101 TFEU.[173] According to the (then) Commissioner for Competition, 'consumer welfare is now well established as the standard the Commission applies when assessing... infringements of the Treaty rules on cartels'.[174] Admittedly, however, the legality of such an approach can be questioned following the judgment of the Court of Justice in *GlaxoSmithKline*,[175] and debate concerning the appropriate welfare standard in EU competition law continues.

This brings one to a crucial point: the debate on whether cartel activity can be interpreted as a form of stealing cannot be divorced from the debate on the appropriate standard to be adopted in antitrust cases (i.e. consumer welfare or total welfare).[176] That is, choice over the standard to be employed affects the viability of the argument on stealing. Neo-classical economists generally prefer a total welfare standard to a consumer welfare standard, as its implementation treats wealth transfers (from consumer to producer, for example) as welfare-neutral.[177] While the 'assumption that wealth transfers are neutral does not necessarily accord with popular assumptions of fairness',[178] this preference has been reflected in the views of some antitrust scholars.[179] Indeed, a number of recent papers have requested competition agencies to adopt this standard in their assessment of allegedly anticompetitive behaviour.[180] By adopting such a standard, the agencies would effectively ignore the distributive consequences of the conduct in question, focusing instead on its alleged efficiency effects, regardless of who benefits from them. The question as to whether the cartelist 'steals' the property of his customer by overcharging him is therefore irrelevant; all that matters is whether total welfare is maximized. By contrast, by adopting a consumer welfare standard (i.e. one which attempts to maximize the

169 See, e.g., Malinauskaite (2007).

170 See Hutchings and Whelan (2006).

171 See, e.g.: European Commission (2011a); European Commission (2008a); and European Commission (2008b). See also: Case C-453/99, *Courage v. Crehan* [2001] ECR I-6297; and Joined Cases C-295–298/04, *Vincenzo Manfredi and others v. Lloyd Adriatico Assicurazioni SpA and others* [2006] ECR I-6619. See also: BIS (2013a); BIS (2012); OFT (2007a); OFT (2007c); and the Draft Consumer Rights Bill, BIS/13/925 (UK), Schedule 7.

172 See: Council of the European Union (2013); European Commission (2013a); and European Commission (2013b).

173 See: Cases T-213/01 and T-214/01, *Österreichische Postsparkasse AG v. Commission* and *Bank für Arbeit und Wirtschaft AG v. Commission* [2006] ECR II-1601, [115]; European Commission (2004c), [13] and [33]; European Commission (1995), 23; Kroes (2005b); and Monti (2001). On this, see also: Marsden and Whelan (2009); and Marsden and Whelan (2006).

174 Kroes (2005b). Cf. Moore (2007).

175 Joined Cases C-501/06 P, etc., *GlaxoSmithKline Services Unltd v. Commission* [2009] ECR I-9291.

176 For an overview of these terms, see Motta (2004). For critical analysis of the debate over the correct welfare standard for antitrust law, see generally: Albaek (2013), 70–4; and Harker (2011).

177 Pittman (2007). See also van den Bergh and Camesasca (2006), 37.

178 Ministry of Economic Development (2010), [10].

179 See, e.g., Hovenkamp (2003), 609. But that is not to say that other scholars have not embraced such a consumer welfare standard for competition policy; see, e.g., Wils (2006a), 189.

180 Pittman (2007). These papers include: Carlton (2007); and Heyer (2006). It is noted that while some of the literature referred to concerns merger analysis, it is nonetheless relevant to the discussion at hand.

consumer surplus and reduce any consumer-to-producer wealth transfers), the enforcement agencies concern themselves with distributive consequences and in the process take a politically motivated decision on who should benefit from intervention in the market, namely in favour of the consumer. Such a choice quite obviously facilitates the argument concerning stealing, as it explicitly vests rights concerning the overcharge in consumers.

By choosing a consumer welfare standard over a total welfare standard, one facilitates the argument that cartel activity can be conceptualized as stealing: such a choice explicitly vests rights concerning the overcharge in consumers. However, there are a number of problematic issues with this type of approach. First, one must establish why consumers should be treated more favourably than producers, a difficult task given that the assumed 'weaker/poorer versus stronger/richer party' analysis may not be valid: '[t]he monopoly yacht manufacturer may be owned by a "blue collar" pension fund'.[181] Indeed, shareholders are ultimately consumers, and therefore no obvious reason exists to prefer consumer surplus to producer surplus.[182] Also, if distributional consequences are to be considered, then presumably poor and rich consumers should not be treated alike; yet, under the consumer welfare standard, this is not the case.[183] Second, a total welfare standard would offer more legal certainty because it does not look to the subjective interests of consumers.[184] Third, compared to the tax system, competition policy is an inefficient instrument for ensuring the redistribution of income.[185] Accordingly, a total welfare standard can be used to maximize efficiency, and any unwanted distributive consequences can be dealt with using the tax system.[186] These arguments reduce the attractiveness of a consumer welfare standard. To the extent that this is so, arguments that cartel activity is akin to stealing would suffer from an inherent limitation.

However, paradoxically, a strong case can be made as to why one should nonetheless use a consumer welfare approach: by maximizing consumer surplus, one is more likely to secure a total-welfare-maximizing outcome than by using the total welfare standard.[187] Intuitively, this is correct, because when firms have a number of profitable strategies at their disposal, a consumer welfare standard may ensure that firms choose the best strategy which will maximize total welfare:

> Under a consumer standard, firms pursue profitable strategies up to the point where consumers are not harmed. If overall profits rise, while consumer surplus does not fall, total welfare must *increase*. [Footnote omitted.] Under a total welfare standard, firms can go past this point—they may find that the most profitable *permissible* strategies are those that harm consumers a lot (ie the very high profits just offset the loss to consumers). In this case, overall total welfare may hardly increase at all.[188]

A consumer welfare standard is also easier to apply, as determining whether consumers have suffered harm, while perhaps difficult, is not as complicated as measuring that harm and then trading if off against gains in profits.[189] Consequently, a consumer welfare standard should be adopted, even absent an express political judgement on the

[181] Calvani (2004b), 3–4. [182] Majumdar (2008).
[183] Farrell and Katz (2006), 11.
[184] Monti (2007) 85. On legal certainty and cartel criminalization, see Chapter 7 of this book.
[185] Monti (2007), 85. See also: Farrell and Katz (2006); and Kaplow and Shavell (1994a). Some scholars would disagree with this assertion; see, e.g., Lande (1999).
[186] Kerber (2008).
[187] See: Lyons (2002), 206; Majumdar (2008); and Nazzini (2009), 396–403.
[188] Majumdar (2008), 145. [189] Majumdar (2008), 145.

desirability of consumer-producer wealth transfers.[190] This pragmatic approach, if accepted, facilitates the conceptualization of cartel activity as stealing and helps to bolster a retribution-based criminalization argument.

The third element, a fundamental violation, will be present in the case of cartel activity, provided of course that: (i) the goods/services represented by the cartel overcharge can be deemed to be the property of the victims; and (ii) the cartelist charges his customer(s) a price which is higher than the competitive price for the product: the cartelist (or more accurately his firm) will keep the overcharge and therefore substantially interfere with the victim's ability to use or possess his property. In fact, if the cartel is successful and the cartelized product is purchased, the victim would be completely incapable of exercising his rights of ownership in the overcharge. One should be aware that a fundamental violation will not be present where the cartel agreement in question is formed but not implemented: by creating a cartel agreement, the cartelists will only have agreed to violate the rights of its customers; actually to violate them, they must put the cartel into practice. Consequently, if the criminal cartel offence is necessarily to capture conduct which amounts to a violation of the moral norm against stealing, its scope should not extend beyond the implementation of a cartel to the mere agreement to implement a cartel.

The final element requires determination of the cartelist's intentions in entering into a cartel in the first place: stealing requires an intention to obtain the overcharge. In order to consider this element, one must first define the concept of intention. In criminal law, intention is generally understood as including two alternative categories: direct intention and indirect (oblique) intention.[191] The defendant *directly* intends a consequence (i.e. capturing an overcharge) if: (i) he wants to bring about that consequence; or (ii) he believes it is possible to achieve an ultimate objective by bringing about that consequence; and (iii) he behaves as he does because of his desire in (i) or his belief in (ii).[192] The literature on criminal intention therefore acknowledges that something done as a means towards another end is deemed to be an intentional act in its own right. By contrast, an *indirect or oblique* intention may be found to exist concerning a given consequence where that particular consequence was recognized by the defendant as a virtually certain consequence of his actions, even when the consequence was neither an ultimate objective nor a means towards an ultimate objective.[193] Importantly, the existence of multiple intentions of the defendant towards a given consequence is not problematic: 'Ignoring extraneous intentions, the criminal law focuses only on the actus reus; and asks, *whatever else he intended*, did D intend that actus?'.[194]

The empirical literature on the intentions of cartelists is relatively sparse,[195] a fact which complicates the issue. Theoretical arguments have tended to fill this void and can help one to analyse this issue. The primary theoretical argument is as follows. By employing economic deterrence theory, one assumes that cartelists are rational economic actors who act in their own interest in order to maximize their own welfare.[196] Accordingly,

[190] As to the standard that has been advocated in the context of US antitrust law, see: Bork (1966) (total welfare standard, despite the fact that he termed it 'consumer welfare'); and Lande (1999) (consumer surplus standard). See also Werden (2007).

[191] See generally: Kaveny (2004); Smith (1974); White (1976); and Williams (1987).

[192] See Simester et al. (2010), 128.

[193] See Ormerod (2008), 98. For English cases incorporating this definition of oblique intention, see: *R v. Woollin* [1999] 1 AC 82; and *R v. D* [2004] EWCA Crim 1391.

[194] See Simester et al. (2010), 138 (emphasis added).

[195] For a general overview, see Parker (2011).

[196] On the plausibility of this assumption in the context of economic activity, see Whelan (2007).

a rational cartelist can be deterred from engaging in a given conduct if the cost to him of such conduct is greater than its benefit, and the existence of a cartel implies that, if rationality is indeed present as assumed, engaging in cartel activity results in a net gain to the cartelist. Following this line of argument, as cartels exist in practice, they must therefore be perceived as profitable to the relevant cartelists.[197] But how exactly are they profitable? They are profitable because the cartelist obtains all or part of the overcharge. The desired objective of maximizing profit (i.e. rationality) therefore manifests itself in a direct intention to obtain all or part of the overcharge. In other words, if rational choice theory holds, the mere existence of cartels dictates that cartelists intend to obtain the overcharge: the overcharge is a means of obtaining profit maximization. But for this to be the case, the assumption of rationality must be a realistic assumption in practice.

Some argue that the available empirical evidence suggests that self-interested calculation is not the sole factor determining adherence to the (competition) law[198] and that complex social and normative factors also affect an individual's decision to cartelize.[199] There may, then, be many different reasons why cartelists act the way they do. According to the available empirical literature, however, cartelists frequently rationalize their conduct in a manner which is consistent with their highly regarded positions in society,[200] for example by claiming their actions were designed to protect their companies (and their employees) in difficult times.[201] It may be too simplistic therefore to argue that, by virtue of rationality, cartelists necessarily act with a given intention.

There are two possible arguments, however, that can nonetheless be employed to attempt to substantiate the claim that cartelists intend to obtain the overcharge. The first is that the conclusions in the available empirical literature on the motivations of cartelists are not always inconsistent with the existence of rationality and therefore do not necessarily undermine the theoretical assumption made in the context of economic deterrence theory. Even if cartelists act with an apparent benevolent intention (e.g., to save jobs), obtaining the overcharge still remains *the means* by which such a benevolent aim is achieved: the cartelist acts because he believes that the benevolent aim can be achieved through cartel activity as such an activity increases profitability by enabling the firm to capture the overcharge. In fact, the same conclusion can hold if the ultimate aim of the cartelist is merely to increase his standing in the firm or to be seen to be doing what other executives in the firm are doing. Understanding intention as capturing both ultimate objective and the means to achieve that objective can therefore facilitate a finding of an intention to capture the overcharge.

The second argument again employs the wide definition of intention noted above, this time focusing on the inclusion of *indirect* intention within that definition. The argument here is that the cartelist was fully aware of the virtually certain result that his actions would occasion: his customers would suffer a fundamental violation of their rights in the overcharge. However, there is a nuance to be understood here. This is due to the requirement of a 'virtually certain' result. When a cartelist *merely enters* into a cartel agreement with his competitors, it is not virtually certain that consumers will be harmed. This is due to the law of demand and the incentives that it places on cartel members to cheat on the cartel. The fact that by lowering their price (i.e. cheating on the cartel) cartelists

[197] Some commentators have proposed a positive relationship between collusion and profitability, positing that lower profits tend to lead to collusion. See, e.g.: Asch and Seneca (1975); and Skilbeck (2003).

[198] See Parker and Nielsen (2008).

[199] Parker (2011). See also Tyler (2006).

[200] See Geis (1995), 155–6 and 163.

[201] See MacCulloch (2007), 362. See also O'Kane (2011b).

may capture more customers may lead to the cartel agreement never being implemented in the first place.[202] Of course, there are numerous examples of cartels that have lasted for many decades irrespective of incentives to cheat.[203] However, the point here is that it does not follow that *every single* cartel will in fact get beyond the stage of agreement and actually result in higher prices to consumers. Therefore, one cannot say with confidence that the creation of a cartel agreement inevitably leads to certain losses for consumers. That said, cartel agreements which have been *implemented* by the cartelists (i.e. by charging higher prices to their customers) will by definition lead to the virtually certain result that is required for a finding of stealing. Therefore, like with the requirement of a fundamental violation, one needs to be careful when defining the precise actions of the cartelist in this context. Where oblique intention alone is relied upon to substantiate the existence of an intention to capture the overcharge, any resulting criminal cartel offence must take account of the nuance identified. In particular, in such an instance, if the criminal cartel offence is necessarily to capture conduct which amounts to a violation of the moral norm against stealing, its scope should not extend beyond the implementation of a cartel to the mere agreement to implement a cartel.

(ii) Cartel activity as deception

A potential alternative explanation for the moral wrongfulness of cartel activity is the concept of deception. As above, deception occurs where (i) a message is communicated, with (ii) an intent to cause a person to believe something that is untrue, and (iii) a person is thereby caused to believe something that is not true.[204] The central issues of concern inherent in the concept are: the actual message that is communicated by the cartelist; the process by which this message leads to a false belief on behalf of a third party; the content of the false belief itself; and the intentions of the cartelist when he communicates the message.

There are three potential scenarios involving the interaction of a cartelist with his customer which are relevant for present purposes. The first scenario relates to the situation where the cartelist *expressly states* to his customer that he *has* colluded. The second scenario exists where the cartelist *expressly states* to his customer that he *has not* colluded. The third scenario arises when the cartelist does not expressly state that cartelization has (or has not) occurred, but nonetheless *fails to disclose* its occurrence to his customer.

The first scenario is the easiest to address. When the cartelist *expressly states* to his customer that he *has* colluded with his competitors, there will be no deception; the cartelist is merely telling the truth. Indeed, the admission effectively ensures that the customer is made aware of the cartel: presumably, the customer would not be led to believe by such an admission that in fact no cartel exists. If there is an admission of the existence of a cartel prior to a sale, then, there is no violation of the moral norm against deception. While this assertion may represent a statement of the obvious, it can nonetheless influence how one designs a criminal cartel offence. For example, the UK Government recently decided to provide for a 'carve out' from the criminal Cartel Offence in Section 188 of the Enterprise Act 2002 for those cartel agreements which are published in a suitable format prior to being implemented 'so that customers and others are aware of them'.[205] Such a

202 Motta (2004), 139.

203 On this, see the extensive literature referenced in De (2010).

204 See Adler (1997), 437.

205 See: BIS (2012), 66; and Section 47 of the Enterprise and Regulatory Reform Act 2013 (contained in Annex II to this book).

'carve out' can be rationalized as an attempt to link cartel activity to immoral behaviour (i.e. deception), particularly given that the UK Government has also decided to remove the definitional element of 'dishonesty' from the UK Cartel Offence.[206]

The second scenario is also relatively unproblematic. Here, however, there will be a violation of the moral norm. The message which is communicated ('I have not engaged in cartel activity') is a verifiable assertion which is literally false.[207] The assertion is verifiable as, irrespective of (legal) issues of evidence, the individual has indeed either cartelized or he has not. If the individual has indeed cartelized, the statement is literally false.[208] The actual message intended to be communicated, then, is a lie. The process by which this communicated message leads to a false belief on the behalf of a third party (i.e. that cartel activity has not occurred) involves the reliance by the third party upon one of the 'core conventions of dialogue': the convention that 'positive assertions of fact are true in the ordinary sense of the words used'.[209] It is this convention which causes the false belief.[210] Furthermore, it is not difficult to argue that, absent a genuine mistake on the part of the cartelist, his ultimate objective in communicating is to mislead the customer. There are certainly incentives for the cartelist to so mislead. Customers are less likely to display 'bad feelings' about the price rise (and are therefore less likely to seek alternative suppliers) if they attribute the price rise to cost increases rather than to collusion; and due to their ignorance of the cartel's existence, customers will not report the cartel to the authorities. One must not forget here that cartel activity is unlawful after all and, if detected, will result in the imposition of significant fines.[211] It should thus be no surprise that, according to the Commission at least, 'the undertakings involved in the gravest antitrust infringements *usually* employ efforts and sometimes sophisticated means to conceal their illegal conduct'.[212] The General Court agrees with this assessment.[213] Alternatively, oblique intention would be present concerning the creation of the false belief if the cartelist is aware that his customers trust him and take his statements at face value. With express statements, then, the criteria concerning deception can be fulfilled relatively easily. But while the second scenario may indeed involve deception, it is unlikely to occur in practice: cases where cartelists provide statements such as 'no need to worry, our prices have not been determined by collusion' will be rare.[214] A possible exception may be where official statements concerning the absence of collusion when preparing tenders are provided to secure government procurement contracts.[215] This occurs in Germany, where bids responding to public calls for tender, or to calls for tender addressed to at least two entities, 'contain either an express or at least an implied representation that the bids are not rigged'.[216]

However, the third scenario is more common in the real world. It also presents a more complicated analysis concerning deception: the message here is more subtle, in that it does not *expressly* comment on the absence or otherwise of cartel activity; and the

[206] See: Whelan (2012b); and Whelan (2011b). Cf. Jones and Williams (2014).

[207] To use the words of Green (2006), 77.

[208] On the concept of 'literal falseness', see Tiersma (1990), 379–80.

[209] Alexander and Sherwin (2003), 403–4.

[210] This convention of dialogue, while problematic when people lie, nonetheless has a positive function: 'If this convention is generally respected, speakers can signal their seriousness by choosing to make assertions, and listeners will have a safe haven of confidence' (Alexander and Sherwin (2003), 403–4).

[211] For EU-level statistics, see generally: Veljanovski (2011); Veljanovski (2009); Veljanovski (2007); and Veljanovski (2006b).

[212] European Commission (2008b), [88] (emphasis added). See also Geis (1995), 154–5.

[213] See Case T-53/03, *British Plasterboard v. Commission* [2008] ECR II-1333, [63].

[214] Whelan (2009b), 280.

[215] See Robinson (2008).

[216] Wagner-von Papp (2011), 165.

mechanism through which the message occasions a false belief is less robust. The message communicated by a cartelist when active in a market is that his (cartelized) goods/services are available for sale. This message is a literal truth: the goods are indeed for sale. This is not a problem though, as literally true statements are capable of being deceptive.[217] What is required is that the message communicated leads to a false belief. The false belief is that cartel activity has not occurred; it is created due to an assumption made by third parties as a result of the communication of the original message. The assumption is that the cartelist is lawfully engaged in normal competition with his competitors. By placing his (cartelized) product on the market and by keeping the cartel secret, the cartelist implies that he has not actually cartelized. A similar point has been argued concerning the common law offence of conspiracy to defraud:

> in many situations today third parties who deal with undertakings that are in fact parties to cartel agreements will proceed on the *assumption* that they are dealing with undertakings that are lawfully engaged in normal competition with each other; and the cartelists will know that that is so and will, in effect, act in a dishonest... manner, if the existence of the cartel is kept secret.[218]

This argument was accepted by the High Court when it ruled that cartel activity per se, that is without aggravating features such as express lies, could be a dishonest practice in law.[219] While the argument was rejected on appeal,[220] it was rejected due to legal precedent[221] and not because the moral concept of dishonesty, or indeed deception, was incapable of accommodating cartel activity.

However, the assertion above concerning the assumptions of consumers is not unproblematic. The reason for this is that there is currently no empirical evidence available to demonstrate directly that consumers do indeed make the assumption that the sellers of goods/services have not colluded. Robust empirical evidence is required to overcome definitively this particular weakness; consumer surveys could be used. This is not to say, however, that the assertion that consumers make such an assumption cannot be supported at present. In fact, two particular points lend support to that assertion.

First, it appears that a majority (60 per cent) of UK citizens surveyed believe that cartel activity is 'dishonest'.[222] Perhaps they find the practice dishonest because they assume that sellers do not *as a matter of course* collude with their competitors. Cartelists may be dishonest because, inter alia, they are acting in a manner that is inconsistent with (what these citizens perceive to be) fair and legitimate business practice. Put differently, if such citizens assumed that *all* sellers actually engaged in cartel activity, would they be as quick to label any given cartelist as dishonest? The answer may well be 'no'. If so, UK citizens would at least be assuming, then, that *some* sellers are not colluding.

Second, the assumption against cartel activity can be transposed to a more general assumption made by consumers: the assumption that, in the absence of contrary evidence, sellers respect the law. Such an assumption could be conceptualized as the popular (rather than the legal) manifestation of the principle of the presumption of innocence.

[217] See Adler (1997).

[218] Lever and Pike (2005), 95. Cf.: Lester (2008), 141–4; and Massey (2006), 179.

[219] See *Norris v. Government of the United States of America and others* [2007] EWHC 71 (Admin), [66]–[67].

[220] See *Norris v. Government of the United States of America and others* [2008] UKHL 16.

[221] Under English jurisprudence the act of rigging bids, for example, has been described as a 'very honest' practice: *Jones v. North* (1875) LR 19 Eq 426, 429. See also Whelan (2009b), where the present author has argued that such jurisprudence reflects an attitude to anticompetitive agreements which is better placed in the late nineteenth and early twentieth centuries, where arguments as to the beneficial effects of such agreements were more readily accepted than they are now.

[222] See Stephan (2008e).

If citizens value the legal manifestation of this principle—which is likely—they may well put it into practice in their daily dealings. If so, consumers may assume that, until contradictory evidence is forthcoming, sellers usually adhere to the cartel law rules and so do not collude. This argument, however, requires citizens actually to be aware that cartel activity is unlawful. Consequently, to the extent that such awareness does not exist, one cannot argue that the more general assumption (concerning adherence to the law) is active.

In any case, it is the secret nature of cartels which provides potential for the existence of any assumption on behalf of consumers concerning the existence of competition between competitors. If this secrecy is not present, for example due to a public statement by the cartelists acknowledging the cartel, then deception should not be found:[223] reasonable publicity as regards the existence of the cartel would effectively turn the third scenario into the first scenario. Deception would be absent, then, if an exemption were expressly granted by the relevant competition authority prior to the cartelist offering his goods for sale, because presumably the public would have (at least constructive) notice of this exemption decision and therefore of the cartel.

The final element that requires consideration is the intention of the cartelist in the third scenario. While an intention to mislead may well be inferred from the conduct of cartelists in those (detected) cartels involving sophisticated methods of concealment,[224] the same issues of empirical assessment of the cartelist's direct intention are nonetheless present in this context as with the moral norm against stealing: the intentions of cartelists have not been determined definitively on the basis of empirical evidence. Likewise, to fill the empirical gap, one can also link the relevant intention (viz., an intention to mislead) to a direct intention which is supported by robust theoretical arguments concerning cartel activity (an intention to make profit). Misleading the customer about the existence of the cartel helps to protect the reputation of the firm and to keep the existence of the cartel secret (thereby protecting the firm from a fine). Causing a false belief may therefore represent a *means* of achieving profit, itself a likely desired end of cartel activity for the majority of cartelists, and hence represents a direct intention in its own right.

An indirect intention to cause a false belief may also exist, although this would not be as clear-cut as the indirect intention identified with stealing. The problem is that the making of an assumption by the customer (regarding the existence of competition) has not been established as an inevitable consequence of offering products on the market, as explained above. Furthermore, if such an assumption were in fact active in practice, the cartelist himself must be aware of it for an indirect intention to be present regarding the false belief. Depending on the closeness of his relationship with his customers, the cartelist may be well placed to appreciate the beliefs, assumptions, and feelings of customers. Customers may reveal by their conduct that they are making the assumption in question. They may express gratitude to the cartelist (or to his representatives) for offering his 'best price' for the product, for example. Customer satisfaction surveys, if taken, may further imply the existence of the assumption (particularly, if customers are generally satisfied with price levels). The point here, however, is that even if the assumption

[223] Cf. Peretz and Lewis (2003) (commenting on the (originally adopted) UK Cartel Offence in Section 188 of the Enterprise Act 2002 and the fact the question of the existence of 'dishonesty' is related to the extent of openness about the alleged cartel).

[224] An EU example is *Gas Insulated Switchgear* (Case COMP/F/38.899), Commission Decision, 24 January 2007, [2008] OJ C5/7. For an additional and interesting example of how those involved in an international cartel try to conceal their activities, see First (2001), 714–15. The fact that cartels often involve sophisticated methods of concealment has been acknowledged in the literature for many years; see, e.g., Watkins (1961), 104.

is inevitably made by customers, it is not inevitable that all cartelists will know about it. There are therefore two inherent limitations of a deception argument based on, inter alia, the indirect intention of the cartelist: the existence of the relevant assumption and the cartelist's awareness of it.

There is a further, final limitation to the argument that cartel activity is akin to deception. It exists for both the second and third scenarios and irrespective of whether direct or indirect intention is at issue. The limitation is that the cartel must have been implemented by the cartelist. It is not sufficient for the cartelist merely to have entered into a cartel agreement. The reason for this is that the message communicated in both scenarios requires the offering of a product *at a cartelized price*. The second scenario requires a false statement that the product on sale is not cartelized; a relevant *false* statement here obviously necessitates that the product actually be overpriced due to a cartel. The third scenario requires the customer to have a *false* belief that a product's price is its competitive price merely through the offering of that product by the cartelist. Again, for the belief to be false, the product in question must in fact be overpriced due to collusion. To link a criminal cartel offence to the violation of a moral norm against deception, then, one must therefore ensure that its actus reus does not include the mere conclusion of a cartel agreement.

(iii) Cartel activity as cheating

Cheating occurs where a natural or legal person has: (i) violated a fair, legitimate, and fairly enforced rule, with (ii) the intent to 'obtain an advantage over a party with whom he is in a cooperative, rule-bound relationship'.[225] The 'rule' in question must also be general, prescriptive, mandatory, conduct-based, and represent a standard.[226] Cartel activity can arguably be interpreted as a form of cheating.[227] The 'rule' is represented by the prohibition on price-fixing, output restriction, market-sharing, and bid-rigging ('the cartel prohibition') in Article 101 TFEU and/or national equivalents. This rule is general in application: it is concerned with *types* of actions (price-fixing, output restrictions, etc.) as opposed to a particular set of actions in a particular set of circumstances.[228] It is prescriptive in that it guides or controls behaviour; it does not seek to describe the actual conduct of market players.[229] The rule is mandatory: it describes what one must not do (e.g., one must not fix prices), not what one is advised not to do in order to achieve a desired result (e.g., one should not fix prices if one wishes to create loyal customers). The cartel prohibition is clearly a conduct rule rather than a decision rule:[230] it is directed at general market players in order to guide *their* behaviour on the market; it is not, by contrast, addressed to competition officials who take decisions concerning the violating behaviour.[231] Furthermore, the actual standard represented by the cartel prohibition reaches sufficient specificity to ensure that it is considered more of a 'rule' in the Dworkinian sense than a 'principle' or a 'policy'.[232] While general in its application,

[225] Green (2006), 57. [226] Green (2006), 58–62.

[227] Cf. Quaid (2012), 194, who argues that cartels are wrong because they violate 'an assumption that honest participants in an economy rely on when they exercise their freedom of action, namely that the ground rules of competition apply to everyone. Cartels deserve to be treated as criminal because they abuse the very economic freedom made possible by the existence of the anticartel rules'.

[228] See Twining and Miers (1991), 123. [229] On this concept, see Schauer (1991), 2.

[230] On the distinction between conduct rules and decision rules, see, e.g., Dan-Cohen (1984).

[231] It is noted that current EU cartel law, in particular Article 101(2) TFEU, contains a decision-based rule: '[a]ny agreements or decisions prohibited pursuant to this Article shall be automatically void'.

[232] On the distinction between these concepts, see Dworkin (1977), 22–8.

the cartel prohibition is nonetheless precise enough to specify a particular outcome or mode of behaviour.

However, to satisfy the first limb of the paradigm of cheating, the cartel prohibition must also be fair, issued by a legitimate authority and enforced in an even-handed manner.[233] The criteria of legitimacy and even-handedness are institution-specific. It is assumed that the relevant authorities are indeed legitimate and that their enforcement of the cartel prohibition would be even-handed.[234] Concerning fairness, what is in question here is whether the *existence* of the rule itself is inherently unfair: by prohibiting cartels, is one acting ipso facto unfairly towards the potential cartelist? It is submitted that one would not be acting unfairly. First, the restriction upon the freedom of action of the potential cartelist is very narrow in scope. While the rule prohibits cartelists from agreeing to fix prices, restrict output, divide markets, or bid-rig (i.e. from cooperating on business decisions), it does not prohibit them from cooperating on business functions, such as research or distribution.[235] Market actors, then, are not prohibited from engaging in cooperative ventures in which their activities are integrated in a manner reasonably expected to generate efficiencies.[236] Second, the power to prevent cooperation on business decisions is not absolute: if market actors are determined to cooperate with their competitors on business decisions, then, provided that the relevant merger control rules[237] are not violated, they may formally merge their respective firms with those of their competitors.[238] Third, if in the unlikely event that the cartel activity leads to efficiencies, the cartelist may be granted an exemption (or may benefit from an exception) from the operation of the cartel prohibition. Whether this is the case will depend upon how the actual cartel offence is drafted. One could, for example, expressly provide for an (automatic) Article 101(3) TFEU-type exception from criminal liability for those (very rare) cartel agreements that possibly generate net gains for consumer welfare.[239] Such an exception would prevent the punishment of a cartelist for engaging in utility-enhancing activity. Fourth, violation of the cartel prohibition rarely occurs through ignorance of the law and the activity involved is relatively easy to comprehend.[240] Unlawfulness is therefore understood by business people.[241] Finally, given the harm caused and the very low probability of an increase in consumer welfare, it is not unreasonable to introduce and maintain the cartel prohibition. For these reasons, the first limb is relatively unproblematic.

Likewise, the second limb of the paradigm of cheating can arguably be fulfilled by the cartel prohibition. In this instance what is at issue is: (i) whether the cartelist and his victim are engaged in a mutually beneficial, cooperative, rule-governed enterprise; and (ii) whether by breaking the rule in question the cartelist intends to gain an advantage over his victims. In order to determine the answers to both of these inquiries, one must first identify the actual victims. Three possible victims present themselves: the (potential) competitors of the cartelists; the customers of the cartelist; and the final consumers of the

233 Green (2006), 63.

234 Institutional restraints, such as those imposed by virtue of human rights law, will help to secure this even-handedness. On (particular aspects of) this, see in particular Chapters 5 and 6 of this book. On the concept of legitimacy in EU cartel law, see Simonsson (2009).

235 See Werden (1998), 714.

236 Werden (1998), 712–15.

237 For the EU-level rules, see Council of the European Union (2004). On these rules, see generally Whish and Bailey (2012), Chapter 21.

238 See Marsden and Waller (2008), 266.

239 See, e.g., the Irish Competition Act 2002, Section 6(4).

240 On this, see Chapter 7, Section C of this book. See also Whelan (2012a).

241 See, e.g., OFT (2001), [2.5].

cartelized product. The mutually beneficial cooperative enterprise within which these parties are organized is represented by the 'market': that is, the commercial mechanism which allows buyers and sellers to exchange goods/services. By entering the market, the potential cartelists (and their victims) have restricted their liberty to some degree—they have implicitly agreed to be bound by the rules of the marketplace. One of the rules of the marketplace is not to engage in cartel activity. So far, so good.

The difficulty, however, is in actually identifying the unfair advantage that the cartelist intends to obtain in breaking the rule. With a *competitor*, it is not immediately obvious what the disadvantage would be. Cartel activity, if successful, will lead to an increase in a product's price. This may be in the interest of the competitor: he can now increase his own price. Moreover, by not changing his price, he will gain a competitive advantage over the cartelists. So, where is the disadvantage? But perhaps this analysis is a little obtuse. One could, for example, conceptualize the disadvantage in terms of the self-restraint exercised by the non-cartelist competitor in deciding not to enter into a cartel, a self-restraint that is exercised to ensure that the market functions correctly and to the benefit of all. Accordingly, the advantage obtained by the cartelist is not one defined as an increase in sales away from a competitor (i.e. a financial gain), but rather as the gain inherent in 'indulging one's will, exercising one's freedoms beyond the restrictions imposed' by the cartel prohibition.[242] The same analysis would hold for the *customer* of a cartelist who is also a firm operating on a market, provided that he did not cartelize the upstream or downstream market: he would be exercising a self-restraint in not violating the rule. He would also suffer a more tangible material disadvantage in terms of the cartel overcharge.[243] But would the unfair disadvantage be present with regard to the *final consumer*? That is a difficult inquiry. Green contends that '[w]hen X cheats, she seeks an advantage by violating a rule that Y is believed to be obeying'.[244] If this analysis is correct, one therefore would have to establish that the cartelist believed that *the consumer* would not be in breach of the cartel prohibition (i.e. that he would be exercising self-restraint by not engaging in cartel activity). But is a final consumer actually exercising any restraint when he—by definition—is incapable of actually engaging in cartel activity?[245] The common-sense answer would probably be 'no'. But perhaps such an analysis would be following too literally the argument of Green and that what really is at issue here is the breach of one in a *set* of different rules of the marketplace; the quid pro quo for expecting adherence to the rule prohibiting cartel activity by the potential cartelist is the consumer's adherence to a different market-based rule, which he is capable of breaching (such as not submitting a vexatious complaint to the antitrust authorities). One can think of an exam situation here to justify such a broad approach to the concept of cheating. Arguably, cheating in the context of an exam is morally wrong not (merely) because one manages to get an advantage over the other exam candidates,

242 To borrow the words of Finnis (1980), 265.

243 It is noted that the customers of the cartelist may 'pass on' the cartel overcharge to their customers. In such a case, the cartelist's customer may still have suffered from the overcharge: due to the law of demand, an increase in his price causes a fall in demand for his product, and possibly a fall in profit.

244 Green (2006), 66.

245 It is true, for example, that intermediate purchasers of goods can be deemed to be 'consumers' for the purposes of the EU antitrust rules: Akman (2010b). In the analysis conducted above, however, the word 'consumer' should be taken as 'final consumer'—that is, the person who purchases and ultimately consumes the product in question. Under EU law, such final individual consumers are not 'undertakings', as they do not use the purchased product in the furtherance of an economic activity; see, e.g., Case T-319/99, *FENIN v. Commission* [2003] ECR II-357, [36]. Therefore, by definition, such entities cannot violate Article 101(1) TFEU, by, for example, entering into collective purchasing agreements with other final individual purchasers.

but because one thereby 'gets one over' other stakeholders in the examination process who are bound to adhere to certain (fairness) rules (such as the examiner and/or those relying upon the exam results). If one accepts this argument, then there is clearly room to consider the exercise of an unfair advantage by the cartelist over not only his competitors and customers, but also the final consumer.

The final element to be examined again concerns the intention of the cartelist. For cheating to be found, the cartelist must have intended to obtain an advantage over another. There were two potential advantages identified above: (i) the overcharge obtained from a customer which is a firm operating on a market (and therefore bound by the EU/national competition rules); and (ii) the advantage of having the freedom to collude with one's competitors. It should be clear that the conclusions from the analysis conducted above concerning the relevant intention for stealing (intention to obtain the overcharge) apply to an analysis of an intention to obtain (i). In short, a strong theoretical argument can be constructed to establish a direct intention to obtain the overcharge; but if one relies upon indirect intention to find the relevant intention, one would be confined to a definition of cartel activity which does not include the mere conclusion of a cartel agreement. The analysis of intention to obtain (ii) (i.e. to exercise the freedom to collude) is far more straightforward, provided that a cartel is entered into or implemented in a wilful manner rather than through mere inadvertence or negligence (i.e. where the cartel actually has a purpose (whatever that might be) rather than being an accident). In this context, it is worth noting that, according to Harding and Joshua, cartel activity inherently involves deliberate action: 'they are by their nature deliberate and specific and any particular cartel activity can be causally traced back to definite discussion on the part of individuals'.[246] Whatever the ultimate objective of a given episode of cartel activity, one thing is clear: exercising one's freedom to engage in that cartel activity is a prerequisite to the achievement of its ultimate objective. To put it another way, one can only obtain the objective *through cartel activity* by first breaking the rule prohibiting cartel activity. Consequently, violating the cartel prohibition (i.e. entering into and/or implementing a cartel) will inevitably be the *means* towards the achievement of any objective of cartel activity (e.g., profit maximization, protecting the firm from competition, fitting in at work, etc.). A direct intention to achieve one's objectives through cartel activity implies a direct intention to engage in cartel activity. This finding is particularly interesting as the direct intention is not confined to situations where the cartel activity is implemented; by contrast, it covers situations where the cartelist has merely entered into a cartel agreement. This is because: (i) the existence of a cartel agreement itself is a necessary prerequisite to the implementation of a cartel (and is therefore one of the means towards the achievement of any objective of cartel activity); and (ii) the mere entering into a cartel agreement violates Article 101(1) TFEU and/or its national equivalents. As a result, a criminal cartel offence which is aimed at capturing conduct which violates the moral norm against cheating could indeed include an actus reus which extends beyond implementation to the initial conclusion of a cartel agreement.

(d) Moral content and cartel activity: the limitations of a retribution-based antitrust criminalization argument

As explained in Chapter 2, retribution theory holds that criminal punishment ought to be justified, not by reference to its ability to prevent future (objectionable) activity,

[246] Harding and Joshua (2010), 331.

but rather because human beings are responsible for their actions and must thus receive what they deserve when they have made what society deems are wrong choices.[247] Such a theory views criminal punishment as a justification in itself for a wrong that has been committed. In order to place the concept of 'cartel activity' as defined by the OECD within a retribution-based criminalization argument, one would therefore have to demonstrate that such an activity is capable of possessing sufficient negative moral content. It is submitted that, given the above analysis, there is an argument that cartel activity is indeed capable of possessing such moral content.

For a start, a mens rea as strict as intention can be chosen without placing cartel activity outside of the criminal law in a de facto sense. In other words, one can ensure the first element in the tripartite framework is fulfilled merely by employing a facilitating feature (i.e. by defining the cartel offence in such a way that culpable behaviour is caught). An example would include the definitional element of an 'intention to subvert the competitive process'. If one does not wish to do that, one can argue that sufficient culpability exists if moral wrongfulness exists, as in this book moral wrongfulness requires violation of at least one moral norm (which, by definition, includes a mental element focused on intention).

Second, cartel activity involves a significant degree of social harmfulness. In short, cartel activity can produce a considerable negative impact upon a socially valuable interest, i.e. the successful operation of a free market. Two limitations of the social harmfulness aspect to cartel activity were identified: (i) the requirement that the operation of a free market should be considered as a socially valuable interest by citizens; and (ii) the fact that the nature of the particular harm engendered by cartel activity presents three difficulties (the harm is 'diluted' across many different victims; cartel activity may be perceived as a 'victimless crime'; and one may not be able in practice to identify the victims even when a cartel is discovered). The first of these limitations is not problematic: most citizens in the EU appear to accept the value of the free market. The second limitation is more challenging for those who seek to construct a retribution-based criminalization argument. In particular, efforts to educate stakeholders in the criminal antitrust regime about its necessity and appropriateness may be hampered by this limitation.[248]

Third, subject to the (problematic) limitations identified, cartel activity can arguably run counter to the moral norms against stealing, deception, and cheating. There is a strong argument that cartel activity can be conceptualized as stealing. To sustain this argument, one must establish that the victims of the cartel activity have rights to the cartel overcharge. The key issue to be decided here is whether a total welfare standard or a consumer welfare standard should be adopted in the context of antitrust law. There is a strong pragmatic argument why a consumer welfare standard should be chosen, even if one believes that wealth transfers from consumers to producers are welfare-neutral. However, even if the relevant rights to the overcharge are created, there is a further limitation of the conceptualization of cartel activity as stealing: due to the requirement of a fundamental violation of these rights, only the actual implementation of a cartel agreement will be captured.

Deception can certainly be present when false statements are offered by the cartelist concerning the non-existence of cartel activity. Deception through non-disclosure also remains a possibility, albeit one with problematic issues. In particular, one must establish that customers actually assume that cartelists compete with their competitors. Without

[247] See Packer (1968), 37.
[248] On these efforts and the practical challenges they present, see Chapter 10, Section C of this book.

firm empirical evidence supporting this assumption, one must rely on (plausible) theoretical arguments, thereby introducing an inherent limitation to the analysis. Moreover, the determination of the intention of the cartelist in remaining silent is not as clear-cut as with false statements, although arguably a direct intention to mislead often exists in this context. There is a further limitation concerning deception through false statements and deception through non-disclosure: the cartel agreement must have been implemented, as the relevant message communicated requires the offering of a product *at a cartelized price*.

The moral norm against cheating also has potential to capture the 'moral wrongfulness' of cartel activity. But problematic issues also exist here. The main difficulty lies in identifying the 'unfair advantage' that the cartelist intends to obtain in breaking the relevant rule. If the 'advantage' is narrowly defined to include a material/financial advantage obtained over another who adheres to that rule, then cheating can only occur against a cartelist's customer who is an undertaking offering goods or services on a market. A wider definition of 'advantage' which includes the mere indulging of one's will beyond the restrictions imposed by the relevant cartel prohibition further facilitates a finding of 'moral wrongfulness' (this time against competitors, customers, *and* final consumers), but does so at the expense of a more rigid link between the cartelist's actions and their impact on other market actors. That said, such an approach allows one to capture the full extent of cartel activity (i.e. entering into a cartel agreement as well as implementing it).

Assuming, then, that one accepts the validity of retribution theory per se,[249] a retribution-based argument can thus be advanced for the introduction and maintenance of personal criminal cartel sanctions. This conclusion obviously rejects the contention that the concept of morality is insufficient as a value basis for prohibiting cartel activity in the criminal law setting. Simonsson has recently argued that morality is insufficient in this regard as any moral outrage occasioned as a result of cartel activity is based solely upon its presumed economic effects, and that if the welfare effects of a given cartel were negligible, then 'the reasoning based on morality would lose all its force'.[250] For that particular author, then, this fact demonstrates that currently the 'real underlying logic is economics, not morality'.[251] Three points can be advanced here in response to this argument which further support a retribution-based criminalization argument. The first is that Simonsson's analysis focuses on the social harmfulness aspect of morality and does not consider two other relevant aspects: culpability and moral wrongfulness. The above analysis, by contrast, considers all of the three relevant aspects and is therefore by definition more inclusive. The second point is that a retribution-based criminalization argument does not rely at all upon popular reactions ('moral outrage') to establish the negative moral quality of cartel activity. Rather, it involves a critical analysis of whether cartel activity is capable of amounting to a violation of prevailing moral norms. The final point is that the current approach to anti-cartel enforcement is not 'cast in stone',[252] to use a reliable metaphor: it could be modified to reflect a theoretical foundation that is based more concretely upon retribution (a theory that is provided for in the jurisprudence of the EU Courts). So while it may be true, as Simonsson contends, that the *current* underlying logic of antitrust enforcement is economics, not morality, it does not necessarily hold that morality is incapable of being relied upon in the context of enforcement. To use the terminology of Harding, anti-cartel enforcement could become

[249] On this, see Chapter 2 of this book.

[250] Simonsson (2009), 126.

[251] Simonsson (2009), 126.

[252] Changing the focus of anti-cartel enforcement policy may bring additional (practical) challenges, however; on this, see Chapter 10, Section B of this book.

'conduct orientated',[253] because, as noted above, cartel activity may be capable of containing a significant amount of negative moral content.

Finally, to be clear, none of the above analysis should be used to suggest that the (potential) negative moral quality of cartel activity actually establishes the *desirability* of choosing retribution theory per se as a foundation for antitrust criminalization. That is a different issue. Once retribution theory is chosen as the basis for the creation of a criminalization argument it is then, and only then, that Green's framework can be employed in any normative sense. So while the elements of the framework help to determine the moral content of any given conduct—and therefore whether essential elements of retribution theory are fulfilled—they do not in and of themselves establish the appropriateness of choosing a retribution-based theory of criminalization in the first place. In short, determining whether one *should* choose retribution theory over, say, deterrence theory in the context of the European antitrust criminalization debate is a different inquiry from determining whether retribution theory *could* be used to criminalize cartel activity.

D. Conclusion

This chapter began by noting that a comprehensive retribution-based argument in favour of (or indeed against) antitrust criminalization has not been established in the literature and that, consequently, the theoretical challenge of retribution in this context has yet to be examined in any great detail. It was further submitted that retribution theory has potential relevance in the European antitrust criminalization debate. It was noted, in particular, that the literature already presents moralistic comments on the nature of cartel activity and that, in the absence of their clarification and verification, such comments engender the risk of introducing emotive sentiment into what should be a critical and objective criminalization debate. Furthermore, to legislators, retribution theory—with its focus on the morality of a given conduct—may actually appear more attractive than deterrence as a justification for criminal antitrust sanctions, especially given the traditional link between the criminal law and immoral behaviour, not to mention the limitations of deterrence theory noted in previous chapters. For such reasons, and others, this chapter examined the challenge offered by retribution theory to antitrust criminalization.

In doing so, this chapter first presented a framework to determine the moral content of any given behaviour. This framework was developed by Green and consists of three elements: culpability; social harmfulness; and moral wrongfulness. By applying this framework to 'cartel activity' (as defined by the OECD), this chapter demonstrated that such conduct can indeed display (negative) moral qualities. If certain implementing features are decided upon—e.g., an appropriate mens rea (that necessarily ensures cartel activity violates one of the relevant moral norms) and/or the provision of rights of ownership in the cartel overcharge—cartel activity is indeed capable of satisfying each of the criteria in the framework. In particular, it causes (or risks causing) significant harm to the free market and it can be conceptualized as a violation of the moral norms against stealing, deception, and/or cheating. It was argued, then, that cartel activity may display sufficient moral content to be put forward for criminalization if retribution theory is chosen as a rationale for punishment.

[253] Harding (2002), 410–12.

This chapter did not set out merely to argue in favour of criminalizing cartel activity for the purposes of retribution; rather, it aimed to analyse the challenge of justifying criminal cartel sanctions by reference to the theory of retribution. As a result, it also examined the limitations of a retribution-based argument in favour of antitrust criminalization. Some of these limitations (e.g., the requirement that citizens value the free-market system) do not weaken a retribution-based argument. Other limitations, however, are more problematic (e.g., the requirement that consumers assume a competitive market). It is submitted that the challenge of overcoming these problematic limitations represents the main theoretical challenge of retribution in the context of antitrust criminalization: a retribution-based criminalization argument can indeed be constructed, as demonstrated above; importantly, however, its actual strength is determined by the extent to which its (problematic) limitations are enduring. Given the extent of the difficulties associated with each of the problematic limitations identified, this theoretical challenge is likely to continue to confront those who argue in favour of antitrust criminalization for reasons of retribution.

As a result of its focus on retribution theory, this chapter did not consider directly the challenge of deterrence theory for antitrust criminalization. However, as noted in Chapter 3, this chapter's findings concerning the challenge of retribution theory for antitrust criminalization are also of crucial importance for a comprehensive understanding of the complexity of the challenge of *deterrence* theory in this context. This chapter has demonstrated that cartel activity can be capable of amounting to immoral conduct. To the extent that this is true, the *deterrence*-based criminalization argument can overcome one of its potential limitations: it can avoid the imposition of personal criminal sanctions for morally neutral conduct, thereby avoiding the disadvantages associated with 'over-criminalization'. That said, as noted above, certain implementing features may be required in order to ensure that a criminal cartel offence inevitably captures immoral behaviour. (For example, to align the criminal cartel offence with a violation of the moral norms against stealing and/or deception (but not cheating), one must ensure that its scope does not extend beyond the implementation of a cartel agreement to its mere creation.) Consequently, specific action may be required for the deterrence-based criminalization argument to overcome the limitation concerning morality: a jurisdiction introducing criminal cartel sanctions for reasons of deterrence which fails to operationalize the implementing features runs the risk of criminalizing conduct that is not morally wrong. To the extent that these implementing features present *additional* hurdles for antitrust prosecutors—for example, by requiring proof to the highest level of culpability in relation to cartel activity—they have a negative effect upon deterrence-related antitrust enforcement efforts: ceteris paribus, a given amount of resources will most likely produce fewer successful prosecutions. In addition, to the extent that capturing 'moral wrongfulness' reduces the scope of the offence (e.g., by requiring that the criminal cartel offence is confined to implementation of a cartel agreement and does not include its mere making) there is scope to argue that deterrence (of the mere making of a cartel agreement) will be undermined. There is a possible tension, then, between the objective of deterrence and the objective of retribution in the context of European antitrust criminalization.

As is evident from the current chapter and from the one which preceded it, there is a limitation that is common to the application of both deterrence theory and retribution theory: the scarcity of robust empirical evidence on the motivations of those who engage in cartel activity. This lack of empirical evidence has an impact upon the justificatory theories in different ways. It leaves the deterrence-based criminalization argument open to the criticism that cartelists may not be as rational as assumed, while it ensures that a retribution-based argument remains vulnerable to the extent that it assumes that cartelists act for a certain purpose (e.g., in order to violate the consumer's right in the overcharge). Consequently, this scarcity of empirical evidence should be addressed: a thorough examination of the motivations of cartelists is vital for a comprehensive understanding of some of the complexities of the theoretical challenges of antitrust criminalization. Until definitive empirical data is forthcoming, assertions that cartel activity inevitably entails 'morally wrongful' conduct remain vulnerable to challenge. Consequently, until such definitive data is presented, the challenge of retribution theory for antitrust criminalization will remain a significant one. Likewise, the complexity of the challenge of deterrence theory for antitrust criminalization will also persist.

PART II

LEGAL CHALLENGES

5

European Antitrust Criminalization and the First Challenge of Due Process: A 'Strengthening of Rights' in Favour of the Accused?

A. Introduction

Irrespective of whether it is pursuing the objective of deterrence or of retribution, any given European antitrust enforcement action must respect the fundamental rights of the accused, including those concerning due process. This remains the case regardless of the nature of the enforcement regime at issue.[1] Indeed, human rights must be respected by the EU authorities when enforcing EU competition law, as well as by national authorities when national-level enforcement is undertaken. Likewise, human rights protections exist in the context of both administrative intervention and criminal intervention, and they extend not only to natural persons, but also to legal persons. In truth, the issue of due process in particular presents many difficult challenges for *all* types of antitrust enforcement regimes, and there is an ever-expanding literature on this very topic.[2] This is not to say, however, that the issue of due process does not present any *unique* challenges for those European jurisdictions which: (i) currently only impose administrative antitrust sanctions; and (ii) wish to introduce personal criminal antitrust sanctions. In fact, the desire to introduce criminal antitrust sanctions in such a situation produces a number of challenges which do not necessarily have to be overcome when only administrative antitrust sanctions are imposed.

Such challenges are the natural result of two distinct contentions. The first contention is that the introduction of criminal antitrust sanctions, including imprisonment, results in a 'strengthening of rights' in favour of the accused.[3] The second contention is that the introduction of criminal antitrust sanctions in a particular jurisdiction does not preclude the imposition of civil/administrative sanctions *alongside* criminal sanctions for a given cartel.[4] Both contentions are analysed in this part of the book (Part II). The current chapter deals with the first contention: the 'strengthening of rights' contention. The chapter which follows, Chapter 6, deals with the second contention: the 'additional dynamic' contention.

The current literature on European antitrust criminalization has at times alluded to the 'strengthening of rights' contention, as well as its possible (negative) effects on

[1] The nature of enforcement is determined by: (i) the level at which enforcement occurs (i.e. EU level versus national level); (ii) the type of enforcement process employed (i.e. administrative/civil versus criminal); and (iii) the legal identity of the defendant (i.e. individual versus corporation).

[2] On the human rights challenges for EU antitrust procedures, see generally: Ameye (2004); Andreangeli (2012); Andreangeli (2008); Andreangeli (2006); Benjamin (2006); MacCormick (2005); and Roth (2006).

[3] On this, see Whelan (2011a).

[4] On this, see Whelan (2010), 177 et seq.

the objectives of antitrust enforcement.[5] According to Spagnolo, for example, one of the drawbacks of antitrust criminalization is that it results in higher standards of proof, and 'hence, lower probability of conviction and deterrence'.[6] Simonsson also notes that the following argument has been considered by the Swedish Government: 'procedural guarantees applicable as regards human rights would be stronger [with criminal antitrust sanctions] than the standard applied in administrative enforcement'.[7] Wilks has pointed out that 'criminal prosecution is very resource intensive' and that 'the standards of proof are such that prosecution is ponderous, uncertain and long drawn out'.[8] For Stucke (admittedly, a US-focused commentator), criminal antitrust prosecutions involve significant additional costs as a result, inter alia, of 'higher evidentiary proof (which presumably involves incremental costs to obtain)'.[9] The reasoning behind such claims is likely to be the following: when the imprisonment of an individual (and with it the inevitable negative impact upon both his reputation and welfare[10]) is a possible outcome of an antitrust investigation, the human rights protections concerning that individual should be at their most robust; protections which would be merely sufficient in relation to the imposition of administrative antitrust sanctions may no longer be adequate when criminal antitrust sanctions are imposed.

The author conducted an initial analysis of this issue in previously published work.[11] This chapter is dedicated to a more detailed and nuanced treatment of the issue. Specifically, by focusing on the 'strengthening of rights' contention, this chapter helps to determine whether in practice the concept of due process obstructs a project of antitrust criminalization which respects the procedural requirements of European human rights law. There are three substantive sections to this chapter; each represents an essential 'step' in the analysis. Section B articulates the legal framework informing the challenges of due process which are analysed;[12] specifically, it highlights how the introduction of criminal cartel sanctions *ensures* the applicability of Article 6 ECHR to antitrust proceedings. Leading on from this, Section C examines whether in applying Article 6 ECHR, one must in fact strengthen certain procedural rights: it examines the *validity* of the 'strengthening of rights' contention. Once the extent of such validity is established, Section D examines the actual *impact* of the 'strengthening of rights' contention. Two inquiries are made in this context, namely, whether: (i) any 'strengthening of rights' required has a potential negative impact upon European antitrust enforcement; and (ii) the European antitrust authorities can compensate for any potential negative impact identified.[13] Taken together, these inquiries determine whether the 'strengthening of

[5] See, e.g., Venit (2008).

[6] Spagnolo (2006), 135. See also: Fingleton et al. (2007), 17; King (2010), 20; Morgan (2010), 71–2; and Reindl (2006), 121 et seq.

[7] Simonsson (2011), 211.

[8] Wilks (2011), 356.

[9] Stucke (2006), 532–3. In fact, this higher standard of proof may explain the DoJ's apparent reticence to pursue criminal antitrust prosecutions in the first half of the twentieth century: Duncan (1953), 99–100.

[10] Of course, actual imprisonment itself is not the only worry for the accused: '[t]he harm that *indictment* brings to the individual may be irremediable even by subsequent dismissal or acquittal': Chadwell (1955), 1139 (emphasis added).

[11] See: Whelan (2010); and Whelan (2011a).

[12] It should be noted that this legal framework is relevant to not only the 'strengthening of rights' contention (which is examined in this chapter), but also the 'additional dynamic' contention (which is examined in Chapter 6 of this book).

[13] One should remember here that these inquiries are particularly relevant to the discussion of *efficient* deterrence through antitrust criminalization carried out in Chapter 3, Section D(b)(iii) of this book. As will become apparent, however, they are also relevant to a project of antitrust criminalization which relies upon retribution theory.

rights' contention is in fact a problematic legal challenge for those who wish to introduce criminal antitrust sanctions (whether for reasons of deterrence or retribution).

B. Step 1: Articulating the Legal Framework

This section articulates the legal framework informing the due process-related challenges which are analysed; specifically, it highlights how the introduction of criminal cartel sanctions *ensures* the applicability of Article 6 ECHR to antitrust proceedings.

(a) Article 6 ECHR

Article 6 ECHR is one of the main European human rights provisions on the issue of due process.[14] Entitled 'right to a fair trial', this provision holds that in the determination of any criminal charge against him, everyone is entitled to a fair and public hearing within a reasonable time by an independent and impartial tribunal established by law.[15] According to its second paragraph, everyone charged with a criminal offence shall be presumed innocent until proven guilty according to the law.[16] Further minimum rights are detailed in its final paragraph;[17] these include, for example, the right to have adequate time and facilities for the preparation of one's defence, the right to examine witnesses, the right to legal assistance, and the right to be informed promptly of the nature and the cause of the accusation at issue. An individual is vested with these rights when notified officially by a competent authority of the fact that he has become subject to a criminal charge;[18] and these rights cover the whole of the criminal proceedings, including any appeal process.[19]

Article 6 ECHR applies by virtue of a 'criminal' charge. The word 'criminal', however, has been interpreted quite liberally and in fact has an autonomous meaning under European human rights law: 'it is independent of the categorizations employed by the national legal systems of the Member States'.[20] In the words of the ECtHR itself, it will 'look behind the appearances and investigate the realities of the procedure in question'.[21] In *Engel*,[22] the ECtHR held that, in determining whether a charge is 'criminal' for the purposes of Article 6 ECHR, one should consider a number of different factors, in particular the classification under national law,[23] the nature of the offence charged, and the nature and severity of the sanction. Later cases identified other relevant factors to be considered, such as the group to whom the law in question applied[24] and whether the law was designed to have a deterrent effect.[25]

14 The EU Charter also contains provisions related to due process: Chapter VI CFR. On the choice of the ECHR over the CFR in this book, see Chapter 1, Section D(a)(v)(3).

15 Article 6(1) ECHR. 16 Article 6(2) ECHR. 17 Article 6(3) ECHR.

18 *Deweer v. Belgium* (1979–80) 2 EHRR 439. According to ECHR jurisprudence, a criminal charge is defined as 'official notification given to an individual by the competent authority of an allegation that he has committed a criminal offence': *Eckle v. Germany* (1983) 5 EHRR 1, [73].

19 *Eckle v. Germany* (1983) 5 EHRR 1, [76].

20 Ovey and White (2006), 159. See also Perroud (2008), 49.

21 *Deweer v. Belgium* (1979–80) 2 EHRR 439, [44].

22 *Engel and others v. the Netherlands* (1979–80) 1 EHRR 647, [82]. See also: *Ezeh and Connors v. United Kingdom* (2004) 39 EHRR 1; *Welsh v. United Kingdom* (1995) 20 EHRR 247, [27]–[35]; and Clements et al. (1999), 158.

23 This factor is merely a starting point and carries less weight than the two factors which follow it: *Öztürk v. Germany* (1984) 6 EHRR 409, [52].

24 *Bendenoun v. France* (1994) 18 EHRR 54, [46]; and *Jussila v. Finland* (2007) 45 EHRR 39, [38].

25 *Tre Traktörer AB v. Sweden* (1991) 13 EHRR 309, [46]; and *Bendenoun v. France* (1994) 18 EHRR 54, [47].

(b) Undeniable application with custodial sanctions

It has been argued many times that the term 'criminal' applies to the types of sanctions provided by administrative competition proceedings at EU level and within the Member States.[26] The ECtHR has recently held that administrative competition proceedings in Italy involved a 'criminal' charge within the scope of Article 6 ECHR.[27] The EU Courts (and some of their Advocates General) also suggest that an infringement of Article 101 TFEU may constitute a 'criminal charge' under Article 6 ECHR, irrespective of its status under EU or national law.[28] While recent jurisprudence may question this assertion,[29] such case law may no longer be sustainable given the *Menarini* judgment of the ECtHR and the similarities between the Italian competition proceedings and those at EU level.[30] In any case, it is undeniable that cartel laws involving personal criminal punishment, including the imposition of custodial sentences, would be within the scope of Article 6 ECHR:

> In a society subscribing to the rule of law, there belong to the 'criminal' sphere deprivations of liberty liable to be imposed as a punishment, except those which by their nature, duration or manner of execution cannot be appreciably detrimental.[31]

Furthermore, and importantly, there is some jurisprudence which suggests that the degree of the protections involved may be different in 'criminal' administrative proceedings when compared with 'traditional criminal' proceedings, i.e. those subject to the procedural law applicable to the investigation and trial of offences classified as criminal offences under domestic law.[32] Domestic human rights protections appear to take a similar approach to this issue in practice. As noted by Mance LJ:

[26] See: Perroud (2008); Riley (2010a), 198; Riley (2000), 270–2; Slater et al. (2008); Wils (2010); Wils (2003a); and Wils (1996). For the purpose of this book, such proceedings are referred to as 'criminal administrative proceedings'; they are not criminal in the 'traditional' sense, but they are nonetheless within the scope of Article 6 ECHR.

[27] *A. Menarini Diagnostics Srl v. Italy*, Application No. 43509/08, ECtHR, 27 September 2011. On this case, see Oliver (2012). For an earlier ruling on the status of (administrative) competition proceedings under Article 6 ECHR, see *Société Stenuit v. France* (1992) 14 EHRR 509 (European Commission on Human Rights only). See also *Jussila v. Finland* (2007) 45 EHRR 39. One should note that the question as to whether (administrative) competition proceedings are included within the autonomous concept of 'criminal' proceedings under Article 6 ECHR is one that is relevant to the discussion on *ne bis in idem* in Chapter 6, Section C(b) of this book.

[28] See: Case T-1/89, *Rhône-Poulenc v. Commission* [1991] ECR II-867 (Vesterdorf AG, 885); Case C-185/95 P, *Baustahlgewebe v. Commission* [1998] ECR I-8422 (Léger AG, [31]); Case C-199/92 P, *Hüls v. Commission* [1999] ECR I-4287, [149]–[150]; Case C-235/92 P, *Montecatini v. Commission* [1999] ECR I-4539, [175]–[176]; Case C-97/08 P, *Akzo Nobel and others v. Commission* [2009] ECR I-8237 (Kokott AG, [39]); and Case C-272/09 P, *KME Germany and others v. Commission*, judgment of 8 December 2011, not yet reported (Sharpston AG, [46] and [51]). Regulation 1/2003 states that fines imposed by the Commission are not of 'a criminal law nature': Council of the European Union (2003), Article 23(5); but, as noted above, the concept of 'criminal' under Article 6 ECHR is autonomous. For some, to term the EU regime as 'administrative' 'stretches to its very limits the concept of "economic regulation of undertakings", which was the peg on which the Commission's enforcement jurisdiction was hung': Joshua (2000a), 20; see also: Forrester (2011), 200; and Massey (2006), 177.

[29] See Case T-276/04, *Compagnie Maritime Belge v. Commission* [2008] ECR II-1277, [66].

[30] See also *Napp Pharmaceutical Holdings Ltd v. Director General of Fair Trading* [2002] CAT 1, [93] and [98], finding that proceedings under the UK Competition Act 1998 are 'criminal' for the purpose of Article 6 ECHR. See also Vesterdorf (2011), 574.

[31] *Engel and others v. the Netherlands* (1979–80) 1 EHRR 647, [82].

[32] See: *A. Menarini Diagnostics Srl v. Italy*, Application No. 43509/08, ECtHR, 27 September 2011; *Jussila v. Finland* (2007) 45 EHRR 39. See also, e.g.: Slater et al. (2008), 3; and Wils (2008a), 160.

The classification of a case as criminal for the purposes of Article 6(3) of the Convention on Human Rights, using the tests established by the Strasbourg jurisprudence, is a classification for the purposes of the Convention only. It entitles the defendant to the safeguards provided expressly or by implication by that Article. It does not make the case criminal for all domestic purposes.[33]

This difference in treatment may be explained in particular by the stigmatizing effect that may be engendered by violation of the 'traditional' criminal law.[34] At any rate, in this book it is assumed that cartel laws which provide for the imposition of *custodial sentences* should attract the most robust of the due process protections inherent in Article 6 ECHR; they should in other words be treated as being equivalent to 'traditional criminal' laws.

C. Step 2: Determining the Validity of the 'Strengthening of Rights' Contention

It follows from the above that an antitrust criminalization project that ensures respect for European human rights is likely to result in the strengthening of procedural rights in favour of the accused: either Article 6 ECHR will henceforth apply for the first time to (criminal) antitrust proceedings; or, in the alternative, if Article 6 ECHR already applies to the (administrative) regime (following the line of reasoning adopted by the ECtHR in *Menarini*), its requirements may become stricter than before, as imprisonment becomes a possible outcome of the proceedings in question. The possible strengthening of such rights is an important issue to analyse. In particular, there is a two-pronged effectiveness-related argument that must be investigated; this argument runs as follows: (i) if such strengthening exists, it may fetter to a degree the investigatory powers of the relevant competition authority; and (ii) if so, in the absence of additional robust and innovative investigatory techniques such strengthening may therefore have negative consequences for the effectiveness of criminal antitrust enforcement. Three crucial aspects of procedural rights are examined directly below (standard of proof, the right to silence, and division of functions) in order to assess the strength of the two-pronged (effectiveness-related) argument.

(a) Aspect 1: standard of proof

The term 'standard of proof' refers to the level of certainty that proof must achieve for a jurisdiction to establish whether or not the law has been infringed.[35] It is often submitted that the introduction of criminal sanctions for cartel activity mandates a higher standard of proof for antitrust offences than that currently applicable in relation to civil/administrative violations—whether at EU or at national level—and that a potential negative impact of criminalization is the raising of the bar, as it were, for antitrust enforcers.[36] Such an argument runs as follows.[37] Under an administrative or civil enforcement regime, competition authorities must prove that the accused (usually

[33] *Han v. Commissioners of Customs and Excise* [2001] 4 All ER 687, [88], and also [84] (Potter LJ).

[34] Cf. *Jussila v. Finland* (2007) 45 EHRR 39, [44].

[35] Parret (2008), 7.

[36] See, e.g.: Fingleton et al. (2007), 17; King (2010), 20; and Morgan (2010), 71–2. See also the discussion in Reindl (2006), 121 et seq.

[37] It is termed 'the standard of proof argument' in this book.

an undertaking) has engaged in an anticompetitive activity,[38] as dictated by the maxim *necessitas probandi incumbit ei qui agit*.[39] When attempting to prove their case, the parties alleging a civil/administrative infringement must establish that it has occurred according to the standards required in a civil/administrative proceeding; they are not held to the same standard of proof as would apply in a criminal case. By introducing criminal sanctions, one ensures the application of a criminal standard of proof, a standard that is necessarily more onerous than its civil/administrative counterpart. Hence, in comparing the effectiveness of civil/administrative antitrust laws with criminal antitrust laws, one must take account of this larger burden being placed on the enforcers in the criminal context: any 'true' measure of the effectiveness of criminalization should take account of the extra enforcement effort that is required to ensure conviction. Taken to an extreme, such an argument could be used to invalidate an argument in favour of criminalization: a criminal conviction may become so difficult to obtain in comparison to a civil/administrative ruling that, in allocating resources to the criminal efforts, in effect one sacrifices successes under a civil/administrative regime in favour of failures under a criminal one. Of course, in practice all would depend upon the relative levels of effectiveness established. But for this particular effect to be operative at all, a crucial factor must be at play: the civil/administrative standard of proof must indeed be less onerous than its criminal counterpart.

It is true that under a civil/administrative regime, a standard of, for example, 'proof on the balance of probabilities' can be deemed to be sufficient. In the *Napp* case, for example, the UK Competition Appeal Tribunal ('CAT') noted that (administrative) offences under the UK Competition Act 1998 ('CA') were to be determined, 'formally speaking', according to 'the civil standard of proof' requiring 'strong and convincing evidence', as opposed to the criminal standard of 'beyond reasonable doubt'.[40] It is also true that, under the national laws of the Member States, a criminal offence can only be made out once it is established to a very high standard of proof that the accused engaged in the alleged behaviour; often the standard of 'beyond reasonable doubt' is employed. Perhaps to state the obvious, according to this standard the proposition being presented by the government must be proven to the extent that there is no 'reasonable doubt' in the mind of a reasonable person that the defendant is guilty;[41] if this is not the case, the accused must be acquitted, even if on the balance of probabilities it is likely that he has committed the antitrust offence. It would thus be clear to any legal commentator that, strictly speaking, a civil standard of 'proof on the balance of probabilities' is indeed less onerous than a criminal standard of 'beyond reasonable doubt'.[42]

But this is not to concede the crucial point of the argument advanced above, viz., that a civil/administrative standard of proof *is of necessity* less onerous than its criminal counterpart. In fact, in practice, particularly in relation to antitrust enforcement, there may be little difference between the so-called 'civil/administrative' standard of proof and that which would apply in the case of a criminal trial.[43] Indeed, statements from the CAT in *Napp* appear to 'muddy the water' a little concerning the traditional understanding of

[38] See, e.g.: Council of the European Union (2003), Article 2; and Case C-199/92 P, *Hüls v. Commission* [1999] ECR I-4287, [45] and [149]–[150].

[39] Literally, 'the necessity of proof lies with he who complains'.

[40] *Napp Pharmaceutical Holdings Ltd v. Director General of Fair Trading* [2002] CAT 1, [108]–[109].

[41] See, e.g., *Woolmington v. DPP* [1935] AC 462, 481.

[42] See, e.g., May and Powles (2004), 79.

[43] See, e.g., Wagner-von Papp (2011), 177–8.

these standards. Notwithstanding its above-noted comments on the standard of proof applicable to the Competition Act 1998, the Tribunal believed that in practice little difference should exist between the civil and the criminal standard in this context:

> whether we are, in technical terms, applying a civil standard on the basis of strong and convincing evidence, or a criminal standard of beyond reasonable doubt, we think in practice the result is likely to be the same. We find it difficult to imagine, for example, this Tribunal upholding a penalty if there were a reasonable doubt in our minds, or if we were anything less than sure that the Decision was soundly based.[44]

Added to this confusing situation are the facts that: (i) 'in most civil law countries [—i.e. in the vast majority of EU countries—] the concept of standard of proof as such is not so well known and certainly not defined by law';[45] and (ii) the EU authorities have relatively little to say on the standard applicable under Article 101 TFEU.[46] Regulation 1/2003 simply refers to the 'requisite legal standard' and does not affect national rules on standard of proof.[47] For the Court of Justice, the Commission must bring forward 'sufficiently precise and coherent proof' upon which it can justify its decision.[48] The European Courts, then, have not actually mandated a standard of proof based on, for example, 'the balance of probabilities' or 'the preponderance of evidence' when a civil/administrative offence is at issue; but it is also true that they have not expressly specified a standard of 'beyond reasonable doubt'. In fact, the GC has recently ruled that the Commission does not have 'to adduce proof beyond reasonable doubt of the existence of an infringement' when it imposes fines.[49] It has been suggested that, given the 'penal nature' of EU cartel law[50] as well as the Court's pronouncement on precision and coherence, 'the standard of proof should be an onerous one, perhaps even that adopted in criminal cases'.[51] Those particular commentators also noted that, since there is no EU criminal law as such, the issue may have to be resolved by reference to (inter alia) fundamental rights.[52]

But this is where the problem lies for present purposes: human rights jurisprudence, at least from Strasbourg, has little to offer. Indeed, while Article 6(2) ECHR places the

[44] *Napp Pharmaceutical Holdings Ltd v. Director General of Fair Trading* [2002] CAT 1, [108]. Admittedly, post-*Napp* case law has 'stressed that the standard of proof is the balance of probabilities, laying less emphasis on the requirement that evidence should be "strong and compelling"': Whish and Bailey (2012), 401, relying upon: *JJB Sports Plc and Allsports Ltd v. OFT* [2004] CAT 17, [195]–[208]; and *Makers UK Ltd v. OFT* [2007] CAT 11, [45]–[52].

[45] Parret (2008), 7.

[46] According to Gippini-Fournier, the concept of 'standard of proof' does not form part of the EU Courts' process of reasoning and judges in the EU Courts decide 'according to the persuasiveness of the evidence without being bound by pre-determined evidentiary or probability "thresholds"': Gippini-Fournier (2010), 187.

[47] Council of the European Union (2003), [5].

[48] Joined Cases 29 and 30/83, *Compagnie Royale Asturienne des Mines SA and Rheinzink GmbH v. Commission* [1984] ECR 1679, [2]. In a relatively recent merger case, the Court of Justice held that the Commission's evidence must be 'accurate, reliable and consistent' and should encompass 'all the information which must be taken into account in order to assess a complex situation and whether evidence can substantiate the conclusions drawn from it': Case C-12/03P, *Commission v. Tetra Laval* [2005] ECR I-987, [39]. For an argument that the general language of this paragraph ensures that the ruling is also relevant for other, non-merger cases, see Legal (2006).

[49] Case T-53/03, *British Plasterboard v. Commission* [2008] ECR II-1333, [64].

[50] See Joined Cases C-89, 104, 114, 116, 117 and 125–9/85, *A. Ahlström Osakeyhtiö and others v. Commission* ('*Woodpulp II*') [1993] ECR I-1307 (Darmon AG, [451]).

[51] Jones and Sufrin (2001), 679. (These comments do not appear in the latest version of Jones and Sufrin (2011), perhaps due to the GC's judgment in Case T-53/03, *British Plasterboard v. Commission* [2008] ECR II-1333.) Cf. Parret (2008), 22.

[52] Jones and Sufrin (2001), 679.

burden on the prosecution to prove its criminal case, it does not actually specify what the standard of proof should be. Furthermore, the European Court of Human Rights itself has taken a 'cautious approach' to this issue, as it has generally done concerning the substantive content of national laws.[53] It appears from analysis of the jurisprudence that the standard of proof under Article 6 ECHR:

> is largely unexplored in [ECtHR] jurisprudence; it is possible that the ECHR requires no more than 'conviction', otherwise undefined, of guilt on the part of the national court.[54]

Indeed, in cases such as *Salabiaku*,[55] the Court, in holding that strict liability offences are not per se unlawful, underlined the fact that 'the prosecution retains the burden of proving whatever it is that the *national court* regards as sufficient for conviction'.[56] So it appears that, given the cautious approach of the Strasbourg Court, it is domestic law that will have the most influence in this area. Consequently, it is by no means inevitable that a criminal standard of 'proof beyond reasonable doubt', for example, will be required across Europe if criminalization were to occur: this concept is not found in the domestic systems of a number of the signatory states to the European Convention.[57]

The 'standard of proof argument' therefore suffers from a serious defect, at least from the perspective of European human rights law: Strasbourg jurisprudence does not mandate a particular standard to apply when Article 6 ECHR is active.[58] There is no 'strengthening of rights' here; and this remains the case irrespective of whether the (administrative) antitrust regime was already subject to Article 6 ECHR. Domestic law, by contrast, will be more influential concerning this issue. The principles of the legal system in question, for example, may dictate a higher standard of proof with antitrust criminalization than that which applies to an administrative antitrust offence. To the extent that such principles so dictate, the 'standard of proof argument' overcomes its first hurdle. However, two points of caveat should be noted, as explained above: (i) the 'standard of proof argument' relies upon national law, not European human rights law (the focus of this chapter); and (ii) the 'standard of proof argument' may be seriously undermined, if not invalidated, when in practice there is little to no difference—at least concerning antitrust proceedings—between the civil/administrative standard and the criminal standard, as is arguably the case in the UK, if not at EU level.

(b) Aspect 2: right to silence

Article 6 ECHR does not expressly mention the right to silence or the right against self-incrimination.[59] Irrespective of this fact, the European Court of Human Rights has itself expressly acknowledged the existence of these fundamental rights: *Funke v. France*.[60] Indeed, it has held that both of these rights are generally recognized international standards which lie 'at the heart of a fair procedure under Article 6'.[61] They are

[53] Bacik (2004), 162.

[54] Buxton (2000), 338–9, relying on Van Dijk and van Hoof (1998), 460.

[55] *Salabiaku v. France* (1991) 13 EHRR 379.

[56] Buxton (2000), 339 (emphasis added).

[57] Buxton (2000), 338–9.

[58] The EU Charter is also vague on this issue; all it states is that the accused should be 'proved guilty according to law': Article 48 CFR.

[59] The 'right to silence' is understood as a composite term encompassing a number of separate rights, including the right not to be compelled to provide self-incriminating evidence; see, e.g.: *R v. Director of Serious Fraud Office, ex p. Smith* [1992] 3 WLR 66; and Ovey and White (2006), 196.

[60] *Funke v. France* (1993) 16 EHRR 297, [44]. However, unlike with its later cases, the Court in *Funke* 'provided no clear justification for recognising these implicit rights/privileges': Mowbray (2001), 298.

[61] *Murray v. United Kingdom* (1996) 22 EHRR 29, [45].

recognized in this manner as they protect the accused against 'improper compulsion by the authorities' and thereby help to avoid miscarriages of justice.[62] The right against self-incrimination, in particular, is closely linked to the presumption of innocence in Article 6(2) ECHR, as it presupposes that criminal prosecutors seek to prove their case against the accused 'without resort to evidence obtained through methods of coercion or oppression in defiance of the will of the accused'.[63] Accordingly, while Article 6 ECHR does indeed protect the right not to incriminate oneself, it does not extend to preventing the use in criminal proceedings of 'material obtained from the accused through the use of compulsory powers but which has an existence independent of the will of the suspect', such as documents acquired pursuant to a warrant: *Saunders v. UK*.[64]

This approach is quite different from that employed at EU level in relation to its own antitrust proceedings.[65] According to the Court of Justice, admittedly in a case decided before the judgment in *Funke*, Article 6 ECHR does not in fact uphold the right not to give evidence against oneself: *Orkem v. Commission*.[66] The Commission is therefore entitled to compel an undertaking to provide all information and documents, even if they may establish the existence of anticompetitive conduct. However, in order to protect principles of EU law, one must protect the rights of the defence; consequently, the Commission may not compel an undertaking to provide answers involving an admission of an infringement which it is incumbent on the Commission to prove.[67] Consequently, leading questions cannot be asked. But so-called 'factual questions' can; and, under EU law, penalties can be imposed upon undertakings for failure to answer such questions.[68] Interestingly, the EU Courts have continued to assert that the interpretation offered by *Orkem* is correct, despite (apparent) contradictory ECtHR case law.[69]

Some have claimed that the Court of Justice's position cannot be upheld in light of the ECtHR jurisprudence. For a start, post-*Funke* one can no longer support the position that Article 6 ECHR does not encompass the right against self-incrimination.[70] Second, the rule in *Orkem* is narrower than that in *Saunders*: under the latter a person is permitted to decline to provide not only directly incriminating information, but also exculpatory remarks and factual information; this is not the case under the former.[71] One could argue, however, that the ECtHR jurisprudence only concerns questions put to natural persons, and not to undertakings, in investigations which can lead to imprisonment or other sanctions for those natural persons.[72] In other words, it could be argued that the judgments in *Funke* and *Saunders* can be distinguished from *Orkem* and *Mannesmannröhren-Werke* on the grounds that the sanctions at issue in the former cases were aimed at individuals, not undertakings, and that the approach of the Court of Justice is in fact consistent—or at least not inconsistent—with ECtHR jurisprudence. In any case, and importantly, the debate on the matter highlights that in practice (and

[62] *Saunders v. United Kingdom* (1997) 23 EHRR 313, [68]. For a detailed assessment of the historical and theoretical basis of the privilege against self-incrimination, see MacCulloch (2006).

[63] *Saunders v. United Kingdom* (1997) 23 EHRR 313, [68]; see also *Heaney and McGuinness v. Ireland* (2001) 33 EHRR 63, [40].

[64] *Saunders v. UK* (1997) 23 EHRR 313, [69].

[65] Cf. Clough (2003), 305.

[66] Case 374/87, *Orkem v. Commission* [1989] ECR 3343.

[67] Case 374/87, *Orkem v. Commission* [1989] ECR 3343, [34]–[35].

[68] The framework for such compulsory powers is provided by Council of the European Union (2003), Articles 18, 23, and 24.

[69] See: Case T-112/98, *Mannesmannröhren-Werke v. Commission* [2001] ECR II-729; and Case C-301/04 P, *SGL Carbon AG v. Commission* [2006] ECR I-5977.

[70] Willis (2001), 314.

[71] Willis (2001), 316.

[72] Wils (2003d), 577.

at EU level at the very least) the right against self-incrimination may be less robust in an administrative setting[73] than a criminal one involving possible custodial sentences. In those jurisdictions where this is the case, the introduction of personal criminal antitrust sanctions necessitates that the (stricter) approach of the ECtHR in *Saunders* be extended to any criminal investigations by national competition authorities.[74]

Such an extension has the potential to restrict the power of the authorities to investigate not only criminal cases, but also administrative cases, as during administrative proceedings individuals would probably refuse to provide incriminating evidence against an undertaking for fear that it may be used against them in later criminal proceedings. This fear needs to be assuaged if the administrative proceedings are not to suffer, something that has arguably been achieved in the UK. The Competition Act 1998, for example, expressly protects an individual's right to silence without compromising the administrative process. It does this by providing that statements compulsorily obtained from an individual in an administrative context[75] cannot be used against him in a later criminal case.[76] But such a pragmatic approach can only really be used to insulate administrative cases (or, at the most, criminal cases against an individual who is not the one being questioned). By protecting the rights of the accused in line with Article 6 ECHR, the power of the authorities to obtain evidence directly from the accused is effectively circumscribed in criminal cases against that accused: they can only use compulsory powers to obtain material from the accused which has an existence independent of his will.

(c) Aspect 3: division of functions

When administrative (as opposed to criminal) sanctions are provided by a given competition law, it is not unusual for the investigating and prosecuting authority also to be vested with an adjudicative function.[77] The competition authority in such a situation will therefore not only gather evidence and present this evidence in proceedings against an individual/undertaking, it will also decide whether the infringement occurred as alleged and, if an infringement has been established, what the resulting sanction should be. The role of the courts in such a scheme is often confined to reviewing the legality of the administrative decision taken; the courts do not exercise the same judicial function as they would in determining whether a criminal offence has been committed. This is the type of system employed at European level, as well as within the majority of the EU Member States.[78]

It has already been explained that, according to jurisprudence from the ECtHR, Article 6 ECHR is capable of applying to proceedings imposing administrative

[73] National law may of course grant more protection against self-incrimination in administrative competition investigations than available under *Orkem v. Commission* or than required under Article 6 ECHR: Wils (2003d), 577. It has been argued, nonetheless, that due to provisions of national law (in the particular case, Section 60 CA) the *Orkem* rule should apply; see: OFT (1999), [6.3]–[6.4]; Riley (2000), 269–70; and Smith (2001).

[74] See Wils (2003d), 577.

[75] That is, under Sections 26–8 CA.

[76] Section 30A CA (introduced by Section 198 EA). There are two very limited exceptions to the rule: (i) in the criminal proceedings the individual makes a statement inconsistent with the earlier statement; or (ii) in the criminal proceedings evidence relating to it is adduced, or a question relating to it is asked, by him or on his behalf: Section 30A CA.

[77] For a general account of the different treatment of a cartel case in an administrative proceeding compared to a criminal proceeding, see ICN (2005), 26–8.

[78] Currently, in only six EU Member States must the relevant NCA bring a case before the national courts in order to have a fine imposed for an alleged violation of the competition law rules: Wils (2013).

sanctions: whether an act or omission is a 'criminal charge' depends upon, inter alia, its classification in domestic law, the nature of the offence, and the nature and severity of the available punishment.[79] Accordingly, administrative competition proceedings in a given Member State may well be within the scope of Article 6 ECHR.[80] If this is the case, these proceedings must be carried out by 'an independent and impartial tribunal'. On its face, a tribunal which possesses the investigatory, prosecutorial, and adjudicative functions in a given proceeding is not an independent and impartial tribunal.[81] According to Roth, in such circumstances the determination of a criminal charge is made in the first instance by a body that does not adhere to the applicable human rights standards.[82] However, under ECtHR jurisprudence a solution to this problem has been found: a 'criminal' administrative proceeding is deemed to satisfy Article 6 ECHR provided that a right of appeal from the original administrative decision to an independent and impartial tribunal, such as the GC, exists.[83] Indeed, this jurisprudence has been adopted by the GC itself in holding that, while the Commission is not an independent and impartial tribunal for the purposes of Article 6 ECHR, the judicial control exercised by the GC over the Commission (through Article 263 TFEU) ensures that its proceedings do not violate due process.[84] This is the case because:

> the addressees of Commission decisions imposing fines can bring an action for annulment before the [GC], which manifestly provides the full guarantees of Article 6(1) ECHR and which undertakes a comprehensive review of the Commission's decisions.[85]

In 2011, the Court of Justice essentially expressed its agreement with this analysis.[86] Although this line of argument has gained acceptance in some of the literature,[87] it nonetheless remains controversial,[88] irrespective of the fact that, according to the jurisprudence (as opposed to the academic literature), the GC, in reviewing the legality of a Commission decision, may be called upon 'to undertake an exhaustive review of both the Commission's substantive findings of fact and its legal appraisal of those facts'.[89]

The problem with introducing personal criminal sanctions, including imprisonment, however, is that, regardless of the merits of the above argument concerning

[79] *Engel and others v. Netherlands* (1979–80) 1 EHRR 647.

[80] See *A. Menarini Diagnostics Srl v. Italy*, Application No. 43509/08, ECtHR, 27 September 2011. See also Forrester (2009), 830. Cf. Lowe (2009), 5–6.

[81] There has been debate on this issue concerning EU-level competition proceedings; see, e.g.: Waelbroeck (2005), 465 et seq.; and Waelbroeck and Fosselard (1994). But to date, incompatibility with Article 6(1) ECHR has not been successfully argued in front of the EU Courts; see, e.g., Joined Cases T-25/95, etc., *Cimenteries CBR and others v. Commission* [2000] ECR II-700, [712]–[724].

[82] Roth (2006), 5.

[83] *Le Compte and others v. Belgium* (1982) 4 EHRR 1, [51]; and *Bryan v. United Kingdom* (1996) 21 EHRR 342, [32]–[47]. See also *A. Menarini Diagnostics Srl v. Italy*, Application No. 43509/08, ECtHR, 27 September 2011.

[84] Case T-348/94, *Enso Española v. Commission* [1998] ECR II-1875, [55]–[65]. See also Roth (2006), 6.

[85] Wils (2004a), 209.

[86] See Cases C-386/10 P, *Chalkor v. Commission*, C-272/09 P, *KME and others v. Commission*, and C-389/10 P, *KME and others v. Commission*, Judgments of 8 December 2011, not yet reported.

[87] See, e.g., Lenaerts and Vanhamme (1997), 559–62.

[88] See, e.g.: Wesseling and van der Woude (2012); Riley (2010a); and Waelbroeck and Fosselard (1994), 133 (it may 'still be doubted whether the control carried by the [GC], as long as it will be limited to manifest errors of fact, will be sufficient to meet the requirements of Article 6').

[89] See: Joined Cases T-25/95, etc., *Cimenteries CBR and others v. Commission* [2000] ECR II-700, [719]; and Case T-342/99, *Airtours v. Commission* [2002] ECR II-2592. See also: Case C-272/09 P, *KME Germany and others v. Commission*, Judgment of 8 December 2011; and Case C-386/10 P, *Chalkor AE Epexergasias Metallon v. Commission*, Judgment of 8 December 2011.

compatibility, an independent and impartial tribunal at the appeal stage only *will not be sufficient* to save a proceeding from violating Article 6 ECHR. In more traditional areas of criminal law or in areas considered criminal under domestic law, the determination of a criminal charge must be made in the first instance by a body that adheres to the applicable human rights standards; the alternative means of satisfying Article 6 ECHR will not be available.[90] There is ECtHR jurisprudence to substantiate this claim. In *De Cubber v. Belgium*, for example, the Court held that jurisprudence such as *Le Compte and others v. Belgium*[91] arose due to the autonomous nature of the term 'criminal' and that 'in its traditional and natural sphere of application'—i.e. outside the context of rulings by 'bodies which, within the national system, [are] not regarded as courts of the classic kind, for the reason that they [are] not integrated within the standard judicial machinery of the country'—Article 6 ECHR cannot be so lenient.[92] Furthermore, in *Findlay v. United Kingdom*, it was held that as the applicant's hearing was concerned with serious charges classified as 'criminal' under both domestic and ECHR law, he was 'entitled to a first instance tribunal which fully met the requirements of Article 6'.[93]

According to this jurisprudence, then, there will be a 'strengthening of rights' with antitrust criminalization, even if the administrative antitrust regime were *already subject* to Article 6 ECHR. Change is therefore required to accommodate the investigation, prosecution, and adjudication of criminal antitrust offences. Specifically, one must separate the adjudicative function from the investigative and prosecutorial functions at first instance as well as on appeal. Quite naturally this will ensure that at least two different bodies are involved in the criminal antitrust enforcement regime: an investigator/prosecutor and an adjudicator. In contrast to the position with the right to silence (and possibly in contrast to the position with the standard of proof), this change does not necessarily fetter the ability of enforcement agencies to secure convictions. Rather, it ensures that the bodies which collect evidence and present it at trial are not the same as those bodies which decide whether or not an offence has been committed. One could argue, however, that the separation of functions increases administrative costs as it ensures a certain degree of inevitable duplication in the acquisition of knowledge on the part of the two distinct bodies; and that this increase in costs can have a negative impact upon the effectiveness of deterrent/retributive objectives: fewer convictions will be achieved with a given amount of resources. But the reality is that any alleged cost increase can be questioned, particularly if internal checks and balances and frequent judicial review are also present when the functions are combined: both internal checks and balances and judicial review require the acquisition of knowledge by entities that are not the entity which investigates initially, and any system that is characterized by either will already incur duplication costs.[94] Furthermore, the separation of functions in this context may actually lead to significant advantages, such as the shortening of the duration of the procedure and improved access to documents.[95] More importantly, Wils notes that such a separation would ensure the avoidance of any 'prosecutorial bias' arising as a result of: (i) confirmation bias; (ii) hindsight bias and the desire to justify past efforts; and (iii) the desire to show a high level of enforcement activity.[96] To the extent that 'effective antitrust enforcement' is concerned with *accurate* adjudicatory decisions,

[90] See Wils (2008a), 160–1.

[91] As already noted, these cases deemed the requirements of Article 6 ECHR to be fulfilled provided that the impartial tribunal existed at appeal level.

[92] *De Cubber v. Belgium* (1985) 7 EHRR 236, [32].

[93] *Findlay v. United Kingdom* (1997) 24 EHRR 221, [79].

[94] Wils (2004a), 222.

[95] See Waelbroeck and Fosselard (1994), 134–9.

[96] Wils (2004a), 214–17. See also Wils (2005a), 161 et seq.

then, a separation of functions would in fact be welcome. It is submitted, therefore, that the requirement to separate functions does not have the potential to undermine the objectives of the criminalization project; the requirement simply ensures that significant (and arguably, beneficial) institutional change be implemented if the due process rights of the accused are not to be violated.

D. Step 3: Determining the Impact of the 'Strengthening of Rights' Contention

This section examines the actual *impact* of the 'strengthening of rights' contention. Two inquiries are made in this context, namely, whether: (i) any 'strengthening of rights' required has a potential negative impact upon European antitrust enforcement; and (ii) the European antitrust authorities can compensate for any potential negative impact identified. Taken together, these inquiries determine whether the 'strengthening of rights' contention is in fact a problematic legal challenge for those who wish to introduce criminal antitrust sanctions (whether for reasons of deterrence or retribution).

(a) Direct implications of the 'strengthening of rights' contention

The conclusions of the analyses undertaken in 'Step 2' above[97] can be summarized briefly as follows. First, the principles of a national legal system, as opposed to European human rights law, may dictate *in theory* a higher standard of proof under antitrust criminalization than that which applies to an administrative antitrust offence; but this may have minimal practical relevance if, in de facto terms, judges see little difference between the civil/administrative antitrust standard and the standard that applies in a criminal trial. Second, by protecting the rights of the accused in line with Article 6 ECHR, the power of the authorities to obtain evidence directly from the accused is effectively circumscribed in criminal cases against that accused: they can only use compulsory powers to obtain material from the accused which has an existence independent of his will. Third, the requirement to separate functions does not have the potential to undermine the objectives of the criminalization project, but merely ensures that significant institutional change be implemented to protect due process rights. The immediate effects of the protection of due process rights upon criminal antitrust enforcement should therefore be relatively clear.

(i) Impact upon the effectiveness of antitrust enforcement

The aspect of due process having the least (negative) impact upon the effectiveness of antitrust enforcement is the division of functions; in fact, there are strong effectiveness arguments in favour of ensuring a strict division of functions *in any type* of antitrust enforcement regime, in particular if accuracy is included in the measure of effectiveness.[98] Next, there is the standard of proof. This aspect may have the potential to raise

[97] Section C of this chapter.

[98] Accuracy will always be included within the measure of effectiveness when the theoretical foundation of retribution is active: only those actually responsible for the existence of a cartel should be punished. Accuracy is also important for the effectiveness of the theoretical foundation of deterrence, but the accuracy does not necessarily have to extend to the finding of culpability, as opposed to the finding of the existence of a cartel, particularly if general deterrence is pursued (as is the case when deterrence is an objective of antitrust enforcement: Baker (2001), 697). Indeed, as argued by the present author

the bar, so to speak, for antitrust enforcers; but all depends upon the principles of the national regime as well as the interpretation of those principles by national judges in the specific case of antitrust. The situation with the right to silence is, relatively speaking, more straightforward than that with the standard of proof: those jurisdictions currently following the approach of the Court of Justice when applying administrative antitrust sanctions will have to strengthen their protections for the accused if personal criminal sanctions, including imprisonment, are introduced. In other words, if the right to silence is to be protected in line with the jurisprudence from Strasbourg, *in the absence of something more*, it will be more difficult post-criminalization for the investigative and prosecutorial authorities to establish that a criminally anticompetitive agreement has been concluded. Of course, if the standard of proof also increases with criminalization, then the additional challenge due to the right to silence may be even greater than otherwise would have been the case: one will have to prove a cartel to a higher degree of probability while respecting a stricter right to silence. It is clear, then, that the challenge presented by the right to silence—and perhaps with the standard of proof—has some potential to undermine the effectiveness of criminal antitrust sanctions: it can impact upon rates of detection and prosecution. Further action is therefore required by the antitrust authorities to ensure that this does not happen.

(ii) Effects are relevant to both of the theoretical justifications

This problem of 'strengthening of rights' can, if left unresolved, have an impact upon both theoretical justifications (deterrence and retribution). Successful detection and prosecution are obvious requisite elements as regards the effectiveness of deterrence; indeed, optimal deterrent enforcement is determined, inter alia, by the probability of detection and prosecution, as noted in Chapter 2. Any negative effect concerning detection and prosecution rates obviously has an impact, ceteris paribus, upon the effectiveness of a deterrent objective. But detection and prosecution are also important for retribution. In other words, if retribution is the operative theoretical justification, it does not follow that detection and prosecution rates are irrelevant in the criminalization debate: one does not resolve the problem of the strengthening of rights by depending upon retribution as a theoretical justification. Indeed, according to some theorists, for retribution to be effective at all, it not only requires the punishment of those who have done wrong, but also their *rooting out*.[99] Following this line of argument, retribution does not merely require the meting out of deserved punishment when an offence is detected, but also the active detection of offences in order to impose deserved punishment. Consequently, a solution is required to the detection problem inherent in the 'strengthening of rights', irrespective of the operative foundational theory.

(b) Compensating for the 'strengthening of rights'

There are two proposed solutions to the problems identified with the required 'strengthening of rights': increasing the severity of punishment; and increasing the detection rates directly.

elsewhere, the failure of deterrence-based theories to account for why the punishment of the innocent should not be allowed remains one of their principal weaknesses: Whelan (2007), 15.

[99] '[F]or a retributionist, the moral culpability of an offender also gives society the *duty* to punish. Retributivism, in other words, is truly a theory of justice such that, if it is true, we have an obligation to set up institutions so that retribution is achieved': Moore (1987), 150. Cf. Yeung (2004), 72–3.

(i) *First proposed solution: increasing the severity of punishment*

One method of responding to the problem with the 'strengthening of rights' relies upon the particular dynamics of deterrence theory: increasing the severity of punishment. According to deterrence theory, if there is a fall in the rate of detection and successful prosecution, there will need to be a corresponding increase in the severity of the punishment imposed in successful cases in order to secure the same level of deterrence.[100] But one must not forget that increasing punishment in this way may be contrary to the concept of proportional justice,[101] because such an increase may result in the imposition of punishment that is not commensurate with the seriousness of the offence, in other words the gravity of the harm and the degree of culpability of the individual.[102] It is submitted, therefore, that whether the severity of punishment could be increased in order to overcome any potential reductions in detection depends upon the choice of theoretical justification: deterrence or retribution. There are two reasons for this. First, an increase in the severity of punishment (to compensate for any fall in detection) is not helpful for retribution theory. It should be remembered that such an increase only affects rates of deterrence and not detection, which is what retribution theory wants to see increased in this context. Second, retribution theory prohibits any increase in severity which results in an undue sanction. This principle of proportionality is central to the punishment theory of retribution; unlike the case with deterrence theory, this principle must be adhered to if retribution is to be achieved. So, even though detection is important for retribution theory—and therefore any reduction in such detection is problematic—we should not compensate for such a reduction (if it exists) with an increase in the severity of the punishment, unlike the situation where deterrence is the operative theoretical justification.

(ii) *Second proposed solution: increasing the detection rates directly*

Fortunately, increasing the severity of the punishment is not the only solution here. In particular, one can use other methods to increase detection rates directly.[103] By avoiding increases in severity, one can attempt to find a solution to the problem of the 'strengthening of rights' which can be employed for both theoretical foundations. One method of increasing detection rates directly is already routinely employed within the Member States, namely, the use of leniency/immunity/amnesty programmes;[104] another, far less common method is the use of bounties.[105] A further option is the increased use of economic evidence to help one to identify those industries that are likely to encourage cartel activity—or indeed to rule out those industries where such activity is unlikely.[106] All three of these techniques aim to overcome one of the main challenges of anti-cartel

[100] See Block and Sidak (1980).

[101] See, e.g.: Article 49(3) CFR, which provides that 'the severity of penalties must not be disproportionate to the criminal offence'; Wils (2006a), 198; and van Zyl Smit and Ashworth (2004).

[102] See Galligan (1981), 164.

[103] On this see generally Hüschelrath (2010).

[104] The terms 'leniency', 'immunity', and 'amnesty' are often used interchangeably and sometimes have different meanings in different jurisdictions; see Beaton-Wells and Fisse (2011b), 379, referencing Hammond (2007), vii–viii. In this book, (unless quotations from others dictate otherwise), the following definitions are adopted: 'immunity' refers to the situation where the informant escapes prosecution altogether in sanction in exchange for information and cooperation; and 'leniency' refers to the situation where the informant receives a reduction in sanction in exchange for information and cooperation. The term 'amnesty' is not employed.

[105] On this, see Kovacic (2007).

[106] See Baker (2000–01), 827–8. The OFT has been particularly keen to develop its capabilities in this regard; see OFT (2005). See also Hüschelrath (2010), 525–8.

enforcement, whether it be criminal or administrative in nature: the inherently secret nature of cartels.[107] In fact, given the respective merits of these techniques a strong case can be made for their use in *any* enforcement regime. If they are to be used as a *solution* to the 'strengthening of rights' problem, however, they must provide *additional* advantages which are only present in a criminal regime. These advantages can be identified with both leniency/immunity and bounties. Furthermore, antitrust criminalization may bring with it unique powers of investigation which have the potential to alleviate further the problem.

1. Leniency/immunity

It is widely accepted that the US 'has led the world' in creating an effective immunity programme that encourages cartelists to expose their cartels by creating a form of the classic 'Prisoner's Dilemma'.[108] In the late 1970s, the US Department of Justice adopted a immunity policy to foster the effective enforcement of the cartel prohibition contained in Section 1 of the Sherman Act 1890. By the early 1990s, however, it was clear that the immunity policy was not working as effectively as it could,[109] and in 1993 the DoJ amended its 'Corporate Leniency Policy' in order to guarantee complete immunity from criminal prosecution for the first corporation to report a cartel and cooperate with the authorities.[110] In 1994, the DoJ also introduced an 'Individual Leniency Policy' in order to encourage individuals to come forward with evidence of cartel activity.[111] A number of years after the adoption of these policies, Spratling, then Deputy Assistant Attorney General at the Antitrust Division of the DoJ, argued that leniency/immunity programmes had become the 'most effective generator of cartel cases' as they are extremely successful at detecting cartel activity.[112] Due to the apparent achievements associated with the DoJ's immunity policies, competition law enforcers in other jurisdictions, including the EU, decided to adopt leniency/immunity policies of their own.[113] To date, more than 50 jurisdictions operate some form of a cartel leniency/immunity programme.[114] In fact, increasingly, leniency/immunity is seen as an 'essential' element of an effective anti-cartel enforcement programme, particularly given the inherently secret nature of cartels.[115] To take the European Commission as an example, it believes that

> it is in the Community interest to reward undertakings involved in this type of illegal practices which are willing to put an end to their participation and co-operate in the Commission's investigation, independently of the rest of the undertakings involved in the cartel. The interests of

[107] Dunphy (2007), 6. The challenge with the inherently secret nature of cartels becomes even more difficult when the 'oligopoly' argument is raised, i.e. where the cartelist presents the effects of the illegal behaviour (i.e. the price increases) as merely resulting from parallel price movements in oligopolistic markets: Riley (2010a), 206.

[108] Schmidt (2006), 232. [109] Gamble (2013), 25. [110] DoJ (1993).

[111] DoJ (1994). [112] Spratling (2001), 799. Cf. Motta and Polo (2003).

[113] Swaak and Arp (2003), 9. See generally Breathnach (2013).

[114] Hammond (2010), 1. For a list of the EU Member States that currently operate such programmes, see <http://ec.europa.eu/competition/ecn/leniency_programme_nca.pdf>.

[115] See, e.g.: Leslie (2004); OECD (2001); Riley (2005a); and Riley (2002). Cf. Gamble (2013), 26, noting Massey (2006) (who argues that the value of the US programmes could be overvalued as other important developments in cartel enforcement occurred during the relevant time period); and OECD (2011), 14–15. Given this (generally perceived) 'essential' quality of leniency, this particular enforcement technique will be examined in more detail in one of the later chapters in this book (Chapter 9) dealing with the practical challenges involved in understanding the complexity of leniency/immunity. What needs to be investigated for the purposes of the current chapter is whether leniency is at least *capable* of providing additional advantages in a criminalized regime in order to compensate for the negative impact of the 'strengthening of rights' contention.

consumers and citizens in ensuring that secret cartels are detected and punished outweigh the interest in fining those undertakings that enable the Commission to detect and prohibit such practices.[116]

The idea here is that one can destabilize a (secret) cartel by providing incentives for whistle-blowing by the cartelists themselves, thereby creating a 'race to the regulator'.[117] These incentives include either a reduction in the potential cartel fine and/or immunity from the imposition of a fine or from prosecution.[118] In exchange for immunity or reductions in fines, cartelists will typically admit their involvement in a cartel, terminate involvement in the cartel (unless such a move would 'tip off' the other cartelists), keep their leniency/immunity arrangement confidential, and cooperate with the antitrust authority by, for example, providing it with evidence to secure fines/convictions against the other parties. Due to their internal dynamics, cartels are inherently vulnerable to such an enforcement strategy.[119]

Leniency/immunity is seen as being superior to other forms of information gathering (e.g., monitoring markets, relying upon third-party information, or using direct force or compulsion against the cartelists), for a number of reasons. Specifically, it can be used to obtain all kinds of information (and not just the physical variety), it reduces search costs, and it does not suffer from the reliability problems of other methods of collection.[120] For Kaplow and Shavell, self-reporting programmes (such as leniency/immunity programmes) have two distinct advantages for society: they save enforcement costs and eliminate risk-bearing costs.[121] Leniency/immunity programmes also incentivize cartelists to preserve evidence of cartel activity as such evidence has an 'economic and strategic value' if whistle-blowing is later deemed to be a viable option for the cartelist.[122] Importantly, leniency/immunity does not raise self-incrimination issues, as, according to the ECtHR, '[p]ersons are always free to incriminate themselves if in doing so they are exercising their own will'.[123] However, leniency/immunity is not advocated as a substitute for other methods of collecting information and evidence; it is merely a complement: 'leniency can only work if the companies and individuals concerned perceive a risk that the competition authorities will detect and establish the antitrust violation without recourse to leniency'.[124] The threat of severe sanctions and a genuine fear of detection are therefore widely understood as 'cornerstones' of an effective leniency/immunity policy.[125] In the literature, there appears to be general agreement on the basic

[116] European Commission (2006b), [3].

[117] There is a growing body of (economic) literature examining the concept of a leniency policy and how it can be optimally designed; see the extensive literature referenced in Beaton-Wells (2013), footnote 16. Some academics, however, have questioned the degree to which leniency (particularly in the absence of personal criminal sanctions) actually contributes to this 'race to the regulator'; see, e.g., Stephan (2008d). It is noted here in any case that it is difficult to determine empirically the impact of leniency policies, as one cannot determine accurately the prevalence of cartels at any given time; see Massey (2006), 184.

[118] See, e.g.: DoJ (1994); DoJ (1993); and European Commission (2006b).

[119] Harding and Joshua (2010), 229.

[120] See Wils (2007a). For a negative view of the reliability of leniency/immunity applicants, see Jacobs (2007), 38.

[121] Kaplow and Shavell (1994b), 584–5.

[122] Harding and Joshua (2010), 254.

[123] Concurring Opinion of Judge Walsh in *Saunders v. UK* (1997) 23 EHRR 313. Interestingly, the Court of Justice has also held that the right against self-incrimination does not prevent the Commission from rewarding undertakings that plead guilty by reducing their fines: Case C-73/02 P, *ThyssenKrupp Acciai speciali Terni SpA v. Commission* [2005] ECR II-6773, [50]. See Berghe and Dawes (2009), 419.

[124] Wils (2007a). See also: Harrington (2006), 14–16; and Massey (2006), 189.

[125] Hammond (2004).

necessary elements of a successful leniency/immunity programme; these include, inter alia: the provision of complete immunity for the first successful applicant; the provision of leniency/immunity in circumstances in which the competition agency has already begun an investigation; and the achievement of the maximum amount of transparency and certainty.[126]

2. Bounties

The problem concerning secrecy may also be alleviated to a degree by the provision of bounties: that is, by the payment of sums of money for information that leads to a sustainable cartel conviction.[127] This method of obtaining information is one that relies not so much upon the desire for revenge,[128] but rather upon the greed or on the financial needs of a given entity.[129] They can be effective in uncovering cartels as they acknowledge that cartel activity may not be beneficial for non-cartelists in a firm and that 'anyone in a firm could have ethical qualms about anticompetitive business conduct'.[130] Bounties could be paid to both undertakings and individuals. Their usage can be understood as a manifestation of a competition authority's commitment to an intelligence-led approach to anti-cartel enforcement.[131] Mechanisms providing for bounties in cartel cases have been introduced in both the UK[132] and South Korea.[133]

According to the Korean Free Trade Commission, their policy in this regard improves their 'capabilities to detect cartel practices and strengthen internal and external monitoring of cartels, which creates distrust among cartel conspirators and, therefore, prevents cartels from being formed'.[134] In South Korea it was felt necessary to introduce such a scheme as its leniency policy was not particularly effective due to cultural behaviour, namely the unwillingness of employees to inform on their colleagues.[135] It was hoped that the attraction of up to $1,000,000 would overcome any cultural aversion to whistle-blowing. The actual amount of reward money to be paid, however, 'will be determined based on the degree of violation (the extent of punishment) and the strength of evidence submitted'.[136]

The UK programme, while not without its issues,[137] works in a similar manner to the South Korean scheme.[138] The OFT can award up to £100,000 for information about cartel activity. A reward is provided at the discretion of the OFT and its amount in any given case depends upon a number of factors, such as the value of the information in terms of what the OFT has been able to achieve from it, the amount of harm to consumer welfare which the information has helped to put an end to, the effort expended by the bounty-seeker in providing the information, and the risks taken in procuring the information. The UK programme is aimed mainly at those with 'inside information' who have not actually participated in cartel activity, although it recognizes that in exceptional circumstances a cartel participant may also be able to obtain the bounty. According to the OFT, an example of such an exceptional circumstance would be 'where the role of the person in the cartel was relatively peripheral—for example that of an

126 See: Bloom (2007); ICN (2009); and OECD (2003c).
127 See generally Kovacic (2007). 128 On this, see Baker (2001), 708.
129 See Spagnolo (2006), 139. 130 OECD (2011), 18. 131 Nikpay (2012), 10.
132 <http://www.oft.gov.uk/OFTwork/competition-act-and-cartels/cartels/rewards>.
133 See Korean Fair Trade Commission (2005a). See also Lee (2003).
134 Korean Fair Trade Commission (2005b). 135 See Kar et al. (2008), 194.
136 Korean Fair Trade Commission (2005a), 1.
137 See: Kar et al. (2008); and Riley (2010b), 270–1.
138 On its potential for success, see Peel (2009).

employee who was occasionally directed by his superiors to attend a cartel meeting and who was not asked to take an active part in decision-making about the cartel'.[139]

According to Riley, the provision of bounties brings with it three distinct advantages.[140] First, it provides the antitrust authorities with a 'second major weapon' after leniency/immunity to detect and terminate cartel activity, hence improving deterrence. Second, there will be more private enforcement of competition law due to the increased number of cartels being detected. And, finally, it may be an attractive method of detecting cartels which does not involve the use of significant (scarce) resources of the authority. More advantages can be added to this list. Like leniency/immunity, the use of bounties may also be superior to other methods of information collection, particularly when rewards are given to those individuals who participated in a given cartel: it can be used to obtain all kinds of information (and not just the physical variety), and it reduces search costs. Moreover, the provision of bounties increases the incentives for individuals to hold on to incriminating evidence, a fact which increases in turn the likelihood that the authorities will detect such evidence.[141]

Some commentators have argued, however, that the importance of bounties can be exaggerated, in particular 'because the secret nature of cartels means that the pool of potential whistleblowers is small'.[142] With bounties there is also the possibility that the entity exercising the adjudicative function (assuming that it understands that the relevant information has been effectively 'bought') would look unfavourably upon the evidence provided, as individuals may be incentivized to falsify documents, to provide false testimony, or simply to exaggerate in order to reap a financial windfall.[143] It is important, therefore, to ensure that the authority has checks in place to ensure the credibility of the bounty-seekers as well as the robustness of the evidence provided. The authority should, for example, ensure that the evidence presented by the bounty-seeker is corroborated as much as possible by other sources, e.g., leniency/immunity applicants. Additional (criminal) sanctions should also be in place to deter the provision of false or misleading evidence in this context.[144] Furthermore, it is not inconceivable that individuals may misunderstand the lawfulness of a given behaviour in their eagerness to obtain a bounty (e.g., by mistaking a legitimate joint venture for a cartel), thereby causing antitrust enforcers to waste scarce resources.[145] However, provided that only the government—and not private parties—can act upon the information provided by the bounty-seeker, the risk of benign conduct being subject to an antitrust enforcement procedure will be very limited: 'the government prosecutor is likely with modest effort to test the basis for the informant's suspicions'.[146] A final point to be made here is that the concept of a bounty has been criticized as creating potential for wasteful over-enforcement. This over-enforcement may occur as individual enforcers could (based on their own individual calculus and assuming rationality on their behalf) 'invest resources to secure the bounty up to that level where, for each of them, expected benefits just exceed expected costs'.[147] As this reasoning will hold for all potential enforcers in the group which wishes to obtain the bounty, these enforcers will, 'on an aggregated level, invest more resources

139 <http://www.oft.gov.uk/OFTwork/competition-act-and-cartels/cartels/rewards>.

140 Riley (2005b), 391.

141 See Aubert et al. (2006).

142 See Ministry of Economic Development (2010), [34].

143 Spagnolo argues (convincingly) that systematic fabrication is unlikely to occur with cartel activity: Spagnolo (2006), 139–40, relying upon Howse and Daniels (1995).

144 Neyrinck (2009), 25.

145 Kovacic (2007), 166.

146 Kovacic (2007), 166.

147 Lewisch (2006), 293.

in enforcement than its social value (as comprised in the bounty)'.[148] Consequently, a cautious approach to the use of bounties is advisable.

3. Employing leniency/immunity and bounties in a *criminal* antitrust regime

It is true that all three of the methods identified (i.e. increased use of economic evidence, leniency/immunity, and bounties) can be employed in an administrative setting. If these methods are already being used to detect administrative offences, then one could argue that one is already benefitting from their (maximum) impact upon detection rates and that their continued use would therefore not really compensate for any increased evidentiary burden imposed, or for any lack of forthcoming information due to the enhanced right to silence, if criminalization were to occur.[149] This may indeed be the case for reliance upon increased economic evidence; but this is not necessarily so with leniency/immunity or with bounties.

In fact, the use of immunity in a criminal regime arguably leads to the discovery of more evidence than would occur in the administrative context.[150] The reason for this should be clear. When only administrative (corporate) sanctions are available, individuals working for a company that has cartelized a market may not be motivated to provide useful information to the antitrust authorities. Indeed, the absence of personal criminal sanctions ensures that the 'involved individuals have little incentive to work hard to recall awkward facts about meetings and understandings', hoping instead for an unpleasant situation to blow over.[151] By contrast, when the individual personally faces not only a hefty fine, but also possible time in a prison cell,[152] there will be an obvious incentive both to come forward quickly in order to secure immunity and to ensure that whatever information is provided is as robust as possible. Under a criminal regime, then, there will tend to be witnesses 'who, with the proper incentives, might be persuaded to come forward with additional evidence... if they can *secure a better deal for themselves*'.[153] Criminal sanctions (with criminal immunity) can be used, in other words, to create a conflict between corporate and private interests.[154] This conflict will not only produce effects in terms of *individual* immunity applications; the number of *corporate* leniency applications is also likely to rise: '[u]ndertakings understand that if they don't make a leniency application, then for fear of personal fines and a jail sentence one or more of their executives will make an individual leniency application'.[155] This fact is very much appreciated by US antitrust enforcers. Hammond clearly understands, for example, that the 'real value and measure of the Individual Leniency Programme is not in the number of individual applications [received by the DoJ]... but in the number of corporate applications it generates'.[156] In short, imprisonment 'could improve the operation of public antitrust leniency programmes because, by shifting corporate officers' expectations toward high personal penalties, top executives of cartel participants are more likely to

[148] Lewisch (2006), 293.

[149] This argument was also noted in Chapter 3, Section D(b)(iii) of this book, in the context of the discussion of *efficient* deterrence through antitrust criminalization.

[150] See Neyrinck (2009), 24. [151] Baker (2001), 709.

[152] Admittedly, one commentator believes that personal punishment falling short of imprisonment (such as director disqualification) could possibly register a similar effect in practice: Ehlermann (2006), 35. While this might be so, it is submitted that the actual extent of the effect is very unlikely to be the same: imprisonment is almost certainly a larger potential cost than a director disqualification order.

[153] Lawrence et al. (2008), 23 (emphasis added). See also Walsh (2009), 32.

[154] Due to the absence of EU-level criminal antitrust sanctions, the European Commission is currently unable to exploit this potential conflict: Joshua (2000a).

[155] Riley (2010a), 205. See also Rodger (2004), 130. Cf. Verma and Billiet (2009), 14.

[156] Hammond (2004), 11.

seek the immunity from prosecution that accompanies awards of corporate amnesty'.[157] According to some informed commentators, this 'basic reality' explains why the big international cartel investigations (concerning lysine, citric acid, carbon rods, and vitamins) were all initiated first in the US before being taken up by other authorities: criminal sanctions in the US lead to a more effective leniency/immunity policy and therefore increased rates of detection.[158] This 'basic reality' may also explain why there was a reported increase in leniency/immunity applications in Australia following that particular jurisdiction's adoption of a criminal cartel law in 2009.[159] Interestingly, some commentators believe that the impact of criminalization upon the operation of (administrative) leniency is so positive that it provides an instrumental justification for the very existence of criminal cartel sanctions; accordingly, 'criminal punishment against managers is sought not as an instrument to penalize these individuals for a fault committed, but as a strong incentive to whistle-blow regarding an involvement of their companies in a cartel'.[160] While such a justification would be consistent with a deterrence-based criminalization argument, it would of course run counter to an objective focused on retribution.

There are two distinct, additional advantages of providing bounties in the context of antitrust criminalization. The first is that the entity exercising the adjudicatory function (e.g., a jury) might consider the use of paid informers to be an 'acceptable evil' when the detection of serious criminal activity is concerned. Such an attitude may not be present when morally neutral, regulatory offences are at issue. This potential advantage, however, would only be present when the entity exercising the adjudicatory function actually considers (criminal) cartel activity to be morally reprehensible. The analysis above concerning how cartel activity can be conceptualized as morally reprehensible,[161] however, ensures that this particular advantage of bounties remains relevant. The second advantage is that criminalization would reduce a potential risk associated with the provision of bounties to those who actually participate in a cartel. The risk here is that, in situations where the same undertakings cartelize a number of different markets, such undertakings could create a system whereby they take turns to whistle-blow and obtain bounties each time one of the cartels is about to be detected by the authorities.[162] Although the risk of this occurring is probably quite low,[163] the creation of the system in question is most unlikely to be attractive when the individuals representing the undertakings face potential terms of imprisonment.[164] For these reasons, as well as the general advantages noted above,[165] the provision of bounties is also a useful method of overcoming the problems associated with cartel secrecy and of compensating for the identified 'strengthening of rights'.

4. Techniques unique to criminal antitrust regimes

It should also not be forgotten that the increased powers of investigation that may be provided by criminalization (such as powers of covert surveillance or wire-tapping) could

157 Connor and Lande (2012), 436.

158 See: Baker (2001), 709; and Bloom (2005), 77.

159 See Ministry of Economic Development (2010), [23], relying upon Ludlow (2009). See also Boberg (2010), 95, relying upon Jacobs (2010). Brazil also appears to have experienced a similar effect when it introduced criminal cartel sanctions; see Tavares de Araujo (2010), 75.

160 Lewisch (2006), 302.

161 See Chapter 4 of this book.

162 Wils (2007a).

163 Some commentators do not believe that such gaming is a 'plausible' outcome; see King (2010), 29.

164 Wils (2007a).

165 See Section D(b)(ii)(2) of this chapter.

supply essential information that would not have been available under an administrative procedure,[166] thereby improving the rate of discovery of (secret) cartels[167] and compensating for the potential reduction in evidence caused by the strengthening of rights. Lowe believes that robust criminal investigative powers are in fact an essential requirement due to human rights guarantees: criminal enforcement 'requires much more extensive investigatory powers... in order to allow the standard of proof to be met in a criminal case'.[168] McFadden agrees and argues that a successful criminal antitrust regime is one which provides its enforcers with adequate investigatory powers, including powers of search and seizure, the power to search private homes, and powers of arrest and detention.[169] Even though the use of such criminal powers should of course be limited due to, inter alia, the privacy rights of an individual—for example, they should only be used when strictly necessary and should not be used in a disproportionate manner—they are nonetheless capable of having a profound and observable impact upon the effectiveness of antitrust enforcement, as evidenced by the US experience with cartels. Indeed, even opponents of criminalization acknowledge that a potential benefit of criminalization is the stronger investigative tools which are made available.[170] According to a former US Assistant Attorney General for Antitrust, US successes in anti-cartel enforcement are due to a number of important factors, including 'the expansion to antitrust of traditional criminal prosecutorial and investigative techniques' by the DoJ and the Federal Bureau of Investigation.[171]

Jurisdictions which have introduced criminal regimes have learned from the experience of the US in this regard.[172] Ireland, for example, in operating a criminal antitrust regime ensures that experienced detectives from the Garda Bureau of Fraud Investigation (i.e. the Irish police) are seconded to the Irish Competition Authority to assist in the assembly of evidence.[173] Ireland is not alone in appreciating the advantages of relying upon the expertise of the police: to varying degrees, quite a number of criminalized regimes depend upon the police to help with on-site searches and raids.[174] The UK, for its part, has ensured that investigative techniques traditionally associated with serious crime are available to facilitate prosecutions under the UK Cartel Offence. Some of these investigative techniques are clearly not available for investigations of the administrative offence contained in the Competition Act 1998.[175] For example, the Chairman of the OFT can only grant authorizations under the Regulation of Investigatory Powers Act 2000 for intrusive surveillance and entry onto or interference with property or with wireless telegraphy under the Police Act 1997 for the purpose of preventing or detecting the Cartel Offence.[176] This phenomenon is also observable in Germany.[177] Indeed, although the administrative investigative powers of the Bundeskartellamt are robust,[178]

[166] See Danagher (2012), 522–33. The introduction of the Cartel Offence in the UK, for example, increased the powers of the antitrust authorities in this manner; see OFT (2004a); and OFT (2004b).

[167] Cf. Ministry of Economic Development (2010), [36]–[38].

[168] Comments of Philip Lowe in Hawk (2007), 121. A similar point has been made in the literature analysing the Australian project to criminalize cartel activity; see, e.g.: Beaton-Wells (2008a), 194; and Hodgekiss (2007), 12.

[169] McFadden (2011). See also ICN (2005), 29.

[170] See: Buccirossi and Spagnolo (2005); King (2010), 19; and Spagnolo (2006), 135.

[171] Baker (2001), 693. Other factors for the apparent US success story include the grand jury system, the leniency programme, and the attitudes of legislators and judges: Baker (2001), 693–4.

[172] See Fingleton et al. (2007).

[173] See, e.g.: Fingleton (2002), 5; and OECD (2000b), 21. See also Massey (2004), 28.

[174] See ICN (2005), 39–40.

[175] Morgan (2010), 72.

[176] OFT (2004b), [1.5].

[177] See generally Vollmer (2006), 259.

[178] Section 46(2) of the Administrative Offences Act ('OWiG').

they do not allow for the antitrust authority to intercept telecommunications.[179] By contrast, such a power can be exercised when the criminal offence of bid-rigging is being investigated.[180]

It should be noted, however, that the introduction of criminal antitrust sanctions does not necessarily *ensure* that certain criminal powers of investigation will be available; implementing measures may need to be taken. In the UK, for example, it was necessary to provide for a maximum term of five years' imprisonment for the UK Cartel Offence to be legally considered to be 'an arrestable offence' under the Police and Criminal Evidence Act 1986, a classification which brought with it a number of important investigatory powers.[181] The exact detail of these implementing measures will of course depend upon the specifics of the national regime in question.

To the extent that such techniques lead to the discovery of information that would not have been discovered under an administrative regime, they quite obviously compensate for any reduction in detection and prosecution resulting from the identified 'strengthening of rights'. It is submitted that, given their more intrusive nature, such techniques may indeed lead to the discovery of evidence that would not be found in an administrative setting. These techniques, then, if used alongside both bounties and leniency/immunity, have some potential to improve the effectiveness of antitrust investigations, something that is crucial to the achievement of both objectives of criminalization, deterrence and retribution, when the human rights of the accused are acknowledged and respected.

E. Conclusion

The issue of due process presents a number of challenges for those who are considering the introduction of criminal antitrust sanctions within the EU. These challenges are the natural result of two distinct contentions: the 'strengthening of rights' contention; and the 'additional dynamic' contention. The former contention holds that protections which would be merely sufficient in relation to the imposition of administrative antitrust sanctions will no longer be adequate when criminal antitrust sanctions are imposed. Both the validity and impact of that particular contention were examined in detail in this chapter in order to investigate the extent of the first aspect of the legal challenge of due process.

The validity of the 'strengthening of rights' contention was established relatively easily. It was noted above that the introduction of criminal cartel sanctions *ensures* the applicability of Article 6 ECHR to antitrust proceedings. A number of consequences flow from this fact. For example, as a result of European human rights law, one must separate the adjudicative function from the investigative and prosecutorial functions at first instance as well as on appeal. In other words, European antitrust criminalization can indeed lead to a 'strengthening of rights' in favour of the accused. Whether this will be so in practice obviously depends upon the legal protections actually guaranteed by a national regime to an accused cartelist *in an administrative proceeding*. The point here, however, is that, as a direct result of the specifics of European human rights law, there is

179 Section 46(3) OWiG.

180 Sections 100a(1) and 100a(2)(1)(r) of the Criminal Procedure Code ('StPO').

181 See OFT (2001), [7.1] and [7.3]. A similar approach was adopted in Ireland concerning its criminal antitrust regime; see Andrews (2002).

some scope for a discord between the protections required by European human rights law in a criminal setting and the protections actually facing an accused cartelist in an administrative setting. Hence, the 'strengthening of rights' contention was deemed to be valid.

The next analytical step undertaken determined the actual impact of the 'strengthening of rights' contention, and hence the extent of the challenge presented by this aspect of the legal requirement of due process. It was noted that, while not every consequence of the 'strengthening of rights' contention is problematic (in fact, some consequences, such as the mandated division of functions, have important advantages for antitrust enforcement), the requirement to 'strengthen' human rights protections nonetheless has the potential to have a negative impact upon antitrust enforcement. In particular, by protecting the rights of the accused in line with Article 6 ECHR, the power of the authorities to obtain evidence directly from the accused is effectively circumscribed in criminal cases against that accused: they can only use compulsory powers to obtain material from the accused which has an existence independent of his will. Overcoming this particular negative impact represents the core legal challenge presented by the 'strengthening of rights' aspect of due process. To overcome the potential negative effects identified, one could either increase the severity of any criminal punishment imposed or increase directly the rate of detection and prosecution of cartels.

The second option noted fits more comfortably with the objectives of both deterrence and retribution: the first option, while improving deterrence, may result in the imposition of an undue sanction, thereby violating the principle of proportionality; the second option, while requiring a particular approach to retribution (i.e. that which mandates that the proportionality principle is merely a restraint on punishment, not a defining feature), does not risk violation of the principle of proportionality, and yet may lead to increased deterrence. To implement the second option, one should adopt an individual criminal immunity policy, provide for bounties, and make full use of criminal methods of investigation. Leniency/immunity and bounties can of course be used in an administrative regime. But their use in a criminal regime brings additional advantages not seen in an administrative regime. Such advantages (along with the advantages of criminal methods of investigation) may have the potential to compensate for any 'strengthening of rights'.

Admittedly, these proposed solutions should not be perceived as panaceas: depending on the particular circumstances, some may well reduce the potential for a problem, but not eliminate the possibility altogether. In addition, leniency/immunity in particular may pose additional practical problems in the context of criminal antitrust enforcement. In this book, in line with its central thesis, these potentially problematic issues will be considered as part of the practical challenges of European antitrust criminalization: Part III of this book. Specifically, Chapter 9 will analyse: (i) the potential for the existence of criminal cartel sanctions to have a negative impact upon administrative leniency policies and whether mechanisms (such as a *criminal* immunity policy) can be put in place to counteract any negative effects; and (ii) the challenges that are unique to the use of a criminal immunity policy to secure successful cartel prosecutions. In analysing (ii) in particular, that chapter highlights that the legal challenges of antitrust criminalization cannot be fully understood in isolation from the practical challenges of such criminalization.

What the current chapter has demonstrated is the complexity of the legal challenge presented by one aspect of due process: the 'strengthening of rights' contention. It has highlighted some enforcement mechanisms that can be employed to meet that challenge, subject to the proviso that additional practical challenges need to be met in putting those enforcement mechanisms into place. To understand the full extent of the legal challenge presented by due process, however, one should also examine the validity and impact of its second contention, the 'additional dynamic' contention. The chapter which follows aims to do just that.

6

European Antitrust Criminalization and the Second Challenge of Due Process: Imposing Criminal Sanctions alongside Civil Sanctions

A. Introduction

The preceding chapter posited that the legal concept of due process presents a number of unique challenges for European antitrust criminalization and that those European jurisdictions which currently only impose administrative antitrust sanctions, and which wish to introduce personal criminal antitrust sanctions, will need to overcome these challenges in order to respect the fundamental rights of the accused. It was submitted that these challenges are the direct result of two distinct contentions: the 'strengthening of rights' contention; and the 'additional dynamic' contention. The validity and impact of the first contention was explored in detail in Chapter 5. It was noted that, provided that the correct mechanisms are in place, the particular legal challenge presented by the required 'strengthening of rights' identified is not necessarily insurmountable. The first contention, then, is not overly problematic: it does not ensure that a project of European antitrust criminalization will inevitably be undermined by the concept of due process. However, to present a more complete picture of the legal challenge of due process for European antitrust criminalization, one should also explore the validity and impact of the second contention: that the introduction of criminal antitrust sanctions in a particular European jurisdiction does not preclude the imposition of civil/administrative sanctions *alongside* criminal sanctions for a given cartel. This chapter aims to conduct such an examination.[1]

It is true that the current (fragmented) literature alludes somewhat to the 'additional dynamic' contention and its potential impact upon European antitrust criminalization. Perrin, for example, argues that, as a result of the concern for European human rights, the fact that criminal antitrust sanctions exist in some EU Member States but not in others (where only administrative sanctions are imposed) impacts negatively on European cooperation in antitrust enforcement.[2] Zuleeg, for his part, questions whether the mere existence of both criminal and administrative antitrust procedures within Europe has the potential to violate the human rights of the accused, in particular his right not to be punished twice for the same conduct.[3] A final example is Nazzini, who considers whether the existence of the UK Cartel Offence introduces human rights-based problems due to the possibility of concurrent criminal and administrative proceedings (aimed at different entities).[4]

Notwithstanding the points raised in all of this particular literature, to date, no in-depth and systematic analysis has been undertaken concerning the validity of the 'additional dynamic' contention and its impact upon a given project of European antitrust criminalization. This situation is regrettable. In truth, a detailed examination of the validity and impact of the 'additional dynamic' contention is desirable for a

[1] For an earlier treatment of this issue by the author, see Whelan (2013b).
[2] Perrin (2006). [3] Zuleeg (2002), 13. [4] Nazzini (2003).

number of reasons. First, even if the 'strengthening of rights' contention is unproblematic, it does not necessarily imply that the 'additional dynamic' contention follows suit: the potential due process-related problems engendered by the (specific/general) employment of criminal antitrust sanctions *instead of* their administrative counterpart are conceptually distinct from those due process-related problems which result from the *co-existence* of criminal and administrative sanctions for a given cartel. Second, the due process-related problems that are unique to the 'additional dynamic' contention deserve consideration in and of themselves. As noted in Chapter 1, the legal requirement to protect the human rights of the accused applies to all of the Member States of the EU due, inter alia, to their respective national constitutions, EU law, and international and regional human rights law. If the 'additional dynamic' contention has the potential to impact negatively on these rights, it is imperative that one is aware of that fact and takes steps to avoid such a negative impact. Third, consideration of the extent of the *validity* of the 'additional dynamic' contention (as opposed to its *impact* upon European antitrust criminalization) is an important inquiry in this context: only by determining such validity can one come to a firm conclusion on the extent of any due process-related problems and whether those problems are likely to continue (if left unaddressed). In other words, if the contention is of limited validity, it follows that one should be less concerned about its impact, and vice versa. Finally, the 'additional dynamic' may impact upon the theoretical justifications for European antitrust criminalization noted in Part I of this book. If a comprehensive understanding of the theoretical challenges of European antitrust criminalization is to be achieved, one should be aware of any such impact, as well as any useful mechanisms to overcome it.

As mentioned above, this chapter aims to examine the validity of the 'additional dynamic' contention, as well as its impact upon a project of European antitrust criminalization which aims to respect the due process rights of the accused. In so doing, this chapter articulates the second legal challenge for European antitrust criminalization presented by the requirement of due process. This chapter is divided into two substantive sections: Sections B and C. Each section represents an essential 'step' in identifying whether the 'additional dynamic' contention is problematic. The first step (Section B) determines the *validity* of the 'additional dynamic' contention: it establishes whether it is necessary to investigate further the actual impact of the 'additional dynamic' contention on a project of European antitrust criminalization. It does so by considering the likelihood and legality of four particular manifestations of the 'additional dynamic' contention. These manifestations reflect the various sanctioning scenarios which can be created when both criminal and administrative antitrust sanctions are employed across the EU. By contrast, the second step (Section C) examines the *impact* of the 'additional dynamic' contention: it examines the specifics of the due process-related challenge presented when personal criminal antitrust sanctions are indeed employed alongside civil/administrative sanctions against undertakings. Three important issues are considered: information exchange; double jeopardy; and concurrent proceedings. When necessary, this section attempts to identify techniques that help antitrust enforcers to meet the challenge of respecting the due process rights of the accused in this context. Finally, some concluding observations are offered.

B. Step 1: Determining the Validity of the 'Additional Dynamic' Contention

The 'additional dynamic' contention holds that the introduction of criminal antitrust sanctions in a particular jurisdiction does not preclude the imposition of civil/

administrative sanctions *alongside* criminal sanctions for a given cartel. The words 'for a given cartel' are important. They have an impact upon the scope of the analysis. For a start, they ensure that the analysis of the 'additional dynamic' contention is not confined to situations involving the imposition of both criminal and administrative sanctions on a given individual: the contention includes situations where only criminal sanctions are imposed on an individual and where only administrative sanctions are imposed on an undertaking *for the same cartel*. Furthermore, they ensure that the analysis is not focused on a single jurisdiction: the contention includes situations where a given jurisdiction imposes criminal sanctions on an individual and a different jurisdiction imposes administrative sanctions on an undertaking *for the same cartel*.

As a result, there are four potential manifestations of the 'additional dynamic' contention: (i) a given national regime imposes both administrative antitrust sanctions on undertakings and criminal antitrust sanctions on individuals; (ii) a given national regime imposes criminal antitrust sanctions on individuals and a different national regime imposes administrative antitrust sanctions on undertakings; (iii) the European Commission imposes administrative antitrust sanctions on undertakings and a given national regime imposes criminal sanctions on individuals; and (iv) the European Commission imposes criminal antitrust sanctions on individuals and a given national regime imposes administrative antitrust sanctions on undertakings. In order to examine the *validity* of the 'additional dynamic' contention, one is therefore required to examine the *likelihood and/or legality* of manifestations (i) to (iv).

(a) Inquiries relevant to the determination of validity

A number of inquiries need to be undertaken in order to examine the likelihood and/or legality of the four identified manifestations of the 'additional dynamic' contention. These inquiries include: (i) whether EU law allows a national regime to adopt both criminal and administrative sanctions; (ii) whether diversity concerning the nature of antitrust sanctions exists across the Member States, and if so, whether such diversity will continue; and (iii) whether the EU can mandate the adoption of (and/or impose) criminal antitrust sanctions. In fact, only by undertaking these inquiries, can one predict the likelihood and/or legality of the four manifestations identified. In so predicting, one can then come to a firm conclusion on the validity of the 'additional dynamic' contention.

(i) National competence to impose criminal and administrative antitrust sanctions

Currently, European law allows Member States to decide on the nature of their antitrust enforcement regime: under EU law, and subject to their own constitutional restraints, Member States can choose whether to impose criminal and/or administrative sanctions for violation of Article 101 TFEU. This is clear from Regulation 1/2003. Recital 16 of Regulation 1/2003, for example, acknowledges the possibility of diversity in the Member States when it provides that 'as regards natural persons, they may be subject to substantially different types of sanctions across the various systems'. Furthermore, Article 5 of the same Regulation explicitly grants the Member States the right to decide on the nature of the antitrust sanction to be imposed for violation of Article 101 TFEU: the national competition authorities may take decisions 'imposing fines, periodic penalty payments or *any other penalty* provided for in their national law'.[5] It is clear from Article 12(3) of Regulation 1/2003 that the 'other penalty' referred to includes individual criminal sanctions.[6] The essence of Article 12(3) is that NCAs may exchange information for the purpose of enforcing Article 101 TFEU, but such information may only be used in evidence to impose *custodial sanctions* on individuals when both the sending and the receiving Member States impose 'sanctions of a similar kind'.[7] Nothing in the Regulation prevents the use of both administrative and criminal sanctions by national regimes for a given cartel. The approach adopted in Regulation 1/2003 reflects the traditional deference of the European institutions to national procedural autonomy.[8] As a result of this deference, and subject to general principles of EU law, such as equivalence and effectiveness,[9] the Member States are given a wide margin of appreciation when it comes to choosing the type of antitrust sanctions they wish to impose. Regulation 1/2003 has not harmonized sanctions and procedures, and Member States decide on the type of sanctions provided for and on their classification as administrative, civil, or criminal according to the general structure of their national law.[10] Under EU law at least, then, both criminal and administrative sanctions remain possible sanctions for violation of Article 101 TFEU.

Even if EU law does not prohibit different types of antitrust sanctions, it does not necessarily follow that national law will be so flexible. In some countries, it may be the case that particular types of sanctions are prohibited by national constitutions. Ireland is an example. In Ireland, sanctions imposed for violation of Article 101 TFEU cannot be administrative sanctions: as a result of Articles 34(1) and 37(1) of the Irish Constitution ('Bunreacht na hÉireann'), and its interpretation by the judiciary,[11] such sanctions must be imposed by courts composed of judges appointed in accordance with the Irish Constitution; antitrust sanctions cannot be imposed by administrative agencies, such as the Irish Competition Authority.[12] However, this situation is not the norm across Europe. The constitutions of Member States do not usually prohibit administrative antitrust sanctions. Hence, national regimes often have the choice between criminal and administrative antitrust sanctions. Accordingly, subject to the (Irish-inspired) caveat above, '[t]he national systems to enforce European competition rules can be designed as a criminal law system, an administrative law system or both'.[13]

5 Emphasis added. Admittedly, Joshua argued in 2002 that (the similarly worded) Article 5 of the then recently proposed implementing Regulation (i.e. the draft of what was to become Regulation 1/2003) did not provide for criminalization at national level: Joshua (2002), 234: 'it is only administrative enforcement, not criminal prosecution in the courts, which is contemplated [in Article 5]'. However, Joshua's argument was based on the fact that Article 3 of the proposed Regulation provided that, when EU competition law was applied by the NCAs, national competition law could not be: criminalization at national level 'certainly does not fit with the Commission's vision of a single legal regime to punish all anti-competitive arrangements with a community dimension' (Joshua (2002), 234). Given that the final version of Article 3 which appeared in Regulation 1/2003 does not exclude national competition law in this way, Joshua's argument concerning the scope of Article 5 is hard to sustain. Cf. Joshua (2003), 628–9. On this, see also Pickford (2002), 39–40.

6 Wils (2006b), 70.

7 On the operation of Article 12(3), see Section C(a) of this chapter.

8 On this, see generally Craig and de Búrca (2011), Chapter 9.

9 See Case 68/88, *Commission v. Greece* [1989] ECR 2925. See generally: Dougan (2012), 78–82; and Steiner et al. (2006), 168 et seq.

10 Lowe (2007), 88.

11 Including cases such as: *Re the Solicitors' Act 1954* [1960] IR 239; and *McDonald v. Bord na gCon (No. 2)* [1965] IR 217.

12 See: Massey (2012); and Massey (2004), 24.

13 Jansen (2004), 258.

(ii) Diversity of antitrust sanctions across the EU

The possibility for different types of antitrust sanctions to exist across the EU is not merely theoretical: diversity of antitrust sanctions is a reality in Europe.[14] In fact, 'there exists a wide variation in the nature and the level of the penalties which can be imposed by the Commission and by the competition authorities of the various Member States'.[15] This is clear from even a cursory examination of the 29 different EU antitrust enforcement regimes (including that at EU level). Indeed, while criminal antitrust sanctions are present in some Member States (such as Ireland, the UK, Denmark, Estonia, and Germany, for example), they are noticeably absent in many others (including, for example, Spain, Sweden, Luxembourg, and Holland).[16] Thus, within the EU, criminal antitrust sanctions exist alongside their administrative counterparts.

This diversity is likely to continue, for a number of reasons. First, for efficiency reasons, criminal antitrust sanctions are unlikely to replace (as opposed to complement) civil/administrative sanctions within a given regime.[17] Second, not all of the legislative bodies or competition authorities of the various Member States may be convinced of the merits of European antitrust criminalization.[18] As was argued in Chapters 3 and 4, such criminalization presents complex theoretical challenges. These challenges may be perceived by a given jurisdiction to be too demanding to be taken on at any given time. Third, the current diversity of cartel sanctions across Europe can be understood as a 'basic philosophical difference' centred on how a given jurisdiction views the phenomenon of cartel activity: some jurisdictions 'regard even the most egregious cartels as an economic phenomenon, to be regulated by administrative law, while others view price-fixing as tantamount to theft'.[19] Diversity will therefore continue to exist in the absence of a consensus on the nature of collusion. A consensus on this issue is not likely to be forthcoming in the immediate future, as the changing of attitudes towards both cartels and the legitimate response of the law to cartel activity takes time, even within a criminalized regime. Fourth, different antitrust authorities may have different priorities. While some Member States have a mature antitrust regime and are better placed to consider the employment of criminal sanctions, others have only been enforcing competition provisions for a number of years.[20] The latter category of antitrust agencies may (wisely) wish to see a 'competition culture' develop in their respective countries before experimenting with criminal sanctions. According to Fingleton et al.,

> cartels should only be criminalised once an agency has an established track record in civil enforcement, merger control and, where possible, in market studies and a sustained flow of outputs in each area. In this way, the agency is more likely to have a sufficient base of experienced and skilled staff to enable it to take on costly criminal investigative work.[21]

It must also be understood here that a strong competition culture and a political commitment to antitrust law is required if criminal antitrust enforcement is to be effective. Fifth, some countries may have more pronounced institutional problems concerning antitrust criminalization than others. Sweden, for example, would have to deal with its

[14] See: European Commission (2009b), [33]; and European Commission (2009c), [203].

[15] Wils (2004b), [190].

[16] See: Perrin (2006), 552–4; and O'Kane (2009a), 325–7.

[17] See, e.g., OFT (2009b), [1.4].

[18] For an insight into the Dutch decision to decriminalize competition law violations, for example, see Kalbfleisch (2006).

[19] Joshua (2006b), 1248.

[20] This is particularly so with the former socialist countries which have become EU Member States in recent years; see generally Cseres (2007).

[21] Fingleton et al. (2007), 22 (footnotes omitted).

legal prohibition on prosecutorial discretion,[22] a problem which did not face the UK or Ireland. Such institutional differences may reduce the attractiveness of criminal sanctions for some jurisdictions. Provided that other Member States remain committed to the imposition of criminal antitrust sanctions, this fact alone ensures continued diversity across the EU. Finally, diversity may continue to exist not only across the EU, but also within a given Member State (i.e. different types of sanctions may co-exist within a given Member State). For reasons of deterrence, those jurisdictions which adopt criminal cartel laws may continue to impose administrative sanctions on undertakings: by maintaining the administrative offences, these jurisdictions ensure that firms would not have an increased incentive to encourage cartel activity among their employees.[23] This is the approach which was adopted in the UK.

(iii) EU competence to mandate (and/or to impose) criminal antitrust sanctions

Traditionally, scholars have argued that only the Member States—and not the European institutions—have the competence to mandate the imposition of criminal sanctions for violation of, what was known as, 'Community' law.[24] Scholarship in the last decade, however, has questioned this particular claim,[25] including in the area of antitrust law. Wils, for example, argued logically that under the (now defunct) EC Treaty framework, not only could the European institutions mandate the introduction of criminal antitrust sanctions in the Member States, but they could also impose such sanctions on individuals at the level of the (then) Community institutions.[26] His argument relied upon the following claims: (i) that criminal EC antitrust sanctions were not expressly *prohibited* by the EC Treaty regime; (ii) that the Commission had broad legislative enforcement powers under Article 83 TEC to establish 'the appropriate regulations or directives to give effect to the principles set out in [Article] 81 [TEC]', principles that inter alia underlined the complete undesirability of hard-core cartels; and (iii) that Article 81 TEC's use of the term 'undertaking' did not preclude individual (criminal) sanctions,[27] as the measures adopted under Article 83 TEC gave effect to the *principles* of Article 81 TEC, not necessarily the Article itself. Wils also noted that, if the above argument failed, Article 308 TEC[28] could also provide a sufficient legal basis for EU-level action on cartel criminalization.[29] In addition, the idea that cartel criminalization could be pursued through EU-level action also found some degree of support in (non-competition law) jurisprudence from the Court of Justice which suggested that the EC pillar could legally require Member States to introduce criminal laws where they were necessary to

[22] See Swedish Competition Authority (2006).

[23] See Chapter 3, Section C(a) of this book.

[24] See Ligeti (2000), 199–200. Indeed, historically EU law has had a relatively minor impact upon matters of criminal law, at least when one considers its impact upon other areas of law: Hirst (2003), 343. See also Baker (1998). That is not to say, however, that 'the "sovereignty" of national criminal law has remained inviolate', to use the words of Sevenster (1992), 39; see, e.g., Goeters (2007), 10–57.

[25] See, e.g., Wasmeier and Thwaites (2004).

[26] See: Wils (2006b); and Wils (2005b).

[27] See Vervaele (1994), 161. See also Case 186/87, *Cown v. Trésor Public* [1989] ECR 195, [221]–[222].

[28] The text of which provided: 'If action by the Community should prove necessary to attain, in the course of the operation of the common market, one of the objectives of the Community, and this Treaty has not provided the necessary powers, the Council shall, acting unanimously on a proposal from the Commission and after consulting the European Parliament, take the appropriate measures'.

[29] Wils (2006b), 95.

ensure the full effectiveness of the rules on environmental protection.[30] Indeed, academics argued that the reasoning of the Court of Justice in those (environmental law) cases could be easily applied to other areas of EU law, including antitrust law.[31] However, the extent to which that particular jurisprudence could be applied to the rules on competition has never been tested in front of the EU Courts.

Importantly, Wils acknowledged that his particular argument would be undermined if the EU Constitution[32] entered into force: the argument relied upon (then) Article 47 TEU and the fact that the EU Treaty provisions on criminal matters had no impact upon the operation of the antitrust provisions of the EC Treaty;[33] the EU Constitution would have integrated the areas covered by the EC Treaty and by the other Titles of the EU Treaty into 'a single Treaty, without any hierarchy of the former over the latter', ensuring that the antitrust provisions would no longer be treated in isolation from (limited) EU powers over criminal matters.[34]

Nonetheless, he argued that, once in force, the provisions of the EU Constitution itself would allow for a (more limited) competence to *mandate* (rather than impose) criminal antitrust sanctions within the Member States.[35] In particular, Article III-271 of the EU Constitution, by providing an express legal basis for criminalization in certain areas,[36] would have effectively prohibited one from using Article III-163 (i.e. the successor to Article 83 TEC) to legislate for criminal antitrust sanctions. Furthermore, by only allowing for 'framework laws' (i.e. 'Directives' in the language of the EC Treaty) to be used to criminalize behaviour, and not 'European laws' (i.e. 'Regulations' under the EC Treaty), Article III-271 would have negatived the argument that criminalization would have been possible at the level of the EU institutions; the institutions, in other words, would not (or, according to Wils, no longer) have had the power to impose criminal sanctions on individuals. If EU-level antitrust criminalization were to have occurred at all, cartel activity would have needed to have been added to Article III-271(1) by a European decision adopted by the Council of the European Union,[37] and it would only have been relevant to the *harmonization* of criminal antitrust sanctions in the Member States.[38] So, in other words, the EU Constitution would have limited the European institutions' power to legislate for criminal antitrust sanctions in two ways: (i) by providing the competence to legislate for criminal matters solely in the context of measures taken concerning judicial cooperation in criminal matters, and not in the context of the antitrust provisions themselves; and (ii) by confining antitrust criminalization to harmonizing measures and the creation of national criminal sanctions—provided, of course, that cartel activity was eventually added to the permissible list in the first place.

[30] See: Case C-176/03, *Commission v. Council* [2005] ECR I-7879; and Case C-440/05, *Commission v. Council* [2007] ECR I-9097. See also: European Commission (2005b); House of Lords (2006); and Cseres et al. (2006b), 15–16.

[31] Hakopian (2010), 160. See also Dawes and Lynskey (2008).

[32] Treaty Establishing a Constitution for Europe [2004] OJ C310/01 ('EU Constitution').

[33] Prior to the adoption of the Lisbon Treaty, the EU and the EC were regarded as 'integrated but separate legal orders': Case T-315/01, *Kadi v. Council and Commission* [2005] ECR II-3649, [120].

[34] Wils (2005b), 158.

[35] See, e.g., Wils (2005b), 158–9.

[36] Article III-271(1) of the EU Constitution does not expressly provide for criminalization of cartels. However, cartels could have been added to the list of permissible areas for criminalization by virtue of the third subparagraph of Article III-271(1) of the EU Constitution.

[37] On the concept of a European decision, see Article I-33 of the EU Constitution (which provides, inter alia, that '[a] European decision shall be a non-legislative act, binding in its entirety. A decision which specifies those to whom it is addressed shall be binding only on them').

[38] Such harmonization would have established 'minimum rules' concerning the definition of criminal offences and sanctions: Article III-271(2) of the EU Constitution.

It is submitted that an identical effect to (i) above has been established with the Lisbon Treaty,[39] the Treaty that was adopted instead of the EU Constitution. Although the Lisbon Treaty actually consists of two founding treaties, it is nonetheless similar in operation to the EU Constitutional Treaty in that it abolished any hierarchy between the amended TEU and the TEC (renamed the TFEU). Indeed, the Lisbon Treaty established one single Union legal order founded on two treaties which have the same value.[40] As a result, the antitrust provisions will therefore have to be interpreted in light of those provisions concerning judicial cooperation on criminal matters. Under the Lisbon Treaty, Union legislative competence in the criminal sphere is provided for in the context of judicial cooperation on criminal matters.[41] Consequently, one cannot argue that Article 103 TFEU (the provision in the TFEU that is equivalent to Article 83 TEC) can be used to legislate for criminal sanctions. Furthermore, for similar reasons, one cannot rely upon Article 352 TFEU (i.e. the successor to Article 308 TEC) as a legal basis for cartel criminalization.[42]

The relevant potential legal bases for cartel criminalization provided in the context of judicial cooperation on criminal matters are Article 83(1) TFEU and Article 83(2) TFEU. It has been argued that each of these particular provisions is *lex specialis* as regards the other,[43] although this is yet to be confirmed by the EU Courts. In any case, concerning the former provision, it is stipulated that, in a certain number of enumerated areas, Directives may be adopted establishing minimum rules concerning the definition of criminal offences and sanctions. Cartel activity is not mentioned, but may be added to this list by virtue of Article 83(1), Paragraph 3 TFEU. For this to happen, the Council of the European Union must unanimously adopt a decision after obtaining the consent of the European Parliament. Using this particular legal basis for cartel criminalization, legislative competence in criminal matters is restricted to the use of Directives and therefore would not cover the criminalization of cartel activity at the level of the EU institutions. In short, then, European antitrust criminalization may be legal under the EU Lisbon Treaty, but, if Article 83(1) TFEU is relied upon as a legal basis, it would be confined to harmonization of the enforcement regimes of the Member States and would be legally possible only if a consensus for such sanctions existed among the Member States themselves—which is something that is currently lacking, as evidenced by the movement towards decriminalization of competition law that has occurred in some Member States.[44]

The other possible legal basis for EU-level action concerning cartel criminalization would be Article 83(2) TFEU, which provides that 'minimum rules with regard to the definition of criminal offences and sanctions' can be introduced by virtue of a Directive provided 'the approximation of criminal laws and regulations of the Member States proves essential to ensure the effective implementation of a Union policy in an area which has been subject to harmonisation measures'. According to Article 83(2) TFEU, the relevant Directive must be adopted by the 'same ordinary or special legislative procedure as was followed for the adoption of the harmonisation measures in question'. As noted by Khan, Article 83(2) TFEU presents some clarity on the legality of EU-mandated criminalization, but its wording 'causes problems'.[45] First of all, there is still considerable debate as to whether criminal sanctions are *essential* to ensure the

[39] See Whelan (2008). [40] See Articles 1(2) and 1(3) TFEU.
[41] See Articles 82–6 TFEU. [42] See Hakopian (2010), 167.
[43] See: Peers (2011), 774; and Peers (2008). See also Hakopian (2010), 162.
[44] See, e.g.: Kalbfleisch (2006); and Wils (2008a), 173. [45] Khan (2012), 84.

effective implementation of EU competition policy,[46] particularly if one interprets this condition as a requirement to demonstrate that criminal sanctions 'can only be used as a measure of last resort where other measures have not been effective'.[47] Given the inherent challenges noted respectively in Chapters 3 and 4 concerning the achievement of deterrence and/or retribution through cartel criminalization, one can indeed question whether this condition would necessarily be met in practice. Added to this is the difficulty of determining what the word 'essential' actually implies.[48] Khan notes a second potential problem: lack of guidance on the meaning of the phrase 'an area which has been subject to harmonisation measures'. For Khan, two interpretations of this phrase are possible: (i) it refers to substantive law; or (ii) it refers to procedural law (i.e. sanctions).[49] With competition law, the substantive law has clearly been harmonized, but it is difficult to argue that harmonization of procedural law (sanctions) has occurred, particularly given the existence of Article 5 of Regulation 1/2003.[50] If the phrase merely refers to sanctions, then Article 83(2) TFEU may not provide a legal basis for EU-level action. However, if it refers to (or at least includes) substantive law, Article 83(2) TFEU can provide a legal basis for cartel criminalization through EU-level action. To be clear, if a legal basis is provided by Article 83(2) TFEU, the resulting Directive would be confined to harmonization of the national enforcement regimes and would need to be adopted according to the same legislative procedure that was employed for the prior harmonization of competition law. That legislative procedure would presumably be the one relevant to Article 103 TFEU (as the harmonizing measure in question would presumably be Regulation 1/2003,[51] which was adopted under Article 83 TEC, the predecessor to Article 103 TFEU). Interestingly, there is an important difference between Article 103 TFEU and Article 83 TEC: the former provision does not contain the phrase 'acting by qualified majority voting'. Indeed, the relevant paragraph of Article 103 TFEU reads as follows: 'The appropriate regulations or directives to give effect to the principles set out in Articles 101 and 102 shall be laid down by the Council, on a proposal from the Commission and after consulting the European Parliament'. However, as Article 16(3) TEU provides the default position of qualified majority voting in the Council, there is no material difference between Article 83 TEC and Article 103 TFEU. If Article 83(2) TFEU can be used as a legal basis for a Directive on criminal sanctions, there would therefore be no need to ensure a consensus in the Council in order to adopt the relevant Directive. Whether this would occur in practice is, of course, a different issue entirely.

At present, then, cartel criminalization within the Member States can be mandated by the EU institutions without a Treaty amendment, provided certain strict conditions are met. Many commentators consider it very unlikely that (national) criminalization through EU-level action would occur in practice,[52] in particular due to contrasting opinions on the necessity and appropriateness of criminal cartel sanctions as well as the inherent link between a Member State's criminal law and its culture, history, and norms.[53]

[46] Khan (2012), 84.

[47] Chambers et al. (2010), 617. For some, it is unquestionable that 'the Commission starts from the assumption that criminal law of this kind should be used as a measure of last resort': Harding and Banach-Gutierrez (2012), 764. See also European Commission (2011b), Section 2.2.1 ('criminal law must always remain a matter of last resort').

[48] See Hakopian (2010), 164–5.

[49] Khan (2012), 84.

[50] Khan (2012), 84. On this, see Wils (2011), 373.

[51] For example, arguably (partial) substantive harmonization of national competition laws occurred due to Article 3 of Regulation 1/2003.

[52] Danagher (2012), 523.

[53] See Safferling (2009), 1385. Cf. Joshua et al. (2008–09), 395.

Daly, however, is less pessimistic, arguing that it may only be a 'matter of time' before a serious proposal is produced to initiate harmonization of criminal cartel sanctions within the EU.[54] For him, while

> such moves might meet with initial resistance, the Commission is likely to argue that international cartels are too difficult to combat on a national basis when their impact is EU-wide and, perhaps ironically, that there are a number of overlapping and misaligned measures already in existence which make prosecution difficult in practice and which should justify some degree of harmonisation.[55]

Such a move by the Commission would represent an underestimation of the significance of the practical problems associated with harmonization of criminal cartel sanctions within the EU. Indeed, as Simonsson has convincingly argued, harmonization in this context would be problematic in practice for a number of reasons, such as the fact that EU law would not require the Member States to resource adequately the criminal cartel regime and the fact that under the current EU enforcement regime the Commission would have a very limited capacity to ensure the uniform and effective application of harmonized cartel criminalization.[56] It is difficult, therefore, to disagree with Simonsson's contention that instead of seeking to introduce criminalization through EU-level action, 'we should use the best aspects of the existing decentralization of competition law to look for an efficient, although geographically uneven, criminalisation system. This would be achieved when a few resourceful Member States step forward and take the lead regionally by criminalising cartels, and by ensuring credible and sustainable enforcement'.[57]

Absent a Treaty amendment, criminalization at the level of the EU institutions (with, for example, the Commission prosecuting cartels and with the EU Courts imposing criminal punishment on individuals) is not possible. For some, this will be bad news. After considering the case for employing criminal cartel sanctions to enforce Article 101 TFEU, Rosochowicz concludes 'that the European Union should introduce criminal sanctions at the European level, in order to compensate for the disparities of the various national systems'.[58] Frese agrees with Rosochowicz,[59] mainly on the basis that national-led criminalization without EU harmonization has the potential for a negative impact on the operation of administrative leniency applications in non-criminalized regimes.[60] For others, however, this will be welcome news. Meiklejohn, for example, believes that criminal enforcement of anti-cartel legislation 'is most effective at the domestic level'.[61] According to Harding and Joshua, for many European citizens, 'criminalization and in particular the use of imprisonment would represent a quantum leap in policy and principle'.[62] Accordingly, such criminalization would likely be viewed as 'an unnecessary intrusion by the Union'.[63] Due to the apparent lack of sufficient broad political support for the project, criminalization at the level of the EU institutions is not a realistic prospect at present.

[54] Daly (2007), 324.
[55] Daly (2007), 324. [56] Simonsson (2011).
[57] Simonsson (2011), 216. See also Whelan (2013c). Cf. Furse (2012), 223.
[58] Rosochowicz (2004), 756. [59] Frese (2005), 31.
[60] On the co-existence of criminal sanctions and administrative leniency policies, see Chapter 9, Section B of this book.
[61] Meiklejohn (2004), 63.
[62] Harding and Joshua (2010), 336. See also Lowe (2007), 96.
[63] Danagher (2013), 19.

(b) Application of findings to the 'four manifestations' to determine the extent of validity

The results of the three inquiries conducted directly above allow one to determine the extent of the validity of the 'additional dynamic' contention. It is submitted that only one out of the four manifestations is invalid. The invalid manifestation in question is the following: the European Commission imposes criminal antitrust sanctions on individuals and a given national regime imposes administrative antitrust sanctions on undertakings. It is clear from the analysis presented concerning EU criminal competence that the European institutions cannot actually impose criminal antitrust sanctions, even if, provided strict conditions are fulfilled, they may be capable of mandating their adoption within the Member States. However, the three remaining manifestations are valid.

The first manifestation (i.e. where a given national regime imposes both administrative antitrust sanctions on undertakings and criminal antitrust sanctions on individuals) occurs within the UK, for example, and is not prohibited under EU law. National law may prohibit administrative sanctions, but this will not be the case in every Member State. The second manifestation (i.e. where a given national regime imposes criminal antitrust sanctions on individuals and a different national regime imposes administrative antitrust sanctions on undertakings) is facilitated by Article 5 of Regulation 1/2003 and is likely given the different priorities facing different Member States, not to mention the current absence of a European consensus about the desirability of criminal antitrust sanctions. Even where the European institutions mandate the adoption of criminal antitrust sanctions for individuals, they are unlikely, due to, inter alia, efficiency reasons, to require the abolition of administrative sanctions. The third manifestation (i.e. where the European Commission imposes administrative antitrust sanctions on undertakings and a given national regime imposes criminal sanctions on individuals) is also valid. This is due, again, to, inter alia, Article 5 of Regulation 1/2003, as well as the fact that the Commission cannot be given the power to impose criminal sanctions: currently, it can only impose administrative sanctions; if it is to continue to enforce EU competition law at all, it will only impose such sanctions. Hence, given that three out of four of its potential manifestations are valid, it is submitted that the 'additional dynamic' contention itself is indeed valid.

C. Step 2: Determining the Impact of the 'Additional Dynamic' Contention

The validity of the 'additional dynamic' contention was established above. This section acknowledges this fact and examines the *impact* of the 'additional dynamic' contention: it examines the specifics of the due process-related challenge presented when personal criminal antitrust sanctions are indeed employed alongside civil/administrative sanctions against undertakings. Three important issues are considered: (i) information exchange; (ii) double jeopardy;[64] and (iii) concurrent proceedings. When necessary, this

[64] While *ne bis in idem* is not, strictly speaking, a formal requirement of 'due process' as enshrined in Article 6 ECHR, it is nonetheless considered in this chapter as it is a formal procedural restriction in favour of the accused which becomes relevant to European antitrust criminalization due to, inter alia, the validity of the 'additional dynamic' contention. In other words, in this chapter, the author adopts a slightly wider definition of the concept of due process than that offered by Article 6 ECHR. As will become apparent, however, the substance of the wider conceptualization of due process is in fact informed by other provisions of the ECHR.

section attempts to identify techniques that help antitrust enforcers to meet the challenge of respecting the due process rights of the accused in this context.

(a) Exchange of information

The effectiveness of an antitrust investigation of a given jurisdiction often depends upon the extent of cooperation and assistance received from foreign states, including other Member States.[65] This is particularly so for cartels: they often cross the boundaries of jurisdictions, as evidenced by recent US and EU cases,[66] and 'an agency may not be aware of a cartel affecting its jurisdiction, while another agency has cognisance of it'.[67] As cartels become increasingly international in nature, cooperation in cartel cases will continue to grow in importance.[68] Cooperation may take many forms, such as the exchange of information and the collection of evidence. According to a former competition official, the importance of cooperation in the form of information exchange 'should not be underestimated'.[69] Information exchange helps, inter alia, to increase rates of detection; it therefore has a positive impact upon both enforcement objectives of antitrust: deterrence and retribution.[70] Thus, such cooperation is valuable and should be facilitated where appropriate.

This is not to suggest, however, that such exchange of information is free from problems in the context of European antitrust criminalization.[71] In fact, a 'due process' problem with the exchange of information between competition authorities may arise when the following three conditions are fulfilled: (i) personal criminal sanctions are imposed in one jurisdiction for cartel activity, and administrative sanctions are imposed in another; (ii) both jurisdictions are investigating a given cartel; and (iii) the jurisdiction imposing criminal sanctions requests from the other jurisdiction information on the cartel that has been collected as a result of its respective investigation. If information collected as a result of the administrative investigation could legally be passed on to the other jurisdiction (and, importantly, that jurisdiction could then use that information in evidence in a criminal trial), it is obvious that potential would exist for a violation of the due process rights of the accused: the collection of evidence in the requested state will presumably have been conducted according to administrative standards and not criminal standards. This potential problem should be neutralized for European antitrust criminalization to be effected in a manner which respects fundamental human rights. It is submitted that EU law (or, more specifically, Regulation 1/2003) has foreseen this potential problem and has dealt with this issue in a relatively reasonable (albeit imperfect) manner.

(i) Regulation 1/2003 and the European Competition Network

As a result of Regulation 1/2003, the European Commission and the national competition authorities cooperate with one another through the European Competition

[65] Perrin (2006), 540.
[66] Such as those relating to the 'Marine Hoses Cartel' and the 'Fuel Surcharges Cartel', for example.
[67] ICN (2007), 7. [68] ICN (2007), 5.
[69] Bloom (2004), 389. On the importance of cooperation in antitrust matters generally, see, e.g.: Brandenburger (2012a); Brandenburger (2012b); Brandenburger (2012c); and Wayland (2012).
[70] On the link between rates of detection and these objectives, see Chapter 5, Section D(a)(ii) of this book.
[71] See Calvani (2003), 423.

Network ('ECN').[72] This network is an official forum for discussion and cooperation in the application and enforcement of EU competition policy.[73] Under EU law, and for the purpose of applying Articles 101 and 102 TFEU, the Commission and the NCAs have the power to provide one another with and use in evidence any matter of fact or of law, including confidential information.[74] Such cooperation, while legal, is not mandatory.[75] There is a narrow exception to the rule that the information exchanged should only be used in evidence for the purpose of applying Article 101 or 102 TFEU and in respect of the subject matter for which it was collected by the transmitting authority:[76] information exchanged under Article 12 may also be used for the application of national competition law, but only where that law 'is applied in the same case and in parallel to Community competition law and does not lead to a different outcome'.[77] This power, a novelty under EU competition law,[78] cannot be undermined by national law.[79] Pursuant to this power, the exchange of information can be either vertical (e.g., from the Commission to the NCAs) or horizontal (i.e. between the NCAs).[80] Consequently, the power to provide information may result in three different scenarios: first, the flow of information from an administrative regime to a criminal regime; second, the flow of information from an administrative regime to another administrative regime; and, third, the flow of information from a criminal regime to an administrative regime.

(ii) Neutralizing potential problems of due process with criminalization within the ECN

For present purposes, it is the first scenario identified directly above which is potentially problematic.[81] As noted previously, if the power to exchange information in this context were unlimited, it is likely that the human rights of individuals accused of a criminal

72 See Council of the European Union (2003), Recital 15 and Chapter IV (in particular Articles 11 and 12). See generally Rose and Bailey (2013), [15.005]–[15.010].

73 See European Commission (2004a), [1]. On cooperation under the ECN, see, e.g.: Rose and Bailey (2013), [15.011]–[15.042]; and Schnichels (2004), 99–121. For analysis of the (successful) functioning of the ECN, see Wils (2013).

74 Council of the European Union (2003), Article 12(1). See also Council of the European Union (2003), Article 11(4) ('[n]ational competition authorities may also exchange between themselves information necessary for the assessment of a case that they are dealing with under [Article 101 TFEU] or [Article 102 TFEU]') and Article 22(1) ('[t]he competition authority of a Member State may in its own territory carry out any inspection or other fact-finding measure under its national law on behalf and for the account of the competition authority of another Member State in order to establish whether there has been an infringement of [Article 101 TFEU] or [Article 102 TFEU]. Any exchange and use of the information collected shall be carried out in accordance with Article 12'). On the situation concerning information exchange prior to the adoption of Regulation 1/2003, see, e.g.: Perrin (2006), 542–3; and van der Woude (2004), 375.

75 For criticism of this, see Kist (2004), 363.

76 See: Council of the European Union (2003), Article 12(2); and Case 85/87, *Dow Benelux v. Commission* [1989] ECR 3137.

77 Council of the European Union (2003), Article 12(1). If Member States wish to exchange information where these conditions are not met, they may need to have in place additional legislative provisions: Jansen (2004), 259.

78 See, e.g., Case C-67/91, *Direccion General de Defensa de la Competencia v. Asociacion Española de Banca Privada (AEB)* [1992] ECR I-4785, [39].

79 See: European Commission (2004a), [27]; and van der Woude (2004), 387.

80 Jansen (2004), 258; and European Commission (2004a), [27].

81 To be sure, that particular scenario (i.e. information flowing from an administrative regime in one jurisdiction to a criminal regime in another) is potentially relevant to two of the three valid manifestations of the 'additional dynamic' contention noted in Section B(b) of this chapter (i.e. the second and third manifestations identified).

offence would be undermined. If the European Commission, in carrying out an administrative investigation, discovered evidence of an individual's participation in a cartel involving harm to UK consumers, for example, it would be allowed to pass that information on to the UK authorities for them to use as evidence in a criminal court against that individual, thus ensuring that the collection of (some of the) evidence was conducted according to administrative standards and not criminal standards. It has already been explained that administrative protections may be less robust than those required in a criminal context, and are in fact so with regard to the Commission's investigations.[82] Allowing information to be exchanged in this way would therefore quite obviously undermine the rights of the accused individual.[83] To avoid this occurring, Regulation 1/2003 contains Article 12(3).

1. Article 12(3) of Regulation 1/2003

Article 12(3) of Regulation 1/2003 states that information exchanged via the ECN can only be used in evidence to impose sanctions upon individuals where:

> — the law of the transmitting authority foresees sanctions of a similar kind in relation to an infringement of Article 101 TFEU or Article 102 TFEU or, in the absence thereof,
>
> — the information has been collected in a way which respects the same level of protection of the rights of defence of natural persons as provided for under the national rules of the receiving authority. However, in this case, the information exchanged cannot be used by the receiving authority to impose custodial sanctions.

In this manner, Regulation 1/2003 accommodates antitrust criminalization in the Member States.[84] Those Member States which have 'sanctions of a similar kind'[85] (e.g., custodial sanctions) are allowed to exchange among themselves, and, importantly, use in evidence against individuals, the information they have collected. The presumption here is that if personal criminal sanctions are imposed in one country, then by virtue of, inter alia, Article 6 ECHR, that country must conduct its investigations in a manner which respects the human rights of the accused.[86] Indeed, if both jurisdictions have custodial sanctions for cartel activity, then the 'procedural safeguards in both systems are considered to be equivalent'.[87] As noted by an official from DG Comp,

> diversity can easily be overstated here. All systems in the EU comply with a high standard of rights of defence. The laws of the Member States are largely based on common traditions. All of them have to comply with the European Convention on Human Rights. So there is a common level of protection that applies at all levels.[88]

[82] The obvious example is the extent of the right against self-incrimination; see, e.g., European Commission (2004a), [28(c)].

[83] See: Wils (2008a), 194; and Wils (2005a), Section 1.2.12.

[84] See also Section B(a)(i) of this chapter.

[85] While there is no case law on this matter, it appears that the fundamental criterion that should be used to determine if the personal sanctions are of a 'similar kind' is whether the sanctions are custodial or non-custodial; see: European Commission (2004a), [28(c)] ('[t]he Council Regulation intends to create a distinction between sanctions which result in custody and other types of sanctions such as fines on individuals and other personal sanctions'); and Blanco (2006), [3.30]. Lowe believes that national qualifications are not relevant and what matters here are material differences (e.g., between financial and custodial sanctions): Lowe (2007), 97.

[86] Cf. Recital 16 of Council of the European Union (2003): 'The rights of defence enjoyed by undertakings in the various systems can be considered as sufficiently equivalent'.

[87] European Commission (2004a), [28(c)]. See also Rose and Bailey (2013), [15.035].

[88] Dekeyser (2005), 12. See also Gauer (2005), 7.

While a 'common' minimum level of protection may well exist, it is also true that some human rights protections may be stronger in one country (due to its national law) than in another, even if both adhere to the requirements of the European Convention.[89] Assume that both requested and requesting state have criminal antitrust sanctions. If the requested state goes no further than the requirements of Article 6 ECHR in its protection of the rights of the accused, then, under Regulation 1/2003, it is that level of protection that is achieved in relation to the information exchanged. However, if the requested state has a level of protection that is more robust than that required by Article 6 ECHR, it is that higher level of protection that is operative concerning the information subject to exchange. To be sure, when both jurisdictions impose criminal sanctions, it is the human rights protections of the requested state that matter: it is irrelevant that the requesting state has in place higher levels of protection than the requested state. Due to the operation of Article 12(3), then, *at the very least* (and assuming that the Member States respect their obligations under European human rights law when collecting evidence) the requirements of Article 6 ECHR will be respected when both jurisdictions impose criminal sanctions on natural persons; but more robust protections may also be secured, depending upon the (national) human rights law of the requested state.

A relatively similar situation is reached where only the requesting state has criminalized its regime: when the transmitting country does not have criminal sanctions and therefore has not necessarily gathered evidence according to criminal standards, such information can only be used as intelligence, not evidence, unless the human rights protections of the receiving country have been respected. It is assumed here that the human rights protections of the receiving country will *at the very least* respect the requirements of Article 6 ECHR. Again, the actual level of protection secured may be higher, and all depends upon the national human rights law of the jurisdiction in question. But this time, of course, the relevant national law is that of the requesting state, not the requested state. There is, however, an extra protection if the requested state does not employ criminal sanctions: if information is used in evidence in the requesting state (i.e. if the information is collected in the requested state in a manner which respects the human rights protections guaranteed in the requesting state), only non-custodial punishment may be imposed.[90] According to the literature, these stricter rules are ostensibly designed to preserve the higher level of protection from which individuals usually benefit in comparison to undertakings.[91]

2. Critically evaluating Article 12(3)

One could argue that, as a direct result of Article 12(3), the due process rights of the accused are adequately protected while: (i) no obstacles are placed in the way of information exchange between criminal antitrust jurisdictions; and (ii) no unreasonable obstacles are placed in the way of information exchange between administrative and criminal antitrust jurisdictions.[92] For this to be the case, one must first accept the logic of the assumption that Article 6 ECHR (or its equivalent) will be protected in the Member States. This is not difficult to do.[93] First, the European Convention, as an international treaty,

[89] Indeed, the ECHR merely represents a minimum level of protection; see, e.g., Evrigenis (1982), 137–8.

[90] This extra level of protection is termed the 'custodial rule' in this book.

[91] Türk (2006), 223.

[92] In this particular context, 'information exchange' includes the possible use of information as evidence in the criminal antitrust regime.

[93] See, e.g., *Hilali v. The Central Court of Criminal Proceedings of Madrid* [2006] EWHC 1239 (Admin), [77].

is binding on all the EU Member States[94] and, although infringements of Article 6 ECHR may occasionally occur in practice, the Member States must nonetheless acknowledge and respect the mandatory nature of rulings addressed to them by the ECtHR.[95] Member States, then, are restrained in their activities by the European Convention.[96] Second, fundamental rights are respected as general principles of EU law, and when Member States act within the scope of EU law they are under the obligation to comply with EU requirements concerning the protection of fundamental rights.[97] Such human rights protections find their inspiration in, inter alia, the European Convention, including Article 6 thereof.[98] Consequently, the assumption appears to be reasonably sound. If so, the exchange of information between two criminal antitrust jurisdictions under Article 12(3) of Regulation 1/2003 is not problematic under European human rights law.[99]

However, the case where information is exchanged between an administrative and a criminal regime is less straightforward. Again, the assumption that Article 6 ECHR will be protected in the Member States is made; and again that assumption appears to be sound. Hence, the human rights of the accused are protected (at least) to the European standard. However, an extra obstacle exists concerning the use in evidence of the information, even where the Article 6 ECHR rights of the accused have been protected: custodial sanctions cannot be imposed. It is not exactly clear why such a rule (the 'custodial rule') is necessary.[100] If the human rights protections of the requesting state are met (i.e. if the information has been collected in a manner which would be acceptable in the context of a criminal trial in the requesting state), then, putting aside the issue of proof concerning such protection, there should be no real issue concerning an imbalance of the requirements of due process between the administrative regime which gathered the information and the criminal one which receives it and uses it in evidence.

It is likely, however, that human rights concerns are not at issue at this point and that politics may have influenced the inclusion of this rule in Article 12(3) of Regulation 1/2003: some Member States may have been concerned about the use of criminal sanctions per se to enforce the EU competition rules and may not have wished to see information collected in their respective jurisdictions being used to send business people to jail in other Member States. For Gauer, the existence of the 'custodial rule' illustrates that 'custodial sanctions for violations of competition law are not a matter of consensus within the Union at present'.[101] Working documents from the Council of the European Union seem to support this view.[102] That said, although one can interpret Article 12(3) as reflecting a degree of 'hostility' towards custodial sanctions,[103] such

94 Gomien (2005), 12. 95 See, e.g., Article 46(1) ECHR.

96 But this is not to say that the signatories must give direct effect to the Convention within national law: *Ireland v. United Kingdom* (1979–80) 2 EHRR 25. In fact, there is 'wide variation' in the extent to which the signatories have given effect to the ECHR in their national laws: Janis et al. (2008), 850.

97 See Chapter 1, Section D(a)(v)(3) of this book.

98 See Article 6(3) TEU. The EU itself has only recently acceded to the ECHR: Article 6(2) TEU, introduced by virtue of the Lisbon Treaty. However, historically, the Court of Justice 'has always indicated its willingness to follow the case-law of the ECtHR': Slater et al. (2008), 3.

99 This is not to say that a wider political issue would not arise, namely: why in the context of information exchange from one criminal antitrust regime to another criminal antitrust regime the accused (presumably a citizen of the requesting state) should not benefit from any higher level of protection that would be operative if the evidence were collected *in the requesting state*. But as that issue is not one which directly concerns the impact of the ECHR, it is outside the scope of this book.

100 Cf. Garzaniti et al. (2004–05), 182. 101 Gauer (2005), 16.

102 See, e.g., Document 11791/02 of 4 September 2002, which was produced by the Competition Working Party to the Permanent Representatives Committee, and which is available at: <http://register.consilium.eu.int>.

103 Perrin (2006), 547.

hostility is less openly reflected in Regulation 1/2003 than in the original Commission proposal for a new implementing Regulation, where it was proposed 'to exclude the use of evidence exchanged for imposing penalties other than pecuniary penalties'.[104] In any case, provided that the assumption about Article 6 ECHR is sound, there is no reason founded in European human rights law for such a strict approach to the issue of information exchange between administrative and criminal regimes. It is submitted that if Regulation 1/2003 is to be reformed,[105] then the (unnecessary) 'custodial rule' should be abolished in the process: to the extent that the threat of imprisonment is more effective in ensuring deterrence than administrative/criminal fines, such a rule reduces in practice the deterrent effect of (criminal) antitrust sanctions, without any justification based upon legality or practicality. The Commission itself has acknowledged that discussions have arisen on the question of whether the 'custodial rule' is 'too far-reaching and is an obstacle to efficient enforcement'.[106] Consequently, for the Commission, it 'may be appropriate to examine whether other options are available, while fully preserving parties' rights of defence'.[107] One possible solution is the abolition of the 'custodial rule' and the use of a 'double barrier', which allows for the information exchanged to be used in evidence to secure custodial sentences provided that: (i) the transmitting authority verifies that the information transmitted can be used in conformity with its rules; and (ii) the receiving authority verifies that the information received can be used in conformity with its rules.[108] Such an approach would deal with the due process-related problem noted above, while ensuring that the impact upon the efficiency and effectiveness of European antitrust enforcement is kept at a minimum.

Nonetheless, it can still be argued that Regulation 1/2003 has foreseen the relevant potential due process-related problem and has dealt with it in a relatively reasonable (albeit imperfect) manner. This point notwithstanding, it has been argued that the *mere co-existence* of criminal and administrative sanctions inevitably places a major obstacle in the way of information exchange within the ECN. For Perrin, in particular, Article 12(3) of Regulation 1/2003 results in 'a considerable fracture in the supposedly unified EU Network into two distinct networks whose *fault-line* is based on the decision of Member States to impose custodial [antitrust] sanctions'.[109] He believes that EU jurisdictions imposing custodial sanctions for antitrust offences 'will find themselves *excluded* from the larger EU Network and demoted to the smaller EU Network of like-minded Member States'.[110] The present author respectfully disagrees with this particular argument, for two reasons. First, the Article 12(3) prohibition on the use of exchanged information to secure custodial sanctions in the receiving state only extends to the use by the *receiving* Member State of such information *in evidence*. Indeed, Member States may legally send information to other Member States (which impose custodial sanctions) in order to facilitate the latter in *its investigation* of a violation of Article 101 TFEU. Furthermore, the receiving Member States (which impose custodial sanctions) are legally entitled to use such information to detect and to obtain proof of—rather than to use as evidence of—a violation. Second, there is no formal or informal punishment mechanism which can be used against those Member States without criminal antitrust sanctions which transfer information to Member States with criminal sanctions where the latter then

[104] European Commission (2000), 21. See also European Commission (2000), 41.

[105] A public consultation on the operation of Regulation 1/2003 was conducted in 2008, but this did not result in any amendments to Regulation 1/2003 being adopted. See <http://ec.europa.eu/competition/consultations/2008_regulation_1_2003/index.html>.

[106] European Commission (2009b), [32].

[107] European Commission (2009b), [32].

[108] See European Commission (2009c), [245].

[109] Perrin (2006), 555.

[110] Perrin (2006), 555. Cf. Blair and Conway (2002), 53.

decide to use that information in evidence to secure custodial sentences. In other words, there is no negative 'fallout' for the sending Member State. Rather, all that Article 12(3) of Regulation 1/2003 does is ensure that the receiving Member State will be restrained in its employment of the information: it does not ensure that such information will not be exchanged in the first place. If information is used in a manner which is inconsistent with Article 12(3) of Regulation 1/2003, it is the receiving Member State—not the sending Member State—which will be at fault, as such. Given these two facts, it is not exactly clear why the mere exchange of information through the ECN will result in the creation of a two-tier entity.

It is conceded, however, that the co-existence of criminal and administrative sanctions is not without its problems, even with the presence of Article 12(3) of Regulation 1/2003. One particular difficulty comes to mind: determining whether information has been collected in a manner which respects 'the same level of protection of the rights of defence of natural persons as provided for under the national rules of the receiving authority'.[111] This inquiry is relevant when a Member State which imposes administrative sanctions sends information to another Member State which is then used in evidence to secure a criminal conviction for cartel activity. In such a situation, it would be open to the defendant to claim that such information should not be used in evidence against him as its collection did not respect the same level of rights protection provided to natural persons in the receiving state. Indeed, for Perrin, the use of information in such a context would 'be highly vulnerable to frequent challenges on the part of defendants who are natural persons'.[112] This is a strong argument: criminal sanctions can be severe; and defendants will likely present whatever (reasonable) claim they can in order to avoid conviction. Nonetheless, whether or not such claims by the defendant would be as frequent as contended by Perrin, it is true that to rule on such a claim, the relevant national judge(s) would be required to evaluate the protections secured in the sending state, an exercise that might be burdened by language difficulties and/or a lack of cooperation on behalf of the sending national competition authority. Reliable information on the procedures and procedural guarantees of other Member States thus increases in importance due to European antitrust criminalization. Obtaining such information in any given case increases the costs associated with enforcement. Challenges by defendants on this ground alone therefore have potential to affect the cost/benefit analyses that need to be undertaken by the authorities when deciding whether to introduce criminal antitrust sanctions for the purpose of economic deterrence:[113] such (likely) challenges can impact upon the efficiency of criminal antitrust enforcement.

(b) *Ne bis in idem*

In Chapter 2, it was explained that the theory of retribution ensures that a person shall be subjected to no more punishment than he deserves for a given wrongful conduct. If cartel activity is criminalized because it is wrong, then, in order to construct a theoretically consistent criminal antitrust regime, one would have to put in place measures to ensure that an individual is indeed protected from excessive punishment for a given wrongful conduct. One such measure could be an express and judicially recognized prohibition on an individual being tried or punished more than once for the same wrongful conduct. As a matter of fact, such a prohibition (*ne bis in idem*) is already enshrined in European

[111] Council of the European Union (2003), Article 12(3). [112] Perrin (2006), 555.
[113] On this, see the discussion in Chapter 3, Section D(b)(iii) of this book.

human rights law. Therefore, one does not have to be in the process of implementing a retribution-focused criminal antitrust regime for such a prohibition to be relevant; a deterrence-based regime would also be required to respect it. As demonstrated further below, the validity of the 'additional dynamic' contention ensures that one should consider the operation of the *ne bis in idem* principle in the context of European antitrust criminalization if one wishes to create a criminal antitrust regime which is not only consistent with the theory of retribution, but is also legally sound.

(i) The basic principle

The principle of *ne bis in idem*, as articulated by Article 4(1) of Protocol No. 7 to the ECHR,[114] restricts the possibility of an individual being tried or punished more than once for the same offence:

> No one shall be liable to be tried or punished again in criminal proceedings under the jurisdiction of the same State for an offence for which [he] has already been finally acquitted or convicted in accordance with the law and penal procedure of that State.

In substance, this provision is effectively the European equivalent of the US double jeopardy clause.[115] From the wording of Article 4(1), it is obvious that the principle only relates to a right not be tried or punished twice in 'criminal proceedings'.[116] It is important to remember here, however, that the term 'criminal' is given an autonomous meaning under the ECHR[117] and that, following the reasoning in *Menarini*,[118] it would cover (administrative) competition proceedings, such as those conducted at EU level by the European Commission. It is also worth noting here that the Court of Justice has itself referred to Article 4 of Protocol No. 7 on a number of occasions when holding that the principle of *ne bis in idem* is a fundamental principle of EU law.[119]

The guarantee enshrined in Article 4 of Protocol No. 7 'becomes relevant on commencement of a new prosecution, where a prior acquittal or conviction has already acquired the force of *res judicata*'.[120] It is obvious that the principle is violated when, for a given course of action, an individual is prosecuted for and convicted of the exact same offence in the second proceedings as that in the first. But Article 4 does not expressly confine itself to situations involving 'the (exact) same offence'; rather, it prohibits 'trial

[114] Protocol No. 7 to the Convention for the Protection of Human Rights and Fundamental Freedoms, as amended by Protocol No. 11, Strasbourg, 22.XI.1984. To date, only four Member States of the Council of Europe have not ratified this protocol; the UK and Germany are among them. See <http://conventions.coe.int/>.

[115] See Wils (2003b).

[116] On this see *Protocol No. 7 to the Convention for the Protection of Human Rights and Fundamental Freedoms—Explanatory Report*, <http://conventions.coe.int/Treaty/en/Reports/Html/117.htm>, [32]: 'Article 4, since it only applies to trial and conviction of a person in criminal proceedings, does not prevent [him] from being made subject, for the same act, to action of a different character (for example, disciplinary action in the case of an official) as well as to criminal proceedings'.

[117] For an express adoption of the autonomous notion of 'criminal' in relation to Article 4 of Protocol No. 7, see *Zolotukhin v. Russia* (2012) 54 EHRR 16, [52].

[118] *A. Menarini Diagnostics Srl v. Italy*, Application No. 43509/08, ECtHR, 27 September 2011.

[119] See, e.g.: Joined Cases T-236, 239, 244–6, 251, and 252/01, *Tokai Carbon v. Commission* [2004] ECR II-1181, [130]; and Joined Cases C-238, 244, 245, 250–2, and 254/99 P, *Limburgse Vinyl Maatschappij and others v. Commission* [2002] ECR I-8375, [59]. Under EU law, the principle comes into effect when unity of facts, unity of offender, and unity of the legal interest protected are present: Case C-213/00 P, *Italcementi v. Commission* [2003] ECR I-123, [338].

[120] *Zolotukhin v. Russia* (2012) 54 EHRR 16, [83].

and punishment "again" for an offence for which the applicant has already been finally acquitted or convicted'.[121] Unfortunately, in the past there have been conflicting judgments on the test to be employed in this context.[122] Early jurisprudence focused on the identity of conduct of the defendant, irrespective of the classification in law given to that conduct.[123] In later judgments, it was held that the same conduct may constitute several offences which may be tried in separate proceedings.[124] It was then held that no one could be tried for or convicted of two nominally different offences which have the same essential elements.[125] In attempting to 'harmonize' these disparate views, the Strasbourg Court, in a 2009 judgment, placed unity of facts at the centre of the inquiry, holding that the principle in Article 4 'must be understood as prohibiting the prosecution or trial of a second "offence" in so far as it arises from identical facts or facts which are substantially the same'.[126] It appears, then, that in following current jurisprudence from Strasbourg, the inquiry should focus on

> those facts which constitute a set of concrete factual circumstances involving the same defendant and inextricably linked together in time and space, the existence of which must be demonstrated in order to secure a conviction or institute criminal proceedings.[127]

Fortunately, there has been no disagreement on the assertion that double prosecution as well as double punishment is prohibited. Consequently, one cannot stay within the principle by simply reducing the amount of the second punishment by that of the first.[128]

The scope of the principle of *ne bis in idem*, as enshrined in Article 4 of Protocol No. 7, remains relatively restricted: the principle only applies to 'acts within the same jurisdiction and does not prevent a person from being convicted for the same offence in a different jurisdiction'.[129] Parallel antitrust prosecutions by the Commission and an NCA, or by the competition authorities of several Member States, would therefore fall outside the scope of this provision. Such prosecutions would not fall outside the concept of 'double jeopardy' as articulated in the EU Charter, however;[130] as provided by Article 50 thereof:

> No one shall be liable to be tried or punished again in criminal proceedings for an offence for which he or she has already been finally acquitted or convicted *within the Union* in accordance with the law.[131]

This particular human rights provision came into effect in December 2009, and, like Article 4(1) of Protocol No. 7, has a direct bearing upon the analysis of the problem of *ne bis in idem* when criminalization occurs in a given Member State. It should be noted, however, that the provisions of the Charter (including Article 50 thereof) are not of general application; in fact, they are addressed to the institutions of the Union and to the Member States 'only when they are implementing Union law'.[132]

121 *Franz Fischer v. Austria*, Application No. 37950/97, ECtHR, 29 May 2001, [25].
122 See generally *Zolotukhin v. Russia* (2012) 54 EHRR 16, [70]–[77].
123 *Gradinger v. Austria*, Application No. 15963/90, ECtHR, 23 October 1995, [55].
124 *Oliveira v. Switzerland* (1999) 28 EHRR 289, [25]–[29].
125 *Franz Fischer v. Austria*, Application No. 37950/97, ECtHR, 29 May 2001, [25].
126 *Zolotukhin v. Russia* (2012) 54 EHRR 16, [82].
127 *Zolotukhin v. Russia* (2012) 54 EHRR 16, [84].
128 *Franz Fischer v. Austria*, Application No. 37950/97, ECtHR, 29 May 2001, [30].
129 Blanco (2006), [4.44].
130 See *Text of the Explanations Relating to the Complete Text of the Charter as Set Out in CHARTE 4487/00 CONVENT 50*, CHARTE 4473/00 CONVENT 49, Brussels, 11 October 2000, <http://www.europarl.europa.eu/charter/pdf/04473_en.pdf>, 45.
131 Article 50 CFR (emphasis added).
132 Article 51(1) CFR.

(ii) European antitrust criminalization and the relevance of ne bis in idem

As with the exchange of information, *ne bis in idem* becomes relevant when personal criminal antitrust sanctions are employed *alongside* civil/administrative sanctions against undertakings. *Ne bis in idem* concerns can be raised with each of the three valid manifestations of the 'additional dynamic' contention. However, as will be explained, Article 4(1) of Protocol No. 7 can only be violated in the case of one of the valid manifestations (i.e. where a given national Member State imposes both criminal antitrust sanctions on individuals and administrative antitrust sanctions on undertakings), while Article 50 CFR can be violated in each of the three valid manifestations.

1. Reasons for the *potential* application of *ne bis in idem*

The reason why *ne bis in idem* becomes relevant at all when administrative antitrust sanctions exist alongside criminal antitrust sanctions for a given cartel is that a broad interpretation has been given to the concept of 'undertaking' and that, consequently, it is always possible in practice for administrative fines to be imposed on individuals. An 'undertaking' is defined in EU competition law as encompassing 'every entity engaged in an economic activity, regardless of the legal status of the entity and the way in which it is financed'.[133] The European authorities, in adopting a functional approach to this concept, have ensured that a broad interpretation of 'undertaking' exists under EU competition law.[134] In fact, the concept has been held to include various entities such as trade associations, agricultural cooperatives, and sporting bodies, as well as companies and partnerships.[135] Importantly for present purposes, *individuals* can be deemed to be undertakings if they carry out an economic activity.[136] It appears that there are two exceptions to this, however: employees[137] and final purchasers.[138] For enforcement reasons, if an infringement of Article 101 TFEU is found, fines are technically imposed upon 'persons'; this is due to Article 299 TFEU: 'Decisions of the Council or of the Commission which impose a pecuniary obligation *on persons* other than States, shall be enforceable'.[139] Indeed, to use the words of the GC, although an 'undertaking' within the meaning of Article 101(1) TFEU

> is not necessarily the same as a company having legal personality, it is necessary for the purposes of applying and enforcing decisions to identify an entity possessing legal personality to be the addressee of the measure.[140]

The Courts have therefore imposed fines upon those legal persons to whom the conduct of the undertaking can be imputed. The point here, however, is that, because Article 299 TFEU only refers to 'persons', such a fine can presumably be enforced not only against 'legal persons', but also against 'natural persons': that is, against individuals.[141] So, as a

[133] Case C-41/90, *Höfner and Elser v. Macrotron* [1991] ECR I-1979, [21].

[134] On the (broad) definition of 'undertaking', see, e.g.: Odudu (2005); Odudu (2006), Chapter 3; Townley (2007); and Wils (2002), Chapter 7.

[135] See the review of the case law in Jones and Sufrin (2011), 126.

[136] See, e.g.: *RAI/UNITEL* (Case IV/29.559), Commission Decision, 15 June 1978, [1978] OJ L157/39 (opera singers); and *Reuter/BASF* (Case IV/28.996), Commission Decision, 26 July 1976, [1976] OJ L254/40 (individual inventors).

[137] Case C-67/96, *Albany International BV v. Stichting Bedrijfspensioenfonds Textielindustrie* [1999] ECR I-5751.

[138] Case T-319/99, *FENIN v. Commission* [2003] ECR II-357, [36].

[139] Emphasis added.

[140] Joined Cases T-305–7, 313–316, 318, 328–9, and 335/94, *Limburgse Vinyl Maatschappij and others v. Commission* [1999] ECR II-945, [978].

[141] See Wils (2002), 176.

direct result of both (i) EU jurisprudence on the concept of an 'undertaking' and (ii) Article 299 TFEU, one is led to support the assertion of Zuleeg that: 'an individually owned firm and a partnership without a distinct legal personality are undertakings in the sense of EU competition law, and may be fined as such'.[142] To the knowledge of the author, however, this has not yet occurred at EU level or indeed in the Member States. Nonetheless, as it remains a legal possibility, it should be addressed if criminalization is to occur in a given EU jurisdiction.

2. Further requirements for the *actual* application of *ne bis in idem*

With criminalization, then, it may happen that for a given (alleged) cartel a natural person in his capacity as an undertaking may be subject to an administrative fine in addition to a criminal fine that could be imposed upon him solely as a natural person: unity with regard to the identity of the defendant is capable of arising when both (corporate) administrative sanctions and (personal) criminal sanctions are available. This is where the principle of *ne bis in idem* may come into play. For this to be the case in practice, two elements *in addition* to unity of defendant need to be present: (i) the existence of (a particular set of) parallel prosecutions; and (ii) the fact that the second prosecution concerns an offence for which an individual has already been finally acquitted or convicted in the first prosecution (which for mere convenience is termed here 'equivalence of offence').

The element concerning the existence of (a particular set of) parallel prosecutions is the least problematic: the 'additional dynamic' contention is valid after all. From Article 4(1) of Protocol No. 7 itself, it is clear that under the European Convention the principle may only be relevant when the administrative fine is imposed by the *same jurisdiction* as that imposing the criminal antitrust sanction. However, with Article 50 of the EU Charter, the principle is extended to include antitrust proceedings in other Member States. Consequently, two different scenarios are also caught by that particular document: parallel antitrust prosecutions by the Commission and a national competition authority, and parallel antitrust prosecutions by the competition authorities of two or more Member States.[143] By contrast, the principle will not be infringed where there are parallel antitrust prosecutions involving a Member State and a non-EU jurisdiction.[144] That is not to say, however, that in the latter scenario one should not ensure that only one prosecution against a given individual results and that the best placed jurisdiction should take the lead as regards prosecution.[145]

The second element, 'equivalence of offence', presents an issue which is a little more complex. According to the latest test advocated by the Strasbourg Court, a factual analysis must be undertaken in any situation where the problem of *ne bis in idem* may arise. Indeed, what is required is an inquiry into the facts which must be demonstrated to secure a conviction or institute criminal proceedings in relation to both the administrative and

142 Zuleeg (2002).

143 The principle is clearly operative in these two scenarios not only when an administrative sanction is imposed alongside a criminal sanction, but also when the two different jurisdictions in question both impose criminal sanctions.

144 It must be remembered here that the foreign jurisdiction may have criminal antitrust sanctions (such as the US) or may employ the same concept of 'undertaking' when imposing an administrative sanction. There are not many non-EU states that employ criminal antitrust sanctions; but there are quite a number which use EU competition law (including its concept of 'undertaking') as an inspiration for the creation and development of their respective antitrust regimes, as can be deduced from Mehta (2006).

145 See: OECD (2003b), 9; and O'Kane (2009b).

the criminal antitrust offence. If these facts are identical or substantially similar, then the principle of *ne bis in idem* will apply. Where the criminal antitrust offence merely adds criminal sanctions to the civil prohibition (i.e. Article 101 TFEU), there is no real problem: the only difference between the administrative and the criminal proceedings for a given cartel will be the outcome (i.e. the nature of the sanction imposed) and not the underlying conduct which is punished; and if the underlying conduct is the same, it follows that the facts which must be demonstrated in order to secure a conviction are also likely to be the same. A different outcome may occur, however, when antitrust criminalization does not imply the mere addition of criminal sanctions: that is, where criminalization involves the creation of a separate stand-alone criminal offence with elements additional to those included within the definition of Article 101 TFEU.[146] Under current jurisprudence, it is true that the test for 'equivalence of offence' no longer focuses on the essential (definitional) elements of the offences and that, therefore, the existence of such additional elements does not ipso facto ensure that *ne bis in idem* concerns become irrelevant.[147] If, however, the additional elements ensure that a different set of concrete factual circumstances surrounding the cartel are relevant to the criminal antitrust offence from those relevant to the administrative antitrust offence, there would be no potential *ne bis in idem* problem. This is a factual inquiry. In practice, and to determine if the principle is operative, the antitrust authority which is conducting the second prosecution must: (i) study the facts relied upon in the previous decision (or judgment); (ii) examine the facts as stated in the indictment (or the Statement of Objections) before it; and (iii) decide whether the facts in both (i) and (ii) are identical or substantially the same. Where they are not, there is no issue with *ne bis in idem*. Where, by contrast, (substantial) factual identity exists, the principle of *ne bis in idem* will apply.

(iii) Dealing with ne bis in idem *in the context of European antitrust criminalization*

Determining that the principle of *ne bis in idem* applies (or would apply) to a given (second) prosecution is one thing; deciding what to do when that is (or would be) the case is quite another. The easiest case to deal with is the situation where the second antitrust prosecution has begun or is about to begin. In this scenario, when the principle is operative, the charge against the individual (or, as the case may be, the undertaking, represented by an individual) should be dropped. The reason for this is clear, at least under ECtHR jurisprudence: double prosecution—and not just double punishment—is prohibited, and one cannot stay within the principle simply by reducing the amount of the second antitrust sanction by that of the first.[148] The situation becomes a little more complicated when neither of the two parallel prosecutions has begun and a decision needs to be made on whether to proceed with a prosecution and, if so, which one—administrative or criminal. (In such a situation, it may also be difficult to establish whether a *ne bis in idem* problem would occur with the two prosecutions: in practice, one

[146] As occurred with the UK Cartel Offence.

[147] Previously, one would have had to consider whether, irrespective of the additional elements in the particular criminal offence, both the administrative and criminal offence contained the same 'essential elements'.

[148] See: *Franz Fischer v. Austria*, Application No. 37950/97, ECtHR, 29 May 2001, [30]; and *Zolotukhin v. Russia* (2012) 54 EHRR 16, [83] ('Article 4 of Protocol No. 7 contains a safeguard against being tried or being liable to be tried again in new proceedings rather than a prohibition on a second conviction or acquittal').

will be precluded from following the three-step methodology noted directly above, and one may therefore have difficulty in determining whether factual identity would exist.) If the prospective criminal and administrative prosecutions will occur in the same Member State, then ultimately it will be the authorities of that Member State which will have to weigh up the relative merits and demerits of the prospective prosecutions. At this point, those authorities will have to consider a number of issues, including resource constraints, likelihood of success, impact upon compliance and, importantly, the degree to which the objectives of the law (e.g., deterrence or retribution) will be achieved.

When another Member State or the European Commission is involved (i.e. when there is a potential violation of the EU Charter rather than of Protocol No. 7 to the ECHR), it will be necessary for the authorities to communicate with one another and to attempt to resolve the issue through dialogue. Identifying and neutralizing any potential *ne bis in idem* problem at the outset would be advisable: it helps to avoid the waste of time and resources engendered when cases are later thrown out of court on human rights grounds. The operation of the ECN may help the authorities in this regard. Indeed, under Regulation 1/2003, the national competition authorities, when acting under Article 101 TFEU, are obliged to inform the Commission (i) after commencing the first formal investigative measure[149] and (ii) no later than 30 days before taking a decision.[150] The other Member States' national competition authorities 'may' also be so informed.[151] Such a flow of information is helpful in that it puts the competition authorities on notice of possible parallel investigations/prosecutions concerning a given cartel, thereby enabling them—in theory at least—to allocate cases among themselves in a manner which eliminates potential *ne bis in idem* problems. That said, there are three difficulties with the employment of the ECN as a mechanism to prevent the emergence of such *ne bis in idem* problems; two concern awareness issues, while the third relates to competence.

The first difficulty is that there is no obligation concerning inter-NCA notifications. The second is that, as a result, inter alia, of the vagueness of Recital 8 of Regulation 1/2003,[152] it may be the case that national competition authorities will not feel obliged to inform the Commission of criminal antitrust cases which involve the imposition of sanctions upon natural persons. Both of these deficiencies have at least some potential to undermine the ability of the ECN to act as a case allocation mechanism: as a result, the authorities of the relevant jurisdictions (including, in some cases, the Commission) may not be aware of the potential parallel investigation and prosecution, and hence the need to discuss appropriate case allocation. One example suffices here: NCA 1 informs the Commission of its (administrative) investigation of Undertaking X (which happens to be an individual); NCA 1 does not inform any other NCA about the investigation; NCA 2 does not inform the Commission (or indeed any NCA) about its prospective criminal case against the individual that makes up Undertaking X. In this scenario, one which arguably respects the obligations of Regulation 1/2003, the *ne bis in idem* problem will only become apparent (if detected) once the second prosecution begins; in other words, the ECN would not have been able to operate effectively and eliminate the *ne bis in idem* concern before it developed. Third, and finally, the NCAs cannot relieve each other of the competence to pursue a given antitrust investigation or prosecution.

149 Council of the European Union (2003), Article 11(3).
150 Council of the European Union (2003), Article 11(4).
151 Council of the European Union (2003), Articles 11(3) and 11(4).
152 On this, see Chapter 8, Section B(b) of this book.

Any resolution of the issue (e.g., in favour of one NCA proceeding with a criminal/administrative prosecution) will therefore require the consent of all relevant NCAs.[153] It is true, however, that the Commission may use Article 11(6) of Regulation 1/2003 to investigate the (individual comprising the) undertaking itself, thereby relieving an NCA of its competence to apply Article 101 TFEU. On its face, then, this power appears useful in preventing the emergence of *ne bis in idem* problems. But this is not necessarily so. For a start, Article 11(6) is likely only to be used in very exceptional circumstances and only where the EU interest so dictates: it is not a panacea when conflict between NCAs develops.[154] Furthermore, Article 11(6) only relieves the NCAs of their competence to apply Article 101 TFEU; it does not relieve criminal courts of their power to impose sanctions for violation of the criminal law when such courts are not NCAs for the purpose of Regulation 1/2003. Moreover, depending on how the national cartel offence is drafted,[155] it may be the case that Article 11(6) will not have any impact on the national proceeding which enforces the offence: Regulation 1/2003 may not actually apply to such a proceeding. Given this situation, it is not inconceivable that potential *ne bis in idem* problems will not be neutralized before the commencement of the parallel prosecutions. This effectively leads one back to the first situation noted above concerning resolution: if parallel antitrust prosecutions are not prevented by the Commission or by the NCAs themselves, then—provided that the criteria for *ne bis in idem* are indeed fulfilled by the (imminent) commencement of the second prosecution—the charges in the second prosecution should be dropped in order for the human rights of the accused to be protected.

(iv) The (negative) consequences of respecting the principle of ne bis in idem

Although the principle of *ne bis in idem* can be rationalized using retribution theory, it does not follow that its existence in a given jurisdiction will be consistent with the theoretical justifications for European antitrust criminalization: it may impact negatively upon deterrence theory. It has already been explained how the principle can lead one to drop the second antitrust prosecution in order to protect the human rights of the accused. This fact alone has the potential to influence the effectiveness of an enforcement policy premised on the achievement of deterrence. The reason for this is as follows. If the enforcement action represented by the first prosecution is indeed an administrative proceeding, it will be the criminal proceeding that will have to be dropped. The administrative antitrust proceeding, then, will be the only proceeding against the individual cartelist (who happens to be an undertaking for the purpose of EU law). In Chapter 3, a number of deficiencies concerning the use of administrative antitrust sanctions alone to secure deterrence were identified, including the inability of the undertaking to pay an optimal fine.[156] As, under the circumstances identified, only an administrative proceeding is legally possible, these deficiencies would continue to be relevant. In short, if the analyses presented in the relevant section of Chapter 3 are indeed sound, then suboptimal deterrence may result when, in order to respect the principle of *ne bis in idem*, only

[153] On the ability of the NCAs to terminate their own antitrust proceedings when there is a parallel proceeding in another Member State concerning the same alleged violation of Article 101 TFEU, see Council of the European Union (2003), Article 13.

[154] For an insight as to when Article 11(6) of Regulation 1/2003 may be used, see European Commission (2004a), Section 3.2.

[155] See Chapter 8, Section B of this book.

[156] See Chapter 3, Section B of this book.

an administrative sanction is imposed for a given cartel. The existence of the principle of *ne bis in idem*, then, further complicates the theoretical challenge of deterrence.

(c) Concurrent proceedings

Three particular manifestations of the 'additional dynamic' contention were deemed to be valid for European antitrust criminalization.[157] All three of these manifestations are relevant to the concept of concurrent proceedings: they are all capable of producing at least two separate antitrust proceedings (one criminal, the other administrative) which take place either simultaneously or within a relatively short period of time of each other. Such concurrent proceedings raise two particular due process-related issues.[158] Such issues will need to be neutralized if antitrust criminalization is to occur in a manner which respects the requirements of the ECHR. However, in neutralizing the due process-related issues, one may potentially impact negatively upon both of the theoretical justifications for criminal antitrust enforcement, deterrence and retribution. How this is so should be understood by those contemplating the introduction of criminal antitrust sanctions.

(i) Two due process-related issues

The first due process-related issue with concurrent proceedings arises due to the fact that the substance of due process rights (at least under the ECHR) is not exactly equivalent as regards both criminal and administrative regimes.[159] Assume that a given antitrust authority is conducting an administrative investigation against an undertaking using its administrative powers. In the course of that administrative proceeding, the antitrust authority uncovers evidence which implicates a particular individual in that cartel. In fact, as a direct result of the evidence uncovered, the antitrust authority decides that it would like to commence a criminal proceeding against the individual concerned. However, if the due process rights protected under the administrative proceeding are not as robust in practice as those which would need to be respected under a criminal proceeding, the evidence collected using the administrative powers could not be used in a criminal court without violating the Article 6 ECHR due process rights of the accused individual.[160] This, then, is the first due process-related issue with concurrent proceedings.[161]

The second due process-related issue with concurrent proceedings is the creation of prejudicial pre-trial publicity.[162] Prejudicial pre-trial publicity may be created if an

157 See Section B(b) of this chapter.

158 The first of these issues, both of which are detailed directly below, is most relevant to the first manifestation of the 'additional dynamic' contention (i.e. where a given Member State imposes both criminal and administrative antitrust sanctions); the second of these issues is equally relevant to all three valid manifestations.

159 See Chapter 5, Section C of this book.

160 Of course, if evidence is collected to a criminal standard and is then used in an administrative proceeding, there would be no human rights-based objection: the strictest of legal guarantees will have been observed and potential prejudice will be absent; see, e.g., Lord Sailsbury, Hansard, House of Lords Debates, 29 July 2002, Volume 638, Column 739.

161 It should be noted that an identical due process-related issue would face the authorities where the evidence collected using administrative powers is found to be relevant for an *already existing* criminal antitrust proceeding against an individual.

162 See Whelan (2012d), 3.

administrative proceeding concerning a given cartel *precedes* any criminal proceedings against an individual cartelist for participation in that cartel. The reason for this should be clear: if a (public) decision is reached in the administrative proceeding that a market has been cartelized by a given undertaking, it may be taken up by the international media, particularly if the market is an important consumer market. The media could be critical of not only the undertakings involved, but also their staff. Consequently, one could argue, such negative publicity may influence potential jurors in a later criminal trial involving an individual employee of that undertaking. In other words, such publicity could engender impartiality in the court to the detriment of that individual's rights under Article 6 ECHR.[163]

(ii) Ensuring consistency with due process

It is clear that, in order to avoid the first due process-related issue with concurrent proceedings, one should not present evidence in a criminal court if it is gathered only to the administrative standard, otherwise one will likely violate Article 6 ECHR. Criminal antitrust proceedings should respect the rights of the accused to a criminal standard *at all stages* of the investigation and prosecution. This is not to say, however, that parallel (criminal and administrative) investigations by the same public antitrust body in a given Member State cannot be conducted.[164] In fact, such parallel enforcement actions can be successfully conducted if mechanisms are in place to avoid the first due process-related issue identified with concurrent proceedings.[165]

The first required mechanism is a system which ensures from the outset that the administrative investigative team is functionally and materially separate from the criminal investigative team.[166] Under this system, each investigative team acquires evidence according to its powers and respects the appropriate level of due process rights (administrative or criminal). What is to be avoided here is the 'fusion' of the investigations (i.e. the treatment of the administrative and criminal investigations as one single investigation into a given cartel), not their parallel advancement (by separate teams within the antitrust enforcement agency).[167] This point appears to have been missed by the authors of the report prepared for the OFT prior to the adoption of the UK Cartel Offence, where they noted when examining the issue of 'parallel investigations' that 'the same investigating officers will be involved in any civil investigation of undertakings as will be involved in the related criminal investigations'.[168] Joshua quickly picked up on this point and posited that their suggestion was 'unlikely to attract universal approbation from human rights lawyers'.[169] In fairness to the OFT, it sought to distance itself from this suggestion and emphasized that different case teams within the organization should operate behind 'ethical walls' to ensure no cross-contamination of the respective investigations and prosecutions.[170]

As implied by the OFT's position on parallel investigations, mechanisms should be in place to ensure that the division of enforcement teams remains solid throughout both

[163] For ECtHR jurisprudence on impartiality contrary to Article 6 ECHR, see, e.g.: *De Cubber v. Belgium* (1985) 7 EHRR 236, [24]; *Gregory v. United Kingdom* (1998) 25 EHRR 577, [45]; *Hauschildt v. Denmark* (1990) 12 EHRR 266, [46]; and *Pullar v. United Kingdom* (1996) 22 EHRR 391, [40].

[164] See Nazzini (2003).

[165] Cf. Pickford (2002), 43, who argues that, although there may be considerable duplications of investigations, 'in order to avoid confusion and claims of unfairness from those accused, the functions of civil and criminal investigation would be best carried out by distinct bodies'.

[166] See ICN (2005), 29.

[167] Nazzini (2003), 485.

[168] OFT (2001), [6.4].

[169] Joshua (2003), 633.

[170] Joshua (2003), 633.

investigations.[171] If different teams within the one authority are pursuing respectively administrative and criminal investigations, it is imperative that 'Chinese walls' are established between these teams.[172] In particular, if information or evidence is to move from one investigative team to another (say, from the administrative team to the criminal team), it should first pass through a screening process involving lawyers who are not part of either investigative team. These lawyers should be qualified to appreciate whether in passing on the relevant information or evidence and allowing it to be used by the respective enforcement team, the rights of the individual accused will be undermined. Where such undermining of rights is likely, the information or evidence in question should not be passed on. Legislation (and/or soft law[173]) could also be adopted in order to provide clarity to antitrust enforcers on legitimate information exchange between investigative teams. Such legislation could detail, for example, the circumstances in which information passed from the administrative team to the criminal team can be legitimately relied upon in court.[174]

Finally, in order to ensure efficiency in enforcement, a formalized decision-making process should be initiated which will determine whether an administrative or criminal proceeding (or both) should be followed in relation to the investigation of a given cartel. The criteria that will inform the final decision could include the amount of commerce affected by the cartel, the duration of the cartel, the role of the accused in the cartel, and the amount of available evidence that would help to ensure that the increased evidentiary requirements under criminal law are met.[175] If, at the outset, it is unclear whether an administrative proceeding should be initiated rather than a criminal one, evidence should be collected to the criminal standard.[176] It is only when it becomes clear that an administrative proceeding should also be initiated (or should take the place of the criminal investigation) that the administrative standards should be deemed relevant in relation to the new proceeding.[177] By having in place a formal structure (composed of experienced investigators and/or prosecutors) which determines whether an investigation should be criminal or administrative (or both), one can ensure that due process is not violated, while nonetheless limiting the amount of resources spent on unnecessary investigative efforts. In particular, one should seek to avoid situations where evidence is initially collected using administrative powers, but which then must be reacquired (if indeed possible) using criminal powers.[178]

It is also clear that, in order to avoid the second due process-related issue with concurrent proceedings, one could ensure that the outcome of the criminal proceeding is decided upon before the outcome in the administrative proceeding:[179] negative publicity concerning a given cartel is less likely to affect a criminal trial in the absence of a

171 See Blake (2008), 13.

172 Frese (2006), 206. See also Joshua and Klawiter (2002), 69. On the (successful) use of 'Chinese Walls' in the UK criminal cartel regime, see Morgan (2010), 72.

173 See, e.g., OFT (2004a), [4].

174 See, e.g., Section 30A CA.

175 OECD (2007b), 29.

176 See Bloom (2002b), 59. It appears that the OFT, when pursuing cartel cases, will routinely ensure that criminal standards are followed, even in the course of an administrative proceeding; see: OFT (2004a), [4.1] and [4.9]; and OFT (2001), [1.20] and [6.25]. Cf. OFT (2013b), [2.46].

177 See Beard (2003), 160.

178 In the UK, documents collected using administrative powers can in fact be used in a criminal proceeding: OFT (2004a), [4.9]; however, subject to very limited exceptions, statements obtained in the course of the administrative proceeding cannot be used in the criminal proceeding: Section 30A CA. If statements have been collected using powers under the Competition Act 1998, the OFT cannot use those statements in a criminal court without repeating the interview under caution (i.e. without consuming additional resources); see OFT (2004a), [4.8].

179 Bloom (2002b), 60. See also Competition and Mergers Review Group (2000), [4.3.17].

prior formal public decision as to the actual existence of the cartel in question. Such an approach was endorsed in the 'Hammond-Penrose Report' when it recommended that:

> criminal proceedings against individuals should precede civil proceedings against undertakings whenever possible... in order that any publicity given to the civil proceedings will not prejudice individuals subject to the related criminal proceedings receiving a fair trial.[180]

But such an approach may not always be possible. For example, the administrative proceeding may take place in a different jurisdiction from the criminal proceeding (such as in another Member State or in front of the European Commission).[181] In such a situation, it may be open to the criminal jurisdiction to request that the administrative proceeding in the other jurisdiction be stayed pending the outcome of the criminal trial; but such a request would not have to be granted by the other jurisdiction (or may not be possible under the law of the respective jurisdiction).[182] This particular issue was noted at the time that the UK Cartel Offence came into effect in the UK.[183] Of particular concern in this context was the fact that it was considered very unlikely that the European Commission, with its 'wider public interest responsibility' to the citizens of the EU Member States, would stay its own administrative anti-cartel enforcement proceedings pending the outcome of a criminal cartel trial in the UK.[184]

One could argue perhaps that this reality may not necessarily be a problem. For a start, as (negative) publicity surrounding cartel decisions is often of limited duration and concerns a subject of limited interest to the public, it cannot be assumed that such publicity automatically becomes prejudicial to a criminal trial.[185] Second, the antitrust authority could simply play down the importance of the administrative proceeding (e.g., by not commenting on it publicly) in order to insulate the criminal antitrust proceeding from negative publicity. In other words, it could attempt to limit the interest of the national media in the administrative proceeding.[186] Third, in order to reduce the negative potential of any publicity, one could simply delay the criminal cartel trial for a short period of time, so as to allow a 'fade effect' to take root.[187] It is conceded, however, that too long of a delay may also bring its disadvantages. For example, the memories of witnesses may also begin to fade with time.[188] Finally, even if one could establish that publicity has some potential to influence decision-makers in the criminal cartel trial, one would still find it difficult to establish a legal challenge to that trial on the basis of a violation of Article 6 ECHR. The reason for this is that under ECtHR jurisprudence, the existence of negative publicity per se is not decisive concerning impartiality: one should

[180] OFT (2001), [1.20]. In fact, the importance of timing in this regard has been officially acknowledged in UK soft law. According to OFT (2004a), [4.6], for example: 'If the OFT decides to institute an administrative procedure under the [Competition Act 1998] against undertakings engaged in a cartel where criminal proceedings are also being considered against individuals in respect of the same cartel, the OFT and the [Serious Fraud Office] will consult on timing'.

[181] OFT (2001), [1.20].

[182] One must remember here that EU law does not give the power to NCAs to relieve another NCA of the competence to pursue a given antitrust investigation or prosecution; see Section C(b)(iii) of this chapter.

[183] See Beard (2003), 160.

[184] See: OFT (2001), [6.10]; Joshua (2003), 634; and Furse (2012), 127.

[185] Cf. Joshua (2002), 238–9.

[186] This observation is particularly relevant when only the first manifestation of the 'additional dynamic' contention is operative: the antitrust authority in such a situation will have more influence over the extent of publicity surrounding the administrative antitrust decision than it would have if it was adopted by a foreign authority (which presumably would have a strong interest in publicizing the outcome of its own investigation).

[187] See Nazzini (2003), 486. [188] Standler (2004), 18.

also consider the effectiveness of measures offered to exclude any legitimate doubt concerning prejudice.[189] Indeed, as stressed by Lord Hope after conducting a survey of Strasbourg jurisprudence on this issue:

> the question is not confined to the residual effect of the publicity on the minds of each of the jurors. Account must also be taken of the part which the judge will play to ensure, so far as possible, that the defendants will receive a fair trial. An examination of the measures which [he] can take under the system which has been laid down for the conduct of criminal jury trials forms an integral part of the whole exercise.[190]

The relevant measures include, in particular, warnings or directions provided to the jury by the trial judge.[191] In order, then, for an argument concerning prejudicial pre-trial publicity to be successful in a criminal cartel case, one would have to convince a court that the available judicial measures are ineffective in protecting against impartiality. This may be difficult to do in practice, even if academic literature supports the argument:[192] indeed, the effectiveness of judicial directions may represent a 'convenient fiction'[193] which the judiciary are generally content to accept.

(iii) Impact upon the theoretical justifications

Due to, inter alia, the existence of the identified techniques for ensuring consistency with due process, concurrent antitrust proceedings do not necessarily violate Article 6 ECHR. This fact provides scope for the achievement of the underlying objectives of the theoretical foundations for European antitrust criminalization: concurrent proceedings followed for reasons of deterrence and/or retribution are not prohibited per se. That said, the required efforts to ensure that concurrent antitrust proceedings are conducted in a manner which is consistent with Article 6 ECHR can impact negatively upon the theoretical justifications for antitrust criminalization in a number of ways.

1. Impact upon deterrence

The main reason that the techniques identified are capable of impacting upon deterrence is that in order to implement these techniques one is required to expend resources. Indeed, additional resources will inevitably be consumed when: (i) evidence collected to an administrative standard is then recollected to a criminal standard; (ii) the investigation respects a (more demanding) criminal standard from the outset instead of an administrative standard (even when, ultimately, an administrative antitrust sanction is the outcome); and (iii) mechanisms, such as 'Chinese walls', are formalized, as staff independent of the investigative teams need to be employed. Such increases in costs are relevant to the theoretical justification of deterrence (as utilized in this book) as such a justification seeks to achieve *economic efficiency*.[194] These additional costs need to be fed into the cost/benefit analysis conducted when deciding whether to introduce criminal antitrust sanctions in the first place.[195] This is not to say that the costs involved in implementing the identified measures inevitably negative the objective of deterrence,

189 *De Cubber v. Belgium* (1985) 7 EHRR 236, [24]. See also *Pullar v. United Kingdom* (1996) 22 EHRR 391, [40].

190 *Montgomery v. H.M. Advocate* [2003] 1 AC 641, 670.

191 See Honess (2002), 720.

192 See, e.g., Fitzpatrick (2010). See also Thomas (2010), demonstrating that a high proportion of jurors do not understand judicial directions fully in the legal terms used by judges.

193 Tanford (1990), 111.

194 See Chapter 2, Section B(b)(i) of this book.

195 See Chapter 3, Section D(b)(iii) of this book.

but rather that such costs will add to one side of the relevant equation which is considered. In short, the additional costs due to the identified techniques further complicate the cost/benefit analysis that needs to be undertaken when employing the justification of deterrence. The real question that remains to be answered is whether the additional costs concerning the techniques can be offset by the increase in benefits (due to marginal deterrence) secured by the introduction of criminal antitrust sanctions. This is a factual issue for any given project of European antitrust criminalization. The point here is that the protection of due process does in fact influence the determination of that particular issue; hence such protection has the potential to impact upon the theoretical justification of deterrence.

2. Impact upon retribution

The techniques which may impact upon the theoretical justification of retribution are those related to the protection against prejudicial pre-trial publicity. It should be noted that, when pursuing the objective of deterrence (and nothing more, such as the protection of the human rights of the accused), one does not necessarily have to protect against negative publicity: (general) deterrence theory per se does not require that only the guilty are punished, unless such (undeserved) punishment is capable of undermining the general level of respect for the law and therefore the deterrent effect of criminal sanctions.[196] In fact, if the population at large believe (due to negative publicity) that an individual is guilty of a criminal cartel offence, his conviction (even if erroneous) may increase their respect for the law (as, according to them at least, 'the law courts got it right') and may increase general deterrence (as a conviction demonstrates that a potential punishment faces a cartelist). With retribution, by contrast, such an approach is prohibited: only *deserved* punishment can be imposed; negative pre-trial publicity which leads to an *erroneous* conviction is inconsistent with this particular theoretical justification. To the extent, then, that the identified techniques concerning the avoidance of prejudicial pre-trial publicity are effective, such techniques can ensure consistency with retribution.

That said, however, one technique in particular could potentially undermine the objective of retribution. The technique in question relates to attempts by the antitrust authority to limit the interest of the national media in the concurrent administrative antitrust proceeding, so as to insulate the criminal antitrust proceeding from negative publicity. The reason that this technique is problematic is that, in order for retribution to be operationalized in the criminal context, the authorities must create awareness of the moral content of cartel activity. The easiest way for the authorities to do this is through the adoption of administrative decisions condemning cartel activity *in conjunction with* the creation of publicity surrounding such decisions. When such publicity is shunned in order to protect the Article 6 ECHR rights of the accused, efforts to create awareness of the moral content of cartel activity will be less successful. This particular problem can be avoided, however, if the administrative antitrust proceeding follows the criminal one. In such a situation, maximum publicity can be created concerning the administrative proceeding (for the purpose of 'norm building') without damaging the sustainability of the criminal conviction. Indeed, it is only when the administrative antitrust proceeding actually precedes the criminal proceeding that the tension between the objective of retribution and the protection of the due process rights of the accused is created.

[196] See Chapter 2, Section C(b) of this book.

D. Conclusion

The issue of due process presents a number of challenges for those who are considering the introduction of criminal antitrust sanctions within the EU. These challenges are the natural result of not only the 'strengthening of rights' contention—which was examined in the previous chapter—but also the 'additional dynamic' contention identified in the present chapter. The latter contention holds that the introduction of criminal antitrust sanctions in a particular European jurisdiction does not preclude the imposition of civil/administrative sanctions alongside criminal sanctions for a given cartel. The validity and impact of the 'additional dynamic' contention were both examined in detail in order to present a more comprehensive understanding of the extent of the legal challenge of due process.

The validity of the 'additional dynamic' contention was established relatively easily. After identifying four possible manifestations of the contention at issue and conducting inquiries concerning these manifestations, this chapter determined that three of these manifestations were valid. Accordingly, the following sentencing scenarios *for a given cartel* comply with EU law: (i) national regimes can impose both administrative antitrust sanctions on undertakings and criminal antitrust sanctions on individuals; (ii) a given national regime can impose criminal antitrust sanctions on individuals and a different national regime can impose administrative antitrust sanctions on undertakings; (iii) the European Commission can impose administrative antitrust sanctions on undertakings and a given national regime can impose criminal sanctions on individuals. Thus, the 'additional dynamic' contention itself was indeed found to be valid.

The next analytical step undertaken determined the actual impact of the 'additional dynamic' contention, and hence the extent of the challenge presented by this aspect of the legal requirement of due process. Three particular issues were considered: the exchange of information between competition authorities; double jeopardy; and concurrent proceedings.

A potential due process issue was identified with the exchange of information from administrative antitrust regimes to criminal antitrust regimes: if such information could be used in evidence in a criminal trial, it could potentially undermine the rights of the accused, as the protections in an administrative regime may not be as robust as those in a criminal regime. EU law has foreseen this problem. Regulation 1/2003 places limitations on the exchange of information within the ECN from administrative to criminal regimes for evidential purposes: Article 12(3). While that particular provision takes care of the problem identified, it arguably goes too far: it prohibits the use of information in evidence to secure custodial sanctions in a receiving (criminal) regime even where the sending (administrative) regime has respected the human rights protections guaranteed in the receiving state. In order to ensure that the objectives of antitrust criminalization are not undermined, this 'custodial rule' should be abolished. Alternative, less strict (but nonetheless effective) protections could also be introduced, such as the use of a 'double barrier'. However, if due process is indeed to be protected, it is necessary to accept an inevitable negative impact upon the efficiency of the criminal antitrust regime: legal appeals questioning whether the relevant collection of information respects the equivalent level of protection of the rights of the accused in the receiving jurisdiction inevitably consume resources. Compensating for this reduction in efficiency (or ensuring that it is no greater than any increase in efficiency secured by criminalization) represents an inherent legal challenge of European antitrust criminalization—at least if the merits of information exchange are as significant as claimed.

The second identified issue of due process concerned 'double jeopardy'. It was argued that this issue becomes relevant due to: (i) the validity of the 'additional dynamic' contention; and (ii) the fact that an individual can in fact constitute an 'undertaking' for the purposes of EU law. The protection against 'double jeopardy' is important in principle for the achievement of retribution, but it is also essential under European human rights law: Article 4(1) of Protocol No. 7 to the ECHR (not to mention Article 50 CFR). Caution must be exercised in order to avoid those relatively rare cases where double jeopardy issues arise when both administrative and criminal sanctions are imposed for a given cartel. Protecting against 'double jeopardy' is least difficult when the second prosecution has not yet begun, but the first prosecution has: the second case against the individual/undertaking should be dropped. When neither of the two parallel prosecutions has begun, the situation becomes problematic, particularly where more than one jurisdiction is involved. In order to secure efficient enforcement as well as fairness (i.e. in order to respect the objectives of both deterrence and retribution), one can use the ECN to resolve the issue. Three limitations were identified with this solution, however: (i) there is no obligation concerning inter-NCA notifications within the ECN; (ii) due to legal ambiguities, NCAs may not feel obliged to inform the Commission of criminal antitrust cases which involve the imposition of sanctions upon natural persons; and (iii) the NCAs cannot relieve each other of the competence to pursue a given antitrust investigation or prosecution. These limitations, then, further contribute to the inherent legal problem of due process.

The final identified issue of due process related to concurrent proceedings. Two potentially problematic matters were identified: (i) the use of administrative powers to collect evidence for a parallel criminal investigation; and (ii) the engendering of prejudicial pre-trial publicity. Techniques can be used to reduce the likelihood of such matters occurring. However, efforts to ensure consistency with due process may have a negative impact upon the effectiveness of the underlying theoretical justifications for European antitrust criminalization. Specifically, such techniques may either increase the costs involved in criminal antitrust enforcement, thereby reducing the possible net (deterrence-based) gain from criminalization, or require the antitrust authority to limit media interest in the (concurrent) administrative proceeding, to the detriment of the objective of retribution. Such limitations of the identified techniques also contribute to the inherent legal problem of due process.

Both the present chapter and the chapter which immediately preceded it examined what can be termed the *procedural aspect* of the human rights-related legal challenge of European antitrust criminalization: they consider how protecting the human rights of the accused impacts on the procedures adopted in this context. Such an examination is only one part of the story, however: the human rights-related legal challenge to European antitrust criminalization also has a *substantive aspect*. The next chapter—the final chapter of Part II—acknowledges this fact and examines that particular aspect of the challenge. In essence, it investigates the restraining influence of the principle of legal certainty on the concept, substance, and existence (or otherwise) of European antitrust criminalization, in order to contribute to a comprehensive understanding of the human rights-related legal challenge of such criminalization.

7

European Antitrust Criminalization and the Challenge of Legal Certainty

A. Introduction

There are sound reasons why one should ensure that the content and scope of any criminal antitrust law can be reasonably understood by potential cartelists, judges, jurors, and the public at large. For a start, comprehensibility is important for the achievement of both of the theoretical justifications analysed in Part I of this book. It is clear that, for a criminal law to deter a given individual from engaging in a given conduct, that individual must understand that the conduct in question is the subject of a criminal law and if carried out will result in criminal punishment. A firm understanding of the prohibited conduct is also important for the achievement of retribution, particularly if such retribution aims to *communicate* the wrongfulness of the behaviour in question to the accused; indeed, without understanding *what* the moral code (i.e. the criminal antitrust offence) actually specifies, one cannot explain to the accused *how* his behaviour has violated this moral code. Furthermore, in a more obvious practical sense, comprehensibility is required to avoid potential jury nullification, as well as to ensure that legal educative efforts are not overburdened. In addition, a clearly defined criminal cartel offence helps to ensure the workability of a criminal immunity policy: 'a clear definition of the offence assists a potential leniency applicant in determining whether or not to take advantage of the programme and thereby provide authorities with the information they are seeking'.[1] A clear, comprehensible criminal antitrust law also results in lower social costs, as, for example, fewer resources are consumed in litigation related to clarification. Such a law may also help to reduce the likelihood of a decrease in society's respect for the institution of the criminal law.

So, for all of the above reasons, comprehensibility is advisable with any project of antitrust criminalization. The point to be established here, however, is that when criminal antitrust sanctions are at issue, such comprehensibility is not *merely advisable* for theoretical or practical reasons, but is in fact a strict *legal* requirement: comprehensibility—as one element of the wider principle of legal certainty—is mandated by European human rights law.[2] This chapter acknowledges this legal reality. In doing so, it analyses the (legal) challenge for criminal antitrust laws presented by the principle of legal certainty.[3]

In order to facilitate this analysis, the basic principle of legal certainty is first set out in detail: Section B. An examination of the challenge of legal certainty for antitrust

[1] See Wardhaugh (2012a), 587.

[2] Legal certainty is also a principle of EU law (see, e.g., Tridimas (2006), Chapter 5) and is enshrined in Article 49 of the Charter of Fundamental Rights of the European Union [2000] OJ C364/1. Relevant EU cases which have considered the principle include: Case 14/86, *Pretore de Salò v. X* [1987] ECR 2545; Case 80/86, *Kolpinghuis Nijmegen BV* [1987] ECR 3969; Case C-168/95, *Criminal Proceedings against Luciano Arcaro* [1996] ECR I-4705; Case C-345/06, *Proceedings Brought by Heinrich* [2009] ECR I-1659; and Cases C-201/09 P and C-216/09 P, *ArcelorMittal Luxembourg v. Commission* and *Commission v. ArcelorMittal Luxembourg SA and others* [2011] ECR I-02239. However, in line with the methodology discussed in Chapter 1, Section D(a)(v)(3) of this book, the focus of the analysis in this chapter will be on the impact of the ECHR.

[3] See also Whelan (2012a).

criminalization is then undertaken from three different perspectives, namely: (i) legal certainty and the concept of a criminal antitrust offence; (ii) legal certainty and the substance of a criminal antitrust offence; and (iii) legal certainty and the existence of a criminal antitrust offence.

The relationship between legal certainty and *the concept* of a criminal antitrust law is analysed first: Section C. The main argument that is examined here posits that, due to the inherently vague nature of the antitrust rules, it would be inappropriate to enforce such rules with criminal sanctions. What is at issue here is whether or not the principle of legal certainty ensures that the concept of a criminal antitrust law per se is incapable of adhering to the requirements of European human rights law. This is an important inquiry, for two reasons. First, if *by definition* the concept of a criminal antitrust law cannot adhere to the principle of legal certainty, it will not be possible to criminalize cartel activity, irrespective of the theoretical robustness of criminal antitrust sanctions. Second, if it is simply impossible to criminalize cartel activity without violating the principle of legal certainty, it follows that all current European criminal cartel laws will be in violation of European human rights law.

Section D approaches the legal challenge at issue from a different perspective; it demonstrates how legal certainty can influence *the substance* of a criminal antitrust offence. Implicitly, this section acknowledges: (a) that it is better to advise the authorities to test a given criminal antitrust law against the legal certainty requirement and adjust it accordingly than to attempt to construct and present to those authorities a definitive design for a criminal antitrust law that is free from legal certainty problems;[4] (b) that it is constructive nonetheless to demonstrate what definitely should not be included in the definition of a criminal antitrust offence for legal certainty reasons; and (c) that the European experience concerning antitrust criminalization should inform such advice. Hence, the section focuses on current Member State legislation (specifically, the UK Cartel Offence (as it was originally drafted)) to highlight a potentially serious pitfall when designing a criminal antitrust law 'from scratch'.

The final substantive section of this chapter considers the impact of the principle of legal certainty upon *the existence* of a criminal antitrust offence: Section E. In particular, it analyses the issue of 'sleeping giants': that is, the use of existing (relatively broad, non-antitrust-specific) criminal laws to impose sanctions for cartel activity. The controversial UK case of *Norris* is particularly instructive in this regard and is therefore analysed in detail. This analysis helps one to provide normative instructions as to how one can deal with the challenge of legal certainty when attempting to awaken the 'sleeping giant' for the first time: i.e. when attempting to assert that a criminal antitrust offence has been in existence as a result of a non-antitrust-specific piece of criminal legislation or common law offence.

B. The Principle of Legal Certainty

Article 7 ECHR provides that no one should be convicted of a retroactive 'criminal offence'[5] nor be subjected to retroactive criminal punishment.[6] This provision, in

[4] Such an acknowledgement is consistent with the limitations imposed upon the scope of this book; see Chapter 1, Section C(b).

[5] As with Article 6 ECHR (see Chapter 5, Section B of this book), the concept of 'criminal charge' in Article 7 ECHR is an autonomous ECHR concept: *Welch v. UK* (1995) 20 EHRR 247, [27]–[28].

[6] The EU Charter contains a similar provision: Article 49 CFR.

incorporating the principle of legal certainty (or 'legality'),[7] holds that a person can only be criminally convicted on the basis of a pre-existing rule of law (*nullem crimen, nulla poena sine lege*)[8] and that 'the criminal law must not be extensively construed to an accused's detriment'.[9] In doing so, Article 7 ECHR not only ensures respect for the rule of law,[10] but also helps to reduce potential costs of litigation.[11] There are two sides to the principle of legality, both of which affect the substance of a criminal law.[12] The first is that legislatures and courts are prohibited from creating or extending the law in order: (i) to criminalize acts or omissions which were not criminal at the time of commission or omission;[13] or (ii) to increase a penalty retroactively. Nonetheless, and in relation to limb (i), the courts may clarify the existing elements of the offence and adapt them to new circumstances which can 'reasonably be brought under the original concept of the offence'.[14] According to the late Lord Bingham, the jurisprudence from Strasbourg establishes that while 'absolute certainty is unattainable, and might entail excessive rigidity', and 'some degree of vagueness is inevitable' (particularly so in common law countries), 'the law-making function of the courts must remain within reasonable limits'.[15] For him, '[i]f the ambit of a common law offence is to be enlarged, it "must be done step by step on a case by case basis and not with one large leap"'.[16] The second aspect of the principle holds that a criminal offence must be clearly defined in law; in other words, it must be possible to predetermine, if necessary with legal advice, what conduct is criminal and what conduct is not solely by reference to the law: Article 7 ECHR 'implies qualitative requirements, notably those of accessibility and foreseeability'.[17] This particular requirement does not imply that the concrete facts giving rise to criminal liability should be stated in the legislation in question; rather, it is sufficient for a general definition to be provided by law for interpretation by the courts.[18] While both of the identified aspects of the principle of legality are distinct, the second is clearly a precondition of the first: the more precision that is brought to bear upon the definition of an offence, the less scope is available for creative judicial interpretation.[19] In any case, they are both relevant to the concept of European antitrust criminalization.

[7] On this principle, see Hall (1960), 225 et seq.

[8] Harris et al. (1995), 274. See: *Kokkinakis v. Greece* (1994) 17 EHRR 397, particularly [52]; and *Baskaya v. Turkey* (2001) 31 EHRR 10, particularly [36].

[9] *Veeber v. Estonia (No. 2)* (2004) 39 EHRR 6, [30]–[31]; and *Kokkinakis v. Greece* (1994) 17 EHRR 397, [52]. See also Greer (2006), 239.

[10] See: Fallon (1997), 7–8; and Hayek (2008), 87.

[11] Buxton (2000), 332.

[12] See Ovey and White (2006), 209. In the UK context, see: *R v. Rimmington* [2006] 1 AC 459, [33]; and *R v. Misra and Srivastava* [2005] Crim App R 328, [29]–[34]. Legality in the sense used here is a requisite of the rule of law; see Hayek (2008), 87. See also: Buxton (2000), 332; and Fallon (1997), 7–8.

[13] See, e.g., *X v. Austria* (1965) 8 Yearbook 190, 198.

[14] *Gay News Ltd and Lemon v. United Kingdom* (1983) 5 EHRR 123, [9].

[15] *R v. Rimmington* [2006] 1 AC 459, [35].

[16] *R v. Rimmington* [2006] 1 AC 459, [35], quoting *R v. Clark (Mark)* [2003] 2 Crim App R 363, [13]. See also *X Ltd and Y v. United Kingdom* (1982) 2 DR 77, [9]; and *SW and CR v. United Kingdom* (1996) 21 EHRR 363.

[17] *SW and CR v. United Kingdom* (1996) 21 EHRR 363, 399. See also Raz (1977).

[18] See generally Dougan (2012), 115.

[19] Ovey and White (2006), 209.

C. Legal Certainty and the Concept of a Criminal Antitrust Offence

To respect Article 7 ECHR, a criminal cartel offence must be clearly defined in law. It must be obvious to a potential cartelist that if he colludes with others and fixes prices, restricts output, allocates markets, or rigs bids, he will be committing a criminal offence and may be subject to criminal punishment. In line with ECtHR jurisprudence, legal certainty may be obtained even when the cartelist requires professional legal help in interpreting the relevant antitrust statute.[20] This is important, because cartelists, as business people, will often have the resources at their disposal to employ a lawyer to investigate whether his past, present, or future conduct is legally questionable. Nonetheless, those opposed to criminalization might argue that, due to their economic foundations, the antitrust rules are not always clear and that, given the severity of imprisonment, it would be unfair to impose criminal sanctions at all for their violation. This type of argument is likely to be raised when criminal cartel sanctions are a novel development in an antitrust regime.[21] While criminal sanctions for cartel activity are now firmly established in the US,[22] antitrust prosecutors received such a criticism as criminal punishment for cartel violations became more common in the early twentieth century.[23] It was argued, for example, that 'the steadily increasing economic emphasis of the [Sherman Act 1890] has rendered the criminal prosecution less and less appropriate' and that 'too many indictments have been returned in areas where the law was unsettled or where the economic complexities of the case were such that [a criminal trial] was highly improper'.[24] In a similar manner, opponents of European antitrust criminalization may argue that the principle of legal certainty does not support the actual concept of a criminal cartel offence.

(a) Contrasting cartel activity with other types of anticompetitive conduct

It is conceded that in some antitrust cases it would indeed be unfair to impose criminal sanctions, in particular due to the uncertainty surrounding the exact content of the law. This would be the case, for example, with abuses of a dominant position under Article 102 TFEU.[25] As noted by de la Torre, '[w]hereas there is general agreement that cartels are "bad", it is sometimes considered that the difference between anti-competitive exclusionary behaviour and legitimate competitive behaviour, which may even benefit the consumer, may in certain cases not be easy to draw'.[26] Recent research of the archives has revealed that, at the time of the negotiations concerning the adoption of what was to become Regulation 17/62,[27] even one of the original drafters of the competition provisions in the EEC Treaty, namely Hans von der Groeben, 'did not think it possible

[20] *Sunday Times v. United Kingdom* (1979–80) 2 EHRR 245, [49]; and *Silver v. United Kingdom* (1983) 5 EHRR 347, [88].

[21] In the early days of the Irish criminal competition law regime, for example, arguments concerning legal certainty can be detected in the literature; see Competition and Mergers Review Group (2000), [2.4] and footnote 76.

[22] See Baker (2001).

[23] See Kramer (1959–60), 532.

[24] Chadwell (1955), 1138–9.

[25] On Article 102 TFEU, see generally O'Donoghue and Padilla (2013).

[26] De la Torre (2010), 365–6.

[27] Council of the European Economic Community (1962).

to impose fines on dominant undertakings under [Article 102 TFEU] as long as no sufficiently detailed rules were laid for their conduct'.[28] The vagueness of that particular provision has in fact been criticized on numerous occasions in the past,[29] and there have been recent efforts by the European Commission to provide some form of guidance on its operation in practice.[30] It appears, however, that the Commission's efforts in this regard have not been entirely successful.[31] Significant uncertainty therefore continues to surround the operation of Article 102 TFEU.[32] Some commentators have in fact (convincingly) argued that at present Article 102 TFEU therefore fails to adhere to the requirements of Article 7 ECHR.[33] For this reason alone,[34] criminal sanctions should not be imposed for anticompetitive unilateral conduct.[35]

But Article 102 TFEU should be contrasted with the cartel law rules contained in Article 101 TFEU. The latter provision captures, inter alia, the behaviour articulated in the 1998 OECD Recommendation.[36] This is the type of behaviour (i.e. agreeing with a competitor to fix prices, share markets, restrict output, and/or rig bids) over which little to no disagreement exists concerning its anticompetitive nature, and indeed for which EU competition law has no tolerance. In fact, if any aspect of EU antitrust law achieves consensus, it is the rules concerning 'hard-core' cartels.[37] Unlike Article 102 TFEU, the substance of the law on 'hard-core' cartels is to all intents and purposes settled.[38] Furthermore, while a cartelist is entitled in law to argue that a cartel should be exempt from unlawfulness by virtue of Article 101(3) TFEU,[39] such an exemption for a 'hard-core' cartel is very unlikely to be provided by EU law.[40] In practice, the fact that business people are aware of the unlawfulness of their cartel activity is often evidenced by the extent to which they are prepared to go to conceal their behaviour from the authorities.[41] The European Commission investigation into the 'Cathode Ray Tubes' cartel, for example, revealed that the investigated companies 'were well aware they were breaking

28 Akman (2009), 297. According to that particular commentator, this fact 'almost implies that the provision was not intended to be enforced': Akman (2009), 297.

29 See, e.g., Temple Lang and O'Donoghue (2005), 39–43.

30 See: European Commission (2009a); and European Commission (2005e). For detailed criticism of both of these documents, see respectively: Akman (2010a); and Akman (2006).

31 See, e.g., Killick and Komninos (2009).

32 See, e.g.: Akman (2010a); and Katsoulacos (2009).

33 See, e.g., Vesterdorf (2011).

34 There may be other reasons not to impose criminal sanctions in Article 102 TFEU cases, such as a lack of moral wrongfulness, the difficulty of meeting criminal standards of proof, or potentially chilling efficient conduct; see, e.g.: Calvani and Calvani (2009), 127; and Massey and Cooke (2011), 128.

35 Some countries have, however, created criminal offences based on unilateral anticompetitive behaviour; ineffective (or non-existent) enforcement is often the result. For analysis of the (unsuccessful) Canadian attempts to impose criminal sanctions for unilateral behaviour, for example, see Scott (2007), 62–4. See also Collins and Eatrides (2003).

36 OECD (1998). See Chapter 1, Section C(a) of this book.

37 It is true that, irrespective of this consensus, 'proper legal advice will always be crucially important in this area': Albors-Llorens (2006), 876. However, the requirement to seek expert legal advice is not necessarily inconsistent with legal certainty: *Sunday Times v. United Kingdom* (1979-80) 2 EHRR 245, [49]; and *Silver v. United Kingdom* (1983) 5 EHRR 347, [88].

38 See generally Whish and Bailey (2012), Chapter 13.

39 See: Case T-17/93, *Matra Hachette SA v. Commission* [1994] ECR II-595; Frese (2006), 211–12; Joshua (2002), 242; and Whish (2009), 150–1.

40 See, e.g.: European Commission (1980), [115]; European Commission (2010b), Article 5(1); and European Commission (2010c), Article 4(1). See also ICN (2005), 14. Cf.: *Reims II* (Case COMP/36.748), Commission Decision, 15 September 1999, [1999] OJ L275/17, [65]; and *Visa International—Multilateral Interchange Fee* (Case COMP/29.373), Commission Decision, 24 July 2002, [2002] OJ L318/17, [79].

41 See, e.g., *Gas Insulated Switchgear* (Case COMP/F/38.899), Commission Decision, 24 January 2007, [2008] OJ C5/7. See also the relevant case studies in Furse (2012), Chapter 6.

the law'.[42] In a document found during the Commission's inspections, the following warning was presented: 'Everybody is requested to keep it as secret as it would be serious damage if it is open to customers or European Commission'.[43] Furthermore, under the old notification regime of Regulation 17/62, it was rare for cartelists to notify their cartel agreements in the hope that they would be granted an exemption: only 4 per cent of the 49 cartels investigated by the European Commission between 1980 and 2004 (when the notification system was abolished) were originally notified by the parties.[44] Unlawfulness had therefore been understood and effectively conceded by the relevant undertakings. Moreover, the 'undisputed illegality' in EU law of cartel activity is demonstrated by the fact that, in the vast majority of appeals against Commission decisions condemning cartels, the legal issues raised were the standard of proof and the amount of the fines imposed.[45] It is true that, irrespective of this consensus on illegality, 'proper legal advice will always be crucially important in this area'.[46] However, the requirement to seek expert legal advice is not necessarily inconsistent with legal certainty.[47] While it would be disingenuous to state that EU cartel law has never been criticized for falling foul of legal certainty requirements, it is true that when such arguments are raised in this context, they almost always concern the size of a potential fine as opposed to the existence of an infringement per se.[48] Finally, while a cartelist is entitled in law to argue that a cartel should be exempt from unlawfulness by virtue of Article 101(3) TFEU,[49] such an exemption for a 'hard-core' cartel is very unlikely to be provided by EU law.[50] In effect rather than in strict legal terms, cartel activity is subject to per se illegality in Europe, much like it is in the US. Such behaviour therefore does not actually involve rambling 'through the wilds of economic theory' under the rule of reason, to use the words of the US Supreme Court.[51] Any arguments that the rule-of-reason approach under Section 1 of the US Sherman Act 1890 conflicts with the rule of law[52] are therefore not transferrable to the cartel rules of Article 101(1) TFEU.

(b) Placing legal certainty in perspective

The argument concerning vagueness in antitrust law should therefore be placed in proper perspective: while relevant to the outer fringes of antitrust activity, as well as to unilateral conduct,[53] it does not necessarily apply to clear-cut violations of European

[42] European Commission (2012).

[43] European Commission (2012).

[44] Günster et al. (2012). For some rare examples of cartel agreements that were notified, see: Skilbeck (2002); and Skilbeck (2003).

[45] Diaz et al. (1999), 336. See also Whish and Bailey (2012), 520–1. A recent, typical example is the (unsuccessful) appeal brought by ICI against a Commission decision imposing a fine upon it of €91 million for its participation in a cartel concerning acrylic glass: Case T-214/06, *Imperial Chemical Industries Ltd v. Commission*, Judgment of 5 June 2012, not yet reported.

[46] Albors-Llorens (2006), 876.

[47] See *Sunday Times v. United Kingdom* (1979–80) 2 EHRR 245, [49].

[48] For examples, see: Geradin and Henry (2005); Joshua and Camesasca (2004); Killick (2005); Korah (1998); Richardson (1999); Stephan (2010a); and van Bael (1995).

[49] See Case T-17/93, *Matra Hachette SA v. Commission* [1994] ECR II-595.

[50] See, e.g.: European Commission (1980), [115]; and ICN (2005), 14.

[51] *United States v. Topco Association* (1972) 405 US 596, 609, footnote 10.

[52] See Stucke (2009).

[53] See, e.g., Easterbrook (2003), 345: 'Aggressive, competitive conduct by any firm, even one with market power, is beneficial to consumers. Courts should prize and encourage it. Aggressive, exclusionary conduct is deleterious to consumers, and courts should condemn it. The big problem lies in this: competitive and exclusionary conduct look alike'.

cartel law, where little confusion exists concerning unlawfulness.[54] The concept of price-fixing, for example, is sufficiently clear as to caution market actors in their business dealings:[55] business people are told simply to refuse to talk to their competitors about prices. Indeed, unlike other (commercial) practices, cartel activity is not a complex concept: at its base, it involves a relatively straightforward, uncontested economic model; in practice, no intricate economic efficiency arguments are offered; and, generally, its effects are direct and observable. Economic analysis, then, does not complicate a prospective cartelist's understanding of the unlawfulness of cartel behaviour.[56] The same is true with the courts' understanding of cartel activity. As noted by Frese, unlike with other areas of competition law, the

> possible complications stemming from the fact that the courts are not adequately equipped to make [economic] analyses and from the possibility that criminal law principles will be breached, will not materialise in these '*by their object*-cases'.[57]

Indeed, economics is of limited application in this context, and 'the questions worthy of debate fall more squarely into the legal domain'.[58] According to Lyons, '[a]lthough econometric evidence can be used to identify suspicious pricing patterns, there is little subtle economics used in identifying a cartel'.[59] In fact, in cartel cases economic theory is only really applied in two situations: (i) to help to determine the optimal fine that is to be imposed by a competition authority; and (ii) to determine the amount of damages that are payable to a private enforcer.[60] Economics is not used to establish a violation of the cartel law rules per se. Such a violation is more often than not proven by incriminating documentary evidence (e.g., e-mails) and witness statements provided by leniency/immunity applicants.[61] In any event, a criminal antitrust provision could be created which does not contain elements requiring an economic assessment.[62] This occurred in the US with Section 1 of the Sherman Act 1890, where the word 'conspiracy' ensures both that the only proof of price-fixing required is proof that the defendant had conspired to fix prices and that an inquiry into whether the defendants actually caused a significant increase in price or reduction in output is immaterial.[63] This particular approach 'largely removes the need for the detailed economic testimony common in civil antitrust actions'.[64] Canada has learned from the US experience and has recently reformed its competition law in order to create a per se criminal offence.[65] Previously, Section 45(1)(c) of the Competition Act 1985 required proof of an 'undue' restriction of competition for a criminal cartel offence to be established, a requirement that engendered considerable

[54] See: Barnett (2006a), 2–3; and Flynn (1967), 1312 et seq.

[55] This point has important consequences for the retribution-based criminalization argument, particularly its reliance on the moral norm against cheating; see Chapter 4, Section C(c)(iii) of this book.

[56] This point was not accepted by the UK Government, however, when it argued that requiring a direct link to EU competition law for violations of the UK Cartel Offence would 'entail a lot of complex argument about economic competition of a sort that would make the prosecution extremely difficult': House of Commons Standing Committee, 18 April 2002, Column 139.

[57] Frese (2006), 205. [58] MacCulloch (2008), 1.

[59] Lyons (2009), 130, relying on Porter (2005). See also OFT (2004a), [2.2].

[60] To be clear, then, situations (i) and (ii) are only relevant once an infringement of the cartel law rules has been established. For two interesting case studies analysing both of these situations, see respectively: Hviid and Stephan (2009); and Møllgaard (2009).

[61] Lyons (2009), 130. [62] Frese (2006), 206.

[63] Posner (2001), 53. For criticism of this approach, see Jacobs (2007), 29 and 32–7.

[64] Barnett (2006b), 3.

[65] See Section 45 of the Competition Act 1985, RSC 1985, c. C-34, as amended. On the recent reform of Canadian criminal cartel law, see: Low and Halladay (2011); and Quaid (2012).

criticism over the years.[66] Interestingly, in the early 1990s, the concept of 'undue' restriction of competition (contained in the predecessor to Section 45(1)(c) of the Competition Act 1985[67]) was subjected to a constitutional challenge on the grounds of vagueness, but this was ultimately unsuccessful in front of the Canadian Supreme Court.[68]

For the above reasons, then, legal certainty arguments concerning the 'inherently vague' nature of the cartel prohibition in Article 101(1) TFEU are not problematic. Admittedly, it does not follow that none of the cartel prohibitions in the national competition laws of the EU Member States (which may have additional (problematic) elements to the cartel prohibition in Article 101(1) TFEU) violates the principle of legal certainty. But this is not problematic for present purposes: the point here is that, by taking the example of the cartel prohibition in Article 101(1) TFEU, one can negative the argument that a cartel prohibition per se violates the principle of legal certainty. The comprehensibility of the cartel prohibition in Article 101(1) TFEU demonstrates that the very concept of a criminal cartel offence within the EU Member States is not prohibited by virtue of Article 7 ECHR.

A final point can be made here concerning the concept of a criminal cartel offence. If, however unlikely, a cartel case did indeed arise involving uncertainty as to unlawfulness, any consequent doubt concerning criminal liability could be resolved through the exercise of prosecutorial discretion; one could ensure that only civil or administrative proceedings result. Such an approach would be consistent with the approach adopted in the US. The US Government, in an attempt to undermine initial criticism concerning uncertainty, requested antitrust enforcers to exercise a reasoned discretion in their use of the power of criminal prosecution: the 'criminal process should be used only where the law is clear and the facts reveal a flagrant offense and plain intent unreasonably to restrain trade'.[69] However, the use of such discretion in this context is not without its own problems—e.g., it may be difficult to respect the principle of equal treatment—and therefore it should be kept to an absolute minimum.[70] To ensure that this is so, a very clear, non-economics-based definition of cartel activity is required. In seeking such a definition, the legislator should be prepared to accept under-inclusivity in the conduct proscribed by the cartel offence, if necessary: one should not rely upon prosecutorial discretion to rectify uncertainty merely to ensure that all potentially harmful horizontal anticompetitive conduct is criminalized. A less inclusive definition which does not rely upon prosecutorial discretion would avoid the pitfalls associated with such a power, and is therefore preferable.[71] In seeking such a definition, one should also be mindful of the (negative) experiences of the relevant EU Member States, in particular that of the UK.

D. Legal Certainty and the Substance of a Criminal Antitrust Offence: Avoiding the Pitfalls of the UK Experience

None of the above should be interpreted as implying that there are no difficulties with the concept of legal certainty when actually choosing a definition for a criminal antitrust offence. That is a different issue. What the above argues is that there are no inherent

66 See Warner and Trebilcock (1992–93).

67 Section 32(1)(c) of Combines Investigation Act 1970, RSC 1970, c. C-23.

68 *R v. Nova Scotia Pharmaceutical Society* [1992] 2 SCR 606.

69 US Attorney General (1955), 349. See also: Baker (2001), 694–5; and Baker (1978).

70 Cf. Committee of Ministers of the Council of Europe (2000); and Committee of Ministers of the Council of Europe (1987).

71 The Canadian authorities recently adopted such an approach in their redrafting of their criminal cartel laws; see generally Low and Halladay (2011).

conceptual difficulties with the idea of cartel activity which would make legal certainty unobtainable: under the current EU rules, economics does not overly complicate the analyses of prospective cartelists and unlawfulness is generally understood. Antitrust criminalization, however, is not necessarily a process of *merely adding* criminal sanctions for violation of the current cartel law rules. Indeed, while criminalization may refer merely to the substitution of criminal for administrative antitrust sanctions, it may also imply the use of the current rules as the basis upon which to create a separate criminal offence. In other words, the criminal offence, while containing the essential concept of cartel activity as articulated by the current EU rules, may nonetheless have different features from the administrative offence. All depends upon the exact definition chosen. This definition in turn will be influenced by the theoretical justification in operation. (For example, retribution theory may dictate a criminal mens rea (e.g., intention or knowledge) which is different to the relevant mental element in an existing civil offence,[72] while deterrence theory may caution against the use of strict liability.[73]) The point here is that by *adding additional elements* to the current cartel law rules—e.g., to ensure consistency with the theoretical justification—one may undermine legal certainty;[74] indeed, extreme care should be taken *in the drafting process* not to turn the current rules into a (stand-alone) criminal antitrust offence which violates human rights prescriptions. The UK experience with the drafting of the (original) UK Cartel Offence provides an important case study in this regard.

(a) The (original) UK Cartel Offence: an argument concerning legal certainty and 'dishonesty'

In 2001, following a public consultation on the issue,[75] the UK Government decided to introduce a criminal Cartel Offence into law in order to create a 'real deterrent' concerning cartel activity.[76] The Enterprise Act ('EA') was passed in 2002, with the relevant sections containing the UK Cartel Offence coming into effect on 20 June 2003.[77] Accordingly, it is a criminal offence for an individual dishonestly to make or implement or cause to be made or implemented a cartel agreement between horizontal competitors. A cartel agreement in this context is confined to agreements relating to price-fixing, market sharing, output restrictions, and bid-rigging. The Cartel Offence is a stand-alone offence which does not require proof of a violation of Article 101 TFEU.[78] Although the Cartel Offence has been on the UK legislative books for more than ten years, to date there has only been one successful criminal prosecution of this offence.[79] The only other prosecution of this offence ended in an embarrassing failure when, due to issues concerning disclosure of evidence, the OFT had to offer no evidence at trial.[80] The OFT's

[72] See Chapter 4, Section C(a) of this book.

[73] See, e.g.: Richardson et al. (1982), 16–17; and Yeung (2004), 85.

[74] There is also an argument that in certain circumstances the non-inclusion of the constitutive elements of the administrative offence in the criminal offence engenders legal certainty problems; on this see below.

[75] DTI (2001b).

[76] DTI (2001c), 20–4.

[77] Sections 188–191 EA. On the UK Cartel Offence, see generally: Beard (2003); Darbishire (2007); Dean (2003); Furse (2012), Chapter 4; Furse and Nash (2004a); Furse and Nash (2004b); Guy (2006); Joshua (2003); Joshua (2002); MacCulloch (2010a); MacCulloch (2007), MacCulloch (2003); Peretz and Lewis (2003); and Stephan (2008c).

[78] Furse and Nash (2004b), 141.

[79] *R v. Whittle and others* [2008] EWCA Crim 2560.

[80] *R v. Burns and others*, Unreported Judgment, Southwark Crown Court, 10 May 2010. See generally: OFT (2010c); and Purnell et al. (2010). On the failure of this case and the lessons learned by the prosecutor in question, see OFT (2010d).

efforts to enforce the UK Cartel Offence have been subjected to considerable criticism,[81] with many in agreement that 'enforcement has some way to go before criminal sanctions against individuals will appear to be an active deterrent'.[82] The UK Government recently conceded that enforcement of the Cartel Offence had been ineffective and that legislative change was required in order to reform the Cartel Offence so that it would become fit for purpose.[83] One of the major changes decided upon by the UK Government was the removal of the 'dishonesty' element from the offence.[84] This particular proposal became part of law when the Enterprise and Regulatory Reform Act 2013 ('ERRA') was adopted. Specifically, Section 47 ERRA reforms the UK Cartel Offence by, inter alia, removing its (original) definitional element of 'dishonesty'; it will come into force on 1 April 2014.[85]

A crucial argument has been raised in the literature concerning the compatibility of the UK Cartel Offence (as originally drafted in 2002) with Article 7 ECHR,[86] which highlights the potential difficulties one faces when drafting a criminal antitrust offence which: first, contains relatively broad definitional elements; and, second, does not contain all of the elements of the current EU (administrative) cartel prohibition. The essential thrust of the argument is that the offence as originally drafted violates the requirement of legal certainty due to its mens rea of 'dishonesty' and the fact that its commission is not linked to a violation of Article 101 TFEU or of Chapter 1 CA. In short, because juries are the ones who decide what is or is not a dishonest practice, and since the potential cartelist does not have EU or UK law to guide him, seeking legal advice on the criminality of his actions may not be as fruitful as he would have wished. While the argument essentially relates to two *practical* issues (the choice of mens rea and the differentiation of the criminal offence from the administrative offence), it may nonetheless have serious implications regarding the restrictive role of European human rights law and the ability of Member States to construct a cartel offence in accordance with human rights; hence, the relevant issues should be considered here.

(i) The definitional element of 'dishonesty'

Central to the legal certainty argument is the definitional element of 'dishonesty'. The test for 'dishonesty' under UK law is provided by the case of *R v. Ghosh*.[87] Accordingly, both subjective and objective analyses are required: the conduct must be (i) dishonest according to the standards of ordinary people and (ii) known by the defendant to be dishonest according to those standards. It was anticipated that the use of 'dishonesty' in the definition of the (original) Cartel Offence would represent a 'significant challenge for the OFT'.[88] MacCulloch argues that 'dishonesty' was employed as an explicit

[81] See, e.g.: Furse (2011); and Joshua (2010).

[82] Morgan (2010), 81.

[83] See BIS (2011), Chapter 6.

[84] See BIS (2012), Chapter 7. On the definitional element of 'dishonesty', see also Chapter 8, Section C(b) of this book.

[85] That said, all references in this chapter to the UK Cartel Offence should be read as references to the *original offence* in Section 188 of the Enterprise Act 2002 (i.e. the offence which actually required proof of 'dishonesty'), unless the context dictates otherwise. For the original text of the UK Cartel Offence and for the text of Section 47 ERRA, see Annex II.

[86] Parkinson (2004). See also the comments of Lord Hunt of Wirral concerning uncertainty in Hansard, House of Lords Debates, 18 July 2002, Column 1537.

[87] *R v. Ghosh* [1982] 2 All ER 689, 696. Although that case concerned the Theft Acts, the test for 'dishonesty' contained therein has been deemed to be of general application: *R v. Lockwood* [1986] Crim LR 244. The case of *R v. George and others* [2010] EWCA Crim 1148 established that the *Ghosh* test applied to the definitional element of 'dishonesty' contained in the original Cartel Offence.

[88] Blake (2008), 12.

element of the Cartel Offence for two main reasons: it helped to ensure compatibility with Article 101(3) TFEU, as well as to delimit the scope of the offence.[89] To these, another reason can be added: the desire to underline the wrongfulness of the cartelist's behaviour.[90] There are merits to each of these three reasons.[91] But, having said that, there is also a major potential problem with the mens rea of 'dishonesty': it could be argued that it is overly broad as a concept and therefore violates *in itself* the legal certainty requirement. The point here is not that legal certainty is violated by bringing a novel set of circumstances (i.e. cartel activity) within a general (non-cartel-specific) offence which employs the mens rea of 'dishonesty'—as occurred in the *Norris* case, examined in Section E below—but rather that such certainty may actually be violated by the inclusion of the mens rea of 'dishonesty' within a *cartel-specific* offence. In other words, what is at issue is the legality of the use of the definitional element of 'dishonesty' per se.

(ii) Legal certainty problems with 'dishonesty'

The problem with the concept of 'dishonesty' is that all depends upon how the jury decides the issue. According to Parkinson, it is for this reason that offences based upon 'dishonesty' alone are incapable of reaching the degree of precision required under Article 7 ECHR:

> It is for juries alone to decide whether or not conduct amounts to being dishonest, applying the tests set out by the Court of Appeal in 1982 in the case of *Ghosh*... Seeking legal advice on such an issue is not likely to be of much assistance, since a lawyer's view as to what a jury may think dishonest is likely to be no better than anyone else's.[92]

In other words, a given cartelist *himself* cannot be sure whether or not in engaging in cartel activity he would actually commit a crime until the jury decides the matter *at a later date*. It is in effect the requirement of the *later* ruling of the jury which is problematic: with this approach, the prospective cartelist would not be able to *foresee*, within reasonable limits, the consequences of his chosen course of action, contrary to the requirements of legal certainty. Indeed, the jury—so the argument runs—is not merely determining whether a crime has been committed, but is also rendering a given act (of cartel activity) criminal due to its willingness to characterize that act as 'dishonest'.

According to its protagonist, this argument gains further strength when the apparent inherent imprecision associated with 'dishonesty' is not rectified or assuaged by additional definitional elements which, taken together, point to criminality: that is, when the underlying conduct of the criminal cartel offence is not deemed to be objectionable in itself irrespective of its alleged honest/dishonest nature.[93] This particular point was accepted by the UK Law Commission in the context of the crime of fraud. Indeed, in its 1999 consultation paper, the Law Commission rejected a general fraud offence with the element of 'dishonesty' at its core; because it would criminalize otherwise unobjectionable behaviour merely by the employment of the concept of 'dishonesty', such an offence would be 'undesirable in principle' and insufficiently certain to satisfy the requirements of the European Convention.[94] According to Parkinson, with the (original) Cartel

[89] MacCulloch (2007), 356.

[90] See, e.g. OFT (2001), [2.5]. On this issue, see Beaton-Wells (2007), 696 et seq. See also Costello (2005): 'dishonesty appropriately captures the genuinely criminal nature of serious cartel conduct'. Cf. Fisse (2008), 8.

[91] In fact, these merits recently persuaded a non-European state (namely, Australia) to consider employing 'dishonesty' in its criminal cartel law; for criticism of this, see, e.g., Fisse (2007a).

[92] Parkinson (2004), 188–9. [93] Parkinson (2004), 189.

[94] Law Commission (1999), [1.23] and [5.9]–[5.53]. For criticism of this paper, see Ormerod (1999). As noted by Parkinson (2004), this approach was followed through in its final report on fraud,

Offence, the criminalization (through the employment of the concept of 'dishonesty') of otherwise unobjectionable behaviour occurs as the commission of the criminal offence is not linked to violation of Article 101 TFEU (or its national equivalent).[95] In other words, as some of the constitutive elements of the administrative cartel offence are not included in the definition of the criminal offence, legal certainty may not exist: the only indicator of criminal behaviour when the administrative offence has not been committed is the concept of 'dishonesty', something which is left for the jury to decipher. As explained by Parkinson,[96] there are two circumstances in which a disconnect can occur between an agreement that violates Section 188 EA (i.e. the criminal offence) and an agreement that necessarily violates Article 101 TFEU or Chapter 1 CA (i.e. the administrative offence): (i) when the agreement subject to the criminal offence does not engender an appreciable restriction of competition;[97] and (ii) where the agreement subject to the criminal offence could obtain an exemption under Article 101(3) TFEU or Section 9 CA.[98] Accordingly, in both of these situations, the potential cartelist does not necessarily have EU or UK competition law (i.e. Article 101 TFEU or Chapter 1 CA) to guide him when seeking legal advice on the criminality of the cartel:[99] in the two situations identified, conduct pointing to criminality would not exist (i.e. there would be no violation of Article 101 TFEU or Chapter 1 CA) and the only gauge for criminality would be the jury's perception of the honest/dishonest nature of the underlying conduct, itself an inherently vague and uncertain concept. Prosecutions in either of the two circumstances identified would therefore be suspect, as 'in each instance a person may not be able to foresee with any reasonable degree of accuracy whether or not a proposed course of action would be decided to be criminal by a jury'.[100]

(b) Evaluating the legal certainty argument

The legal certainty argument presented above concerning 'dishonesty' can be evaluated by conducting three separate investigations. These investigations concern whether: (i) when employing the definitional element of 'dishonesty', one must also employ a definitional element that 'points to criminality' in order to respect Article 7 ECHR; (ii) cartel activity as defined in the (original) UK Cartel Offence actually fails to point to such criminality;

where the Law Commission recommended a 'dishonesty'-based offence that contained an actus reus which pointed itself to criminality: Law Commission (2002). For analysis of this report, see Scanlan and Kiernan (2003).

95 One should note here the comments of MacDonald and Thompson (2003), 96: 'in deciding what are the standards of ordinary honest people, and in evaluating whether or not the accused considered [his] actions to be honest by those standards, one important factor will be whether or not the agreement has already been found to be, or is potentially unlawful as a matter of competition law'. See also DTI (2001b), [7.31].

96 Parkinson (2004), 188.

97 For Article 101 TFEU or Chapter 1 CA to apply, there must be an 'appreciable' restriction of competition; see, e.g.: Case 5/69, *Völk v. Vervaecke* [1969] ECR 295; and European Commission (2001b), particularly [7]. (Cf. Case C-226/11, *Expedia Inc. v. Autorité de la Concurrence and others*, Judgment of 13 December 2012, not yet reported.) However, the European Commission's de minimis Notice (as opposed to the de minimis doctrine itself) does not apply to hard-core restrictions of competition, such as price-fixing and market sharing: European Commission (2001b), [11].

98 A disconnect may also be engendered when the agreement subject to the criminal offence does not affect trade between Member States: Article 101 TFEU would not be violated; see, e.g., *IB v. The Queen* [2009] EWCA Crim 2575, [18].

99 See also Pickford (2002), 36.

100 Parkinson (2004), 189.

and (iii) the argument has implications which extend further than the legal validity of the (original) UK Cartel Offence.

(i) 'Dishonesty' and the apparent requirement to point to criminality

Parkinson's argument concerning incompatibility with the ECHR was not conceded by the UK legislature when the original Cartel Offence was adopted. In actual fact, the argument does not appear even to have been presented during the parliamentary passage of the Enterprise Bill.[101] In addition, the vast majority of those commentating on the initial development of a criminal cartel regime within the UK did not seem to appreciate the legal certainty issue presented by the use of 'dishonesty' in this context. In a 2001 report prepared for the OFT which analysed how cartel criminalization could be implemented within the UK, for example, Hammond and Penrose posited that use of the element of 'dishonesty' in any future cartel offence should lead to a criminal offence which is 'sufficiently clearly defined as to satisfy the requirements of Article 7 ECHR'.[102] A report prepared by the OFT for the OECD shortly after the UK Cartel Offence came into effect stated that '[b]y adopting a different definition [in the UK Cartel Offence] from that in existing anti-trust legislation, any possible problems relating to... legal certainty have been avoided'.[103] Ironically, legal certainty issues were later used to support the eventual removal of 'dishonesty' from the Cartel Offence.[104] Unfortunately, a legal certainty argument has not been tested in front of the courts in the UK concerning the original Cartel Offence. It is submitted here that, if legal certainty arguments were raised in relation to the original Cartel Offence,[105] they would have an uphill struggle, so to speak, in order to be successful. For a start, a case based upon Article 7 ECHR is very difficult to sustain in front of the ECtHR or the domestic courts: the offence must be 'very loosely defined indeed'.[106] Furthermore, while legal certainty arguments are not unknown in the context of an offence based upon the relatively vague notion of 'dishonesty',[107] they have not yet succeeded solely on the basis of the employment of this concept in the definition of an offence. It was held by Judge Mercer in *R v. Pattni and others*,[108] for example, that 'dishonesty' as interpreted in *Ghosh* did not necessarily render the common law offence of cheating unascertainable. All elements of the definition need to be considered and the mere existence of the definitional element of 'dishonesty' is not sufficient to invalidate a criminal offence on legal certainty grounds.

[101] See, however, the comments of Lord Hunt of Wirral concerning uncertainty in Hansard, House of Lords Debates, 18 July 2002, Column 1537.

[102] OFT (2001), [1.11]. [103] OECD (2003b), 95. [104] See BIS (2011), 64.

[105] To be clear: irrespective of Section 47 ERRA, the original Cartel Offence will remain the appropriate offence for a criminal prosecution in the UK when the (dishonest) cartel activity was allegedly committed between 20 June 2003 and 1 April 2014. Consequently, it is still theoretically possible for a legal certainty argument to be pursued at a later date in front of the courts concerning the original Cartel Offence. (Interestingly, the OFT has recently charged an individual for an (alleged) offence under the original version of Section 188 EA; see OFT (2014).)

[106] See Ovey and White (2006), 214–15. See also Buxton (2000), 332: 'it is very difficult to discern in the ECHR jurisprudence any general principle that the criminal law must be accessible and certain above a very modest level; and where certainty of criminal law has come into issue in ECHR questions, the standards required by the Convention jurisprudence have been distinctly undemanding'.

[107] Indeed, there are English cases concerning offences based upon 'dishonesty', public mischief, or conspiring to corrupt public morals where inconsistency with the principle of legality (due to uncertainty) has been (unsuccessfully) argued: *Shaw v. DPP* [1962] AC 220; *Knuller Ltd v. DPP* [1973] AC 435; and *R v. Pattni and others* [2001] Crim LR 570.

[108] *R v. Pattni and others* [2001] Crim LR 570.

As noted by the ECtHR in the case of *Hashman and Harrup v. United Kingdom*,[109] 'dishonesty' is 'but one element of a more comprehensive definition of the proscribed behaviour' in the UK Theft Acts. This statement has been interpreted as the 'distinguishing mark' between conduct proscribed by, for example, the Theft Acts (which is assumed to be in conformity with legal certainty) and conduct such as behaving *contra bonos mores* (which in the case at issue was held to be in violation of legal certainty requirements).[110] It is arguable that such an approach lends a degree of support to the position of the Law Commission in its 1999 consultation paper (arguing against a *general* 'dishonesty' offence)[111] and therefore to the argument advanced by Parkinson regarding the (original) Cartel Offence: the 'comprehensive definition' referred to by the Court may imply that other elements in the offence point to the criminality of the conduct, and that on this basis one may be able to foresee, within reasonable limits, the consequences of one's chosen course of action, irrespective of the definitional element of 'dishonesty'. Admittedly, this may be a stretch too far for a quotation that is, for practical purposes, an *obiter dictum* in a case where the issue of 'dishonesty' was not considered directly. Nonetheless, even if one accepts this point (i.e. that the other definitional elements may 'save' the 'dishonesty'-based offence if they point to criminality), it does not necessarily follow that Parkinson's argument is unassailable: one must still analyse his assertion that the underlying conduct in the (original) Cartel Offence does not point to criminality.

(ii) Failure to point to criminality

It is true that Section 188 EA does not require an appreciable restriction of competition and does not explicitly provide an exemption, unlike Article 101(3) TFEU or Section 9 CA. This part of Parkinson's argument, then, is logically correct: in theory, one can commit the (original) Cartel Offence without violating either Article 101 TFEU or Chapter 1 CA. It is submitted, however, that it does not necessarily follow that in such circumstances one is presented with definitional elements (in this context, those elements apart from 'dishonesty') which do not point to criminality. Violation of a pre-existing administrative offence (in this case, the competition law rules in Article 101 TFEU or in Chapter 1 CA) is *merely one method* of pointing to criminality in the context of a criminal antitrust offence; another method can also be employed: subject to certain inherent limitations, one can conceptualize cartel activity, as defined in the criminal offence (but again, and to be sure, minus the element of 'dishonesty'), as being inherently wrongful in a moral sense. It was argued in Chapter 4 of this book how this can be done: cartel activity can be viewed as a violation of any one of the moral norms of stealing, deception, or cheating if certain implementing measures are taken.[112] It is submitted here that consideration of the applicability of these norms to the underlying conduct in the (original) Cartel Offence helps one to determine the objectionable nature—or otherwise—of the conduct and therefore to establish whether the definitional elements of the Cartel Offence minus 'dishonesty' point to

[109] *Hashman and Harrup v. United Kingdom* (2000) 30 EHRR 241, [39].

[110] Ovey (2000), 186.

[111] Ovey (2000), 186.

[112] These implementing features attempt to capture the essence of the social norms of stealing, deception, or cheating. They include, for example, the adoption of a sufficiently culpable mens rea, the incorporation of particular elements concerning the rationale behind cartel activity (e.g., intention to obtain an unlawful advantage, to mislead, or to deprive), and the granting of rights of ownership in the overcharge. For more detail, see Chapter 4 of this book.

criminality.[113] This is in turn helps one to verify whether the (original) Cartel Offence meets the requirements of legal certainty encompassed by Article 7 ECHR.

In the case of the (original) Cartel Offence, cheating (i.e. rule breaking) is unlikely to have occurred in the two situations identified by Parkinson: in those situations, by definition the administrative offence will not have been committed.[114] One could perhaps argue that the rule in question was broader than that contained in the administrative offence, such as a mere prohibition on price-fixing, output restriction, market-sharing, and bid-rigging. In other words, the rule at issue need not contain a requirement concerning 'an appreciable restriction of competition'. But this only gets one so far. What is also required is the existence of an intention to obtain an unfair advantage through breach of this rule. This element is not present in Section 188 EA, and on this ground alone the Cartel Offence can arguably be distinguished from the moral norm of cheating. Likewise, the moral norm of deception can be distinguished from the underlying conduct of the Cartel Offence: while in practice a cartelist may indeed intend to mislead his customers (by, e.g., allowing them to assume that the price offered is the competitive price), an intention to cause a person to believe something that is untrue is not actually required by Section 188 EA, and so may not actually be present. Finally, the moral norm of stealing may also be inapplicable, again on the grounds that the relevant implementing measure is not present. In this instance, an *intentional* violation of another's rights of ownership in something that is capable of being bought or sold (i.e. the consumer surplus) may not necessarily be present when the (original) Cartel Offence is committed. Consequently, Parkinson's argument concerning the legality of the (original) Cartel Offence may have some value: the underlying conduct of the Cartel Offence in itself (and in the absence of the element of 'dishonesty') is not necessarily objectionable in the two situations articulated by Parkinson, due, inter alia, to the absence of the features required to ensure violation of the moral norms against stealing, deception, or cheating (which were identified in Chapter 4 above).

However, an important caveat should be mentioned here. If cartel activity *inevitably* fulfils the content represented by (some of) the facilitating features, then the absence of such facilitating measures in the definition of the (original) Cartel Offence would not lend support to Parkinson's argument. If, for example, cartelists *by definition* aim to obtain an unfair advantage and/or mislead customers, the moral norms against cheating and/or deception can be fulfilled; violation of the (original) Cartel Offence, then, would inevitably involve conduct pointing to criminality even where the express element of 'dishonesty' is put to one side. As mentioned in Chapter 4 above,[115] there is a lack of empirical data on the specific motivations of cartelists and thus this counter-argument to Parkinson's claim cannot be definitively established.

(iii) Implications of the legal certainty argument

To the extent identified directly above, Parkinson's argument may sway those legislators seeking a definition of a criminal antitrust offence that is acceptable under Article 7 ECHR; in other words, it may deter other law-makers from adopting a *'dishonesty'-based*

[113] It should be remembered here that, irrespective of the fact that the discussion in Chapter 4, Section C of this book reaches a relatively technical level, a major advantage of the 'social norms' approach to moral wrongfulness is its comprehensibility to the average citizen: Green (2006), 44.

[114] To be clear, this is because either: (i) there is no 'appreciable' restriction of competition; or (ii) the cartel in question is excepted from unlawfulness due to the presence of efficiencies.

[115] See Chapter 4, Section C(c)(i) of this book.

criminal antitrust offence. In any case, the argument, however technical, highlights the difficulties one may face when trying to create a criminal law which explicitly underlines the wrongful nature of cartel activity (by focusing on its dishonest quality), while at the same time protecting the human rights of the accused. As illustrated in Chapter 4, the employment of the concept of 'dishonesty' is not actually required in order to underline the moral wrongfulness of cartel activity. If, however, 'dishonesty' is used, for legal certainty reasons one should ensure that the additional definitional elements of the offence clearly point to criminality. In order to do this, one should: (i) link the commission of the criminal antitrust offence to the commission of the administrative offence contained in Article 101 TFEU or in the equivalent national provision (i.e. ensure that every violation of the criminal offence constitutes a violation in itself of the administrative offence); or (ii) ensure that at least one of the moral norms against stealing, deception, or cheating is necessarily encompassed by the criminal antitrust offence. Failure to follow either of these recommendations could lead to a situation where the legality of the ('dishonesty'-based) cartel-specific offence is questionable under European human rights law, as is arguably the case with the original UK Cartel Offence—at least in the two situations identified by Parkinson.

E. Legal Certainty and the Existence of a Criminal Antitrust Offence: The Issue of 'Sleeping Giants'

The issue of whether 'sleeping giants' exist in the criminal laws of the Member States—whether, that is, pre-existing criminal laws can be interpreted in novel ways to capture cartel activity—is an issue particularly relevant to the debate on antitrust criminalization. For various reasons, legislators may not wish to adopt criminal antitrust laws. They may be reluctant to antagonize the business community, for example.[116] Or they may decide that their limited resources are better allocated to the fight against more serious or morally questionable activities. They may underestimate the harm caused by cartel activity.[117] There may even be disagreement on the legal definition to be employed, or the exact conduct to be criminalized.[118] Even if criminal antitrust laws exist, their temporal jurisdictions might not extend to past cartel activity.[119] In these particular circumstances, it may be others who take the lead in developing the (criminal) antitrust regime. Prosecutors, for example, when faced with an apparent lack of specific criminal antitrust laws, may decide to characterize cartel activity in terms of an already existing, relatively broad criminal offence such as fraud[120] or conspiracy to defraud.[121] If and when this occurs, it is imperative that the authorities respect the principle of legal certainty and that they insulate themselves from challenges to their action on the grounds

[116] On antitrust sanctions and the reaction of business, see Parker (2006).

[117] See OECD (2000a), 20.

[118] As occurred in Australia prior to its adoption of a new criminal cartel law in the summer of 2009; see, e.g., Fisse (2008).

[119] The UK Cartel Offence, e.g., only applies to conduct occurring after 20 June 2003; see the Enterprise Act 2002 (Commencement No. 3, Transitional and Transitory Provisions and Savings) Order 2003, SI 2003/1397.

[120] As noted by one eminent commentator, there is an argument that Section 4 of the Fraud Act 2006 may be infringed by certain forms of cartel activity: Whish (2009), 415. But for an argument that that legislation should not cover cartel activity, see Corker and Smith (2007).

[121] This occurred in the UK in the (unsuccessful) case taken by the UK Serious Fraud Office ('SFO') against generic drugs manufacturers; see *R v. GG Plc and others* [2008] UKHL 17.

of a violation of Article 7 ECHR. A challenge on such grounds may negative the argument that cartel activity was illegal irrespective of silence from the legislature; it may in other words affect the actual existence of the criminal antitrust sanction, as has occurred in the UK in the *Norris* case.[122]

(a) Legal certainty determining the (non-)existence of criminal antitrust sanctions: the *Norris* case

The *Norris* case is interesting in that it was a foreign authority—namely, the US Government—which claimed that cartel activity was already proscribed by the criminal law of England and Wales prior to the entry into force of the UK Cartel Offence on 20 June 2003. The facts of this case can be summarized as follows. In September 2004, Mr Ian Norris, a British national, was indicted by a US grand jury on four counts, one of which alleged that Mr Norris conspired with others to operate a price-fixing agreement in relation to different carbon products in a number of different countries, including the US, contrary to Section 1 of the US Sherman Act 1890.[123] On the basis of this indictment, the US authorities sought to extradite Mr Norris from the UK. The problem, however, was that 'dual criminality' was required for extradition to occur: Section 137(2) of the Extradition Act 2003. In other words, the price-fixing agreement in question would also have to have been proscribed by UK criminal law at the time it was concluded. As the alleged cartel was outside the temporal scope of the UK Cartel Offence, the US authorities argued that the cartel nonetheless violated UK criminal law, as it amounted to a conspiracy to defraud. For District Judge Evans, the conduct which was alleged in the indictment did indeed constitute an extradition offence, as argued by the US Government; accordingly, he held that Mr Norris could legally be extradited. Mr Norris appealed to the High Court and then to the UK House of Lords (now the Supreme Court);[124] the latter allowed the appeal in part, and held that Mr Norris should not be extradited to face price-fixing charges in the US.[125]

One of Mr Norris's main arguments in his appeals to both the High Court and the House of Lords was that the conduct alleged in his indictment, namely mere price-fixing, would not have constituted a criminal offence under the law of England and Wales at the time that it was allegedly committed. It was accepted by all parties that the conduct would not have been subject to criminal punishment under statutory law; nonetheless, the US Government was persistent in its claim that the conduct would have amounted to a common law conspiracy to defraud, as price-fixing in itself, due to its secretive nature, was inherently dishonest. Such a claim was bolstered by a recent article published by Sir Jeremy Lever QC and John Pike arguing that price-fixing could indeed be a common law offence if it 'involves the use of dishonest means and prejudices, or carries a risk of prejudice to, another's rights, to the knowledge of the parties to the agreement that they had no right to do so'.[126] For Lever and Pike:

[122] *Norris v. Government of the United States of America and others* [2007] EWHC 71 (Admin) (High Court); and *Norris v. Government of the United States of America and others* [2008] UKHL 16 (House of Lords). On this case, see generally: Joshua (2008a); Joshua (2008b); Joshua (2008c); Stephan (2008b); Stephan (2008c); and Whelan (2009b).

[123] See Second Superseding Indictment, US District Court, Eastern District of Pennsylvania, *United States of America v. Ian P. Norris*, Criminal No. 03-632, 28 September 2004.

[124] In the remainder of this chapter, the judicial body in question is referred to as the 'House of Lords'.

[125] *Norris v. Government of the United States of America and others* [2008] UKHL 16.

[126] Lever and Pike (2005), 93.

> in many situations today third parties who deal with undertakings that are in fact parties to cartel agreements will proceed on the *assumption* that they are dealing with undertakings that are lawfully engaged in normal competition with each other; and the cartelists will know that that is so and will, in effect, act in a dishonest and therefore criminal manner, if the existence of the cartel is kept secret.[127]

In contrast to the High Court,[128] the House of Lords was not prepared to accept this argument, much to the relief of the appellant.

A number of judicial precedents were relied upon by Mr Norris to highlight that the judiciary had not treated price-fixing agreements as criminal under the common law. In *Jones v. North*, for example, the appellant underlined the traditional tolerance for such agreements; indeed, in that particular case the act of rigging bids was described as a 'very honest' practice.[129] The case of *Adelaide Steamship*[130] was also used to support this argument. In that case, it was held that no contract was ever an offence under the common law merely because it was in restraint of trade.[131] What mattered was that the parties to an agreement entered into that agreement in order to further their own interests and not to harm the interests of others.[132] In the context of such pre-existing case law, the appellant sought to argue that something more was required than mere secrecy. For him, although there were some cases that were supportive of the existence of a common law conspiracy to defraud by fixing prices,[133] they could be distinguished on the basis that they involved some form of 'positive' deception, beyond mere secrecy.[134] Price-fixing per se, then, would not be caught by such case law. This argument was ultimately accepted by the Law Lords. According to their interpretation of the applicable jurisprudence,[135] an agreement to fix prices was not criminal under the common law, 'unless there were aggravating features such as fraud, misrepresentation, violence, intimidation or inducement of a breach of contract'.[136] While the common law recognized that agreements in restraint of trade may indeed be unreasonable and therefore against the public interest and so void and unenforceable, such agreements were not actionable or indictable in the absence of such 'aggravating features'.[137]

Importantly for present purposes, their Lordships held that even if it had otherwise been open to them to decide that price-fixing in itself could now amount to a common law offence, they would have been prevented from doing so due to the principle of legal certainty.[138] Specifically, the 'consistent message' of Parliament and the judiciary, through legislation and case law respectively, reinforced by both ministerial statements and textbooks, was that price-fixing per se was not capable of constituting a crime. Given

[127] Lever and Pike (2005), 95.

[128] See *Norris v. Government of the United States of America and others* [2007] EWHC 71 (Admin), [66]–[67].

[129] *Jones v. North* (1875) LR 19 Eq 426, 429.

[130] *Attorney General of the Commonwealth of Australia v. Adelaide Steamship Co. Ltd* [1913] AC 781.

[131] *Attorney General of the Commonwealth of Australia v. Adelaide Steamship Co. Ltd* [1913] AC 781, 797.

[132] *Attorney General of the Commonwealth of Australia v. Adelaide Steamship Co. Ltd* [1913] AC 781, relying on *Mogul Steamship Co. Ltd v. McGregor, Gow & Co.* [1892] AC 25.

[133] Such as: *R v. De Berenger* (1814) 105 All ER 536; *R v. Lewis* (1869) Cox CC 404; and *Scott v. Brown, Doering, McNab & Co.* [1892] 2 QB 724.

[134] *Norris v. Government of the United States of America and others* [2007] EWHC 71 (Admin), [54].

[135] Namely: *Mogul Steamship Co. Ltd v. McGregor, Gow & Co.* [1892] AC 25; *Attorney General of the Commonwealth of Australia v. Adelaide Steamship Co. Ltd* [1913] AC 781; *North Western Salt Co. Ltd v. Electrolytic Alkali Co. Ltd* [1913] 3 KB 422; and *Rawlings v. General Trading Co.* [1921] 1 KB 635.

[136] *Norris v. Government of the United States of America and others* [2008] UKHL 16, [17].

[137] For criticism of this reasoning, see: Joshua (2008a), 12; and Whelan (2009b), 277.

[138] *Norris v. Government of the United States of America and others* [2008] UKHL 16, [55].

this context, it would have been contrary to the principle of legal certainty to hold that price-fixing in itself could amount to a dishonest practice and therefore a conspiracy to defraud. Even if a recent shift in public perception concerning price-fixing could be established,[139] which on the facts it could not, criminalization would be hard to reconcile with the jurisprudence of the ECtHR denying courts the ability to criminalize conduct merely because it was wrong rather than right according to the majority of contemporary fellow citizens.[140]

It was undisputed that there has not been a criminal prosecution for price-fixing per se under UK common law. This was not enough, however, to rule in favour of Mr Norris. What needed to be examined was whether mere price-fixing could 'reasonably be brought under the original concept of the [common law] offence'.[141] According to the late Lord Bingham, the jurisprudence from Strasbourg established that while 'absolute certainty is unattainable, and might entail excessive rigidity', and while 'some degree of vagueness is inevitable', particularly so in common law countries, 'the law-making function of the courts must remain within reasonable limits'.[142] The question, then, was whether it would be reasonable to bring price-fixing into the common law offence of conspiracy to defraud. It is submitted that in that particular case it would not have been reasonable to do so and that the ruling of the House of Lords is correct in this regard. It is undeniable that there was a 'consistent message' of the UK authorities that price-fixing per se was not capable of constituting a crime. This is clear from, inter alia, parliamentary debates, ministerial statements, and the research of experienced legal scholars. As stated by the House, there 'was no reported case, indeed, it would appear, no unreported case, no textbook, no article which suggested otherwise'.[143] Even if Mr Norris retained some of the best lawyers in the UK when he allegedly engaged in cartel activity, it is almost certain that he would have been advised then that what he was allegedly doing or contemplating was not criminal according to the common law of England and Wales.[144] It is here, in fact, that the judgment of the House of Lords on the conspiracy to defraud issue makes most sense.[145] Indeed, such is its strength that it may even have been preferable for their Lordships to have dealt with the conspiracy to defraud issue by analysing whether legal certainty would have been violated without considering the concept of 'dishonesty', particularly given the possible negative consequences of their ruling on this concept for the operation of the UK Cartel Offence.[146]

(b) Application of the lessons learned in *Norris*

The judgment in *Norris* demonstrates the perils one faces when attempting to awaken a 'sleeping giant' and use novel interpretations of existing laws to ensure that anticompetitive

139 On this, see Stephan (2008e).

140 *Norris v. Government of the United States of America and others* [2008] UKHL 16, [57], quoting *Hashman and Harrup v. United Kingdom* (2000) 30 EHRR 241, [38].

141 *Gay News Ltd and Lemon v. United Kingdom* (1983) 5 EHRR 123, [9].

142 *R v. Rimmington* [2006] 1 AC 459, [35].

143 *Norris v. Government of the United States of America and others* [2008] UKHL 16, [55]. On the importance of publicly accessible, identifiable sources for legal certainty, see *Fothergill v. Monarch Airlines Ltd* [1981] AC 251, 279.

144 Interestingly, a leading authority on EU cartel law submitted to the author that had he been consulted on the matter at any time during the 1980s, the 1990s, or the early 2000s, he would have advised his client that price-fixing was indeed 'dodgy' in a criminal sense under UK law.

145 For detailed criticism of other aspects of the 'conspiracy to defraud issue', see Whelan (2009b), 276–8.

146 See: Lester (2008), 139–40; Riley (2010b), 278; and Whelan (2009b), 278. Cf. Joshua (2011), 138.

conduct is subject to criminal sanctions.[147] While arguments can indeed be made as to why criminalization should occur,[148] it does not follow that such criminalization should proceed on an unprincipled basis.[149] Human rights considerations in particular need to be accommodated in whatever approach to criminalization is adopted.[150] Specifically, as revealed by the *Norris* case, criminalization by virtue of awakening a 'sleeping giant', if it is to occur, must take note of (inter alia) the principle of legal certainty: the authorities must be very careful in assuming that existing laws are capable of catching cartel activity per se when such a situation has never arisen before and when cartel activity in itself has consistently been perceived as being outside of the scope of the criminal law. Without such caution, criminal enforcement efforts will be undermined, resulting in a waste of resources and a possible reduction in the current level of respect for the law.

The central issue in this context is the *reasonableness* of applying a broadly defined criminal offence to a very novel set of circumstances, namely those relating to cartel activity. This inquiry in any given case will of course be one of fact. It will be decided according to an objective standard. Therefore, it is the opinion of the common, ordinary person as to whether it is reasonable to bring a given (anticompetitive) conduct within the original concept of the offence in question that matters; the subjective views of a competition authority or of a domestic or foreign prosecutor, for example, are not determinative. Different jurisdictions or courts may differ in their opinion concerning (objective) reasonableness, as seen in the respective judgments of the High Court and of the House of Lords in the *Norris* case. Different outcomes concerning legal certainty arguments are therefore possible. But, as suggested by the approach of the House of Lords—an approach, it must be remembered, that is grounded in European human rights jurisprudence—the greater the degree of (prior) consensus of the legal community on the apparent lawfulness of a given behaviour, the more likely that it will be considered unreasonable for judges to bring that behaviour within the original concept of a given ('sleeping-giant-type') offence. Where no reported or unreported case, no textbook, no article, or indeed no publicly available PhD thesis suggests anything other than lawfulness, the more difficult the antitrust prosecutor's case becomes.

It appears, then, that an authority contemplating awakening a 'sleeping giant' in the context of cartel activity has two immediate choices: either it leaves the 'giant' sleeping for good (i.e. it refuses to apply the broadly defined criminal offence to a very novel set of circumstances for fear of violating legal certainty requirements) or it awakens it very slowly. In the latter case, if the 'awakening' is to be successful, it is imperative that some form of advance notice be given to market operators that a criminal antitrust law already exists and may be used against them. Such notice should only concern itself with contemplated conduct rather than with conduct that has already occurred, otherwise the efforts to improve legal certainty will be in vain: what matters is that the rules be ascertainable at the time the individual actually decides on his future (competitive/anticompetitive) conduct. In other words, if notice is effected, it will only remove or reduce legal certainty concerns for conduct which occurs *after* the provision of notice. Accordingly,

[147] It should be noted that the UK is not the only Member State to attempt to awaken a 'sleeping giant'. Indeed, a number of years ago the German authorities attempted to make more accessible the criminal prosecution of price-fixing agreements and competition law violations under the general rules on fraud in the German Criminal Code ('StGB'); see Gotting and Lampert (2003). In fact, since 1992, the German general criminal fraud provision (Section 263 StGB) can be applied to bid-rigging, provided that the rigged price is higher than what the hypothetical competitive price would have been: Wagner-von Papp (2011), 165.

[148] See Part I of this book.

[149] Whelan (2007).

[150] Whelan (2010).

prosecutors should avoid bringing charges against those who allegedly engaged in cartel activity prior to the provision of notice as to the encompassing effect of a 'sleeping giant'.

Care should also be taken to ensure that contradictory statements do not emanate from the authority wishing to effect notice, or indeed from any other governmental authority that could help to inform legal advisers' opinions as to the lawfulness or otherwise of cartel activity under a 'sleeping-giant-type' offence. In the UK, immediately prior to the entry into force of the Cartel Offence, quite a number of statements were offered by the legislature, government agencies, and the OFT about the *introduction* of criminal antitrust sanctions in Section 188 EA;[151] these sorts of statements obviously did not help the US Government in the *Norris* case, where it argued that a criminal antitrust sanction already existed prior to 20 June 2003. In fact, they helped Lord Bingham to reach his conclusion about the 'consistent message' of Parliament, reinforced by both ministerial statements and textbooks, concerning lawfulness.[152] While the consistent message of a given single authority may be relatively easy to produce, problems arise when various different authorities or government agencies are involved. In such a case, it may be difficult for the government to present a united front on the issue. There may, for example, be differences in principle: one agency may not agree with the interpretation of the law offered by another. Differences may also be caused by the fact that some government agencies/departments may be 'captured' by business (which may be opposed to the use of criminal antitrust sanctions). If a united front is not presented—say, where the competition authority claims that a 'sleeping giant' covers cartel activity and ministers and/or their government departments claim the opposite—the chances of allaying legal certainty concerns through the use of notice will be significantly reduced. While the provision of notice in such an instance is not without merit—informed legal practitioners will at least be aware of the debate and should advise their clients of that fact, thereby allowing them to evaluate the advisability of their (future) conduct—it will not be fully effective. In such a situation, it might be preferable to let the 'sleeping giant' lie and to concentrate one's efforts on trying to introduce a new law through Parliament which expresses explicitly its applicability to cartel activity.

If the provision of notice is chosen as a way forward (e.g., where no conflicting statements from the legislature or from government agencies on existing criminality are reasonably foreseeable), it could be effected through the use of seminars, public meetings, the publication of guidelines for businesses, competition advocacy, or any of a wide range of activities, including the sponsorship and publication of PhD theses. The provision of notice through such means would not be a significant departure from current practice: at present in the UK, for example, in addition to guidance documents, senior OFT officials occasionally provide information to market actors by 'speaking publicly and candidly about enforcement efforts'.[153] It must be understood that the provision of notice is not law-making per se; the authorities are not creating a new criminal antitrust offence. Rather, they are putting business people on notice of the fact that such a criminal law already exists and may be used against them; in other words, they are trying to ensure that a future prosecution (of future anticompetitive conduct) does not collapse

[151] For examples, see: Bloom (2002a), 6 ('the Enterprise Bill [footnote omitted] *introduces* a new criminal offence for cartels' (emphasis added)); DTI (2001b), [7.2.4] ('the government is... concerned to ensure that *introducing a new criminal offence* does not cause significant divergence from European Law' (emphasis added)); and OFT (2001) (referring in its title to 'The Proposed Criminalisation of Cartels in the UK'). Academics generally supported this view; see, e.g., Furse and Nash (2004a), ix ('For the first time in over 200 years those found guilty of engaging in certain specified commercial arrangements... face the prospect of individual prosecution, fines, and in some cases imprisonment').

[152] See *Norris v. Government of the United States of America and others* [2008] UKHL 16, [46].

[153] O'Kane (2009a), 33.

due to lack of legal certainty. Furthermore, the authorities should allow a period of time to pass in order for the notice to take root and grow, so to speak. Indeed, if Lever and Pike's article had appeared prior to the alleged cartel activity in the *Norris* case[154]—and had received as much attention as it did in the mid 2000s[155]—it is very possible that the Law Lords might have come to a different conclusion on legal certainty. At any rate, their assertion in *Norris* that no textbook/legal article suggested anything other than lawfulness in the context of conspiracy to defraud—a statement that was, if not determinative, at least highly supportive of their conclusion on legal certainty—would have been impossible to advance.

While helpful, then, the provision of notice—whether effected directly through intervention of the authorities themselves or indirectly through the scholarship of legal commentators—is not a panacea for the legal certainty problems with 'sleeping giants'. Even if notice is provided as to the intentions of the authorities, and/or their or the legal community's understanding of the current law, it does not necessarily follow that legal certainty will be established. Notice does not necessarily establish reasonableness with regard to bringing a given (anticompetitive) conduct within the original concept of the offence in question; if effective at all, it merely reduces the likelihood of unreasonableness being found. In other words, irrespective of notice, a sufficient (definitional) link should still exist between the specifics of the offence and the cartel activity in question. It must also be noted that the provision of advance notice may not be possible in practice prior to the awakening of the 'sleeping giant'. *Norris* again provides an example of how this can happen. In that case, it was the US authorities (after submitting an extradition request) which adopted a novel interpretation of conspiracy to defraud, thereby forcing the courts of England and Wales to consider the issue before any effort was taken by the British authorities to provide notice of its intentions or of its understanding of conspiracy to defraud as it applies to cartel activity.[156] Given the current attitude of the US Government to (international) cartels,[157] as well as its evident desire to seek the extradition of foreign nationals,[158] it is not unlikely that its authorities would attempt to awaken a 'sleeping giant' in another Member State in the future.[159] One should understand here that officials from the DoJ were apparently hoping that a ruling in *Norris* that cartel activity could amount to a form of 'fraud' could set a precedent for extraditions from

[154] One should remember in this regard that their article 'was not only published after the 2002 [Enterprise] Act, but a number of years after the activities complained of in [the indictment] had ended. So it is not as if even an astute reader of legal articles in this area of law could have informed [himself] at the relevant time [i.e. between late 1989 and May 2000] of the possibility of [his] price fixing activities attracting criminal sanctions': *Norris v. Government of the United States of America and others* [2008] UKHL 16, [60].

[155] Not only was the article quoted in both the High Court and the House of Lords—although admittedly as a result of the *Norris* case itself—it was also the subject of a number of specialized conferences in respectable legal fora. One example would be 'Cartel Agreements, Criminal Conspiracy and the Statutory "Cartel Offence"', held on 22 February 2005, at the British Institute of International and Comparative Law ('BIICL'), London.

[156] Admittedly, however, the SFO did later attempt to rely upon the same argument as that relied on in *Norris*, i.e. that mere price fixing could amount to a conspiracy to defraud, in front of the English courts; this was also rejected by the House of Lords: *R v. GG Plc and others* [2008] UKHL 17. On this, see Lester (2008), 137–8.

[157] See, e.g.: Hammond (2010); and Garrett (2011), 1819–25.

[158] See, e.g.: Joshua et al. (2008–09); Joshua (2006a); Joshua (2005); and O'Kane (2011a), 418.

[159] It should be remembered here that cartel activity engaged in outside of the US will fall within US jurisdiction if it has substantial and reasonably foreseeable effects in the US market: *United States v. Nippon Papers Industries Co. Ltd* (1997) 109 F.3rd 1 (1st Circuit). On this, see: Lee (1998); and Reynolds et al. (1998).

other jurisdictions that 'had not criminalized cartel behaviour as such'.[160] Therefore the concept of awakening a 'sleeping giant' may not be confined to a common law offence, as in *Norris*, but could extend at a later date to a statutory offence from a civil jurisdiction. If the US authorities were to attempt once more to awaken a 'sleeping giant' in another Member State, it is very likely that the defendant would raise the issue of legal certainty to try to avoid serving time in a US federal prison. Consequently, the analysis above remains relevant, even after the resolution of the conspiracy to defraud issue in the UK-specific case of *Norris*.

F. Conclusion

European human rights law requires legal certainty in the context of punishment for the commission of a criminal antitrust offence. The principle of legal certainty imposes a number of different imperatives: legislatures and courts are prohibited from creating or extending the law in order to criminalize acts or omissions which were not criminal at the time of commission or omission or to increase a penalty retroactively; and a criminal offence must be clearly defined in law. This principle presents a challenge for those wishing to introduce a criminal antitrust offence. There are three potential elements to this particular legal challenge.

The first element of the legal challenge under investigation requires the demonstration that the principle of legal certainty does not prohibit in any absolute sense the imposition of criminal antitrust sanctions. It was argued above that the European cartel law rules are not inherently vague to a degree that would ensure inevitable legal certainty problems and that therefore their enforcement could encompass the use of criminal sanctions. Indeed, while relevant to the outer fringes of antitrust activity, the argument that legal certainty prohibits criminal antitrust sanctions does not necessarily apply to clear-cut violations of European cartel law, where little confusion exists concerning unlawfulness. Meeting this element of the challenge, then, is relatively undemanding.

The second element of the legal challenge at issue concerns the substance of the criminal antitrust law: one must be careful in designing the criminal antitrust law that the principle of legal certainty is not violated. Whether a given criminal antitrust law adheres to legal certainty requirements is a factual issue. In order to respect the relevance of the applicable justificatory theories for antitrust criminalization and the variety of ways in which they can be implemented, this chapter did not attempt to construct a definitive, legally certain cartel offence. Rather, it attempted to present the lessons learned from the European experience with criminal antitrust sanctions. The UK Cartel Offence was chosen as the case study. Relying upon this case study, the current chapter argued that to avoid problems with legal certainty, one should avoid the employment of the definitional element of 'dishonesty' if a stand-alone offence (i.e. one that does not require violation of Article 101 TFEU) is to be created. The validity of that argument, however, depended to a large degree upon whether one operationalized any of the norms noted in Chapter 4 concerning stealing, deception, or cheating.

The final element of the legal challenge under examination only becomes relevant when one attempts to impose criminal antitrust sanctions by awakening a 'sleeping giant': that is, by employing a non-antitrust-specific criminal law. This issue was raised directly in the *Norris* case. That particular case was therefore informative concerning

[160] Joshua et al. (2008–09), 355.

normative instructions on the use of 'sleeping giants'. The provision of notice, including its limitations, was analysed in this context. In particular, it was emphasized that the provision of notice (whether effected directly through intervention of the authorities themselves or indirectly through the scholarship of legal commentators), while useful, is not a panacea for the legal certainty problems with 'sleeping giants'. Notice does not necessarily establish reasonableness with regard to bringing a given (anticompetitive) conduct within the original concept of the offence in question; irrespective of notice, a sufficient (definitional) link should still exist between the specifics of the offence and the cartel activity in question. Finally, it was noted that, while applicable to other situations where the awakening of a 'sleeping giant' is attempted (i.e. where criminalization is actively pursued by the authorities of a given European jurisdiction), this warning becomes increasingly relevant as the US Government continues to pursue its hard-line approach to international cartels and to seek extradition of accused individuals from the European jurisdictions.

PART III
PRACTICAL CHALLENGES

8

European Antitrust Criminalization and the First Challenge of Design: Defining the Criminal Cartel Offence

A. Introduction

The effectiveness of a criminal cartel regime in achieving its objectives in practice depends upon a number of different factors. These factors include: the existence of a well-resourced, dedicated investigator and prosecutor; the provision of adequate powers of investigation for the relevant enforcers; the willingness of judges (and, where relevant, juries) to convict cartelists; the existence of political and public support; and the imposition of corporate fines in addition to custodial sentences.[1] One of the most important factors impacting upon effectiveness, however, is the actual definition of the criminal cartel offence.[2] The recent experiences with the UK Cartel Offence demonstrate that a poorly drafted cartel offence can be detrimental to the operation of a successful criminal cartel regime. In that particular instance, if one is to take the comments of officials from the OFT at face value, the inclusion within the UK Cartel Offence of the definitional element of 'dishonestly' agreeing with another to make or implement (or cause to be made or implemented) a cartel arrangement proved to be too difficult for the OFT to overcome in practice, resulting in a relatively poor enforcement record.[3] More specifically, 'the definition of the offence, and particularly the need to prove dishonesty on the part of defendants' was criticized as 'artificially' limiting 'the scope of cases that can be brought' and making 'those cases disproportionately difficult to prove'.[4] What needs to be ensured, in fact, is that the criminal cartel offence is designed in such a way as to facilitate the achievement of its enforcement objectives (deterrence and/or retribution) in practice, while respecting the relevant legalities. This is not an easy task. To ensure that resources are not wasted on an ineffective regime, it would be best for the issue of definition to be considered very early on in the process of antitrust criminalization, 'preferably at the same time that the general question of whether to criminalize is considered'.[5]

This book has already considered a number of different issues that are relevant to the process of creating an acceptable definition for a criminal cartel offence. In Chapter 1, it was noted that the OECD's definition of 'cartel activity' in its 1998 Recommendation would be employed in this book as a working definition of 'cartel activity'. The reason for this was that the OECD definition has a number of important merits: 'clarity and simplicity, while covering what are agreed to be the principal categories of anti-competitive strategy, but also linking the agreement of anti-competitive purpose with its material realisation'.[6] It also limits the definition of 'cartel activity' to agreements, concerted

1 Wils (2006b), 87–90. See also the discussion in Chapter 10 of this book.

2 See: Harding (2002), 417; and Harding and Joshua (2010), 340–2.

3 See: Branch (2013), 15; and Nikpay (2012), 19–23. See also Riley (2010b), 277.

4 BIS (2011), [6.6].

5 Beaton-Wells (2009), 3–4.

6 Harding (2004), 279. Cf. ICN (2005), 11–12.

practices, or arrangements that are horizontal in nature, thereby ensuring that their vertical counterparts (which often display efficiency-enhancing properties) are excluded. By relying upon the OECD's definition, Chapter 1 established the general concept of 'cartel activity' to be utilized in this book. Chapter 4 employed that particular definition and analysed the moral qualities of cartel activity, in the process considering the potential for a retribution-based criminalization argument. In doing so, it provided an examination of the issues of culpability and moral wrongfulness. As explained in Chapter 4, both of these issues have the potential to affect the mens rea of the criminal cartel offence: to ensure sufficient culpability in a criminal cartel offence (in order for retribution to be achieved), certain choices need to be made concerning the level of mens rea and its target; and to ensure that the criminal cartel offence necessarily encompasses the moral wrongfulness of cartel activity, one could design the cartel offence in such a way that it captures the violation of any of the norms against stealing, deception, or cheating. For its part, Chapter 7 acknowledged that there is a legal requirement for European law-makers to ensure that, in creating a criminal cartel offence, sufficient clarity exists in its definition so that individuals will know in advance whether their anticipated conduct will violate the criminal law. As was demonstrated in that chapter, this requirement can restrict the choices that can be made regarding the definition of the cartel offence.

As noted in Chapter 1,[7] this book does not attempt to provide a definitive definition to be used in any European jurisdiction that is considering introducing criminal cartel sanctions. The author has left that particular task to legislators. It is hoped, however, that such legislators will find the analyses contained in this book to be of use. What this book aims to do in fact is to provide analysis of the main theoretical, legal, and practical challenges for European antitrust criminalization. Admittedly, the book would not fulfil this aim if it did not consider some of the most significant challenges that need to be met when designing a criminal cartel offence within Europe; hence the motivation for the current chapter. What remain to be considered in this book concerning the definition of a criminal cartel offence are the following two problematic issues, both of which must be understood (if not resolved) by legislatures that are serious about the effective enforcement of their criminal cartel laws.

First, the impact of Regulation 1/2003 on the design and operation of a national cartel offence needs to be articulated. This is an issue which is unique to the EU Member States. It is also a very important one. Other jurisdictions clearly have the option of designing their criminal cartel offences from 'basic principles',[8] but, as will become apparent below, such an option may be restricted in practice in the EU Member States if Regulation 1/2003 applies to the enforcement of the national criminal cartel law. The extent to which Regulation 1/2003 impacts upon the definition of the national cartel offence clearly needs to be understood by those who wish to ensure that the national cartel offence achieves its objectives in practice: the definition of the offence in question is, as noted above, crucial to the effectiveness of cartel criminalization. In addition to this, there may be additional good reasons not related to the definition of the offence why one might wish to ensure that Regulation 1/2003 does not apply to the enforcement of the national cartel offence.[9] If so, conscientious legislators should know what is required in drafting the offence to avoid the operation of Regulation 1/2003: with that knowledge, the option of circumventing Regulation 1/2003 will be available to them (should they

[7] See Chapter 1, Section C(b) of this book.

[8] See, e.g., Ministry of Economic Development (2010), [4.3].

[9] See Whelan (2012b), 598–9.

wish to pursue it). There are therefore two sub-issues here: (i) assuming Regulation 1/2003 applies to the enforcement of the national cartel offence, how does it impact on the definition and operation of the cartel offence in question?; and (ii) how should a national criminal cartel offence be designed to avoid the application of Regulation 1/2003 (and its impact on the design and operation of the criminal cartel offence)? This subject has received scant treatment in the literature on European antitrust criminalization. Given the importance of this matter, this situation should be rectified.

Second, the legislature which is responsible for drafting a given national criminal cartel law is required to make a decision about how to deal with 'acceptable' (i.e. legitimate and/or efficiency-enhancing) cartel activity. If the OECD definition of cartel activity noted in Chapter 1 were to be used to construct a national criminal cartel offence, it is likely that the resulting offence would be too broadly drawn.[10] One of the reasons for this is that some types of cartels may generate efficiencies that ultimately benefit consumers and that can only be created through the cartel activity or agreement in question. While this is a rare occurrence, the fact of the matter is that civil competition regimes often provide for the legal possibility of an exemption or exception for cartel activity that provides net benefits to society. This is the case with Article 101 TFEU, for example. If one reads the 1998 OECD Recommendation in full, one can see that there is in fact express recognition that 'acceptable' cartel activity may exist:

> the hard core cartel category does not include agreements, concerted practices, or arrangements that (i) are reasonably related to the lawful realisation of cost-reducing or output-enhancing efficiencies, (ii) are excluded directly or indirectly from the coverage of a Member country's own laws, or (iii) are authorised in accordance with those laws.[11]

The challenge for the drafters of a criminal cartel offence is how to ensure that 'acceptable' cartel activity is carved out of the criminal offence without making the offence unworkable in practice. This is an important issue and one which has troubled a number of jurisdictions which have contemplated the introduction of criminal cartel sanctions; hence it deserves treatment in a book dedicated to the analysis of the practical challenges of antitrust criminalization.

What is deemed in this book to be the 'first (practical) challenge of design' for European antitrust criminalization encompasses both of the problematic issues noted directly above. This chapter aims to contribute to the current literature by analysing 'the first (practical) challenge of design'. It is divided into two substantive sections and a conclusion. Section B considers the potential (negative) impact of Regulation 1/2003 on the design and operation of a national criminal cartel offence and what can be done to reduce the scope for such impact in this context. In doing so, it: (i) makes the assumption that Regulation 1/2003 applies to the enforcement of a given national cartel offence and examines how it can impact upon the definition and the operation of the national criminal cartel offence; and (ii) analyses the assumption made concerning the application of Regulation 1/2003 and, in the process, examines how the national criminal cartel offence can be designed so as to reduce the scope for any impact of the Regulation in question. Section C considers how the issue of 'acceptable' cartel activity can be dealt with in the context of European antitrust criminalization. In doing so, it articulates the central dilemma regarding the issue of 'acceptable' cartel activity by explaining how EU competition law currently deals with this issue and why that approach may not be ideal in a criminal law setting. It then critiques the role that the definitional element of 'dishonesty' can play in resolving the issue of 'acceptable' cartel activity and examines the recent

[10] Pickford (2002), 36. [11] OECD (1998), [2(b)].

UK consultation on the reform of the UK Cartel Offence in order to propose an additional (workable) mechanism for ensuring that a criminal cartel offence is not too broadly drafted. Finally, Section D provides a number of conclusions on both of the problematic issues considered and hence articulates 'the first (practical) challenge of design' in this context.

B. Controlling the Potential (Negative) Impact of Regulation 1/2003

This section considers the (negative) impact of Regulation 1/2003 on the design and operation of a national criminal cartel offence and what can be done to reduce the scope for such an impact in this context. It is divided into two sub-sections. Sub-section (a) makes the assumption that Regulation 1/2003 applies to the enforcement of a given national cartel offence and examines how it can impact upon the definition and the operation of the national criminal cartel offence. Sub-section (b) analyses the assumption made in the earlier sub-section and, in the process, examines how the national criminal cartel offence can be designed so as to reduce the scope for any impact of Regulation 1/2003.

(a) Regulation 1/2003's potential impact on the definition and operation of the national criminal cartel offence

Regulation 1/2003 was adopted in order, inter alia, to decentralize the enforcement of EU competition and to clarify the relationship between the enforcement of EU competition law and the enforcement of national competition law. Regulation 1/2003 abolished the centralized notification and authorization system established under Regulation 17/62 and replaced it with a system whereby Articles 101 and 102 TFEU would be directly applicable in full,[12] with the Commission, the NCAs, and the national courts having the power to apply those particular provisions of EU law.[13] The main underlying rationales for the 'modernization' of EU competition law through Regulation 1/2003 were to increase the application of Articles 101 and 102 TFEU at Member State level and to allow the Commission to prioritize its resources in those particular areas of competition policy where it can contribute significantly to the enforcement of the EU competition law rules.[14] Regulation 1/2003 provides some scope for a potential (problematic) impact on the definition of the national criminal cartel offence as a result of its Article 3. The actual operation of the national criminal cartel offence can also arguably be (negatively) influenced as a result of, inter alia, Articles 11(6) and 35 of the Regulation.[15]

[12] Council of the European Union (2003), Recital 4 and Article 1.

[13] See, e.g., Council of the European Union (2003), Articles 4, 5, and 6.

[14] De Smijter and Kjølbye (2007), 89–91.

[15] Other articles of Regulation 1/2003 also have the potential to impact negatively upon the operation of the criminal cartel offence, such as the article imposing an obligation on the NCAs to inform the Commission in writing after commencing the first formal investigative measure in applying Article 101 TFEU: Article 11(3). See, e.g., European Commission (2005a), 3–4. However, it is submitted that Articles 11(6) and 35 provide a sufficient illustration of the potential (problematic) impact of Regulation 1/2003 for present purposes. In addition, there may be disadvantages for the criminalized regime if Regulation 1/2003 *does not apply*; for example: 'it would not be possible to use Articles [sic.] 12 or 22 of the Regulation as a legal basis for exchanging information with and/or requesting or granting assistance in investigations to other competition authorities': Lowe (2007), 97. This point is not

(i) Impact on definition: Article 3

Article 3(1) of Regulation 1/2003 provides that when the NCAs or national courts apply 'national competition law' to agreements, decisions by associations of undertakings, or concerted practices[16] within the meaning of Article 101(1) TFEU *which may affect trade between Member States* within the meaning of that provision, they shall also apply Article 101 TFEU to such agreements, etc. As a result, when there is no effect on trade, Member States may apply their national competition laws without applying Article 101 TFEU; but when there is an actual or potential effect on trade and Member States are applying their national competition law to the agreement, etc., then they must also apply Article 101 TFEU to that agreement, etc. This particular rule ensures that parallel application of both EU competition law and national competition law is legally possible following the adoption of Regulation 1/2003,[17] just like it had been under Regulation 17/62.[18] It also ensures that 'the EU competition rules are applied to all cases within their scope and are not avoided by applying only national law'.[19] According to Recital 8 of Regulation 1/2003, Article 3(1) helps to ensure 'the effective enforcement of the Community competition rules and the proper functioning of the cooperation mechanisms contained in this Regulation'.

From Article 3(1) of Regulation 1/2003 it is clear that the concept of 'effect on trade' plays a central role in determining the jurisdictional extent of EU competition law: it is the concept that draws the 'boundary line' between national competition enforcement where EU competition law does not play a part and national competition law enforcement where EU competition law must play a part.[20] Given that the concept of 'effect on trade' has only a jurisdictional role to play, it 'has been interpreted broadly, although it is accepted that the EU has no jurisdiction over cases in which the effects of an agreement . . . are confined to one Member State'.[21] According to the Court of Justice, to establish the requisite effect on trade 'it must be possible to foresee with a sufficient degree of probability on the basis of a set of objective factors of law or of fact that the agreement in question may have an influence, direct or indirect, actual or potential, on the pattern of trade between Member States'.[22] According to Marco Colino, as a practical issue 'it will not be difficult to show that most transactions of any real size are capable of affecting trade between Member States', and that an 'extreme reading' of the Court of Justice's pronouncements on this concept 'would permit the application of EU law to almost any situation'.[23]

Article 3(2) of Regulation 1/2003 contains the so-called 'convergence rule', whereby the application of national competition law may not lead to the prohibition of agreements, etc. which may affect trade between Member States but which do not restrict

developed here, however, as the aim of this section is to analyse the *negative* impact of Regulation 1/2003 on the enforcement of the national criminal cartel offence.

16 In the remainder of this chapter, the phrase 'agreements, decisions by associations of undertakings or concerted practices' has been shorted to 'agreements, etc.'.

17 De Smijter and Kjølbye (2007), 96.

18 See Case 14/68, *Walt Wilhelm v. Bundeskartellamt* [1969] ECR 1, [9] (where it was held that national competition law enforcement could occur so long as it did not 'prejudice the full and uniform application of Community law or the effects of measures taken or to be taken to implement it').

19 Rose and Bailey (2013), 64. See also Wils (2005a), 41.

20 Case 22/78, *Hugin Kassaregister AB and Hugin Cash Registers Ltd v. Commission* [1979] ECR 1869, [17].

21 Jones and Sufrin (2011), 178.

22 Case 56/65, *Société La Technique Minière Ulm v. Maschinenbau* [1966] ECR 235, 249. See also European Commission (2004b).

23 Marco Colino (2011), 52–3.

competition within the meaning of Article 101(1) TFEU, which fulfil the conditions of Article 101(3) TFEU, or which are covered by a Regulation for the application of Article 101(3) TFEU (a so-called 'block exemption Regulation'). This effectively means that if there is an effect on trade and national competition law is being applied alongside EU competition law, then national competition law cannot treat agreements, etc. more strictly than EU competition law. Article 3(2) is a 'directly applicable rule that can be relied on before national courts, which implies that any measure adopted in breach of that rule would be inapplicable and unenforceable'.[24] The decentralization of the enforcement of the EU competition law rules is therefore 'compensated with the obligation imposed on national courts to set aside divergent national rules where the jurisdictional criteria of Community law are met'.[25] The idea here is that Article 3(2) 'eliminates legal uncertainty coming out of concurrent application of national and Community law and directly contradicts fears of renationalisation' of competition law rules in the EU.[26] That said, Article 3(2) does not prevent stricter national competition laws from being applied to unilateral conduct, and there are further exceptions provided in Article 3(3).[27]

Assuming that Regulation 1/2003 applies to the criminal cartel offence, it is arguable that Articles 3(1) and 3(2) can influence the content of a national criminal cartel offence, if only in those circumstances where there is an effect on trade due to the cartel in question. The argument runs as follows. If there is an effect on trade between Member States due to the cartel which forms the substance of the criminal prosecution, then the national authority enforcing the cartel offence must also apply Article 101 TFEU: Article 3(1). In doing so, the national authority cannot allow for the application of the national cartel offence to result in a stricter prohibition of the cartel than would occur under Article 101 TFEU: Article 3(2). If the (criminal) cartel in question would not have violated the prohibition in Article 101(1) TFEU, would have fulfilled the criteria of Article 101(3) TFEU, or would have been covered by a block exemption, then it could not form the subject matter for the national criminal sanction. EU law, in other words, can ensure that the national cartel offence is restricted in its application when there is an effect on trade: the scope of the national cartel offence can be affected.

This particular argument, if accepted, is problematic for national criminal cartel enforcement for a number of reasons. First, it makes the concept of 'effect on trade' relevant in a criminal trial. If EU competition law would be less strict in terms of prohibiting the cartel than the national cartel offence, it would be in the interests of the defendant to argue that his cartel had an actual or potential effect on trade, in the hope that the criminal judge would apply the 'convergence rule' in Article 3(2) in his favour. In fact, given how broadly this concept is defined, it is not unlikely that a defendant would try to rely upon it to secure a more lenient treatment in the criminal courts. This should be avoided. Indeed, the undesirability of having the effect on trade criterion analysed in a court of law was one of the reasons why the parallel application of national and EU competition law is allowed[28] and why the Commission's original legislative proposal for exclusive application of Article 101 TFEU to agreements, etc. having an effect on trade was not followed.[29] Second, it opens the way for economic arguments to be made in the context

[24] European Commission (2009c), 49. [25] Boskovits (2010), 99.

[26] Pijetlovic (2004), 360.

[27] Article 3(3) will be considered below when the assumption that Regulation 1/2003 applies to a cartel offence is considered; see Chapter 8, Section B(b) of this book.

[28] See De Smijter and Kjølbye (2007), 98.

[29] See European Commission (2000), Article 3.

of a criminal trial, something that the legislator may have been keen to avoid in drafting the criminal cartel offence in such a way that it does not require a finding of a violation of Article 101 TFEU. In particular, it brings in the Article 101(3) 'defence' through the back door (if it is not expressly contained in the national criminal cartel offence)[30] and (on the assumption that the national criminal cartel offence does not contain a de minimis requirement) also provides additional scope for a defendant to argue that the cartel in question would not have had an appreciable effect on competition, as only agreements, etc. with an appreciable effect on competition are prohibited under Article 101(1) TFEU.[31] Harding and Joshua seem to acknowledge this type of problem when they posit that, with the enforcement of the UK Cartel Offence, 'there is still some possibility that the defence in criminal proceedings could exploit a potential "Euro-defence" (i.e. raise some doubt as to whether there was a violation of Article 101)'.[32] Finally, by allowing Regulation 1/2003 to dictate the content of the cartel offence (in particular, by requiring it to provide a defence in the form of Article 101(3) TFEU), the criminalized jurisdiction may be restricted in its ability to generate a moral norm against cartel activity in the hope that cartelists will internalize the norm, thereby reducing the cost of criminal cartel enforcement. When a defence along the lines of Article 101(3) TFEU is provided, it may well foster an (arguably already existing) perception among EU citizens that competition law enforcement (including its criminal variant) is about 'satisfying somewhat technical and arcane regulations rather than about preventing conspiracies that cost EU consumers large amounts of money'.[33] The existence of Article 101(3) TFEU as a defence in a criminal cartel regime communicates the message that the criminality of cartel activity (in particular its moral wrongfulness) is ambiguous.

(ii) Impact on operation: Articles 11(6) and 35

Article 11(6) of Regulation 1/2003 contains the European Commission's power to withdraw a case from the national competition authorities. The provision stipulates that the 'initiation by the Commission of proceedings for the adoption of a decision under Chapter III [of Regulation 1/2003] shall relieve the competition authorities of the Member States of their competence to apply' Articles 101 and 102 TFEU. It further provides that if an NCA is 'already acting on a case, the Commission shall only initiate proceedings after consulting' with that NCA. As noted in Recital 35 of Regulation 1/2003, the effects of Article 11(6) apply to all NCAs (which can include courts), but there is an exception to the general rule: 'where a prosecuting authority brings a case before a separate judicial authority, Article 11(6) should apply to the prosecuting authority subject to the conditions of Article 35(4)'. Article 35(4) therefore ensures that Member States can arrange their national procedures 'so as formally to avoid the Commission withdrawing a case from a national court in circumstances where cases are brought before the court

30 Cf. Furse (2012), 122.

31 To prove a violation of Article 101(1) TFEU, the relevant enforcer is required to demonstrate that the restriction of competition involved is an 'appreciable' one; see: Case 5/69, *Völk v. Vervaecke* [1969] ECR 295; and European Commission (2001b), particularly [7].

32 Harding and Joshua (2010), 348. Admittedly, while their comment is located in a section in their book entitled 'Problems at the interface with European law', it may be explained on the basis that a Euro-defence could be understood as flowing merely from the use of the definitional element of 'dishonesty' in the UK Cartel Offence (rather than from Articles 3(1) and (2) of Regulation 1/2003). Either way, their anxiety about the existence of a Euro-defence is equivalent in nature to that identified above.

33 Massey (2004), 32.

by a prosecutor'[34] (as a criminal cartel case would surely be). In addition, Article 11(6) does not apply to courts if they are acting as review courts: Article 35(3). Guidance on the operation of Article 11(6) is provided in the Commission Notice which is dedicated to the issue of cooperation with the NCAs.[35]

The existence of Article 11(6), which is generally understood to be 'central to the functioning of Regulation 1/2003',[36] can be rationalized on the basis of the consistent application of the EU competition law rules: 'If the competition rules are to be applied consistently and, at the same time, the network [i.e. the ECN] is to be managed in the best possible way, it is essential to retain the rule that the competition authorities are automatically relieved of their competence if the Commission initiates its own proceedings'.[37] From a reading of the Regulation as a whole (including Article 3(1) thereof), it is clear that Article 11(6) relieves the NCA not only of its power to enforce EU competition law, but also of its power to enforce national competition law.[38] However, following the conclusion of the Commission's proceedings, there is a revival of the relevant NCA's jurisdiction to apply both EU competition law and its national law,[39] subject to the obligation in Article 16 of Regulation 1/2003 not to adopt a decision which runs counter to the findings of the Commission.[40] The ability of the Commission under Article 11(6) to restrict the competence of the NCAs to enforce competition law is 'a powerful weapon' and one which gives the Commission 'considerable leverage over an NCA when it disapproves of the decision it is about to adopt'.[41] That said, to this author's knowledge, Article 11(6) has not been used to date to 'correct' the approach of a Member State.[42]

If Regulation 1/2003 applies to the enforcement of a national cartel offence, then Article 11(6) of the Regulation has the potential to influence the operation of that national offence.[43] Specifically the Commission, in theory at least, would hold the power to relieve the prosecuting authority of its competence to lead a criminal cartel prosecution in front of a criminal court, in effect bringing the national criminal proceedings to an end. This is a relatively uncomplicated conclusion, provided of course that the assumption is correct that Regulation 1/2003 applies to the enforcement of the national cartel offence in the first place. However, when *private* criminal prosecutions are allowed under the national regime, the situation becomes more complicated. Indeed, it might be argued that it is at least questionable whether Article 11(6) could bring the national criminal proceedings to a close when a private criminal prosecution is at issue concerning the national cartel offence: the private prosecutor would not exactly be a 'competition authority' in the literal sense of the phrase and would therefore not be subject to the dictates of Article 11(6), which relieves the *competition authorities of the Member States* of their competence to apply Article 101 TFEU. It would all depend on whether: (a) the criminal court would be deemed to be a national competition authority for the purposes of Article 11(6) of Regulation 1/2003; and (b) Article 35(4) of that Regulation would be applicable in the context of a private prosecution. The criminal court could certainly

[34] De Smijter and Kjølbye (2007), 162. It seems in fact that Article 35(4) 'was introduced to accommodate the sensitivities of certain Member States where the first decision-maker is a court': De Smijter and Kjølbye (2007), 162.

[35] See European Commission (2004a), [50]–[57].

[36] Whish and Bailey (2012), 265.

[37] Council of the European Union (2003), Recital 17.

[38] Case C-17/10, *Toshiba Corp. v. Czech Competition Authority*, Judgment of 14 February 2012, not yet reported, [72] et seq.

[39] See Case C-17/10, *Toshiba Corp. v. Czech Competition Authority*, Judgment of 14 February 2012, not yet reported, [79]–[80].

[40] Rose and Bailey (2013), 1173.

[41] Jones and Sufrin (2011), 1162.

[42] See also European Commission (2009c), 76–7.

[43] Wils appears to agree: Wils (2006b), 73.

be a national competition authority, as Article 35(1) of the Regulation provides that the designated authorities 'may include courts'. Whether a given national criminal court would be a designated national competition authority would, of course, depend on the actions of the Member State in question regarding its designation of its national competition authorities.[44] In addition, it seems very likely, given its wording, that Article 35(4) would not be relevant, therefore allowing for Article 11(6) to apply directly to the criminal court in the context of a private prosecution (provided that the court were a designated authority for the purpose of that latter Article). Article 35(4) essentially provides that, where the 'authority' prosecuting the case is separate from the judicial authority deciding the case, then the direct effects of Article 11(6) shall be limited to that authority prosecuting the case. But Article 11(6), as was noted, only applies to the 'competition authorities of the Member States'. Relying upon this fact, one can argue that the term 'authority' in Article 35(4) actually means a (public) national competition authority, and therefore that Article 35(4) has no bearing on the operation of Article 11(6) in the context of a private criminal investigation. To this author, this seems the most sensible interpretation.

The argument that Article 11(6) can influence the operation of a criminal cartel offence may not be a mere academic argument. Its effects can possibly be detected in the approach to criminal cartel enforcement adopted in Ireland, a jurisdiction with a criminal cartel offence that is clearly based upon the specific wording of Article 101(1) TFEU. Massey and Cooke note that Irish criminal cartel enforcement has focused entirely on relatively localized businesses, and that this particular enforcement policy is unlikely to change for a number of reasons, chief of which is the potential impact of Regulation 1/2003 when larger, perhaps EU-wide cartels are prosecuted.[45] While Massey and Cooke do not mention Article 11(6) and instead focus their energies on highlighting that Article 3 of Regulation 1/2003 will require the enforcement of Article 101 TFEU alongside the national cartel offence contained in Section 4 of the Competition Act 2002 (if there is an effect on trade between Member States), their analysis can nonetheless be extended to Article 11(6). In short, the focus on domestic cartels could well be explained by a desire to avoid the cooperation mechanisms in Regulation 1/2003 (which come into play as a result of Article 3 thereof), including the specific cooperation mechanism contained in Article 11(6).

Another provision of Regulation 1/2003 that can impact upon the operation of a national cartel offence is Article 35(1). That particular Article provides that the 'Member States shall designate the competition authority or authorities responsible for the application of [Articles 101 and 102 TFEU] in such a way that the provisions of [Regulation 1/2003] are effectively complied with'. The argument here is that if the criminal courts are not in fact designated as competition authorities for the purposes of Regulation 1/2003, and EU competition law must be applied if the national cartel offence is being enforced (due to the existence of an effect on trade), then those criminal courts will not have the jurisdiction to apply EU competition law and therefore will not have the jurisdiction to apply the national cartel offence. This type of argument was presented by counsel in the prosecution by the UK Office of Fair Trading of BA executives accused of fixing fuel surcharges on long-haul flights contrary to Section 188 of the Enterprise Act 2002.[46] It relies upon the assumption that only those national

44 If the criminal court is not a 'designated' competition authority under Regulation 1/2003, another issue arises: whether the criminal court could in fact enforce Article 101 TFEU at all. This issue is considered directly below.

45 Massey and Cooke (2011), 128. See also Furse (2012), 187.

46 *IB v. The Queen* [2009] EWCA Crim 2575, [19].

competition authorities and/or national courts designated as competition authorities for the purpose of Regulation 1/2003 have the competence to enforce the provisions of EU competition law. The Court of Appeal in the *IB* case rejected the defendants' argument that the Crown Court did not have the jurisdiction to rule on whether the UK Cartel Offence was committed due to the fact that the Crown Court had not been designated as a competition authority for the purposes of Regulation 1/2003.[47] In so ruling, the Court of Appeal noted that there was nothing in the Regulation itself which states that only a designated competition authority has the competence to enforce EU competition law and that it 'makes excellent sense' for the directly effective Regulation to enable the Member States to enforce the EU competition law rules without the need for domestic legislation.[48] While this appears to be a sensible approach to the issue, it is obviously not the end of the matter for European antitrust criminalization. Only a ruling from the Court of Justice in a preliminary reference request would put this question to rest once and for all. If it were required to rule on this issue, it would be advised to follow the lead of the Court of Appeal, particularly if it wished to see national criminal cartel enforcement develop without complicating matters by requiring the designation of the Member States' criminal courts as national competition authorities.

(b) Dealing with the potential impact through legislative drafting

To minimize the problematic impact of Regulation 1/2003 on the content and the operation of the national criminal cartel offence, one could, from the outset, base the criminal cartel offence completely on the cartel prohibition in Article 101(1) TFEU and allow for a defence based on Article 101(3) TFEU. In other words, one could link the cartel offence to the EU-level cartel prohibition, thereby avoiding the operation of the 'convergence rule' in a criminal trial. This would ensure that from the very creation of the criminal cartel offence one can be certain of its elements and of any potential defence to its commission. Regulation 1/2003, then, would not throw up nasty surprises for the prosecution in the context of a criminal trial, such as providing for the introduction of the defence of Article 101(3) TFEU through the back door when an effect on trade between Member States can be identified. This, of course, brings with it the disadvantage of dealing with such a defence in a criminal trial as well as the requirement to prove, inter alia, that the cartel agreement had an appreciable effect on competition. It introduces the potential, then, for economic evidence to be considered as part of the criminal trial, something that legislatures can be keen to avoid.[49] Indeed, creating a national 'stand-alone' criminal cartel offence (applicable to individual cartelists) which does not include an exemption/exception-type defence and which does not contain a de minimis requirement acknowledges in effect that Article 101 TFEU 'is ill-suited to form the basis of a criminal charge'[50] and helps to ensure that the criminal cartel offence is underpinned by moral norms which are simple and unequivocal, i.e. of the 'thou shalt not' variety, thereby facilitating educative efforts.[51] In fact, for related reasons, Ireland has been criticized for not adopting such an approach when it introduced criminal antitrust sanctions.[52] To avoid any argument concerning lack of competence based on Article 35(1) of Regulation 1/2003, the criminalized jurisdiction would also be advised to designate the

[47] *IB v. The Queen* [2009] EWCA Crim 2575, [38].
[48] *IB v. The Queen* [2009] EWCA Crim 2575, [38].
[49] See, e.g.: BIS (2012), [6.9]; and DTI (2001b), [7.30].
[50] Joshua (2001).
[51] See Stucke (2006), 527.
[52] Massey (2004), 38.

criminal courts as national competition authorities for the purposes of the Regulation. Of course, all of these measures are also inherently limited in that they do not remove the (theoretical) possibility for the Commission to use Article 11(6) to take jurisdiction over the criminal cartel case from the criminal court.

Central to the potential impact of Regulation 1/2003 is the concept of effect on trade. Where there is no effect on trade between Member States due to the cartel under investigation, then the EU competition law rules will not be applied (even if Regulation 1/2003 itself applies to the enforcement of the national cartel offence) and the problems due to the potential application of Regulation 1/2003 could be avoided. If one were very concerned about the negative impact of Regulation 1/2003, one might be inclined to argue for the creation of a criminal cartel offence that only applies to those cartels which do not have an effect on trade. But such an approach would be on very dodgy legal ground, so to speak. This is due to the principle of equivalence,[53] a general principle of EU law which, broadly speaking, ensures that the penalties provided under national law for the violation of Article 101 TFEU 'must at least be equivalent in effectiveness and dissuasiveness to the sanctions they provide for comparable violations of their national laws'.[54] Where criminal sanctions for violation of Article 101 TFEU were not available (due to the existence of an effect on trade) and such sanctions would be available under national competition law (albeit only when there is no effect on trade), the criminal cartel law would arguably violate the principle of effectiveness contrary to the dictates of EU law, provided of course that the criminal cartel offence could be understood as a violation comparable to Article 101 TFEU for the purposes of that particular principle. This would only be so, of course, where it can be established that imprisonment for cartel activity is a more effective and dissuasive sanction than the (non-custodial) sanction provided in national law for violation of Article 101 TFEU.[55]

If one wished to avoid the impact of Regulation 1/2003 without running the risk of violating the principle of equivalence, one could simply follow the (apparent) Irish enforcement policy and ensure that the cartels prosecuted by the authority are always local in nature and do not have an effect on trade. This would ensure autonomy in practice for the criminalized jurisdiction over the content and operation of the criminal cartel offence, but unfortunately it would also bring with it a number of problems concerning the achievement of the underlying criminal enforcement objectives. For a start, if business executives are aware of such an enforcement policy, then they will be incentivized to engage in cartel activity on a large scale (which ensures an obvious effect on trade) as they will know that criminal sanctions will not be pursued against them. This clearly reduces the deterrent effect of the law. Indeed, as noted during the Committee stage of the passage of the UK Cartel Offence through Parliament:

> Running the risk of sending small offenders to prison or fining them heavily, and of subjecting large offenders to civil rather than criminal sanctions makes a nonsense of the deterrence argument.[56]

Such a policy would also cause problems with the achievement of retribution, as the most serious cartels (i.e. those with an effect on trade and, therefore, presumably with

[53] See, e.g., Case C-231/96, *Edilizia Industriale Siderurgica Srl (Edis) v. Ministero delle Finanze* [1998] ECR I-4951, [36].

[54] Wils (2006b), 72.

[55] On the effectiveness of imprisonment as a method of achieving the underlying enforcement aims of antitrust law, see Chapters 3 and 4 of this book.

[56] Nigel Waterson MP, House of Commons Debates, 10 April 2002, Column 152. This point is also made in Joshua (2011), footnote 83.

the highest degrees of social harmfulness) would not be subjected to criminal punishment, unlike the less serious, localized cartels. Such an enforcement policy would clearly not be ideal. What would be better would be for the criminalized jurisdiction to ensure that Regulation 1/2003 did not apply at all to the enforcement of the national criminal cartel offence.

All of the above discussion of the potential impact of Regulation 1/2003 has proceeded on the assumption that Regulation 1/2003 would apply to the enforcement of the national cartel offence in the first place. It is clear that the impact of Article 3, 11(6), or 35 will only be felt if the Regulation actually applies to the enforcement of the national criminal cartel offence: if the national cartel offence is not subject to Regulation 1/2003, then of course it is not subject to its Articles, and the problems of the impact of Regulation 1/2003 will not exist. In order to provide an insight into how one should draft a criminal cartel offence in order to avoid the application of Regulation 1/2003, one should of course understand when that particular Regulation would indeed apply to a criminal cartel offence; indeed, with this knowledge one can try to shape the national cartel offence so that Regulation 1/2003 does not apply to it, thereby avoiding the problems associated with Articles 3, 11(6), and 35. For this reason, the assumption in question needs to be analysed in detail.

Central to the resolution of the issue as to whether Regulation 1/2003 applies to the enforcement of a national cartel offence are Recitals 8 and 9 and Article 3(3) of the Regulation. Recital 8 provides, inter alia, that Regulation 1/2003 'does not apply to national laws which impose criminal sanctions on natural persons except to the extent that such sanctions are the means whereby competition rules applying to undertakings are enforced'.[57] Recital 9 states that Regulation 1/2003, which has been adopted to implement Articles 101 and 102 TFEU,

> does not preclude Member States from implementing on their territory national legislation, which protects other legitimate interests provided that such legislation is compatible with general principles and other provisions of Community law. In so far as such national legislation pursues predominantly an objective different from that of protecting competition on the market, the competition authorities and courts of the Member States may apply such legislation on their territory.

Article 3(3) provides, inter alia, that without prejudice to general principles and other provisions of EU law, Articles 3(1) and 3(2) of Regulation 1/2003 'do not preclude the application of provisions of national law that predominantly pursue an objective different from that pursued by' Articles 101 and 102 TFEU.

One possible reading of these provisions is that a national criminal cartel offence which only applies to individuals and which, therefore, does not apply to undertakings (corporations) is not subjected at all to Regulation 1/2003. This is the position adopted by the OFT in its understanding of whether Regulation 1/2003 applies to the enforcement of the UK Cartel Offence,[58] a position that appears to be supported by a number of academics.[59] The argument depends upon a rather restricted and literal interpretation of the relevant sentence in Recital 8. The OFT argued in effect that as the Cartel Offence only targets individuals, it is not a means by which competition rules applying to undertakings are enforced;[60] consequently, as a result of Recital 8, Regulation 1/2003 does not

[57] For the purpose of this chapter, this phrase is referred to as 'the relevant sentence in Recital 8'.

[58] See OFT (2004c), [4.21]–[4.22]. See also Bloom (2002b), 59, who at the time was the Director of Competition Enforcement at the OFT, commenting on a draft of Regulation 1/2003 (that contained the same phrase as the relevant sentence in Recital 8).

[59] See, e.g.: Riley (2003), 606–7; and Furse and Nash (2004a), 9–10. See, however, Furse's reconsideration of this issue in Furse (2012), 124 et seq.

[60] OFT (2004c), [4.21].

apply to it.[61] The point here is that the term 'means whereby competition rules applying to undertakings are enforced' is understood as implying a requirement that undertakings be subjected to the criminal cartel offence alongside individuals. Where undertakings cannot be made subject to criminal proceedings for cartel activity, so the argument runs, the criminal cartel offence cannot be understood as a 'means whereby competition rules applying to undertakings are enforced'. This interpretation has the advantage of simplicity: if one wishes to avoid any impact of Regulation 1/2003 on the operation and content of the national criminal cartel offence, all one has to do is to ensure that it applies to individuals and not to undertakings. However, such an interpretation can be criticized on the basis that it not only ignores the fact that undertakings can in some circumstances be constituted by a mere individual (provided they are carrying out an economic activity),[62] but also that it gives too much importance to what is admittedly merely a Recital (as opposed to an Article) in the Regulation. In addition, this type of interpretation of the applicability of Regulation 1/2003 in this context would clearly not be acceptable to those who wish to see the Commission have the power to influence the operation of competition policy in the Member States (even when it is dictated towards individuals as such, rather than undertakings). Indeed, in a 2004 letter addressed to the Director General of the Swedish Competition Authority, the then Director General of DG Competition set out the Commission's thinking on the applicability of Regulation 1/2003 to a proposed Swedish national cartel offence and in the process expressly disavowed the interpretation favoured by the OFT, noting that it 'fail[s] to find any support for such conclusion in the Regulation'.[63]

Another possible reading of the relevant provisions in Regulation 1/2003 is provided by Wils, who argues that the relevant sentence in Recital 8

> merely specifies, with regard to national laws which impose criminal sanctions on natural persons, what already follows from Article 3(3) of Regulation 1/2003, namely that Article 3(1) and (2) of this Regulation do not preclude the application of provisions of national law that predominantly pursue an objective different from that pursued by [Articles 101 and 102 TFEU].[64]

What Wils in effect proposes is that one should interpret the relevant sentence in Recital 8 (which he admittedly, and rightly, finds hard to understand[65]) to mean nothing more than that the national criminal cartel offence must have the same predominant objective as Articles 101 and 102 TFEU for Regulation 1/2003 to apply to it.[66] Wils offers four points in support of his broad interpretation of the true meaning of the phrase 'means whereby competition rules applying to undertakings are enforced'.[67] First, the relevant sentence in Recital 8 is located at the end of the first of the two recitals which accompany Article 3 of Regulation 1/2003.[68] Second, the phrase 'competition rules applying to undertakings' is used in the chapter and section headings which cover Articles 101 and 102 TFEU.[69] Third, it is clear from Article 5, read alongside Article 12(3) of Regulation

[61] OFT (2004c), [4.22].

[62] See, e.g.: *RAI/UNITEL* (Case IV/29.559), Commission Decision, 15 June 1978, [1978] OJ L157/39 (opera singers); and *Reuter/BASF* (Case IV/28.996), Commission Decision, 26 July 1976, [1976] OJ L254/40 (individual inventors). See also the discussion in Chapter 6, Section C(b)(ii)(1) of this book.

[63] European Commission (2005a), 3.

[64] Wils (2006b), 74.

[65] Wils (2005a), 42.

[66] Finding 'difficulty seeing how one could consider that the UK cartel offence predominantly pursues an objective different from that pursued by [Article 101 TFEU]', Wils believes that the UK Cartel Offence should 'be considered a means whereby competition rules to undertakings are enforced': Wils (2006b), 74.

[67] See Wils (2005a), 43.

[68] Wils (2005a), 43.

[69] Wils (2005a), 43.

1/2003, that the Regulation 'applies in principle to all types of penalties which national law may provide for violations of [Articles 101 and 102 TFEU], including criminal sanctions on natural persons'.[70] Finally, the purpose of Article 3 of Regulation 1/2003 (i.e. ensuring that the NCAs or national courts do not circumvent the application of Regulation 1/2003 and, in particular, its cooperation mechanisms) would be undermined if a narrow interpretation of the relevant sentence in Recital 8 were adopted.[71] The European Commission appears to favour Wils's approach. Indeed, it has argued that a Swedish proposal to introduce individual criminal cartel sanctions would have the same objective as the enforcement of Article 101 TFEU and that, therefore, 'the sanctioning of individuals [for cartel activity] would appear to be a means to influence the behaviour of the undertakings', a fact that ensures the applicability of Regulation 1/2003 to the future enforcement of the proposed cartel offence.[72]

There are potential problems, however, with Wils's approach. The first is that Recital 8 and Article 3(3) seem to perform different functions, and therefore interpreting the former of these provisions by relying upon the latter can be questioned. The sentence in Recital 8—whatever it may mean—actually takes the enforcement of the national cartel offence outside of the scope of Regulation 1/2003 as a whole. Article 3(3) does not do this: if its conditions are fulfilled, it merely takes the enforcement of the criminal cartel offence outside of the scope of Articles 3(1) and 3(2). In practice, there may be little difference of course: by removing the requirement to enforce EU competition law, Article 3(3) provides the scope for the national criminal cartel law enforcer to avoid enforcing EU law, thereby ensuring the irrelevance of Regulation 1/2003. Nonetheless, if Recital 8 is indeed to be interpreted in the manner suggested by Wils, one can legitimately inquire why the Regulation should actually contain the statement that Articles 3(1) and 3(2) of Regulation 1/2003 'do not preclude the application of provisions of national law that predominantly pursue an objective different from that pursued by' Articles 101 and 102 TFEU. The answer, however, might lie in the fact that a Recital does not have the same force of law as an Article and that the Article in question is in one respect more extensive than the relevant sentence in Recital 8:[73] it ensures that national laws that predominantly pursue an objective different from that pursued by Articles 101 and 102 TFEU are not subjected to Articles 3(1) and 3(2), *irrespective of whether they impose criminal sanctions on individuals*.

More problematic, however, and particularly so for those who wish to draft a criminal cartel offence to ensure that it lies outside the scope of Regulation 1/2003, is the issue of 'predominant objective'. In fact, Wils's approach begs the question as to what the predominant objective of the provisions of EU competition law actually is. If the predominant objective of EU competition law is to prevent anticompetitive behaviour from occurring in an economy, then it would be very difficult to demonstrate that a criminal cartel offence does not pursue the same objective. If so, the application of Regulation 1/2003 to the enforcement of the national cartel offence would be difficult to avoid (when the cartel activity in question affects trade between Member States). However, by having a rather restricted approach to the identification of the predominant objective of EU competition law, one can ensure that there is sufficient scope to allow for the creation of a national criminal cartel offence that does not engage the operation of Regulation 1/2003—even if one adopts Wils's broad approach to the interpretation of the relevant sentence in Recital 8.

[70] Wils (2005a), 43. [71] Wils (2005a), 43.
[72] European Commission (2005a), 3. [73] Cf. De Smijter and Kjølbye (2007), 111.

What is required, then, if one is to follow Wils's interpretation is a definitive statement on what the predominant purpose of the EU competition rules actually is for the purpose of the relevant provisions (Recitals 8 and 9 and Article 3(3)) in Regulation 1/2003. The EU Courts have not provided a ruling on this issue, but there is an English case that can be useful in this context: *IB v. The Queen*.[74] In that particular case, the Court of Appeal held that the UK Cartel Offence is not a 'national competition law' within the meaning of Article 3(1) of Regulation 1/2003. In coming to this conclusion, the Court held that the test for determining what is a 'national competition law' for this purpose is not 'as broad as whether the law in question pursues the objective of preventing anti-competitive practices'.[75] For it, the mere fact that a national criminal cartel offence is designed to prevent anticompetitive behaviour does not ensure that that particular offence would be considered a 'national competition law' within the meaning of Article 3(1).[76] What is in fact required in order for a criminal cartel offence to be a 'national competition law' is for the enforcement of that criminal offence to have a direct impact on the *validity* of an agreement, decision by an association of undertakings, or concerted practice made by an undertaking: imprisonment of an individual must be part of the process of ruling upon the invalidity of an agreement, etc. made by an undertaking.[77] When, in enforcing a criminal cartel offence, no decision is required from the criminal court on the validity of the underlying cartel agreement, then, according to the Court of Appeal, that criminal cartel offence would not be a 'national competition law' and therefore would not be subject to Article 3(1) of Regulation 1/2003. In coming to this conclusion, the Court highlighted that the aim of Regulation 1/2003 in directly enforcing EU competition law rules is to avoid 'the risk of "limping" agreements, which are enforceable in one jurisdiction and not in another'.[78]

The ruling of the Court of Appeal on the definition of a 'national competition law' could arguably be used for present purposes in order to inform the test as to what the 'predominant objective' of a criminal cartel offence must be in order for Regulation 1/2003 as a whole to apply to its enforcement.[79] In short, if the criminal cartel offence does not require a ruling on the validity of an agreement, etc. entered into by an undertaking, then one can argue that it does not pursue the same predominant objective of the EU competition law rules, and that therefore its enforcement should not be subjected to Regulation 1/2003. This approach would operationalize the interpretation of Recital 8 offered by Wils without allowing for an overly broad definition of the predominant objective of the EU competition law rules (such as the protection of competition on the market). Importantly, such an interpretation of the predominant objective of the EU competition law rules finds some support in Regulation 1/2003 as well as official statements from the Commission. From the first three sentences of Recital 8 of Regulation

[74] *IB v. The Queen* [2009] EWCA Crim 2575. On this case, see: Osepciu (2009); and Whelan (2009c).

[75] *IB v. The Queen* [2009] EWCA Crim 2575, [35].

[76] *IB v. The Queen* [2009] EWCA Crim 2575, [24].

[77] See *IB v. The Queen* [2009] EWCA Crim 2575, [34], [35], and [38].

[78] *IB v. The Queen* [2009] EWCA Crim 2575, [34].

[79] Indeed, the possible link between the term 'national competition law' and the relevant sentence in Recital 8 has been noted in the literature. It has been argued, for example, that if criminal sanctions imposed on natural persons are indeed 'the means whereby competition rules applying to undertakings are enforced', then the relevant provision of national criminal law 'can be classified as belonging to national competition law within the meaning of Article 3': Böge and Bardong (2008), 1546. See also the definition of 'national competition law' put forward in the revised Presidency compromise proposal for a Directive on rules governing national damages actions for infringement of the EU competition law provisions: Council of the European Union (2013), Annex, Article 4(2).

1/2003, for example, it is clear that the 'convergence rule' in Article 3(2) is rationalized on the basis of creating a 'level playing field' for agreements, etc. within the internal market, as has been confirmed by the Commission itself.[80] The point here is that the objective of creating such a 'level playing field' can only be achieved if the enforcement of competition rules requires a ruling on the validity of the underlying agreement, etc. entered into by the undertaking. This type of logic may have found some support in the literature. De Smijter and Kjølbye argue, for example, that a 'criminal offence that applies irrespective of any findings of an infringement on the part of undertakings [which, if Article 101(1) TFEU is involved, inevitably brings with it a ruling on the enforceability of the agreement etc. due to Article 101(2) TFEU] is... deemed not to belong to the sphere of national competition law'.[81] For them, then, criminal sanctions against natural persons will not be the means of enforcing competition rules against undertakings if the criminal offence applies 'irrespective of any finding of an infringement on the part of undertakings'.[82]

However, this approach is not without its problems. One can plausibly argue that the predominant objective of Article 101 TFEU is to ensure that a 'level playing field' exists across the EU concerning anticompetitive agreements, etc. But one cannot easily do so when the Treaty provision in question is Article 102 TFEU, the provision that prohibits an abuse of a dominant position. The reason for this is that a finding of a violation of Article 102 TFEU by an NCA does not automatically render unenforceable any agreement which is deemed to underlie an abuse of a dominant position.[83] One may well posit that Article 102 TFEU is irrelevant when analysing cartel agreements and therefore that its apparent role regarding the declaration of invalidity would also be irrelevant. But this would be missing the point: Article 102 TFEU is relevant when determining what the predominant objective of the EU competition law rules actually is. If one looks at the wording of Article 3(3) of Regulation 1/2003, one can see that it states that Articles 3(1) and (2) do not preclude 'the application of provisions of national law that predominantly pursue an objective different from *that* pursued by Articles [101] *and* [102 TFEU]'.[84] The use of the word 'that' rather than 'those' combined with the use of the word 'and' rather than 'or' to connect Articles 101 and 102 TFEU seems to suggest that there is one predominant objective of the EU competition rules.[85] If so, it is this particular objective which would inform the test to be used when applying Wils's approach to the relevant sentence in Recital 8. Given that Article 102 TFEU does not necessarily rule on the enforceability of agreements, etc. (unlike Article 101 TFEU), one may be forced to admit that the relevant objective is wider than the ruling on validity and may in fact be as wide as the 'protection of competition on the market'[86] or 'the maintenance of effective competition within the common market'.[87] If this is so, one is inevitably led back to the problems associated with Wils's original (overly broad) contention concerning the logical implication of his approach to interpreting the relevant sentence in Recital 8.

[80] European Commission (2009c), 49.

[81] De Smijter and Kjølbye (2007), 111.

[82] De Smijter and Kjølbye (2007), 111.

[83] That is not to say, however, that a party to a contract with a dominant undertaking cannot argue in a civil case that clauses in the contract are prohibited by Article 102 TFEU and are therefore void and unenforceable; see, e.g.: Jones and Sufrin (2011), 265; and *English Welsh and Scottish Railway Ltd v. E. ON UK Plc* [2007] EWHC 599.

[84] Emphasis added.

[85] See also Case 6/72, *Continental Can v. Commission* [1973] ECR 215, [25] ('Articles [101] and [102 TFEU] seek to achieve the *same aim* on different levels, *viz.* the maintenance of effective competition within the same market' (emphasis added)).

[86] See Council of the European Union (2003), Recital 9.

[87] Case 6/72, *Continental Can v. Commission* [1973] ECR 215, [11].

The legal position on the applicability of Regulation 1/2003 to a national criminal cartel offence has yet to be definitively explained by the Court of Justice. Given the different possible explanations that can be offered regarding its application, it is obvious that a cautious approach to this issue is warranted. Nonetheless, subject to the specifics of the (rational) interpretation of the legal situation that is chosen as being relevant, useful advice can be formulated and provided to national legislators who wish to design criminal cartel offences in such a manner that avoids the potential application of Regulation 1/2003. If one adopts the interpretation of the OFT, all the national legislature has to do to avoid the application of Regulation 1/2003 to the national criminal cartel offence is to ensure that undertakings (as opposed to individuals) cannot be subjected to a criminal prosecution for commission of the criminal cartel offence. If one is not swayed by the OFT's argument, one could find inspiration from Wils and create a criminal cartel offence that does not pursue the same predominant objective as the EU competition law rules. As noted above, this of course begs the question as to what that predominant objective might be. If one were to take inspiration from the Court of Appeal in the *IB* case concerning this issue, one could design the criminal cartel offence so that it does not inevitably involve a finding by the criminal court on the validity of the underlying agreement, etc. that is entered into by undertakings. As explained above, such a restrictive approach to the issue of 'predominant objective' can be questioned.

If one wished to have a more robust approach in defining the criminal cartel offence so that it is not subjected to Regulation 1/2003, then in addition to delinking the criminal cartel offence from a finding of invalidity regarding the agreement, etc., one could design the offence in such a way that one can plausibly argue that its predominant objective is not 'the protection of competition on the market' or 'the maintenance of effective competition within the common market'. This might be difficult to do, particularly if the rationale for the introduction of criminal cartel sanctions is the achievement of deterrence of anticompetitive behaviour. One possible way of 'engineering' a different predominant objective for the criminal cartel offence from that involving the prevention of anticompetitive behaviour (and with it the protection of the market) would be to create the cartel offence on the basis of an explicit moral concept.[88] According to Lord Bingham, the punishment of immoral (anticompetitive) behaviour can be understood as being conceptually distinct from the punishment of cartel activity for the purposes of enforcing competition rules:

> in a case involving dishonest misstatement in connection with price-fixing, it would be the punishment of the dishonesty not price-fixing which would be the 'objective' of the criminal [cartel] law.[89]

Leading on from this, one could, for example, define the criminal cartel offence in such a manner that it requires the cartelist to 'dishonestly' agree with another to engage in cartel activity. However, as will be explained directly below, such an approach is not without its own significant problems. Alternatively, one could create a criminal cartel offence that necessarily captures the moral wrongfulness of cartel activity by creating an express link between cartel activity and the violation of one or more of the norms against stealing, deceiving, and cheating.[90] For example, before imposing criminal cartel sanctions, one could require proof that the cartelist intended to mislead customers. Admittedly, such an

[88] See Whelan (2012b), 599–600.

[89] *Norris v. Government of the United States of America and others* [2008] UKHL 16, [51]. See also Furse (2012), 126, noting a similar point that was made in *R v. GG Plc and others* [2008] UKHL 17.

[90] See Chapter 4, Section C(c) of this book.

approach, while operationalizing the justificatory theory of retribution more fully, could easily run counter to the achievement of deterrence: additional definitional elements present *additional* hurdles for antitrust enforcers, and ceteris paribus, a given amount of resources will most likely produce fewer successful prosecutions if a criminal cartel offence requires proof of additional definitional elements. Moreover, the 'engineering' process may not work in practice: depending on the rules of legal interpretation in existence in a given jurisdiction, its judicial authorities may look beyond the exact definition in the cartel offence to green and white papers, consultation documents, responses to consultation documents, legislative debates, draft legislation, etc., all of which may reveal that a predominant purpose to the introduction of a criminal cartel offence is in fact to prevent anticompetitive conduct in order to protect the functioning of markets.[91]

C. Resolving the Issue of 'Acceptable' Cartel Activity

This section considers how the issue of 'acceptable' cartel activity can be dealt with in the context of European antitrust criminalization. It is divided into three sub-sections. Sub-section (a) articulates the central dilemma regarding the issue of 'acceptable' cartel activity by explaining how EU competition law currently deals with this issue and why that approach may not be ideal in a criminal law setting. Sub-section (b) critiques the role that the definitional element of 'dishonesty' can play in resolving the issue of 'acceptable' cartel activity. Finally, Sub-section (c) examines the recent UK consultation on the reform of the Cartel Offence in order to propose an additional (workable) mechanism for ensuring that a criminal cartel offence is not too broadly drafted.

(a) The central dilemma

'Acceptable' cartel activity can be understood as the type of activity that would fulfil the definition of cartel activity offered by the OECD in Paragraph 2(a) of its 1998 Recommendation,[92] but which a competition regime would not wish to prohibit because the activity in question pursues a legitimate purpose and/or generates net efficiencies for consumers. There are at least two ways in which what might be deemed to be 'acceptable' cartel activity is regulated by the EU competition law rules. The first involves the employment of the doctrine of 'commercial ancillarity'; the second involves the application of the exception criteria in Article 101(3) TFEU. Each of these techniques brings problems in the context of European cartel criminalization.

As noted by Whish and Bailey, there are a number of judgments from the EU Courts that demonstrate that 'it is possible to argue successfully that restrictions which are necessary to enable the parties to an agreement to achieve a legitimate commercial purpose fall outside Article 101(1) TFEU'.[93] This alone has the potential to influence how one might approach drafting a national criminal cartel offence, particularly if one is

[91] See, e.g., the analysis of the Court of Appeal concerning the travaux préparatoires of the UK Cartel Offence in *IB v. The Queen* [2009] EWCA Crim 2575, [21]–[23].

[92] OECD (1998), [2(a)]: 'an anticompetitive agreement, anticompetitive concerted practice, or anticompetitive arrangement by competitors to fix prices, make rigged bids (collusive tenders), establish output restrictions or quotas, or share or divide markets by allocating customers, suppliers, territories, or lines of commerce'.

[93] Whish and Bailey (2012), 129. Examples include: Case 161/84, *Pronuptia de Paris GmbH v. Pronuptia de Paris Irmgard Schillgallis* [1986] ECR 353; and Case 250/92, *Gøttrup-Klim Grovvareforening and others v. Dansk Landbrugs Grovvareselskab AmbA (DLG)* [1994] ECR I-5641.

concerned about the issue of so-called 'acceptable' cartel activity. Admittedly, it is true that Whish and Bailey consider what they have termed 'commercial ancillarity' only when analysing whether contractual restrictions are anticompetitive *by effect* (rather than by object).[94] One may be inclined to argue, then, that, when cartel activity as defined in Paragraph 2(a) of the OECD's 1998 Recommendation forms the substance of the national criminal cartel offence, the doctrine of 'commercial ancillarity' becomes irrelevant on the basis that the activity covered by that part of the Recommendation (price-fixing, bid-rigging, output reductions, and market sharing) are restrictions *by object* under EU competition law. But this would be missing the point. The 'commercial ancillarity' case of *Remia BV and Verenidge Bedrijven and Nutricia v. Commission*,[95] for example, demonstrates that use of the OECD's definition in Paragraph 2(a) to create a national cartel offence could possibly ensure that 'acceptable' cartel activity under the EU competition rules can actually fall within the scope of that criminal cartel offence. In that particular case, the Court of Justice, in ruling on a non-compete clause in an agreement for the sale of a business, held that while such a non-compete clause could be within the scope of Article 101(1) TFEU[96]—and, if so, void—it would fall outside Article 101(1) TFEU if it is 'necessary for the transfer' of the business concerned and if its 'duration and scope' is 'strictly limited to that purpose'.[97] An agreement of a (potential) competitor not to compete in a given market could plausibly be understood as an agreement to reduce capacity (as one competitor will not be supplying a market) or as an agreement to divide markets (in this case, with one undertaking completely conceding a market to another). In other words, a non-compete clause could fall within the prohibited activity in the definition of cartel activity contained in Paragraph 2(a) of the OECD's Recommendation.[98] Hence, the EU doctrine of 'commercial ancillarity' remains relevant even when one is focusing on by-object agreements in the context of European antitrust criminalization.

As explained previously, Article 101(3) TFEU is the provision of EU competition law that provides an exception to the prohibition in Article 101(1) TFEU for those agreements, etc. that meet its four criteria,[99] all of which must be fulfilled.[100] The burden of proving that the exception criteria are fulfilled lies upon the undertaking or undertakings seeking to defend the agreement, etc.[101] It is clear from the case of *Matra Hachette*[102] that no type of anticompetitive agreement is excluded as a matter of law from the application of Article 101(3) TFEU, and therefore there is no legal rule that would prevent an undertaking seeking to rely upon an agreement, etc. from arguing that the criteria in Article 101(3) TFEU are fulfilled concerning that agreement, etc. Consequently, unlike the case with Section 1 of

[94] Other scholars do likewise, such as: Jones and Sufrin (2011), 227–31; and Lorenz (2013), 99–100.

[95] Case 42/84, *Remia BV and Verenidge Bedrijven and Nutricia v. Commission* [1985] ECR 2545.

[96] Case 42/84, *Remia BV and Verenidge Bedrijven and Nutricia v. Commission* [1985] ECR 2545, [17].

[97] Case 42/84, *Remia BV and Verenidge Bedrijven and Nutricia v. Commission* [1985] ECR 2545, [20].

[98] Of course, one could argue that the inclusion of the term 'anticompetitive' in OECD (1998), [2(a)] could help to ensure that the non-compete clause would not be subject to criminal penalties; in doing so one could in fact rely upon the very reasoning of the Court of Justice in Case 42/84, *Remia BV and Verenidge Bedrijven and Nutricia v. Commission* [1985] ECR 2545, particularly [19]. But this begs the question as to what 'anticompetitive' means (e.g., by effect or by object) and indeed whether a finding of 'anti-competitiveness' is inherent in a finding of an agreement, etc. that includes one or more of the prohibited activities (i.e. price-fixing, bid-rigging, restricting output, and market sharing).

[99] For the text of Article 101(3) TFEU, see Annex I of this book.

[100] See, e.g., Joined Cases 43 and 63/82, *VBVB and VVVB v. Commission* [1984] ECR 19, [61].

[101] Council of the European Union (2003), Article 2.

[102] Case T-17/93, *Matra Hachette SA v. Commission* [1994] ECR II-595, [85].

the Sherman Act 1890,[103] EU competition law does not really have a per se approach to the illegality of certain agreements, etc.[104] This particular feature of EU competition law is not a mere legal technicality. For example, up until October 2008, a block exemption was in place which exempted horizontal price-fixing concerning containerized cargo carried by international liner conferences.[105] In addition, there are a (limited) number of cases where the criteria of Article 101(3) TFEU were deemed to be fulfilled in practice by the Commission even when instances of fixing of prices were identified.[106] In *Reims II*,[107] the Commission ruled upon the application of Article 101(3) TFEU to an agreement fixing the price paid by one postal operator for the onward delivery of letters in the sphere of operation of another postal operator. After noting that the agreement was technically a price-fixing agreement,[108] albeit with 'unusual characteristics',[109] the Commission nonetheless found that the agreement fulfilled the conditions in Article 101(3) TFEU.[110] In doing so, it highlighted that the agreement in fact created a number of advantages for consumers, such as 'a substantial increase in the quality of post-border mail services'.[111] In a later decision, the Commission granted an individual exemption (under the now defunct Regulation 62/17) to the multilateral interchange fee (i.e. the fee that was paid in order to process credit card transactions) that was agreed between issuing and acquiring banks that formed part of the Visa network.[112] Dealing with these types of decisions is a challenge for advocates of European antitrust criminalization.

It can be argued that a central feature of an effective criminal cartel law is the absence of a requirement to analyse and prove any economic effects in a market in order to find an infringement. There are three particular reasons for this. First of all, despite the robustness of the economic theory underlying the definition of a market,[113] it can be notoriously difficult to establish the boundaries of a market in practice,[114] and particularly so when one must do this to a criminal standard of proof. Second, forcing criminal courts to undertake complex economic analyses 'runs counter to our notions of the relative institutional competence of criminal courts as compared with a specialized administrative agency'.[115] This issue can

[103] See, e.g., *United States v. Socony-Vacuum Oil Co.* (1940) 310 US 150. Cf. Calvani and Calvani (2009), 135–6.

[104] Harding and Joshua (2002), 936.

[105] Council of the European Communities (1986), Articles 3, 4, and 5.

[106] See generally Whish and Bailey (2012), 153–5. Admittedly, these cases 'were far from being classic cartel cases: rather they concerned network industries in which prices were "fixed" between participants in a network that supplied services to one another (the price fixing was business to business, or "B to B"), whereas "hard-core" price fixing involves the fixing of prices to customers (business to customer, or "B to C"). It is interesting to note that, in these decisions, the Commission considered that the agreements restricted competition *by effect* rather than *by object*: in other words it did not treat the restrictions as hard-core': Whish and Bailey (2012), 154.

[107] *Reims II* (Case COMP/36.748), Commission Decision, 15 September 1999, [1999] OJ L275/17.

[108] *Reims II* (Case COMP/36.748), Commission Decision, 15 September 1999, [1999] OJ L275/17, [62]–[63].

[109] *Reims II* (Case COMP/36.748), Commission Decision, 15 September 1999, [1999] OJ L275/17, [65].

[110] *Reims II* (Case COMP/36.748), Commission Decision, 15 September 1999, [1999] OJ L275/17, [69]–[90].

[111] See, e.g., *Reims II* (Case COMP/36.748), Commission Decision, 15 September 1999, [1999] OJ L275/17, [70] and [77].

[112] *Visa International—Multilateral Interchange Fee* (Case COMP/29.373), Commission Decision, 24 July 2002, [2002] OJ L318/17.

[113] See, e.g., European Commission (1997).

[114] See, e.g., Jones and Sufrin (2011), 63.

[115] Warner and Trebilcock (1992–93), 690. On the problems encountered in Canada when prosecutors had to prove an 'undue' lessening of competition in order to impose criminal cartel sanctions, see: Jacobs (2007), 29; and Scott (2007), 70–1.

become particularly problematic when a jury (as opposed to a panel of criminal judges) is required to rule on the fulfilment of economic criteria in order to determine whether a criminal cartel offence has been made out on the facts presented to it.[116] If the offence itself did not involve an economic analysis, but a defence along the lines of Article 101(3) TFEU was created that needed to be proven by the defendant, this problem would still exist, even if the relevant standard applicable to the defence was lower than beyond reasonable doubt (such as on the balance of probabilities): the decision-maker would still be required to come to a conclusion about whether the economic argument is made out by the defendant, in the knowledge that a lack of such a defence may result in serious punishment being imposed upon the convicted cartelist. This may be very difficult for the decision-maker to do.[117] Furthermore, it may inject a degree of inconsistency into the law, as it 'leaves open the possibility of inconsistent findings between criminal and civil proceedings arising as a result of differences in economic judgement between a lay jury [and, it is submitted, a non-specialized panel of criminal judges] and a specialist "civil" tribunal'.[118] Third, by requiring economic assessments to be made in order to determine if a criminal cartel offence has been committed, a criminalized jurisdiction would be creating a very fine—and some may argue inappropriate—distinction between criminal conduct and non-criminal conduct.[119] To alleviate these problems, a per se offence could be created that does not depend upon economic analyses.[120] This has been recognized by the Competition Committee of the OECD, which notes that:

> Relying on the general competition law definition of anticompetitive conduct can hinder criminal enforcement... if there is no recognition of a *per se* cartel offence. Otherwise, elements of a competition law violation such as market definition, entry barriers, and effects on competition may have to be proven under criminal standards, making it exceedingly difficult to obtain criminal convictions in courts.[121]

A per se cartel offence would not require the criminal enforcer to prove harm to competition and prevents a defendant from claiming an efficiency justification, in the process providing certainty concerning the legality of specific conduct.[122]

The problem with the solution of a per se cartel offence is that it would not allow for the implementation of the mechanisms of EU competition law that deal with 'acceptable' cartel activity. The reason for this is that both 'commercial ancillarity' and Article 101(3) TFEU involve economic assessments. Going back to the case of *Remia BV and Verenidge Bedrijven and Nutricia v. Commission*,[123] for example, one can see that the central factor in determining whether the non-compete clause falls within Article 101(1) TFEU was the issue of the counterfactual: in order to determine whether non-compete clauses come within the prohibition in Article 101(1) TFEU, 'it is necessary to examine what would be the state of competition if those clauses did not exist'.[124] This is an inquiry that involves an economic assessment of the market in question. Of course, with Article 101(3) TFEU, one only has to look at its criteria to understand that they necessarily involve economic assessments. For example, the decision-maker is required to consider, inter alia, whether the agreement, etc. would have led to an improvement in

116 Joshua (2002), 242. Cf. Massey (2012), 159.

117 Cf. De Smijter and Kjølbye (2007), 111.

118 Pickford (2002), 43.

119 Pickford (2002), 37.

120 Jenny (2011), vi–vii.

121 OECD (2007b), 13. See also the comments of Farmer in Marsden et al. (2013), 615.

122 ICN (2005), 14.

123 Case 42/84, *Remia BV and Verenidge Bedrijven and Nutricia v. Commission* [1985] ECR 2545.

124 Case 42/84, *Remia BV and Verenidge Bedrijven and Nutricia v. Commission* [1985] ECR 2545, [18].

the production or distribution of goods or to the promotion of technical or economic progress. Another problem with the per se approach is that it would result in a 'chilling effect' on 'acceptable' cartel activity (however rare it might be) to the detriment of consumer welfare. In addition, it would introduce an element of unfairness into the criminal process: it would 'be wholly inequitable (not to say undermining of the competition regime) to subject the executives responsible for concluding such agreements to criminal penalties if their activities were entirely lawful for the purposes of civil competition law'.[125] Consequently, one is faced with an apparent dilemma concerning the treatment of 'acceptable' cartel activity under the criminal law: by implementing the EU mechanisms for dealing with such cartel activity, one creates significant problems for the criminal cartel regime (due to the necessity of undertaking economic assessments); and, by pursuing a per se offence (in order for the criminal cartel offence to avoid these problems), one is forced to renounce the identified EU mechanisms for dealing with 'acceptable' cartel activity. Given this context, it is advisable to consider methods of drafting the criminal cartel offence in order to resolve this apparent dilemma. An ideal solution would involve the 'carve out' of 'acceptable' cartel activity from the criminal cartel offence in a manner that does not depend upon the decision-maker in a criminal trial undertaking economic analyses.

(b) 'Dishonesty' and its potential role

In 2001, the British Government decided that in order for its competition law regime to be effective at deterring cartels, it would be necessary for criminal sanctions to be imposed against individuals. In the document that advocated the introduction of criminal cartel sanctions, it was noted that it might be difficult to define the offence in such a way that there would be a clear distinction between legitimate agreements and illegitimate ones.[126] In that same document, the following was also noted:

> the Government recognises the need to define carefully the criminal offence so as to make it clear that only individuals actively involved in agreements which could never be exempt would be caught. The Government has no desire to criminalise involvement in benign agreements which would not be unlawful under existing competition law.[127]

In pursuing this policy, the Government believed that it was presented with two options: (i) it could make it a criminal offence for an individual to participate in a cartel agreement where the agreement in question also involves a violation of either Article 101 TFEU or Chapter 1 of the Competition Act 1998;[128] or (ii) it could avoid a direct link to a finding of a violation of Article 101 TFEU or Chapter 1 of the Competition Act 1998, instead defining the offence as the dishonest participation in cartel activity.[129] Interestingly, it was noted that if Option (ii) were followed, a defendant 'could use as his defence the claim that he honestly believed he was acting in accordance with [Article 101 TFEU] or Chapter 1'.[130] Option (ii) was understood, then, to be a possible method of ensuring that 'acceptable' cartel activity did not lead to the imposition of criminal punishment.[131]

After being persuaded of the merits of Option (ii)—which were set out in, inter alia, a document prepared for the OFT by Sir Anthony Hammond QC and Roy Penrose OBE[132]—the Government decided to rely upon the definitional element of 'dishonesty'

125 Pickford (2002), 36.
126 DTI (2001b), [7.22].
127 DTI (2001b), [7.26].
128 DTI (2001b), [7.29].
129 DTI (2001b), [7.31].
130 DTI (2001b), [7.31].
131 Cf. MacCulloch (2007), 356.
132 OFT (2001), [1.9]–[1.12] and [2.1]–[2.11].

to pursue its objective of distinguishing between legitimate and illegitimate cartel activity. Consequently, and as was noted in Chapter 7,[133] the original text of Section 188 of the Enterprise Act 2002[134] made it a criminal offence in the UK for an individual to *dishonestly* make or implement or cause to be made or implemented a cartel agreement between horizontal competitors. In order for this definitional construct to be proven, one must demonstrate that the constituent components of the *Ghosh* test[135] have been fulfilled.[136] Accordingly, both subjective and objective analyses are required: the cartel conduct must be (i) dishonest according to the standards of ordinary people and (ii) known by the defendant to be dishonest according to those standards.

It is submitted that there is indeed scope for the *Ghosh* test effectively to carve out 'acceptable' cartel activity from the UK Cartel Offence: the defendant could indeed try to argue that the conduct would not have been unlawful under national or EU competition rules and that, ipso facto, he would not have fulfilled the first part of the *Ghosh* test.[137] This logic could be applied not only to cartel activity that fulfils the exception criteria in Article 101(3), but also to cartel activity that falls outside the scope of Article 101(1) TFEU due to the fact that, for example, it fulfils the criteria of the 'ancillarity doctrine'.[138] The problem, however, is that if one accepts this point, one must also acknowledge that there is a conflict between the various objectives of including the definitional element of 'dishonesty' in the criminal cartel offence in the first place.[139] The other relevant objective here (in addition to dealing effectively with 'acceptable' cartel activity) is the objective of avoiding the presentation of complex economic evidence in front of a criminal court (and jury).[140] Hammond and Penrose argue, for example, that the employment of the definitional element of 'dishonesty' would 'go a long way to preclude a defence argument that the activity being prosecuted... might have economic benefits or is an activity which might have attracted exemption domestically or under [EU] law'.[141] But for 'dishonesty' to carve out 'acceptable' cartel activity, it will be necessary for the defendant to argue that ordinary people would not find that activity to be dishonest *because it is not unlawful under EU/national competition law*, and in order to substantiate that argument the defendant will be required to put forward economic evidence which demonstrates that an exception under Article 101(3) TFEU (or the national equivalent) would be forthcoming. In short, the use of 'dishonesty' does not preclude the presentation of complex economic evidence and may in fact encourage it if the defendant is serious about avoiding a custodial sentence.[142] This point has been accepted by the UK Department for Business, Innovation and Skills ('BIS'),[143] as well as by a judge who was required to a give a preliminary ruling in a UK Cartel Offence prosecution.[144] The reality, then, is that the employment of the definitional element of 'dishonesty' does not

133 Chapter 7, Section D(a) of this book.

134 To be clear, and as was also noted in Chapter 7, Section D(a) of this book, Section 47 of the Enterprise and Regulatory Reform Act 2013 removes the dishonesty element from the UK Cartel Offence.

135 *R v. Ghosh* [1982] 2 All ER 689, 696.

136 *R. v. George and others* [2010] EWCA Crim 1148 established that the *Ghosh* test applied to the definitional construct of 'dishonesty' contained in the original Cartel Offence.

137 Cf. Dobbin and Peretz (2005), 182.

138 This point was noted by Hammond and Penrose; see OFT (2001), [2.9].

139 Whelan (2013f). 140 See DTI (2001b), [7.30]. 141 OFT (2001), [2.5].

142 In fairness to Hammond and Penrose, they do not say that dishonesty would *completely* preclude the presentation of economic evidence.

143 BIS (2011), [6.13]. See also BIS (2012), [7.5].

144 See Nikpay (2012), 22, who notes that the judge in question 'was persuaded that expert economic evidence was potentially relevant to the issue of dishonesty'.

resolve the dilemma noted above; in fact, it merely provides another way for economic evidence to be used to carve 'acceptable' cartel activity out of the criminal cartel offence.

Importantly, and in addition, 'dishonesty' as a definitional element in an antitrust offence is not without its own significant problems,[145] including problems of legal certainty.[146] Stephan succinctly summarizes one of the main problems as follows:

> It was thought that incorporating the moral element of 'dishonesty' into the [UK Cartel Offence] would harden public attitudes. However, this has not happened in the absence of regular convictions and may be problematic because dishonesty necessitates a contemporary moral judgement on the part of the jury and therefore relies on attitudes being sufficiently hardened in the first place.[147]

In other words, the use of the definitional construct of 'dishonesty' engenders a problem of the 'chicken and egg' variety: one wishes to have criminal prosecutions in order to harden attitudes to cartel activity; but by arguing that cartel activity is dishonest (according to the standards of ordinary people), one in effect presupposes the existence of such hardened attitudes. Furthermore, it may be possible for defendants to advance dubious defences in the context of the analysis of 'dishonesty';[148] the accused cartelists may allege, for example, that they were acting to protect employment or that they were acting in the best interests of some other category of person, such as shareholders.[149] Indeed, for Black, 'few people, perhaps, will see anything dishonest in the practice where the purpose is to preserve jobs, and a vigorous entrepreneur may see nothing dishonest in it in any circumstances'.[150] It has also been argued that defendants 'might rely on mistake of law as a way of denying that their conduct was dishonest'[151] and that the element of 'dishonesty' may in practice result in a requirement to waive professional privilege in order to demonstrate such a mistake, thus involving an unacceptable incursion into the rights of the defendant.[152] Added to this is the very real possibility that there may be huge variations in what different people think amounts to dishonest behaviour.[153] For Joshua, if the aim of including the element of 'dishonesty' within a cartel offence is to confine liability to the most serious cartels, then the criterion is 'entirely misconceived'.[154] Beaton-Wells and Fisse are particularly sceptical of the appropriateness of using the concept of 'dishonesty' in the context of cartel criminalization, arguing that it

> serves no useful purpose as an element of a cartel offence, is uncertain in meaning, creates avenues for unmeritorious denials of liability and, in terms of deterrence and public education, is false and misleading as a label or signal.[155]

These problems and criticisms were deemed to be so acute that the Australian authorities eventually decided to abandon the use of 'dishonesty' in their (draft)[156] criminal antitrust legislation[157] and the UK Parliament recently adopted legislation to remove

145 See generally: Elliott (1982); Fisse (2007a); Halpin (1996); Harding and Joshua (2002); Joshua (2011); MacCulloch (2007); and Scanlan (2002).

146 See the discussion in Chapter 7, Section D of this book.

147 Stephan (2008c), 32.

148 See: Harding and Joshua (2002), 938; and MacCulloch (2007), 362.

149 Parkinson (2004), 189. See also Fisse (2007a), 262.

150 Black (2010), 128.

151 Gray (2008), 377.

152 See, e.g., Pickford (2002), 38.

153 See, e.g., Connor (2009), discussing the 'Honesty Lab' research conducted by Finch and Fafinski.

154 Joshua (2011), 142. On this, see also: Fisse (2007a), 241–4; and Fisse (2007b), 52–3.

155 Beaton-Wells and Fisse (2008c), 1.

156 The definitional element of 'dishonesty' only appeared in draft criminal antitrust legislation in Australia; see Trade Practices Amendment (Cartel Conduct and Other Measures) Bill 2008 (Exposure Draft Bill, January 2008) (Australia), Sections 44ZZRF and 44ZZRG.

157 On this, see Senate Standing Committee on Economics (2009), [3.14]–[3.18].

the 'dishonesty' element from the UK Cartel Offence. Given the above, including the fact that the definitional element of 'dishonesty' does not resolve the central dilemma under examination, it would not be advisable for legislatures contemplating introducing criminal cartel sanctions to draft their criminal cartel offence with such a definitional element.[158]

(c) The BIS consultation and its proposed solution

In March 2011, BIS published its consultation document *A Competition Regime for Growth: A Consultation on Options for Reform*.[159] The overall objective of that particular consultation was to ensure that the competition regime in the UK becomes even more effective at supporting economic growth.[160] Chapter 6 of the Consultation Document focused on the UK Cartel Offence.[161] It acknowledged that the deterrent effect of the Cartel Offence has been weaker than what was intended:[162] there has only been one case which has led to convictions.[163] One of the identified reasons for this scarcity of convictions was the current definition of the offence, particularly its use of 'dishonesty'.[164] Consequently, the four different options for reform which were suggested in the Consultation Document all focused on potential changes to the current definition in the criminal offence.[165] Option 1 proposed the removal of the 'dishonesty' element and the introduction of guidance for prosecutors. Option 2 advocated the removal of the 'dishonesty' element and the carve-out from the offence of a set of 'white-listed' agreements. Option 3 wished to replace the 'dishonesty' element of the offence with a 'secrecy' element. Finally, Option 4 recommended the removal of the 'dishonesty' element from the offence and the 'carve out' from the UK Cartel Offence of agreements that are made openly.

One year after the publication of its Consultation Document, and after receiving more than 100 responses, BIS published its Final Report on the consultation.[166] In Chapter 7 of the Final Report, the UK Government committed itself to the adoption of Option 4 from the Consultation Document. In doing so, it provided clarification on what is meant by agreements which are 'made openly': they are agreements which are published in a suitable format before they are implemented, so that customers and others can be deemed to be (constructively) aware of them.[167] The Final Report also notes that only a small number of respondents agreed that Option 4 should be adopted.[168] It appears from a reading of all of the publicly available responses (110 in total) that in fact only three respondents advocated the adoption of Option 4: the Office of Fair Trading; the ESRC Centre for Competition Policy; and the author.[169] Irrespective of this limited support, a version of Option 4 is contained within Section 47 of the Enterprise and Regulatory Reform Act 2013 ('ERRA').[170] In essence, Section 47(5) ERRA ensures that an individual does not commit the Cartel Offence if:

(a) in a case where the arrangements would (operating as the parties intend) affect the supply in the United Kingdom of a product or service, customers would be given relevant information

158 Admittedly, a number of scholars would disagree with this statement, including: Bailin (2011); Corker (2011); Gray (2008); and Purnell and Winter (2011).

159 BIS (2011).

160 BIS (2011), [1.3].

161 Enterprise Act 2002, Section 188.

162 BIS (2011), [6.5].

163 The 'Marine Hoses' case: *R v. Whittle and others* [2008] EWCA Crim 2560.

164 BIS (2011), [6.6].

165 See BIS (2011), [6.19]–[6.53].

166 BIS (2012).

167 BIS (2012), 66.

168 BIS (2012), [7.22].

169 Whelan (2012b), 590.

170 For the full version of the text, see Annex II of this book.

about the arrangements before they enter into agreements for the supply to them of the product or service so affected,

(b) in the case of bid-rigging arrangements, the person requesting bids would be given relevant information about them at or before the time when a bid is made, or

(c) in any case, relevant information about the arrangements would be published, before the arrangements are implemented, in the manner specified at the time of the making of the agreement in an order made by the Secretary of State.

That same provision clarifies that 'relevant information about the arrangements' means:

(a) the names of the undertakings to which the arrangements relate, (b) a description of the nature of the arrangements which is sufficient to show why they are or might be arrangements of the kind to which section 188(1) applies, (c) the products or services to which they relate, and (d) such other information as may be specified in an order made by the Secretary of State.[171]

It is submitted here that the adoption of Option 4 (as reflected in Section 47 of ERRA) is an astute move by the UK Parliament,[172] and one that helps to deal effectively with the issue of 'acceptable' cartel activity. Rationalizing the removal of 'dishonesty' from the offence has been done directly above. What needs to be considered here, then, is why the 'carve out' of agreements made openly would be a reasonable way of dealing with the issue of 'acceptable' cartel activity. First, one should understand that a criminal cartel offence that prohibits price-fixing, output restrictions, market sharing, and bid-rigging while allowing for a 'carve out' of agreements made openly would not require a decision-maker to assess the economic effects of an agreement to find that the offence has been committed. In short, BIS's Option 4 avoids the presentation of complex economic evidence in a trial. However, it also provides scope for the operation of the 'commercial ancillarity' doctrine as well as for the operation of Article 101(3) TFEU. In short, Option 4 can indirectly provide immunity from criminal sanctions for those who conclude agreements that would benefit from an exception under Article 101(3) TFEU and for those who believe that the doctrine of 'commercial ancillarity' would be fulfilled under the EU competition law rules. If cartelists genuinely believe that their cartel agreement would benefit from an exception (as it would fulfil the criteria of Article 101(3) TFEU) or that it would fulfil the criteria specified by the Court of Justice in implementing the 'commercial ancillarity' doctrine, all they have to do to avoid criminal sanctions is to publish publicly the agreement prior to its implementation or to notify the competition authority of its existence prior to implementation. Accordingly, no economic evidence needs to be presented to a jury for an Article 101(3)-type exception to be operationalized or for the 'commercial ancillarity' doctrine to be applied. What is necessary is that *before coming to any agreement* the cartelists analyse the agreement contemplated and make their decision (based on legal advice if necessary) whether those methods of dealing with 'acceptable' cartel activity would be applicable to it under (civil) EU competition law. If so, and they wish to conclude and to implement the agreement, they should publish the agreement (prior to implementation) and avoid criminal sanctions. If they are correct in their analyses about ancillarity or Article 101(3) TFEU, the undertakings for whom they work will also avoid administrative sanctions, such as fines. If the rules of EU competition law would not deem the cartel to be 'acceptable' cartel activity, the cartelists can then decide: (i) to conclude and publish the agreement (in the process subjecting the

[171] A consultation on the content of the above-noted order of the Secretary of State was conducted in late 2013; see BIS (2013b), Chapter 2.

[172] See: Whelan (2012b); and Whelan (2011b). For an alternative view, see, e.g., Patel (2012).

cartel to possible civil competition law enforcement, but avoiding criminal liability for themselves); (ii) to conclude and then implement the agreement without publishing it (subjecting themselves to possible criminal liability); or (iii) to abandon their attempts to reach agreement altogether so that criminal and/or administrative sanctions will not result.

Critics might say that cartelists will 'short circuit' the criminal antitrust regime by routinely making public all of their cartel agreements, thereby nullifying the deterrent effect of the criminal cartel sanctions. This is unlikely, as presumably the cartelist wishes to see the cartel actually work in practice (and not receive fines and/or the negative publicity that would presumably follow). If so, they would be reluctant to bring the cartel to the attention of those who enforce the administrative cartel prohibitions. However, if (in the very unlikely case that) cartelists do decide to make their (clearly unlawful) agreement public merely to avoid criminal sanctions, the following positive effect would register: the veil of secrecy surrounding the cartel would be pierced, thereby increasing the rate of detection of unlawful cartels for the purposes of the enforcement of Article 101 TFEU or a national equivalent (and with it the deterrent effect of the administrative offence). This increase in the rate of detection (if it were to occur) would undermine the need for criminal sanctions to deter cartel activity in the first place (as the optimal fine would be reduced significantly). Hence, the 'short circuiting' if it were to occur (which, again, is unlikely anyway) would not be overly problematic—at least when deterrence is the underlying objective of the criminal cartel sanctions. In addition, if such 'short circuiting' were to occur, its impact on the achievement of retribution is not as powerful as one might first imagine. In particular, the carve out of agreements made openly is in fact required in order to ensure consistency between cartel activity subjected to criminal sanctions and the violation of the moral norm against deception. As was noted in Chapter 4,[173] the implementation of a form of BIS's Option 4 in Section 47 ERRA can without difficulty be rationalized as an attempt to link cartel activity to immoral behaviour (i.e. deception), particularly given that the UK Government has also decided to remove the definitional element of 'dishonesty' from the UK Cartel Offence.

The 'carve out' from the criminal cartel offence of agreements made openly is not a novel idea. Warner and Trebilcock proposed something very similar to BIS's Option 4 in the early 1990s in the context of their critique of the (then extant) Canadian approach to criminal cartel enforcement.[174] After noting that 'a *per se* criminal prohibition for naked price-fixing cannot be formulated with complete precision, and will unavoidably target potentially pro-competitive arrangements', those scholars identify a characteristic of naked price-fixing agreements in addition to their lessening of competition: the fact that they are 'generally covert'.[175] They therefore advocate a refocusing of the criminal cartel prohibition on the 'covertness of horizontal arrangements',[176] and propose a per se criminal cartel offence with legislation expressly providing that such an offence would not be committed where 'the accused has filed a notification with the [Canadian Bureau of Competition Policy] either prior to the time at which the arrangement takes effect, or within 30 days of the execution of the arrangement, whichever is earlier'.[177] The central rationale for their proposal is that covert forms of price-fixing 'become self-defeating through the act of filing a notification before the arrangement is acted

173 Chapter 4, Section C(c)(ii) of this book.
174 Warner and Trebilcock (1992–93).
175 Warner and Trebilcock (1992–93), 716.
176 Warner and Trebilcock (1992–93), 716.
177 Warner and Trebilcock (1992–93), 717.

upon'.[178] Importantly, their proposal ensures that any cartel agreements which may have 'positive welfare effects can easily escape the risk of criminal sanctions by the election of the parties themselves'.[179]

The use of BIS's Option 4 as the basis for dealing with 'acceptable' cartel activity is not without its detractors. In the course of the public consultation on the reform of the UK Cartel Offence, it was noted by some contributors that Option 4 might

> create conflict with legitimate commercial confidentiality and could capture legitimate and lawful joint venture and specialisation agreements that are exempt from the civil prohibitions on the basis of their countervailing economic benefits, but that have not been made public.[180]

In addition, concerns were raised during the passage of the ERRA 2013 through Parliament that Option 4 would effectively reintroduce a notification and authorization system into competition enforcement in the UK,[181] and with it the inevitable administrative inefficiencies and burdens that will result.[182] It is submitted, however, that these particular concerns should not rule out the use of Option 4 as a method of dealing with 'acceptable' cartel activity. For a start, the impact on confidentiality is likely to be minimal and, in any case, can be rationalized as a minor, reasonable interference with the freedom of business people in the interests of dealing appropriately with the issue of 'acceptable' cartel activity while maintaining an effective criminal cartel regime. The author supports the views of BIS when it notes that:

> In the rare cases where businesses operate arrangements that (absent disclosure) would fall within the scope of the offence but that nevertheless offer countervailing benefits, it is reasonable to require a limited disclosure of those provisions so as to bring them outside the scope of the offence (other elements of the arrangements could remain confidential).[183]

In short, for Option 4 to work well in practice the information that should be disclosed when a cartel is formed does not have to be extensive and protecting the confidentiality of some (if not most) of the specifics of the arrangement would remain possible. Second, the 'carve out' of agreements made openly (i.e. published in a suitable format prior to their implementation) is not equivalent to a notification and authorization regime as it does not require any action on behalf of the competition authorities: the mere fact that an agreement has been published in a suitable format *automatically* removes the cartelists from the sphere of criminal law. There is therefore no resultant administrative burden on the authority. This is very different from a state of affairs where a ruling by the competition authority on the validity of an agreement is actually required in order to provide clarification of the legal situation. What the 'carve out' really amounts to in practice is a form of criminal immunity that is granted prior to the implementation of a cartel agreement that leaves open the possibility of later civil/administrative action by the competition authority.[184] It is submitted in fact that such a 'carve out' engenders more advantages than disadvantages and should be an option favoured by those jurisdictions that are serious about dealing with hard-core cartel activity, but do not wish to prohibit

[178] Warner and Trebilcock (1992–93), 718.

[179] Warner and Trebilcock (1992–93), 718.

[180] BIS (2012), [7.24].

[181] See, e.g., the comments of Chi Onwurah MP in Hansard, House of Commons Debates, 10 July 2012, Columns 553–4.

[182] On the inefficiencies of the authorization procedure that used to exist at EU level under Regulation 17/62, see, e.g.: Jones and Sufrin (2004), 1045–6; and Wils (2005a), 10–11.

[183] BIS (2012), 66.

[184] See, e.g., Warner and Trebilcock (1992–93), 719.

cartel activity that (according to the EU competition law rules) pursues a legitimate purpose or may produce net benefits for consumers.[185]

D. Conclusion

One of the most important practical issues which has the potential to undermine the effectiveness of criminal antitrust enforcement is the issue as to how to define the criminal cartel offence. While this book does not attempt to provide a definitive definition to be used in any European jurisdiction that is considering introducing criminal cartel sanctions, it does aim to analyse some of the most important practical issues for antitrust criminalization. Consequently, this chapter analysed two very important issues concerning the definition of the criminal cartel offence: (i) the potential (negative) impact of Regulation 1/2003 on the design and operation of a national criminal cartel offence and what can be done to reduce the scope for such impact in this context; and (ii) how to deal with 'acceptable' (i.e. legitimate and/or efficiency-enhancing) cartel activity in the context of European antitrust criminalization. Taken together, these two issues represent the 'first (practical) challenge of design' examined by this book.

If Regulation 1/2003 applies to the enforcement of the national cartel offence, then there is a clear case that that particular Regulation can impact upon both the definition and the operation of the criminal offence. The definition of the criminal cartel offence could be affected as a result of Article 3 of Regulation 1/2003. Where there is an effect on trade between Member States (and the Regulation applies to the enforcement of the criminal cartel offence), the antitrust enforcers must also apply EU competition law, and in doing so they cannot prohibit agreements under national law which would not be prohibited under EU competition law. Arguably, this feature of competition law enforcement restricts the scope of a criminal cartel offence in that (when there is an effect on trade) the criminal offence cannot capture cartel activity which would not have violated the prohibition in Article 101(1) TFEU, would have fulfilled the criteria of Article 101(3) TFEU, or would have been covered by a block exemption. This situation is problematic for three reasons: (i) it makes the concept of 'effect on trade' relevant in a criminal trial; (ii) it allows for (potentially confusing) economic arguments to be made in a criminal trial; and (iii) it restricts the ability of a jurisdiction to generate a moral norm against cartel activity, as citizens may perceive the criminal cartel offence as focusing on the technical and arcane regulation of trade rather than on preventing conspiracies that cost consumers significant amounts of money. For their part, Articles 11(6) and 35 have the potential to impact negatively on the operation of the criminal cartel offence. If Regulation 1/2003 applies to the enforcement of the national criminal cartel offence, then, under Article 11(6) thereof, the Commission would have the power to relieve the national criminal cartel enforcer of its power to prosecute cartelists for their commission of the criminal cartel offence. There is also the possibility that Article 35(1) of the Regulation could also be used to argue that, if the national criminal enforcer is not a

[185] It is true, as explained above, that the UK has reformed its Cartel Offence in order to carve out agreements made openly. To be clear, however, this is not to say that the UK criminal cartel regime does not suffer from problems in legislative design. In actual fact, the ERRA 2013 also introduced a number of new defences to the commission of the Cartel Offence, one of which (the defence of seeking legal advice) may prove to be particularly troublesome due to its obvious potential to undermine the workability of the offence. On this, see, e.g.: Branch (2013), 20–1; MacCulloch (2013); Stephan (2013); and Whelan (2013e).

designated NCA under Regulation 1/2003, then it would not have jurisdiction to prosecute an individual for an alleged commission of the criminal cartel offence.

One could eliminate the possibility for a later 'surprise' restriction of the scope of the national criminal cartel offence by linking the offence to a violation of Article 101(1) TFEU and by providing a defence along the lines of Article 101(3) TFEU. In addition, one can also designate the criminal prosecutor as an NCA under Regulation 1/2003. However, while this approach would avoid certain nasty surprises for the prosecution during a criminal trial, and would avoid arguments centred on a lack of jurisdiction due to Article 35 of Regulation 1/2003, it would also facilitate the introduction of economic evidence in a trial (something that legislators are keen to avoid) and would not deal with the Article 11(6) issue. Alternatively, one could design the criminal cartel offence so that it only applied to situations where there was no effect on trade between Member States. However, such an approach would be legally questionable. A policy of only pursuing cases with no effect on trade would be preferable, but such an option brings with it disadvantages in terms of achieving deterrence and/or retribution.

The best option would be to design the criminal cartel offence in such a manner that Regulation 1/2003 would not apply to it at all. This is a difficult thing to do, as it is not exactly clear when the Regulation will and will not apply concerning the enforcement of a national criminal cartel offence. This is due to, inter alia, the ambiguous nature of the relevant sentence in Recital 8 of Regulation 1/2003. Two alternative interpretations of when Regulation 1/2003 will not apply were identified: (i) when undertakings (as opposed to individuals) cannot be subjected to a criminal prosecution for commission of the criminal cartel offence; or (ii) when the criminal cartel offence does not pursue the same predominant objective as the EU competition law rules. If one is persuaded by the former interpretation, then all that one needs to do to avoid the impact of Regulation 1/2003 is to ensure that only individuals can be convicted of the criminal cartel offence. If the later interpretation is preferred, then one is required: (i) to take a (supportable) decision regarding the predominant objective of EU competition law; and (ii) to design the criminal cartel offence in such a way that its predominant objective can be distinguished from that of the EU competition law rules. One way of doing this might be to argue that the predominant objective of the EU competition rules is 'the protection of competition on the market' and that this is not pursued by the creation of a criminal cartel offence that is linked to an explicit moral concept, such as one of the norms against stealing, deception, or cheating.

This chapter also addressed the second aspect of the 'first (practical) challenge of design': the issue of dealing with 'acceptable' cartel activity. It first identified the central dilemma in this context by explaining how EU competition law currently deals with this issue and why that approach may not be ideal in a criminal law setting. EU competition law deals with the issue by virtue of the 'commercial ancillarity' doctrine and through Article 101(3) TFEU. Both of these mechanisms involve the conducting of assessments of the economic effects of the cartel in question. This is unfortunate, as a central feature of an effective criminal cartel law is the absence of a requirement to analyse and prove any economic effects in a market in order to find an infringement. An ideal solution to this issue would be the 'carve out' of 'acceptable' cartel activity from the criminal cartel offence in a manner that does not require the decision-maker in a criminal trial to undertake economic analyses.

The definitional element of 'dishonesty' was considered as one method of ensuring that 'acceptable' cartel activity is 'carved out' of the offence without the need for economic analysis. It was demonstrated that this particular definitional element is less than ideal: for 'dishonesty' to carve out 'acceptable' cartel activity, it will be necessary for the defendant to argue that ordinary people would not find that activity to be dishonest *because it is not unlawful under EU/national competition law* and in order to substantiate that argument the defendant will be required to put forward *economic* evidence which demonstrates that, for example, an exception under Article 101(3) TFEU (or the national equivalent) would be forthcoming. In addition to this failing, the definitional element of 'dishonesty' presents a number of problematic features, such as allowing for the presentation of dubious 'defences' in a criminal trial. Its inclusion in a criminal cartel offence is therefore not advisable.

Fortunately, one can identify an alternative method of 'carving out' so-called 'acceptable' cartel activity from the criminal cartel offence without the need for a decision-maker to conduct economic analyses in a criminal trial: the mechanism of 'carving out' cartel agreements that are published in an appropriate format prior to their implementation. This mechanism has recently been adopted in the UK. A criminal cartel offence that prohibits price-fixing, output restrictions, market sharing, and bid-rigging while allowing for a 'carve out' of agreements that are published would not require a decision-maker to assess the economic effects of an agreement to find that the offence has been committed. Importantly, however, it also provides scope for the operation of the 'commercial ancillarity' doctrine as well as for the operation of Article 101(3) TFEU: if cartelists genuinely believe that their cartel agreement would benefit from an exception (as it would fulfil the criteria of Article 101(3) TFEU) or that it would fulfil the criteria specified by the Court of Justice in implementing the 'commercial ancillarity' doctrine, all they have to do to avoid criminal sanctions is to publish publicly the agreement prior to its implementation or to notify the competition authority of its existence prior to implementation. One should understand that the 'carve out' of agreements made openly is not equivalent to the operation of a notification and authorization regime as it does not require any action on behalf of the competition authorities: the mere fact that an agreement has been published in a suitable format *automatically* removes the cartelists from the sphere of criminal law. There is, therefore, no resultant administrative burden on the authority. In fact, as argued above, such a 'carve out' engenders more advantages than disadvantages and should be an option favoured by those jurisdictions that are serious about dealing with hard-core cartel activity, but do not wish to prohibit activity that pursues a legitimate purpose or may produce net benefits for consumers.

9

European Antitrust Criminalization and the Second Challenge of Design: Understanding the Complexities of Leniency/Immunity

A. Introduction

It is clear that a successful antitrust criminalization project does not depend solely on the existence of a well-defined criminal cartel offence. This is true regardless of whether the underlying enforcement objective is deterrence or retribution. Common to the achievement of both of these objectives is the requirement to bring successful prosecutions when cartel activity actually occurs in a market. Successful detection and prosecution are obvious requisite elements as regards the effectiveness of deterrence; indeed, optimal deterrent enforcement is determined by, inter alia, the probability of detection and prosecution, as noted in Chapter 2. To put it another way, 'harsh penalties represent a hollow threat unless there is also vigorous, timely, and successful enforcement'.[1] For deterrence to work in practice, potential cartelists must understand that by engaging in cartel activity they actually risk going to prison as a result. The mere publication of new legislation that ultimately is not enforced effectively will not achieve deterrence in the long term: the existence of the criminal cartel offence must be complemented with efficient enforcement mechanisms and strategies in order to produce the desired results. While not as obvious as it is with deterrence, such an assertion is also relevant to retribution theory. According to some leading theorists, for retribution to be effective at all, it not only requires the punishment (through successful trials) of those who have done wrong, but also their *rooting out*.[2] Following this line of argument, retribution does not merely require the meting out of deserved punishment when an offence is detected, but also the active detection of offences in order to impose deserved punishment. Like deterrence, then, retribution is not achieved by the mere creation of a well-defined criminal cartel offence: further action by the authorities is required. Consequently, the practical challenge of antitrust criminalization is not confined to the design of the criminal cartel offence itself; rather, it also encompasses the identification of any desirable enforcement mechanisms and strategies.

When determining the correct enforcement mechanisms and strategies for criminal cartel law, one must understand that cartel activity is inherently secret. In non-criminalized anti-cartel regimes within the EU, cartel activity not only remains unlawful, but is also sanctioned severely. In that particular atmosphere, cartelists have developed sophisticated methods of concealment in order to avoid (administrative) punishment.[3] When

[1] Klawiter and Driscoll (2009), 75.

[2] '[F]or a retributionist, the moral culpability of an offender also gives society the *duty* to punish. Retributivism, in other words, is truly a theory of justice such that, if it is true, we have an obligation to set up institutions so that retribution is achieved': Moore (1987), 150. Cf. Yeung (2004), 72–3.

[3] An EU example is *Gas Insulated Switchgear* (Case COMP/F/38.899), Commission Decision, 24 January 2007, [2008] OJ C5/7. For an additional and interesting example of how those involved in an international cartel try to conceal their activities, see First (2001), 714–15. The fact that cartels often

criminal cartel sanctions are introduced into an anti-cartel regime, it would be no surprise if efforts to conceal cartel activity and to keep the (criminal) antitrust enforcers at bay actually increase. If individuals are intent on engaging in cartel activity irrespective of the existence of criminal sanctions, they may well decide to be extra careful in this regard, as the risks they are taking are significantly higher, encompassing as they do the risk of losing one's liberty. To enforce actively the criminal cartel offence, antitrust enforcers must pierce this veil of secrecy. The challenge for those who advocate criminal cartel sanctions is to determine how this can be done effectively. One obvious mechanism that can be used to do this is the provision of criminal immunity for the first self-reporting cartelist. In Chapter 5, it was explained that in theory criminal immunity can bring additional advantages to administrative leniency/immunity, provided of course that criminal sanctions exist in the first place. The granting of criminal immunity, however, is not without its own particular problems, and these problems should be understood by those who wish to have a full understanding of the practical challenge of European antitrust criminalization.

Another aspect of the practical challenge of European antitrust enforcement is to ensure that the introduction of criminal sanctions in a given Member State does not impact negatively upon those (effective) detection methods that are already in existence in the administrative competition regimes across Europe. There are a number of mechanisms that can be used to detect cartel activity. Competition authorities can rely upon both proactive and reactive tools to detect cartel activity.[4] Proactive methods include the use of economics (involving examination of collusion factors, industry studies, and market screening), industry monitoring, and agency cooperation, while reactive methods include complaints, external information (from whistle-blowers or informants), and leniency/immunity applications.[5] Leniency/immunity is perceived as being an extremely important mechanism to detect cartels. It would be unfortunate if the introduction of criminal cartel sanctions were to impact negatively upon the operation of administrative leniency/immunity programmes, particularly given that, as was noted above, the detection of cartel activity is intrinsically linked to the achievement of both deterrence and retribution. Understanding this issue and responding to it effectively constitutes the main practical challenge concerning the preservation of already-existing mechanisms. Leniency/immunity, then, is also at the heart of this additional aspect of the practical challenge of European antitrust criminalization.

What is deemed in this book to be the 'second challenge of design' for European antitrust criminalization encompasses both of the issues noted directly above. Specifically, it involves articulating and overcoming the unique challenges of *criminal* immunity for cartelists and responding to the challenge of ensuring peaceful co-existence of both administrative leniency/immunity and criminal cartel sanctions. A systematic analysis that focuses on both aspects of this practical challenge is absent from the current literature.[6] This situation is regrettable. Failure by policy-makers and legislators to understand and respond to the 'second challenge of design' may ensure the creation and maintenance of a criminal cartel regime that fails to meet its objectives.[7] Such failure would certainly have negative

involve sophisticated methods of concealment has been acknowledged in the literature for many years; see, e.g., Watkins (1961), 104.

[4] See generally ICN (2011b). [5] See Hüschelrath (2010).

[6] See, however: Frese (2006); Massey (2006); and MacCulloch and Wardhaugh (2012).

[7] This has arguably occurred in Hungary, where the criminalization of public procurement and concession cartels occurred 'without having solved problems such as cooperation between the police and the competition authority, rival procedures for the same infringement and *primacy of application for leniency*': Cseres (2007), 494 (emphasis added). Greece has also experienced a number of practical problems with cartel criminalization, particularly concerning the design of its immunity policy; see, e.g., Brisimi and Ioannidou (2011).

budgetary implications for a jurisdiction and, as a result, has the potential to undermine any existing public support for competition regulation within that jurisdiction.

This chapter aims to contribute to the literature on European cartel criminalization by providing a systematic analysis of the challenge of design posed for such criminalization by the investigative mechanism of leniency/immunity. In doing so, it considers both aspects of the 'second challenge of design': peaceful co-existence of administrative leniency/immunity and criminal sanctions; and the unique challenge of criminal immunity. Importantly, it also identifies how the specifics of this particular practical challenge impact upon the achievement of the underlying enforcement objectives of antitrust criminalization (deterrence and retribution). Consequently, this chapter, in conjunction with Chapters 8 and 10, not only presents a detailed analysis of the practical challenge of leniency/immunity in the criminal context, but also contributes to the articulation of the extent of any dynamic interaction between this practical challenge and the theoretical and legal challenges analysed respectively in Parts I and II of this book.

In order to achieve its aims, this chapter is divided into two substantive sections and a conclusion. Section B considers the potential for the existence of criminal cartel sanctions to have a negative impact upon administrative leniency/immunity policies and whether any mechanisms (such as a *criminal* immunity policy) can be put in place to counteract any negative effects. Section C looks at the issue of design from a different angle and makes the assumption that a criminal immunity policy is part of the enforcement armoury of the criminal enforcer. In particular, it considers the challenges that are unique to the use of a criminal immunity policy to secure successful cartel prosecutions. Finally, Section D provides a number of conclusions on the complexities of leniency/immunity for European antitrust criminalization and hence articulates 'the second (practical) challenge of design' in this context.

B. The Co-Existence of Administrative Leniency/Immunity and Criminal Sanctions

This section analyses the specific challenge of ensuring a peaceful co-existence between criminal cartel sanctions and administrative leniency/immunity[8] programmes. Specifically, this section acknowledges the importance of administrative leniency for competition law enforcement (Sub-section (a)), analyses the argument that the introduction of criminal cartel sanctions has the potential to undermine the effectiveness of administrative leniency policies (Sub-section (b)), and considers whether mechanisms can be put in place to protect administrative leniency policies from any negative effect identified (Sub-section (c)).

(a) Acknowledging the importance of administrative leniency/immunity

In Chapter 5, it was noted that there is the potential for a 'strengthening of rights' to occur when a competition law regime introduces criminal sanctions (in addition to or in place of administrative sanctions) for cartel activity and that leniency is one very useful method of investigation that can be used to help to overcome any negative impact

[8] In order to avoid excessive repetition, in this chapter all references to 'leniency' should also be understood to include a reference to 'immunity', unless the context dictates otherwise. References to 'immunity' do not necessarily imply an additional reference to 'leniency'.

upon the enforcement objectives occasioned by this particular 'strengthening'. Due to the particular research question pursued in Chapter 5, the purpose of the analysis of leniency in that chapter was to establish whether there are certain additional advantages to the employment of immunity in a criminal context (i.e. advantages that do not exist in an administrative setting where fines are only imposed upon corporate entities). The reason for the focus on *additional* advantages was that leniency programmes can be used (and indeed have been used) in administrative regimes: their usefulness is not confined to a criminalized cartel regime. The use of leniency in an administrative setting can also be seen as being superior to other forms of information gathering in that setting (e.g., monitoring markets, relying upon third-party information, or using direct force or compulsion against the cartelists): it can be used to obtain all kinds of information (and not just the physical variety); it reduces search costs; and it does not suffer from the reliability problems of other methods of collection.[9] One should understand here in fact that, while robust empirical evidence supporting (or indeed refuting) their effectiveness is relatively scarce,[10] leniency programmes have become a 'prominent element' of modern antitrust enforcement (including its administrative variety)[11] and that competition law enforcers are extremely keen to ensure that the effectiveness of such programmes is not undermined by other enforcement initiatives (whether undertaken in the competition law enforcers' own jurisdictions or in another state).

One such enforcement initiative is the current push at EU level and in some EU Member States towards increased private enforcement of competition law,[12] where it is feared that (forced) disclosure of administrative leniency material (by a competition authority or a leniency applicant) in the course of civil proceedings may undermine the incentives of undertakings to apply for leniency.[13] The EU case of *Pfleiderer*[14] highlights this particular fear.[15] In that case, the Court of Justice was asked, in the context of a request for a preliminary ruling under Article 267 TFEU, whether the provisions of EU competition law ensure that parties adversely affected by a cartel should not 'be given access to leniency applications or to information and documents voluntarily submitted in that context by applicants for leniency which the national competition authority of a Member State has received, pursuant to a national leniency policy'.[16] Ultimately, the Court ruled that it would be for the national courts and tribunals to decide on a case-by-case basis, on the basis of national law, after weighing the interests protected by EU law, whether access should be granted.[17] In coming to this conclusion, the Court noted that

[9] See Wils (2007a).

[10] See, however: Brenner (2009) (finding evidence that agencies with a leniency programme are better informed about cartel activity than they would have been without such a programme); Miller (2009) (who demonstrates that statistical tests are consistent with the assertion that leniency improves deterrence and detection rates); and Stephan (2008d) (finding that, at EU level in the time period under discussion, leniency was predominantly awarded in cases where cartels were failing or had already failed). See also Hüschelrath (2010), 524 (highlighting that there is limited evidence to determine the relative importance of reactive and proactive methods to detect cartels).

[11] Harding and Joshua (2010), 229.

[12] See, e.g.: Council of the European Union (2013); European Commission (2013a); European Commission (2013b); European Commission (2008a); European Commission (2008b); European Commission (2005c); and European Commission (2005d).

[13] On this, see generally: Canenbley and Steinvorth (2011); and Caruso (2010).

[14] Case C-360/09, *Pfleiderer AG v. Bundeskartellamt* [2011] ECR I-05161.

[15] So, too, does the following (later) case: C-536/11, *Bundeswettbewerbsbehörde v. Donau Chemie AG and others*, Judgment of 6 June 2013, not yet reported. However, as the *Pfleiderer* judgment provides sufficient context for the discussion that follows, the case of *Donau Chemie* is not considered.

[16] Case C-360/09, *Pfleiderer AG v. Bundeskartellamt* [2011] ECR I-05161, [18].

[17] Case C-360/09, *Pfleiderer AG v. Bundeskartellamt* [2011] ECR I-05161, [33].

the effectiveness of leniency programmes could be compromised 'if documents relating to a leniency procedure were disclosed to persons wishing to bring an action for damages, even if the national competition authorities were to grant to the applicant for leniency exemption, in whole or in part, from the fine which they could have imposed'.[18] The central point is that the leniency applicant cannot be granted immunity from a civil proceeding (damages claim) and would think twice about applying for leniency if the information provided in the course of a leniency application could later be used to facilitate such a civil proceeding.[19] The (later) English case of *National Grid*[20] also demonstrates this particular fear of competition enforcers. In that case, the European Commission was invited to provide observations to the High Court of England and Wales on both the relevance and applicability of the *Pfleiderer* judgment to the case before the court (which involved the applicant's seeking of access to documents held by the defendant which could or would contain leniency material).[21] In its observations, the Commission stated that

> there appears to exist a general perception amongst potential leniency applicants that disclosure of their corporate [leniency] statements would particularly disadvantage them in actions for damages compared to those parties that did not cooperate by exposing them to greater liability. The Commission therefore respectfully submits that this particular factor augurs in favour of non-disclosure of leniency documents.[22]

For the Commission, then, the protection of the leniency application process is of extremely high importance, even where the exercise of a Treaty right is concerned (i.e. the right to claim damages for loss due to cartel activity[23]).[24] National competition authorities across the EU have displayed a similar attitude towards their (administrative) leniency programmes.[25] Such is the Commission's commitment to the protection of administrative leniency programmes that it recently proposed a Directive which provides, inter alia, that Member States would have the obligation to ensure that national courts cannot order a party to litigation or a third party to disclose 'corporate leniency statements' for the purpose of private actions for damages for violation of the competition law rules.[26] While aspects of this particular proposal were later modified, an equivalent approach concerning the disclosure of leniency statements is present in the latest version of the proposal: the revised Presidency compromise proposal of 3 December 2013.[27]

18 Case C-360/09, *Pfleiderer AG v. Bundeskartellamt* [2011] ECR I-05161, [26].

19 On the general ramifications of the *Pfleiderer* case, see, e.g.: Cauffman (2011a); and Cauffman (2011b).

20 *National Grid v. ABB* [2012] EWHC 869 (Ch).

21 On this, see generally Gamble (2013), 37–9.

22 European Commission (2011c), [18].

23 On this, see: Case C-453/99, *Courage v. Crehan* [2001] ECR I-6297, [24] and [26]; and Joined Cases C-295–8/04, *Vincenzo Manfredi and others v. Lloyd Adriatico Assicurazioni SpA and others* [2006] ECR I-6619, [59] and [61].

24 See, e.g., European Commission (2013a), 3.

25 See, e.g., ECN (2012a).

26 European Commission (2013b), Article 6(1). Article 4(14) of the proposed Directive stipulates that '"leniency corporate statement" means an oral or written presentation voluntarily provided by, or on behalf of, an undertaking to a competition authority, describing the undertaking's knowledge of a secret cartel and its role therein, which was drawn up specifically for submission to the authority with a view to obtaining immunity or a reduction of fines under a leniency programme concerning the application of Article 101 of the Treaty or the corresponding provision under national law; this does not include documents or information that exist irrespective of the proceedings of a competition authority ("pre-existing information")'.

27 See Council of the European Union (2013), Annex, Articles 4(15), 4(16), and 6(5).

The importance ascribed to administrative leniency policies is a crucial factor in the European criminalization debate and impacts upon the specifics of the practical challenge of designing an effective criminal cartel regime. In fact, a number of commentators fear that the use of criminal cartel sanctions has the potential to undermine administrative leniency programmes within the EU,[28] with some even arguing that national-level criminalization should not occur due to the negative impact it would potentially have on the operation of administrative leniency.[29] To understand fully the challenge of design posed for European antitrust criminalization by the investigative mechanism of leniency, one must first identify why the potential exists for a negative impact of criminal sanctions upon administrative leniency policies in the EU, before determining whether mechanisms can be put in place to counteract any potential negative impact.

(b) The potential negative impact of criminal sanctions upon administrative leniency/immunity programmes

It is clear from the literature that commentators believe that some potential exists for criminal cartel sanctions to impact negatively upon administrative leniency policies.[30] It is also obvious that the potential for negative effect is not confined to a situation where the criminal sanctions and the administrative leniency policy exist in the same jurisdiction. The potential negative effect may also occur in practice if the administrative leniency policy in question exists in one jurisdiction and the criminal cartel sanctions exist in another.[31] Cartel conduct can (and often does) extend beyond the borders of nation states and can register its impact in a number of different jurisdictions simultaneously.[32] Indeed, 'given globalisation, it is likely that a cartel in one jurisdiction may have knock-on effects in another, through re-exporting or the use of cartelised products as parts in finished goods'.[33] A particular cartel could therefore be investigated in more than one state at any given time, and administrative cartel proceedings (involving leniency applicants) could be in existence in one state and criminal cartel proceedings in another. While this does not complicate the identification of the potential for a negative effect, it certainly has an impact on the ability of the state with the administrative leniency policy (and no criminal sanctions) to create a workable solution to the issue, as will become apparent below.

There are at least four (good) reasons for the existence of a potential negative impact of criminal sanctions upon administrative leniency policies within the EU. The first reason is the fact that companies (or, more accurately, the relevant decision-making units within companies) applying for administrative leniency may actually care about what happens to their employees. They may not wish to apply for administrative leniency (at EU level or within a Member State) if, by doing so, they would expose their employees to potential jail sentences in another Member State or in another jurisdiction (such as the US).[34] One should understand here that cartel activity, if successful, directly benefits the company,[35] and that, following discovery, the employees who are responsible for the cartel activity may have convinced the management of the company that they were only doing what was necessary to ensure that the business obtained maximum returns

28 Harding and Joshua (2010), 352. 29 See Frese (2005), 30.

30 See, e.g.: Billiet (2009), 18; Carmeliet (2011–12), 479; Joshua and Klawiter (2002), 70; Letsike (2013), 6 et seq.; McFadden (2011), 15; and Schroeder and Heinz (2006), 162–3.

31 Cf. Shaffer and Nesbitt (2011). 32 See generally Connor and Helmers (2007).

33 Paulis (2004), [3].

34 Reynolds and Anderson (2006), 89. 35 Aubert (2009), 3.

for shareholders. This type of problem was recognized in the UK when it criminalized (dishonest) cartel activity in June 2003. According to the (then) Deputy Director of the Office of Fair Trading's Cartels Group,

> it was recognised from the outset that if undertakings thought that by applying to the OFT for immunity they would be exposing their employees and directors to the risk of criminal prosecution, this would have a serious chilling effect on the OFT's immunity policy and, therefore, on its ability to uncover cartels.[36]

The second reason is that individuals within a firm which is contemplating applying for leniency may fear for their own exposure to criminal cartel sanctions.[37] This fear impacts upon an individual's preparedness to cooperate with a leniency application or to pursue such an application on behalf of the firm.[38] The second reason is similar to the first, but recognizes that, in some instances at least, the individuals applying for leniency on behalf of the firm may actually be the individuals within that firm who have engaged in the cartel activity for which the firm is applying for leniency. While such a situation may occur with any size or type of business, it is more likely with a family-owned business or a relatively small-sized business than with a multinational corporation. In such a situation, it is very unlikely that an individual will risk being sent to prison merely to ensure the business is not subjected to an administrative fine. The third reason why undertakings would be hesitant to apply for administrative leniency if their employees would be subject to criminal law exposure is that undertakings may well need the cooperation of their employees who have engaged in cartel activity in order to be certain that they can provide the necessary documentation and information to secure the benefit of the leniency policy.[39] Such cooperation would surely not be provided if the employees were to risk being exposed to criminal liability.

At this point, and before considering the fourth reason why criminal cartel sanctions can impact negatively upon administrative leniency policies, one should explain why an administrative leniency application could theoretically lead to the exposure of an individual to a criminal process. One reason for increased exposure would simply be the existence of a final, published administrative decision finding the existence of a cartel (which, it must be understood, usually results from an administrative leniency application): the existence of such a decision may lead the relevant criminal investigator to focus on the cartelized market in question and, provided any rules on limitation are not prohibitive, could eventually result in the pressing of criminal charges against individuals. Obviously, exposure could also occur if the entity receiving the leniency application were the same entity that would be responsible for investigating and/or prosecuting the criminal cartel offence. In the alternative, exposure might also be likely if the entity operating the administrative leniency policy exists within the same jurisdiction as the criminal cartel investigator, as it may feel an obligation to report the fact that an application has been made to its national competition law enforcement counterpart. If, however, the administrative leniency policy is operated by a different jurisdiction from the jurisdiction with the relevant criminal cartel sanctions, exposure to criminal sanctions may nonetheless occur if the entity operating the administrative leniency programme passes on the leniency application itself (or the mere fact that it has been made) to the other (criminalized) jurisdiction. In order to put in place mechanisms satisfying an undertaking contemplating applying for administrative leniency that its employees

[36] Blake (2008), 14. [37] See, e.g., Joshua (2002), 236.
[38] Cf. Levy and O'Donoghue (2004), 96. [39] See Arp and Swaak (2002), 64.

will not be exposed to criminal sanctions for the cartel, one must take account of these different ways of creating criminal law exposure.

The fourth and final reason for a potential negative impact of criminal sanctions upon leniency programmes is the fear that by applying for administrative leniency a corporation would be increasing its risk of exposure to private damages actions.[40] This fear is similar to the fear expressed in the *Pfleiderer* litigation noted above. The difference here, however, is that there is an additional route for the private litigant to obtain disclosure of the relevant leniency documents: depending on the specific legalities of the criminal cartel regime, those documents may need to be disclosed to the criminal defendant in order to protect his rights of defence, and therefore may eventually be referred to in open court resulting in public disclosure for the purposes of a civil proceeding.[41] This problem has also been acknowledged by the OFT[42] and represents an additional complication to the '*Pfleiderer* problem'. According to the OFT, if a prosecution is commenced in the UK, under applicable law,[43] criminal disclosure 'will inevitably include material provided by the leniency applicant, and would typically include application statements (whether written or transcripts of oral statements), where such statements are capable of having an impact on issues arising in the criminal case'.[44] The worry of the applicant for administrative leniency is that the disclosure of these documents to the accused could facilitate a later compensation claim against it in a civil court (which may involve treble damages if the civil claim is heard in a US court).[45] The disclosure of the applicant's statements would be particularly worrying to administrative leniency applicants as they may contain aspects of the application not pursued by the prosecuting authority 'or the applicant's own analysis of the emerging details of the cartel at the time of the application, and there is therefore a potential risk that any unnecessary disclosures may put leniency applicants at a disadvantage relative to non-leniency parties'.[46] For cartel criminalization to be effective, then, one must put in place mechanisms to allay (as best one can) the above-noted fears of administrative leniency applicants.

(c) Identifying mechanisms to counteract any negative impact

(i) Creating a criminal immunity policy

One of the most obvious ways to help to counteract the potential negative impact of criminal cartel sanctions upon administrative leniency programmes would be to introduce a *criminal* immunity programme in the criminalized regime. This particular mechanism has been put in place in many criminalized cartel regimes, including, for example, the US,[47] Canada,[48] Australia,[49] Ireland,[50] and the UK.[51] As with its administrative counterpart, there are of course many different ways of designing a criminal immunity policy.[52] However, the central feature of such a programme would generally be the granting of automatic criminal immunity for the first individual to self-report, admit

40 See Zingales (2008), 15. 41 Cf. Purnell et al. (2010), 322.

42 OFT (2013b), [7.14].

43 Namely, the Criminal Procedure and Investigations Act 1996, as amended by the Criminal Justice Act 2003.

44 OFT (2013b), [7.11]. 45 See Furse (2012), 145. 46 OFT (2013b), [7.7].

47 DoJ (1994). 48 The Competition Bureau (2010).

49 Commonwealth Director of Public Prosecutions (1992), Annexure B.

50 The Competition Authority (2001). 51 See generally OFT (2013b).

52 See generally: ICN (2009); and Zingales (2008). On the general requisites of an effective (criminal) leniency policy, see OECD (2007b), 12.

guilt, and cooperate with the authorities, if by doing so that individual would enable the authorities to take forward a credible (administrative/criminal) investigation. If the individual is not the first to report, or if an investigation is already in progress when the applicant reports, the criminal immunity policy could provide for a discretionary immunity from prosecution, as occurs in the UK. In such a case, additional requirements could be imposed, such as the requirement that the applicant provide significant value to the investigation. Alternatively, the authorities may wish to create a rapid 'race to the regulator' and therefore may choose to design a criminal immunity policy that only applies to those who have 'won' the race outright. In such situations, the existence of a system of plea-bargaining could provide scope for a reduction in sentence for those who fall outside of the criminal immunity programme, but who wish to cooperate with the authorities. However the immunity programme is designed, it is imperative that transparency surrounding its operation exists.[53]

Criminal immunity policies are generally perceived to be *essential* in a criminalized regime in order to protect the administrative leniency policy:[54] they help to reassure the undertaking that its employees have a route out of potential criminal proceedings against them. This represents a different rationale for the existence of criminal immunity policies than that presented in Chapter 5. In that particular chapter, it was noted that criminal immunity policies are *advisable* as their existence may engender additional advantages over administrative leniency which help to overcome the extra enforcement burdens created by virtue of cartel criminalization (e.g., a 'strengthening' of human rights in favour of the accused[55]). In the context under discussion, however, criminal immunity is understood as an effective way to ensure that exposure to criminal sanctions (however it may have occurred otherwise) does not transpire in practice,[56] thereby allaying the fears of those undertakings that are worried about their employees and, as a result, fortifying the (jealously guarded) administrative leniency policy.

There are, however, two significant drawbacks to the 'solution' of employing a criminal immunity policy to counteract the negative effect of criminal sanctions on administrative leniency policies. The first is that, given its application to breaches of criminal (cartel) law as opposed to administrative (cartel) law, the criminal immunity policy may conflict with the principle of mandatory prosecution, which exists in some EU Member States.[57] This principle holds that if sufficient evidence exists concerning the commission of a criminal offence, then the public authorities must take enforcement action;[58] no discretion can therefore be exercised over the prosecutorial decision. This principle appears to exclude the possibility of criminal immunity: the authorities cannot promise to ignore the crimes of those who have decided to whistle-blow. However, as noted by Wils, four points need to be remembered here:[59] (i) the principle only prohibits immunity from prosecution, not immunity from the imposition of criminal punishment arising due to prosecution;[60] (ii) depending upon the specifics of the legal regime, the principle can

[53] See Spratling (1999). [54] See Lowe (2007), 95. [55] See Chapter 5 of this book.

[56] If the criminalized cartel regime also allows for private criminal prosecutions, it would be advisable not only to create a criminal leniency policy, but also to ensure that a private criminal prosecution cannot proceed without the consent of the entity granting the criminal immunity; see DTI (2001b), [7.51]. Such a move would also help to prevent vexatious private prosecutions: Fingleton et al. (2007), 21.

[57] See Zingales (2008), 14. This argument has been made in relation to Sweden, for example. See: Swedish Competition Authority (2006); and Holm (2006). Germany also has this particular issue; see Vollmer (2006), 259.

[58] Mansfield and Peay (1987), 17. [59] See Wils (2008a), 143–4.

[60] In other words, the principle only prohibits criminal immunity, not criminal leniency (where a prosecution is brought, but a reduced punishment (perhaps to zero) is imposed).

often be displaced by legislation; (iii) the Council of Europe has been actively encouraging its members to introduce and/or expand the principle of discretionary prosecution; and (iv) the main objective motivating the principle (i.e. equal treatment)[61] can still be achieved if transparency is a feature of the criminal immunity policy. Furthermore, in jurisdictions where the principle exists, there are often 'various and extensive' exceptions to the requirement of mandatory prosecution.[62] Consequently, the issue is not overly problematic: the principle of mandatory prosecution does not in fact completely tie the hands of the authorities; rather, it merely: (i) dictates that, in the absence of further legislative action, criminal leniency should be provided instead of criminal immunity; or (ii) requires legislative action in order to provide a legitimate base for a policy that allows for immunity from prosecution. For undertakings that care about their employees, approach (ii) is preferable to approach (i). The reason for this is that approach (i), unlike (ii), requires an individual to stand trial and the mere fact that an individual is subjected to a criminal process (even if the outcome is a conviction with no punishment) is likely to have significant negative effects on an individual's life: the 'harm that *indictment* brings to the individual may be irremediable even by subsequent dismissal or acquittal'.[63]

The second drawback of criminal immunity concerns the extent to which the investigating antitrust authorities can actually *guarantee* immunity for applicants. If a system is not in place whereby applicants fulfilling the requirements of the criminal immunity policy are *guaranteed* full immunity, then such applicants may be very hesitant to come forward with their evidence.[64] This may be the case even where the application can be made on a no-name, hypothetical basis or where guarantees are made (by the prosecutor) that any evidence provided as a result of such an application will not be used against the applicant in the case of a refusal to grant immunity; indeed, in both cases the applicant will still be vulnerable to prosecution. The absence of a system whereby a guarantee of immunity can be granted (provided the necessary criteria are fulfilled) has the potential not only to impact upon the effectiveness of the criminal regime, but it may also undermine the operation of any parallel administrative regime.[65] This point was not initially appreciated by the UK authorities. For example, in the 2001 'White Paper' that proposed the introduction of criminal cartel sanctions in the UK, it was recommended that the OFT would only have a *discretion* not to prosecute those cartelists who self-reported a cartel.[66] This proposal was (rightly) criticized at the time on the basis that it would 'do nothing to encourage wrongdoers to come forward. Only a guarantee of non-prosecution will do so'.[67] Indeed, for Venit, nothing short of an 'iron clad assurance' that an administrative leniency applicant will not face potential criminal antitrust sanctions will be sufficient to ensure the integrity of the administrative leniency procedure.[68] Failure to deal effectively with this issue can result in a 'paradox', as 'strengthening the sanction system might make it harder to detect cartels'.[69] Unfortunately, it is

[61] On the motivations behind the principle, see Tak (2004). Interestingly, one of the motivations is apparently the theory of deterrence: Tak (2004), 9. If this is so, there may be even less to worry about concerning the principle of mandatory prosecution in the context of antitrust criminalization: when deterrence is the operative foundational theory, the very use of criminal antitrust sanctions—and their effective implementation through, inter alia, an individual leniency programme—is directed towards achieving deterrence, and so would be consistent with this particular concern of the principle of mandatory prosecution.

[62] See Wagner-von Papp (2011), 176.

[63] Chadwell (1955), 1139 (emphasis added).

[64] See: Frese (2006), 201; and Joshua (2002), 236. Cf. MacCulloch and Wardhaugh (2012), 18–19.

[65] See: Kelly (2010), 329–30; and Lavoie (2012), 152.

[66] DTI (2001b), [7.50].

[67] Smith (2001), 292.

[68] Venit (2008).

[69] Norgen (2007), 56.

well recognized that there are 'inherent difficulties in "guaranteeing" absolute immunity from prosecution'.[70] In particular, a system guaranteeing (conditional) immunity in this context may be difficult to put in place when the investigating antitrust authority (i.e. the body receiving the immunity application) is not the body which will be making the final prosecutorial decision.[71] Institutional traditions or politics will be relevant here: it is not unlikely in such a situation that the prosecuting authority will be reluctant to delegate its prosecutorial discretion to the investigating body and to bind itself to the latter's decisions. Wils proposes two potential solutions to this problem. Either one can impose the criminal immunity policy of the investigating authority upon the prosecuting authority by virtue of a higher legislative act, or one could ensure that the prosecuting authority is involved in the introduction and application of the policy.[72] The first proposed solution is obviously the most coercive: it requires the prosecuting authority to respect the decision of the investigating body; however, it requires legislative action and risks alienating the prosecuting authority. The second proposed solution is less likely to cause friction between the two relevant entities; however, it still requires the consent of the prosecuting authority, a consent that may be difficult to obtain for political reasons. A further solution would be for the prosecuting authority to agree to accord 'serious weight' to recommendations for immunity that are proposed by the investigating body.[73] Although not without its own problems concerning certainty and transparency, this final proposed solution may provide a 'workable level of comfort' that will relieve the concerns of potential immunity applicants.[74] It may act as a middle ground between the other two proposed solutions. Whichever solution is chosen, however, it is imperative that the different authorities possess 'a shared philosophy about the seriousness of cartel conduct, shared priorities toward prosecuting cartel activity and open and constant communication'.[75]

(ii) Linking the criminal immunity policy and the administrative leniency/immunity policy

At this point, one should note that the *mere existence* of a criminal immunity policy in the criminalized regime may not be enough to allay the above-noted (employee-focused) fears of the undertaking contemplating applying for administrative leniency. For companies seriously concerned about their employees, it would not be enough for them to apply for administrative leniency knowing that a criminal immunity policy also exists. The reasons for this are as follows. In order to secure the additional advantages of criminal immunity noted in Chapter 5, the authorities would be advised to design the criminal immunity policy to ensure a conflict between employees and their company. One way of doing this would be to ensure that guaranteed criminal immunity should only be provided to an employee if he were the first person to reveal the existence of the cartel to the authorities. In other words, in order to incentivize individuals to come forward quickly, one could ensure that an undertaking's application for administrative leniency

[70] Guy (2006), 251.

[71] This is the case, e.g., in Scotland, where the OFT investigates cartel activity and the Lord Advocate decides whether to prosecute an individual for commission of the UK Cartel Offence contained in the Enterprise Act 2002.

[72] Wils (2008a), 144. See also Kovacic (2011), 53.

[73] This represents the solution chosen in Scotland. See: OFT (2009a); and Shearing and Fonyonga (2009).

[74] Young et al. (2009).

[75] ICN (2009), [3.12].

would preclude an application by an individual for criminal immunity for the same cartel. If the criminal immunity policy is designed in this way, then the undertaking's application for administrative leniency would—in the absence of some other mechanism—actually preclude an application for criminal immunity by one of its employees. In a similar vein, the rule requiring the applicant for criminal immunity to be the first to confess would ensure that the application for criminal immunity of *one employee* in a company would preclude a similar application concerning the same cartel by *any other employee* in that company. This would not be acceptable to an undertaking that cares about all of its employees involved in the cartel activity in question. In addition, the undertaking may wish to help its employees with any immunity application (and/or legal fees) and may prefer to see a possibility for joint (administrative and criminal) applications in order to save costs. These particular factors lead one to a crucial point: the need for a link between administrative leniency programmes and the granting of criminal immunity.[76] In order to ensure that applications for administrative leniency are not 'chilled' by the existence of criminal cartel sanctions, one must not only create a criminal immunity policy in the criminalized jurisdiction, but, ideally, also ensure that criminal immunity automatically extends to the (cooperating) employees of those undertakings that have successfully applied for 'full' administrative leniency (i.e. a reduction of a fine to zero Euros).[77]

Linking administrative leniency for an undertaking with criminal immunity for its employees raises additional challenges to those already inherent in ensuring the existence of a successful criminal immunity policy. The reason for this is that the jurisdiction operating the relevant criminal immunity policy may not be the same jurisdiction that is operating the applicable administrative leniency policy. To take an example, an undertaking may be contemplating applying for administrative leniency at EU level, but may be worried about exposing its employees to criminal sanctions in Ireland or in Estonia. In such a situation, it is very difficult to ensure that a successful application for administrative leniency would also eliminate any criminal exposure of the undertaking's employees. When the administrative regime in question is indeed the EU-level regime, a number of possibilities for resolution of this issue can be identified: (i) Article 4(3) TEU (the Treaty article which contains the 'principle of sincere cooperation' between the Union and the Member States) could be used to require the national criminal investigator/prosecutor to refrain from prosecuting the (cooperating) employees of the undertaking to which the Commission has granted full administrative leniency; (ii) the EU could adopt legislation establishing that the grant of full administrative leniency by the Commission precludes the imposition of national criminal cartel sanctions; (iii) the Commission could adopt a non-binding resolution recommending that the Member States do not bring criminal cartel prosecutions against the (cooperating) employees of the undertaking to which the Commission has granted full administrative leniency; and (iv) national criminal prosecutors could formally agree not to bring criminal charges against the (cooperating) employees of the undertaking to which the Commission has granted full administrative leniency.[78] Clearly, when the administrative regime in question is not the Commission, the first three of the proposed solutions will not be relevant and one is only left with mechanism (iv) as a possible solution.

76 See Stephan (2008c), 32–3. See also the comments of Guersent in Hawk (2004), 128.

77 The UK authorities have expressly acknowledged this fact; see: Blake (2008), 14–16; Fingleton et al. (2007), 21; and OFT (2013b), [1.8]. The Greek authorities have also done so; see Brisimi and Ioannidou (2011), 172. Not all commentators agree with this approach, however; see MacCulloch and Wardhaugh (2012), 17–18 (who argue that decoupling the administrative policy from the criminal immunity policy ensures that an individual applicant 'has a real independent engagement with the process' which helps to ensure that the evidence generated through immunity is 'credible and robust').

78 Levy and O'Donoghue (2004), 97–8.

While the first of these proposed solutions has been mooted in a number of academic publications,[79] it has yet to be tested in front of the EU Courts. A question mark therefore hangs over its effectiveness at dealing with the issue identified; as noted by Levy and O'Donoghue, Article 4(3) TEU

> would need to be expansively interpreted to restrict the application of criminal sanctions at the national level. It is uncertain whether the Community courts would be sympathetic to such an interpretation.[80]

The second solution would require a firm legal basis in the Treaty framework. The most obvious candidate for a potential legal basis is Article 103 TFEU. Article 103(1) TFEU provides, inter alia, that Regulations and Directives may be adopted to give effect to the principles set out in Article 101 TFEU. Article 103(2)(e) TFEU clarifies that the Regulations and Directives referred to in Article 103(1) TFEU shall be designed to determine, inter alia, the relationship between national laws, on the one hand, and Article 101 TFEU and/or the provisions adopted under Article 103(1) TFEU, on the other. The issue here is to determine whether an EU measure establishing that the grant of full administrative leniency by the Commission precludes the imposition of national criminal cartel sanctions could reasonably be interpreted as a measure determining the relationship between national laws and Article 101 TFEU and/or a measure adopted under Article 103(1). This is quite debateable. The adoption of a Regulation using Article 103 TFEU as a legal basis would in any case require political support in (a qualified-majority of) the Member States. Given how jealously the Member States attempt to protect their sovereignty (and particularly so when criminal law is at issue), 'it seems unlikely that a binding EU measure seeking to limit the enforcement of national criminal laws would receive the necessary support of the Member States'.[81] The second identified solution is therefore not entirely realistic. The third solution proposed is also problematic: it would not 'give sufficient legal certainty to potential applicants'.[82] The fourth solution is, however, the 'most realistic'[83] and has essentially been adopted in the UK.

The UK approach is quite instructive and is as follows.[84] An undertaking that is contemplating applying for administrative leniency under the EU leniency programme and is worried about exposing its employees to criminal exposure in the UK is advised also to apply to the OFT for administrative leniency. If the undertaking fulfils the requirements for 'Type A immunity',[85] there will be a granting of 'blanket immunity' to its current and former employees and directors. If 'Type A immunity' is not available, the OFT may still be able to convince the undertaking (on the basis of the hypothetical facts submitted) that the case would not be the type of case that the OFT would pursue with a criminal investigation. If the OFT is not prepared to give such an assurance, it may nonetheless grant criminal immunity to the relevant employees and directors if the undertaking qualifies for full leniency under the EU leniency programme. The OFT makes it clear that, in such a situation, criminal immunity may still be available even if

79 See, e.g., Reynolds and Anderson (2006), 89.
80 Levy and O'Donoghue (2004), 98.
81 Levy and O'Donoghue (2004), 98.
82 Levy and O'Donoghue (2004), 98.
83 Levy and O'Donoghue (2004), 98.
84 See OFT (2013b), [8.1]–[8.5].
85 To obtain 'Type A immunity', the undertaking must be the first applicant, there must be no pre-existing investigation, and the information must give the OFT a sufficient basis for taking forward a credible investigation. In addition, the undertaking must also: (i) accept participation in a cartel activity (which by definition is a breach of the law); (ii) provide the OFT with all relevant information, documents, and evidence; (iii) maintain continuous and complete cooperation throughout the investigation; (iv) refrain from further participation in the cartel activity; and (v) not have coerced another to take part in the cartel. See OFT (2013b), 11.

another undertaking had obtained 'Type A immunity' in the UK for the cartel and had thereby also obtained 'blanket' criminal immunity for its employees and directors. It is also important to understand that 'blanket' criminal immunity is *not guaranteed* when the undertaking has not obtained 'Type A immunity' in the UK, but has obtained full administrative leniency at EU level: the OFT will 'normally' be prepared to grant criminal immunity to individuals when their undertaking obtains full administrative leniency under the EU leniency policy; it is not obliged to do so. One of the reasons for not guaranteeing immunity in this context is to avoid any attempts by applicants to 'game the system' by using a (successful) leniency application to the European Commission as a mere device to procure criminal immunity when it would not otherwise be available.[86] The best option for the undertaking, then, is to make concurrent (or near concurrent) applications for leniency in both the UK and at EU level.[87]

The UK approach, while very useful in dealing with the potential conflict between criminal sanctions and administrative leniency, is not a perfect solution to the problem. For a start, it does not take account of administrative leniency applications in other Member States: it only deals with a (successful) application for full leniency at EU level. Administrative leniency programmes in other Member States may therefore be compromised if undertakings are unable to secure 'Type A immunity' in the UK. The logical response to this would be to ensure that undertakings do everything they can to secure 'Type A immunity' in the UK, such as reporting a cartel as early as possible. Admittedly, such an answer would not deal with those undertakings that are deemed to be 'coercers' for the purpose of the UK policy. A more robust approach would perhaps be to allow for 'blanket' criminal immunity to be 'normally' provided to undertakings that have obtained full administrative leniency in other Member States. It is likely, however, that criminal prosecutors would be unwilling to accept such a restraint on their ability to prosecute criminal cartel activity as they may be less concerned about the integrity of the leniency programmes of other Member States than they would be about the integrity of the EU-level leniency programme. In addition to this, the UK approach requires concurrent (or near concurrent) applications to be made. This feature of the solution can be criticized on the basis that it requires the expenditure of significant legal cost and effort.[88] One could avoid this expenditure if criminal prosecutors in all of the criminalized cartel regimes across Europe formally agreed in a publicly available Notice that national criminal prosecutions would not be brought against the employees of undertakings that had obtained full administrative leniency at EU level (or indeed within the Member States). Apart from issues of forum-shopping and a potential race to the bottom (which is likely to be particularly acute if administrative leniency in one Member State were sufficient to ensure criminal immunity in another),[89] obtaining consensus on this approach across the EU could be difficult, not least due to the presence of the principle of mandatory prosecution in some Member States, as explained above. However:

> Were it possible to reach agreement on the non-enforcement of criminal sanctions in circumstances where a successful leniency application had been made to the Commission or an NCA, a declaration to that effect in a Notice jointly agreed by the Commission and NCAs would likely

86 OFT (2013b), [8.6]. See also Nikpay (2012), 30–1. 87 OFT (2013b), [8.7].

88 See Harding and Joshua (2010), 239. For a general criticism of the cost implications of concurrent leniency applications, see Schwab and Steinle (2008), 527.

89 Admittedly, the existence of the 'ECN Model Leniency Programme' may reduce somewhat the intensity of the 'race to the bottom'; see ECN (2012b).

give business people a sufficient degree of comfort that criminal sanctions under national law would not be imposed on individuals who had assisted in the preparation of such an application.[90]

Where such a Notice is not created, and the UK approach were adopted throughout the EU by criminalized regimes, the Member State operating an administrative leniency policy may find itself unable to counteract any negative effect on its policy due to the existence of criminal sanctions in another Member State.

A final issue with the UK approach is that undertakings that have 'discovered' that they are part of a cartel but have not been able to secure immunity at EU level (because, for example, they are not the first through the door) may refuse to cooperate with the Commission and obtain a reduction in a potential fine under its leniency policy due to the worry about increased criminal exposure of their employees. The OFT believes that, in such a situation, applicants for EU-level leniency should not be concerned that an approach to the Commission will increase their employees' criminal exposure.[91] Two reasons are advanced: (i) the existence of information safeguards in Regulation 1/2003 and the ECN Notice; and (ii) the OFT's commitment to internal information barriers.[92] As a result of Article 12 of Regulation 1/2003,[93] information received by the OFT from the Commission cannot be used in evidence in a criminal trial against an individual. This could provide some reassurance to undertakings. Critics may reply that the information exchanged could be used as *intelligence* to initiate or develop a criminal investigation. According to the OFT,[94] this argument is unsustainable, due to the impact of, inter alia, paragraphs 37 to 42 of the ECN Notice.[95] Paragraph 39 of the Notice provides that information concerning a case initiated on the basis of a leniency application (which could include the mere fact that leniency has been applied for by a particular undertaking) submitted to the ECN 'will not be used by other members of the network as the basis for starting an investigation on their own behalf whether under the competition rules of the Treaty or, in the case of NCAs, under their national competition law or other laws'.[96] This would not, however, prevent the leniency information from being used to further an *already existing* criminal proceeding. Nonetheless, the OFT believes that it would be 'contrary to the spirit' of the ECN Notice to use leniency-derived information in this manner.[97] Furthermore, information voluntarily submitted by a leniency applicant will only be transmitted to another member of the ECN if the leniency applicant has given its consent, the receiving NCA has also received a leniency application from the applicant relating to the same infringement, or the receiving NCA gives a written commitment that the information transmitted to it will not be used 'to impose' sanctions on the leniency applicant or on any employee or former employee of the leniency applicant.[98] The verb 'to impose' is rather vague. It could be interpreted to mean that the NCA cannot use leniency information voluntarily submitted by the leniency applicant as either intelligence in a criminal case or evidence in a criminal trial. However, it could also be reasonably interpreted to mean *merely* that the leniency information voluntarily submitted could not be used as *evidence* in a criminal trial, a fact which would not reassure the undertaking that cares about its employees, particularly if a criminal

[90] Levy and O'Donoghue (2004), 98–9.

[91] OFT (2013b), [8.8].

[92] OFT (2013b), [8.8].

[93] On this generally, see Chapter 6, Section C(a) of this book.

[94] OFT (2013b), [8.9]–[8.12].

[95] European Commission (2004a).

[96] The reference to 'other laws' is important, particularly if criminal cartel offences are deemed not to be 'national competition laws' in this context, as per the *IB* case. On this, see: Chapter 8, Section B(b) of this book; and *IB v. The Queen* [2009] EWCA Crim 2575.

[97] OFT (2013b), footnote 102.

[98] European Commission (2004a), [40]–[41].

investigation is already underway (but does not yet encompass these employees). While the OFT seems to prefer the first interpretation, it seeks to provide further reassurance to the potential leniency applicant: it will use 'an internal information barrier' between staff having access to the leniency information and staff investigating the same cartel activity under Section 188 EA.[99] It is submitted that such an approach is a reasonable one that should reassure the undertaking applying for administrative leniency when full immunity from a fine is not possible.

An important point that needs to be made about the linking of criminal immunity to administrative leniency is that the linkage should not be 'complete': the criminal immunity policy should also be capable of standing apart from the administrative leniency policy. In order to secure the additional advantages of criminal immunity noted in Chapter 5, a criminal immunity policy needs to ensure that a conflict can exist between an undertaking and its employees. If the criminal immunity policy is only allowed to come into effect when administrative leniency has been applied for by the undertaking, these advantages would not be secured. To be clear, there must be a possibility for individuals to seek and obtain criminal immunity without having to involve cooperation of the undertaking. This may sound like an obvious point, but it was overlooked in Greece when criminal cartel sanctions were introduced in that jurisdiction in 2009, a fact which contributed to their ineffectiveness.[100]

A final issue that needs to be considered concerning linkage is whether a successful application by an individual for criminal immunity should lead to a guarantee for administrative leniency for the firm. In the UK, as in other criminalized regimes, there is currently no provision for administrative leniency for a company to follow criminal immunity for an individual.[101] Such a linkage is not required to protect the administrative leniency policy: given that what can impact upon the effectiveness of the administrative leniency policy is the potential for criminal exposure of its employees, the administrative leniency policy is adequately protected by securing criminal immunity through an administrative leniency application. Of course, one could argue that an individual may be deterred from reporting a cartel if he understood that by doing so his company would be exposed to a large fine and his colleagues in the company would be exposed to criminal sanctions. This issue impacts upon the effectiveness of the criminal immunity policy rather than the administrative one. The response would be twofold. First, the cartelist who fears for his company and colleagues could approach the company management and convince it to apply for administrative leniency for the company and with it criminal immunity for its employees (assuming that were possible). Second, the potential detriment to be suffered by the individual if he were not to self-report quickly (i.e. imprisonment) is likely to outweigh any (sentimental) attachment he feels to his firm or his colleagues (who incidentally might be about to seek criminal immunity themselves). The potential races between employees in the same company, not to mention between the employees and the company itself, are fostered when administrative leniency does not follow criminal immunity.

(iii) Dealing with the issue of criminal disclosure

Neither of the two solutions noted above (viz., the creation of a criminal immunity programme and the linking of the criminal immunity policy with administrative leniency)

99 OFT (2013b), [8.12]. 100 Brisimi and Ioannidou (2011), 174.
101 See Lawrence et al. (2008), 38.

would deal with the '*Pfleiderer*-type' problem, where undertakings are worried that applications for administrative leniency will lead to criminal cartel trials and therefore to increased exposure of the undertakings to private actions due to the disclosure requirements which are unique to the criminal process. It is difficult to provide a broad perspective on this problem as the criminal disclosure requirements will be specific to each EU Member State. Nonetheless, a number of points can be advanced here that can help to inform the debate on this particular aspect of the potential conflict between the existence of criminal cartel sanctions and the effectiveness of administrative leniency programmes.

The first point that should be made is that, even if disclosure of leniency-derived material in the course of a criminal trial were to remain a possibility, the undertaking would still have a significant incentive to apply for leniency. The worst that can happen to the undertaking, if its fears were to become reality, is that it has to pay compensation to a private party (which, admittedly, may involve the payment of treble damages in the US). If the other 'solutions' to the hesitancy of the undertaking are put in place, the undertaking—provided it acts quickly and can fulfil the relevant requirements—will not have to worry about the fate of its employees under the criminal law. Exposure to compensation payments involves a different risk assessment for the undertaking (that cares about its employees) from that undertaken when custodial sentences are a potential issue.[102] When the only negative consequence for a company is the payment of compensation, it would be a very high risk strategy not to apply for leniency, particularly given the large size of cartel fines, the fact that by self-reporting the undertaking can avoid having to pay (all or a significant portion of) the fine, and the fact that a decision not to self-report does not provide any guarantee of protection from civil liability, as the cartel could nonetheless be exposed by, for example, other participants in the cartel.[103]

The first point notwithstanding, there are a number of steps that could be taken by the authorities in order to reassure the undertaking contemplating applying for administrative leniency. For example, Member States could pass legislation to ensure that joint and several (civil) liability does not apply to successful leniency applicants[104] and/or they could only allow awards of multiple damages for cartel activity (if they exist) to be imposed on those cartelists who have not received leniency/immunity.[105] Such special treatment of the successful leniency applicant has some potential to influence an undertaking to self-report, even where it risks exposure to private actions: it reduces the maximum (negative) impact of the private action. Importantly, and irrespective of these mechanisms, the European authority that accepts the undertaking's leniency application

102 McFadden makes a similar point when he argues that an individual will not be put off from applying for criminal leniency, even where an immunity against private actions against that individual cannot be provided: McFadden (2011), 15 ('The fact that they may face the prospect of paying damages to the victims of their anticompetitive conduct appears comparatively trivial to the consequences of criminal conviction which include imprisonment, disqualification from holding a directorship, severe fines, public opprobrium, potential exclusion from public contracts and travel restrictions (due to having a criminal record). The balance appears to favour immunity from criminal sanction in return for paying to your victims the damages you owe').

103 Cf. *National Grid v. ABB* [2012] EWHC 869 (Ch), [37].

104 To deal specifically with worries about civil disclosure (as opposed to criminal disclosure) of leniency material, the European Commission proposed EU legislation to remove joint and several liability in the EU Member States for successful leniency applicants for injury caused to those other than their direct or indirect purchasers (with the exception of where the claimants demonstrate that they cannot obtain full compensation from the other undertakings that participated in the same infringement of competition law). See: European Commission (2013a), 16; and European Commission (2013b), [28] and Article 11(2). See also Council of the European Union (2013), Annex, [29], and Article 11(2).

105 Both of these 'solutions' have been implemented in the US; see Harrison and Bell (2005–06), 225.

(or hears about it through the ECN) should do its utmost to keep the details of the application (including the mere fact that it has been made) confidential and out of the public domain. The US authorities follow this practice and do their best to provide an 'ironclad assurance' of confidentiality for all immunity applicants.[106] More specifically, the US Department of Justice has the following policy:

> The Division holds the identity of leniency applicants and the information they provide in strict confidence, much like the treatment afforded to confidential informants. Therefore, the Division does not publicly disclose the identity of a leniency applicant or information provided by the applicant, absent prior disclosure by, or agreement with, the applicant, unless required to do so by court order in connection with litigation.[107]

This type of approach should be followed by those antitrust enforcers that are serious about protecting the integrity of their leniency policies.[108] Such an approach does not necessarily prevent the leniency information from becoming public once it has been disclosed (by virtue of a court order) to the accused in a criminal trial. Further action will likely be required to ensure that public disclosure does not occur through the use of leniency information in open court by the criminal accused. The US DoJ has been particularly successful in ensuring that information supplied by an immunity applicant does not become public in this manner as a result of its ability to avoid a high proportion of criminal cartel trials due to the existence of the system of plea-bargaining.[109] In the absence of a system of plea-bargaining, the authority's mission to keep leniency information from becoming public (through criminal trials) is more difficult. This will be particularly so where, as under the law of England and Wales, the antitrust enforcer is required to take all reasonable steps to ensure that it, or third parties over which it has control, disclose(s) material information to the criminal accused (which may include requiring the leniency applicant to waive legal professional privilege in order to obtain leniency in the first place[110]). Where leniency information has been disclosed to the criminal accused and a (public) criminal trial is to occur, it would be in the antitrust authorities' interest to apply for any available protective orders to ensure that there is no public disclosure of the leniency material in open court.

C. The Unique Challenges of Criminal Immunity

The employment of criminal immunity brings with it a number of unique challenges for antitrust law enforcers. Three particular challenges are noteworthy and should be

106 Hansen et al. (2012), 13.

107 Hammond and Barnett (2008), Question No. 32.

108 See Arp and Swaak (2002), 64.

109 Hansen et al. (2012), 13. Between 1996 and 2005, e.g., 84 per cent of federal criminal antitrust convictions in the US were obtained through guilty pleas; see Warin et al. (2006), 2.

110 In the UK Cartel Offence case of *R v. George and others*, Unreported Judgment, Southwark Crown Court, 7 December 2009, the trial judge, Owen J, held that the OFT should have pressed (through warning of a possible revocation of leniency) for disclosure of material belonging to a successful leniency applicant which was covered by legal professional privilege in order to perform its duty to the criminal accused: [31]–[32]. This judgment has not (yet) been tested on appeal, but for some it was seen as a worrying development; see Nikpay (2012), 7. Furse argues that one solution to the judgment (if it is upheld) 'would be to separate out the prosecution of the cartel offence from the authority applying a leniency programme in the context of civil enforcement': Furse (2012), 145. Interestingly, following a public consultation, the OFT recently decided not to include a waiver of legal professional privilege as a condition of participation in its leniency/immunity programmes; see: OFT (2013a), [6.1]–[6.18]; and OFT (2013b), [3.15]–[3.23]. On the (problematic) issue of waiver of privilege in this context, see O'Kane (2012), 55–60.

analysed in detail: dealing with the employment of an 'immunized witness' in a criminal cartel trial (Sub-section (a)); ensuring that cultural opposition to criminal immunity does not exist (Sub-section (b)); and reconciling criminal immunity policies with the theoretical justifications for criminal cartel sanctions (Sub-section (c)). These challenges are examined in turn.

(a) The Problem of an 'Immunized Witness'

It is clear that criminal immunity may lead to the presentation of an 'immunized witness' in front of a criminal court. As noted by MacCulloch, by turning 'Queen's Evidence' in return for immunity from prosecution, individual whistle-blowers not only cooperate with the authorities, they also become their 'key witnesses' at trial.[111] This unique feature of criminal immunity may lead to tension between the 'immunized witness' and the prosecution, tension which is not apparent with administrative leniency: 'immunized witnesses', while attempting to fulfil the immunity conditions (which will surely involve admitting all elements of the criminal cartel offence), nonetheless may wish to play down their culpability (and, in the process, the criminality of cartel activity) to the outside world (including the jury, where this is a standard feature of the criminal regime in question); by contrast, the prosecution actually aims to employ the witness to underline the culpability of the cartelists on trial.[112] This is indeed a potential problem with the use of criminal immunity: given human nature, and the fact that the 'immunized witness' may have more in common with the defendants than antitrust officials (itself signalled by their willingness to breach the cartel law rules in the first place), it is not inconceivable that such a tension will exist.

However, a number of methods could be employed to minimize the impact of this potential problem at trial. One could, for example, make immunity conditional upon a successful outcome at trial. But this would be the 'nuclear option'. It might well ensure that (when they are forthcoming) 'immunized witnesses' underline the criminality of their conduct in front of any jury, but it would no doubt reduce the likelihood of an immunity application being made by such witnesses in the first place. Thus, as it may cause more problems than it solves, this is not really an attractive option for antitrust enforcers. This is particularly so when such enforcers rely to a considerable degree on immunity applications to detect cartel activity. Alternatively, one could impose a different additional condition on the 'immunized witness': that, with the exception of truthful responses to questions under oath, he may not make public statements which have the potential to jeopardize the sustainability of a conviction against the defendant(s). Such a condition is justifiable in principle: after all, the 'immunized witness' is not forced to perjure himself, for example, and, as a reward for *voluntarily* restricting his right to self-expression, he will not face criminal punishment. However, the condition may be difficult to police in practice. How, for example, does one prove that an 'immunized witness' in putting forward under oath an opinion which undermines the case of the prosecution, and which puts the 'immunized witness' in a better light, has actually lied under oath about that opinion? For example, if an 'immunized witness' is asked under oath by defence counsel whether he believes cartel activity to be dishonest/immoral, and, for reasons of vanity, he answers in the negative (even though in fact he believes it to be dishonest/immoral), what can the prosecution do? They would need to prove that the opinion was not actually held by the 'immunized witness' in order to revoke the

[111] MacCulloch (2010b). [112] MacCulloch (2010b).

immunity. But how would this be done in practice? One must remember here that the actions of the 'immunized witness' (i.e. engaging in cartel activity) will lend support to the alleged (in this case, false) opinion of the 'immunized witness' (i.e. that cartelization is not wrong). Given this inherent difficulty, it may be better for the antitrust officials to consider a different method of dealing with the conflict identified.

An alternative method of so doing would be to ensure that the definition of the criminal cartel offence is designed in such a way as to minimize the discomfort of the 'immunized witness' in admitting that he had voluntarily breached the criminal law. Furse has noted, concerning the originally enacted UK Cartel Offence (which required proof of 'dishonesty' on behalf of the accused), that the

> very fact that an applicant is required to admit personal dishonesty to secure comfort from the risk of prosecution may, it has been suggested, serve to deter leniency applications.[113]

To avoid any negative impact on leniency and to reduce potential for conflict between the 'immunized witness' and the prosecution, one can design the criminal cartel offence in a manner that captures the inherent criminality of cartel activity without containing express definitional elements that require the 'immunized witness' to admit to being a less than decent member of society. Words such as 'fraudulently', 'dishonestly', 'deceptively', or 'deceitfully' should therefore be avoided.

One would also be advised to avoid the sole reliance upon an 'immunized witness' to construct a case against the defendant.[114] This is the most sensible option. One should also understand here that the credibility of the immunity applicant will almost certainly be questioned by the defendant's lawyers at trial and that experience in the US demonstrates that questions surrounding the credibility of immunity applicants can in fact lead to failure at trial.[115] The information provided by immunity applicants may not be entirely accurate.[116] The General Court has acknowledged this issue; for it,

> some caution as to the evidence provided voluntarily by the main participants in an unlawful cartel is understandable, since those participants might tend to play down the importance of their contribution to the infringement and maximise that of others.[117]

Where the cartel is a bilateral one in which the immunity applicant is equally implicated in alleged cartel activity, issues regarding reliability of the 'immunized witness' are particularly likely to arise.[118] Avoiding the sole reliance upon an 'immunized witness' helps to ensure that additional support for the prosecution's case is an integral part of their trial strategy from the outset, thereby reducing the potential of setbacks due to the self-interested testimony of the 'immunized witness'. Just as important, however, is the fact that such a strategy also helps to ensure that, when a case comes to trial, it is as robust as possible. Indeed, by also relying upon other available (non-immunized) witnesses, and upon other sources of verifiable incriminating evidence,[119] the prosecution not only acknowledges (and, to a degree, responds to) the identified criticism concerning a potential conflict between its interests and those of the 'immunized witness', but also reduces the odds of their case unravelling at trial. Hence, this option should be followed by all

[113] Furse (2012), 118. [114] MacCulloch (2010b).

[115] See Bunzel and Miller (2009). [116] See generally Gamble (2013), 27–8.

[117] Case T-448/07, *YKK Corp., YKK Holding Europe BV and YKK Stocko Fasteners GmbH v. Commission*, Judgment of 27 June 2012, not yet reported, [54]. See also the Australian case of *ACCC v. Leahy Petroleum Pty Ltd* (2007) 160 FCR 321, 136.

[118] OFT (2010d), 2. See also Corker (2011).

[119] Such evidence could be obtained using investigative techniques unique to criminal enforcement. On this, see Chapter 5, Section D(b)(ii)(4) of this book.

conscientious criminal antitrust prosecutors. In addition to avoiding sole reliance on an 'immunized witness', the prosecution should rigorously test the value of the criminal immunity applicant's narrative and the evidence provided. Corroboration of the immunity applicant's story by other evidence is particularly important.[120] The actual extent of existing documentary evidence can also be revealing, as implied by the following 'rule of thumb' developed by the General Court:

> where a person admits that he committed an infringement and thus admitted the existence of facts going beyond those whose existence could be directly inferred from the documentary evidence, that implies, *a priori*, in the absence of special circumstances indicating otherwise, that that person had resolved to tell the truth. Thus, statements which run counter to the interests of the declarant must in principle be regarded as particularly reliable evidence.[121]

The approach of the OFT in this context is also instructive here and should be quoted at length:

> Bearing in mind that there may be strong financial and personal incentives for undertakings and individual witnesses to present the conduct as falling within the scope of the leniency policy, the OFT's investigation must robustly assess the probative value of information provided by the leniency applicant, including witness evidence from employees and directors. The OFT will need to probe any changes in story or inconsistencies, look for independent corroborative material where possible, and pursue any lines of enquiry which call into question evidence from the leniency applicant. Where there is a clear dispute over the facts of the case between the leniency applicant and another alleged party to the cartel, the OFT will consider carefully both parties' accounts before deciding which it regards to be the most credible.[122]

MacCulloch and Wardhaugh go even further than this and suggest that, due to the inherent tension between the prosecution and the 'immunized witness', the latter should be treated as a hostile witness from the very beginning.[123] They also underline the sensibleness of Killick's proposal that all 'immunized witnesses' should provide evidence under oath to the investigating body at an early stage in the process: this approach would allow the investigator to test the witness's testimony against any evidence uncovered by the authority.[124] An enforcement agency that is serious about prosecuting criminal cartel cases using leniency-derived information would be advised to take these suggestions on board.

(b) The issue of cultural opposition

In the year 2000, the Competition Law and Policy Committee of the OECD reported that some of its members' competition authorities had encountered the attitude that in seeking public assistance with the enforcement of cartel law, 'it would not be appropriate for an employee to "blow the whistle" on hard core cartel activity since it is not a serious violation'.[125] This opposition can be understood as a cultural opposition to the notion of 'whistle-blowing'. Leniency, as a form of whistle-blowing, is not immune from claims that it can run counter to cultural norms in a given jurisdiction. According to Lee, the 'cultural values of citizens could affect the performance of leniency programs to a certain

[120] See: Case T-448/07, *YKK Corp., YKK Holding Europe BV and YKK Stocko Fasteners GmbH v. Commission*, Judgment of 27 June 2012, not yet reported, [56]; and OFT (2001), [5.11].
[121] Case T-448/07, *YKK Corp., YKK Holding Europe BV and YKK Stocko Fasteners GmbH v. Commission*, Judgment of 27 June 2012, not yet reported, [55].
[122] OFT (2013b), [5.27].
[123] MacCulloch and Wardhaugh (2012), 18.
[124] MacCulloch and Wardhaugh (2012), 14, referencing Killick (2008), 7.
[125] See OECD (2000a), 20.

extent'.[126] It is submitted here that the idea of cultural opposition, while worth noting, is not overly problematic with administrative leniency policies within the EU.[127] There are two reasons for this. First, it seems that since the beginning of the twenty-first century, granting (administrative) leniency has become an increasingly acceptable practice across Europe. The vast majority of EU countries already have in place a leniency programme and—at least from the (limited) available evidence[128]—these programmes do not appear to be suffering from cultural opposition concerning their usage. Most authorities highlight how useful leniency is in practice, and when criticizing current policies they are primarily concerned with establishing incentives and clarity, rather than with overcoming popular opposition.[129] Second, cultural norms concerning whistle-blowing can be reshaped through education. A number of EU Member States have engaged in efforts to educate their citizens about cartel activity and the need for whistle-blowing to uncover cartels. Indeed, both the Dutch Competition Authority and the Swedish Competition Authority are aware of the value of educative efforts here and have produced videos on this topic which are available via 'YouTube'.[130] In this context, it is vitally important to highlight the social harmfulness of cartel activity.

While cultural opposition may not be overly problematic with administrative leniency within the EU, it does not follow that cultural opposition is not an issue with criminal immunity. The potential unique consequence of a criminal trial (i.e. imprisonment) could be the motivating factor in ensuring this divergence: popular opposition may exist due to the perceived unacceptability of allowing one (criminal) culprit to go free at the expense of another, who ultimately goes to prison. This issue has been noted in the literature. It was noted above that criminal immunity works most effectively if the authorities can automatically grant full immunity to the first self-confessing cartelist. According to Joshua, such an automatic grant of full immunity is 'disturbing to British concepts of the public interest'.[131] Joshua is not the only commentator to express these types of anxieties. Edghill, for example, notes that when criminal immunity is used to protect a confessing cartelist and to ensure that the non-cooperating cartelist(s) ultimately pay(s) 'the criminal price' (i.e. suffering a custodial sentence), a 'moral conundrum' is created, particularly given that both the immunity applicant and the convicted cartelist display moral culpability in entering into the cartel in the first place.[132] In a similar manner, the 'fairness' of using criminal immunity in order to punish 'only half the perpetrators so severely' was also called into question by some of those commenting on the (ultimately unsuccessful) English criminal cartel case concerning the fixing of fuel surcharges in long-haul passenger flights.[133] The available empirical evidence also suggests that in the UK 'weak' support exists concerning the implementation of criminal immunity for cartel activity: only 37 per cent of individuals surveyed were in favour of it, while 38 per cent were against.[134] Cultural opposition in this context—assuming that it is as strong as argued by some—could manifest itself in a reluctance to acknowledge the credibility

126 Lee (2008), 48.

127 It seems, however, that cultural opposition to leniency has been problematic in some non-European jurisdictions, such as Korea; see Kar et al. (2008), 194.

128 Some countries, e.g., Ireland, do not inform the public of the number of leniency applications received.

129 See, e.g.: Norgen (2007); and Swedish Competition Authority (2006).

130 See respectively: <http://www.youtube.com/watch?v=5diFAaJdweI&feature=related>; and <hhtp://www.youtube.com/watch?v=_r99qzC8aHA>.

131 Joshua (2002), 236.

132 See Edghill (2011), 5.

133 Stephan (2011b), 453, referencing: Preston (2007); and Sunderland (2007).

134 Stephan (2008e), 141.

of the evidence provided by the successful criminal immunity applicant or to convict on the basis of such evidence, particularly if a jury is involved in the criminal proceedings.

There may be ways of overcoming any potential cultural opposition. It is clear that education and competition advocacy have significant roles to play here. Lee, for example, suggests that, for leniency programmes to be accepted, there is a need for 'competition advocacy directly focusing on citizens' values'.[135] If Lee is correct, then it would be in the criminalized jurisdiction's interest to highlight how cartel activity can be understood as a violation of *currently existing* moral norms. The analyses in Chapter 4 would therefore be very useful in determining the content of such education and competition advocacy. Interestingly, Stephan has argued that:

> If cartel infringements are perceived to be *too serious*, public attitudes may strongly oppose the use of such detection mechanisms as they allow some guilty parties to go unpunished and allow the sanction on others to be substantially reduced.[136]

This would suggest that educating the population on the immorality (i.e. culpability, social harmfulness, and moral wrongfulness) of cartel activity would be counter-effective: accordingly, the more serious cartel activity is perceived to be, the more opposition there will be to criminal immunity. It is submitted, however, that (within limits) the opposite could actually be true: when cartel activity is conceptualized as 'immoral' in the minds of the general population *and* understood to be very difficult to detect absent a leniency programme, there may well be an increased willingness to accept the 'necessary evil' of whistle-blowing in this context. Lee implicitly accepts this analysis:

> in a culture that regards a cartel as a form of cooperation rather than a conspiracy or crime, an informer is nothing but a betrayer. If cartels are not sanctioned severely enough due to the cultural resilience, only a few will dare to be betrayers.[137]

In any case, effective education and advocacy concerning the immorality of cartel activity is not without its own problems, as will be examined in Chapter 10. Furthermore, a need to be cautious will remain, even where educative efforts have had some pay-off. Intelligent case prioritization and case management is vital in ensuring that cultural opposition to criminal immunity does not flare up at trial. Most importantly, prosecutors should understand that the prosecution of bilateral cartels (where one side goes free due to a grant of immunity and the other is prosecuted, perhaps due to being slow, rather than unwilling, to cooperate) are prone to this type of problem. Corker describes the risk eloquently, when he states that:

> the court may regard the prosecution with distaste taking account of the fact that pragmatism has apparently scored over principle and that the accused have palpably been singled out for prosecution whilst the others happened to do a deal which meant they escaped justice so long as they heaped blame on the accused. Whilst these problems may also infect a more multi-party case, the mirror-image issue is unlikely to be as pronounced.[138]

It should also be clear that any potential for cultural opposition further underlines the necessity to avoid the sole reliance upon an 'immunized witness' to construct a case against the defendant, particularly in bilateral cartel cases.

(c) The impact upon the theoretical justifications

A successful (administrative) leniency programme has three effects: (i) it increases the detection rate of cartel activity; (ii) it reduces the potential sanction facing a given (as yet,

135 Lee (2008), 49.
136 Stephan (2008e), 124 (emphasis added).
137 Lee (2008), 48–9.
138 Corker (2011). See also MacCulloch and Wardhaugh (2012), 16.

undetected) cartelist; and (iii) it ensures that the reduction in the potential sanction is *more than* compensated for by the increase in the detection rate.[139] Provided that effect (iii) is present, an administrative leniency programme would actually increase deterrence.[140] The existence of administrative leniency programmes can therefore be reconciled with the objective of deterrence. Importantly, the existence of criminal immunity can also be reconciled with the criminal justificatory theory of deterrence. For a start, as was explained above, criminal immunity can be understood as being essential in order to protect the administrative leniency policy. To the extent that its existence does so, a criminal immunity policy contributes to the achievement of deterrence: it ensures that criminal cartel sanctions do not disrupt the operation of an already existing and apparently successful detection technique. In addition to this, as was implied in Chapter 3 and was analysed in Chapter 5, criminal immunity policies generate their own additional advantages concerning the detection of cartels: they create additional 'races to the regulator'. Admittedly, they also reduce the potential sanction facing a given (as yet, undetected) cartelist. But provided that the reduction in the potential sanction is *more than* compensated for by the increase in the detection rate, criminal immunity can also contribute to the achievement of deterrence in its own right. Of course, in order for this to occur, the authorities must meet the unique challenges of criminal immunity and take heed of the relevant advice offered above.

While it is not difficult to reconcile deterrence theory with the existence of criminal immunity policies, the same cannot be said for retribution. The OECD alludes to this issue when it notes that:

> because leniency programmes remove some or all of the punishment for committing competition law violations, they clash with the objective of persuading society that those violations are morally wrong.[141]

In fact, one can argue that retribution is at odds with the very existence of a criminal immunity programme: as a result of immunity, people who have done wrong are not being punished.[142] Fortunately, there are a number of ways of responding to this argument. First, one could adopt a particular variant of retribution theory as the underlying justificatory theory of criminalization, namely, the variant that holds that the proportionality principle merely limits the *maximum punishment* that can be legitimately imposed rather than defines the *exact amount* of punishment which must be imposed for a given conduct.[143] The immunity policy would be consistent with such a variant of retribution theory: it would not result in the imposition of undue punishment. Second, to reduce (further) the possibility of conflict with the theoretical justification of retribution, one could ensure that the criminal antitrust immunity policy does not allow the 'ringleader' of a cartel (i.e. the most blameworthy of the cartelists) to claim immunity from prosecution.[144] This type of approach forms an integral part of the US immunity programme.[145] In order to be guaranteed immunity in that jurisdiction, an individual applicant must demonstrate that he 'did not coerce another party to participate in the illegal activity and clearly was not the leader in, or originator of, the

139 See generally, Wils (2007a). 140 See: OECD (2002a); and OECD (2001).
141 OECD (2011), 13. 142 See Harding and Joshua (2010), 250.
143 On this, see: Morris (2000), 181–3; and Chapter 2, Section B(c)(ii) of this book.
144 Wils (2008a), 140.
145 See DoJ (1994). The European Commission's leniency programme has a similar (although not completely equivalent) provision whereby 'coercers' of cartel activity are excluded from achieving a 100 per cent reduction of their cartel fine; see European Commission (2006b), [13].

activity'.[146] Such an approach would reduce somewhat the deterrence effects associated with criminal immunity (as there will be less potential immunity applicants, not to mention the fact that cartel members will know that they can trust the 'ringleader' not to apply for immunity[147]), but it would also be more acceptable to those who advocate the punishment theory of retribution (including those who advocate the less flexible variant). Third, one could also argue that immunity applicants redeem themselves somewhat by cooperating completely with antitrust officials, and therefore deserve less punishment than they otherwise would have done.[148] Arguably, one can conceptualize an application for immunity (and the inevitable confession of guilt that it requires) to be an 'acknowledgment of responsibility' and therefore a manifestation of remorse.[149] To the extent that any remorse is genuine, there is less of a need to communicate society's disapproval to the immunity applicant: he has already 'learned his lesson' and has, as a result, tried to rectify the consequences of his actions. Of course, if remorse is not genuine, and an application for immunity is simply a cynical strategic move (i.e. it is done merely to avoid punishment), this argument would not be sustained. Finally, one could argue, as Lippke does, that a 'principle of scope' should be a guiding principle of retributive justice, and that, accordingly, to achieve retribution the criminal justice system should convict and punish more rather than fewer offenders.[150] The argument here would be that as the existence of criminal immunity allows more cartels to be detected, it ensures that more guilty individuals are subjected to the criminal process and punished than would have been in the absence of such a programme. Even though some people (viz., the successful immunity applicants) do not receive criminal punishment for their wrongful acts of cartel activity, this fact must be accepted in order to ensure that the 'principle of scope' is adhered to: immunity becomes a necessary evil in order to ensure that as many cartelists are possible are punished under the criminal law.

D. Conclusion

This chapter aimed to contribute to the literature on European cartel criminalization by providing a systematic analysis of the challenge of design posed for such criminalization by the investigative mechanism of leniency/immunity. In this book, this particular challenge has been termed the 'second (practical) challenge of design' and is comprised of two elements, both of which have been analysed in detail: ensuring the peaceful co-existence of administrative leniency/immunity and criminal sanctions; and the unique aspects of the challenge of *criminal* immunity for cartel activity.

It is clear that administrative leniency policies are an important part of the competition law enforcement landscape and that they can be particularly effective at piercing the veil of secrecy that typically surrounds cartel activity. It is clear also that commentators believe that some potential exists for criminal cartel sanctions to impact negatively upon administrative leniency policies. Four reasons for the existence of a potential negative impact were identified above: (i) companies may actually care about what happens to

[146] DoJ (1994). If he fails to do so, the individual may nonetheless be granted immunity if the DoJ decides to use its discretion to provide it.

[147] On the negative impact of this fact on deterrence, see Leslie (2006b), 478–9.

[148] On this, see Wils (2008a), 139.

[149] Cf. Harding and Joshua (2010), 253.

[150] Lippke (2006), 6.

their employees and may be hesitant to apply for administrative leniency if by doing so they would expose their employees to criminal sanctions; (ii) individuals within a firm which is contemplating applying for leniency may be hesitant to advocate their company's applying for leniency if it would lead to their exposure to criminal sanctions; (iii) firms may well need the cooperation of their employees who have engaged in cartel activity if they are to benefit from the leniency policy, and such cooperation would be unlikely if it would lead to the individuals' being exposed to criminal sanctions; and (iv) firms may fear that by applying for leniency it would be increasing their risk of exposure to private damages actions as their corporate statements may eventually become public through their disclosure to the accused (and eventually their use in open court) in the context of a criminal prosecution.

This chapter identified three mechanisms that can be useful in resolving any conflict between administrative leniency programmes and criminal sanctions. The first mechanism identified was the creation of a criminal immunity programme for cartel activity. Such a policy would help to reassure firms contemplating applying for administrative leniency that their employees have a route out of potential criminal proceedings against them. There are drawbacks to this solution, however, such as the impact of the principle of mandatory prosecution and the fact that the investigating antitrust authorities may not be able to *guarantee* immunity for applicants (particularly when it is not the prosecuting authority). Potential solutions to these problems include: using criminal leniency instead of criminal immunity where the principle of mandatory prosecution is applicable; where possible, using legislation to remove the principle of mandatory prosecution for criminal cartel offences; imposing the criminal immunity policy of the investigating authority upon the prosecuting authority through legislation; involving the prosecuting authority in the introduction and application of the immunity policy; and requiring the prosecuting authority to give 'serious weight' to recommendations for immunity that are proposed by the investigating body.

The second mechanism which is designed to resolve any conflict between administrative leniency programmes and criminal sanctions is the linking of the criminal immunity policy with the administrative leniency policy. In order to ensure that applications for administrative leniency are not 'chilled' by the existence of criminal cartel sanctions, one must not only create a criminal immunity policy in the criminalized jurisdiction, but, ideally, also ensure that criminal immunity automatically extends to the (cooperating) employees of those undertakings that have successfully applied for 'full' administrative leniency (i.e. a reduction of a fine to zero Euros). A significant problem may exist here, however: the jurisdiction operating the relevant criminal immunity programme may not be the same jurisdiction that is operating the applicable administrative leniency policy. A number of potential solutions to this issue can be identified, the most useful of which is allowing the national criminal prosecutors to decline to bring charges against the (cooperating) employees of the firms to which the authorities of another jurisdiction (e.g., the Commission) have granted full administrative immunity. Such a solution is not without its own issues, however, such as the need for concurrent (or near concurrent) applications and the difficulty of convincing criminal prosecutors not to take forward a criminal cartel case in order to protect the integrity of a foreign administrative leniency programme (as opposed to a domestic one).

The third mechanism identified that can be useful in resolving any conflict between administrative leniency programmes and criminal sanctions involves dealing with the issue of criminal disclosure. Although the issue of criminal disclosure can be overstated in this context, there are a number of steps that could be taken by the authorities in order to reassure the undertaking contemplating applying for administrative leniency. For example, administrative leniency applications should be kept confidential and out of the public domain and, if corporate statements are destined to be employed in a criminal trial, the relevant authorities should apply for any available protective orders to ensure that there is no public disclosure of the material in open court.

The employment of a *criminal* immunity programme for cartel activity brings with it a number of unique challenges for antitrust law enforcers. Three particular challenges were identified and analysed in detail above: (i) dealing with the employment of an 'immunized witness' in a criminal cartel trial; (ii) ensuring that cultural opposition to criminal immunity does not exist; and (iii) reconciling criminal immunity policies with the theoretical justifications for criminal cartel sanctions.

The problem with an 'immunized witness' is that: (i) the prosecution aims to employ the witness to underline the culpability of the cartelists on trial; and (ii) the witness, while attempting to fulfil the immunity conditions (including admitting all elements of the criminal cartel offence), may nonetheless wish to play down their culpability (and, in the process, the criminality of cartel activity) to the outside world (including the jury, where appropriate). This chapter identified a number of methods that can be used to minimize the impact of the potential problem with 'immunized witnesses' at trial. The 'nuclear' option is to make immunity conditional upon a successful outcome at trial; but this option reduces significantly the attractiveness of applying for criminal immunity in the first place. Alternatively, one could restrict the ability of the cartelist to make public statements which have the potential to jeopardize the sustainability of convictions; but this would be difficult to police in practice. A more practical option would be to design the criminal cartel offence so that it does not contain definitional elements that the 'immunized witness' would have a discomfort in admitting to at trial (such as 'fraudulently', 'deceitfully', etc.). In any case, one would be advised to avoid the sole reliance upon an 'immunized witness' to construct a case against the accused, particularly where the cartel is a bilateral one.

The use of a criminal immunity policy in a criminalized jurisdiction has the potential to engender cultural opposition. For example, the wider public may perceive it as unfair that some (equally culpable) cartelists walk free at the expense of others going to prison. There is some empirical support for the existence of this type of cultural opposition. In order to overcome such opposition, one must engage in educative efforts and competition advocacy. If the immoral aspects of cartel activity are understood in addition to how difficult it is to detect cartel activity, it is more likely that citizens will come to accept the 'necessary evil' of criminal immunity programmes. Intelligent case prioritization and case management also have their roles to play.

Finally, as demonstrated by this chapter, one can reconcile criminal immunity policies with the theoretical justifications for criminal cartel sanctions. A criminal leniency programme has a direct impact on the potential sanction facing a prospective cartelist: it reduces the sanction. However, such a programme will also increase the rate of detection of cartels. Provided that the reduction in punishment is more than compensated for by the increase in the detection rate, the criminal immunity policy will be successful in increasing the deterrence of cartel activity. One should also understand here that a criminal leniency policy creates additional 'races to the regulator' than an administrative one, as individuals can be punished severely if they fail to be the first to apply for immunity. It is arguable that criminal immunity can impact negatively upon the other objective of cartel criminalization: retribution. However, this issue is not problematic if: (i) one adopts a version of retribution theory that merely limits the maximum amount of punishment that can be imposed by the state; (ii) one does not allow 'ringleaders' to benefit from the programme; (iii) one accepts that, by coming forward and revealing the cartel to the authorities, the cartelist redeems himself and therefore has earned a more lenient treatment; or (iv) one accepts that a principle of scope should exist when pursuing retribution and that in practice this principle is fulfilled with a criminal leniency policy.

10

European Antitrust Criminalization and the Third Challenge of Design: Identifying the Desirable Enforcement Strategies

A. Introduction

Chapters 8 and 9 of this book considered respectively two particular aspects of the practical challenge of European antitrust criminalization: designing the cartel offence and understanding the complexities of leniency/immunity in the context of cartel criminalization. While extremely important in themselves, these two aspects do not represent the totality of the practical challenge of European antitrust criminalization. Responding to those particular aspects of the practical challenge will not necessarily ensure that the criminal cartel regime will be effective in practice. In fact, more is required from the relevant authorities in order to ensure that the theoretical objectives of cartel criminalization are achieved. Well-thought-out enforcement strategies need to be in place in addition to a well-defined criminal cartel offence and an effective criminal immunity programme. Identifying and examining the most important of these strategies represents the third and final aspect of the practical challenge of design for European antitrust criminalization that is analysed in this book.

Fortunately, the current literature provides some guidance on what is required in order for a criminal cartel regime to be effective in practice. Wils, for example, notes that there are five conditions for effective criminal enforcement: (i) there must be a well-resourced, dedicated investigator and prosecutor; (ii) adequate powers of investigation should be provided to the relevant enforcers; (iii) judges and juries must be willing to convict; (iv) political and public support must be in existence; and (v) corporate fines should also be employed.[1] Lowe concurs with Wils on this and, in addition, highlights the need for an effective immunity programme for individuals (in addition to a corporate immunity programme) in order to prevent an adverse effect on any existing administrative procedure punishing undertakings for cartel activity.[2] Some scholars have looked to the US in a bid to understand what might be needed in Europe to ensure effective criminal antitrust enforcement. Calvani, for example, explains that US successes in the criminal enforcement of Section 1 of the Sherman Act 1890 are due in large part to a number of important features of the US system that are not related to the definition of the relevant criminal offence.[3] These features include: treating the criminal cartel offence as a serious offence (i.e. a felony) and therefore providing for a significant maximum term of imprisonment for its commission; using FBI agents to assist in cartel investigations; employing criminal investigative techniques; creating an individual immunity

[1] Wils (2006b), 87–90.

[2] Lowe (2007), 95. The concept of leniency/immunity has been considered in Chapter 9 of this book.

[3] Calvani (2004a), 7–8.

programme; and providing the judiciary with sentencing guidelines.[4] To this list should be added the reliance upon plea-bargaining,[5] the existence of the grand jury process,[6] the evident willingness of the Antitrust Division of the US Department of Justice ('DoJ') to seek international cooperation for the criminal enforcement of international cartels,[7] as well as a general (eventual) acceptance by the public that cartel activity violates social norms.[8] While it would be naïve in the extreme to assume that (apparent) US successes in anti-cartel enforcement can be achieved in Europe by the mere transposition of their enforcement mechanisms and techniques,[9] it is clear, however, that an understanding of the US approach can inform the debate on the extent of the practical challenge of European antitrust criminalization.[10] Some aspects of the US approach to cartel criminalization will therefore be touched upon in the analyses conducted in this chapter.

The current literature, while informative, can nonetheless be criticized for failing to provide a systematic, detailed analysis of the extent of what is here termed the 'third (practical) challenge of design' for European antitrust criminalization: the identification of important enforcement strategies that help to ensure that the criminal cartel regime is effective in practice. With some notable exceptions,[11] the vast majority of the literature relevant to the practical aspects of the criminalization debate either focuses on the issue of the definition of the criminal cartel offence or comments on the practical problems inherent *in a given* criminal cartel regime. Relatively little room is reserved for a more generally applicable analysis of the third challenge of design or for consideration of the impact of specific criminal enforcement strategies upon both of the identified theoretical justifications for criminal cartel sanctions. Given that a failure to understand and respond to the totality of the practical challenge of European antitrust criminalization may engender significant setbacks for the relevant stakeholders, this situation is regrettable and should be rectified.

This chapter aims to contribute to the literature on European antitrust criminalization by analysing important enforcement strategies that help to ensure that the criminal cartel regime is effective in practice. It is divided into four substantive sections and a conclusion. Section B details a particular issue that needs to be understood (and avoided) by serious criminal antitrust officials when they rely upon 'moral leveraging' to enforce the criminal cartel offence: the so-called 'compliance trap'. In doing so, this chapter also explains the importance of creating and fostering political and public support for the criminal cartel regime. Section C examines the strategic issue of ensuring sufficient support from important stakeholders in the cartel criminalization project. The (problematic) stakeholders that are examined are the general public, potential jury members, and the judiciary. In analysing the issue under consideration, this section details the main difficulties concerning the achievement of stakeholder support, as well as the strategies that can be adopted to help to overcome these difficulties. Section D is dedicated to the institutional design of a criminal cartel regime. Specifically, it examines the strategic issue of which entity/entities should exercise the investigative and/or prosecutorial functions in

[4] Calvani (2004a), 7–8.
[5] See, e.g., Hammond (2006).
[6] See Baker (2011), 39–40.
[7] See, e.g., Hammond (2010), 14–16.
[8] On the development of US criminal antitrust enforcement norms, see generally: Kovacic (2011); and Kovacic (2006), 49–53.
[9] Beaton-Wells and Ezrachi (2011b), 20.
[10] One should also acknowledge that the US approach to the practicalities of criminal cartel enforcement has already influenced the approaches of some EU Member States that have criminalized cartel activity (Ireland, in particular); see, e.g., Calvani (2004a).
[11] Such as: Calvani and Calvani (2009), 137–40; Frese (2006); Massey (2006); Stephan (2011c); and Wils (2006b), 87–90.

a criminal cartel regime. Section E focuses on the concept of international cooperation. In particular, it considers the importance of such cooperation for those criminalized regimes that are serious about tackling the most harmful cartels, the difficulties engendered in this context by criminal antitrust enforcement, as well as strategies that can be adopted in order to overcome these difficulties. Finally, Section F provides concluding remarks on the third (practical) challenge of design for European cartel criminalization.

B. Avoiding the 'Compliance Trap'

It was noted in Chapter 2 that retribution ('punishment') appears to be an established aim of the enforcement of EU competition law and that this aim has been pursued to varying degrees in the European Commission's antitrust enforcement policy. In particular, it was noted that the 1998 Fining Guidelines could arguably be placed within a retributive framework. This is less so for the latest (2006) Fining Guidelines. Nonetheless, some retributive elements can be found in those Guidelines. For example, the concepts of cardinal and ordinal proportionality can be loosely transposed to its methodology: the basic amount of a fine is set according to the gravity of the violation (itself determined by a percentage of the volume of sales in the affected market);[12] aggravating and mitigating circumstances may increase or decrease the fine respectively.[13] As argued in Chapter 2, retribution (or at least something approaching it) is not a completely alien concept in EU antitrust law.

Even so, one must nonetheless acknowledge the following qualification concerning the current status of retribution theory in this context: the identified retributive features of EU anti-cartel enforcement focus upon the nature of the *cartel agreement itself*, and not upon the nature of the actual *conduct* of the undertaking.[14] This distinction reflects the analysis of Harding when he argued that, in the context of cartels, EU antitrust enforcement was largely 'outcome orientated', while its US counterpart was primarily 'conduct orientated'.[15] In Harding's view, in US antitrust law, there is a focus on the collusive character of cartel activity, and censure is present due to the element of conspiracy in the definition of the offence[16] and its interpretation by the judiciary.[17] Cartel activity is thus conceptualized as an activity which is—by virtue of its given definition—immoral. As explained by Sullivan, Section 1 of the Sherman Act 1890

> aims at bad conduct, at conspirators who deliberately decide on evil, who eschew competition, who plan and execute action to strike market forces and who, conscious of their own wrongdoing, take precautions to hide their own conduct or disguise it.[18]

[12] European Commission (2006a), [21].

[13] European Commission (2006a), [28]–[29].

[14] This is not to say, however, that culpability is irrelevant for EU antitrust enforcement: even though it is not essential for a finding of a violation of Article 101 TFEU, culpability (intention/negligence) is in fact required in order for the Commission to impose a fine. On this, see Chapter 4, Section C(a) of this book.

[15] Harding (2002), 410–12.

[16] Section 1 of the Sherman Act 1890 states that '[e]very contract, combination in the form of trust or otherwise, or *conspiracy*, in restraint of trade or commerce among the several States, or with foreign nations' shall be illegal: 15 USC §§ 1–7 (2000 & Supp IV, 2004) (emphasis added). On this element of conspiracy, see Cooper and Dedjinou (2005), 181–2. For an overview of US state antitrust criminal laws, see Farmer (2008).

[17] Harding (2002), 410. See also: Beaton-Wells (2007), 698; and Stucke (2006), 503.

[18] Sullivan (1991), 311.

This 'bad actor' theory emphasizes conduct and attitude; it 'encapsulates the idea of deliberate, planned, conspiratorial action, done with a clear awareness of the illegal nature of what is intended'.[19] In contrast, the current European approach is concerned primarily with the market impact of a given conduct (i.e. its outcome)[20] and not the inherent nature of that conduct. With EU anti-cartel enforcement, then, the main focus of its retributive aim is on the nature of the agreement (e.g., whether or not it is a hard-core cartel agreement), not the bad character of the undertaking (e.g., whether or not it 'conspired' with others). Consequently, the European (administrative) offence can be interpreted as an 'offence of outcome'.[21]

This is an important distinction. For a start, it helps to explain one of the crucial differences between the US model of antitrust enforcement and the model which is applied in most of Europe: the existence of personal criminal sanctions for hard-core cartel activity.[22] As the moral basis of the censure is apparent under US law, there can be a clear (retribution-based) foundation for the use of criminal sanctions: the existence of a *conspiracy* between the cartelists 'for their own gain to strike out on a forbidden course which adversely affects the public'.[23] More importantly, however, it introduces a potential limitation to a retribution-based argument for criminal cartel sanctions. Specifically, the classification of EU antitrust enforcement as 'outcome orientated' rather than 'conduct orientated' ensures that the imposition of individual criminal sanctions for morally wrongful *conduct* would be inconsistent with current enforcement practice. In other words, a change in the focus of antitrust enforcement is required in order to operationalize a retribution-based foundation for antitrust criminalization.

It is true that the current approach to anti-cartel enforcement is not 'cast in stone' and that it could be modified to reflect a theoretical foundation which is based more concretely upon retribution. Indeed, the introduction of criminal sanctions for cartel activity would *in itself* represent a significant change in the enforcement focus of European competition law, particularly where retribution is the underlying theoretical objective. As noted in Chapter 6, cartel criminalization can legally occur in the Member States: Article 5 of Regulation 1/2003 allows for national criminal enforcement and such enforcement would arguably be consistent with the 'punishment' objective noted by the EU Courts.[24] Nonetheless, the available literature suggests that a change from an 'outcome-orientated' enforcement policy to a 'conduct-orientated' one may engender some (practical) problems.[25] These problems should be understood by those seeking a full understanding of the practical challenge of European antitrust criminalization. The work of Parker (2006) is particularly enlightening here: it explores the difficulties which faced the Australian antitrust authority, the ACCC, when it attempted to harden citizens' attitudes to cartel activity through the use of explicitly moral language combined with tough (albeit administrative) enforcement efforts. The main difficulty is what is termed 'the compliance trap'; it occurs where 'there is a lack of political support for the

19 Harding (2002), 410. See also Sullivan (1991), 320.

20 A fact acknowledged from the very foundation of the (then) EEC regime; see Thorelli (1959), 234.

21 Harding (2002), 412.

22 See Harding and Joshua (2003), Chapter 2. See also Joshua and Jordan (2003–04), 650–1.

23 Sullivan (1991), 320. Cf. Flynn (1967), 1315; and *United States v. Alton Box Board Co.* [1977-1] Trade Cases (CCH) ¶ 61,336 (N.D. Ill. 1977), 71,166–667.

24 See, e.g.: Case 41/69, *ACF Chemiefarma v. Commission* [1970] ECR 661, [173]; Case T-329/01, *Archer Daniels Midland v. Commission* [2006] ECR II-3255, [141]; and Case C-289/04 P, *Showa Denko v. Commission* [2006] ECR I-5859, [16].

25 See, e.g., MacCulloch (2007), 360.

moral seriousness of the law it must enforce'.[26] When the antitrust activities of business offenders are condemned for their immoral qualities, such offenders may interpret the moral leveraging of antitrust enforcement as 'unfair or stigmatizing'.[27] These bad feelings in turn can lead businesses actively to lobby for the political emasculation of the regulator, a process which may eventually lead to the regulator's being forced to adopt a more lenient approach to cartel activity.[28] For Parker, it 'is a trap because, in the absence of external political support, there is nothing the regulator can do to escape'.[29]

In Australia, a softening of enforcement did not occur, but this was due mainly to the strong leadership of the then Chairman of the ACCC, Allan Fels.[30] The point here is that in criminalizing cartel activity (and thereby adopting a 'conduct-orientated' enforcement policy), jurisdictions risk their antitrust authorities' falling into 'the compliance trap'. To avoid this, significant political support for antitrust enforcement is required prior to any 'moral leveraging', as is a dedicated, strong leadership at the relevant antitrust authority. Clearly, it should be the strategy of any serious criminal antitrust enforcer to avoid the 'compliance trap' that can be occasioned with the imposition of criminal cartel sanctions. If significant political support or leadership concerning the criminalization of cartel activity is lacking in a given Member State, then the introduction and maintenance of criminal cartel sanctions would be a very 'hasty' move and one that is likely to fail. Where some political support can be detected, it would be wise to foster such support before allowing any dedicated leader(s)—if necessary from a foreign jurisdiction with a strong criminal cartel regime[31]—to pursue rigorously individual cartelists. Furthermore, given that public support is necessary for political support,[32] the strategies noted below concerning the creation of public support should also be utilized.

The above discussion on enforcement focus centred on retribution theory and the fact that the enforcement of a criminal cartel offence created to achieve retribution can lead to the 'compliance trap'. The reason for the focus on retribution is that enforcement of a criminal cartel offence designed to achieve retribution will *by definition* involve 'moral leveraging'; hence, the potential for the 'compliance trap'. The employment of deterrence theory to justify cartel activity does not necessarily involve efforts to employ 'moral leveraging': one could use deterrence theory to create a criminal cartel offence that is morally neutral. That said, the 'compliance trap' is not irrelevant for deterrence theory. For a start, the mere use of the criminal law to enforce cartel law may bring with it moral overtones, particularly in a regime that is not suffering from a significant degree of 'over-criminalization'. In addition, provided cartel activity could be linked to immoral behaviour,[33] one could underline the immorality of cartel activity when enforcing a criminal cartel law for reasons of deterrence: underlining the immoral aspects of cartel activity in this manner helps to create/reinforce norms concerning such conduct with a possible result of the internalization of the norm and a reduction in enforcement costs (to the benefit of efficient deterrence). Consequently, criminal antitrust enforcers should try to avoid the 'compliance trap' whatever the underlying theoretical justification for cartel criminalization actually is in their respective regimes.

[26] Parker (2006), 591. [27] Parker (2006), 592. [28] Parker (2006), 593.
[29] Parker (2006), 593. [30] See generally Brenchley (2003).
[31] Over the last number of years, e.g., the Irish Competition Authority has employed several high-profile US competition lawyers/former officials in an effort to boost, inter alia, its enforcement capabilities.
[32] Beaton-Wells (2008b), 230. [33] On this, see Chapter 4 of this book.

C. Ensuring Support from Stakeholders

The 'compliance trap' noted above demonstrates the need for effective leadership, political support, and (to the extent that political support follows it) public support for an antitrust criminalization project to be successful. It is clear, in fact, that support from all stakeholders in the project is vitally important to its success. Indeed, it is not enough for antitrust academics and law-makers alone to agree that a deterrence-based and/or retribution-based criminalization argument display(s) sufficient merit in order to implement a project of antitrust criminalization: 'achieving broad community support is critical'.[34] In the absence of such support, one risks the provision of insufficient resources for antitrust enforcement efforts and/or nullification of the law.[35] As Beaton-Wells observes,

> without broad-ranging acceptance and support domestically, the rhetoric of regulators in local and international fora may not be sufficient to secure the effective enforcement of criminal provisions. Absent such enforcement, these provisions have little prospect of achieving their primary objective, that is to change business norms and behaviour so as to reduce significantly the incidence of serious cartel conduct.[36]

While Beaton-Wells's observation focuses on the objective of deterrence, a similar line of argument can be applied to the achievement of retribution. Sufficient support from stakeholders, then, is a crucial issue in the European antitrust criminalization debate. For this reason, this section examines the strategic issue of ensuring sufficient support from important stakeholders in the cartel criminalization project. The (problematic) stakeholders that are examined are the general public, potential jury members (for those (few) European jurisdictions with trial by jury), and the judiciary.[37] In analysing the issue under consideration, this section details the main difficulties concerning the achievement of stakeholder support (Sub-section (a)), as well as the strategies that can be adopted to help to overcome these difficulties (Sub-section (b)).

(a) The difficulty of securing stakeholder support

As explained in Chapter 4, the nature of cartel activity is challenging in three respects: (i) the harm is often 'diluted' across many different victims; (ii) the individual (as opposed to the aggregate) loss may be minimal; and (iii) the identity of the victims may be difficult to determine. When, for these reasons, cartel activity is perceived as a 'victimless crime',[38] it can be very difficult to get the attention of the general public concerning this conduct, particularly if the media are also disinterested.[39] This can result in a low level of support from the public concerning the existence of criminal cartel sanctions. Added to this is the fact that cartelists may attempt to convince the public that their conduct, as an economic activity, was aimed at the achievement of social objectives, such as the protection of employment.[40] The words of an Australian cartelist are illustrative of this problem:

34 King (2010), 1. See also: Cseres et al. (2006b), 5; King (2010), 27; and Kovacic (2006), 41–2.
35 On the latter phenomenon, see Block and Sidak (1980), 1134.
36 Beaton-Wells (2008b), 206.
37 The issue of support from the regulator/enforcer is examined in a later section of this chapter that considers the design of the criminal enforcement agency/agencies; see Section D.
38 See Massey (2004), 32.
39 See, e.g., Evans and Lundman (1983).
40 On the possible legal implications of this argument, see MacCulloch (2007), 361–2.

The key reason for us to enter into [cartel] arrangements was not to make profits, but for survival and to retain jobs. . . . I put the interest of the business and the employees above my own personal risk. I thought I was acting in the national interest.[41]

Moreover, it is possible that any desired tendency towards reproach may be assuaged by an admiration for economic and business success;[42] in fact, '[t]he affluent and elite context of business crime and cartel activity may even add a kind of glamour to the public perception of the subject'.[43] It is certainly clear that cartel activity is not as worrying to citizens as crimes such as murder, rape, or burglary.[44] Cartels, as a manifestation of corporate wrongdoing, 'simply do not yet give rise to the personal horror that we equate with so many other criminal acts against people and property'.[45] There may be a 'false view' in society that corporate wrongdoing is more closely aligned with legitimate conduct than traditional crime.[46] Consequently, newspaper editors may hesitate to provide decent coverage of criminal cartel trials. One should also understand here that support could be particularly difficult to drum up if the process of criminalization is a top-down process rather than a bottom-up one.[47] There may be a further problem regarding the securing of public support for cartel criminalization in that some jurisdictions may display a cultural propensity towards business collaboration;[48] expecting citizens to view cartel activity in this context as immoral (in order to support criminalization) may result in the antitrust prosecutors coming up against the problem of 'sticky norms' noted in Chapter 3.[49] Added to this situation is the fact that, technically speaking, exemptions (or more accurately 'exceptions') may be available under national and/or European law for cartels that are deemed to be beneficial to society.[50] Indeed, while such an exemption for a 'hard-core' cartel is very unlikely to be provided by EU law in any given case,[51] a cartelist is nonetheless entitled in law to argue that a cartel should be exempt from unlawfulness by virtue of Article 101(3) TFEU.[52] The (remote) possibility of a legal exemption for a given cartel may ensure that the immorality of cartel activity (or at least its social harmfulness) is not unequivocal in the minds of the public.[53] The existence of such exemptions may well have fostered a perception among EU citizens that European competition law is about 'satisfying somewhat technical and arcane regulations rather than about preventing conspiracies that cost EU consumers large amounts of money'.[54]

A lack of public support for cartel criminalization may impact negatively upon the extent of political support, resulting in fewer resources being dedicated to criminal cartel enforcement and/or less robust investigative powers being granted to the enforcement agency/agencies. This is a universal problem that can affect all types of legal systems.

41 Parker et al. (2004), 47. 42 Harding (2006), 199.

43 Harding (2006), 199. See also Reiner (2002), 395–6.

44 Stephan (2009b). See also King (2010), 14.

45 Castle and Writer (2002), 23. See, however, the discussion in Stucke (2006), 500 et seq.: '[US] surveys suggest moral opprobrium toward antitrust violations'.

46 Wells (2001), 25.

47 According to Harding (2006), the movement towards the criminalization of cartel activity in Europe is a top-down process.

48 Stephan (2010b). 49 On this, see Kahan (2000).

50 See, e.g., Article 101(3) TFEU. See also ICN (2005), 13.

51 See, e.g.: European Commission (1980), [115]; European Commission (2010b), Article 5(1); European Commission (2010c), Article 4(1); and Schaub (2001), 76. See also ICN (2005), 14. Cf.: *Reims II* (Case COMP/36.748), Commission Decision, 15 September 1999, [1999] OJ L275/17, [65]; and *Visa International—Multilateral Interchange Fee* (Case COMP/29.373), Commission Decision, 24 July 2002, [2002] OJ L318/17, [79].

52 See: Case T-17/93, *Matra Hachette SA v. Commission* [1994] ECR II-595; Frese (2006), 211–12; Joshua (2002), 242; and Whish (2009), 150–1.

53 See Stucke (2006), 527. 54 Massey (2004), 32.

Ceteris paribus, those legal systems which utilize trial by jury in criminal cases are, however, more vulnerable to a negative impact than those that do not: weak public support will generally be reflected in weak support for cartel criminalization among jury members. If jury support for the concept of criminal cartel sanctions is weak, there is a strong potential for jury nullification to occur. This problem has been acknowledged by commentators on cartel criminalization. Clough, for example, has asked whether criminalization will 'bring competition law into disrepute, not only in this country [the UK] but in the rest of Europe, if the criminalization doesn't work, because juries have not yet been educated to consider cartels to be the equivalent of theft'.[55] Jacobs is even more pessimistic, believing that

> where citizens have an awareness of the value generated by an economic activity and its social importance, where they view the participants as basically decent people, and where they comprehend the pressures of the economic environment that motivate the challenged conduct, they are not nearly as likely as antitrust enforcers to be doctrinaire. Jurors frequently won't consider the conduct so pernicious as to warrant treating it as a crime. Indeed, any reasonable excuse to move the classification of that conduct emotionally back along the spectrum toward a mere civil violation, or even legally-neutral behavior, can be attractive to jurors as an alternative to severe punishment.[56]

It seems from experience in Ireland that, in appropriate cases, juries are in fact prepared to convict cartelists and to subject them to the possibility of a custodial sentence.[57] A case in point is the conviction on 3 May 2012 of Mr Pat Hegarty for his involvement in a cartel in the home-heating oil market.[58] Mr Hegarty became one of the few individuals to be convicted of cartel activity by a jury in Ireland (the vast majority of convictions for 'hard-core' cartel activity to date being secured through guilty pleas) and was sentenced to two years in prison.[59] Although his prison sentence was suspended, Mr Hegarty also received a fine of €30,000. The fact that in Ireland cartelists have been convicted following a trial by jury undermines somewhat the argument of those who feel that jury nullification is an inevitable part of the process of cartel criminalization. On the basis of this case, one can argue that cartel activity is an activity that jurors can understand: determining the existence of a cartel does not involve sophisticated economic analysis that is beyond the comprehension of ordinary citizens.[60] Moreover, one can also argue that, by convicting Mr Hegarty (and others), the relevant jurors have demonstrated either that they believe cartel activity is inherently wrong or that the existence of such a belief regarding wrongfulness is unnecessary, even when the imposition of *criminal* sanctions is at issue. Either of these explanations would be acceptable to advocates of cartel criminalization. It is submitted, however, that the Irish example does not lay the matter to rest. One successful criminal case is clearly not enough to demonstrate that nullification would not be an issue in a recently criminalized cartel regime in Europe that employs trial by jury in criminal cases. In fact, given that the phenomenon of nullification is arguably present even in the context of US criminal antitrust enforcement (where it is regularly claimed that social norms have hardened towards cartel activity),[61]

[55] Clough (2003), 305. [56] Jacobs (2007), 30.

[57] See: Gorecki and McFadden (2006), 639–40; and Whelan (2013d).

[58] *DPP v. Hegarty*, Unreported Judgment, the Circuit Criminal Court, Galway, 3 May 2012.

[59] See <http://www.tca.ie/en/Enforcing-Competition-Law/Criminal-Court-Cases/Home-Heating-Oil.aspx>.

[60] Cf. Nettle (2011), 221.

[61] According to Warin et al. (2006), the fact that defendants in criminal antitrust cases (with a conviction rate of 49 per cent) fare better at trial than other criminal defendants (with a conviction rate of 80 per cent) is due in part to the fact that 'juries may view antitrust offences as less contemptible than other crimes'.

all countries that employ trial by jury in criminal cases should be advised to put in place strategies to avoid the issue of jury nullification if they wish to ensure an effective project of cartel criminalization. Of particular importance is the response to the challenge of 'communicating the issues and evidence *clearly and succinctly* to the jury in such a way that the evidence can be understood'.[62]

Unfortunately for those who advocate the introduction of criminal cartel sanctions, securing the necessary support from the judiciary can also be difficult: judges themselves may display reluctance concerning the imposition of custodial sentences for economic crimes committed by 'respectable' members of society.[63] This phenomenon is a manifestation of the 'compliance model' of enforcement, a model which assumes that there is a difference between corporate offenders and traditional offenders—corporate offenders engage in 'otherwise socially productive activities and are capable of being socially responsible'.[64] This particular model of enforcement is 'premised on cooperative models of persuasion, education, strategies of self-regulation and the belief that prosecution should be a last resort'.[65] Indeed, in Ireland, a jurisdiction which has introduced criminal antitrust sanctions, such 'hesitation to convict and imprison corporate offenders still exists',[66] a fact displayed in the judiciary's relatively lenient treatment of cartelists.[67] Japan has also experienced a similar phenomenon: in that jurisdiction, courts 'have assessed fines and imposed prison sentences, but no one has actually served any prison time yet as the result of a competition law conviction because the sentences have been suspended'.[68] Canada has had criminal antitrust sanctions on its books for many years and its judiciary has also been reluctant to impose custodial sentences. Scott believes that this reluctance can be explained by two factors: (i) the stipulation in the Canadian Criminal Code that offenders should not be incarcerated if a less restrictive punishment is appropriate; and (ii) the view that cartel crime does not deserve the same punishment as violent crime.[69] Even the US has experienced a degree of judicial hesitation regarding the imposition of custodial sentences for cartel activity.[70] In the 1980s, for example, it was argued that, in the antitrust context, imprisonment was an 'inferior penalty' due to judicial reluctance to impose such punishment.[71] If judicial reluctance persists in a criminal antitrust regime, the long-term deterrent effect of the law may be exaggerated (i.e. there may be an overestimation of the benefits of criminal sanctions): 'a criminal offence only packs a significant deterrent punch if convicted defendants serve custodial sentences'.[72] Furthermore, depending on how one conceptualizes it, the objective of retribution would fail to be achieved if the judiciary refuse to impose upon convicted cartelists sentences that are commensurate with both the gravity of the (actual/potential) harm caused by their actions and the degree of their culpability in engaging in cartel activity.

(b) Strategies to secure stakeholder support

The strategies designed to secure sufficient stakeholder support should aim: (i) to create considerable public support for the existence of criminal cartel sanctions; (ii) to avoid jury

[62] Gordon (2010), 17 (emphasis in the original).
[63] See Stephan (2008c), 27–30. See also Harding (2006), 201. [64] Gray (2006), 877.
[65] Gray (2006), 877. [66] Curtis and McNally (2007), 49.
[67] See generally <http://www.tca.ie/EN/Enforcing-Competition-Law/Criminal-Court-Cases.aspx>.
[68] OECD (1999), 25. See also Sanekata and Wilks (1996) (in Japan 'criminal sanctions against individuals have become an inherited treasure sword—used only for decoration').
[69] Scott (2007), 77. [70] See: Baker (2001), 706; and Whalley (1988), 575.
[71] Breit and Elzinga (1986), 57. [72] Stephan (2008c), 27.

nullification from becoming a noticeable feature of the criminal cartel regime; and (iii) to overcome judicial hesitancy to the imposition of custodial sentences on convicted cartelists.

(i) Securing general support for criminal cartel sanctions

To secure support from the general public for any type of antitrust regime (whether it be administrative or criminal in nature), one must engage in well-resourced educative efforts that underline the negative qualities of anticompetitive conduct. As noted by the OECD, 'improving public knowledge about the nature of [cartel activity] and the harm that it causes would bolster popular support for more effective action against it'.[73] More specifically, 'regulators have to be able to develop an effective outreach programme to the media, political class, and public to explain why price-fixing is so damaging and why heavy penalties are required'.[74] Such educative efforts could be conducted through workshops, public awareness campaigns, news releases, television interviews, and media publicity.[75] They could even involve the introduction of novel aspects to the national educational curricula.[76] To secure support for the *criminal* antitrust regime, however, one must go further and demonstrate not only that anticompetitive conduct can be harmful (and should therefore be sanctioned), but also that a deterrence-based and/or a retribution-based criminalization argument(s) is/are robust. In particular, one must demonstrate convincingly that cartel criminalization ensures that all citizens (as consumers) receive significant benefits, benefits that cannot be secured through the use of non-criminal sanctions.

An important (and arguably unique) aspect of any educative drive regarding the need for criminalization would be the articulation of the moral wrongfulness of cartel activity. This would be the case irrespective of whether deterrence or retribution is the underlying theoretical justification. The reason for this is that the general population may well believe that there should be some link between a crime and morally wrongful behaviour; and, if so, the public may not react well to legislative initiatives that can be interpreted as moves towards 'over-criminalization'. Alternatively, viewed from a different perspective: it may be easier to get people to accept criminal cartel sanctions when—in addition to demonstrating that they are needed to ensure deterrence of harmful behaviour—such sanctions are directed towards those who have done something that is 'morally wrong'. Given this context, some may argue that, irrespective of their extent, future educative efforts are inherently limited: there could be a problem with 'sticky norms' in some European jurisdictions when it comes to conceptualizations of the moral wrongfulness of cartel activity. This problem of resistance to change can occur when there is a wide disparity between the views of the criminal law and those of society in general as regards the moral character of a given conduct.[77] It is submitted that the issue with 'sticky norms' may not be overly problematic, even in those jurisdictions with an apparent cultural propensity towards collusion. This is so for two reasons. First, if cartel activity is widespread in a country, it does not necessarily follow that all citizens actually condone such behaviour; all it means is that *business people* either: (i) do not see anything wrong

[73] OECD (2002b), 5. [74] Riley (2007), 2.

[75] OECD (2005), 18–20. In order to promote 'cartel awareness', the ICN's Cartel Working Group has 'collected examples of public messages and materials used by competition agencies in their own cartel-related outreach efforts'; see <http://www.internationalcompetitionnetwork.org/working-groups/current/cartel/awareness.aspx>.

[76] The Antitrust Section of the American Bar Association has developed a four-part antitrust curriculum for use in high-school classrooms across the US; see <http://www.abanet.org/publiced/antitrust/>.

[77] See generally Green (2004), 507–8.

with such behaviour; or (ii) they know others would perceive it as wrong behaviour (if they understood what collusion involves), but they have not internalized the norm themselves. In other words, in such countries, a *social* (as opposed to a *business*) norm does not necessarily exist concerning the acceptance of cartel activity. If so, there will be no social norm that is 'sticky'. Second, as noted in Chapter 4, the conceptualization of cartel activity as 'morally wrongful' does not depend upon the creation of *new* social norms; rather, it can apply the concept of cartel activity to *already established* norms. The norms against cheating, deception, and stealing are likely to be widely accepted by European citizens, even if they do not necessarily refrain in every instance from their violation. These norms are certainly not as controversial as other potential norms, such as those relating to sexual or religious practices. So what would arguably be at issue in those jurisdictions with a cultural propensity towards collusion is not a substitution of one (newly created) moral norm for another one, but rather the employment of an already established, accepted norm to interpret the desirability of certain harmful (widespread) practices. In others words, if citizens understood the immoral quality of cartel activity, they would not be as likely to ignore the current practices of businesses in those jurisdictions with a cultural propensity towards collusion. Another point that undermines any alleged problematic limitation upon educative efforts is the fact that one of the advantages of employing a norms-based approach to understand the moral wrongfulness of cartel activity is that the norms involved are relatively easy to understand and apply in daily life: 'Even people who have never had occasion to read a single page of moral philosophy are capable of making finely grained distinctions about, say, what properly constitutes cheating or stealing'.[78] Understanding the immoral quality of cartel activity, then, is actually facilitated as a result of the mere employment of these norms: as a direct result of the employment of Green's framework, the immoral quality of cartel activity should become comprehensible to the average citizen.

The educative efforts noted above should continue throughout the development of the criminalized regime, in recognition of the fact that it can take a considerable period of time to develop a norm accepting the existence of criminal cartel sanctions.[79] The timing of the introduction of criminal sanctions also needs to be correct in order to secure considerable support for the criminalization project. As noted by Brisimi and Ioannidou:

> Timely intervention is crucial; otherwise, a vicious circle is created; the lack of moral condemnation of cartel activity reinforces itself through the lack of educational efforts or through the unavailability of information regarding enforcement activities.[80]

A general competition culture needs to be in place prior to criminalization,[81] and any attempt to introduce criminal sanctions without the existence of that competition culture will surely be perceived as 'premature', particularly by industry lobbies.[82] What is important is that the measures in a civil competition regime 'should be given time to prove their worth before a decision is taken on criminalisation'.[83] The input of experts in competition law, as well as the general opinion of the public (obtained through

[78] Green (2006), 44.

[79] On the 'long period of time' it took the US to achieve the 'goal of obtaining broader moral and legal support for increased penalties for individual cartelists', see Dixon (2012). See also Kovacic (2003–04), 416–25.

[80] Brisimi and Ioannidou (2011), 168.

[81] See Smith (2001), 291.

[82] See Joshua (2002), 231.

[83] See Blair and Conway (2002), 54.

representative surveys[84]), is vital in order to determine whether such a competition culture exists prior to criminalization. The input of experts in particular is also important in drafting a criminal competition law which would be capable of achieving the support of the wider public: their input may help to ensure that the criminal cartel offence actually 'captures the criminality' of cartel activity. What needs to be ensured here, then, is an open, well-publicized consultation on cartel criminalization prior to the adoption of criminal cartel sanctions (or indeed prior to the (final) decision by policy-makers that the adoption of such sanctions would be the best way forward for a given competition regime). This consultation should ideally involve: the publication of a detailed discussion document (created by a competent entity that has recognized experience in drawing up detailed reports, such as a national law reform commission or equivalent), which sets out the justifications for criminalization as well as any drawbacks or challenges; the active encouragement of submissions on the discussion document from the 'epistemic' competition law community and the wider public; the later publication of a draft bill containing the criminal cartel offence (if criminal sanctions have been decided upon) which has been influenced by the (informed) submissions received and/or international best practice; the provision of opportunities to comment on the draft bill and any later amendments; and the encouragement of interested parties to provide 'evidence' to parliamentary committees during the bill's passage through Parliament. The publication of all relevant documents/submissions on a special (micro-)website which is regularly updated throughout the process would also be a good idea. This type of process (or something similar) would help to establish some public support for criminalization prior to its occurrence and/or would make it less likely that a criminal cartel offence would be created that would not be accepted by the general population. Unfortunately, this strategy has not always been adopted by regimes contemplating cartel criminalization; in fact, it seems that a number of jurisdictions that have recently criminalized cartel activity (or that have reformed their criminal cartel laws) have been somewhat deficient in their approach to public consultation and/or to the fostering of public debate on cartel criminalization.[85] The notable exception to this trend is New Zealand, where the consultation process[86] and the official documents informing that process[87] have been particularly robust and professional.

Following criminalization, in order to overcome any potential limitations due to the nature of cartel activity, the authorities must act carefully and sensibly in their educative efforts. In particular, they need to be clever in their prioritization strategies regarding criminal antitrust prosecutions. One should understand here that the actual securing of prosecutions is clearly central to the creation and/or maintenance of support for cartel criminalization.[88] The early cases in particular are very important, as they may set sentencing precedents.[89] For Stephan, there are two key elements to a clever strategy of gaining public support: (i) an initial focus on public procurement involving bid-rigging; and (ii) an initial focus on cartels selling to final consumers. For him:

[84] For examples, see: Beaton-Wells (2012); Beaton-Wells et al. (2010); Parker and Platania-Phung (2012); and Stephan (2008e).

[85] For (considerable) criticism of the UK and Australian processes, e.g., see Beaton-Wells (2008a). For criticism of the Greek and Canadian processes, see respectively: Brisimi and Ioannidou (2011), 161; and Quaid (2012), 168.

[86] For a description, see Hamilton and Scott (2013), 188.

[87] See, e.g.: King (2010); and Ministry of Economic Development (2010).

[88] See Morgan (2010), 79. [89] Calvani and Calvani (2009), 137.

Public procurement cases involving bid-rigging provide a useful way of side-stepping the victim hurdle faced in most cartel cases. As tax payers, every reader and viewer automatically becomes a victim paying artificially inflated prices. The direct victims—especially schools, hospitals and the military—are also more likely to capture the popular imagination and spark public outrage.... Cartels selling to final consumers are also likely to be more newsworthy; members of the public can immediately identify the products, the companies involved and can even determine whether they are potential victims.[90]

As noted by Stephan himself, sufficient support for this type of strategy can be found in the US antitrust cases involving bid-rigging in the supply of milk to school children and in the supply of equipment to the military,[91] cases which helped to foster current US public support for criminal antitrust punishment.[92] This strategy also appears to have been adopted in Germany, where the specific offence of bid-rigging has been created.[93] Indeed, as some have acknowledged, there is a very good reason to start the process of antitrust criminalization with an offence focused on bid-rigging: 'in the case of public procurement, the tax-payers' money and usually large stakes are involved'.[94] Obtaining public money through rigged bids is an activity that is easily regarded by society as 'contemptible'.[95] If a decision is made not to restrict the definition of cartel activity in the criminal legislation to bid-rigging, it is still vitally important to choose the right cases.[96] The criminal cartel enforcers should not 'debase the currency': they should only pursue 'serious cases where serious penalties are appropriate'.[97] While determining what is 'serious' is a complex endeavour, it would no doubt involve inquiries regarding the importance of the market involved for consumers, the culpability of the accused, the extent to which the accused attempted to disguise his conduct, the overall value of the market concerned, the percentage of the market affected by the cartel, the alleged price rise (in percentage terms), etc. The creation of a formal list of prioritization criteria or principles could be useful in ensuring the focus on 'serious' cases is maintained.[98] However, care must be taken when a strategy of selective enforcement is pursued. As Harding and Joshua are quick to point out, 'a distinction should be drawn between a selective enforcement policy, on the one side, and one that is vacillating and uncertain on the other'.[99] In order to avoid the perception that one's enforcement policy is 'vacillating and uncertain' rather than merely 'selective' and focused on 'serious' cartel activity, one should be acutely aware of the 'dangers of loss of credibility' that may occur when an enforcement agency clearly determines that a cartel is serious (by, e.g., taking administrative enforcement action against it) 'yet gives no explanation, or an unconvincing explanation, for not bringing criminal proceedings'.[100] Clear explanations regarding prioritization in practice are required in order to prevent any negative perceptions of the competition law community or of the wider public.

[90] Stephan (2011c), 391. According to Skilbeck, however, consumer goods industries tend to be the most competitive, and intermediate, homogenous products are the most suitable for cartel behaviour: Skilbeck (2002). If true, Stephan's strategy will inevitably be limited: it will tend to focus on a small number of cartels, to the exclusion of the vast majority.

[91] See, e.g.: Snyder (1990); and Whalley (1990–91), 153.

[92] See Kovacic (2011), 66.

[93] See Section 298 of the German Criminal Code ('StGB').

[94] Wagner-von Papp (2011), 180.

[95] See Kovacic (2006), 52.

[96] See, e.g.: Nikpay (2012), 10–11; and Reindl (2006), 127.

[97] Calvani and Calvani (2009), 138.

[98] In 2008, the OFT developed a set of prioritization principles: OFT (2008). These principles are applicable to the UK Cartel Offence: OFT (2013b), [2.47]. On the merits and demerits of the exercise of discretion and prioritization in public antitrust enforcement generally, see Wils (2011).

[99] Harding and Joshua (2010), 339.

[100] Fisse (2009), 5.

It is also important to ensure that publicity is created when criminal cartel convictions are obtained.[101] After each successful criminal cartel trial, the antitrust enforcers should prepare and release detailed press releases and appear on television and radio if possible, in the process explaining the nature of cartel activity, the holding of the criminal court, and the benefits for consumers of the criminalization policy. Barnett, in arguing that publicizing convictions is one of the 'seven steps to better cartel enforcement', posits that one should not forget

> that criminal anti-cartel enforcement is a government function, and government resources are always scarce. Antitrust enforcers should not be shy about publicizing the fact that anti-cartel enforcement is, on a dollar-for-dollar basis, among the best uses of law enforcement resources from the standpoint of consumer welfare.[102]

Publicizing successful criminal cartel cases also helps to achieve deterrence: it brings home to potential cartelists the fact that detection and (successful) prosecution will be a possible outcome of their decision to engage in cartel activity.[103] It also serves a retributive function: by highlighting the existence of the criminal judgment, the enforcer helps to facilitate the communication of society's disapproval of the convicted cartelist's conduct that is inherent in the conviction (if it is justified upon the basis of retribution). In addition to creating such publicity after each criminal case, it is also important for the authority to keep a public record of cartel convictions. This would not only help academics to have a better command of the important statistics that are necessary to evaluate the deterrent effect of sanctions,[104] but it would also contribute to the creation (or, more appropriately, the reinforcement) of a competition culture that involves the imposition of severe sanctions for anticompetitive behaviour.[105]

(ii) Avoiding jury nullification

The above-noted strategies to obtain general public support for criminal cartel sanctions are of obvious relevance to the creation of a strategy to ensure that jury nullification is not a significant feature of the criminalized regime: after all, subject to certain conditions, juries are drawn from the general (adult) population. In short, educating the population about cartel activity helps to reduce the potential for jury nullification.[106] Correctly drafted criminal cartel offences can also help to reduce the scope for jury nullification, particularly if one ensures that the definition of the offence does not require the jury to rely upon their views of the moral wrongfulness of cartel activity.[107] In addition, there are a number of other mechanisms that can be used to reduce the possibilities for jury nullification.

The criminal court should have adequate powers to assist the jury in understanding complex issues at trial. In Australia, for example, Section 23EC of the Federal Court of Australia Act 1976 empowers judges 'to order such things as it thinks appropriate in the circumstances to be given to the jury to assist the jury to understand the issues during trial'.[108] What is very important in the context of a criminal cartel trial is the production of a 'road map' that will help jury members to understand and appreciate the significance of the evidence as it is presented.[109] This lesson has recently been taken on board

101 Kovacic (2003–04), 422. 102 Barnett (2006b), 10. 103 Barnett (2006b), 10.
104 See Chapter 3, Section D(b)(i)(2) of this book.
105 See Brisimi and Ioannidou (2011), 160. 106 Cf. Clough (2003), 305.
107 On issues concerning the definition of the cartel offence, see Chapter 8 of this book.
108 Gordon (2010), 17.
109 Gordon (2010), 17.

in Ireland.[110] On 3 July 2012, the Irish Minister for Jobs, Enterprise and Innovation signed a commencement order bringing into effect Section 10 of the Competition Act 2002. Section 10 allows for certain documents to be made available to juries in competition cases (such as transcripts of opening and closing speeches, transcripts of the judge's charge to the jury, and any charts, diagrams, graphics, schedules, or agreed summaries of evidence produced at the trial). This step arguably reduces the potential for jury nullification in future cases in Ireland because any confused juror may seek the benefit of Section 10 of the Competition Act 2002: the trial judge now has the power to make available documents which help to reduce a juror's possible confusion. Model jury instructions for criminal cartel cases could also be created to reduce the potential for jury confusion.[111] These instructions could focus on various issues, such as the content of the criminal cartel offence, what needs to be proven, what does not need to be proven, and the applicable standard of proof.[112]

Choosing the correct type of case is also of importance in avoiding jury nullification. As noted in Chapter 9, prosecutors should understand that the prosecution of bilateral cartels where one side goes free due to a grant of immunity and the other is prosecuted (perhaps due to being slow, rather than unwilling, to cooperate) may present particular difficulties. If a jury has to decide on whether a cartel offence has been committed, nullification may occur in such cases if the jury feels that it would be unfair to impose punishment on only one side of the cartel arrangement.[113] Bilateral cartels with a successful leniency/immunity applicant therefore do not present the best type of cases to be prosecuted in front of a jury. Admittedly, bilateral cartels can have a significant impact on consumer welfare, and a prosecution policy that effectively provides criminal immunity for such cartels would be deficient. That said, prosecutors need to be careful with such cases and only prosecute them when leniency information can be corroborated from other sources, the cartel conduct is clear and unambiguous, and/or it is immediately obvious that the accused appreciated the criminal nature of his conduct by, for example, engaging in active efforts to disguise the conduct. Bringing cases where there is an actual effect in the market (e.g., a price rise) which is unequivocally due to the cartel, even when such an effect does not need to be proven in order to establish commission of the cartel offence, can also help to overcome the jury's hesitancy to convict in cartel cases.[114]

To avoid issues with nullification, one could also follow a strategy of initiating summary prosecutions instead of prosecutions on indictment when the criminal cartel offence has been committed. While this approach would eliminate the jury from the process, and thereby solve the problem of jury nullification, it would not be a good strategy to follow, for two reasons. First, the criminal courts dealing with summary cases may be ill-equipped to handle criminal cartel cases, as such 'litigation is not the fare of these courts, where the dockets are crowded with summary criminal cases such as disorderly conduct and small civil actions'.[115] Second, and perhaps more importantly, the likely sanctions of a summary case would not be sufficient to secure deterrence: 'the existence of "small cartel" cases with "small penalties" debases the currency of the sanction'.[116] A similar point could be made with regard to the achievement of retribution: summary

110 See Whelan (2013d).
111 Beaton-Wells and Fisse (2008c), 34.
112 For an example of model jury instructions, see ABA Section of Antitrust Law (2009).
113 MacCulloch and Wardhaugh (2012), 16–17.
114 Cf. Calvani and Carl (2013), 311–12.
115 Calvani and Carl (2013), 311.
116 Calvani and Carl (2013), 311.

cases do not communicate society's disapproval of cartel activity as well as prosecutions on indictment.

A related, and final, option that could be employed to deal with jury nullification would be the abolition of trial by jury altogether for cartel offences.[117] This option is clearly the nuclear one. Assuming that it was not deemed to be unconstitutional or in violation of fundamental human rights, this option would have to be implemented by legislation. There is precedent in the UK for such a move.[118] However, given the difficulties experienced by the UK Government when it tried to ensure the adoption of legislation bringing into force Section 43 of the Criminal Justice Act 2003,[119] it is clearly a challenging option to pursue in practice. In particular, the advantages of the system of trial by jury may be perceived by law-makers to be such that its abolition for certain offences would not be fair to the criminal accused.[120] Furthermore, where legislation does provide for the possibility of trial by jury to be circumvented, judicial interpretation of the relevant legislation may be overly restrictive,[121] thereby reducing the attractiveness of this potential solution to the issue of jury nullification. Consequently, this option is not likely to be enthusiastically pursued by policy-makers.

(iii) Dealing with judicial reluctance

As with jury nullification, the strategies designed to achieve general public support for cartel criminalization are also important in overcoming judicial reluctance to impose custodial sentences upon convicted cartelists: judges are consumers after all, and benefit from a robust approach to cartel law enforcement; appreciating this fact helps to strengthen their resolve to deal severely with such activity when individuals have been found guilty of criminal cartel offences. There is an additional strategy that can help to foster judicial acceptance of the need for custodial sentences; it involves the use of 'signalling' the need for custodial sentences to the judiciary by the legislature.

One way of signalling the need for custodial sentences is through the creation of a relatively high maximum custodial sentence that can be imposed for cartel activity. A maximum sentence of, say, five or seven years might perform this particular function, particularly if it is accompanied by educative efforts directed at the public (and, therefore, in part at least, at the judiciary). If, following the conviction of a number of individuals for cartel activity, the judiciary remain reluctant to impose custodial sentences, the legislature could raise the maximum sentence in order to signal its disapproval of the sentencing record of the court and to signal further the need for significant custodial sentences. The approach recently adopted by the legislature in Ireland followed this

117 See: Furse and Nash (2004a), 91–2; and Ministry of Economic Development (2010), 14 and 83–5.

118 See Part 7 of the Criminal Justice Act 2003.

119 Section 43 of the Criminal Justice Act 2003 would allow for the prosecution to apply to a judge of the Crown Court for a criminal trial relating to certain fraud offences to be conducted without a jury. For this provision to enter into force, a statutory instrument needs to be adopted, subject to an affirmative resolution by each House of Parliament: Section 330(5)(b) of the Criminal Justice Act 2003. This has not occurred to date, despite the Government's best efforts; on this issue, see, e.g.: Broadbridge (2009), 6–7; and Slapper and Kelly (2013), 544–6.

120 On the advantages (and disadvantages) of trial by jury, see, e.g.: Davies et al. (2010), 314–19; and Joyce (2013), 209 et seq.

121 See, e.g., the following judgments concerning the interpretation of Section 44 of the Criminal Justice Act 2003 (which allows for criminal trials to be conducted without a jury when there is a danger of jury tampering): *J, S, M v. R* [2010] EWCA Crim 1755; and *KS v. R* [2010] EWCA Crim 1756.

strategy.[122] On 3 July 2012, the Competition (Amendment) Act 2012 came into effect in the Republic of Ireland. This particular piece of legislation amended Ireland's competition regime (which is enshrined in the Irish Competition Act 2002, as amended) in a number of significant ways. As a result of these amendments, those individuals convicted on indictment of a criminal cartel offence in Ireland now face a higher maximum custodial sentence: the maximum sentence is now ten years, rather than the five years that previously applied. Section 2(h) of the Competition (Amendment) Act 2012 also provides that Section 1(1) of the Probation of Offenders Act 1907—which allows a court to find the facts proven and nonetheless dismiss the charge at issue—shall not apply to criminal cartel offences in Ireland. A number of cartelists convicted of offences under the Competition Act 2002 had previously received the benefit of the Probation of Offenders Act 1907[123] and none had actually served a custodial sentence, although a number of individuals had received suspended sentences. The Competition (Amendment) Act 2012 can easily be interpreted as an attempt by the Irish legislature to perform a signalling effect towards the Irish judges, who are being encouraged to be stricter in future in the sentencing of cartelists. Specifically, the custodial sentencing reforms in the 2012 Act can be understood as an implicit plea by the legislature to the judiciary to (at least in very serious cases) abandon the practice of systematically imposing suspended sentences on convicted cartelists.[124]

The point here is that, provided the judiciary *understand the seriousness of cartel activity*, they may well respond to this type of legislative encouragement. Understanding of the seriousness of cartel activity and of other anticompetitive activity can be fostered to a degree by judges' participation in discussions and conferences organized by the Association of European Competition Law Judges.[125] Fortunately for those who advocate cartel criminalization, there appears to be some judicial support for the use of criminal cartel sanctions in Ireland.[126] A current Justice of the Irish Supreme Court, for example, has expressly stated his ('strong') agreement with the current author's assessment that cartels represent a fundamental violation of prevailing moral norms and therefore deserve serious criminal punishment.[127] Mr Justice McKechnie has also stated in *Manning* that he anticipated that the serving of a custodial sentence was near at hand.[128] Two years later in *Duffy*, McKechnie J reiterated this particular point, claiming that 'if the first generation of carteliers have escaped prison, the second and present generation almost certainly will not'.[129] If other judges were as receptive to the need for criminal cartel sanctions as McKechnie J appears to be,[130] there is the potential for the signalling function of the Competition (Amendment) Act 2012 to have some effect in practice.

[122] See generally Whelan (2013d). In addition, Canada has recently introduced legislation restricting the sentencing discretion of judges by removing their ability to impose non-custodial conditional sentences for individuals convicted of cartel activity; see: Berra (2012); and the Safe Streets and Communities Act 2012. This move can also be understood as a form of signalling on behalf of the Canadian legislature to the Canadian judiciary.

[123] An example includes the *Grain Imports* case, where in October 2004 the Circuit Court in Dundalk applied the Probation of Offenders Act 1907 to three convicted parties; see <http://www.tca.ie/EN/Enforcing-Competition-Law/Criminal-Court-Cases/Grain-Imports-.aspx>.

[124] On this practice, see Curtis and McNally (2007).

[125] See <http://www.aeclj.com>.

[126] See, e.g., McNally (2010).

[127] See *DPP v. Duffy and Duffy Motors (Newbridge) Ltd* [2009] IEHC 208, [25].

[128] *DPP v. Manning*, Unreported Judgment, High Court, 9 February 2007.

[129] *DPP v. Duffy and Duffy Motors (Newbridge) Ltd* [2009] IEHC 208, [67].

[130] Judge Groarke appeared to agree with these comments of Mr Justice McKechnie when sentencing Mr Hegarty for his commission of a criminal cartel offence in *DPP v. Hegarty*, Unreported Judgment, Circuit Criminal Court, Galway, 3 May 2012; see <http://www.tca.ie/images/uploaded/documents/Hegarty%20sentencing.pdf>, 14.

Admittedly, there are limitations to this type of signalling by the legislature. For a start, in the absence of mandatory sentences, there is no obligation on the judiciary to actually take heed of the encouragement of the legislature. Second, merely increasing the maximum sentence for a criminal cartel offence does not provide judges with any formal framework according to which they can determine the custodial sentence to impose upon convicted cartelists. A stronger form of signalling can be adopted to overcome these drawbacks: the use of (cartel-offence-specific) sentencing guidelines,[131] such as exist in the US.[132] When these sentencing guidelines are mandatory, rather than discretionary, their effect is strongest. Until the Supreme Court ruled otherwise in January 2005,[133] the US federal courts for a number of years had treated the US Sentencing Guidelines as mandatory, a fact that helped to overcome initial judicial reluctance to impose custodial sentences for cartel activity.[134] As explained by Joshua, by identifying

> the conduct as meriting imprisonment, the [US] legislators altered the previously deeply-engrained view of many judges that the defendants appearing before them were not criminals but the type of person they would meet at the country club or charity fundraiser. With the judges having no choice but to hand down jail terms, public, legal and business circles came more readily to regard the conduct in question as unalloyed criminality.[135]

However, the use of mandatory sentencing guidelines is not without its own problems. As the experience of the US demonstrates, mandatory guidelines may not be constitutionally acceptable in some jurisdictions. Added to this is the fact that they may cause judicial resentment, in particular due to the significant interference with judicial independence represented by such guidelines.[136] That said, if a jurisdiction wishes to implement mandatory sentences (and is not legally prevented from doing so), it needs to be very careful. If the penalties imposed are very high from the outset, and sufficient education about the nature of cartel activity has not been provided, one risks engendering some of the disadvantages associated with 'over-criminalization',[137] as well as potential inefficiencies in the enforcement regime.[138] If such an option is decided upon, it is preferable, therefore, to increase the penalties slowly but surely;[139] this would at least allow some time for acceptance of a criminal cartel law to develop within society.

A compromise solution to the problem of ineffective signalling would be the creation of discretionary sentencing guidelines. These types of guidelines would not cause the judiciary as much concern as mandatory guidelines as, quite clearly, they do not restrict their independence in sentencing to anywhere near the same extent as the latter do. Importantly, empirical evidence—admittedly from the US rather than Europe—supports the view that judges tend to 'respond to congressional sentiment for changing the harshness of sanctions even if such changes are not mandated'.[140] If this phenomenon is present in Europe, then

131 For examples of how these guidelines can operate in practice, see, e.g., Gorecki and Maxwell (2013c).

132 See, e.g.: US Sentencing Commission (2012), §2R1.1; and Zweifach and Creizman (2008).

133 See *United States v. Booker* (2005) 543 US 220.

134 Baker (2009), 160. See also: Calvani and Carl (2013), 316; and Klawiter and Driscoll (2009), 75 (the US Sentencing Guidelines 'set forth a definite, transparent, and consistent process for sentencing individual offenders and increased the number and duration of antitrust prison sentences significantly. This represented a turning point in antitrust enforcement').

135 Joshua (2003), 640 (footnotes omitted).

136 See OECD (2008), 35.

137 On this, see Chapter 3, Section D(a) of this book. US commentators acknowledged this potential problem when the US Sentencing Commission first published sentencing guidelines for criminal antitrust offences in the 1980s; see Cohen (1989), 37–8.

138 See: Klawiter and Driscoll (2009); and Cohen and Scheffman (1989–90), 356–7.

139 The US increased its criminal antitrust penalties over time; see Harrison and Bell (2005–06), 209–18.

140 Cohen (1989), 44.

(discretionary) guidelines on sentencing ranges could serve their signalling purpose without acting as an inappropriate restriction of judicial independence. Of course, developing such guidelines is not likely to be without difficulty. Clearly, there is a tension between 'too much predictability and too much fettering of the discretion of the Courts'.[141] What is crucial is that the balance is correct, so that 'the sentencing guidelines or methodology provides a reasonably acceptable framework within which sentences are determined while at the same time leaving the Court sufficient flexibility to reflect the facts of the case'.[142] Provided that they can achieve such a balance,[143] discretionary guidelines could also help to build support for the criminal competition regime more generally, as they reduce the potential for convicted individuals to complain to the media about the arbitrary nature of any punishment imposed by a court. Indeed, an absence of such guidelines can lead to frustrations with a system that can be interpreted as 'unclear and, more importantly, subjective or arbitrary'.[144] The ability of such guidelines to help to create legal certainty should be appreciated. The Irish Competition Authority, in advocating the adoption of such guidelines in Ireland for criminal cartel offences, has been keen to point out that such guidelines can help to provide legal certainty to the general public and competition law practitioners.[145] Unfortunately, the Irish legislature has to date refused to adopt such guidelines.[146] It is submitted that other jurisdictions across Europe that are considering introducing criminal cartel sanctions should give serious thought to the idea of introducing discretionary sentencing guidelines for criminal cartel cases if they wish to use their best endeavours to ensure that judicial reluctance does not undermine the objectives of cartel criminalization.

D. Designing the Enforcement Agency/Agencies

It is axiomatic to state that, for cartel criminalization to be effective in practice, sufficient resources need to be expended on the creation of the criminal antitrust enforcement agency/agencies (or criminal unit within an existing agency) and that the annual budget for criminal cartel enforcement should be adequate in order for the agency/agencies to meet the relevant criminal law enforcement objectives.[147] Indeed, where antitrust criminalization has failed in the past, one can often detect a failure to resource adequately the relevant enforcement agencies.[148] In short, the mistake of under-funding criminal enforcement efforts needs to be avoided, and the securing of political support for cartel criminalization can help enormously in this regard.[149] Another related area where mistakes can be made concerns the actual institutional design of a (well-resourced) criminal cartel regime. A very important decision that obviously needs to be made at the outset of any proposed change from an administrative cartel regime to a criminal one concerns the make-up and (respective) role(s) of

141 Gorecki and Maxwell (2013b), 247.

142 Gorecki and Maxwell (2013b), 247.

143 For a (convincing) argument that the current US Sentencing Guidelines provide a solid basis upon which one can construct guidelines which achieve the correct balance, see Gorecki and Maxwell (2013a).

144 Scott (2007), 83.

145 The Competition Authority (2007), [2.47].

146 See Calvani and Carl (2013), 319.

147 Wils (2006b), 87.

148 Even in the US, there were enforcement failures in the early days of the development of the criminal antitrust regime due to a lack of resources; see Furse (2012), 55 (when the Sherman Act 1890 'was first introduced the legislature did not focus on enforcement mechanisms, the power to enforce the new law simply being passed to the Attorney General with no additional funds or resources made available to support enforcement, and the first attempt to enforce the new legislation was a crushing failure for the Government').

149 See Beaton-Wells (2008b), 220.

the criminal antitrust enforcement agency/agencies.[150] In particular, what needs to be decided is the issue as to who will exercise the investigative and the prosecutorial functions in the criminalized regime.[151] Of course, there are many different ways of organizing the distribution of these particular functions in a criminalized cartel regime. For example, both functions could be exercised by a competition authority (which is also responsible for administrative enforcement), a specialist economic-crime unit, or a general criminal prosecutor's office. Alternatively, the functions could be separated, with the competition authority undertaking the investigative function and a (special/general) prosecutor exercising the prosecutorial role.

There are four important strategic questions that need to be answered when choosing the design of the criminal cartel enforcement apparatus in a given jurisdiction. The first is whether an existing competition authority (which is responsible, say, for the investigation of administrative competition law offences, including abuse of dominance) should exercise the investigative function in a criminal cartel regime. Assuming that the answer to the first question is in the positive, the second question is whether the competition authority should share the investigative function with another (special/general) agency. Assuming again that the answer to the first question is in the positive, and irrespective of the answer to the second question, the third question is whether the competition authority should also be able to prosecute a cartel offence. Assuming that the answer to the third question is also in the positive, the fourth and final question is whether it should exercise its prosecutorial function alone or in conjunction with another (special/general) prosecutor. The answers to these questions are by no means obvious, as each approach has its own particular advantages and disadvantages.

There are clear advantages to allowing the (traditionally administrative) competition agency to exercise the investigatory function in a criminalized cartel regime. That agency's extensive knowledge and experience of economics, the general operation and structure of cartels, and the law of cartels would be an obvious asset for an agency which is tasked with fulfilling the investigative function of a criminal cartel case.[152] So, too, is the agency's presumed knowledge of the harmfulness and seriousness of cartels and its dedication to ensuring that markets work well for consumers. An agency's experience with running a (successful) administrative leniency/immunity programme would also be beneficial for a criminal cartel investigator, particularly given the need for a criminal immunity programme for cartel activity.[153] Indeed, if the agency has exercised administrative functions for quite a number of years, and therefore has acquired significant experience in anti-cartel enforcement, there is a firm case for advocating their involvement in the investigation of a criminal cartel. In fact, some have argued that it is essential that the administrative agency has an 'established track record in civil enforcement, merger control and, where possible, in market studies and a sustained flow of outputs in each area' before even contemplating exercising a criminal investigative function.[154] By taking this advice, the competition authority is 'more likely to have a sufficient base of experienced and skilled staff to enable it to take on costly criminal work'.[155] The stronger the 'track record' established by the competition agency, the stronger the case for its involvement in the investigative function. Admittedly, there are important procedural

150 See, e.g., Beaton-Wells (2009), 41–2.

151 As noted in Chapter 5, Section C(c) of this book, in order to adhere to the dictates of the ECHR, the other relevant enforcement function (i.e. the adjudicative function) would need to be performed by a criminal court and that court would not be able to perform the other functions of enforcement (i.e. the investigative and prosecutorial functions).

152 See OECD (2007b), 28.

153 See Chapter 9 of this book.

154 Fingleton et al. (2007), 22 (footnotes omitted).

155 Fingleton et al. (2007), 22.

differences between an administrative investigation and a criminal one, differences that are driven by divergent human rights standards in the respective enforcement proceedings.[156] Consequently, and irrespective of the enforcement experience of the administrative agency, there would be an obvious need for detailed training in criminal procedural law prior to the creation of the criminal investigative function.[157] Staff would also need to be trained in the use of (novel) criminal investigative techniques (such as, e.g., the use of covert surveillance).[158] A thorough understanding of the legal restraints operating when such techniques are employed would need to be established in the agency. One should also understand here that, in comparison to cases involving abuse of dominance or anticompetitive mergers, (criminal) cartel cases should generally be staffed with fewer economists and more individuals with specialist investigative skills and prosecutorial experience. As Calvani and Calvani note:

> Good cartel cases may be difficult to investigate, but the facts cannot be complicated. Cartel cases that depend on subtle linkages and a vast amount of evidence are hard to bring and harder to win. What is required is a mating of good criminal investigative talent and prosecutorial skills. Thus the skills of detectives and prosecutors with experience in embezzlement cases are likely to be more valuable than those with experience in abuse of dominance.[159]

An agency may well decide to recruit experienced criminal investigators as part of its investigative staff, but, in response to this, the argument could be made that 'to import criminal investigators would not only be divisive and undermine the morale of the present investigative complement, it would also be disjointed and lack continuity' within the respective competition agency.[160] Whether this would occur in a given agency would be for the management to determine; but outside recruitment would certainly be a possible option. Any additional training or additional staff recruitment may well be costly and certainly will take time to become effective, but it should be understood that any cartel criminalization project would be 'a long-term, front-end loaded investment'.[161] Provided this is understood and that significant political support exists for the criminalization venture, there should be relatively few difficulties in securing the relevant funding for such training. Fostering cooperation with the police is also important if a competition law enforcer is to become an effective criminal law enforcer.[162] In Ireland, for example, the Competition Authority investigates criminal cartel activity and has understood the need for cooperation with the Irish police; in fact, it has 'embedded' members of the police within its structure.[163] This strategic decision—in addition to a number of others, such as the decision to recruit forensic investigators as part of its cartel investigation teams—has helped the Irish Competition Authority to prosecute successfully a significant number of criminal cartel cases.[164] Of course, if administrative competition powers will continue to be exercised by the criminal cartel agency, it is also imperative that additional mechanisms be put in place to ensure that the rights of the accused are protected without a noticeable negative impact upon the overall effectiveness of the competition regime apparatus. These mechanisms were detailed in Chapter 6.[165]

156 See generally Chapter 5 of this book.

157 See, e.g., OFT (2001), [1.14].

158 On these techniques, see generally Chapter 5, Section D(b)(ii)(4) of this book.

159 Calvani and Calvani (2009), 139.

160 OFT (2001), [4.11].

161 See Reindl (2006), 115.

162 Of course, cooperation with the police may also be necessary in order to perform administrative investigatory functions, such as conducting dawn raids; see, e.g., ICN (2005), 39.

163 Gorecki and McFadden (2006), 635.

164 See <http://www.tca.ie/EN/Enforcing-Competition-Law/Criminal-Court-Cases.aspx>. See also: Calvani and Carl (2013); and Massey and Cooke (2011).

165 See Chapter 6, Section C(c)(ii) of this book.

Given the steep learning curve that would be facing a competition agency taking on a criminal investigative function for the first time,[166] there is a supportable case for allowing another experienced criminal enforcement agency to provide additional help with criminal investigations to the competition agency. For example, in the UK, it was proposed in the 2001 'Hammond and Penrose Report' that criminal cartel investigations would be undertaken by the OFT 'under the guidance and direction of an SFO [Serious Fraud Office] case controller who would be experienced in criminal law'.[167] The advantage of this approach is that the 'domain-specific expertise and experience'[168] of the competition agency can be combined with the considerable criminal investigative experience of another specialist agency. In the early days of criminal cartel enforcement, such guidance could ensure that mistakes are not made by the competition agency that would not be made by a seasoned criminal investigative body, thus helping to ensure that any existing public and political support for criminal cartel enforcement is not lost through embarrassing, unprofessional actions of the competition authority. In addition, the experienced criminal investigative body may have particular specialist knowledge (e.g., about financial markets or the operation of the Stock Exchange) or skills (e.g., dealing effectively with forensic accounting) that may be lacking in the competition agency.[169] Admittedly, such an approach can result in conflict if the competition authority displays a different enforcement culture from the other agency and/or if its caseload priorities diverge from those of its counterpart. The input of an additional agency could also complicate the operation of any criminal immunity programme. However, by putting a formal agreement in place concerning the respective investigative roles of the competition agency and the other (special/general) agency[170] and by clearly allocating responsibility for the operation of the immunity programme, one can reduce somewhat the potential for conflict.

Whether a competition authority should be allowed to exercise the prosecutorial function is a more difficult issue. A number of arguments in favour of allowing it to exercise that particular function can be found in the literature. The first is that the competition authority would be more likely to be dedicated to prosecuting cartel activity than a general public prosecutor's office. As Tavares de Araujo notes, 'it is quite natural for an antitrust authority to set anti-cartel enforcement as a top priority, but not as natural for criminal authorities that usually are involved with the investigation of other serious crimes to do the same'.[171] This negative effect has in fact manifested itself in criminalized cartel regimes where general prosecutors were responsible for criminal cartel enforcement. One of the reasons for the failure of criminal antitrust enforcement in Austria (a failure that would lead to eventual decriminalization[172]), for example, was the fact that the efforts of the relevant prosecutors were completely insufficient, due mainly to a general disinterest in criminal cartel enforcement and a realization that taking such cases involves the accumulation of human capital that, given the low number of criminal cartel cases, would not be of much use in future.[173] Likewise, in the Netherlands, when cartel activity was a criminal offence, public prosecutors 'did not seem to show much interest in the enforcement of competition rules'.[174] All that is required for a criminal

166 See OFT (2010d), 10: 'At the outset of the [criminal] case [*R v. Burns and others*], the OFT had only recently recruited and begun to expand the staff with appropriate skills and experience and they were relatively few in number at that time. A steep learning curve could have been anticipated'.

167 OFT (2001), [1.14].

168 To borrow the words of Beaton-Wells (2009), 28.

169 See, e.g., OFT (2003), 5.

170 For an example, see OFT (2003).

171 Tavares de Araujo (2010), 76.

172 However, bid-rigging would remain a criminal offence.

173 Lewisch (2006), 297.

174 Kalbfleisch (2006), 313.

cartel case to get pushed down even further in the pile in the public prosecutor's office is a serious violent crime, like a murder or rape.[175] When the prosecutor only has the function of prosecuting cartel cases, this effect would not occur. A second reason advanced is that, quite apart from their dedication to criminal antitrust enforcement, general prosecutors—at least initially—may feel ill-equipped to take on cartel cases due to their unfamiliarity with competition law issues. Therefore, they may be more cautious in bringing cases.[176] This type of hesitancy was also one of the reasons for the failure of cartel criminalization in the Netherlands.[177] The third reason for involvement of the competition authority (which is responsible for the investigation of cartel activity) in the exercise of the prosecutorial function is the desire to ensure the operation of an effective criminal immunity programme.[178] As noted in Chapter 9, a system guaranteeing (conditional) immunity in the context of criminal cartel enforcement may be difficult to put in place when the investigating antitrust authority (i.e. the body receiving the immunity application) is not the body which will be making the final prosecutorial decision. When the investigating authority is also the prosecutorial authority, it is easier to provide such guarantees, as the coordination of immunity programmes and decisions to prosecute between two separate agencies will not be needed.[179] This is to the benefit of the number of immunity applications submitted and, consequently, of the detection rate of cartel activity; hence, the desire in some quarters to ensure that the competition authority exercises the prosecutorial function. The final reason as to why it might be a good reason to allow the competition authority to exercise the prosecutorial function concerns the (assumed) political independence of the competition authority. The point here is that 'there might be concerns that a government could instruct a public prosecutor not to pursue a case, whereas it might not have such an authority over an independent competition agency'.[180]

There are two clear disadvantages, however, to involving a competition authority in the prosecution of criminal cartel cases. The most obvious one is the competition authority's lack of expertise in prosecuting criminal cases in court. While such expertise could be acquired, it 'may not always be cost effective to build up staff for prosecution of criminal cases, especially if it is expected that there will not be many such cases'.[181] The criminal case pursued by the OFT against individuals involved in the fixing of fuel surcharges on long-haul flights demonstrates well the problem of lack of prosecutorial experience.[182] In that particular case, the OFT in failing to discharge its obligations of disclosure to the criminal accused, as well as its 'general deference to resistance' from counsel of the successful leniency applicant (Virgin Atlantic) to disclose witness interviews and other materials held by the leniency applicant, 'committed an error unlikely to be seen from a seasoned criminal prosecutor'.[183] Although the OFT was quick to admit its mistakes and to learn from them,[184] its failure to secure convictions in this case has clearly had a negative impact upon its reputation as a serious and competent criminal antitrust enforcer,[185] a fact admitted by the OFT itself.[186] Another reason to keep the (investigating) competition authority away from the prosecutorial function is to ensure that bias does not creep into the system. Dividing the investigative and prosecutorial functions provides 'checks and balances'. Wils notes that when different enforcement

175 See Fingleton (2003), 309. 176 See Baker (2012), 10.
177 Kalbfleisch (2006), 313. 178 See Baker (2012), 10. 179 OECD (2003b), 23.
180 OECD (2007b), 28. Cf. Beaton-Wells (2009), 28. 181 OECD (2003b), 24.
182 *R v. Burns and others*, Unreported Judgment, Southwark Crown Court, 10 May 2010.
183 Purnell et al. (2010), 325. 184 See OFT (2010d).
185 See: Furse (2011), 227; and Lane (2012), 1003. 186 OFT (2010d), 9.

functions are exercised by one agency, 'prosecutorial bias' can occur due to: (i) confirmation bias; (ii) hindsight bias and the desire to justify past efforts; and (iii) the desire to show a high level of enforcement activity.[187] If, however, the investigating competition authority must convince a public prosecutor to go forward with a case, this arrangement may 'limit criminal cases to those where criminal prosecution is really warranted',[188] thereby avoiding this problem.[189]

If the competition authority is provided with the ability to prosecute criminal cartel cases, a final decision needs to be made regarding the prosecutorial function: should it be shared with another (special/general) body? In the early days of criminal cartel enforcement, oversight and technical assistance from a more seasoned prosecutor could also be helpful, provided that a close working relationship can be established without causing friction between the two prosecutors. The fact that there would be a possibility for a more experienced prosecutor to take on a cartel prosecution (after the investigation by the competition authority is completed) is certainly advantageous, in that it could avoid a situation where the competition authority finds itself 'out of its depth' when faced with an increasingly complex and difficult case. The creation of detailed (cartel law-specific) case selection criteria applicable to the more experienced prosecutor could help to ensure that a decision about the more appropriate prosecutor could be taken at an early stage of the investigation.[190] An early decision about the more appropriate prosecutor would reduce the potential for later disruptions and delays (particularly given that the prosecutor would be required to have an excellent qualitative command of the facts of the (complex, difficult) case and a detailed understanding of the credibility of witnesses, and the strengths and weaknesses of the available evidence). The major disadvantage with the existence of two prosecutorial bodies is the increased difficulty of operating a criminal immunity policy which guarantees immunity from prosecution to the individuals who meet the relevant criteria. There are ways, however, of dealing with this difficulty, as explained in Chapter 9 of this book.[191]

E. Securing International Cooperation

European jurisdictions that wish to operate an effective criminal cartel regime should be advised that their vision for criminal antitrust enforcement should ideally extend beyond their national borders and become international in scope. The reason for this is that the most harmful of cartels will often themselves be international in scope, and for cartel law enforcement to impact effectively upon such cartels, an international approach is warranted. For Griffin, for example, a 'common characteristic of an international cartel is its power to control prices on a worldwide basis effective almost immediately'.[192] It is often extremely difficult to take enforcement action against such a cartel without cooperation

[187] Wils (2004a), 214–17. See also Wils (2005a), 161 et seq. To be clear, while Wils's analysis focuses specifically on the separation of the investigative and prosecutorial functions from the adjudicative one, the points made in the context of his analysis can be easily transposed to a discussion focusing on the separation of the investigative and prosecutorial functions from one another.

[188] OECD (2003b), 24.

[189] Admittedly, *internal* checks and balances can be established (such as a 'Devil's Advocate' panel charged with casting a 'fresh set of eyes' over the case) by the single agency exercising the investigative and prosecutorial functions, a fact which reduces somewhat the strength of this argument; see ICN (2005), 36.

[190] For an example, see OECD (2003b), 96.

[191] See Chapter 9, Section B(c)(i) of this book.

[192] Griffin (2000), 10.

from the antitrust authorities located in other jurisdictions.[193] Indeed, following a deepening of international cooperation in competition law over the last couple of decades,[194] it is now widely accepted that cooperation between jurisdictions is central to an effective anti-cartel policy,[195] particularly if one is concerned about tackling international cartels. Such cooperation can take many forms, including the coordination of surprise inspections, the exchange of information, the provision of enforcement advice, the exercise of positive comity, the collection of evidence, and the interviewing of individuals.[196] Given that cooperation between national bodies can clearly 'enhance the prospects of catching and successfully prosecuting' those engaged in international cartel activity,[197] it should be no surprise that there have been a number of (relatively successful) multilateral initiatives to encourage cooperation between competition authorities, the most obvious being the creation of the International Competition Network ('the ICN') in 2002.[198]

The criminalization of cartel activity brings with it particular disadvantages regarding the need for cooperation and the possible lack of desire of other (non-criminalized) jurisdictions to provide such cooperation when the incarceration of individuals remains a possible outcome of enforcement proceedings. Joshua explained the predicament eloquently when he commented on the initial proposal for the adoption of a criminal cartel offence in the UK. After noting that global cartels do the most damage to the UK economy and that (international) cartel members are 'likely to "deep-six" any evidence in the United Kingdom or meet only abroad',[199] he stated that:

> Given the incomprehension generated in many European countries at the idea of jailing price-fixers, there is not likely to be a rush of support at official level for conducting evidence searches for the British authorities in a cartel case. And nothing is likely to inflame national sensitivities more than attempts to investigate suspected crime inside its territory without going through the local authorities. It is a criminal offence in some countries for foreign investigators to attempt to conduct inquiries or gather evidence. Even such an innocuous-seeming act as interviewing a witness without official permission can result in arrest, deportation and denial of further assistance.[200]

This situation, if unchecked, would not bode well for the successful operation of a cartel offence: 'it would make a nonsense of the law if [cartelists] could avoid detection by meeting or keeping all the evidence abroad'.[201] In addition to this is the problem of prosecuting overseas executives. Where criminal cartel sanctions do not exist in the jurisdiction where the overseas executive is located, there will be no chance of extradition, as this invariably requires 'dual criminality', i.e. that the alleged conduct be a crime in both the requesting and requested state.[202] Furthermore, given the fact that in a criminalized cartel regime the potential punishment of a convicted cartelist is a period of time in prison, it is unlikely that such executives will self-surrender (from a regime where there are no criminal cartel sanctions). If the executive is located in another EU Member State, one might be tempted to consider whether the European Arrest Warrant would be of help in securing personal jurisdiction over the individual.[203] Unfortunately, as it currently stands, that particular instrument of EU law would not be of any help to the criminalized regime: with the exception of a number of generic offences (which do not

[193] See Tierno Centella (2010), 498. [194] See Calvani (2005).
[195] See ICN (2011a). On cooperation in antitrust law, see generally Terhechte (2011), Chapter 2.
[196] See generally ICN (2007). [197] Gray (2008), 376.
[198] See <http://www.internationalcompetitionnetwork.org/>. See also Lugard (2011).
[199] Joshua (2002), 240. [200] Joshua (2002), 241. [201] Joshua (2002), 240.
[202] See Furse (2006), 482. On the common features of international extradition regimes, see Girardet (2010), 288–9.
[203] Council of the European Union (2002).

include cartel activity), 'dual criminality' is also required in both the requesting and the requested Member State.[204] Admittedly, the list of offences for which dual criminality is not required could be amended to include a cartel offence,[205] but given that such a move would require the consent of all the Member States, it is unlikely to occur any time soon.

If other jurisdictions could eventually be persuaded to criminalize cartel activity, two particular ways of alleviating the difficulty of international cartels on a bilateral basis could be created. The first solution would be to ensure that legal arrangements are in place that would allow for the extradition of the overseas executive. Most likely, this will involve the extension of an already existing extradition treaty to cartel activity. This solution, quite clearly, would aim to ensure that the executive located in the requested state could be legally coerced back to the prosecuting jurisdiction, thereby enhancing the enforcement of criminal cartel law in that country (to the benefit of deterrence and/or retribution).[206] The second solution would be the adoption of a mutual legal assistance treaty ('MLAT') between the two jurisdictions providing for cooperation on cartel cases (or the extension of an already-existing MLAT to the prosecution of cartel activity[207]). This type of arrangement would facilitate the collection of evidence, the production of records, and/or the questioning of witnesses located in the requested state to the benefit of criminal cartel enforcement in the requesting state.[208] Such are the perceived potential advantages of MLATs in this regard that it has been argued that the mere fact that an MLAT can be created between two criminalized regimes is an important factor in itself for justifying the actual existence of criminal cartel sanctions.[209]

Admittedly, each of these solutions is inherently limited due to the principle of 'dual criminality'. The fact that extradition invariably requires 'dual criminality' has already been noted above. With MLATs, the situation is similar, but not equivalent: 'sometimes dual criminality is not a requirement for the application of MLATs, thus their use might in theory be extended into the area of competition law enforcement even if only one of the parties to the agreement is a criminal jurisdiction as regards competition law'.[210] It seems, however, that the general (if not universal) principle with MLATs is that 'dual criminality' is indeed required: it represents the rule, rather than the exception.[211] This fact explains why some commentators have argued that, traditionally, MLATs have not been particularly useful to the US in criminal competition enforcement:[212] when those arguments were advanced, there were very few jurisdictions with criminal cartel offences on their legislative books. It also brings one to an important point about the strategy that a criminalized regime should adopt to ensure effectiveness. Such a regime should engage in advocacy in order to convince other jurisdictions of the desirability of introducing criminal cartel sanctions.[213] Once criminal sanctions have been adopted in (an)other jurisdiction(s), then the adoption of the two solutions noted above is facilitated.[214]

204 See: Joshua (2003), 636; and O'Kane (2011a).

205 See Council of the European Union (2002), Article 2(3).

206 Cf. O'Kane (2011a), 418.

207 Prior to the adoption of a criminal cartel offence in the UK, the UK authorities removed a side letter provision that had ensured that the US-UK Mutual Legal Assistance Treaty excluded antitrust assistance; see: Barnett (2006a), 11; and Schoneveld (2003), 439.

208 See, e.g., ABA Section of Antitrust Law (2011), 117. See also Scott (2007), 80.

209 See, e.g., Jenny (2011), v.

210 ICN (2007), 15. Examples include: the US-Spain and the US-Italy MLATs; see ICN (2007), 15.

211 See ICN (2007), 15.

212 See, e.g., Victor (2004), 84.

213 The US has been particularly enthusiastic about pursuing such a strategy; see, e.g., Masoudi (2007).

214 This reality was noted by the Ministry of Economic Development in New Zealand in the Discussion Document which it published prior to the tabling of legislation to introduce criminal cartel sanctions in that jurisdiction; see Ministry of Economic Development (2010), [41] and [45].

Convincing another jurisdiction to introduce criminal cartel sanctions is not going to be easy, particularly given that, currently, no international consensus exists concerning the need for criminal cartel sanctions (even if there is consensus on the harmful nature of cartel activity).[215] One should also understand that cartel criminalization is usually a domestic issue, relying on national social norms, and thus may not be amenable to a multinational trend in its favour.[216] Given this reality, focusing on the most important bilateral trading relationships for the criminalized regime might be a priority, as demonstrated by the recent move in New Zealand to introduce criminal cartel sanctions after their introduction in Australia.[217] While justifying cartel criminalization on the basis of the actions of one's close trading partners (or indeed on the basis of developing international practice) is questionable on theoretical grounds,[218] the points to be made here are: (i) what the (already) criminalized regime wishes to see is the existence of criminal cartel sanctions in the other jurisdiction, however they are 'sold' to the stakeholders in that jurisdiction; and (ii) that demonstrating that close trading partners have made the move to cartel criminalization may well make it easier for a jurisdiction to 'sell' the idea of criminal cartel sanctions to its own stakeholders (particularly where there is a distinct similarity between its social and legal norms and those of the criminalized regime). If these points are accepted, it would be advisable for a criminalized jurisdiction to focus the majority of its advocacy efforts on its close trading partners before turning to multilateral fora to convince the wider world of the desirability of introducing criminal cartel sanctions. It is important to avoid pressurizing the other jurisdiction into adopting criminal sanctions when that jurisdiction is at a stage in the development of its competition law when criminalization would be inappropriate.[219] Any attempt 'to implant a criminalization regime into a non-receptive environment risks leading to "unenforced criminalization", the social cost of which may be higher than the mere lack of criminalization'.[220] A cynic might reply that all that is required for extradition to work is the adoption of a criminal cartel offence and the putting into place of legal measures to allow for extradition to occur: 'unenforced criminalization' is therefore not problematic (at least for the requesting state). The reasoning there would be that 'dual criminality' does not require active enforcement; it simply requires the criminal cartel offence to be in existence in both the requesting and the requested state.[221] However, this analysis would miss the bigger picture. For a start, the task of convincing other jurisdictions of the desirability of introducing criminal cartel sanctions becomes more difficult if the (resource-intensive) failures of 'unenforced criminalization' are evident in jurisdictions that have been previously convinced by the criminalized jurisdiction's rhetoric. Furthermore, the use of an MLAT in particular requires the expenditure of considerable resources by the requested state; to justify the expenditure of such resources, the requested state needs to demonstrate to its stakeholders that the imposition of criminal sanctions (in the other jurisdiction) is justifiable.

Central to a successful advocacy strategy is the articulation of solid theoretical justifications for antitrust criminalization and the demonstration that the criminalized regime has been successful in prosecuting criminal cartel cases. Focusing initially on local cartels (as opposed to global ones) can help to demonstrate the ability of the criminalized regime to prosecute cartel activity successfully. Once the message about the benefits of

215 See Ezrachi and Kindl (2011), 420.

216 See Ezrachi and Kindl (2011), 420.

217 See, e.g.: Boberg (2010), 98–9; and Hamilton and Scott (2013), 187–8.

218 See, e.g.: Clarke and Bagaric (2003), 208; and Hoel (2008), 108.

219 On the importance of the timing of cartel criminalization, see Fingleton et al. (2007), 21.

220 Ezrachi and Kindl (2011), 434.

221 See Girardet (2010), 287.

criminalization has been heard (and acted upon) by other jurisdictions, there will be increased potential for criminal enforcement action against bi-national or global cartels. If, however, at an early stage the criminalized regime wishes to prosecute international (as opposed to local) cartels, then, in order to demonstrate effectiveness, it could make use of the novel strategy adopted by the UK in 2008 in the *Marine Hoses* case.[222] In doing so, the criminalized regime in question would be taking the advice of Calvani and Calvani when they suggest that competition enforcement agencies embarking on a criminal cartel programme should 'piggyback where possible' on the enforcement efforts of the US.[223] In the *Marine Hoses* case,[224] three UK nationals were arrested in Texas by US antitrust prosecutors investigating price-fixing and bid-rigging in the marine hose market. All three of the UK nationals confessed their involvement in the (international) cartel and entered into a plea-bargain with the DoJ.[225] According to the terms of this plea-bargain, the three individuals would be allowed to travel back to the UK where they would plead guilty to the UK Cartel Offence. In addition, they would waive their right to contest extradition back to the US if the sentence served in the UK were less than that agreed to in the plea-agreements. The effect of the arrangement 'was that, assuming that the individuals were convicted in the United Kingdom for a term not less than the term of imprisonment specified in their respective plea-agreements, they would not be required to return to the United States to serve time in custody'.[226] When the individuals arrived back in London, they pleaded guilty to the UK Cartel Offence, as agreed. Unfortunately for them, the trial judge imposed higher sentences than those stated in the plea-agreements;[227] however, on appeal these sentences were reduced to the sentences in those agreements.[228] This particular novel arrangement allowed the OFT to prosecute its first (and to date only) successful criminal (international) cartel case, thus helping to demonstrate that criminal enforcement can be effective in the UK, even where an international cartel is at issue. While some commentators argued that the US DoJ handed the case to the OFT 'on a plate', the UK authorities are keen to point out that this was not what occurred and that the convictions in that case were due, in part at least, to effective enforcement activities of the OFT.[229] Admittedly, replication of this particular approach may be difficult, but according to some informed commentators, 'there will be opportunities for joint investigations [between the US and the UK], and these may give rise for similar outcomes'.[230] Moreover, one should be aware that the criminal courts in the newly criminalized jurisdiction may not take too kindly to the fact that a plea-agreement of the type in *Marine Hoses* could easily be interpreted as an attempt to

[222] *R v. Whittle and others* [2008] EWCA Crim 2560.

[223] Calvani and Calvani (2009), 139–40.

[224] On this, see generally: Furse (2012), 202–14; Lucraft et al. (2009); and MacCulloch (2010a), 286–92.

[225] The three plea-agreements in question are available at: <http://www.justice.gov/atr/cases/f228500/228582.pdf>; <http://www.justice.gov/atr/cases/f228500/228585.pdf>; and <http://www.justice.gov/atr/cases/f228500/228588.pdf>.

[226] Tassopoulou (2009), 41.

[227] *R v. Whittle and others*, Sentencing Remarks, Southwark Crown Court, 11 June 2008, <http://www.oft.gov.uk/shared_oft/prosecutions/remarks.pdf>.

[228] *R v. Whittle and others* [2008] EWCA Crim 2560, [32]. To be clear, the sentences were reduced on the basis that they were excessive on the facts. They were not reduced due to the existence of the plea-agreement. The reason that the sentences after the appeal were equivalent to the sentences in the plea-agreement was that the appellants only requested a reduction in their sentences to the levels indicated in the plea-agreement and no more.

[229] See Nikpay (2012), 2–3.

[230] Calvani and Calvani (2009), 140.

restrict the court's sentencing discretion.[231] A very cautious approach to the reliance upon such novel plea-agreements is therefore warranted.

F. Conclusion

This chapter proceeded on the assumption that well-thought-out enforcement strategies need to be in place in order for a criminal cartel regime to be effective in practice. Specifically, it articulated the 'third (practical) challenge of design' for European antitrust criminalization: it examined the important strategies that need to be put in place in order to ensure the actual achievement of the underlying enforcement objectives of antitrust criminalization. These strategies were categorized into four distinct imperatives: (i) avoiding the 'compliance trap'; (ii) securing sufficient support from stakeholders in the project of antitrust criminalization; (iii) designing effectively the criminal antitrust enforcement agency/agencies; and (iv) securing international support for the enforcement efforts of the criminalized cartel regime.

The 'compliance trap' occurs when political support for the moral seriousness of the law which an (antitrust) authority must enforce is lacking. When the antitrust activities of business offenders are condemned by antitrust enforcers for their immoral qualities (as they would be when criminal sanctions are imposed upon them), such offenders may interpret this particular form of moral leveraging of antitrust enforcement to be unfair or stigmatizing and, therefore, may actively lobby for the political emasculation of the regulator, a process which can eventually force the regulator to adopt a more lenient approach to enforcement. Without external political support, the regulator can do little to escape this 'trap'. While the 'compliance trap' is most relevant when retribution theory is at issue, it can also occur when the underlying enforcement theory is that of (economic) deterrence. To avoid this 'trap', political support is required for the criminal antitrust regime, as is effective, strong leadership in the criminal enforcement agency. Given that political support follows public support, any strategy designed to avoid the 'compliance trap' should attempt to create public support for the criminal cartel regime.

Support from all stakeholders in a project of antitrust criminalization is vitally important to its success. Indeed, without such support, one risks the provision of insufficient resources for antitrust enforcement efforts and/or nullification of the law. Unfortunately, securing support from the public is particularly difficult due to the characteristics of both cartel activity and cartelists, as well as the type of harm at issue. In addition, weak public support will generally be reflected in weak support for cartel criminalization among jury members in those European jurisdictions which employ trial by jury. The judiciary may also be hesitant to send convicted cartelists to jail, believing that there is an inherent, material difference between corporate offenders and traditional offenders.

To secure public support for cartel criminalization, the authorities must engage in considerable educative efforts regarding the nature of cartel activity. Such educative efforts could be conducted through workshops, public awareness campaigns, news releases,

[231] Cf., e.g., *R v. Whittle and others* [2008] EWCA Crim 2560, [27]–[28]: 'Whilst each applicant through counsel has invited us to reduce the terms imposed by the judge, none has invited us to reduce the terms below the period specified in the agreement into which he entered. It follows that this court has not had the benefit of the kind of argument from counsel to which it is accustomed; we emphasise this is through no fault of theirs. They were acting upon their instructions and their instructions were imposed upon them by the terms of the plea agreements. We have our doubts as to the propriety of a US prosecutor seeking to inhibit the way in which counsel represent their clients in a UK court, but having heard no argument on the subject we shall express no concluded view'.

television interviews, and media publicity. To secure support for the criminal antitrust regime, one must demonstrate not only that anticompetitive conduct can be harmful, but also that a deterrence-based and/or a retribution-based criminalization argument(s) is/are robust. What also needs to be ensured is a well-publicized, well-designed public consultation on cartel criminalization prior to the adoption of criminal cartel sanctions. Following criminalization, the authorities need to be clever in their prioritization strategies regarding criminal antitrust prosecutions. Two key elements to a clever strategy of gaining public support are: (i) an initial focus on public procurement involving bid-rigging; and (ii) an initial focus on cartels selling to final consumers. Furthermore, criminal antitrust enforcers should only pursue serious cases where severe penalties are appropriate. The creation of a formal list of prioritization criteria or principles could help in this regard. After each successful criminal cartel trial, the antitrust enforcers should also release detailed press releases and appear on television and radio in order to explain the nature of cartel activity, the holding of the criminal court, and the benefits for consumers of cartel criminalization.

To prevent jury nullification, jurisdictions should ensure that their criminal courts have adequate powers to assist the jury in understanding complex issues at trial. What is particularly important is the production of a 'roadmap' that will help jurors to understand and appreciate the significance of the evidence as it is presented. The creation of model jury instructions could also be useful. Criminal antitrust enforcers should understand that bilateral cartels with a successful leniency/immunity applicant do not present ideal cases to be prosecuted in front of a jury; such cases should only be prosecuted when leniency information can be corroborated from other sources, the cartel conduct is clear and unambiguous, and/or it is immediately obvious that the accused appreciated the criminal nature of his conduct. The strategies of only prosecuting summary cases or of circumventing the use of the jury are inherently limited; the former should be avoided, and the latter is unlikely to be successful, particularly when law-makers have a strong attachment to the tradition of trial by jury.

Overcoming judicial reluctance can be achieved through the use of 'signalling' by the legislature of the need for custodial sentences for convicted cartelists. Creating a high maximum sentence may perform this function, but if it fails, the legislature could raise the maximum sentence in order to signal its disapproval of the sentencing record of the court. However, this approach suffers from two inherent limitations: (i) judges do not have to take notice of the signalling; and (ii) it does not provide a methodology according to which an actual custodial sentence can be determined. Mandatory sentencing guidelines overcome these inherent drawbacks, but they may represent an inappropriate interference with judicial independence. Discretionary guidelines can be a compromise solution to the problem. They would not only provide a framework according to which judges could justify a chosen custodial sentence, but they also help to build support more generally, as they reduce the potential for convicted individuals to complain to the media about the arbitrary nature of any criminal punishment imposed.

When one is designing the criminal antitrust enforcement landscape, four strategic questions need to be considered: (i) whether an existing competition authority should exercise the investigative function in a criminal cartel regime; (ii) if so, whether the competition authority should share the investigative function with another (special/general) agency; (iii) whether the competition authority should also be able to prosecute a cartel offence; and (iv) if so, whether it should exercise its prosecutorial function alone or in conjunction with another (special/general) prosecutor. In answering these questions, one should understand that each approach has its own particular advantages and disadvantages: there is no ideal way to allocate the investigative and prosecutorial functions. It may be the case that a competition authority will be more dedicated to the investigation of cartel activity than a general criminal investigative agency. But the competition authority would need to acquire significant new skills if it is to avoid committing embarrassing mistakes that a seasoned investigator would not. When it comes to the prosecutorial function, a competition authority could well be out of its depth in a criminal court, a fact attested to by recent failings of the OFT in the UK. While a general prosecutor's office may have a limited appetite for cartel law enforcement, if it were to pursue a criminal cartel prosecution, it would be more likely to be successful than a competition authority that is new to the environment of a criminal court.

The criminalization of cartel activity brings with it a particular disadvantage that needs to be addressed: the need for international cooperation combined with the possible lack of desire of other (non-criminalized) jurisdictions to provide such cooperation when imprisonment could occur. If, however, other jurisdictions could eventually be persuaded to criminalize cartel activity, two particular ways of alleviating the difficulty of international cartels on a bilateral basis could be created: (i) the extension of extradition treaties to cartel offences; and (ii) the use of MLATs to facilitate the collection of evidence, the production of records, and/or the questioning of witnesses located abroad. Central to this strategy is convincing other countries to adopt criminal cartel laws. Demonstrating one's criminal enforcement successes at home is a prerequisite for advocating the adoption of criminal cartel laws abroad. Focusing initially on local cartels may be the best way to create such successes, unless the jurisdiction in question wishes to 'piggy-back' on US enforcement efforts. It would also be advisable for a criminalized jurisdiction to focus the majority of its advocacy efforts on its close trading partners before turning to multilateral fora to convince the wider world to criminalize cartel activity. Either way, it is vital to avoid pressurizing other jurisdictions into adopting criminal sanctions when those jurisdictions are not ready for cartel criminalization. Finally, it should go without saying that any advocacy efforts would be most effective if criminalized jurisdictions could articulate clearly the theoretical, legal, and practical challenges of antitrust criminalization and demonstrate convincingly that they have been able to meet those types of challenges in the real world. It is hoped that the analyses contained in this book would provide some help to them in fulfilling that advocacy function.

CONCLUSION

11

Concluding Remarks on the Theoretical, Legal, and Practical Challenges of European Antitrust Criminalization

A. Introduction

The first chapter of this book introduced the concept of European antitrust criminalization and established that continued debate on this particular concept is advisable for those concerned about the enforcement of Article 101 TFEU. Three reasons were advanced as to why continued debate is required. First of all, it was noted that, currently, a consensus is lacking on some of the central issues in the debate. In particular, important stakeholders in the process of antitrust criminalization (such as legislators, antitrust officials, and academics) have failed to reach agreement concerning the necessity and appropriateness of personal criminal antitrust sanctions. Added to that is the fact that some EU Member States have already introduced personal criminal sanctions for cartel activity. If the authorities in these jurisdictions are intent on pursuing criminal antitrust cases, it is imperative that they are capable of: (i) justifying the employment of personal criminal punishment; (ii) demonstrating that in imposing such punishment they are respecting the rule of law; and (iii) putting in place the correct practical measures that will ensure that the employment of criminal antitrust punishment actually achieves its aims, while maintaining its legitimacy. Given that the question as to whether—and, indeed, how—these requirements can be fulfilled remains to be conclusively answered; continued debate is necessary. Furthermore, and importantly, there are a number of specific deficiencies in the literature which need to be addressed if the relevant authorities are to make informed decisions as to whether to introduce (or to continue to maintain) personal criminal sanctions for cartel activity.

The aim of this book is to contribute to the European antitrust criminalization debate by addressing the deficiencies in the literature on the employment within the EU of personal criminal sanctions for cartel activity. Three categories of deficiencies in the current literature were identified in this book: theoretical, legal, and practical.[1] The first (theoretical) category contains those deficiencies related to the analysis of the application of justificatory theories of criminal punishment to cartel activity. The second (legal) category encompasses those deficiencies related to the analysis of the legal restraints facing those who wish to introduce individual criminal antitrust sanctions. The third (practical) category concerns those deficiencies related to the identification and articulation of the desirable practical mechanisms and features for a criminal antitrust regime within the EU.

Specifically, the theoretical deficiencies in the literature include: (i) a lack of analysis of a number of the potential limitations of the application of deterrence theory to justify the employment of criminal antitrust sanctions within the EU; and (ii) a lack of

[1] See Chapter 1, Section B.

analysis concerning the relevance and the strength of any plausible alternative arguments in favour of European antitrust criminalization (i.e. those not built upon deterrence theory). By contrast, the legal deficiencies relate to a lack of: (i) a thorough and comprehensive examination of the restraining influence of due process on a project of European antitrust criminalization; and (ii) detailed scholarship which specifically focuses on the restraining influence of legal certainty on a project of European antitrust criminalization. The practical deficiencies relate to: (i) a lack of analysis of the potential (negative) impact of Regulation 1/2003 on the actual design and operation of a national criminal cartel offence (and what can be done to reduce the scope for such impact in this context); (ii) a failure to articulate clearly how, in a process of antitrust criminalization, one can ensure that 'acceptable' (i.e. legitimate and/or efficiency-enhancing) cartel activity is not subjected to criminal sanctions; (iii) a failure to provide a detailed, systematic analysis that focuses on the practical challenges of leniency/immunity for European antitrust criminalization; and (iv) a failure to provide a systematic, detailed analysis of the important enforcement strategies that help to ensure that the criminal cartel regime is effective in practice. In order to rectify all three of the identified categories of deficiencies, this book considered (what were termed) 'the theoretical, legal, and practical challenges' of European antitrust criminalization.

The findings of this book concerning these theoretical, legal, and practical challenges are collated and outlined briefly in this, the final, chapter of the book. There are four substantive sections to this chapter and a conclusion. Section B sets out the specifics of the theoretical challenges presented by both deterrence and retribution in the context of European antitrust criminalization. Section C details the legal challenges for European antitrust criminalization which are created by the requirements of due process and legal certainty. Section D details the practical challenges involved in: designing a criminal cartel offence; ensuring peaceful co-existence between a criminal cartel regime and administrative leniency/immunity; operating a criminal immunity programme; and determining an effective enforcement strategy in the context of European antitrust criminalization. Section E acknowledges the 'linking function' of the current chapter[2] and clarifies the extent to which the theoretical, legal, and practical challenges are interrelated. To conclude, Section F presents some suggestions for possible future research in this area.

B. Antitrust Criminalization Presents Difficult Theoretical Challenges

This book identified two potentially relevant justificatory theories for the employment of criminal punishment in antitrust law: deterrence and retribution.[3] These theories were deemed to be of potential relevance for European antitrust criminalization as, inter alia: the current literature on criminal cartel sanctions focuses to varying degrees on both of these theories; and the objectives of deterrence and retribution are currently pursued by the EU antitrust enforcers. Consequently, the theoretical challenges of deterrence and retribution for antitrust criminalization formed the substance of the analysis in Part I of this book. This section sets out the specifics of the challenges presented to European antitrust enforcement by those two particular justificatory theories of criminalization.

[2] On this function, see Chapter 1, Section E(d).

[3] See Chapter 2, Section B.

(a) The challenge of deterrence theory

This book identified and examined the theoretical challenge of deterrence for European antitrust criminalization.[4] In doing so, it demonstrated that a strong deterrence-based criminalization argument can be constructed concerning cartel activity: imprisonment helps, inter alia, to overcome the significant problems associated with optimally deterrent cartel fines, in particular: inability to pay; difficulties with individual (financial) responsibility; and proportional justice. The employment of criminal antitrust sanctions would also ensure that European anti-cartel enforcement would no longer lack adequate condemnation of offenders (as an instrumental factor in ensuring deterrence). Arguably, then, deterrence theory can be relied upon as a foundation for antitrust criminalization, and this justificatory theory is therefore relevant to the discussions which were conducted in this book concerning the legalities to be adhered to and the practicalities to be resolved in criminalizing cartel activity.

However, as demonstrated in Chapter 3 of this book, the deterrence-based criminalization argument is not as robust as some legal commentators would have one believe; in fact, it suffers from a number of potential limitations. Specifically, the case in favour of the employment of criminal antitrust sanctions to deter cartel activity is vulnerable to the extent that one can demonstrate that: (i) cartel activity is morally neutral conduct; (ii) undertakings are risk averse; (iii) undertakings/individuals do not act rationally; and (iv) personal criminal sanctions are incapable of generating more benefits than costs.

If cartel activity is understood as being morally neutral conduct, a number of problematic issues may arise when a deterrence-based criminalization argument is pursued. For a start, it has been argued that applying the criminal law to morally neutral/ambiguous conduct is not only unjust, but also counterproductive, in that by unfairly labelling offenders as criminals, the moral authority of the law is undermined, resulting as a consequence in a weakening of the deterrent value of criminal sanctions. Some even contend that applying the criminal sanction to morally neutral conduct in fact 'decriminalizes' the criminal law, and taken to its extreme either results in nullification or, more subtly, a changing of people's attitudes towards the meaning of criminality. For them, the criminal law should be concerned solely with conduct which unequivocally attracts the moral opprobrium of society; it should, in other words, concentrate on traditional crimes and not morally neutral conduct. They argue that, in the absence of such a restraint, the criminal law may begin to lose its legitimacy.

Regarding the issue of risk aversion, one can posit the following regarding a deterrence-based antitrust criminalization argument. If the corporate entity facing the cartel fine is a risk-seeker, there will be no problem here for the deterrence-based criminalization argument. In fact, if the corporate entity facing the cartel fine is a risk-seeker, there would be an even stronger case for criminal sanctions in the context of a deterrence-based criminalization argument. If, however, the corporate entity facing the cartel fine is risk averse, the figure of 150 per cent of annual turnover may represent an overestimation of the optimal fine. If this overestimation can be established, the deterrence-based criminalization argument will be somewhat weakened: the practical problems with imposing the optimal fine will be less pronounced. The current lack of empirical data on the extent to which corporate entities are risk averse therefore produces an inherent limitation of the deterrence-based criminalization argument.

[4] See Chapter 3.

By relying on the assumption that potential offenders act rationally when deciding to break the law, a deterrence-based criminalization argument is open to the criticism that it does not adequately reflect reality. Detractors could argue that rationality is not a dominant feature of the human condition, that many factors influence how people order their behaviour, and that, consequently, one cannot adequately predict how people will act in given situations. In response, one might argue that, while this sort of criticism may indeed have value when analysing the existence of crimes of passion, it loses its potency somewhat when applied to economic offences that are committed after long periods of deliberation by educated, intelligent, and otherwise morally functional persons. An economic approach to sanctions in the antitrust context is more attractive than in others, as executives are no doubt more likely to undertake a cost/benefit analysis of their (market) behaviour—especially concerning its economic impact on the firm for which they work—than the ordinary citizen unconnected in a direct way with the dynamics of business. Furthermore, some have argued that the more competitive the environment, the more likely it is that actors act rationally. At least in a business context, where the environment can generally be considered to be competitive, one could argue that the concern with rationality may be subject to overstatement. What is really needed here, however, is the provision of significant robust empirical data that demonstrates the extent to which rationality is indeed a realistic characteristic of cartelists. Without such data, the deterrence-based criminalization argument is inherently limited.

In order to establish a strong deterrence-based criminalization argument, one must be able to demonstrate that the introduction and maintenance of criminal sanctions generates more benefits than costs. This is not an easy task; in fact, it is one of the most difficult challenges facing those who advocate the imposition of criminal punishment to deter cartel activity. The problem here is that one does not have accurate measurements of the exact costs and benefits of criminal antitrust sanctions. Nonetheless, there are arguments supporting the assertion that criminal sanctions are at least *capable* of generating more benefits than costs. For example, useful methods of increasing the benefits and reducing the costs of criminal enforcement exist. They relate to, inter alia: reducing the severity of custodial sentences; obtaining cooperation from cartelists (through, e.g., plea-bargaining); and imposing costs upon the convicted cartelist. However, there are additional problems with the employment of these mechanisms. These include: the fact that some may feel that long prison sentences would more adequately reflect society's condemnation of cartel activity than relatively short ones; the risk of undermining the procedural guarantees for the defendant, not to mention the risk of placing pressure on innocent people to plead guilty; and the existence of reluctance on behalf of the judiciary concerning the imposition of punishment for economic crimes committed by 'respectable' members of society.

This book submits that all four of these specific limitations together form the main theoretical challenge of deterrence as the basis for European antitrust criminalization and that, given the extent of the (above-examined) difficulties associated with each of the identified limitations, this challenge will continue to confront those who argue in favour of European antitrust criminalization for reasons of deterrence.

(b) The challenge of retribution theory

This book also examined the challenge offered by retribution theory to antitrust criminalization.[5] In doing so, it first presented a framework to determine the moral content

[5] See Chapter 4.

of any given behaviour. This framework was developed by Green and consists of three elements: culpability; social harmfulness; and moral wrongfulness. By applying this framework to 'cartel activity' (as defined by the OECD), this book demonstrated that such conduct can in fact display (negative) moral qualities and that, therefore, a retribution-based argument for cartel criminalization can be advanced.

For a start, a mens rea as strict as intention can be chosen without placing cartel activity outside of the criminal law in a de facto sense. In other words, one can ensure that the first element in the tripartite framework is fulfilled merely by employing a facilitating feature (i.e. by defining the cartel offence in such a way that culpable behaviour is caught). An example would include the definitional element of an 'intention to subvert the competitive process'. If one does not wish to do that, one can argue that sufficient culpability exists if moral wrongfulness exists, as in this book moral wrongfulness requires violation of at least one moral norm (which, by definition, includes a mental element focused on intention).

Second, cartel activity involves a significant degree of social harmfulness. In short, it can produce a considerable negative impact upon a socially valuable interest, i.e. the successful operation of a free market. Two limitations of the social harmfulness aspect to cartel activity were identified: (i) the requirement that the operation of a free market should be considered as a socially valuable interest by citizens; and (ii) the fact that the nature of the particular harm engendered by cartel activity presents three difficulties (the harm is 'diluted' across many different victims; cartel activity may be perceived as a 'victimless crime'; and one may not be able in practice to identify the victims even where a cartel is discovered). The first of these limitations is not problematic: most citizens in the EU appear to accept the value of the free market. The second limitation is more challenging for those who seek to construct a retribution-based criminalization argument. In particular, efforts to educate stakeholders in the criminal antitrust regime about its necessity and appropriateness may be hampered by this limitation.[6]

Third, subject to the (problematic) limitations identified, cartel activity can arguably run counter to the moral norms against stealing, deception, and cheating. There is a strong argument that cartel activity can be conceptualized as stealing. To sustain this argument, one must establish that the victims of the cartel activity have rights to the cartel overcharge. The key issue to be decided here is whether a total welfare standard or a consumer welfare standard should be adopted in the context of antitrust law. There is a strong pragmatic argument why a consumer welfare standard should be chosen, even if one believes that wealth transfers from consumers to producers are welfare-neutral. However, even if the relevant rights to the overcharge are created, there is a further limitation of the conceptualization of cartel activity as stealing: due to the requirement of a fundamental violation of these rights, only the actual implementation of a cartel agreement will be captured.

Deception can certainly be present when false statements are offered by the cartelist concerning the non-existence of cartel activity. Deception through non-disclosure also remains a possibility, albeit one with problematic issues. In particular, one must establish that customers actually assume that cartelists compete with their competitors. Without firm empirical evidence supporting this assumption, one must rely on (plausible) theoretical arguments, thereby introducing an inherent limitation to the analysis. Moreover, the determination of the intention of the cartelist in remaining silent is not as clear-cut as with false statements, although arguably a direct intention to mislead

[6] On these efforts and the practical challenges they present, see Chapter 10, Section C.

often exists in this context. There is a further limitation concerning deception through false statements and deception through non-disclosure: the cartel agreement must have been implemented, as the relevant message communicated requires the offering of a product *at a cartelized price*.

The moral norm against cheating also has the potential to capture the 'moral wrongfulness' of cartel activity. But problematic issues also exist here. The main difficulty lies in identifying the 'unfair advantage' that the cartelist intends to obtain in breaking the relevant rule. If the 'advantage' is narrowly defined to include a material/financial advantage obtained over another who adheres to that rule, then cheating can only occur against a cartelist's customer who is an undertaking offering goods or services on a market. A wider definition of 'advantage' (i.e. one which includes the mere indulging of one's will beyond the restrictions imposed by the relevant cartel prohibition) further facilitates a finding of 'moral wrongfulness' (this time against competitors, customers, *and* final consumers), but does so at the expense of a more rigid link between the cartelist's actions and their impact on other market actors. That said, such an approach allows one to capture the full extent of cartel activity (i.e. entering into a cartel agreement as well as implementing it).

As should be clear, this book did not set out merely to argue in favour of criminalizing cartel activity for the purposes of retribution; rather, it aimed to analyse the challenge of justifying criminal cartel sanctions by reference to the theory of retribution. As a result, it also highlighted the limitations of a retribution-based argument in favour of antitrust criminalization. Some of these limitations (e.g., the requirement that citizens value the free-market system) do not weaken a retribution-based argument. Other limitations, however, are more problematic. It is submitted that the challenge of overcoming the problematic limitations identified represents the main theoretical challenge of retribution in the context of antitrust criminalization: a retribution-based criminalization argument can indeed be constructed, as demonstrated in Chapter 4; importantly, however, its actual strength is determined by the extent to which its (problematic) limitations are enduring. Given the extent of the difficulties associated with each of the problematic limitations identified, this theoretical challenge is likely to continue to confront those who argue in favour of antitrust criminalization for reasons of retribution.

C. Antitrust Criminalization Must Overcome Complicated Legal Challenges

Two types of legal challenge were deemed to be of central importance[7] and were critically analysed in detail in Part II of this book: due process; and legal certainty. While both of the challenges identified are human rights-related, they differ in terms of their focus: one challenge is procedural in perspective (due process), the other is substantive (legal certainty). This section details the legal challenges for European antitrust criminalization which are created by the requirements of due process and legal certainty.

(a) The challenge of due process

The issue of due process presents a number of challenges for those who are considering the introduction of criminal antitrust sanctions within the EU. These challenges are the natural result of two distinct contentions: the 'strengthening of rights' contention;

[7] See Chapter 1, Section D(a)(v)(2).

and the 'additional dynamic' contention. The former contention holds that protections which would be merely sufficient in relation to the imposition of administrative antitrust sanctions will no longer be adequate when criminal antitrust sanctions are imposed. The latter contention, by contrast, holds that the introduction of criminal antitrust sanctions in a particular European jurisdiction does not preclude the imposition of civil/administrative sanctions alongside criminal sanctions for a given cartel. The validity and impact of both of these contentions were examined in this book in order to analyse the legal challenge of due process for European antitrust criminalization.

(i) The 'strengthening of rights' contention

This book established the validity of the 'strengthening of rights' contention.[8] The introduction of criminal cartel sanctions *ensures* the applicability of Article 6 ECHR to antitrust proceedings. A number of consequences flow from this fact. For example, as a result of European human rights law, one must separate the adjudicative function from the investigative and prosecutorial functions at first instance as well as on appeal. In other words, European antitrust criminalization can indeed lead to a 'strengthening of rights' in favour of the accused. Whether this will be so in practice obviously depends upon the legal protections actually guaranteed by a national regime to an accused cartelist *in an administrative proceeding*. The point relevant to this book, however, is that, as a direct result of the specifics of European human rights law, there is some scope for a discord between the protections required by European human rights law in a criminal setting and the protections actually facing an accused cartelist in an administrative setting. Hence, the 'strengthening of rights' contention was deemed to be valid.

This book also determined the actual impact of the 'strengthening of rights' contention, and hence the extent of the challenge presented by this aspect of the legal requirement of due process. It was noted that, while not every consequence of the 'strengthening of rights' contention is problematic, the requirement to 'strengthen' human rights protections nonetheless has the potential to have a negative impact upon antitrust enforcement. In particular, by protecting the rights of the accused in line with Article 6 ECHR, the power of the authorities to obtain evidence directly from the accused is effectively circumscribed in criminal cases against that accused: they can only use compulsory powers to obtain material from the accused which has an existence independent of his will. To overcome the potential negative effects identified, one could either increase the severity of any criminal punishment imposed or increase directly the rate of detection and prosecution of cartels.

The second option noted fits more comfortably with the objectives of both deterrence and retribution: the first option, while improving deterrence, may result in the imposition of an undue sanction, thereby violating the principle of proportionality; the second option, while requiring a particular approach to retribution, does not risk violation of the principle of proportionality, and yet may lead to increased deterrence. To implement the second option, one should adopt an individual criminal immunity policy, provide for bounties, and make full use of criminal methods of investigation. Leniency/immunity and bounties can of course be used in an administrative regime. But their use in a criminal regime brings *additional* advantages not seen in an administrative regime. Such advantages (along with the advantages of criminal methods of investigation) may have the potential to compensate for any 'strengthening of rights'.

[8] See Chapter 5.

Admittedly, these proposed solutions should not be perceived as panaceas: depending on the particular circumstances, some may well reduce the potential for a problem, but not eliminate the possibility altogether. In addition, immunity in particular may pose additional practical problems in the context of criminal antitrust enforcement. In this book, in line with its central thesis, these potentially problematic (practical) issues were considered as part of the *practical* challenges of European antitrust criminalization: Part III of this book. The analyses conducted in this book on the 'strengthening of rights' contention in fact highlight, then, that the legal challenges of antitrust criminalization cannot be fully understood in isolation from the practical challenges of such criminalization.

(ii) The 'additional dynamic' contention

This book then proceeded to analyse the 'additional dynamic' contention.[9] Its validity was also established relatively easily. After identifying four possible manifestations of the contention at issue and conducting inquiries concerning these manifestations, this book determined that three of these manifestations were valid. Accordingly, the following sentencing scenarios *for a given cartel* are possible under EU law: (i) national regimes can impose both administrative antitrust sanctions on undertakings and criminal antitrust sanctions on individuals; (ii) a given national regime can impose criminal antitrust sanctions on individuals and a different national regime can impose administrative antitrust sanctions on undertakings; (iii) the European Commission can impose administrative antitrust sanctions on undertakings and a given national regime can impose criminal sanctions on individuals. Thus, the 'additional dynamic' contention itself was indeed found to be valid.

This book also determined the actual impact of the 'additional dynamic' contention, and hence the extent of the challenge presented by this aspect of the legal requirement of due process. Three particular issues were considered: (i) the exchange of information between competition authorities; (ii) double jeopardy; and (iii) concurrent proceedings.

A potential due process issue was identified with the exchange of information from administrative antitrust regimes to criminal antitrust regimes: if such information could be used in evidence in a criminal trial, it could potentially undermine the rights of the accused, as the protections in an administrative regime may not be as robust as those in a criminal regime. EU law has foreseen this problem. Regulation 1/2003 places limitations on the exchange of information within the ECN from administrative to criminal regimes for evidential purposes: Article 12(3). While that particular provision takes care of the problem identified, it arguably goes too far: it prohibits the use of information in evidence to secure custodial sanctions in a receiving (criminal) regime even where the sending (administrative) regime has respected the human rights protections guaranteed in the receiving state. In order to ensure that the objectives of antitrust criminalization are not undermined, this 'custodial rule' should be abolished. Alternative, less strict (but nonetheless effective) protections could also be introduced, such as the use of a 'double barrier'. However, if due process is indeed to be protected, it is necessary to accept an inevitable negative impact upon the efficiency of the criminal antitrust regime, as one must allow for defendants to question the procedures adopted in the foreign jurisdiction. Compensating for this reduction in efficiency represents an inherent legal challenge of European antitrust criminalization.

[9] See Chapter 6.

The second identified issue of due process concerned 'double jeopardy'. It was argued that this issue becomes relevant due to: (i) the validity of the 'additional dynamic' contention; and (ii) the fact that an individual can in fact constitute an 'undertaking' for the purposes of EU law. Protecting against 'double jeopardy' is least difficult when the second prosecution has not yet begun, but the first prosecution has: the second case against the individual/undertaking should be dropped. When neither of the two parallel prosecutions has begun, the situation becomes problematic, particularly where more than one jurisdiction is involved. In order to secure efficient enforcement as well as fairness, one can use the ECN to resolve the issue. However, three limitations were identified with this solution: (i) there is no obligation concerning inter-NCA notifications within the ECN; (ii) due to legal ambiguities, NCAs may not feel obliged to inform the Commission of criminal antitrust cases which involve the imposition of sanctions upon natural persons; and (iii) the NCAs cannot relieve each other of the competence to pursue a given antitrust investigation or prosecution. These limitations, then, further contribute to the inherent legal problem of due process.

The final identified issue of due process related to concurrent proceedings. Two potentially problematic matters were examined: (i) the use of administrative powers to collect evidence for a parallel criminal investigation; and (ii) the engendering of prejudicial pre-trial publicity. Techniques can be used to reduce the likelihood of such matters occurring. However, efforts to ensure consistency with due process may have a negative impact upon the effectiveness of the European antitrust criminalization. Specifically, such techniques may either increase the costs involved in criminal antitrust enforcement or require the antitrust authority to limit media interest in the (concurrent) administrative proceeding. Such limitations of the identified techniques also contribute to the inherent legal problem of due process.

(b) The challenge of legal certainty

European human rights law requires legal certainty in the context of punishment for the commission of a criminal antitrust offence. The principle of legal certainty presents a challenge for those wishing to introduce such an offence. As identified in this book, there are three potential elements to this particular legal challenge.[10]

The first element of the challenge of legal certainty requires the demonstration that the principle of legal certainty does not prohibit in any absolute sense the imposition of criminal antitrust sanctions. It was argued that the European cartel law rules are not inherently vague to a degree that would ensure inevitable legal certainty problems and that, therefore, their enforcement could encompass the use of criminal sanctions. Indeed, while relevant to the outer fringes of antitrust activity, the argument that legal certainty prohibits criminal antitrust sanctions does not necessarily apply to clear-cut violations of European cartel law, where little confusion exists concerning unlawfulness. Meeting this element of the challenge, then, is relatively undemanding.

The second element concerns the substance of the criminal antitrust law: one must be careful in designing such a law not to violate the principle of legal certainty. Relying upon the case study of the UK Cartel Offence, this book argued that to avoid problems with legal certainty, one should avoid the employment of the definitional element of 'dishonesty' if a stand-alone offence is to be created. The validity of that particular recommendation,

[10] See Chapter 7.

however, depended to a large degree upon whether one operationalized any of the norms noted in Chapter 4 concerning stealing, deception, or cheating.

The final element concerns the actual existence of criminal antitrust sanctions. This particular element of the legal challenge at issue becomes relevant when one attempts to impose criminal antitrust sanctions by awakening a 'sleeping giant': i.e. by employing a non-antitrust-specific criminal law. The case of *Norris* was informative concerning normative instructions on the use of 'sleeping giants'. The provision of notice, including its limitations, was analysed in this context. In particular, it was emphasized that the provision of notice, while useful in dealing with the challenge at issue, is not a panacea for the legal certainty problems with 'sleeping giants'. Notice does not necessarily establish reasonableness with regard to bringing a given (anticompetitive) conduct within the original concept of the offence in question; irrespective of notice, a sufficient (definitional) link should still exist between the specifics of the offence and the cartel activity in question. Without this (definitional) link, one will inevitably violate the principle of legal certainty through the waking of a 'sleeping giant'.

D. Antitrust Criminalization Must Overcome Complicated Practical Challenges

Part III of this book examined the extent to which European antitrust criminalization must overcome complicated practical challenges. It submitted that one of the most important practical issues which has the potential to undermine the effectiveness of criminal antitrust enforcement is the issue of how to define the criminal cartel offence. This book analysed two very important issues concerning the definition of such an offence: (i) the potential (negative) impact of Regulation 1/2003 on the design and operation of a national criminal cartel offence and what can be done to reduce the scope for such impact in this context; and (ii) how to deal with 'acceptable' (i.e. legitimate and/or efficiency-enhancing) cartel activity in the context of European antitrust criminalization. Taken together, these two issues represent the 'first (practical) challenge of design' examined by this book. This book also aimed to contribute to the literature on European cartel criminalization by providing a systematic analysis of the challenge of design posed for such criminalization by the investigative mechanism of leniency/immunity. In this book, this particular challenge has been termed the 'second (practical) challenge of design' and comprises two elements, both of which have been analysed in detail: (i) ensuring the peaceful co-existence of administrative leniency/immunity and criminal sanctions; and (ii) the unique aspects of the challenge of *criminal* immunity for cartel activity. This book also proceeded on the assumption that well-thought-out enforcement strategies need to be in place in order for a criminal cartel regime to be effective in practice. Specifically, in addition to the two practical challenges already outlined, it articulated the 'third (practical) challenge of design' for European antitrust criminalization: it examined the important strategies that need to be put in place in order to ensure the actual achievement of the underlying enforcement objectives of antitrust criminalization. These strategies were categorized into four distinct imperatives: (i) avoiding the 'compliance trap'; (ii) securing sufficient support from stakeholders in the project of antitrust criminalization; (iii) designing effectively the criminal antitrust enforcement agency/agencies; and (iv) securing international support for the enforcement efforts of the criminalized cartel regime.

(a) The first challenge of design—defining the criminal cartel offence

If Regulation 1/2003 applies to the enforcement of the national cartel offence, then there is a clear case that that particular Regulation can impact upon both the definition and the operation of the criminal offence. The definition of the criminal cartel offence could be affected as a result of Article 3 of Regulation 1/2003. Arguably, this provision of EU competition law may restrict the scope of a criminal cartel offence in that (when there is an effect on trade) the criminal offence cannot capture cartel activity which would not have violated the prohibition in Article 101(1) TFEU, would have fulfilled the criteria of Article 101(3) TFEU, or would have been covered by a block exemption. This situation is problematic for three reasons: (i) it makes the concept of 'effect on trade' relevant in a criminal trial; (ii) it allows for (potentially confusing) economic arguments to be made in a criminal trial; and (iii) it restricts the ability of a jurisdiction to generate a moral norm against cartel activity, as citizens may perceive the criminal cartel offence as focusing on the technical and arcane regulation of trade, rather than on preventing conspiracies that cost consumers significant amounts of money. For their part, Articles 11(6) and 35 have the potential to impact negatively on the operation of the criminal cartel offence. If Regulation 1/2003 applies to the enforcement of the national criminal cartel offence, then, under Article 11(6) thereof, the Commission would have the power to relieve the national criminal cartel enforcer of its power to prosecute cartelists for their commission of the criminal cartel offence. There is also the possibility that Article 35(1) of the Regulation could be used to argue that, if the national criminal enforcer is not a designated NCA under Regulation 1/2003, then it would not have jurisdiction to prosecute an individual for an alleged commission of the criminal cartel offence.

One could eliminate the possibility for a later 'surprise' restriction of the scope of the national criminal cartel offence by linking the offence to a violation of Article 101(1) TFEU and providing a defence along the lines of Article 101(3) TFEU. In addition, one can also designate the criminal prosecutor as an NCA under Regulation 1/2003. However, while this approach would avoid certain nasty surprises for the prosecution during a criminal trial, and would avoid arguments centred on a lack of jurisdiction due to Article 35 of Regulation 1/2003, it would also facilitate the introduction of economic evidence in a trial (something that legislators are keen to avoid) and would not deal with the Article 11(6) issue. Alternatively, one could design the criminal cartel offence so that it only applied to situations where there was no effect on trade between Member States. However, such an approach would be legally questionable. A policy of only pursuing cases with no effect on trade would be preferable, but such an option brings with it disadvantages in terms of achieving deterrence and/or retribution.

The best option would be to design the criminal cartel offence in such a manner that Regulation 1/2003 would not apply to it at all. This is a difficult thing to do, as it is not exactly clear when the Regulation will and will not apply concerning the enforcement of a national criminal cartel offence. This is due to, inter alia, the ambiguous nature of the relevant sentence in Recital 8 of Regulation 1/2003. Two alternative interpretations of when Regulation 1/2003 will not apply were identified: (i) when undertakings (as opposed to individuals) cannot be subjected to a criminal prosecution for commission of the criminal cartel offence; or (ii) when the criminal cartel offence does not pursue the same predominant objective as the EU competition law rules. If one is persuaded by the former interpretation, then all one needs to do to avoid the impact of Regulation 1/2003 is to ensure that only individuals can be convicted of the criminal cartel offence. If the latter interpretation is preferred, then one is required: (i) to take a (supportable) decision regarding the predominant objective of EU competition law; and (ii) to design the criminal cartel offence in such a way that its predominant objective can be distinguished from that of the EU competition law rules.

This book also addressed the issue of dealing with 'acceptable' cartel activity. It first identified the central dilemma in this context by explaining how EU competition law currently deals with this issue and why that approach may not be ideal in a criminal law setting. EU competition law deals with the issue by virtue of the 'commercial ancillarity' doctrine and through Article 101(3) TFEU. Both of these mechanisms involve the conducting of assessments of the economic effects of the cartel in question. This is unfortunate, as a central feature of an effective criminal cartel law is the absence of a requirement to analyse and prove any economic effects in a market in order to find an infringement. An ideal solution to this issue would be the 'carve out' of 'acceptable' cartel activity from the criminal cartel offence in a manner that does not rely upon the decision-maker in a criminal trial undertaking economic analyses.

The definitional element of 'dishonesty' was considered as one method of ensuring that 'acceptable' cartel activity is 'carved out' of the offence without the need for economic analysis. It was demonstrated that this particular definitional element is less than ideal: for 'dishonesty' to carve out 'acceptable' cartel activity, it will be necessary for the defendant to argue that ordinary people would not find that activity to be dishonest *because it is not unlawful under EU/national competition law*, and in order to substantiate that argument the defendant will be required to put forward *economic* evidence which demonstrates that, e.g., an exception under Article 101(3) TFEU (or the national equivalent) would be forthcoming. In addition to this failing, the definitional element of 'dishonesty' presents a number of problematic features, such as allowing for the presentation of dubious 'defences' in a criminal trial. Its inclusion in a criminal cartel offence is therefore not advisable.

Fortunately, one can identify an alternative method of 'carving out' so-called 'acceptable' cartel activity from the criminal cartel offence without the need for a decision-maker to conduct economic analyses in a criminal trial: the mechanism of 'carving out' cartel agreements that are published in an appropriate format prior to their implementation. This mechanism has recently been adopted in the UK. A criminal cartel offence that prohibits price-fixing, output restrictions, market sharing, and bid-rigging while allowing for a 'carve out' of agreements that are published would not require a decision-maker to assess the economic effects of an agreement to find that the offence has been committed. Importantly, however, it also provides scope for the operation of the 'commercial ancillarity' doctrine, as well as for the operation of Article 101(3) TFEU: if cartelists genuinely believe that their cartel agreement would benefit from an exception (as it would fulfil the criteria of Article 101(3) TFEU) or that it would fulfil the criteria specified by the Court of Justice in implementing the 'commercial ancillarity' doctrine, all they have to do to avoid criminal sanctions is to publish publicly the agreement prior to its implementation or to notify the competition authority of its existence prior to implementation. One should understand that the 'carve out' of agreements made openly (i.e. published in a suitable format prior to their implementation) is not equivalent to a notification and authorization regime as it does not require any action on behalf of the competition authorities: the mere fact that an agreement has been published in a suitable format *automatically* removes the cartelists from the sphere of criminal law. There is, therefore, no resultant administrative burden on the authority. In fact, such a 'carve out' engenders more advantages than disadvantages and should be an option favoured by those jurisdictions that are serious about dealing with hard-core cartel activity, but do not wish to prohibit activity that pursues a legitimate purpose or may produce net benefits for consumers.

(b) The second challenge of design—understanding the complexities of leniency/immunity

It is clear that administrative leniency policies are an important part of the competition law enforcement landscape and that they can be particularly effective at piercing the veil of secrecy that typically surrounds cartel activity. It is also clear that commentators believe that some potential exists for criminal cartel sanctions to impact negatively upon administrative leniency policies. Four reasons for the existence of a potential negative impact were identified: (i) companies may actually care about what happens to their employees and may be hesitant to apply for administrative leniency if by doing so they would expose their employees to criminal sanctions; (ii) individuals within a firm which is contemplating applying for leniency may be hesitant to advocate their company's applying for leniency if it would lead to their exposure to criminal sanctions; (iii) firms may well need the cooperation of their employees who have engaged in cartel activity if they are to benefit from the leniency policy, and such cooperation would be unlikely if it would lead to the individuals' being exposed to criminal sanctions; and (iv) firms may fear that by applying for leniency they would increase their risk of exposure to private damages actions, as their corporate statements may eventually become public through their disclosure to the accused (and eventually their use in open court) in the context of a criminal prosecution.

This book identified three mechanisms that can be useful in resolving any conflict between administrative leniency programmes and criminal sanctions. The first mechanism identified was the creation of a criminal immunity programme for cartel activity. Such a policy would help to reassure firms contemplating applying for administrative leniency that their employees have a route out of potential criminal proceedings against them. There are drawbacks to this solution, however, such as the impact of the principle of mandatory prosecution and the fact that the investigating antitrust authorities may not be able to *guarantee* immunity for applicants (particularly when it is not the prosecuting authority). Potential solutions to these problems include: using criminal leniency instead of criminal immunity where the principle of mandatory prosecution is applicable; where possible, using legislation to remove the principle of mandatory prosecution for criminal cartel offences; imposing the criminal immunity policy of the investigating authority upon the prosecuting authority through legislation; involving the prosecuting authority in the introduction and application of the immunity policy; and requiring the prosecuting authority to give 'serious weight' to recommendations for immunity that are proposed by the investigating body.

The second mechanism which is designed to resolve any conflict between administrative leniency programmes and criminal sanctions is the linking of the criminal immunity policy with the administrative leniency policy. In order to ensure that applications for administrative leniency are not 'chilled' by the existence of criminal cartel sanctions, one must not only create a criminal immunity policy in the criminalized jurisdiction, but, ideally, also ensure that criminal immunity automatically extends to the (cooperating) employees of those undertakings that have successfully applied for 'full' administrative leniency (i.e. a reduction of a fine to zero Euros). However, a significant problem may exist here: the jurisdiction operating the relevant criminal immunity programme may not be the same jurisdiction that is operating the applicable administrative leniency policy. A number of potential solutions to this issue can be identified, the most useful of which is allowing the national criminal prosecutors to decline to bring charges against the (cooperating) employees of the firms to which the authorities of another jurisdiction (e.g., the Commission) have granted full administrative immunity. Such a solution is not without its own issues, however, such as the need for concurrent (or near concurrent) applications and the difficulty of convincing criminal prosecutors not to take forward a criminal cartel case in order to protect the integrity of a foreign administrative leniency programme (as opposed to a domestic one).

The third mechanism identified that can be useful in resolving any conflict between administrative leniency programmes and criminal sanctions involves dealing with the issue of criminal disclosure. Although the issue of criminal disclosure can be overstated in this context, there are a number of steps that could be taken by the authorities in order to reassure the undertaking contemplating applying for administrative leniency. For example, administrative leniency applications should be kept confidential and out of the public domain and, if corporate statements are destined to be employed in a criminal trial, the relevant authorities should apply for any available protective orders to ensure that there is not public disclosure of the material in open court.

The employment of a *criminal* immunity programme for cartel activity brings with it a number of unique challenges for antitrust law enforcers. Two examples include: dealing with the employment of an 'immunized witness' in a criminal cartel trial; and ensuring that cultural opposition to criminal immunity does not exist. The problem with an 'immunized witness' is that: (i) the prosecution aims to employ the witness to underline the culpability of the cartelists on trial; and (ii) the witness, while attempting to fulfil the immunity conditions (including admitting all elements of the criminal cartel offence), may nonetheless wish to play down their culpability (and, in the process, the criminality of cartel activity) to the outside world (including the jury, where appropriate). This book identified a number of methods that can be used to minimize the impact of the potential problem with 'immunized witnesses' at trial. The 'nuclear' option is to make immunity conditional upon a successful outcome at trial; but this option reduces significantly the attractiveness of applying for criminal immunity in the first place. Alternatively, one could restrict the ability of the cartelist to make public statements which have the potential to jeopardize the sustainability of convictions; but this would be difficult to police in practice. A more practical option would be to design the criminal cartel offence so that it does not contain definitional elements that the 'immunized witness' would have a discomfort in admitting to during a trial (such as 'fraudulently', 'deceitfully', etc.). In any case, one would be advised to avoid the sole reliance upon an 'immunized witness' to construct a case against the accused, particularly where the cartel is a bilateral one. The use of a criminal immunity policy in a criminalized jurisdiction has the potential to engender cultural opposition. For example, the wider public may perceive it as unfair that some (equally culpable) cartelists walk free at the expense of others going to prison. There is some empirical support for the existence of this type of cultural opposition. In order to overcome such opposition, one must engage in educative efforts and competition advocacy. If the immoral aspects of cartel activity are understood in addition to how difficult it is to detect cartel activity, it is more likely that citizens will come to accept the 'necessary evil' of criminal immunity programmes. Intelligent case prioritization and case management also have their roles to play.

(c) The third challenge of design—identifying the desirable enforcement strategies

The 'compliance trap' occurs when political support for the moral seriousness of the law which an (antitrust) authority must enforce is lacking. When the antitrust activities of business offenders are condemned by antitrust enforcers for their immoral qualities (as they would be when criminal sanctions are imposed upon them), such offenders may interpret this particular form of moral leveraging of antitrust enforcement to be unfair or stigmatizing and, therefore, may actively lobby for the political emasculation of the regulator, a process which can eventually force the regulator to adopt a more lenient approach to enforcement. Without external political support, the regulator can do little to escape this 'trap'. While the 'compliance trap' is most relevant when retribution theory is at issue, it can also occur when the underlying enforcement theory is that of (economic) deterrence. To avoid this 'trap', political support is required for the criminal antitrust regime, as is effective, strong leadership in the criminal enforcement agency. Given that political support follows public support, any strategy designed to avoid the 'compliance trap' should attempt to create public support for the criminal cartel regime.

Support from all stakeholders in a project of antitrust criminalization is vitally important to its success. Indeed, without such support, one risks the provision of insufficient resources for antitrust enforcement efforts and/or nullification of the law. Unfortunately, securing support from the public is particularly difficult due to the characteristics of both cartel activity and cartelists, as well as the type of harm at issue. In addition, weak public support will generally be reflected in weak support for cartel criminalization among jury members in those European jurisdictions which employ trial by jury. The judiciary may also be hesitant to send convicted cartelists to jail, believing that there is an inherent, material difference between corporate offenders and traditional offenders.

To secure public support for cartel criminalization, the authorities must engage in considerable educative efforts regarding the nature of cartel activity. Such educative efforts could be conducted through workshops, public awareness campaigns, news releases, television interviews, and media publicity. To secure support for the criminal antitrust regime, one must demonstrate not only that anticompetitive conduct can be harmful, but also that a deterrence-based and/or a retribution-based criminalization argument(s) is/are robust. What also needs to be ensured is a well-publicized, well-designed public consultation on cartel criminalization prior to the adoption of criminal cartel sanctions. Following criminalization, the authorities need to be clever in their prioritization strategies regarding criminal antitrust prosecutions. Two key elements to a clever strategy of gaining public support are: (i) an initial focus on public procurement involving bid-rigging; and (ii) an initial focus on cartels selling to final consumers. Furthermore, criminal antitrust enforcers should only pursue serious cases where severe penalties are appropriate. The creation of a formal list of prioritization criteria or principles could help in this regard. After each successful criminal cartel trial, the antitrust enforcers should also release detailed press releases and appear on television and radio in order to explain the nature of cartel activity, the holding of the criminal court, and the benefits for consumers of cartel criminalization.

To prevent jury nullification, jurisdictions should ensure that their criminal courts have adequate powers to assist the jury in understanding complex issues at trial. What is particularly important is the production of a 'road map' that will help jurors to understand and appreciate the significance of the evidence as it is presented. The creation of model jury instructions could also be useful. Criminal antitrust enforcers should understand that bilateral cartels with a successful leniency/immunity applicant do not present ideal cases to be prosecuted in front of a jury; such cases should only be prosecuted when leniency information can be corroborated from other sources, the cartel conduct is clear and unambiguous, and/or it is immediately obvious that the accused appreciated the criminal nature of his conduct. The strategies of only prosecuting summary cases or circumventing the use of the jury are inherently limited; the former should be avoided, and the latter is unlikely to be successful, particularly when law-makers have a strong attachment to the tradition of trial by jury.

Overcoming judicial reluctance can be achieved through the use of 'signalling' by the legislature of the need for custodial sentences for convicted cartelists. Creating a high maximum sentence may perform this function, but if it fails, the legislature could raise the maximum sentence in order to signal its disapproval of the sentencing record of the court. However, this approach suffers from two inherent limitations: (i) judges do not have to take notice of the signalling; and (ii) it does not provide a methodology according to which an actual custodial sentence can be determined. Mandatory sentencing guidelines overcome these inherent drawbacks, but they may represent an inappropriate interference with judicial independence. Discretionary guidelines can be a compromise solution to the problem. They would not only provide a framework according to which judges could justify a chosen custodial sentence, but they would also help to build support more generally, as they would reduce the potential for convicted individuals to complain to the media about the arbitrary nature of any criminal punishment imposed.

When one is designing the criminal antitrust enforcement landscape, four strategic questions need to be considered: (i) whether an existing competition authority should exercise the investigative function in a criminal cartel regime; (ii) if so, whether the competition authority should share the investigative function with another (special/general) agency; (iii) whether the competition authority should also be able to prosecute a cartel offence; and (iv) if so, whether it should exercise its prosecutorial function alone or in conjunction with another (special/general) prosecutor. In answering these questions, one should understand that each approach has its own particular advantages and disadvantages: there is no ideal way to allocate the investigative and prosecutorial functions. It may be the case that a competition authority will be more dedicated to the investigation of cartel activity than a general criminal investigative agency. But the competition authority would need to acquire significant new skills if it is to avoid committing embarrassing mistakes that a seasoned investigator would not. When it comes to the prosecutorial function, a competition authority could well be out of its depth in a criminal court, a fact attested to by recent failings of the OFT in the UK. While a general prosecutor's office may have a limited appetite for cartel law enforcement, if it were to pursue a criminal cartel prosecution it would be more likely to be successful than a competition authority that is new to the environment of a criminal court.

The criminalization of cartel activity brings with it a particular disadvantage that needs to be addressed: the need for international cooperation combined with the possible lack of desire of other (non-criminalized) jurisdictions to provide such cooperation when imprisonment could occur. If, however, other jurisdictions could eventually be persuaded to criminalize cartel activity, two particular ways of alleviating the difficulty of international cartels on a bilateral basis could be created: (i) the extension of extradition treaties to cartel offences; and (ii) the use of MLATs to facilitate the collection of evidence, the production of records, and/or the questioning of witnesses located abroad. Central to this strategy is convincing other countries to adopt criminal cartel laws. Demonstrating one's criminal enforcement successes at home is a prerequisite for advocating the adoption of criminal cartel laws abroad. Focusing initially on local cartels may be the best way to create such successes, unless the jurisdiction in question wishes to 'piggy-back' on US enforcement efforts. It would also be advisable for a criminalized jurisdiction to focus the majority of its advocacy efforts on its close trading partners before turning to multilateral fora to convince the wider world to criminalize cartel activity. Either way, it is vital to avoid pressurizing other jurisdictions into adopting criminal sanctions when those jurisdictions are not ready for cartel criminalization.

E. The Theoretical, Legal, and Practical Challenges of European Antitrust Criminalization Cannot Be Analysed in Isolation

This section clarifies the extent to which the theoretical, legal, and practical challenges of European antitrust criminalization are interrelated. In doing so, it: (i) emphasizes the potential 'points of contact' between the two theoretical challenges identified; (ii) underlines the extent to which the legal challenges further complicate the theoretical challenges under examination; and (iii) articulates any additional links between the theoretical and legal challenges and the practical challenges.

(a) Links between the theoretical challenges

Each justificatory theory for criminal punishment under examination in this book pursues a conceptually distinct objective. With deterrence, one aims to prevent the future occurrence of a particular conduct. With retribution, by contrast, one aims to punish those who have committed moral wrongs. The general inquiries relevant to each theory will therefore differ: the application of deterrence theory requires investigation of whether conduct can be influenced by the criminal law; the application of retribution theory necessitates an examination of the moral quality of a given conduct. Nonetheless, in certain contexts, a number of 'points of contact' between the theories may be encountered: the results of specific inquiries related to, say, deterrence theory can also impact on the application of retribution theory, and vice versa. As demonstrated in this book, two such 'points of contact' can be detected when the justificatory theories are applied to the concept of cartel activity.

The first 'point of contact' concerns the moral content of cartel activity. Here, it should be understood that the findings in this book concerning the challenge of retribution theory for European antitrust criminalization are of crucial importance for a comprehensive understanding of the complexity of the challenge of *deterrence* theory in this context. This book has demonstrated that cartel activity may be capable of amounting to immoral conduct. To the extent that this is true, the *deterrence*-based criminalization argument can overcome one of its potential limitations: it can avoid the imposition of personal criminal sanctions for morally neutral conduct, thereby avoiding the disadvantages associated with 'over-criminalization'. However, as noted in Chapter 4, certain implementing features may be required in order to ensure that a criminal cartel offence captures immoral behaviour (e.g., the legislature must create an appropriate mens rea, which may be as strict as intention to distort competition). Consequently, specific action may be required for the deterrence-based criminalization argument to overcome the limitation concerning morality. To the extent that the relevant implementing features present *additional* hurdles for antitrust prosecutors—e.g., by requiring proof to the highest level of culpability in relation to cartel activity—they have a negative effect upon deterrence-related antitrust enforcement efforts: ceteris paribus, a given amount of resources will most likely produce fewer successful prosecutions. The results, then, of specific inquiries related to retribution theory and cartel activity also impact on the application of deterrence theory in this context. More specifically, the results of the particular inquiries undertaken in this book demonstrate that there is a possible tension between the objective of deterrence and the objective of retribution in the context of European antitrust criminalization.

The second 'point of contact' is the common requirement for empirical evidence on the motivations of cartelists and on whether or not they act rationally. The deterrence-based criminalization argument requires rationality on behalf of cartelists.[11] While the retribution-based argument does not necessarily require rationality, it is strengthened to the extent that such rationality exists.[12] Indeed, if cartelists pursue cartels because it is profitable to do so, the retribution-based argument may overcome one of its potential limitations: its underlying assumptions (concerning the cartelist's intention to obtain an unlawful advantage, intention to mislead, and/or intention to deprive) become more realistic. So, for both theoretical challenges, then, the empirical evidence in question is important. In other words, the results of a specific inquiry related to deterrence theory and cartel activity (i.e. that concerning the existence or otherwise of rationality on the behalf of cartelists) also impact on the application of retribution theory in this context. As far as this author is aware, this particular link between the justificatory theories has not yet been acknowledged in the literature on antitrust criminalization.

(b) Links between the theoretical and legal challenges

Efforts to meet the legal challenges of European antitrust criminalization identified in this book can at times further complicate the theoretical challenges one faces with such criminalization. The exact circumstances in which this is the case should be understood by those European jurisdictions considering the introduction and/or the continued maintenance of criminal antitrust sanctions. It is imperative that the human rights of the accused are protected within the EU.[13] These rights must be respected even when they impact negatively upon the theoretical justifications for criminal antitrust sanctions. One cannot merely ignore the human rights of the accused in order to ensure that the objectives of antitrust criminalization are achieved. Consequently, where there is a negative impact upon the theoretical justifications, one may have to implement appropriate mechanisms or techniques which can help to compensate for such a negative impact *while nonetheless respecting the rights of the accused.*

The fact that the 'strengthening of rights' contention of due process identified in this book is valid impacts upon both of the theoretical foundations. In particular, if the right to silence is to be protected in line with ECtHR jurisprudence, *in the absence of something more*, it will be more difficult post-criminalization for the investigative and prosecutorial authorities to prove a cartel. As the achievement of both deterrence and retribution depend upon the detection of cartel activity, both of these objectives can be undermined as a result. In order to compensate for such an effect, one can attempt to increase detection rates directly by, inter alia, employing a criminal immunity policy. Unfortunately, the employment of such a policy brings with it difficult practical issues concerning its implementation, as noted above. In addition, and importantly, a criminal leniency policy itself has the potential to impact (both positively and negatively) upon the achievement of the objectives of antitrust criminalization, as explained below.[14]

The (valid) 'additional dynamic' contention of due process may also influence the operation of the theoretical justifications. This is true for all of the three contexts analysed: (i) information exchange; (ii) *ne bis in idem*; and (iii) concurrent proceedings. If due process is indeed to be protected, it will be necessary to accept an inevitable negative impact upon the efficiency of the criminal antitrust regime if information exchanged between different jurisdictions is to be used in evidence: legal appeals questioning whether the relevant collection of information respects the equivalent level of

[11] See Chapter 3, Section D(b)(ii). [12] See Chapter 4, Section C(c)(i).
[13] On this, see Chapter 1, Sections D(a)(v)(1) and D(a)(v)(2).
[14] See Chapter 11, Section E(c).

protection of the rights of the accused in the receiving jurisdiction inevitably consume resources. This particular cost, then, represents another factor which must be taken into account when applying economic deterrence theory to cartel activity. In other words, the actual cost of protecting due process in the context of information exchange between an administrative antitrust regime and a criminal one complicates further the theoretical challenge of deterrence. The situation with *ne bis in idem* is similar, at least as regards the potential impact upon the effectiveness of deterrence. Fortunately, retribution theory can provide a solid rationale for the avoidance of 'double jeopardy': prohibiting double punishment for a given infraction of the moral code can help to prevent the imposition of a disproportionate sanction. The principle of *ne bis in idem* can therefore lead to results consistent with retribution theory. However, when *ne bis in idem* becomes a formal principle of the legal system and must be followed irrespective of the theoretical justification for antitrust criminalization, there may be negative knock-on effects in terms of the objective of deterrence. The reason for this is that the principle can lead one to drop the second (criminal) antitrust prosecution in order to protect the human rights of the accused. In such a case, the (first) administrative antitrust proceeding will be the only proceeding against the individual cartelist (who happens to be an undertaking for the purpose of EU law). The identified deficiencies concerning the use of administrative sanctions alone to secure deterrence would therefore be relevant:[15] sub-optimal deterrence may be occasioned. Finally, solving issues of due process with concurrent proceedings can also add to the theoretical challenges of antitrust criminalization. The techniques identified to reduce the likelihood of due process-related problems occurring may either increase the costs involved in criminal antitrust enforcement, thereby reducing the possible net (deterrence-based) gain from criminalization, or require the antitrust authority to limit media interest in the (concurrent) administrative proceeding, to the detriment of the objective of retribution.

Likewise, the principle of legal certainty may also impact upon both of the theoretical justifications. For a start, legal certainty requires the existence of comprehensibility concerning the criminal antitrust offence. If achieved, such comprehensibility not only satisfies the requirements of legal certainty, but also helps to secure the objectives of deterrence and retribution. Indeed, for a criminal law to deter a given individual from engaging in a given conduct, that individual must understand the actual specifics of the criminalized conduct in question. Furthermore, without understanding *what* the moral code actually specifies, one cannot explain to the accused *how* his behaviour has violated this moral code, to the detriment of the 'communicative function' variant of retribution theory. In this particular regard, then, legal certainty can be helpful for the theoretical justifications. However, as demonstrated by the *Norris* case, legal certainty can become problematic when it calls into question the very existence of a criminal antitrust offence: by prohibiting the waking of 'sleeping giants', legal certainty undermines the objectives inherent in the process of 'waking', i.e. deterrence and/or retribution. To reduce the chances of this happening, one can wake the 'sleeping giant' slowly through the use of notice. However, caution must be exercised here: notice is not a panacea for legal certainty problems, as explained above.[16] Finally, legal certainty becomes an issue when actually designing the criminal cartel offence. In fact, it may impact directly upon the definitional elements chosen to operationalize retribution theory in practice. In particular, the concept of 'dishonesty' should not be used in a stand-alone criminal cartel offence unless the implementing

[15] On this, see Chapter 3, Section B.
[16] See Chapter 7, Section E(b).

features of the retribution-based criminalization argument are also employed. If they *are* employed, one can avoid legal certainty problems. However, as explained above,[17] the use of such implementing features may also render the achievement of deterrence more difficult in practice. Hence, efforts to secure legal certainty in the definition of a criminal cartel offence may engender a tension between both of the potential objectives of European antitrust criminalization: deterrence and retribution.

(c) Additional links between the theoretical and legal challenges and the practical challenges

The two sub-sections directly above illustrate quite a number of links between the challenges under investigation in this book. However, further links between the challenges can be identified. For example, a link between all three of the different types of challenges examined can be identified regarding the use of a criminal immunity policy. As argued in Chapter 5, the validity of the 'strengthening of rights' contention ensures that the theoretical challenges of European antitrust criminalization become more difficult, and that in order to overcome this additional difficulty one would be advised to implement a particular practical measure: a criminal immunity policy. One must understand, though, that a criminal immunity policy has the potential itself to impact negatively upon the theoretical justifications. A criminal immunity programme has a direct impact on the potential sanction facing a prospective cartelist: it reduces the sanction (to zero). By itself, this can be problematic for deterrence. However, such a programme will also increase the rate of detection of cartels. Provided that the reduction in punishment is more than compensated for by the increase in the detection rate, the criminal immunity policy will be successful in increasing the deterrence of cartel activity. One should also understand here that a criminal immunity policy creates additional 'races to the regulator' than an administrative one, as individuals can be punished severely if they fail to be the first to apply for immunity. It is also arguable that criminal immunity can impact negatively upon the other objective of cartel criminalization: retribution. The reason is that some cartelists will escape punishment if a policy of criminal immunity is pursued. However, this issue is not problematic if one: (i) adopts a version of retribution theory that merely limits the maximum amount of punishment that can be imposed by the state; (ii) does not allow 'ringleaders' to benefit from the programme; (iii) accepts that, by coming forward and revealing the cartel to the authorities, the cartelist redeems himself and therefore has earned a more lenient treatment; or (iv) accepts that a principle of scope should exist when pursuing retribution and that in practice this principle is fulfilled with a criminal immunity policy. Consequently, the interaction between the three types of challenges in this context is not one that inevitably leads to problems for European antitrust criminalization.

An additional link between all three of the types of challenges can also be found regarding the definition of the criminal cartel offence. It was explained in Chapter 8[18] that Regulation 1/2003 can have a negative impact upon the content (definition) and operation of a national criminal cartel offence. For example, arguably, that Regulation could in certain circumstances ensure that a defence along the lines of Article 101(3) TFEU applies in the context of a criminal trial. In order to avoid such a negative impact, one must understand how one can draft the national cartel offence in order to avoid the application of Regulation 1/2003. This book demonstrated that there is an argument

[17] See Chapter 4, Section D.

[18] See Chapter 8, Section B(a).

that Regulation 1/2003 does not apply to a national criminal cartel offence when that criminal offence does not pursue the same predominant objective as the EU competition law rules.[19] In addition, if this is so, and one wished to avoid the application of Regulation 1/2003, one is required: (i) to take a (supportable) decision regarding the predominant objective of EU competition law; and (ii) to design the criminal cartel offence in such a way that its predominant objective can be distinguished from that of the EU competition law rules. The point here is that one way of doing this might be to argue that: (i) the predominant objective of the EU competition rules is 'the protection of competition on the market' (something that is not very difficult to do); and (ii) this is not pursued by the creation of a criminal cartel offence that is linked to an explicit moral concept, such as one of the norms against stealing, deception, or cheating. This sort of argument illustrates the dynamic link between the three types of challenges: theoretical, legal, and practical. By designing the national cartel offence in such a way that retribution is facilitated (i.e. by responding to the practical challenge of designing the cartel offence by relying upon a specific theoretical justification for criminal punishment), one can arguably ensure that the challenge of avoiding the application of Regulation 1/2003 is met in a manner that is legally robust.

Finally, this book demonstrated the importance of securing support for the criminalized/criminalizing cartel regime if that regime is to be effective in practice in achieving its objectives of deterrence and/or retribution. Due to the nature of (international) cartel activity, support is not only required from stakeholders (e.g., the general public, jury members, and the judiciary) located in the criminalized regime (or the jurisdiction contemplating criminalizing cartels), but also from those located in other jurisdictions, in particular if one wishes to see those other jurisdictions introduce criminal cartel sanctions in the future. Therefore, while advocacy efforts should be directed primarily at entities in the criminalized jurisdiction (or the jurisdiction contemplating criminalizing cartels), they should also be undertaken in the knowledge that other important jurisdictions (such as trading partners) may be influenced in a positive manner (i.e. as a result of such advocacy efforts, other jurisdictions may introduce their own criminal cartel laws, a process which may strengthen domestic criminal cartel enforcement). This brings one to a final point about the link between the three types of challenges: their importance for advocacy efforts. Indeed, it should go without saying that any advocacy efforts would be most effective if criminalized jurisdictions (or jurisdictions contemplating criminalizing cartels) could articulate clearly the theoretical, legal, and practical challenges of antitrust criminalization and demonstrate convincingly that they have been able (or would be able) to meet all three of those types of challenges in the real world. It is hoped that the analyses contained in this book would provide some help to jurisdictions in this regard.

F. Final Comments: Suggestions for Future Research

This book aimed to fill certain identified lacunae in the literature on European antitrust criminalization. Interestingly, however, the research conducted for this book revealed the existence of further gaps in the (empirical) literature which were not necessarily to be addressed by the actual research questions posed by this book. It is submitted that the topics underlying these particular gaps in the literature represent fruitful topics for future research. Importantly for present purposes, such research would not only enlighten those immediately interested in the respective topics, but would in turn also

[19] See Chapter 8, Section B(b).

help one to appreciate better the theoretical, legal, and practical challenges of European antitrust criminalization. The lacunae in question should therefore be mentioned specifically in a book which analyses directly such theoretical, legal, and practical challenges. This book, then, ends with a note for the future: it hopes to encourage relevant academics to engage in further study in a number of different areas.

Specifically, five different research questions should be addressed by future researchers. First, more detailed, reliable empirical evidence on the motivations of cartelists and whether or not they act in accordance with the rationality assumption of deterrence theory is required. Such evidence would be of direct use in determining whether the application of economic deterrence theory to cartel activity is in fact appropriate: i.e. it would help to determine if a particular assumption underlying deterrence theory is realistic in the context of anticompetitive behaviour. As mentioned directly above, however, such empirical research would also be useful for the purposes of applying retribution theory to cartel activity.

Second, detailed qualitative and quantitative research concerning the usefulness of information exchange within the ECN would also be useful. The results of such research could be used to put the due process-related problem with information exchange (as well as its solution) into perspective: compensating for the reduction in efficiency to ensure due process is protected in the context of information exchange represents an inherent legal challenge of European antitrust criminalization *only if* the merits of information exchange are as significant as claimed.

Third, empirical evidence should be generated concerning whether (and, if so, the extent to which) consumers actually assume that their suppliers are not engaged in cartel activity with their competitors. The results of such research would help one to understand more fully the limitations of the argument that cartel activity inevitably involves deception on the part of cartelists. In other words, it would help to determine more accurately the strength of a retribution-based argument for the introduction of criminal cartel sanctions.

Fourth, empirical studies on the extent to which risk aversion is a characteristic of corporate entities need to be pursued. Such studies would help one to come to firmer conclusions on the extent of the challenge of deterrence theory: they would provide evidence that would help one to determine whether the current formulation of the optimal cartel fine (at 150 per cent of annual turnover) is realistic.

Finally, empirical evidence on the cultural sensitivity of perceptions of (and attitudes towards) cartel activity among the citizens of the different EU Member States would be welcome. Such evidence would help one to come to firmer conclusions on the extent of the challenge of retribution theory: it would reveal whether some Member States inevitably have a more difficult task in conveying the immoral content of cartel activity to their citizens than that facing others.

This is not to suggest, however, that the (other) empirical evidence actually relied upon in this book should be considered to be definitive. In fact, as acknowledged in Chapter 3, an argument based on empirical evidence is inherently vulnerable: current empirical evidence in support of different elements of an argument may eventually be called into question, if not completely undermined, by later (more robust) empirical evidence. Empirical research on cartel-specific data (e.g., cartel duration and cartel overcharges) should therefore continue; such empirical evidence should be frequently tested and updated. In the absence of fresh empirical research on cartel activity, one risks presenting an unrealistic picture of the effectiveness or otherwise of current European antitrust enforcement. Such an unrealistic picture would in turn distort the analyses of the theoretical challenges of European antitrust criminalization, a result which runs counter to one of the principal objectives of this book.

ANNEXES AND BIBLIOGRAPHY

ANNEX I

Text of Article 101 TFEU

Article 101 TFEU (ex Article 81 TEC)

1. The following shall be prohibited as incompatible with the internal market: all agreements between undertakings, decisions by associations of undertakings and concerted practices which may affect trade between Member States and which have as their object or effect the prevention, restriction or distortion of competition within the internal market, and in particular those which:
   (a) directly or indirectly fix purchase or selling prices or any other trading conditions;
   (b) limit or control production, markets, technical development, or investment;
   (c) share markets or sources of supply;
   (d) apply dissimilar conditions to equivalent transactions with other trading parties, thereby placing them at a competitive disadvantage;
   (e) make the conclusion of contracts subject to acceptance by the other parties of supplementary obligations which, by their nature or according to commercial usage, have no connection with the subject of such contracts.
2. Any agreements or decisions prohibited pursuant to this Article shall be automatically void.
3. The provisions of paragraph 1 may, however, be declared inapplicable in the case of:
   — any agreement or category of agreements between undertakings,
   — any decision or category of decisions by associations of undertakings,
   — any concerted practice or category of concerted practices,

which contributes to improving the production or distribution of goods or to promoting technical or economic progress, while allowing consumers a fair share of the resulting benefit, and which does not:

(a) impose on the undertakings concerned restrictions which are not indispensable to the attainment of these objectives;
(b) afford such undertakings the possibility of eliminating competition in respect of a substantial part of the products in question.

ANNEX II

Text of the (Original) UK Cartel Offence and Section 47 of the Enterprise and Regulatory Reform Act 2013

Text of the (Original) UK Cartel Offence in the Enterprise Act 2002

188 Cartel offence

(1) An individual is guilty of an offence if he dishonestly agrees with one or more other persons to make or implement, or to cause to be made or implemented, arrangements of the following kind relating to at least two undertakings (A and B).

(2) The arrangements must be ones which, if operating as the parties to the agreement intend, would—
   (a) directly or indirectly fix a price for the supply by A in the United Kingdom (otherwise than to B) of a product or service,
   (b) limit or prevent supply by A in the United Kingdom of a product or service,
   (c) limit or prevent production by A in the United Kingdom of a product,
   (d) divide between A and B the supply in the United Kingdom of a product or service to a customer or customers,
   (e) divide between A and B customers for the supply in the United Kingdom of a product or service, or
   (f) be bid-rigging arrangements.

(3) Unless subsection (2)(d), (e) or (f) applies, the arrangements must also be ones which, if operating as the parties to the agreement intend, would—
   (a) directly or indirectly fix a price for the supply by B in the United Kingdom (otherwise than to A) of a product or service,
   (b) limit or prevent supply by B in the United Kingdom of a product or service, or
   (c) limit or prevent production by B in the United Kingdom of a product.

(4) In subsections (2)(a) to (d) and (3), references to supply or production are to supply or production in the appropriate circumstances (for which see section 189).

(5) 'Bid-rigging arrangements' are arrangements under which, in response to a request for bids for the supply of a product or service in the United Kingdom, or for the production of a product in the United Kingdom—
   (a) A but not B may make a bid, or
   (b) A and B may each make a bid but, in one case or both, only a bid arrived at in accordance with the arrangements.

(6) But arrangements are not bid-rigging arrangements if, under them, the person requesting bids would be informed of them at or before the time when a bid is made.

(7) 'Undertaking' has the same meaning as in Part 1 of the 1998 Act.

189 Cartel offence: supplementary

(1) For section 188(2)(a), the appropriate circumstances are that A's supply of the product or service would be at a level in the supply chain at which the product or service would at the same time be supplied by B in the United Kingdom.

(2) For section 188(2)(b), the appropriate circumstances are that A's supply of the product or service would be at a level in the supply chain—
   (a) at which the product or service would at the same time be supplied by B in the United Kingdom, or
   (b) at which supply by B in the United Kingdom of the product or service would be limited or prevented by the arrangements.

(3) For section 188(2)(c), the appropriate circumstances are that A's production of the product would be at a level in the production chain—
  (a) at which the product would at the same time be produced by B in the United Kingdom, or
  (b) at which production by B in the United Kingdom of the product would be limited or prevented by the arrangements.
(4) For section 188(2)(d), the appropriate circumstances are that A's supply of the product or service would be at the same level in the supply chain as B's.
(5) For section 188(3)(a), the appropriate circumstances are that B's supply of the product or service would be at a level in the supply chain at which the product or service would at the same time be supplied by A in the United Kingdom.
(6) For section 188(3)(b), the appropriate circumstances are that B's supply of the product or service would be at a level in the supply chain—
  (a) at which the product or service would at the same time be supplied by A in the United Kingdom, or
  (b) at which supply by A in the United Kingdom of the product or service would be limited or prevented by the arrangements.
(7) For section 188(3)(c), the appropriate circumstances are that B's production of the product would be at a level in the production chain—
  (a) at which the product would at the same time be produced by A in the United Kingdom, or
  (b) at which production by A in the United Kingdom of the product would be limited or prevented by the arrangements.

Section 47 of the Enterprise and Regulatory Reform Act 2013

47 Cartel offence

(1) Section 188 of the 2002 Act (cartel offence) is amended as follows.
(2) In subsection (1), omit 'dishonestly'.
(3) Omit subsection (6).
(4) After subsection (7) insert—

'(8) This section is subject to section 188A.'

(5) After that section insert—

'188A Circumstances in which cartel offence not committed

(1) An individual does not commit an offence under section 188(1) if, under the arrangements—
  (a) in a case where the arrangements would (operating as the parties intend) affect the supply in the United Kingdom of a product or service, customers would be given relevant information about the arrangements before they enter into agreements for the supply to them of the product or service so affected,
  (b) in the case of bid-rigging arrangements, the person requesting bids would be given relevant information about them at or before the time when a bid is made, or
  (c) in any case, relevant information about the arrangements would be published, before the arrangements are implemented, in the manner specified at the time of the making of the agreement in an order made by the Secretary of State.
(2) In subsection (1), "relevant information" means—
  (a) the names of the undertakings to which the arrangements relate,
  (b) a description of the nature of the arrangements which is sufficient to show why they are or might be arrangements of the kind to which section 188(1) applies,

(c) the products or services to which they relate, and
(d) such other information as may be specified in an order made by the Secretary of State.

(3) An individual does not commit an offence under section 188(1) if the agreement is made in order to comply with a legal requirement.

(4) In subsection (3), "legal requirement" has the same meaning as in paragraph 5 of Schedule 3 to the Competition Act 1998.

(5) A power to make an order under this section—
(a) is exercisable by statutory instrument,
(b) may be exercised so as to make different provision for different cases or different purposes, and
(c) includes power to make such incidental, supplementary, consequential, transitory, transitional or saving provision as the Secretary of State considers appropriate.

(6) A statutory instrument containing an order under this section is subject to annulment in pursuance of a resolution of either House of Parliament.'

(6) After section 188A (as inserted by subsection (5) above) insert—

'188B Defences to commission of cartel offence

(1) In a case where the arrangements would (operating as the parties intend) affect the supply in the United Kingdom of a product or service, it is a defence for an individual charged with an offence under section 188(1) to show that, at the time of the making of the agreement, he or she did not intend that the nature of the arrangements would be concealed from customers at all times before they enter into agreements for the supply to them of the product or service.

(2) It is a defence for an individual charged with an offence under section 188(1) to show that, at the time of the making of the agreement, he or she did not intend that the nature of the arrangements would be concealed from the CMA.

(3) It is a defence for an individual charged with an offence under section 188(1) to show that, before the making of the agreement, he or she took reasonable steps to ensure that the nature of the arrangements would be disclosed to professional legal advisers for the purposes of obtaining advice about them before their making or (as the case may be) their implementation.'

(7) After section 190 of the 2002 Act insert—

'190A Cartel offence: prosecution guidance

(1) The CMA must prepare and publish guidance on the principles to be applied in determining, in any case, whether proceedings for an offence under section 188(1) should be instituted.

(2) The CMA may at any time issue revised or new guidance.

(3) Guidance published by the CMA under this section is to be published in such manner as it considers appropriate.

(4) In preparing guidance under this section the CMA must consult—
(a) the Director of the Serious Fraud Office;
(b) the Lord Advocate; and
(c) such other persons as it considers appropriate.'

(8) The amendments made by subsections (1) to (6) apply only in relation to agreements falling within section 188(1) of the 2002 Act which—
(a) are made after the commencement of this section, and
(b) relate to arrangements made or to be made after that commencement.

ANNEX III

Diagrammatical Representation of the Social Harm Due to Cartel Activity

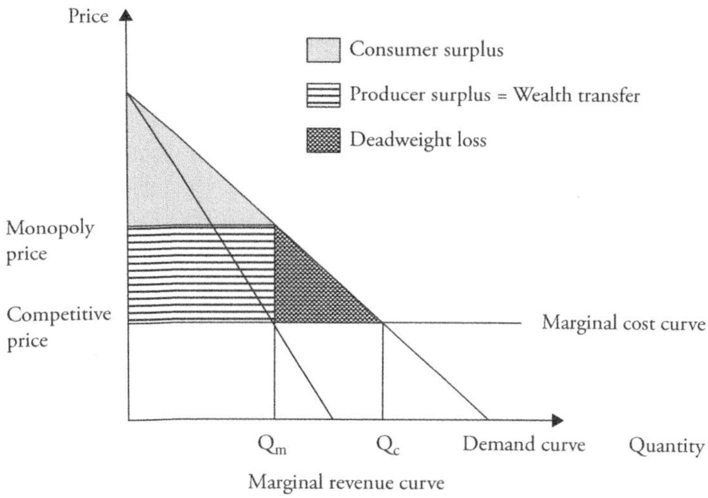

Source: Akman (2012).

Bibliography

ABA Section of Antitrust Law (2011), *Competition Laws Outside the United States*, American Bar Association, Chicago.

ABA Section of Antitrust Law (2009), *Model Jury Instructions in Criminal Antitrust Cases*, American Bar Association, Chicago.

Abrantes-Metz, R. and Sokol, D. (2013), 'Antitrust Corporate Governance and Compliance', Minnesota Legal Studies Research Paper No. 13-18, April 2013, <http://papers.ssrn.com/sol3/papers.cfm?abstract_id=2246564>.

Adler, J. (1997), 'Lying, Deceiving or Falsely Implicating' (1997) 94 *Journal of Philosophy* 435.

Akman, P. (2012), *The Concept of Abuse in EU Competition Law: Law and Economic Approaches*, Hart Publishing, Oxford.

Akman, P. (2010a), 'The European Commission's Guidance on Article 102 TFEU: From *Inferno* to *Paradiso*?' (2010) 73(4) *Modern Law Review* 605.

Akman, P. (2010b), 'Consumer versus Customer: The Devil in the Detail' (2010) 37(2) *Journal of Law and Society* 315.

Akman, P. (2009), 'Searching for the Long-Lost Soul of Article 82 EC' (2009) 29(2) *Oxford Journal of Legal Studies* 267.

Akman, P. (2006), 'Article 82 Reformed? The EC Discussion Paper on Exclusionary Abuses' [2006] *Journal of Business Law* 816.

Albaek, S. (2013), 'Consumer Welfare in EU Competition Policy', in Heide-Jorgensen, C., Bergqvist, C., Neergaard, U., and Troels Poulsen, S. (eds), *Aims and Values in Competition Law*, DJØF Publishing, Copenhagen.

Albors-Llorens, A. (2006), 'Horizontal Agreements and Concerted Practices in EC Competition Law: Unlawful and Legitimate Contacts between Competitors' (2006) 51(4) *Antitrust Bulletin* 837.

Alexander, L. and Sherwin, E. (2003), 'Deception in Morality and Law' (2003) 22 *Law and Philosophy* 393.

Alfter, M. and Young, J. (2005), 'Economic Analysis of Cartels—Theory and Practice' (2005) 26(10) *European Competition Law Review* 546.

Allen, F. (1981), 'The Morality of Means: Three Problems in Criminal Sanctions' (1981) 42 *University of Pittsburgh Law Review* 737.

Alvey, J. (1999), 'A Short History of Economics as a Moral Science' (1999) 2(1) *Journal of Markets and Morality* 53.

Ameye, E. (2004), 'The Interplay between Human Rights and Competition Law in the EU' (2004) 25(6) *European Competition Law Review* 332.

Andenaes, J. (1974), *Punishment and Deterrence*, University of Michigan Press, Ann Arbor, Michigan.

Anderson, J.L. (1999), 'Annulment Retribution: A Hegelian Theory of Punishment' (1999) 5 *Legal Theory* 363.

Andreangeli, A. (2012), 'Competition Law and Human Rights: Striking a Balance between Business Freedom and Regulatory Intervention', in Lianos, I. and Sokol, D. (eds), *The Global Limits of Competition Law*, Stanford University Press, Stanford.

Andreangeli, A. (2008), *EU Competition Enforcement and Human Rights*, Edward Elgar Publishing, Cheltenham.

Andreangeli, A. (2006), 'The Impact of the Modernisation Regulation on the Guarantees of Due Process in Competition Proceedings' (2006) 31(3) *European Law Review* 342.

Andrews, P. (2002), '"Modernisation"—Irish Style' (2002) 23(9) *European Competition Law Review* 469.

Arbault, F. (2003), 'La Politique de la Commission en Matière d'Amendes Antitrust: Recent Développements, Perspectives d'Avenir' [2003] 2 *Competition Policy Newsletter* 1.

Arlen, J. (1994), 'The Potentially Perverse Effects of Corporate Criminal Liability' (1994) 23 *Journal of Legal Studies* 833.

Arp, D.J. and Swaak, C. (2002), 'A Tempting Offer: Immunity from Fines for Cartel Conduct Under the European Commission's New Leniency Notice' (2002) 16 *Antitrust* 59.

Asch, P. and Seneca, J. (1975), 'Characteristics of Collusive Firms' (1975) 23(3) *Journal of Industrial Economics* 223.

Ashurst (2004), 'Study on the Conditions of Claims for Damages in Case of Infringement of EC Competition Rules', Brussels, 31 August 2004, <http://ec.europa.eu/competition/antitrust/actionsdamages/comparative_report_clean_en.pdf>.

Ashworth, A. (2009), *Principles of Criminal Law*, 6th edn, Oxford University Press, Oxford.

Ashworth, A. (2008), 'Conceptions of Overcriminalization' (2008) 5 *Ohio State Journal of Criminal Law* 407.

Ashworth, A. (2005), *Sentencing and Criminal Justice*, Cambridge University Press, Cambridge.

Ashworth, A. (2004), *Principles of Criminal Law*, 4th edn, Oxford University Press, Oxford.

Ashworth, A. (2000), 'Is the Criminal Law a Lost Cause?' (2000) 116 *Law Quarterly Review* 225.

Ashworth, A. (1989), 'Criminal Justice and Deserved Sentences' [1989] *Criminal Law Review* 340.

Ashworth, A. and Redmayne, M. (2010), *The Criminal Process*, 4th edn, Oxford University Press, Oxford.

Aubert, C. (2009), 'Managerial Effort Incentives and Market Collusion', Toulouse School of Economics Working Paper No. 09-127, December 2009.

Aubert, C., Rey, P., and Kovacic, W. (2006), 'The Impact of Leniency and Whistle-Blowing Programmes on Cartels' (2006) 24(6) *International Journal of Industrial Organization* 1241.

Audretsch, D. (1989), 'Legalized Cartels in West Germany' (1989) 34(3) *Antitrust Bulletin* 579.

Australian Industry Group (2002), 'Submission to Committee of Enquiry into the Competition Provisions of the Trade Practices Act 1974, and their Administration', Public Submission 109, Trade Practices Act Review.

Aylward, G. (2007), 'Crime and Punishment: Custodial Sentences for Hard Core Cartels: An Ideological Revolution in Embryonic Form', Thesis, College of Europe, Bruges.

Ayres, I. and Braithwaite, J. (1992), *Responsive Regulation: Transcending the Deregulation Debate*, Oxford University Press, Oxford.

Bacik, I. (2004), 'Criminal Law', in Kilkelly, U. (ed.), *ECHR and Irish Law*, Jordans, Bristol.

Bagaric, M. and Amarasekara, K. (2000), 'The Errors of Retributivism' (2000) 24 *Melbourne University Law Review* 124.

Bailey, D. (2009), 'Common Concepts of Competition Law', in Adams, J., Aitman, D., Lever, J., and Allan, B. (eds), *Butterworths Competition Law Service*, LexisNexis Butterworths, London.

Bailin, A. (2011), 'Doing Away with Dishonesty' (2011) 10(3) *Competition Law Journal* 169.

Baker, D. (2012), 'Deterring Cartels—The Criminalization Dimension', 15th Annual Irish European Law Forum, Dublin, 23 March 2012.

Baker, D. (2011), 'Punishment for Cartel Participants in the US: A Special Model?', in Beaton-Wells, C. and Ezrachi, A. (eds), *Criminalising Cartels: A Critical Interdisciplinary Study of an International Regulatory Movement*, Hart Publishing, Oxford.

Baker, D. (2009), 'An Enduring Antitrust Divide across the Atlantic Over Whether to Incarcerate Conspirators and When to Restrain Abusive Monopolists' (2009) 5(1) *European Competition Journal* 145.

Baker, D. (2004), 'Revisiting History—What Have We Learned About Private Antitrust Enforcement That We Would Recommend To Others?' (2004) 16(4) *Loyola Consumer Law Review* 379.

Baker, D. (2001), 'The Use of Criminal Law Remedies to Deter and Punish Cartels and Bid-Rigging' (2001) 69 *George Washington Law Review* 693.

Baker, D. (1981), 'To Make the Penalty Fit the Crime: How to Sentence Antitrust Felons, Remarks before the Tenth New England Antitrust Conference', 20 November 1977, published in Clabault, J. and Block, M. (eds), *Sherman Act Indictments, 1955–1980*, Federal Legal Publications, New York.

Baker, D. (1978), 'To Indict or Not to Indict: Prosecutorial Discretion in Sherman Act Enforcement' (1978) 63 *Cornell Law Review* 405.

Baker, D. and Reeves, B. (1977), 'The Paper Label Sentences: Critique' (1977) 86 *Yale Law Journal* 619.

Baker, E. (1998), 'Taking European Criminal Law Seriously' [1998] *Criminal Law Review* 361.

Baker, J. (2000–01), 'New Horizons in Cartel Detection' (2000–01) 69 *George Washington Law Review* 824.

Ball, H. and Friedman, L. (1964), 'The Use of Criminal Sanctions in the Enforcement of Economic Legislation' (1964) 17 *Stanford Law Review* 197.

Banks, C. (2004), *Criminal Justice Ethics: Theory and Practice*, SAGE Publications Inc., Los Angeles.

Barennes, M. and Wolf, G. (2011), 'Cartel Recidivism in the Mirror of EU Case Law' (2011) 2(5) *Journal of European Competition Law & Practice* 423.

Barnett, B. (2009), 'Criminalization of Cartel Conduct—The Changing Landscape', Joint Federal Court of Australia/Law Council of Australia (Business Law Section) Workshop, Adelaide, 3 April 2009.

Barnett, T. (2007), 'Global Antitrust Enforcement', Georgetown Law Global Antitrust Enforcement Symposium, Washington DC, 26 September 2007.

Barnett, T. (2006a), 'Criminal Enforcement Of Antitrust Laws: The U.S. Model', Fordham Competition Law Institute's Annual Conference on International Antitrust Law and Policy, New York, 14 September 2006.

Barnett, T. (2006b), 'Seven Steps to Better Cartel Enforcement', 11th Annual EU Competition Law & Policy Workshop, European Union Institute, Florence, 2 June 2006.

Baucus, M. and Near, J. (1991), 'Can Illegal Corporate Behavior Be Predicted? An Event History Analysis' (1991) 34 *Academy of Management Journal* 9.

Bauer, J. (2004), 'Reflections on the Manifold Means of Enforcing the Antitrust Laws: Too Much, Too Little, or Just Right?' (2004) 16 *Loyola Consumer Law Review* 303.

Bean, P. (1981), *Punishment: A Philosophical and Criminological Inquiry*, Martin Robertson, Oxford.

Beard, D. (2003), 'The Cartel Criminal Offence' (2003) 2(2) *Competition Law Journal* 156.

Beaton-Wells, C. (2013), 'The ACCC Immunity Policy for Cartel Conduct: Due for Review', Melbourne Legal Studies Research Paper No. 654, Melbourne Law School, 4 May 2013.

Beaton-Wells, C. (2012), 'Criminal Sanctions for Cartels—The Jury is Still Out', in Ezrachi, A. (ed.), *Research Handbook on International Competition Law*, Edward Elgar Publishing, Cheltenham.

Beaton-Wells, C. (2009), 'Australia's Criminalization of Cartels—Will It Be Contagious?', 4th ASCOLA Conference, More Common Ground for International Competition Law?, Washington, 16–17 June 2009.

Beaton-Wells, C. (2008a), 'The Politics of Cartel Criminalisation: A Pessimistic View from Australia' (2008) 29(3) *European Competition Law Review* 185.

Beaton-Wells, C. (2008b), 'Criminalising Cartels: Australia's Slow Conversion' (2008) 31 *World Competition* 205.

Beaton-Wells, C. (2007), 'Capturing the Criminality of Hard Core Cartels: The Australian Proposal' (2007) 31(3) *Melbourne University Law Review* 675.

Beaton-Wells, C. and Ezrachi, A. (eds) (2011a), *Criminalising Cartels: A Critical Interdisciplinary Study of an International Regulatory Movement*, Hart Publishing, Oxford.

Beaton-Wells, C. and Ezrachi, A. (2011b), 'Criminalising Cartels: Why Critical Studies?', in Beaton-Wells, C. and Ezrachi, A. (eds), *Criminalising Cartels: A Critical Interdisciplinary Study of an International Regulatory Movement*, Hart Publishing, Oxford.

Beaton-Wells, C. and Fisse, B. (2011a), 'US Policy and Practice in Pursuing Individual Accountability for Cartel Conduct: A Preliminary Critique' (2011) 56(2) *Antitrust Bulletin* 277.

Beaton-Wells, C. and Fisse, B. (2011b), *Australian Cartel Regulation: Law, Policy and Practice in an International Context*, Cambridge University Press, Cambridge.

Beaton-Wells, C. and Fisse, B. (2008a), 'Criminal Cartels: Individual Liability and Sentencing', 6th Annual University of South Australia Trade Practices Workshop, 17–18 October 2008.

Beaton-Wells, C. and Fisse, B. (2008b), 'Criminalising Serious Cartel Conduct: Issues of Law and Policy' (2008) 36 *Australian Business Law Review* 166.

Beaton-Wells, C. and Fisse, B. (2008c), 'The Australian Criminal Cartel Regime: A Model for New Zealand?', Legal Studies Research Paper No. 413, Melbourne Law School, 2 August 2008.

Beaton-Wells, C. and Haines, F. (2010), 'The Australian Conversion: How the Case for Cartel Criminalisation Was Made' (2010) 1 *New Journal of European Criminal Law* 499.

Beaton-Wells, C. and Haines, F. (2009), 'Making Cartel Conduct Criminal: A Case Study of Ambiguity in Controlling Business Behaviour' (2009) 42(2) *The Australian and New Zealand Journal of Criminology* 218.

Beaton-Wells, C., Haines, F., Parker, C., and Platania-Phung, C. (2010), 'Report on a Survey of the Australian Public Regarding Anti-Cartel Law and Enforcement', Melbourne Law School, December 2010.

Beaton-Wells, C. and Parker, C. (2013), 'Justifying Criminal Sanctions for Cartel Conduct: A Hard Case' (2013) 1(1) *Journal of Antitrust Enforcement* 198.

Beccaria, C. (1767), *On Crimes and Punishment*, Cambridge University Press, Cambridge, 1995 (first published in English in 1767).

Beckenstein, A. and Landis-Gabel, H. (1982), 'Antitrust Compliance: Results of a Survey of Legal Opinion' (1982) 52 *Antitrust Law Journal* 459.

Becker, G., Grossman, M., and Murphy, K. (1991), 'Rational Addiction and the Effect of Price on Consumption' (1991) 81(2) *American Economic Review* 237.

Becker, G. and Murphy, K. (1988), 'A Theory of Rational Addiction' (1988) 9 *Journal of Political Economy* 675.

Becker, G. (1978), *The Economic Approach to Human Behavior*, University of Chicago Press, Chicago.

Becker, G. (1968), 'Crime and Punishment: An Economic Approach' (1968) 76 *Journal of Political Economy* 169.

Benjamin, V. (2006), 'The Application of EC Competition Law and the European Convention on Human Rights' (2006) 27(12) *European Competition Law Review* 693.

Benn, S.I. (1958), 'An Approach to the Problems of Punishment' (1958) 33 *Philosophy* 325.

Bennett, B. (2009), 'Criminalization of Cartel Conduct: The Changing Landscape', Joint Federal Court of Australia/Law Council of Australia (Business Law Section) Workshop, Adelaide, Australia, 3 April 2009, <http://www.justice.gov/atr/public/speeches/247824.htm#N_1>.

Bentham, J. (1789), *Introduction to the Principle of Morals and Legislation*, Oxford University Press, Oxford, 1996 (first published in 1789).

Bentham, J. (1838), 'The Principles of Penal Law', in Bowring, J. (ed.), *The Works of Jeremy Bentham*, Thoemmes Continuum, Bristol, 1997 (first published in 1838).

Berghe, P. and Dawes, A. (2009), '"Little Pig, Little Pig, Let Me Come In": An Evaluation of the European Commission's Powers of Inspection in Competition Cases' (2009) 30(9) *European Competition Law Review* 407.

Berman, M. (2007), 'On the Moral Structure of White Collar Crime' (2007) 5(1) *Ohio State Journal of Criminal Law* 301.

Bernstein, A. (2005), 'Whatever Happened to Law and Economics?' (2005) 64 *Maryland Law Review* 303.

Berra, S. (2012), 'Prison Made Mandatory for Canadian Antitrust Convicts', Global Competition Review, 21 November 2012, <http://globalcompetitionreview.com/news/article/32590/prison-made-mandatory-canadian-antitrust-convicts/>.

Beyleveld, D. (2000), 'Deterrence Research and Deterrence Policies', in Ashworth, A. and von Hirsch, A. (eds), *Principled Sentencing: Readings on Theory and Policy*, Hart Publishing, Oxford.

Billiet, P. (2009), 'How Lenient is the EC Leniency Policy? A Matter of Certainty and Predictability' (2009) 30(1) *European Competition Law Review* 14.

BIS (2013a), *Private Actions in Competition Law: A Consultation on Options for Reform—Government Response*, January 2013.

BIS (2013b), *Competition Regime: Draft Secondary Legislation—Part Two*, September 2013.

BIS (2012), *Growth Competition and the Competition Regime: Government Response to Consultation*, March 2012.

BIS (2011), *A Competition Regime for Growth: A Consultation on Options for Reform*, March 2011.

Bishop, S. and Walker, M. (2010), *The Economics of EC Competition Law: Concepts, Application and Measurement*, 3rd edn, Sweet & Maxwell, London.

Black, O. (2010), *Conceptual Foundations of Antitrust*, Cambridge University Press, Cambridge.

Blair, C. and Conway, L. (2002), *Enterprise Bill (Bill 115 of 2001–02) Commons Library Research Paper*, Research Paper 02/21, House of Commons, 4 April 2002.

Blair, R. (1985), 'A Suggestion for Improved Antitrust Enforcement' (1985) 30(2) *Antitrust Bulletin* 433.

Blake, S. (2008), 'Criminal and Civil Cartel Enforcement: Issues and Challenges for Advisors and Authorities—Perspective of the Authority' (2008) 7(1) *Competition Law Journal* 9.

Blanco, L.O. (ed.) (2006), *EC Competition Procedure*, 2nd edn, Oxford University Press, Oxford.

Block, M. and Sidak, J. (1980), 'The Cost of Antitrust Deterrence: Why Not Hang a Price Fixer Every Now and Then?' (1980) 68 *Georgetown Law Journal* 1131.

Bloom, M. (2007), 'Despite Its Great Success, the EC Leniency Program Faces Great Challenges', in Ehlermann, C.D. and Atanasiu, I. (eds), *European Competition Law Annual 2006: Enforcement of Prohibition of Cartels*, Hart Publishing, Oxford.

Bloom, M. (2005), 'The Great Reformer: Mario Monti's Legacy in Article 81 and Cartel Policy' (2005) 1(1) *Competition Policy International* 55.

Bloom, M. (2004), 'Exchange of Confidential Information Among Members of the EU Network of Competition Authorities: Possible Consequences of a Relatively Broad Scope for Exchange of Confidential Information on National Procedural Law and Antitrust Rules', in Ehlermann, C.D. and Atanasiu, I. (eds), *European Competition Law Annual 2002: Constructing the EU Network of Competition Authorities*, Hart Publishing, Oxford.

Bloom, M. (2002a), 'Key Challenges in Public Enforcement', British Institute of International and Comparative Law, London, 17 May 2002.

Bloom, M. (2002b), 'Response: A Significant Step Forward: The UK Criminalization Initiative' (2002) 17 *Antitrust* 59.

Boberg, A. (2010), 'Fixing the Price at Liberty: The Case for Imprisoning Price-Fixers in New Zealand' (2010) 16 *Auckland University Law Review* 81.

Bolotova, Y. and Connor, J. (2008), 'Cartel Sanctions: An Empirical Analysis', 3 April 2008, <http://papers.ssrn.com/sol3/papers.cfm?abstract_id=1116421>.

Boonin, D. (2008), *The Problem of Punishment*, Cambridge University Press, New York.

Bork, R. (1966), 'Legislative Intent and the Policy of the Sherman Act' (1966) 9 *Journal of Law and Economics* 7.

Boskovits, K. (2010), 'Modernization and the Role of National Courts: Institutional Choices, Power Relations, and Substantive Implications', in Lianos, I. and Kokorris, I. (eds), *The Reform of EC Competition Law: New Challenges*, Kluwer Law International, Amsterdam.

Böge, U. and Bardong, A. (2008), 'Article 3: Relationship between Articles 81 and 82 of the Treaty and National Competition Laws', in Hirsch, G., Montag, F., and Jürgen Säcker, F. (eds), *Competition Law: European Community Practice and Procedure—Article-by-Article Commentary*, Sweet & Maxwell, London.

Braithwaite, J. (1989), *Crime, Shame and Reintegration*, Cambridge University Press, Cambridge.

Braithwaite, J. and Makkai, T. (1991), 'Testing an Expected Utility Model of Corporate Deterrence' (1991) 25 *Law and Society Review* 7.

Branch, S. (2013), 'Enforcement Investigations—Now and Under the New Regime', Law Society Evening Session, Competition Section, 2 July 2013.

Brandenburger, R. (2012a), 'Intensification of International Cooperation: The Antitrust Division's Recent Efforts', The American Chamber of Commerce, Brussels, 17 February 2012.

Brandenburger, R. (2012b), 'The Many Facets of International Cooperation at the Antitrust Division', International Bar Association's Midyear Conference, Madrid, 15 June 2012.

Brandenburger, R. (2012c), 'International Cooperation: Taking a Broader View', 29th American Chamber of Commerce Annual EU Competition Policy Conference, Brussels, 6 December 2012.

Brannman, L. and Klein, J.D. (1992), 'The Effectiveness and Stability of Highway Bid-Rigging', in Audretsch, D. and Siegfried, J. (eds), *Empirical Studies in Industrial Organization: Essays in Honor of Leonard W. Weiss*, Kluwer Academic Publishers, Dordrecht.

Braum, S. (2012), 'Taking a Chance on Per Se Cartel Crime?' (2012) 3(2) *New Journal of European Criminal Law* 112.

Breathnach, S. (2013), 'Sweetening the Carrot: The Role of Leniency Programmes in the Fight Against Cartels' (2013) 34(1) *European Competition Law Review* 12.

Breit, W. and Elzinga, K. (1989), *The Antitrust Casebook: Milestones in Economic Regulation*, Dryden, New York.

Breit, W. and Elzinga, K. (1986), *Antitrust Penalty Reform: An Economic Analysis*, American Enterprise Institute for Public Policy Research, Washington DC.

Breit, W. and Elzinga, K. (1976), *The Antitrust Penalties*, Yale University Press, New Haven, CT.

Brenchley, F. (2003), *Allan Fels: A Portrait of Power*, Wiley-Blackwell, Brisbane.

Brenner, S. (2009), 'An Empirical Study of the European Corporate Leniency Policy' (2009) 27 *International Journal of Industrial Organization* 639.

Brickey, K. (1982), 'Criminal Liability of Corporate Officers for Strict Liability Offences—Another View' (1982) 35(6) *Vanderbilt Law Review* 1337.

Brisimi, V. and Ioannidou, M. (2011), 'Criminalizing Cartels in Greece: A Tale of Hasty Developments and Shaky Grounds' (2011) 34(1) *World Competition* 157.

Broadbridge, S. (2009), *Recent Developments Concerning Juries*, SN/HA/2876, House of Commons Library, Home Affairs Section, 19 May 2009.

Bromberg, W. (1965), *Crime and the Mind: A Psychiatric Analysis of Crime and Punishment*, Macmillan Company, New York.

Brunt, M. (1990), '"Market Definition" Issues in Australian and New Zealand Trade Practices Litigation' (1990) 18 *Australian Business Law Review* 86.

Bryant, P. and Eckhard, E. (1991), 'Price-Fixing: The Probablity of Getting Caught' (1991) 73(3) *Review of Economics and Statistics* 531.

Buccirossi, G. and Spagnolo, P. (2005), 'Optimal Fines in the Era of Whistleblowers—Should Price Fixers Still Go To Prison?', Lear Research Paper No. 05-01, 12 December 2005, <http://papers.ssrn.com/sol3/papers.cfm?abstract_id=871726>.

Bucy, P. (1991), 'Indemnification of Corporate Executives Who Have Been Convicted of Crimes: An Assessment and Proposal' (1991) 24 *Indiana Law Review* 279.

Bunzel, R. and Miller, H. (2009), 'Defending "Last Man Standing": Trench Lessons from the 2008 Criminal Antitrust Trial *United States v. Swanson*', *Antitrust Source*, June 2009.

Burns, J. (1958), *A Study of the Antitrust Laws, Their Administration, Interpretation and Effect*, Central Book Company, New York.

Bussmann, K. (2003), 'Causes of Economic Crime and the Impact of Values: Business Ethics as a Crime Prevention Measure', November 2003, <http://bussmann2.jura.uni-halle.de/econcrime/Bussmann2003-Causes_of_EconCrime.pdf>.

Buxton, R. (2000), 'The Human Rights Act and the Substantive Criminal Law' [2000] *Criminal Law Review* 331.

Cairns Committee (1955), *Collective Discrimination: A Report on Exclusive Dealing, Collective Boycotts, Aggregated Rebates and Other Discriminatory Trade Practices*, Cmd 9505.

Calkins, S. (2007), 'Coming to Praise Criminal Antitrust Enforcement', in Ehlermann, C.D. and Atanasiu, I. (eds), *European Competition Law Annual 2006: Enforcement of Prohibition of Cartels*, Hart Publishing, Oxford.

Calkins, S. (1997), 'Corporate Compliance and the Antitrust Agencies' Bi-Modal Penalties' (1997) 60 *Law and Contemporary Problems* 127.

Calvani, T. (2006), 'Cartel Penalties and Damages in Ireland: Criminalization and the Case for Custodial Sentences', in Cseres, K., Schinkel, M. P., and Vogelaar, F. (eds), *Criminalization of Competition Law Enforcement: Economic and Legal Implications for the EU Member States*, Edward Elgar Publishing, Cheltenham.

Calvani, T. (2005), 'Conflict, Cooperation, and Convergence in International Competition' (2005) 72 *Antitrust Law Journal* 1127.

Calvani, T. (2004a), 'Enforcement of Cartel Law in Ireland', in Hawk, B. (ed.), *Annual Proceedings of the Fordham Corporate Law Institute 2003*, Juris Publishing Inc., New York.

Calvani, T. (2004b), 'Competition Penalties and Damages in a Cartel Context: Criminalisation and the Case for Custodial Sentences', Irish Centre for European Law, 13 December 2004.

Calvani, T. (2003), 'Devolution and Convergence in Competition Enforcement' (2003) 24(9) *European Competition Law Review* 415.

Calvani, T. and Calvani, T.H. (2011), 'Cartel Sanctions and Deterrence' (2011) 56(2) *Antitrust Bulletin* 185.

Calvani, T. and Calvani, T.H. (2009), 'Custodial Sanctions for Cartel Offences: An Appropriate Sanction in Australia?' (2009) 17 *Competition and Consumer Law Journal* 119.

Calvani, T. and Carl, K. (2013), 'The Competition Act 2002, Ten Years Later: Lessons from the Irish Experience of Prosecuting Cartels as Criminal Offences' (2013) 1(2) *Journal of Antitrust Enforcement* 296.

Camilli, E.L. (2006), 'Optimal Fines in Cartel Cases and the Actual EC Fining Policy' (2006) 2(4) *World Competition* 575.

Cane, P. (2002), *Responsibility in Law and Morality*, Hart Publishing, Oxford.

Canenbley, C. and Steinvorth, T. (2011), 'Effective Enforcement of Competition Law: Is There a Solution to the Conflict Between Leniency Programmes and Private Damages Actions?' (2011) 2(4) *Journal of European Competition Law & Practice* 315.

Capel, T. (2007), 'To What Extent are Criminal Sanctions for Infringements of Articles 81 and 82 EC Necessary or Appropriate and is there a Case and a Basis for Criminalisation of Articles 81 and 82 at an EC Level?', winner of the LSEG Horsfall Turner Essay Competition 2007, 30 October 2007 (copy in the possession of the author).

Carlton, D. (2007), 'Does Antitrust Need to be Modernized?' (2007) 21(3) *Journal of Economic Perspectives* 155.

Carlton, D. and Perloff, M. (2005), *Modern Industrial Organization*, 4th edn, Pearson, Boston.

Carmeliet, T. (2011–12), 'How Lenient is the European Leniency System? An Overview of Current (Dis)incentives to Blow the Whistle' (2011–12) 48(3) *Jura Falconis Jg* 463.

Caruso, A. (2010), 'Leniency Programmes and the Protection of Confidentiality: The Experience of the European Commission' (2010) 1(6) *Journal of European Competition Law & Practice* 453.

Cass, R. and Hylton, K. (2000–01), 'Antitrust Intent' (2000–01) 74 *Southern California Law Review* 657.

Castle, L. and Writer, S. (2002), 'More Than a Little Wary: Applying the Criminal Law to Competition Regulation in Australia' (2002) 10 *Competition and Consumer Law Journal* 1.

Cauffman, C. (2011a), 'The Interaction of Leniency Programmes and Actions for Damages' (2011) 7(2) *Competition Law Review* 181.

Cauffman, C. (2011b), 'Access to Leniency-Related Documents after *Pfleiderer*' (2011) 34(4) *World Competition* 597.

Cavanagh, E. (2005), 'Antitrust Remedies Revisited' (2005) 84 *Oregon Law Review* 147.

Chadwell, J. (1955), 'Antitrust Administration and Enforcement' (1955) 53 *Michigan Law Review* 1133.

Chambers, D., Davies, G., and Monti, G. (2010), *European Union Law*, 2nd edn, Cambridge University Press, Cambridge.

Chemtob, S. (2000), 'Antitrust Deterrence in the United States and Japan', Conference on Competition Policy in the Global Trading System: Perspectives from Japan, the United States, and the European Union, Washington DC, 23 June 2000, <http://www.usdoj.gov/atr/public/speeches/5076.pdf>.

Clarke, J. (2012), 'The Increasing Criminalization of Economic Law—A Competition Law Perspective' (2012) 19(1) *Journal of Financial Crime* 76.

Clarke, J. (2005), 'Criminal Penalties for Contraventions of Part IV of the Trade Practices Act' (2005) 10(1) *Deakin Law Review* 141.

Clarke, J. and Bagaric, M. (2003), 'The Desirability of Criminal Penalties for Breaches of Part IV of the Trade Practices Act' (2003) 31 *Australian Business Law Review* 192.

Clements, L., Mole, N., and Simmonds, A. (1999), *European Human Rights: Taking a Case under the Convention*, 2nd edn, Sweet & Maxwell, London.

Clough, M. (2003), 'Problems of Criminalisation', in Hutchings, M. and Andenas, M. (eds), *Competition Law Yearbook 2002*, British Institute of International and Comparative Law, London.

Coase, R. (1992), 'The Institutional Structure of Production' (1992) 82 *American Economic Review* 713.

Coffee, J. (1992), 'Paradigms Lost: The Blurring of the Criminal and Civil Law Models—And What Can Be Done About It' (1992) 101 *Yale Law Journal* 1875.

Coffee, J. (1991), 'Does "Unlawful" Mean "Criminal"?: Reflections on the Disappearing Tort/Crime Distinction in American Law' (1991) 71 *Boston University Law Review* 193.

Coffee, J. (1981), '"No Soul to Damn: No Body to Kick": An Unscandalised Inquiry into the Problem of Corporate Punishment' (1981) 79 *Michigan Law Review* 387.

Coffee, J. (1980), 'Corporate Crime and Punishment: A Non-Chicago View of the Economics of Criminal Sanctions' (1980) 17 *American Criminal Law Review* 419.

Cohen, M. (1989), 'The Role of Criminal Sanctions in Antitrust Enforcement' (1989) 7(4) *Contemporary Policy Issues* 36.

Cohen, M. and Scheffman, D. (1989–90), 'The Antitrust Sentencing Guideline: Is the Punishment Worth the Costs?' (1989–90) 27 *American Criminal Law Review* 331.

Collins, P. and Eatrides, V. (2003), 'An Analysis of the Proposal to Decriminalize the Anti-Competitive Pricing Practices under the Competition Act' (2003) 26(3) *World Competition* 381.

Combe, E. and Monnier, C. (2011), 'Fines Against Hard Core Cartels in Europe: The Myth of Over-Enforcement' (2011) 56(2) *Antitrust Bulletin* 235.

Combe, E., Monnier, C., and Legal, R. (2008), 'Cartels: The Probability of Getting Caught', Bruges European Economic Research Papers, Paper 12, March 2008, <http://www.coleurope.eu/sites/default/files/research-paper/beer12.pdf>.

Comino, V. (2006), 'Civil or Criminal Penalties for Corporate Misconduct: Which Way Ahead?' (2006) 34 *Australian Business Law Review* 428.

Committee of Ministers of the Council of Europe (2000), *The Role of Public Prosecution in the Criminal Justice System*, Recommendation Rec(2000)19, 6 October 2000.

Committee of Ministers of the Council of Europe (1987), *Recommendation No. R (87)18 of the Committee of Ministers to Member States Concerning the Simplification of Criminal Justice*, 17 September 1987.

Commonwealth Director of Public Prosecutions (1992), *Prosecution Policy of the Commonwealth* (as amended in March 2009).
Competition and Mergers Review Group (2000), *Report of the Competition and Mergers Review Group*, March 2000, Dublin.
Conley, J.M. and O'Barr, W.M. (1997), 'Crime and Custom in Corporate Society: A Cultural Perspective on Corporate Misconduct' (1997) 60 *Law and Contemporary Problems* 5.
Connor, J. (2013), 'Cartel Fine Severity and the European Commission' (2013) 34(2) *European Competition Law Review* 58.
Connor, J. (2011), 'Problems with Prison in International Cartel Cases' (2011) 56(2) *Antitrust Bulletin* 311.
Connor, J. (2010), 'Recidivism Revealed: Private International Cartels 1990–2009' (2010) 6(2) *Competition Policy International* 101.
Connor, J. (2007a), *Studies in Industrial Organisation: Global Price Fixing*, 2nd edn, Springer, New York.
Connor, J. (2007b), 'Overcharges: Legal and Economic Evidence' (2007) 22 *Research in Law and Economics* 59.
Connor, J. (2006), 'Optimal Deterrence and Private International Cartels', Purdue University, Working Paper.
Connor, J. (2004), 'Price-Fixing Overcharges: Legal and Economic Evidence', American Antitrust Institute ('AAI') Working Paper No. 04-05, November 2004, <http://papers.ssrn.com/sol3/papers.cfm?abstract_id=1103516>.
Connor, J. (2003), 'Private International Cartels: Effectiveness, Welfare and Anti-Cartel Enforcement', Staff Paper No. 03-12, Department of Agricultural Economics, Purdue University, 5 November 2003.
Connor, J. (2001), 'Global Price Fixing: Our Customers are the Enemies' (2001) 24 *Studies in Industrial Organization*, <http://ssrn.com/abstract=287638>.
Connor, J. and Bush, D. (2008), 'How to Block Cartel Formation and Price Fixing: Using Extraterritorial Application of the Antitrust Laws as a Deterrence Mechanism', 29 March 2008, <http://papers.ssrn.com/sol3/papers.cfm?abstract_id=1156469>.
Connor, J. and Helmers, C. (2007), 'Statistics on Modern Private International Cartels, 1990–2005', American Antitrust Institute, Working Paper No. 07-01.
Connor, J. and Lande, R. (2012), 'Cartels as Rational Business Strategy: Crime Pays' (2012) 34 *Cardozo Law Review* 427.
Connor, J. and Lande, R. (2005), 'How High Do Cartels Raise Prices? Implications for Optimal Cartel Fines' (2005) 80 *Tulane Law Review* 513.
Connor, J. and Miller, D. (2013), 'Determinants of EC Antitrust Fines for Members of Global Cartels', 6 March 2013, <http://ssrn.com/abstract=2229358>.
Connor, J. and Miller, D. (2010), 'Determinants of EC Antitrust Fines for Members of Global Cartels', ESRC Centre for Competition Policy, University of East Anglia, 18 February 2010.
Connor, J., Foer, A., and Udwin, S. (2010), 'Criminalizing Cartels: An American Perspective' (2010) 1(2) *New European Journal of Competition Law* 199.
Connor, S. (2009), 'Sexes Differ over Dishonesty Says New Study', *The Guardian*, 7 September 2009.
Cooper, K. and Dedjinou, A. (2005), 'Antitrust Violations' (2005) 42 *American Criminal Law Review* 179.
Cooter, R. (1984), 'Prices and Sanctions' (1984) 84 *Columbia Law Review* 1523.
Cooter, R. and Ulen, T. (2004), *Law and Economics*, Pearson Addison Wesley, US.
Corker, D. (2011), 'Redefining the Criminal Cartel Offence' (2011) 10(10) *Competition Law Insight* 14.
Corker, D. and Smith, A. (2007), 'Cartels: Who's Liable?' (2007) 157 *New Law Journal* 1593.
Costello, P. (2005), 'Criminal Penalties for Serious Cartel Behaviour', Press Release from the Treasurer of Australia, 2 February 2005.

Council of the European Communities (1986), Council Regulation (EEC) No. 4056/86 of 22 December 1986 Laying Down Detailed Rules for the Application of Articles 85 and 86 of the Treaty to Maritime Transport, [1986] OJ L378/1.

Council of the European Economic Community (1962), Regulation 17/62 of 6 February 1962: First Regulation Implementing Articles 85 and 86 of the Treaty, [1962] OJ 13/204.

Council of the European Union (2013), Proposal for a Directive of the European Parliament and of the Council on Certain Rules Governing Actions for Damages under National Law for Infringements of the Competition Law Provisions of the Member States and of the European Union—Adoption of the General Approach, 17317/13, Brussels, 3 December 2013.

Council of the European Union (2004), Council Regulation (EC) No. 139/2004 of 20 January 2004 on the Control of Concentrations Between Undertakings (the EC Merger Regulation), [2004] OJ L124/1.

Council of the European Union (2003), Council Regulation (EC) No. 1/2003 of 16 December 2002 on the Implementation of the Rules on Competition Laid Down in Articles 81 and 82 of the Treaty, [2003] OJ L1/1.

Council of the European Union (2002), Council Framework Decision 2002/584/JHA of 13 June 2002 on the European Arrest Warrant and the Surrender Procedures between Member States, [2002] OJ L190/1.

Cowan, A. (1992), 'Scarlet Letters for Corporations? Punishment by Publicity under the New Sentencing Guidelines' (1992) 65 *Southern California Law Review* 2387.

Craig, P. and De Búrca, G. (2011), *EU Law—Text, Cases and Materials*, 5th edn, Oxford University Press, Oxford.

Crane, D. (2007), 'Antitrust Modesty' (2007) 105 *Michigan Law Review* 1193.

Craycraft, C., Craycraft, J., and Gallo J. (1997), 'Antitrust Sanctions and a Firm's Ability to Pay' (1997) 12 *Review of Industrial Organisation* 171.

Cseres, K. (2007), 'Multi-Jurisdictional Competition Law Enforcement: The Interface between European Competition Law and the Competition Laws of the New Member States' (2007) 3(2) *European Competition Journal* 465.

Cseres, K., Schinkel, M. P., and Vogelaar, F. (eds) (2006a), *Criminalization of Competition Law Enforcement: Economic and Legal Implications for the EU Member States*, Edward Elgar Publishing, Cheltenham.

Cseres, K., Schinkel, M. P., and Vogelaar, F. (2006b), 'Law and Economics of Criminal Antitrust Enforcement: An Introduction', in Cseres, K., Schinkel, M. P., and Vogelaar, F. (eds), *Criminalization of Competition Law Enforcement: Economic and Legal Implications for the EU Member States*, Edward Elgar Publishing, Cheltenham.

Curcio, A.A. (1996), 'Painful Publicity—An Alternative Punitive Damage Sanction' (1996) 45 *DePaul Law Review* 341.

Curtis, M. and McNally, J. (2007), 'The Classic Cartel—Hatchback Sentence?' (2007) 4(1) *Competition Law Review* 41.

Daboub, A., Rasheed, A., Priem, R., and Gray, D. (1995), 'Top Management Team Characteristics and Corporate Illegal Activity' (1995) 20 *Academy of Management Review* 138.

Daly, K. (2007), 'Cartels and Deterrence—Creeping Criminalisation and the Class Action Boom' (2007) 1(2) *Bloomberg European Business Law Journal* 315.

Danagher, L. (2013), 'Criminal Cartels: A Lesson in Restricting Harmonisation' (2013) 6(1) *Global Competition Litigation Review* 18.

Danagher, L. (2012), 'The Criminalisation of Cartels: A European and Trans-Atlantic Perspective' (2012) 33(11) *European Competition Law Review* 522.

Dan-Cohen, M. (1984), 'Decision Rules and Conduct Rules: On Acoustic Separation in Criminal Law' (1984) 97 *Harvard Law Review* 625.

Darbishire, A. (2007), 'Aspects of the Section 188 Cartel Offence', Central Law Training Conference, 27 February 2007.

Darbyshire, P. (2000), 'The Mischief of Plea Bargaining and Sentencing Rewards' [2000] *Criminal Law Review* 895.

Davies, M., Croall, H., and Tyrer, J. (2010), *Criminal Justice*, 4th edn, Pearson, Harlow.

Dawes, A. and Lynskey, O. (2008), 'The Ever-Loner Arm of EC Law: The Extension of Community Competence into the Field of Criminal Law' (2008) 45 *Common Market Law Review* 140.

De, O. (2010), 'Analysis of Cartel Duration: Evidence from EC Prosecuted Cartels' (2010) 17(1) *Journal of the Economics of Business* 33.

Dean, N. (2003), 'Creating a Stir' (2003) 153 *New Law Journal* 910.

de Broca, H. (2006), 'The Commission Revises Its Guidelines for Setting Fines in Antitrust Cases' [2006] 3 *Competition Policy Newsletter* 2.

Dekeyser, K. (2005), 'Q & A on Modernisation', Global Competition Review, February 2005.

de la Serre, E.B. and Lagathu, E. (2013), 'The Law on Fines Imposed in EU Competition Proceedings: Faster, Higher and Harsher' (2013) 4(4) *Journal of European Competition Law & Practice* 325.

de la Serre, E.B. and Winckler, C. (2012), 'A Landmark Year for the Law on Fines Imposed in EU Competition Proceedings' (2012) 3(4) *Journal of European Competition Law & Practice* 351.

de la Torre, F.C. (2010), 'The 2006 Guidelines on Fines: Reflections on the Commission's Practice' (2010) 33(3) *World Competition* 359.

Denvil, W.J. (2010), 'What Happens to Executives Who Are Sanctioned for Their Involvement in Cartels?', <http://www.cardozolawreview.com/content/34-2/Connor.Lande.34.2/DenvilStudy.pdf>.

De Smijter, E. and Kjølbye, L. (2007), 'The Enforcement System under Regulation 1/2003', in Faull, J. and Nikpay, A. (eds), *The EC Law of Competition*, 2nd edn, Oxford University Press, Oxford.

Diamond, J. (1996), 'The Myth of Morality and Fault in Criminal Law Doctrine' (1996) 34 *American Criminal Law Review* 111.

Diaz, F.E.G., Kirk, D., Flores, F.P., and Verkleij, C. (1999), 'Horizontal Agreements', in Faull, J. and Nikpay, A. (eds), *The EC Law of Competition*, Oxford University Press, Oxford.

DiMento, J. (1989), 'Can Social Science Explain Organizational Noncompliance and Environmental Law?' (1989) 45(1) *Journal of Social Issues* 109.

Dixon, M. (2012), 'A Tension in the US Approach to International Cartel Enforcement: At What Point Does Aggressive Pursuit of Individuals Undercut the Corporate Leniency Program?' (2012) 8(1) *Competition Law International* 82.

Dobbin, C. and Peretz, C. (2005), 'The Cartel Offence', in Ward, T. and Smith, K. (eds), *Competition Litigation in the UK*, Sweet & Maxwell, London.

DoJ (1994), *Leniency Policy for Individuals*, US Department of Justice, 10 August 1994, <http://www.usdoj.gov/atr/public/guidelines/0092.pdf>.

DoJ (1993), *Corporate Leniency Policy*, US Department of Justice, 10 August 1993, <http://www.usdoj.gov/atr/public/guidelines/0091.pdf>.

DoJ and INS (1996), *Memorandum of Understanding Between the Antitrust Division United States Department of Justice and the Immigration and Naturalization Service United States Department of Justice*, 15 March 1996.

Dougan, M. (2012), 'From the Velvet Glove to the Iron Fist: Criminal Sanctions for the Enforcement of Union Law', in Cremona, M. (ed.), *Compliance and the Enforcement of EU Law*, Oxford University Press, Oxford.

Dressler, J. (2001), *Understanding Criminal Law*, Lexis Publishing, New York.

DTI (2001a), *Peer Review of the UK Competition Policy Regime*, prepared for DTI by PricewaterhouseCoopers, 18 April 2001, <http://www.berr.gov.uk/files/file32812.pdf>.

DTI (2001b), *A World Class Competition Regime*, Cm 5233, July 2001.

DTI (2001c), *'Productivity and Enterprise—A World Class Competition Regime': Government's Response to Consultation*, December 2001.

Duff, A. (2001), *Punishment, Communication and Community*, Oxford University Press, Oxford.

Duff, A. (1999), 'Punishment, Communication and Community', in Matravers, M. (ed.), *Punishment and Legal Theory*, Hart Publishing, Oxford.

Duff, A. and Garland, D. (1994), 'Introduction: Thinking about Punishment', in Duff, A. and Garland, D. (eds), *A Reader on Punishment*, Oxford University Press, Oxford.

Duncan, J. (1953), 'The "Big Case"—When Tried Criminally' (1953) 4 *Western Reserve Law Review* 99.

Dunphy, P. (2007), 'Variable Geometry Europe—Patching Together What Works in the Fight Against Hard-Core Cartels: Carrots, Sticks, Custody and Leniency', February 2007, <http://papers.ssrn.com/sol3/papers.cfm?abstract_id=1024983>.

Dworkin, R. (1977), *Taking Rights Seriously*, Harvard University Press, Cambridge, MA.

Easterbrook, F. (2003), 'When Is It Worthwhile to Use Courts to Search for Exclusionary Conduct?' [2003] 2 *Columbia Business Law Review* 345.

Easterbrook, F. (1985), 'Detrebling Antitrust Damages' (1985) 28 *Journal of Law and Economics* 445.

Easterbrook, F. (1983), 'Criminal Procedure as a Market System' (1983) 12(2) *Journal of Legal Studies* 289.

Easton, S. and Piper, C. (2005), *Sentencing and Punishment: The Quest for Justice*, Oxford University Press, Oxford.

ECN (2012a), 'Protection of Leniency Material in the Context of Civil Damages Actions', Resolution of the Meeting of Heads of the European Competition Authorities, 23 May 2012, <http://ec.europa.eu/competition/ecn/leniency_material_protection_en.pdf>.

ECN (2012b), *ECN Model Leniency Programme*, as revised in November 2012, <http://ec.europa.eu/competition/ecn/mlp_revised_2012_en.pdf>.

Edghill, K. (2011), 'Is the UK Cartel Offence Dead or Is There a Problem with Immunity?: The Role of Immunity as a Prosecutorial Tool in Criminal Cartel Offences in the United Kingdom and Australia', 9th Annual University of South Australia Competition and Consumer Workshop, Adelaide, 15 October 2011.

Ehlermann, C.D. (2006), 'Criminal Competition Law Enforcement: Taking Stock on the Debate', in Cseres, K., Schinkel, M. P., and Vogelaar, F. (eds), *Criminalization of Competition Law Enforcement: Economic and Legal Implications for the EU Member States*, Edward Elgar Publishing, Cheltenham.

Ehlermann, C.D. and Atanasiu, I. (eds) (2003), *European Competition Law Annual 2001: Effective Private Enforcement of EC Antitrust Law*, Hart Publishing, Oxford.

Elliott, D. (1982), 'Dishonesty in Theft: A Dispensable Concept' [1982] *Criminal Law Review* 395.

Ellison, J. (2011), 'Individual Deterrence and Competition Disqualification Orders' (2011) 10(1) *Competition Law Journal* 65.

Elzinga, K. and Breit, W. (1973), 'Antitrust Penalties and Attitudes Toward Risk: An Economic Analysis' (1973) 86 *Harvard Law Review* 693.

European Commission (2013a), Proposal for a Directive of the European Parliament and of the Council on Certain Rules Governing Actions for Damages under National Law for Infringements of the Competition Law Provisions of the Member States and of the European Union—Explanatory Memorandum, Strasbourg, 11 June 2013, COM(2013) 404 final, 2013/0185 (COD).

European Commission (2013b), Proposal for a Directive of the European Parliament and of the Council on Certain Rules Governing Actions for Damages under National Law for Infringements of the Competition Law Provisions of the Member States and of the European Union, Strasbourg, 11 June 2013, COM(2013) 404 final, 2013/0185 (COD).

European Commission (2013c), *DG Competition Management Plan 2013*, Brussels, <http://ec.europa.eu/atwork/synthesis/amp/doc/comp_mp_en.pdf>.

European Commission (2012), 'Antitrust: Commission Fines Producers of TV and Computer Monitor Tubes € 1.47 Billion for Two Decade-Long Cartels', Press Release, IP/12/1317, 5 December 2012.

European Commission (2011a), Public Consultation—Towards a Coherent European Approach to Collective Redress, SEC(2011) 173 final, Brussels, 4 February 2011.

European Commission (2011b), Towards an EU Criminal Policy: Ensuring the Effective Implementation of EU Policies through Criminal Law, COM(2011) 573 final, Brussels, 20 September 2011.

European Commission (2011c), '*National Grid v. ABB*: Observations of the European Commission Pursuant to Article 15(3) of Regulation 1/2003', 3 November 2011, <http://ec.europa.eu/competition/court/amicus_curiae_2011_national_grid_en.pdf>.

European Commission (2010a), *DG Competition Management Plan 2010*, Brussels, 12 May 2010, <http://ec.europa.eu/competition/publications/annual_ management_plan/amp_2010_en.pdf>.

European Commission (2010b), Commission Regulation (EU) No. 1217/2010 of 14 December 2010 on the Application of Article 101(3) of the Treaty on the Functioning of the European Union to Certain Categories of Research and Development Agreements, [2010] OJ L335/36.

European Commission (2010c), Commission Regulation (EU) No. 1218/2010 of 14 December 2010 on the Application of Article 101(3) of the Treaty on the Functioning of the European Union to Certain Categories of Specialisation Agreements, [2010] OJ L335/43.

European Commission (2009a), Communication from the Commission—Guidance on the Commission's Enforcement Priorities in Applying Article 82 of the EC Treaty to Abusive Exclusionary Conduct by Dominant Undertakings, C(2009) 864 final, Brussels, 9 February 2009.

European Commission (2009b), Communication from the Commission to the European Parliament and the Council—Report on the Functioning of Regulation 1/2003, COM(2009) 206 final, Brussels, 29 April 2009.

European Commission (2009c), Commission Staff Working Paper Accompanying the Communication from the Commission to the European Parliament and the Council—Report on the Functioning of Regulation 1/2003, SEC(2009) 574 final, Brussels, 29 April 2009.

European Commission (2008a), White Paper—Damages Actions for Breach of the EC Antitrust Rules, COM(2008) 165 final, Brussels, 2 April 2009.

European Commission (2008b), Commission Staff Working Paper Accompanying the White Paper—Damages Actions for Breach of the EC Antitrust Rules, SEC(2008) 404, Brussels, 2 April 2009.

European Commission (2006a), Guidelines on the Method of Setting Fines Imposed Pursuant to Article 23(2)(a) of Regulation No. 1/2003, [2006] OJ C210/02.

European Commission (2006b), Commission Notice on Immunity from Fines and Reduction of Fines in Cartel Cases, [2006] OJ C298/17.

European Commission (2005a), DG Competition's Reply to Questions Raised by the Swedish Competition Authority with Regard to SOU 2004:131, Brussels, 29 April 2005.

European Commission (2005b), Communication from the Commission to the European Parliament and the Council on the Implications of the Court's Judgment of 13 September 2005 (Case C-176/03, *Commission v. Council*), COM(2005) 583 final/2, Brussels, 24 November 2005.

European Commission (2005c), Green Paper—Damages Actions for Breach of the EC Antitrust Rules, COM(2005) 672 final, Brussels, 19 December 2005.

European Commission (2005d), Commission Staff Working Paper—Annex to the Green Paper—Damages Actions for Breach of the EC Antitrust Rules, COM(2005) 672 final, Brussels, 19 December 2005.

European Commission (2005e), DG Competition Discussion Paper on the Application of Article 82 of the Treaty to Exclusionary Abuses, Brussels, December 2005.

European Commission (2004a), Commission Notice on Cooperation within the Network of Competition Authorities, [2004] OJ C101/03.

European Commission (2004b), Guidelines on the Effect on Trade Concept Contained in Articles 81 and 82 of the Treaty, [2004] OJ C101/07.

European Commission (2004c), Guidelines on the Application of Article 81(3) of the Treaty, [2004] OJ C101/08.

European Commission (2001a), *XXXIst Report on Competition Policy*, Office for Official Publications of the European Communities, Luxembourg.

European Commission (2001b), Commission Notice on Agreements of Minor Importance Which Do Not Appreciably Restrict Competition under Article 81(1) of the Treaty Establishing the European Community (De Minimis), [2001] OJ C368/07.

European Commission (2000), Proposal for a Council Regulation on the Implementation of the Rules on Competition Laid Down in Articles 81 and 82 of the Treaty and Amending Regulations (EEC) No. 1017/68, (EEC) No. 2988/74, (EEC) No. 4056/86 and (EEC) No. 3975/87, COM(2000) 582 final, Brussels, 27 September 2000.

European Commission (1998), Guidelines on the Method of Setting Fines Imposed Pursuant to Article 15(2) of Regulation No. 17 and Article 65(5) of the ECSC Treaty, [1998] OJ C9/3

European Commission (1997), Commission Notice on the Definition of Relevant Market for the Purposes of Community Competition Law, [1997] OJ C372/5

European Commission (1995), *XXVth Report on Competition Policy*, Brussels.

European Commission (1983), *XIIIth Report on Competition Policy*, Brussels.

European Commission (1980), *Xth Report on Competition Policy*, Brussels.

Evans, S. and Lundman, R. (1983), 'Newspaper Coverage of Corporate Price-Fixing' (1983) 21 *Criminology* 529.

Evenett, S., Levenstein, M., and Suslow, V. (2001), 'International Cartel Enforcement: Lessons from the 1990s' (2001) 24 *World Economy* 1221.

Evrigenis, D. (1982), 'Recent Case-Law of the European Court of Human Rights under Article 8 and 10 of the ECHR' (1982) 3 *Human Rights Law Journal* 121.

Ezrachi, A. and Kindl, J. (2011), 'Cartels as Criminal? The Long Road from Unilateral Enforcement to International Consensus', in Beaton-Wells, C. and Ezrachi, A. (eds), *Criminalising Cartels: A Critical Interdisciplinary Study of an International Regulatory Movement*, Hart Publishing, Oxford.

Fallon, R. (1997), '"The Rule of Law" as a Concept in Constitutional Discourse' (1997) 97 *Columbia Law Review* 1.

Farmer, S. (2013), 'Real Crime: Criminal Competition Law' (2013) 9(3) *European Competition Journal* 599.

Farmer, S. (2008), 'State Criminal Antitrust Enforcement', Penn State Legal Studies Research Paper No. 10-2008, 4 August 2008, <http://papers.ssrn.com/sol3/papers.cfm?abstract_id=1207582>.

Farrell, J. and Katz, M. (2006), 'The Economics of Welfare Standards in Antitrust' (2006) 2(2) *Competition Policy International* 3.

Fehr, E. and Fischbacher, U. (2004), 'Social Norms and Human Cooperation' (2004) 8(4) *Trends in Cognitive Sciences* 185.

Feinberg, J. (1984), *The Moral Limits of the Criminal Law: Harm to Others*, Oxford University Press, Oxford.

Feinberg, J. (1970), *Doing and Deserving: Essays in the Theory of Responsibility*, Princeton University Press, Princeton, NJ.

Feinberg, R. (1985), 'The Enforcement and Effects of European Competition Policy: Results of a Survey of Legal Opinion' (1985) 23 *Journal of Common Market Studies* 373.

Fels, A. (2002), 'The Trade Practices Act and World's Best Practice: Proposals for Criminal Penalties for Hard-Core Collusion', Current Issues In Regulation: Enforcement and Compliance, University of South Australia, Melbourne, 2–3 September 2002.

Fingleton, J. (2003), 'Criminal Enforcement—The Irish Experience', in Hutchings, M. and Andenas, M. (eds), *Competition Law Yearbook 2002*, British Institute of International and Comparative Law, London.

Fingleton, J. (2002), 'Speech by The Chairperson of the Competition Authority, John Fingleton, on the Commencement of the Competition Act 2002', Dublin, 1 July 2002.

Fingleton, J., Girard, M.B., and Williams, S. (2007), 'The Fight against Cartels: Is a "Mixed" Approach to Enforcement the Answer?', in Hawk, B. (ed.), *International Antitrust Law & Policy: Fordham Corporate Law 2006*, Juris Publishing, New York.

Finnis, J. (1980), *Natural Law and Natural Rights*, Clarendon Press, Oxford.

Finnis, J. (1972), 'Meaning and Ambiguity in Punishment (and Penology)' (1972) 10 *Osgoode Hall Law Journal* 1.

First, H. (2001), 'The Vitamins Case: Cartel Prosecutions and the Coming of International Competition Law' (2001) 68 *Antitrust Law Journal* 711.

Fisse, B. (2009), 'Recent OFT Decisions Illustrate Fundamental Flaws in UK Cartel Law', <http://www.brentfisse.com/images/Fisse_Recent_OFT_Cartel_Decisions_041009.pdf>.

Fisse, B. (2008), 'Defining the Australian Cartel Offences: Disaster Recovery', Competition Law Conference, Sydney, 24 May 2008, <http://www.brentfisse.com/images/Fisse_Defining_the_Australian_Cartel_Offences_240608.pdf>.

Fisse, B. (2007a), 'The Cartel Offence: Dishonesty?' (2007) 35 *Australian Business Law Review* 235.

Fisse, B. (2007b), 'The Australian Cartel Criminalisation Proposals: An Overview and Critique' (2007) 4(1) *Competition Law Review* 51.

Fisse, B. (1983), 'Reconstructing Corporate Criminal Law: Deterrence, Retribution, Fault, and Sanctions' (1983) 56 *Southern California Law Review* 1141.

Fisse, B. and Braithwaite, J. (1993), *Corporations, Crime and Accountability*, Cambridge University Press, Cambridge.

Fisse, B. and Braithwaite, J. (1983), *The Impact of Publicity on Corporate Offenders*, State University of New York Press, Albany, NY.

Fitzgerald, P. (1960), 'A Concept of Crime' [1960] *Criminal Law Review* 257.

Fitzpatrick, P. (2010), 'The British Jury: An Argument for the Reconstruction of the Little Parliament' (2010) 6(1) *Cambridge Student Law Review* 1.

Flynn, J. (1967), 'Criminal Sanctions under State and Federal Antitrust Law' (1967) 45 *Texas Law Review* 1301.

Foer, A. (2006), 'The Goals of Antitrust: Thoughts on Consumer Welfare in the US', in Marsden, P. (ed.), *Handbook of Research in Trans-Atlantic Antitrust*, Edward Elgar Publishing, Cheltenham.

Foer, A. (2003), 'The Third Leg of the Antitrust Stool: What the Business Schools Have to Offer to Antitrust' (2003) 47 *New York Law School Law Review* 21.

Foer, A. and Cuneo, J. (eds) (2010), *The International Handbook on Private Enforcement of Competition Law*, Edward Elgar Publishing, Cheltenham.

Forrester, I. (2011), 'A Challenge for Europe's Judges: The Review of Fines in Competition Cases' (2011) 36(2) *European Law Review* 185.

Forrester, I. (2009), 'Due Process in EC Competition Cases: A Distinguished Institution with Flawed Procedures' (2009) 34(6) *European Law Review* 817.

Fox, E. (2006), 'Cartels: A United States Story, and a Research Programme for the World', in Cseres, K., Schinkel, M. P., and Vogelaar, F. (eds), *Criminalization of Competition Law Enforcement: Economic and Legal Implications for the EU Member States*, Edward Elgar Publishing, Cheltenham.

Francis, A. (2008), 'The Economics of Sexuality: The Effects of HIV/AIDS on Homosexual Behaviour in the United States' (2008) 27(3) *Journal of Health Economics* 675.

Frese, M. (2006), 'The Negative Interplay between National Custodial Sanctions and Leniency', in Cseres, K., Schinkel, M. P., and Vogelaar, F. (eds), *Criminalization of Competition Law Enforcement: Economic and Legal Implications for the EU Member States*, Edward Elgar Publishing, Cheltenham.

Frese, M. (2005), 'Anti-Cartel Enforcement in Community Law Context: Considerations on Sanctions and Leniency', University of Amsterdam/Amsterdam Center for Law and Economics Conference, Amsterdam.

Froeb, L., Koyah, R., and Werden, G. (1993), 'What is the Effect of Bid Rigging on Prices?' (1993) 42 *Economic Letters* 419.

Furse, M. (2012), *The Criminal Law of Competition in the UK and in the US: Failure and Success*, Edward Elgar, Cheltenham, UK and Northampton, MA.

Furse, M. (2011), 'The New Cartel Offence: "Great for a Headline But Not Much Else?"' (2011) 32(5) *European Competition Law* 223.

Furse, M. (2006), 'Issues Relating to the Enforcement and Application of Criminal Laws in Respect of Competition', in Marsden, P. (ed.), *Handbook of Research in Trans-Atlantic Antitrust*, Edward Elgar Publishing, Cheltenham.

Furse, M. and Nash, S. (2004a), *The Cartel Offence*, Hart Publishing, Oxford.

Furse, M. and Nash, S. (2004b), 'Partners in Crime: The Cartel Offence in the UK' (2004) 15(5) *International Company and Commercial Law Review* 138.

Galligan, D. (2007), *Law in Modern Society*, Oxford University Press, Oxford.

Galligan, D. (1981), 'The Return to Retribution in Penal Theory', in Tapper, C. (ed.), *Crime, Proof and Punishment: Essays in Memory of Sir Rupert Cross*, Butterworths, London.

Gallo, J., Dau-Schmidt, K., Craycraft, J., and Parker, C. (1994), 'Criminal Penalties under the Sherman Act: A Study of Law and Economics' (1994) 16 *Research in Law and Economics* 25.

Gamble, R. (2013), 'The Cartel Penumbra: Where Public and Private Enforcement Policies Intersect' (2013) 42 *Common Law World Review* 23.

Gamble, R. (2011), 'Speaking (Formally) with the Enemy' (2011) 32(9) *European Competition Law Review* 449.

Garoupa, N. and Stephen, F. (2006), 'Law and Economics of Plea-Bargaining', July 2006, <http://ssrn.com/abstract=917922>.

Garrett, B. (2011), 'Globalized Corporate Prosecutions' (2011) 97(8) *Virginia Law Review* 1775.

Garzaniti, L., Gudofsky, J., and Moffat, J. (2004–05), 'Dawn of a New Era? Powers of Investigation and Enforcement under Regulation 1/2003' (2004–05) 72 *Antitrust Law Journal* 159.

Gauer, C. (2005), 'Due Process in the Face of Divergent National Procedures and Sanctions', Antitrust Reform in Europe: A Year in Practice Papers, Brussels, 9–11 March 2005.

Gazal-Ayal, O. (2006), 'Partial Ban on Plea Bargains' (2006) 27(5) *Cardozo Law Review* 2295.

Geis, G. (1995), 'The Heavy Electrical Equipment Antitrust Cases of 1961', in Geis, G., Meier, R.F., and Salinger, L.M. (eds), *White Collar Crime*, 3rd edn, Free Press, New York.

Geradin, D. and Henry, D. (2005), 'The EC Fining Policy for Violations of Competition Law: An Empirical Review of the Commission Decisional Practice and the Community Courts' Judgments' (2005) 1(2) *European Competition Journal* 401.

Geradin, D., Layne-Farrar, A., and Petit, N. (2012), *EU Competition Law and Economics*, Oxford University Press, Oxford.

Gerber, D.J. (2001), *Law and Competition in Twentieth Century Europe: Protecting Prometheus*, Oxford University Press, Oxford.

Gerla, H. (1988), 'A Micro-Microeconomic Approach to Antitrust Law: Games Managers Play' (1988) 86 *Michigan Law Review* 892.

Gert, B. (1988), *Morality: A New Justification of the Moral Rules*, Oxford University Press, New York.

Ginsburg, D. and Wright, J. (2010), 'Antitrust Sanctions' (2010) 6(2) *Competition Policy International* 3.

Gippini-Fournier, E. (2010), 'The Elusive Standard of Proof in EU Competition Cases' (2010) 33(2) *World Competition* 187.

Girardet, P. (2010), '"What If Uncle Sam Wants You?": Principles and Recent Practice Concerning US Extradition Requests in Cartel Cases' (2010) 1(4) *Journal of European Competition Law & Practice* 286.

Glaeser, E. and Sacerdote, B. (2000), 'The Social Consequences of Housing', National Bureau of Economic Research Working Paper No. 8034, December 2000, <http://www.nber.org/papers/w8034>.

Gneezy, U. and Rustichini, A. (2004), 'Incentives, Punishment, and Behavior', in Camerer, C., Loewenstein, C., and Rabin, M. (eds), *Advances in Behavioral Economics*, Princeton University Press, Princeton, NJ.

Goeters, H. (2007), *New Criminal Law Developments in the Community Legal Order*, Swedish Institute for European Policy Studies, Stockholm, February.

Gomien, D. (2005), *Short Guide to the European Convention on Human Rights*, Council of Europe, Strasbourg.

Gordon, M. (2010), 'Criminalisation of Cartel Conduct—Can Commercial Competition Litigators Become Criminal Defence Lawyers? Are Pre-Trial and Trial Issues Different in Criminal Proceedings and, If So, How Might They Be Dealt With?', October 2010, <http://www.fedcourt.gov.au/publications/judges-speeches/justice-gordon/Gordon-J-201010.pdf>.

Gorecki, P. and Maxwell, S. (2013a), 'The US and Ireland Approach to Sentencing in Cartel Cases: The *Citroen* Case', ESRI Working Paper No. 447, January 2013.

Gorecki, P. and Maxwell, S. (2013b), 'Sentencing in Criminal Cartel Cases in Ireland: The *Duffy* Judgment' (2013) 34(5) *European Competition Law Review* 239.

Gorecki, P. and Maxwell, S. (2013c), 'Alternative Approaches to Sentencing in Cartel Cases: The European Union, Ireland and the United States' (2013) 9(2) *European Competition Journal* 341.

Gorecki, P. and McFadden, D. (2006), 'Criminal Cartels in Ireland: The Heating Oil Case' (2006) 27(11) *European Competition Law Review* 631.

Gotting, S. and Lampert, T. (2003), 'Opening Shot for Criminalisation of German Competition Law? Federal High Court Judgment Simplifies Options for Prosecuting Competition Law Violations as Fraud under German Penal Code' (2003) 24(1) *European Competition Law Review* 30.

Grannon, E. and Kownacki, N. (2012), 'Are Antitrust Violations Crimes Involving Moral Turpitude?' (2012) 36(3) *The Champion* 40.

Grasmick, H. and Bursik, R. (1990), 'Conscience, Significant Others, and Rational Choice: Extending the Deterrence Model' (1990) 24 *Law and Society Review* 837.

Gray, A. (2008), 'Criminal Sanctions for Cartel Behaviour' (2008) 8(2) *Queensland University of Technology Law and Justice Journal* 364.

Gray, G. (2006), 'The Regulation of Corporate Violations: Punishment, Compliance, and the Blurring of Responsibility' (2006) 46 *British Journal of Criminology* 875.

Green, S. (2006), *Lying, Cheating, and Stealing: A Moral Theory of White-Collar Crime*, Oxford University Press, Oxford.

Green, S. (2004), 'Moral Ambiguity in White Collar Criminal Law' (2004) 18 *Notre Dame Journal of Law, Ethics and Public Policy* 501.

Green, S. (1997), 'Why It's a Crime to Tear a Tag off a Mattress: Overcriminalization and the Moral Content of Regulatory Offences' (1997) 46 *Emory Law Journal* 1535.

Greenfield, K. (2002), 'Using Behavioural Economics to Show the Power and Efficiency of Corporate Law as Regulatory Tool' (2002) 35 *University of California Davis Law Review* 581.

Greer, S. (2006), *The European Convention on Human Rights—Achievements, Problems and Prospects*, Cambridge University Press, Cambridge.

Griffin, J. (2000), 'An Inside Look at a Cartel at Work: Common Characteristics of International Cartels', American Bar Association, Section of Antitrust Law, 48th Annual Spring Meeting, Washington DC, 6 April 2000.

Guersent, O. (2004), 'The Fight against Secret Horizontal Agreement in the EC Competition Policy', in Hawk, B. (ed.), *Annual Proceedings of the Fordham Corporate Law Institute 2003*, Juris Publishing Inc., New York.

Günster, A., Carree, M., and van Dijk, M.A. (2012), 'Do Cartels Undermine Economic Efficiency?', December 2011, <http://www.aeaweb.org/aea/2012conference/program/retrieve.php?pdfid=510>.

Guy, D. (2006), 'The UK's Experience with Criminal Law Sanctions', in Cseres, K., Schinkel, M. P., and Vogelaar, F. (eds), *Criminalization of Competition Law Enforcement: Economic and Legal Implications for the EU Member States*, Edward Elgar Publishing, Cheltenham.

Haines, F. and Beaton-Wells, C. (2012), 'Ambiguities in Criminalising Cartels: A Political Economy' (2012) 52 *British Journal of Criminology* 953.

Hakopian, G. (2010), 'Criminalisation of EU Competition Law Enforcement—A Possibility after Lisbon?' (2010) 7(1) *Competition Law Review* 157.

Hall, J. (1960), *General Principles of Criminal Law*, Bobbs-Merrill, Indianapolis, IN.

Hall, R. and Lieberman, M. (2007), *Microeconomics: Principles and Applications*, Cengage Learning, Mason, OH.

Halpin, A. (1996), 'The Test for Dishonesty' [1996] *Criminal Law Review* 283.

Hamilton, L. and Scott, P. (2013), *Guide to Competition Law*, LexisNexis, Wellington, NZ.

Hammond, S. (2010), 'The Evolution of Criminal Antitrust Enforcement over the Last Two Decades', 24th National Institute on White Collar Crime, Miami, Florida, 25 February 2010.

Hammond, S. (2007), 'Preface: US Department of Justice', in Arquit, K., Buhart, J., and Antoine, O. (eds), *Leniency Regimes*, 2nd edn, European Lawyer, London.

Hammond, S. (2006), 'The US Model of Negotiated Plea Agreements: A Good Deal with Benefits for All', OECD Competition Committee, Working Party No. 3, Paris, 17 October 2006.

Hammond, S. (2004), 'Cornerstones of an Effective Leniency Program', ICN Workshop on Leniency Programs, Sydney, Australia, 22–3 November 2004.

Hammond, S. and Barnett, B. (2008), 'Frequently Asked Questions Regarding the Antitrust Division's Leniency Program and Model Leniency Letters', 19 November 2008, <http://www.justice.gov/atr/public/criminal/239583.htm>.

Hampton, J. (1991), 'A New Theory of Retribution', in Frey, R.G. and Morris, C.W. (eds), *Liability and Responsibility: Essays in Law and Morals*, Cambridge University Press, Cambridge.

Hansen, M., Crocco, L., and Kennedy, S. (2012), 'Challenges to International Cartel Enforcement and Multi-Jurisdictional Leniency Applications—Disclosure of Leniency Applicant Statements and Materials', ABA International Cartel Workshop, Vancouver, 1–3 February 2012.

Harding, C. (2012), 'Hard Core Cartel Conduct as Crime: The Justification for Criminalisation in the European Context' (2012) 3(2) *New Journal of European Criminal Law* 138.

Harding, C. (2011a), 'Cartel Deterrence: The Search for Evidence and Argument' (2011) 56(2) *Antitrust Bulletin* 345.

Harding, C. (2011b), 'Recidivism, Criminalisation and the Growth of the Anti-Cartel Enforcement Industry', in Beaton-Wells, C. and Ezrachi, A. (eds), *Criminalising Cartels: A Critical Interdisciplinary Study of an International Regulatory Movement*, Hart Publishing, Oxford.

Harding, C. (2010), 'A Pathology of Business Cartels: Original Sin or the Child of Regulation?' (2010) 1 *New Journal of European Criminal Law* 44.

Harding, C. (2006), 'Business Collusion as a Criminological Phenomenon: Exploring the Global Criminalisation of Business Cartels' (2006) 14 *Critical Criminology* 181.

Harding, C. (2004), 'Forging the European Cartel Offence: The Supranational Regulation of Business Conspiracy' (2004) 12 *European Journal of Crime, Criminal Law and Criminal Justice* 275.

Harding, C. (2002), 'Business Cartels as Criminal Activity: Reconciling North American and European Models of Regulation' (2002) 9(4) *Maastricht Journal of European and Comparative Law* 393.

Harding, C. and Banach-Gutierrez, J.B. (2012), 'The Emergent EU Criminal Policy: Identifying the Species' (2012) 37(6) *European Law Review* 758.

Harding, C. and Joshua, J. (2010), *Regulating Cartels in Europe*, 2nd edn, Oxford University Press, Oxford.

Harding, C. and Joshua, J. (2002), 'Breaking Up the Hard Core: The Prospects for the Proposed Cartel Offence' [2002] *Criminal Law Review* 933.

Harford, T. (2008), *The Logic of Life—Uncovering the New Economics of Everything*, Little, Brown & Co., London.

Harker, M. (2011), 'Antitrust Law and Administrability: Consumer Versus Total Welfare' (2011) 34(3) *World Competition* 433.

Harrington, J. (2006), 'Behavioral Screening and the Detection of Cartels', 11th Annual EU Competition Law and Policy Workshop, European University Institute, Florence, 2–3 June 2006, <http://www.econ.jhu.edu/People/Harrington/Florence.pdf>.

Harris, D.J., O'Boyle, M., and Warbrick, C. (1995), *Law of the European Convention on Human Rights*, London, Butterworths.

Harrison, G. and Bell, M. (2005–06), 'Recent Enhancements in Antitrust Criminal Enforcement: Bigger Sticks and Sweeter Carrots' (2005–06) 6 *Houston Business and Tax Law Journal* 206.

Hart, H.L.A. (1968), *Punishment and Responsibility*, Clarendon Press, Oxford.

Hart, H.L.A. (1959–60), 'Prolegomenon to the Principles of Punishment' (1959–60) 60 *Proceedings of the Aristotelian Society* 1.

Hart, H. M. (1958), 'The Aims of the Criminal Law' (1958) 23 *Law and Contemporary Problems* 401.

Hawk, B. (ed.) (2007), *International Antitrust Law & Policy: Fordham Corporate Law 2006*, Juris Publishing, New York.

Hawk, B. (ed.) (2004), *Annual Proceedings of the Fordham Corporate Law Institute 2003*, Juris Publishing, New York.

Hayek, F.A. (2008), *The Road to Serfdom*, Routledge, Abingdon, New York, 1944 (reprinted in 2008).

Heimler, A. and Mehta, K. (2012), 'Violations of Antitrust Provisions: The Optimal level of Fines for Achieving Deterrence' (2012) 35 *World Competition* 103.

Henning, P. (2008), 'The DNA of White-Collar Crime' (2008) 11(2) *New Criminal Law Review* 323.

Heyer, K. (2006), 'Welfare Standards and Merger Analysis: Why Not the Best?' (2006) 2(2) *Competition Policy International* 29.

Hirst, M. (2003), *Jurisdiction and the Ambit of the Criminal Law*, Oxford University Press, Oxford.

Hodgekiss, C. (2007), 'Criminalising Cartels: A Slow Conversion? Comments', 5th Annual University of South Australia Trade Practices Workshop, October 2007.

Hoel, A. (2008), 'Crime Does Not Pay But Hard-Core Cartel Conduct May: Why It Should Be Criminalised' (2008) 16 *Trade Practices Law Review* 102.

Holm, C. (2006), 'Competition Law Enforcement in Sweden and in the EU—Present Trends', in Hawk, B. (ed.), *Annual Proceedings of the Fordham Corporate Law Institute 2005*, Juris Publishing, New York.

Honess, T.M. (2002), 'Empirical and Legal Perspectives on the Impact of Pre-Trial Publicity' [2002] *Criminal Law Review* 719.

House of Lords (2006), *The Criminal Law Competence of the European Community*, House of Lords Select Committee on European Union, 42nd Report of Session 2005–06, London.

Hovenkamp, H. (2005a), *The Antitrust Enterprise: Principle and Execution*, Harvard University Press, Cambridge, MA and London.

Hovenkamp, H. (2005b), *Federal Antitrust Policy: The Law of Competition and Its Practice*, 3rd edn, Thompson/West, St Paul, MN.

Hovenkamp, H. (2003), 'Antitrust Violations in Securities Markets' (2003) 28 *Iowa Journal of Corporate Law* 607.

Howse, R. and Daniels, R.J. (1995), 'Rewarding Whistleblowers: Costs and Benefits of an Incentive-Based Compliance Strategy', in Daniels, R. and Morck, R. (eds), *Corporate Decision-Making in Canada*, University of Calgary Press, Calgary.

Hughes, P. (2008), 'Directors' Personal Liability for Cartel Activity under UK and EC Law: A Tangled Web' (2008) 29(11) *European Competition Law Review* 632.

Husak, D. (2004), 'The Criminal Law as Last Resort' (2004) 24 *Oxford Journal of Legal Studies* 207.

Hüschelrath, K. (2010), 'How Are Cartels Detected? The Increasing Use of Proactive Methods to Establish Antitrust Infringements' (2010) 1(6) *Journal of European Competition Law & Practice* 522.

Hutchings, M. and Whelan, P. (2006), 'Consumer Interest in Competition Law Cases' (2006) 16(5) *Consumer Policy Review* 180.

Hviid, M. and Stephan, A. (2009), 'The Graphite Electrodes Cartel: Which Fines Deter?', in Lyons, B. (ed.), *Cases in European Competition Policy—The Economic Analysis*, Cambridge University Press, Cambridge.

Hylton, K. (2003), *Antitrust Law: Economic Theory and Common Law Evolution*, Cambridge University Press, Cambridge.

ICN (2011a), 'ICN Roundtable on Enforcement Cooperation Roundtable Report & Questionnaire Response Summary', Washington DC, 29 March 2011, <http://www.internationalcompetitionnetwork.org/uploads/library/doc793.pdf>.

ICN (2011b), *Compilation of 'Good Practices' from the Anti-Cartel Enforcement Manual of the ICN Cartel Working Group*, Cartel Working Group, Subgroup 2: Enforcement Techniques, April 2011.

ICN (2009), 'Drafting and Implementing an Effective Leniency Program', in ICN, *Anti-Cartel Enforcement Manual*, ICN.

ICN (2007), *Co-operation between Competition Agencies in Cartel Investigations*, Report to the ICN Annual Conference, Moscow, May 2007.

ICN (2005), *Defining Hard Core Cartel Conduct—Effective Institutions, Effective Penalties*, Report Prepared by the ICN Working Group on Cartels, ICN 4th Annual Conference, Bonn, 6–8 June 2005.

ICPAC (2000), *Final Report to the Attorney General and Assistant Attorney General for Antitrust*, International Competition Policy Advisory Committee to the Assistant Attorney General for Antitrust, Antitrust Division, Washington DC.

Jacobs, L. (2007), 'Criminal Enforcement of Antitrust Laws—Problems with the US Model', in Hawk, B. (ed.), *International Antitrust Law & Policy: Fordham Corporate Law 2006*, Juris Publishing, New York.

Jacobs, M. (2010), 'Attack on Cartels as Tip-Offs Climb', *Australian Financial Review*, 18 January 2010.

Janis, M., Kay, R., and Bradley, A. (2008), *European Human Rights Law—Text and Materials*, 3rd edn, Oxford University Press, Oxford.

Jansen, O. (2004), 'The Systems of International Cooperation in Administrative and Criminal Matters in Relation to Regulation EC 1/2003', in Dannecker, G. and Jansen, O. (eds), *Competition Law Sanctioning in the European Union*, Kluwer Law International, The Hague.

Jenny, F. (2011), 'Foreword', in Beaton-Wells, C. and Ezrachi, A. (eds), *Criminalising Cartels: A Critical Interdisciplinary Study of an International Regulatory Movement*, Hart Publishing, Oxford.

Jephcott, M. (2005), *Horizontal Agreements and EU Competition Law*, Richmond Law & Tax Ltd, Richmond.

Jolls, C., Sunstein, C., and Thaler, R. (1998), 'A Behavioral Approach to Law and Economics' (1998) 50 *Stanford Law Review* 147.

Jones, A. and Sufrin, B. (2011), *EU Competition Law: Text, Cases and Materials*, 4th edn, Oxford University Press, Oxford.

Jones, A. and Sufrin, B. (2004), *EC Competition Law: Text, Cases and Materials*, 2nd edn, Oxford University Press, Oxford.

Jones, A. and Sufrin, B. (2001), *EC Competition Law: Text, Cases and Materials*, 1st edn, Oxford University Press, Oxford.

Jones, A. and Williams, R. (2014), 'The UK Response to the Global Effort Against Cartels: Is Criminalization Really the Solution?' (2014) *Journal of Antitrust Enforcement*, forthcoming.

Joshua, J. (2011), 'D.O.A: Can the UK Cartel Offence be Resuscitated?', in Beaton-Wells, C. and Ezrachi, A. (eds), *Criminalising Cartels: A Critical Interdisciplinary Study of an International Regulatory Movement*, Hart Publishing, Oxford.

Joshua, J. (2010), 'Shooting the Messenger: Does the UK Criminal Cartel Offense Have a Future?', *Antitrust Source*, August 2010.

Joshua, J. (2008a), '*Norris v. the United States*: A Stalking Horse for the Cartel Offence?' (2008) 7(2) *Competition Law Insight* 11.

Joshua, J. (2008b), 'Dishonesty After *Norris*' (2008) 7(4) *Competition Law Insight* 13.

Joshua, J. (2008c), 'Implications of *Norris* for UK-US Extradition and Future UK Cartel Prosecutions', *Antitrust Source*, June 2008.

Joshua, J. (2006a), 'The Brave New World of Extradition: A North Atlantic Treaty Alliance Against Cartels', in Marsden, P. (ed.), *Handbook of Research in Transatlantic Antitrust*, Edward Elgar Publishing, Cheltenham.

Joshua, J. (2006b), 'The European Cartel Enforcement Regime Post-Modernization: How Is It Working?' (2006) 13(6) *George Mason Law Review* 1247.

Joshua, J. (2005), 'Extradition: The DOJ's New Foreign Policy Weapon' (2005) 4(10) *Competition Law Insight* 12.

Joshua, J. (2003), 'The UK's New Cartel Offence and Its Implications for EC Competition Law: A Tangled Web' (2003) 28(5) *European Law Review* 620.

Joshua, J. (2002), 'A Sherman Act Bridgehead in Europe, or a Ghost Ship in Mid-Atlantic? A Close Look at the United Kingdom Proposals to Criminalise Hardcore Cartel Conduct' (2002) 23(5) *European Competition Law Review* 231.

Joshua, J. (2001), 'Flawed Thinking About Price Fixers', *Financial Times*, London, 2 August 2001.

Joshua, J. (2000a), 'Leniency in US and EU Cartel Cases' (2000) 14 *Antitrust* 19.

Joshua, J. (2000b), 'The Criminalisation of Antitrust Leniency and Enforcement: The Carrot and the Stick—A View from Europe', International Bar Association, Amsterdam.

Joshua, J. and Camesasca, P. (2004), 'EC Fining Policy against Cartels after the *Lysine* Rulings: The Subtle Secrets of X' [2004] *European Antitrust Review* 5.

Joshua, J., Camesasca, P., and Jung, Y. (2008–09), 'Extradition and Mutual Legal Assistance Treaties: Cartel Enforcement's Global Reach' (2008–09) 75 *Antitrust Law Journal* 353.

Joshua, J. and Jordan, S. (2003–04), 'Combinations, Concerted Practices and Cartels: Adopting the Concept of Conspiracy in European Community Competition Law' (2003–04) 24 *Northwestern Journal of International Law and Business* 647.

Joshua, J. and Klawiter, D. (2002), 'The UK "Criminalization" Initiative' (2002) 16 *Antitrust* 67.

Joyce, J. (1989), 'The Effect of Firm Organizational Structure on Price-Fixing Deterrence' (1989) 7(4) *Contemporary Policy Issues* 19.

Joyce, P. (2013), *Criminal Justice—An Introduction*, 2nd edn, Routledge, London.

Kadish, S. (1963), 'Some Observations on the Use of Criminal Sanctions in Enforcing Economic Regulations' (1963) 30 *University of Chicago Law Review* 423.

Kahan, D. (2000), 'Gentle Nudges vs. Hard Shoves: Solving the Sticky Norms Problem' (2000) 67 *University of Chicago Law Review* 607.

Kahan, D. (1997), 'Social Influence, Social Meaning, and Deterrence' (1997) 83 *University of Virginia Law Review* 349.

Kahan, D. and Posner, E. (1999), 'Shaming White-Collar Criminals: A Proposal for Reform of the Federal Sentencing Guidelines' (1999) 42 *Journal of Law and Economics* 365.

Kalbfleisch, P. (2006), 'Criminal Competition Law Sanctions in the Netherlands', in Cseres, K., Schinkel, M. P., and Vogelaar, F. (eds), *Criminalization of Competition Law Enforcement: Economic and Legal Implications for the EU Member States*, Edward Elgar Publishing, Cheltenham.

Kant, I. (1785), *Foundations of the Metaphysics of Morals*, Liberal Arts Press, New York, 1959 (first published in German in 1785).

Kaplow, L. and Shavell, S. (1994a), 'Why the Legal System Is Less Efficient Than Income Tax in Redistributing Income' (1994) 23 *Journal of Legal Studies* 667.

Kaplow, L. and Shavell, S. (1994b), 'Optimal Law Enforcement with Self-Reporting of Behaviour' (1994) 102 *Journal of Political Economy* 583.

Kar, N., Tsaacs, D., Masterson, J., and Rickards, J. (2008), 'UK: OFT Payments to Whistleblowers—A Step Too Far?' (2008) 2 *Concurrences* 192.

Karier, T. (1985), 'Unions and Monopoly Profits' (1985) 67 *Review of Economics and Statistics* 34.

Kathuria, S. (2007), 'The Bargain Has Been Struck: A Case for Plea Bargaining in India' (2007) 19(2) *Student Bar Review* 55.

Katsoulacos, Y. (2009), 'Some Critical Comments on the Commission's Guidance Paper on Article 82 EC' [2009] 1 *Global Competition Policy*.

Katyal, N. (1997), 'Deterrence's Difficulty' (1997) 95 *Michigan Law Review* 2386.

Katz, M. and Rosen, H. (1998), *Microeconomics*, 3rd edn, McGraw-Hill, Boston.

Kaveny, M.C. (2004), 'Inferring Intention from Foresight' (2004) 120 *Law Quarterly Review* 81.

Kelly, L. (2010), 'The Introduction of a "Cartel Offence" into South African Law' (2010) 21(2) *Stellenbosch Law Review* 321.

Kerber, W. (2008), 'Should Competition Law Promote Efficiency?', in Drexl, J., Idot, L., and Moneger, J. (eds), *Economic Theory and Competition Law*, Edward Elgar Publishing, Cheltenham.

Khan, A. (2012), 'Rethinking Sanctions for Breaching EU Competition Law: Is Director Disqualification the Answer?' (2012) 35(1) *World Competition* 77.

Killick, J. (2008), 'Leniency, Incentives to Lie and Due Process: The Lessons of the *Stolt-Nielsen* Case' (2008) 7(6) *Competition Law Insight* 5.

Killick, J. (2006), 'The 2006 Fining Guidelines: Two Steps Forward but One Step Back?' (2006) 5(9) *Competition Law Insight* 5.

Killick, J. (2005), 'Is It Now Time for a Single Europe-Wide Fining Policy? An Analysis of the Fining Policies of the Commission and the Member States', Working Paper No. 07, Competition Law Scholars' Forum Working Paper Series, April 2005.

Killick, J. and Komninos, A. (2009), 'Schizophrenia in the Commission's Article 82 Guidance Paper: Formalism alongside Increased Recourse to Economic Analysis' [2009] 1 *Global Competition Policy*.

King, D. (2010), 'Criminalisation of Cartel Behaviour', Ministry of Economic Development Occasional Paper 10/01, New Zealand, January 2010.

Kist, A.W. (2004), 'Exchange of Information: Scope and Limits Seen From the Perspective of the National Competition Authorities', in Ehlermann, C.D. and Atanasiu, I. (eds), *European Competition Law Annual 2002: Constructing the EU Network of Competition Authorities*, Oxford, Hart Publishing.

Klawiter, D. and Driscoll, J. (2009), 'Sentencing Individuals in Antitrust Cases: The Proper Balance' (2009) 23(2) *Antitrust* 75.

Klein, J. (1999a), 'Luncheon Address', International Anti-Cartel Enforcement Conference, Washington DC, 30 September 1999.

Klein, J. (1999b), 'The War against International Cartels: Lessons from the Battlefront', 26th Annual Conference on International Antitrust Law and Policy, Fordham Corporate Law Institute, New York, 14 October 1999.

Klick, J. and Stratmann, T. (2008), 'Abortion Access and Risky Sex Among Teens: Parental Involvement Laws and Sexually Transmitted Diseases' (2008) 24 *Journal of Law Economics and Organization* 2.

Kolasky, W. (2004), 'Criminalising Cartel Activity: Lessons for the US Experience', Global Competition Law Centre, Brussels, 29 September 2004.

Kolasky, W. (2002), 'Antitrust Compliance Programs: The Government Perspective', Corporate Compliance 2002 Conference, Practising Law Institute, San Francisco, 12 July 2002.

Korah, V. (1998), 'Europe Needs Tough, Clear Competition Sanctions', *European Voice*, 8–14 January 1998.

Korean Fair Trade Commission (2005a), 'KFTC's Launch of Reward System for Informants', April 2005, <http://www.ftc.go.kr/data/hwp/rewardsystem.doc>.

Korean Fair Trade Commission (2005b), 'KFTC News—July 2005', July 2005, <http://eng.ftc.go.kr/files/bbs/2008/kftcnews(2005july).doc>.

Korobkin, R. and Ulen, T. (2000), 'Law and Behavioral Science: Removing the Rationality Assumption from Law and Economics' (2000) 88 *California Law Review* 1051.

Kortmann, C., Fleuren, J., and Voermans, W. (2006), *Constitutional Law of 10 New EU Member States*, Kluwer, Deventer.

Kovacic, W. (2011), 'Criminal Enforcement Norms in Competition Policy: Insights from US Experience', in Beaton-Wells, C. and Ezrachi, A. (eds), *Criminalising Cartels: A Critical Interdisciplinary Study of an International Regulatory Movement*, Hart Publishing, Oxford.

Kovacic, W. (2007), 'Bounties as Inducements to Identify Cartels', in Marsden, P., Hutchings, M., and Whelan, P. (eds), *Current Competition Law V*, British Institute of International and Comparative Law, London.

Kovacic, W. (2006), 'Competition Policy and Cartels: The Design of Remedies', in Cseres, K., Schinkel, M. P., and Vogelaar, F. (eds), *Criminalization of Competition Law Enforcement: Economic and Legal Implications for the EU Member States*, Edward Elgar Publishing, Cheltenham.

Kovacic, W. (2003–04), 'The Modern Evolution of US Competition Policy Enforcement Norms' (2003–04) 71 *Antitrust Law Journal* 377.

Kraakman, R. (1984), 'Corporate Liability Strategies and the Cost of Legal Controls' (1984) 93 *Yale Law Journal* 857.

Kramer, V. (1959–60), 'Criminal Prosecutions for Violations of the Sherman Act: In Search of a Policy' (1959–60) 48 *Georgetown Law Journal* 531.

Kroes, N. (2009), 'Tackling Cartels—A Never-Ending Task', SPEECH/09/454, Brasilia, 8 October 2009.

Kroes, N. (2006), 'Delivering on the Crackdown: Recent Developments in the European Commission's Campaign Against Cartels', SPEECH/06/595, Florence, 13 October 2006.

Kroes, N. (2005a), 'Taking Competition Seriously—Antitrust Reform in Europe', International Bar Association/European Commission Conference: Antitrust Reform in Europe: A Year in Practice, SPEECH/05/157, Brussels, 10 March 2005.

Kroes, N. (2005b), 'European Competition Policy: Delivering Better Markets and Better Choices', SPEECH/05/512, European Consumer and Competition Day, London, 15 September 2005.

Lamond, G. (2007), 'What Is Crime?' (2007) 27(4) *Oxford Journal of Legal Studies* 609.

Lande, R. (1999), 'Proving the Obvious: The Antitrust Laws Were Passed to Protect Consumers (Not Just to Increase Efficiency)' (1999) 50 *Hastings Law Journal* 959.

Lande, R. (1993), 'Are Antitrust "Treble" Damages Really Single Damages?' (1993) 54 *Ohio State Law Journal* 115.

Lande, R. and Davis, J. (2011), 'Comparative Deterrence from Private Enforcement and Criminal Enforcement of the US Antitrust Laws' [2011] 2 *Brigham Young University Law Review* 315.

Lande, R. and Davis, J. (2010), 'Comparative Deterrence from Private Enforcement and Criminal Enforcement of the US Antitrust Laws', University of Baltimore, Legal Studies Research Paper No. 2010-08, March 2010.

Landes, W. (1983), 'Optimal Sanctions for Antitrust Violations' (1983) 50 *University of Chicago Law Review* 652.

Lane, R. (2012), 'Competition Law' (2012) 61(4) *International and Comparative Law Quarterly* 991.

Lanzillotti, R. (1996), 'The Great School Milk Conspiracies of the 1980s' (1996) 11 *Review of Industrial Organization* 413.

Lavoie, C. (2012), 'South Africa's Corporate Leniency Policy', in Moodaliyar, K. and Roberts, S. (eds), *The Development of Competition Law and Economics in South Africa*, HSRC Press, Cape Town, SA.

Law Commission (2010), *Criminal Liability in Regulatory Contexts: A Consultation Paper*, Consultation Paper No. 195, London.

Law Commission (2002), *Fraud*, Law Com No. 276, London, July 2002.

Law Commission (1999), *Legislating the Criminal Code, Fraud and Deception: A Consultation Paper*, Consultation Paper 155, London, March 1999.

Law Reform Commission of New South Wales (2003), *Sentencing Corporate Offenders*, Report 102, Sydney.

Lawrence, J., O'Kane, M., Rab, S., and Nakhwal, J. (2008), 'Hardcore Bargains: What Could Plea Bargaining Offer in UK Criminal Cartel Cases?' (2008) 7(1) *Competition Law Journal* 17.

Lee, I. (1999), 'Non-Cooperative Tacit Collusion, Complementary Bidding and Incumbency Premium' (1999) 15 *Review of Industrial Organization* 115.

Lee, K.J. (2008), 'Culture and Competition: National and Regional Levels' (2008) 21(1) *Loyola Consumer Law Review* 33.

Lee, M. (1998), '*US v. Nippon Paper*: Extending the Criminal Provisions of the Sherman Act to Foreign Conduct Producing a Substantial Intended Effect in the US' (1998) 33 *Wake Forest Law Review* 189.

Lee, N.J. (2003), 'Korea's Whistleblower Protection and Reward System', in Asian Development Bank and OECD, *Controlling Corruption in Asia and the Pacific—Papers Presented at the 4th Regional Anti-Corruption Conference of the ADB/OECD Anti- Corruption Initiative for Asia and the Pacific, Kuala Lumpur, 3–5 December 2003*, Asian Development Bank, Manila, <http://www.oecd.org/dataoecd/28/19/38225653.pdf>.

Legal, H. (2006), 'Standards of Proof and Standards of Judicial Review in EU Competition Law', Annual Proceedings of the Fordham Corporate Law Institute, International Antitrust and Policy, Juris Publishing, New York.

Lenaerts, K. and Vanhamme, J. (1997), 'Procedural Rights of Private Parties in the Community Administrative Process' (1997) 34 *Common Market Law Review* 531.

Leslie, C. (2008), 'Cartels, Agency Costs, and Finding Virtue in Faithless Agents' (2008) 49(5) *William and Mary Law Review* 1621.

Leslie, C. (2006a), 'Antitrust Damages and Deadweight Loss' (2006) 51(3) *Antitrust Bulletin* 521.

Leslie, C. (2006b), 'Antitrust Amnesty, Game Theory and Cartel Stability' (2006) 31 *Journal of Corporation Law* 453.

Leslie, C. (2004), 'Trust, Distrust and Antitrust' (2004) 82(3) *Texas Law Review* 515.

Lester, M. (2008), 'Prosecuting Cartels for Conspiracy to Defraud' (2008) 7(2) *Competition Law Journal* 135.

Letsike, T. (2013), 'The Criminalising of Cartels—How Effective Will the New Section 73A of the Competition Amendment Act Be?', Competition Commission, Competition Tribunal, Mandela Institute & University of Johannesburg Seventh Annual Competition Law, Economics & Policy Conference, Johannesburg, 5–6 September 2013.

Levenstein, M. and Suslow, V. (2006), 'Cartel Bargaining and Monitoring: The Role of Information Sharing', in *The Pros and Cons of Information Sharing*, Konkurrensverket, Stockholm.

Levenstein, M. and Suslow, V. (2004), 'Studies of Cartel Stability: A Comparison of Methodological Approaches', in Grossman, P. (ed.), *How Cartels Endure and How They Fail, Studies of Industrial Collusion*, Edward Elgar Publishing, Cheltenham.

Lever, J. and Pike, J. (2005), 'Cartel Agreements, Criminal Conspiracy and the Statutory "Cartel Offence": Parts I & II' (2005) 26(2) *European Competition Law Review* 90.

Levine, D. (2010), 'Antitrust Convictions Don't Mean End of Job for Some Executives', *The Recorder*, 12 April 2010.

Levy, N. and O'Donoghue, R. (2004), 'The EU Leniency Programme Comes of Age' (2004) 27(1) *World Competition* 75.

Lewisch, P. (2006), 'Enforcement of Antitrust Law: The Way from Criminal Individual Punishment to Semi-Penal Sanctions in Austria', in Cseres, K., Schinkel, M. P., and Vogelaar, F. (eds), *Criminalization of Competition Law Enforcement: Economic and Legal Implications for the EU Member States*, Edward Elgar Publishing, Cheltenham.

Ligeti, K. (2000), 'European Criminal Law: Administrative and Criminal Sanctions as Means of Enforcing Community Law' (2000) 41(3–4) *Acta Juridica Hungaria* 199.

Liman, A. (1977), 'The Paper Label Sentences: A Critique' (1977) 86 *Yale Law Journal* 619.

Lippke, R. (2006), 'Retributivism and Plea Bargaining' (2006) 25(2) *Criminal Justice Ethics* 3.

Lipsky, A.B. (2009), 'Managing Antitrust Compliance through the Continuing Surge in Global Enforcement' (2009) 75 *Antitrust Law Journal* 965.

Lipsky, A.B. (1992), 'Deterring Cartel Behavior: Harmonies and Disharmonies, Problems and Solutions' (1992) 60 *Antitrust Law Journal* 563.

Loewy, A. (1988), 'Culpability, Dangerousness and Harm: Balancing the Factors on Which Our Criminal Law Is Predicated' (1988) 66 *North Carolina Law Review* 283.

Lorenz, M. (2013), *An Introduction to EU Competition Law*, Cambridge University Press, Cambridge.

Loughlin, J. (1979–80), '*Mens Rea* and Felony Violations under the Sherman Act' (1979–80) 11 *Loyola University Law Journal* 176.

Low, D.M. and Halladay, C. (2011), 'Redesigning a Criminal Cartel Regime: The Canadian Conversion', in Beaton-Wells, C. and Ezrachi, A. (eds), *Criminalising Cartels: A Critical Interdisciplinary Study of an International Regulatory Movement*, Hart Publishing, Oxford.

Lowe, P. (2009), 'Cartels, Fines, and Due Process' [2009] 2 *Global Competition Policy*.

Lowe, P. (2007), 'Preventing and Sanctioning Anticompetitive Conduct: Effective Use of Administrative and Criminal Sanctions, Leniency Programmes and Private Action in the EU', in Hawk, B. (ed.), *International Antitrust Law & Policy: Fordham Corporate Law 2006*, Juris Publishing, New York.

Lowe, P. (2003), 'What's the Future for Cartel Enforcement?', Understanding Global Cartel Enforcement, Brussels, 11 February 2003.

Lucraft, M., Payne, T., and Rawlings, D. (2009), 'Case Comment—The Dunlop Three: The Cartel Offence Makes Its Debut' [2009] 1 *Archbold News* 7.

Ludlow, M. (2009), 'Cartel Crackdown Sparks Whistleblowers' Chorus', *Australian Financial Review*, 1–2 August 2009.

Lugard, P. (ed.) (2011), *The International Competition Network at Ten: Origins, Accomplishments and Aspirations*, Intersentia, Cambridge.

Lusty, G. (2010), 'Refining the Anti-Cartel Tool Kit: Complements to Corporate Fines' (2010) 9(3) *Competition Law Journal* 338.

Lynch, G. (1997), 'The Role of Criminal Law in Policing Criminal Misconduct' (1997) 60(3) *Law and Contemporary Problems* 23.

Lyons, B. (ed.) (2009), *Cases in European Competition Policy—The Economic Analysis*, Cambridge University Press, Cambridge.

Lyons, B. (2002), 'Could Politicians Be More Right Than Economists? A Theory of Merger Standards', University of East Anglia, Centre for Competition and Regulation Working Paper CCR 02-1, May 2002.

MacCormick, N. (2005), 'Human Rights and Competition Law: Possible Impact of the Proposed EU Constitution' (2005) 2(4) *SCRIPT-ed* 445.

MacCulloch, A. (2013), 'Get Out of Jail Free: S 188B(3) of the Enterprise Act 2002', 15 November 2013, <http://whoscompeting.wordpress.com/2013/11/15/get-out-of-jail-free-s-188b3-of-the-enterprise-act-2002/>.

MacCulloch, A. (2012), 'The Cartel Offence: Defining an Appropriate "Moral Space"' (2012) 8(1) *European Competition Journal* 73.

MacCulloch, A. (2010a), 'The Cartel Offence: Is Honesty the Best Policy?', in Rodger, B. (ed.), *Ten Years of UK Competition Law Reform*, Dundee University Press, Dundee.

MacCulloch, A. (2010b), 'Leniency, Immunity and the Moral Maze', Seminar Presentation, ESRC Centre for Competition Policy, University of East Anglia, 15 October 2010 (copy in the possession of the author).

MacCulloch, A. (2009), 'Cartels: Deterrence, Leniency and Criminalisation', in Rodger, B. and MacCulloch, A. (eds), *Competition Law and Policy in the EC and UK*, 4th edn, Routledge Cavendish, Abingdon.

MacCulloch, A. (2008), 'Cartel Revolution and Evolution' (2008) 5(1) *Competition Law Review* 1.

MacCulloch, A. (2007), 'Honesty, Morality and the Cartel Offence' (2007) 28(6) *European Competition Law Review* 355.

MacCulloch, A. (2006), 'The Privilege against Self-Incrimination in Competition Investigations: Theoretical Foundations and Practical Implications' (2006) 26(2) *Legal Studies* 211.

MacCulloch, A. (2003), 'The Cartel Offence and the Criminalisation of UK Competition Law' [2003] *Journal of Business Law* 616.

MacCulloch, A. and Wardhaugh, B. (2012), 'The Baby and the Bathwater—The Relationship in Competition Law between Private Enforcement, Criminal Penalties, and Leniency Policy', ESRC Centre for Competition Policy Annual Conference, University of East Anglia, 14 June 2012.

MacDonald, K. and Thompson, R. (2003), 'Dishonest Agreements' (2003) 2(2) *Competition Law Journal* 94.

Macrory, R. (2006), *Regulatory Justice: Sanctioning in a Post-Hampton World*, Consultation Document, London, May 2006.

Majumdar, A. (2008), 'The Role of A Consumer Harm Test in Competition Policy' (2008) 20(2) *Loyola Consumer Law Review* 144.

Malinauskaite, J. (2007), 'The Development of "Consumer Welfare" and Its Application in the Competition Law of the European Community and Lithuania' (2007) 18(10) *International Company and Commercial Law Review* 354.

Mankiw, N. (2008), *Essentials of Economics*, Cengage Learning, US.

Mansfield, G. and Peay, J. (1987), *The Director of Public Prosecutions: Principles and Practices for the Crown Prosecutor*, Tavistock Publications, London.

Manzini, P. (2008), 'European Antitrust in Search of the Perfect Fine' (2008) 31 *World Competition* 3.

Marco Colino, S. (2011), *Competition Law of the EU and UK*, 7th edn, Oxford University Press, Oxford.

Marsden, P. and Waller, S.W. (2008), 'Antitrust Marathon II' (2008) 4(1) *European Competition Journal* 213.

Marsden, P. and Whelan, P. (2009), 'The "Consumer Welfare" Standard as a Form of Substantive Protection for Consumers under European Competition Law', in Ezrachi, A. and Bernitz, U. (eds), *Own Labels, Branded Goods and Competition Policy: The Changing Landscape of Retail Competition*, Oxford University Press, Oxford.

Marsden, P. and Whelan, P. (2006), '"Consumer Detriment" and its Application in EC and UK Competition Law' (2006) 27(10) *European Competition Law Review* 569.

Marsden, P., Waller, S.W., and Fabbio, P. (2013), 'Antitrust Marathon V: When in Rome—Public and Private Enforcement of Competition Law' (2013) 9(3) *European Competition Journal* 503.

Markham, J. (2012), 'Does Criminalization of Cartels Work?' (2012) 3(2) *New Journal of European Criminal Law* 115.

Masoudi, G. (2007), 'Cartel Enforcement in the United States (and Beyond)', Cartel Conference, Budapest, 16 February 2007.

Massey, P. (2012), 'Criminalising Competition Law Offences—A Review of Irish Experience' (2012) 3(2) *New Journal of European Criminal Law* 153.

Massey, P. (2006), 'Criminalization and Leniency: Will the Combination Favourably Affect Cartel Stabilisation?', in Cseres, K., Schinkel, M. P., and Vogelaar, F. (eds), *Criminalization of Competition Law Enforcement: Economic and Legal Implications for the EU Member States*, Edward Elgar Publishing, Cheltenham.

Massey, P. (2004), 'Criminal Sanctions for Competition Law: A Review of Irish Experience' (2004) 1(1) *Competition Law Review* 23.

Massey, P. and Cooke, J. (2011), 'Competition Offences in Ireland: The Regime and Its Results', in Beaton-Wells, C. and Ezrachi, A. (eds), *Criminalising Cartels: A Critical Interdisciplinary Study of an International Regulatory Movement*, Hart Publishing, Oxford.

Matikkala, J. (2009), 'Criminal Law and Competition Infringements' (2009) 54 *Scandinavian Studies in Law* 269.

May, R. and Powles, S. (2004), *Criminal Evidence*, 5th edn, Sweet & Maxwell, London.

McFadden, D. (2011), 'Some Thoughts on Criminalising Cartels', 'European Competition Day', Hungarian Academy of Sciences, Budapest, 30 May 2011.

McGowan, L. (2010), *The Antitrust Revolution in Europe: Exploring the European Commission's Cartel Policy*, Edward Elgar Publishing, Cheltenham.

McGowan, L. and Morgan, E. (2012), '"Today's Softness is Tomorrow's Nightmare": Intensifying the Fight against Cartels in Brussels and Bonn' (2012) 34(6) *Journal of European Integration* 603.

McNally, J. (2010), 'Case Comment: *DPP v Duffy and Duffy Motors (Newbridge) Limited*' (2010) 1(2) *Irish Journal of Legal Studies* 116.

Mehta, P. (ed.) (2006), *Competition Regimes in the World—A Civil Society Report*, CUTS International, Jaipur.

Meiklejohn, S.D. (2004), 'You Can't Legislate Perfection: The Virtues of Experimentation in the Design of Antitrust Enforcement Regimes', in Hawk, B. (ed.), *Annual Proceedings of the Fordham Corporate Law Institute 2003*, Juris Publishing, New York.

Mill, J.S. (1859), *On Liberty*, Oxford World's Classics, Oxford, 1998 (first published in 1859).

Miller, N. (2009), 'Strategic Leniency and Cartel Enforcement' (2009) 99 *American Economic Review* 750.

Milligan, T. (2007), 'Book Review: *Lying, Cheating, and Stealing: A Moral Theory of White-Collar Crime*, Stuart Green, Oxford University Press, 2006' [2007] 1 *Criminal Law and Philosophy* 333.

Ministry of Economic Development (2010), 'Cartel Criminalisation', Discussion Document, Wellington, New Zealand, January 2010.

Mitchell, L. (1999), 'Understanding Norms' (1999) 49 *University of Toronto Law Journal* 177.

Møllgaard, P. (2009), 'Assessment of Damages in the District Heating Pipes Cartel', in Lyons, B. (ed.), *Cases in European Competition Policy—The Economic Analysis*, Cambridge University Press, Cambridge.

Monti, M. (2007), *European Competition Law*, Cambridge University Press, Cambridge.

Monti, M. (2001), 'The Future for Competition Policy in the European Union', SPEECH/01/340, London, 9 July 2001.

Monti, M. (2000), 'Fighting Cartels: Why and How?', 3rd Nordic Competition Policy Conference, Stockholm, 11–12 September 2000.

Moore, M. (2007), 'Is Competition Law Really Concerned with Consumer Welfare? An Analysis of the Objectives of European Competition Law in the 21st Century', LLM Thesis, Swansea University.

Moore, M. (1987), 'The Moral Worth of Retribution', in Schoeman, F. (ed.), *Responsibility, Character, and the Emotions: New Essays in Moral Psychology*, Cambridge University Press, Cambridge, 1987, reprinted in Ashworth, A. and von Hirsch, A. (eds), *Principled Sentencing: Readings on Theory and Policy*, Hart Publishing, Oxford, 2000.

Morgan, E. (2010), 'Criminal Cartel Sanctions under the UK Enterprise Act: An Assessment' (2010) 17(1) *International Journal of the Economics of Business* 67.

Morris, H. (2000), 'Desert as a Limiting Principle', in Ashworth, A. and von Hirsch, A. (eds), *Principled Sentencing: Readings on Theory and Policy*, Hart Publishing, Oxford.

Morris, H. (1995), 'Persons and Punishment', in Baird, R. and Rosenbaum, S. (eds), *Punishment and the Death Penalty: The Current Debate*, Prometheus Books, Amherst, NY.

Morris, N. (1994), '"Dangerousness" and Incapacitation', in Duff, A. and Garland, D. (eds), *A Reader on Punishment*, Oxford University Press, Oxford.

Motta, M. (2008), 'On Cartel Deterrence and Fines in the European Union' (2008) 29(4) *European Competition Law Review* 209.

Motta, M. (2004), *Competition Policy: Theory and Practice*, Cambridge University Press, Cambridge.

Motta, M. and Polo, M. (2003), 'Leniency Programmes and Cartel Prosecutions' (2003) 21(3) *International Journal of Industrial Organisation* 347.

Mowbray, A. (2012), *Cases, Materials and Commentary on the European Convention on Human Rights*, Oxford University Press, Oxford.

Mowbray, A. (2001), *Cases and Materials on the European Convention on Human Rights*, Butterworths, London.

Nazzini, R. (2009), 'Welfare Objective and Enforcement Standard in Competition Law', in Ezrachi, A. and Bernitz, U. (eds), *Own Labels, Branded Goods and Competition Policy: The Changing Landscape of Retail Competition*, Oxford University Press, Oxford.

Nazzini, R. (2003), 'Criminalisation of Cartels and Concurrent Proceedings' (2003) 24(10) *European Competition Law Review* 483.

Nelson, R. and Winter, S. (1982), *An Evolutionary Theory of Economic Change*, Harvard University Press, Cambridge, MA.

Nettle, G. (2011), 'Criminalization of Cartel Conduct: Commentary' (2011) 18 *Competition & Consumer Law Journal* 213.

New Zealand Ministry of Commerce, 'Penalties, Remedies and Court Processes under the Commerce Act 1986', Discussion Document, Wellington, January 1998, <http://www.med.govt.nz/templates/Page____9120.aspx>.

Neyrinck, N. (2009), 'Granting Incentives, Deterring Collusion: The Leniency Policy', Working Paper No. 2/2009, Institut d'Études Juridiques Européenne, <http://www.droit.ulg.ac.be/ieje/fileadmin/IEJE/WP/working-paper-2-2009.pdf>.

Nikpay, A. (2012), 'UK Cartel Enforcement—Past, Present, Future', Law Society Anti-Trust Section, London, 11 December 2012.

Norgen, C. (2007), 'Criminal Enforcement of Antitrust Laws', in Hawk, B. (ed.), *International Antitrust Law & Policy: Fordham Corporate Law 2006*, Juris Publishing, New York.
O'Dea, W. (1998), 'White Collar Criminals Are Getting Clean Away', *Sunday Independent*, Ireland, 12 April 1998.
O'Donoghue, R. and Padilla, J. (2013), *The Law And Economics of Article 102 TFEU*, 2nd edn, Hart Publishing, Oxford.
Odudu, O. (2006), *The Boundaries of EC Competition Law—The Scope of Article 81*, Oxford University Press, Oxford.
Odudu, O. (2005), 'The Meaning of Undertaking within Article 81 EC' (2005) 7 *Cambridge Yearbook of European Legal Studies* 209.
OECD (2011), *Roundtable on Promoting Compliance with Competition Law*, OECD Competition Committee, DAF/COMP(2011)4.
OECD (2008), *Policy Roundtables—Plea Bargaining*, OECD Competition Committee, DAF/COMP(2007)38.
OECD (2007a), *Remedies and Sanctions in Abuse of Dominance Cases*, Competition Committee, DAF/COMP(2006)19.
OECD (2007b), 'Cartels: Sanctions Against Individuals' (2007) 9(3) *OECD Journal of Competition Law and Policy* 7.
OECD (2005), *Hard Core Cartels: Third Report on the Implementation of the 1998 Council Recommendation*, OECD Competition Committee.
OECD (2003a), *Second Report on Effective Action against Hard Core Cartels*, OECD Competition Committee.
OECD (2003b), *Cartels: Sanctions against Individuals*, OECD Competition Committee.
OECD (2003c), *Hard Core Cartels—Recent Progress and Challenges Ahead*, OECD Competition Committee.
OECD (2002a), *Fighting Hard Core Cartels: Harm, Effective Sanctions and Leniency Programmes*, OECD Competition Committee.
OECD (2002b), *Report on the Nature and Impact of Hard Core Cartels and Sanctions against Cartels under National Competition Laws*, OECD Competition Committee.
OECD (2001), *Report on Leniency Programmes to Fight Hard Core Cartels*, OECD Competition Committee.
OECD (2000a), *Report on Hard Core Cartels*, OECD Competition Committee.
OECD (2000b), *OECD Country Studies: Ireland—The Role of Competition Policy in Regulatory Reform*, OECD Competition Committee.
OECD (1999), 'Regulatory Reform in Japan—The Role of Competition Policy in Regulatory Reform', OECD Competition Committee.
OECD (1998), *Recommendation of the OECD Council Concerning Effective Action against Hard Core Cartels*, adopted by the Council at its 921st Session on 25 March.
OECD (1995), *Competition Policy and Efficiency Claims in Horizontal Agreements*, OECD Competition Committee.
OFT (2014), 'Man Faces Charge in Criminal Cartel Investigation', OFT Press Release, 04/14, 27 January 2014, <http://www.oft.gov.uk/news-and-updates/press/2014/04-14>.
OFT (2013a), *Applications for Leniency and No-Action in Cartel Cases—OFT's Detailed Guidance on the Principles and Process: Summary of the Responses to the OFT's Consultation and Supplementary Consultation*, OFT 1495resp, July 2013.
OFT (2013b), *Applications for Leniency and No-Action in Cartel Cases—OFT's Detailed Guidance on the Principles and Process*, OFT 1495, July 2013.
OFT (2010a), *Director Disqualification Orders in Competition Cases—Summary of Responses to the OFT's Consultation, and OFT's Conclusions and Decision Document*, OFT 1244, May 2010.
OFT (2010b), *Director Disqualification Orders in Competition Cases—An OFT Guidance Document*, OFT 510, June 2010.

OFT (2010c), 'OFT Withdraws Criminal Proceedings against Current and Former BA Executives', OFT Press Release, 47/10, 10 May 2010, <http://www.oft.gov.uk/news-and-updates/press/2010/47-10#.Uf57LCBwbIU>.

OFT (2010d), *Project Condor Board Review*, London, December 2010, <http://www.oft.gov.uk/shared_oft/board/2010/Project_Condor_Board_Review.pdf>.

OFT (2009a), *Memorandum of Understanding between the Office of Fair Trading (OFT) and the National Casework Division (NCD), Crown Office, Scotland*, OFT 546, June 2010.

OFT (2009b), *An Assessment of Discretionary Penalties Regimes*, OFT 1132, October 2009.

OFT (2008), *OFT Prioritisation Principles*, OFT 953, October 2008.

OFT (2007a), *Private Actions in Competition Law: Effective Redress for Consumers and Business*, OFT 916, April 2007.

OFT (2007b), *The Deterrent Effect of Competition Enforcement by the OFT*, OFT 962, November 2007.

OFT (2007c), *Private Actions in Competition Law: Effective Redress for Consumers and Business—Recommendations from the Office of Fair Trading*, OFT 916resp, November 2007.

OFT (2005), *Predicting Cartels*, OFT 773, March 2005.

OFT (2004a), *Powers for Investigating Criminal Cartels*, OFT 515, January 2004.

OFT (2004b), *Covert Surveillance in Cartel Investigations—Code of Practice*, OFT 738, August 2004.

OFT (2004c), *Modernisation—Understanding Competition Law*, OFT 442, December 2004.

OFT (2003), *Memorandum of Understanding between the Office of Fair Trading and the Director of the Serious Fraud Office*, OFT 547, October 2003.

OFT (2001), *The Proposed Criminalisation of Cartels in the UK—A Report prepared for the Office of Fair Trading by Sir Anthony Hammond KCB QC and Roy Penrose OBE QPM*, OFT 365, November 2001.

OFT (1999), *Powers of Investigation*, OFT 404, March 1999.

O'Kane, M. (2012), 'International Cartel Criminalisation and Leniency: Recent Lessons from the UK and Global Comparisons' (2012) 8(2) *Competition Law International* 55.

O'Kane, M. (2011a), 'International Cartels, Concurrent Criminal Prosecutions and Extradition: Law, Practice and Policy', in Beaton-Wells, C. and Ezrachi, A. (eds), *Criminalising Cartels: A Critical Interdisciplinary Study of an International Regulatory Movement*, Hart Publishing, Oxford.

O'Kane, M. (2011b), 'Does Prison Work for Cartelists?—The View from Behind Bars' (2011) 56(2) *Antitrust Bulletin* 483.

O'Kane, M. (2009a), *The Law of Criminal Cartels: Practice and Procedure*, Oxford University Press, Oxford.

O'Kane, M. (2009b), 'Practical Issues Arising from Concurrent Criminal Prosecutions in the UK and Overseas', Criminalising Cartels: A Critical Interdisciplinary Workshop on an International Regulatory Movement, Centre for Competition Law and Policy, Oxford, 12 November 2009 (copy in the possession of the author).

O'Kane, M. (2008), 'A New Dimension in International Cartel Enforcement', International Cartels Conference 2008, British Institute of International and Comparative Law, London, 26 February 2008.

Oliver, P. (2012), '"Diagnostics"—A Judgment Applying the Convention of Human Rights to the Field of Competition' (2012) 3(2) *Journal of European Competition Law & Practice* 163.

Ormerod, D. (2008), *Smith and Hogan—Criminal Law*, 12th edn, Oxford University Press, Oxford.

Ormerod, D. (1999), 'A Bit of a Con? The Law Commission's Consultation Paper on Fraud' [1999] *Criminal Law Review* 789.

Ormerod, P. (2006), 'Shun the Rational Agent to Rebuild Economics', *Financial Times*, London, 6 November 2006.

Osepciu, L. (2009), 'Crown Court Has Jurisdiction to Try the Cartel Offence', December 2009, <http://monckton.com/docs/library/IBLODEC09.pdf>.

Ovey, C. (2000), 'Case and Comment: *Hashman and Harrup v. United Kingdom*' [2000] *Criminal Law Review* 185.

Ovey, C. and White, R.C.A. (2010), *Jacobs & White, The European Convention on Human Rights*, 5th edn, Oxford University Press, Oxford.

Ovey, C. and White, R.C.A. (2006), *Jacobs & White, The European Convention on Human Rights*, Oxford University Press, Oxford.

Packer, H. (1968), *The Limits of the Criminal Sanction*, Oxford University Press, London.

Packer, K. (2011), 'A Cautionary Tale: How a Competition Law Breach Led to a Jail Term for One BA Exec', 22 September 2011, <http://www.legalweek.com/legal-week/analysis/2110631/cautionary-tale-exec-consequences-competition-law-infringement>.

Padfield, N. (2006), *Criminal Law*, Oxford University Press, Oxford.

Parker, C. (2013), 'The War on Cartels and the Social Meaning of Deterrence' (2013) 7(2) *Regulation & Governance* 174.

Parker, C. (2012), 'Economic Rationalities of Governance and Ambiguity in the Criminalization of Cartels' (2012) 52(5) *British Journal of Criminology* 974.

Parker, C. (2011), 'Criminalisation and Compliance: The Gap Between Rhetoric and Reality', in Beaton-Wells, C. and Ezrachi, A. (eds), *Criminalising Cartels: A Critical Interdisciplinary Study of an International Regulatory Movement*, Hart Publishing, Oxford.

Parker, C. (2006), 'The "Compliance Trap": The Moral Message in Regulatory Enforcement' (2006) 40 *Law & Society Review* 591.

Parker, C., Ainsworth, P., and Stepanenko, N. (2004), 'The Impact of ACCC Enforcement Activity in Cartel Cases', The Australian National University Centre for Competition and Consumer Policy, Working Paper, ACCC Enforcement and Compliance Project, May 2004.

Parker, C., Haines, F., Kotey, J., Nankivell J., and Round, D. (2011), 'The Cartel Project—Report on Interviews with Civil Respondents in Cartel Cases', University of Melbourne, December 2011, <http://cartel.law.unimelb.edu.au/go/project-news/litigant-interviews>.

Parker, C. and Nielsen, V.L. (2011), 'Deterrence and the Impact of Calculative Thinking on Business Compliance with Competition and Consumer Regulation' (2011) 56(2) *Antitrust Bulletin* 377.

Parker, C. and Nielsen, V.L. (2008), 'How Much Does It Hurt? How Australian Businesses Think About the Costs and Gains of Compliance and Non-Compliance with the Trade Practices Act' (2008) 32 *Melbourne University Law Review* 554.

Parker, C. and Platania-Phung, C. (2012), 'The Deterrent Impact of Cartel Criminalisation: Supplementary Report on a Survey of Australian Public Opinion Regarding Business People's Views on Anti-Cartel Laws and Enforcement', Melbourne Law School, 12 January 2012.

Parker, J. (1989), 'Criminal Sentencing Policy for Organizations: The Unifying Approach of Optimal Penalties' (1989) 26 *American Criminal Law Review* 513.

Parkinson, S. (2004), 'The Cartel Offence under the Enterprise Act 2002' (2004) 25(6) *Company Lawyer* 187.

Parret, L. (2008), 'Sense and Nonsense of Rules on Proof in Cartel Cases', Tilburg Law and Economics Center Discussion Paper DP 2008-004, January 2008, <http://ssrn.com/abstract=1088959>.

Pate, H. (2003), 'Anti-Cartel Enforcement: The Core Antitrust Mission', 3rd Annual Trans-Atlantic Dialogue, British Institute of International and Comparative Law, London, 16 May 2003.

Patel, R. (2012), 'The Removal of Dishonesty from the Cartel Offense and the Publication Defense: A Panacea?' (2012) 5(1) *Competition Policy International* 1.

Paternoster, R. and Simpson, S. (1996), 'Sanction Threats and Appeals to Morality: Testing a Rational Choice Model of Corporate Crime' (1996) 30 *Law and Society Review* 549.

Paulis, E. (2004), 'International Cooperation against Cartels', ACCC Conference on Cracking Cartels, Sydney, 24 November 2004.

Peel, M. (2009), 'OFT Targets Directors Ignoring Price-Fixing', *Financial Times*, London, 15 July 2009.

Peel, M. (2008), 'BA Sales Chief on Price-Fixing Charge to Join Board', *Financial Times*, London, 28 November 2008.

Peers, S. (2011), *EU Justice and Home Affairs Law*, 3rd edn, Oxford University Press, Oxford.

Peers, S. (2008), 'EC Criminal Law in the Treaty of Lisbon' (2008) 33 *European Law Review* 516.

Peretz, G. and Lewis, J. (2003), 'Go Directly to Jail: Losing Badly in "Monopoly"' (2003) 153 *New Law Journal* 99.

Perrin, B. (2006), 'Challenges Facing the EU Network of Competition Authorities: Insights from a Comparative Criminal Law Perspective' (2006) 31(4) *European Law Review* 540.

Perroud, T. (2008), 'The Impact of Article 6(1) ECHR on Competition Law Enforcement: A Comparison between France and the United Kingdom' [2008] 1 *Global Antitrust Review* 48.

Pesendorfer, M. (2000), 'A Study of Collusion in First-Price Auctions' (2000) 67 *Review of Economic Studies* 381.

Pew Global Attitudes Project (2003), *Views of a Changing World, Second Major Report of the Pew Global Attitudes Project*, June 2003, <http://pewglobal.org/files/pdf/185.pdf>.

Pickford, M. (2002), 'The Introduction of a New Economic Crime' (2002) 1(1) *Competition Law Journal* 35.

Pijetlovic, K. (2004), 'Reform of EC Antitrust Enforcement: Criticism of the New System is Highly Exaggerated' (2004) 25(6) *European Competition Law Review* 356.

PIPA (2008), 'Erosion of Support for Free Market System: Global Poll', The Program on International Policy Attitudes, 15 April 2008, <http://www.worldpublicopinion.org/pipa/pdf/apr08/Free_Markets_April08_pr.pdf>.

Pittman, R. (2007), 'Consumer Surplus as the Appropriate Standard for Antitrust Enforcement' (2007) 3(2) *Competition Policy International* 205.

Polinsky, A. and Shavell, S. (2000), 'The Economic Theory of Public Enforcement of the Law' (2000) 38(1) *Journal of Economic Literature* 45.

Polinsky, A. and Shavell, S. (1993), 'Should Employees Be Subject to Fines and Imprisonment Given the Existence of Corporate Liability?' (1993) 13 *International Review of Law and Economics* 239.

Porter, R. (2005), 'Detecting Collusion' (2005) 26(2) *Review of Industrial Organization* 147.

Porter, R. and Zona, J.D. (1999), 'Ohio School Milk Markets: An Analysis of Bidding' (1999) 30 *RAND Journal of Economics* 263.

Posner, E. (2000), *Law and Social Norms*, Harvard University Press, Cambridge, MA.

Posner, E. (1996), 'Law, Economics and Inefficient Norms' (1996) 144 *University of Pennsylvania Law Review* 1697.

Posner, R. (2001), *Antitrust Law: An Economic Perspective*, 2nd edn, University of Chicago Press, Chicago.

Posner, R. (1992), *Economic Analysis of Law*, Little, Brown & Co., Boston.

Posner, R. (1985), 'An Economic Theory of the Criminal Law' (1985) 85 *Columbia Law Review* 1193.

Posner, R. (1980a), 'The Value of Wealth: A Comment on Dworkin and Kronman' (1980) 9 *Journal of Legal Studies* 243.

Posner, R. (1980b), 'Optimal Sentences for White-Collar Criminals' (1980) 17 *American Criminal Law Review* 409.

Posner, R. (1979–80), 'Optimal Sentences for White-Collar Criminals' (1979–80) 17 *American Criminal Law Review* 409.

Posner, R. (1979a), 'The Chicago School of Antitrust Analysis' (1979) 127 *University of Pennsylvania Law Review* 925.

Posner, R. (1979b), 'Utilitarianism, Economics and Legal Theory' (1979) 8 *Journal of Legal Studies* 103.

Posner, R. (1976), *Antitrust Law: An Economic Perspective*, University of Chicago Press, Chicago.

Prakke, L. and Kortmann, C. (eds) (2004), *Constitutional Law of 15 EU Member States*, Kluwer, Deventer.

Prentice, R. (2003), 'Chicago Man, K-T Man, and the Future of Behavioral Law and Economics' (2003) 56 *Vanderbilt Law Review* 1663.

Preston, R. (2007), 'Where's Branson's Apology', BBC News, 1 August 2007, <http://www.bbc.co.uk/blogs/thereporters/robertpeston/2007/08/wheres_bransons_apology.html>.

Purnell, N. and Winter, I. (2011), 'It Takes Two to Lie: One to Lie and One to Listen: Should Dishonesty Remain the Critical Ingredient in Price Fixing Cartel Offences?', Cloth Fair Chambers.

Purnell, N., Bellamy, C., Kar, N., Piccinin, D., and Sahathevan, P. (2010), 'Criminal Cartel Enforcement—More Turbulence Ahead? The Implications of the *BA/Virgin* Case' (2010) 9(3) *Competition Law Journal* 313.

Pyle, D. (1983), *The Economics of Crime and Law Enforcement*, Macmillan, London.

Quaid, J. (2012), 'Making Sense of the Shift in Paradigm on Cartel Enforcement: The Case for Applying a Desert Perspective' (2012) 58(1) *McGill Law Journal* 149.

Ramage, S. (2008), 'Criminal Cartels' [2008] *Criminal Lawyer* 5.

Ramcharan, B.G. (2008), *Contemporary Human Rights Ideas*, Taylor & Francis, New York.

Rawls, J. (1967), 'Two Concepts of Rules', in Foot, P. (ed.), *Theories of Ethics*, Oxford University Press, London.

Rayment, B. (2004), 'Disqualification as a Director for Breaches of Competition Law' (2004) 3(3) *Competition Law Journal* 201.

Raz, J. (1977), 'The Rule of Law and Its Virtue' (1977) 93 *Law Quarterly Review* 195.

Reeves, A. (2010), 'Behavioural Antitrust: Unanswered Questions on the Horizon', *Antitrust Source*, June 2010.

Reindl, A. (2006), 'How Strong is the Case for Criminal Sanctions in Cartel Cases?', in Cseres, K., Schinkel, M. P., and Vogelaar, F. (eds), *Criminalization of Competition Law Enforcement: Economic and Legal Implications for the EU Member States*, Edward Elgar Publishing, Cheltenham.

Reiner, R. (2002), 'Media Made Criminality: The Representation of Crime in the Mass Media', in Maguire, M., Morgan, M., and Reiner, R. (eds), *The Oxford Handbook of Criminology*, Oxford University Press, Oxford.

Renfrew, C. (1977), 'The Paper Label Sentence: An Evaluation' (1977) 86 *Yale Law Journal* 590.

Reynolds, M. and Anderson, D. (2006), 'Immunity and Leniency in EU Cartel Cases: Current Issues' (2006) 27(2) *European Competition Law Review* 82.

Reynolds, R.M., Sicilian, J., and Wellman, P.S. (1998), 'The Extraterritorial Application of the US Antitrust Laws to Criminal Conspiracies' (1998) 19(3) *European Competition Law Review* 151.

Richardson, G., Ogus, A., and Burrows, P. (1982), *Policing Pollution: A Study of Regulation and Enforcement*, Clarendon Press, Oxford.

Richardson, R. (1999), 'Guidance without Guidance—A European Revolution in Fining Policy? The Commission's New Guidelines on Fines' (1999) 20(7) *European Competition Law Review* 360.

Riley, A. (2011), 'Modernising Cartel Sanctions: Effective Sanctions for Price-Fixing in the European Union' (2011) 32(11) *European Competition Law Review* 551.

Riley, A. (2010a), 'The Modernisation of EU Anti-Cartel Enforcement: Will the Commission Grasp the Opportunity?' (2010) 31(5) *European Competition Law Review* 191.

Riley, A. (2010b), 'Outgrowing the European Administrative Model? Ten Years of British Anti-Cartel Enforcement', in Rodger, B. (ed.), *Ten Years of UK Competition Law Reform*, Dundee University Press, Dundee.

Riley, A. (2007), 'Editorial—Developing Criminal Cartel Law: Dealing with the Growing Pains' (2007) 4(1) *Competition Law Review* 1.

Riley, A. (2005a), 'The Consequences of the European Cartel Busting Revolution' (2005) 12(1) *Irish Journal of European Law* 3.

Riley, A. (2005b), 'Beyond Leniency: Enhancing Enforcement in EC Antitrust Law' (2005) 28(3) *World Competition* 377.

Riley, A. (2003), 'EC Antitrust Modernisation: The Commission Does Very Nicely—Thank You! Part 1: Regulation 1 and the Notification Burden' (2003) 24(11) *European Competition Law Review* 604.

Riley, A. (2002), 'Cartel Whistleblowing: Toward an American Model?' (2002) 9 *Maastricht Journal of European and Comparative Law* 67.

Riley, A. (2000), '*Saunders* and the Power to Obtain Information in Community and United Kingdom Competition Law' (2000) 25(3) *European Law Review* 264.

Robinson, J. (2008), 'Safe for Now', Bird & Bird, 12 March 2008, <http://www.twobirds.com/english/publications/articles/Safe_for_Now.cfm>.

Robinson, P. (2002), 'Mens Rea', in Dressler, J. (ed.), *Encyclopaedia of Crime and Justice*, 2nd edn, Macmillan Reference, US.

Robinson, P. (1996), 'The Criminal-Civil Distinction and the Utility of Desert' (1996) 76 *Boston University Law Review* 202.

Rodger, B. (2005), 'Competition Law Compliance Programmes: A Study of Motivations and Practice' (2005) 28(3) *World Competition* 349.

Rodger, B. (2004), 'The Competition Act and the Enterprise Act Reforms: Sanctions and Deterrence in UK Competition Law', in Dannecker, G. and Jansen, O. (eds), *Competition Law Sanctioning in the European Union*, Kluwer Law International, The Hague.

Rosati, F. and Ehmer, C. (2009), 'Science, Myth and Fines: Do Cartels Typically Raise Prices by 25%?' (2009) *Concurrences*, No. 4-2009, No. 28832.

Rose, V. and Bailey, D. (eds) (2013), *Bellamy & Child—European Union Law of Competition*, 7th edn, Oxford University Press, Oxford.

Rosenboom, N. (2012), 'Career Development after the Cartel Prosecution: Cartel Versus Non-Cartel Manager' (2012) 8 *Journal of Competition Law and Practice* 145.

Rosochowicz, P. (2004), 'The Appropriateness of Criminal Sanctions in the Enforcement of Competition Law' (2004) 25(12) *European Competition Law Review* 752.

Roth, P. (2006), 'Ensuring That Effectiveness of Enforcement Does Not Prejudice Legal Protection. Rights of Defence. Fundamental Rights Concerns', EU Competition Law and Policy Workshop, European University Institute, Florence, 3 June 2006.

Sadurski, W. (1985), *Giving Punishment Its Due*, D. Reidel, Dordrecht, the Netherlands.

Safferling, C. (2009), 'Europe as Transnational Law—A Criminal Law for Europe: Between National Heritage and Transnational Necessities' (2009) 10 *German Law Journal* 1383.

Sakkers, E. and Ysewyn, J. (2008), *European Cartel Digest*, Wolters Kluwer, the Netherlands.

Salinger, M. (2010), 'Behavioural Economics, Consumer Protection and Antitrust' (2010) 6(1) *Competition Policy International* 65.

Salinger, M. (1984), 'Tobin's Q, Unionization and the Concentration of Profits Relationship' (1984) 15 *RAND Journal of Economics* 159.

Samuel, G. (2009), 'Corporate Thieves Can Expect Jail Time', *Australian Financial Review*, 22 July 2009.

Sanekata, K. and Wilks, S. (1996), 'The Fair Trade Commission and the Enforcement of Competition Policy in Japan', in Doern, G.B. and Wilks, S. (eds), *Comparative Competition Policy: National Institutions in a Global Market*, Oxford University Press, Oxford.

Sayre, F. (1933), 'Public Welfare Offenses' (1933) 33 *Columbia Law Review* 55.

Scanlan, G. (2002), 'Dishonesty in Corporate Offences: A Need for Reform?' (2002) 23 *Company Lawyer* 114.

Scanlan, G. and Kiernan, P. (2003), 'Fraud and the Law Commission: The Future of Dishonesty' (2003) 24(1) *Company Lawyer* 4.

Schaub, A. (2001), 'Continued Focus on Reform: Recent Developments in EC Competition Policy', in Hawk, B. (ed.), *International Antitrust Law and Policy*, Juris Publications, New York.

Schauer, F. (1991), *Playing by the Rules*, Oxford University Press, Oxford.

Scherer, F. and Ross, D. (1990), *Industrial Market Structure and Economic Performance*, 3rd edn, Houghton Mifflin, Boston.

Scheuner, U. (1975), 'Fundamental Rights in European Community Law and in National Constitutional Law' (1975) 12 *Common Market Law Review* 171.

Schinkel, M. P. (2007), 'Effective Cartel Enforcement in Europe' (2007) 30(4) *World Competition* 539.

Schmidt, J. (2006), 'Keeping US Courts Open to Foreign Antitrust Plaintiffs: A Hybrid Approach to the Effective Deterrence of International Cartels' (2006) 31 *Yale Journal of International Law* 211.

Schnichels, D. (2004), 'The Network of Competition Authorities: How Will It Work in Practice?', in D. Geradin (ed.), *Modernisation and Enlargement: Two Major Challenges for EC Competition Law*, Intersentia, Antwerp.

Schoneveld, F. (2003), 'Cartel Sanctions and International Competition Policy: Cross-Border Cooperation and Appropriate Forums for Cooperation' (2003) 26(3) *World Competition* 433.

Schonsheck, J. (1994), *On Criminalization: An Essay in the Philosophy of the Criminal Law*, Kluwer Academic Publishers, Dordrecht.

Schroeder, D. and Heinz, S. (2006), 'Requests for Leniency in the EU: Experience and Legal Puzzles', in Cseres, K., Schinkel, M. P., and Vogelaar, F. (eds), *Criminalization of Competition Law Enforcement: Economic and Legal Implications for the EU Member States*, Edward Elgar Publishing, Cheltenham.

Schwab, A. and Steinle, C. (2008), 'Pitfalls of the European Competition Network—Why Better Protection of Leniency Applications and Legal Regulation of Case Allocation Is Needed' (2008) 29(9) *European Competition Law Review* 523.

Scott, S. (2007), 'Criminal Enforcement of Antitrust Laws: The US Model—A Canadian Perspective', in Hawk, B. (ed.), *International Antitrust Law & Policy: Fordham Corporate Law 2006*, Juris Publishing, New York.

Senate Standing Committee on Economics (2009), *Trade Practices Amendment (Cartel Conduct and Other Measures) Bill 2008*, Canberra, Australia, February 2009.

Sevenster, H. (1992), 'Criminal Law and EC Law' (1992) 29 *Common Market Law Review* 29.

Shaffer, G. and Nesbitt, N. (2011), 'Criminalising Cartels: A Global Trend?' (2011) 12 *Sedona Conference Journal* 313.

Shavell, S. (1987), 'The Optimal Use of Nonmonetary Sanctions as a Deterrent' (1987) 77 *American Economic Review* 584.

Shearing, L. and Fonyonga, A. (2009), 'Procedure: Office of Fair Trading/Scottish Crown Office—Cartel Offence—Application in Scotland' (2009) 30(10) *European Competition Law Review* 172.

Sher, G. (1987), *Desert*, Princeton University Press, Princeton, NJ.

Simester, A.P. (ed.) (2005), *Appraising Strict Liability*, Oxford University Press, Oxford.

Simester, A.P., Spencer, J.R., Sullivan, G.R., and Virgo, G.J. (2010), *Simester and Sullivan's Criminal Law: Theory and Doctrine*, 4th edn, Hart Publishing, Oxford.

Simonsson, I. (2011), 'Criminalising Cartels in the European Union: Is There a Case for Harmonisation?', in Beaton-Wells, C. and Ezrachi, A. (eds), *Criminalising Cartels: A Critical Interdisciplinary Study of an International Regulatory Movement*, Hart Publishing, Oxford.

Simonsson, I. (2009), *Legitimacy in EC Cartel Law*, Doctoral Thesis, Department of Law, Stockholm University.

Simpson, S. (2002), *Corporate Crime, Law, and Social Control*, Cambridge University Press, Cambridge.

Skeel, D.A. (2001), 'Shaming in Corporate Law' (2001) 149 *University of Pennsylvania Law Review* 1811.

Skilbeck, J. (2003), 'Cartels: Where Is the Case for Criminal Sanctions?' (2003) 4(2) *World Economics Journal* 1.

Skilbeck, J. (2002), 'So What *Exactly* Is Wrong with Cartels? An Economic Perspective' (2002) 1(3) *Competition Law Journal* 226.

Slapper, G. and Kelly, D. (2013), *The English Legal System*, 14th edn, Routledge, London.

Slater, D., Thomas, S., and Waelbroeck, D. (2008), 'Competition Law Proceedings before the European Commission and the Right to a Fair Trial: No Need for Reform?', The Global Competition Law Centre Working Papers Series, GCLC Working Paper 04/08.

Smith, G. (2001), 'Criminalising UK Competition Law: A Step Too Far?' (2001) 12(12) *International Company and Commercial Law Review* 291.

Smith, J. (2002), *Smith and Hogan—Criminal Law*, Butterworths, London.

Smith, J. (1974), 'Intention in Criminal Law' (1974) 27 *Current Legal Problems* 93.

Smith, T.F. (2005), 'Comments for the Antitrust Modernization Commission Hearing on Criminal Antitrust Remedies', 3 November 2005, <http://govinfo.library.unt.edu/amc/commission_hearings/pdf/Smith_Statement.pdf>.

Smuda, F. (2014), 'Cartel Overcharges and the Deterrent Effect of EU Competition Law' (2014) 10(1) *Journal of Competition Law and Economics* 63.

Snyder, E. (1990), 'The Effect of Higher Criminal Penalties in Antitrust Enforcement' (1990) 33(2) *Journal of Law and Economics* 439.

Sonnenfeld, J. (1981), 'Executive Apologies for Price-Fixing: Role Biased Perceptions of Causality' (1981) 24(1) *Academy of Management Journal* 192.

Sonnenfeld, J. and Lawrence, P. (1978), 'Why Do Companies Succumb to Price-Fixing?' (1978) 56(4) *Harvard Business Review* 145.

Soper, P. (1985), 'The Moral Value of Law' (1985) 84 *Michigan Law Review* 63.

Spagnolo, S. (2006), 'Criminalization of Cartels and Their Internal Organisation', in Cseres, K., Schinkel, M. P., and Vogelaar, F. (eds), *Criminalization of Competition Law Enforcement: Economic and Legal Implications for the EU Member States*, Edward Elgar Publishing, Cheltenham.

Spivack, G. (1963), 'The System of Enforcement', in British Institute of International and Comparative Law, *Comparative Aspects of Antitrust Law in the US, the UK and the EEC*, BIICL, London.

Spratling, G. (2001), 'Detection and Deterrence: Rewarding Informants for Reporting Violations' (2001) 69 *George Washington Law Review* 798.

Spratling, G. (1999), 'Transparency in Enforcement Maximises Co-operation from Antitrust Offenders', Fordham Corporate Law Institute 26th Annual Conference on International Antitrust Law & Policy, Fordham University School of Law, New York, 15 October 1999.

Standler, R. (2004), 'Pre-Trial Publicity Prevents a Fair Trial in the US', 21 February 2004, <http://www.rbs2.com/pretrial.pdf>.

Steel, A. (2010), 'What's To Know? The New Cartel Offence' (2010) 32(1) *University of South Wales Law Journal* 216.

Steel, A. (2006), 'Book Review: *Lying, Cheating, and Stealing: A Moral Theory of White-Collar Crime*, Stuart Green, Oxford University Press, 2006' (2006) 29(3) *University of New South Wales Law Journal* 349.

Steiner, J., Woods, L., and Twigg-Flesner, C. (2006), *EU Law*, 9th edn, Oxford University Press, Oxford.

Stelzer, I. (2001), *Lectures on Regulatory and Competition Policy*, Institute of Economic Affairs, London.

Stephan, A. (2013), 'The UK's Revised Cartel Offence: The Need for a Purposive Approach to the "Seeking Legal Advice" Defence', ESRC Centre for Competition Policy, December 2013.

Stephan, A. (2012), 'Why Morality Should be Excluded from the Cartel Criminalisation Debate' (2012) 3(2) *New Journal of European Criminal Law* 126.

Stephan, A. (2011a), 'Disqualification Orders for Directors Involved in Cartels' (2011) 2(6) *Journal of European Competition Law & Practice* 529.

Stephan, A. (2011b), 'How Dishonesty Killed the Cartel Offence' [2011] *Criminal Law Review* 446.

Stephan, A. (2011c), 'Cartel Criminalisation: The Role of the Media in the "Battle for Hearts and Minds"', in Beaton-Wells, C. and Ezrachi, A. (eds), *Criminalising Cartels: A Critical Interdisciplinary Study of an International Regulatory Movement*, Hart Publishing, Oxford.

Stephan, A. (2010a), 'Yes European Competition Law Enforcement is Open to Abuse, But at Least Firms in Europe Can Appeal', CCP Competition Policy Blog, February 2010, <http://competitionpolicy.wordpress.com/2010/02/25/yes-european-competition-law-enforcement-is-open-to-abuse-but-at-least-firms-in-europe-can-appeal/>.

Stephan, A. (2010b), 'Cartel Laws Undermined: Corruption, Social Norms, and Collectivist Business Cultures' (2010) 37(2) *Journal of Law and Society* 345.

Stephan, A. (2009a), 'Will the Recession Make Cartels More Likely and Cartel Enforcement More Difficult?' (2009) 16 *ESRC Centre for Competition Policy Newsletter* 5.

Stephan, A. (2009b), 'Cartel Criminalisation: The Role of the Media in the "Battle for Hearts and Minds"', Criminalising Cartels: A Critical Interdisciplinary Workshop on an International Regulatory Movement, Centre for Competition Law and Policy, Oxford, 12 November 2009 (copy in the possession of the author).

Stephan, A. (2009c), 'See No Evil: Cartels and the Limits of Antitrust Compliance Programs' (2010) 31 *Company Lawyer* 231.

Stephan, A. (2009d), 'The Direct Settlement of EC Cartel Cases' (2009) 58 *International and Comparative Law Quarterly* 627.

Stephan, A. (2008a), 'Enhancing Deterrence in European Cartel Enforcement', Doctoral Thesis, University of East Anglia, January 2008.

Stephan, A. (2008b), 'That Unsettling Feeling: Secret Price-Fixing is Not in Itself Dishonest?' (2008) 14 *ESRC Centre for Competition Policy Newsletter* 5.

Stephan, A. (2008c), 'Lame Duck or Black Mamba: Can the UK Cartel Offence Enhance Deterrence?', ESRC Centre for Competition Policy Working Paper 08-19, November 2008, <http://www.ccp.uea.ac.uk/public¢les/workingpapers/CCP08-19.pdf>.

Stephan, A. (2008d), 'An Empirical Assessment of the European Leniency Notice' (2008) 5(3) *Oxford Journal of Competition Law & Economics* 537.

Stephan, A. (2008e), 'Survey of Public Attitudes to Price-Fixing and Cartel Enforcement in Britain' (2008) 5(1) *Competition Law Review* 123.

Stephan, A. (2006), 'The Bankruptcy Wildcard in Cartel Cases' (2006) 5 *Journal of Business Law* 511.

Stevenson, B. and Wolfers, J. (2007), 'Marriage and Divorce: Changes and Their Driving Forces', National Bureau for Economic Research Working Paper No. 12944, March 2007, <http://www.nber.org/papers/w12944>.

Stone, C. (1991), 'Sentencing the Corporation' (1991) 71 *Boston University Law Review* 383.

Stucke, M. (2012), 'Is Intent Relevant?' (2012) 8 *Journal of Law, Economics and Policy* 801.

Stucke, M. (2011), 'Am I a Price-Fixer? A Behavioural Economics Analysis of Cartels', in Beaton-Wells, C. and Ezrachi, A. (eds), *Criminalising Cartels: A Critical Interdisciplinary Study of an International Regulatory Movement*, Hart Publishing, Oxford.

Stucke, M. (2009), 'Does the Rule of Reason Violate the Rule of Law?' (2009) 42(5) *UC Davis Law Review* 1375.

Stucke, M. (2007), 'Behavioural Economists at the Gate: Antitrust in the 21st Century' (2007) 38 *Loyola University Chicago Law Journal* 513.

Stucke, M. (2006), 'Morality and Antitrust' [2006] 3 *Columbia Business Law Review* 443.

Suchman, M. (1997), 'On Beyond Interest: Rational, Normative and Cognitive Perspectives in the Social Scientific Study of Law' [1997] 3 *Wisconsin Law Review* 475.

Sullivan, T. (ed.) (1991), *The Political Economy of the Sherman Act: The First One Hundred Years*, Oxford University Press, New York.

Summers, S. (2012), 'What Should the Dishonesty Element of the UK Cartel Offence Be Replaced With?' (2012) 11(1) *Competition Law Journal* 53.

Sunderland, R. (2007), 'OFT Defends "Snitch Policy"', *Observer*, London, 5 August 2007.

Sunstein, C., Schkade, D., and Kahneman, D. (2000), 'Do People Want Optimal Deterrence?' (2000) 29 *Journal of Legal Studies* 237.

Sutinen, J. and Kuperan, K. (1999), 'A Socio-Economic Theory of Regulatory Compliance' (1999) 26 *International Journal of Social Economics* 174.

Swaak, C. and Arp, D.J. (2003), 'A Tempting Offer: Immunity from Fines for Cartel Conduct under the European Commission's New Leniency Notice' (2003) 24(1) *European Competition Law Review* 9.

Swedish Competition Authority (2006), 'Criminal Enforcement of Antitrust Laws', Fordham Law Seminar, New York, 14 September 2006.

Szockyj, E. (1998–99), 'Imprisoning White-Collar Criminals?' (1998–99) 23 *Southern Illinois University Law Journal* 485.

Tak, J.P. (2004), 'Introduction', in Tak, J.P. (ed.), *Tasks and Powers of the Prosecution Services in the EU Member States: Volume I*, Wolf Legal Publishers, Nijmegen.

Tanford, J.A. (1990), 'The Law and Psychology of Jury Instructions' (1990) 69 *Nebraska Law Review* 71.

Tassopoulou, I. (2009), 'Case Comment: Anti-Competitive Agreements: Marine Hose—Cartel' (2009) 30(3) *European Competition Law Review* 41.

Tavares de Araujo, M. (2010), 'Improving Deterrence of Hard-Core Cartels' (2010) 6(2) *Competition Policy International* 69.

Temple Lang, J. and O'Donoghue, R. (2005), 'The Concept of an Exclusionary Abuse under Article 82 EC', in *GCLC Research Papers on Article 82 EC*, Global Competition Law Centre, College of Europe, Bruges, July 2005.

Terhechte, J.P. (2011), *International Competition Enforcement Law Between Cooperation and Convergence*, Springer, Heidelberg.

The City of London Law Society's Competition Law Committee (2012), 'Memorandum Submitted by the City of London Law Society's Competition Law Committee', ERR 31, July 2012, <http://www.publications.parliament.uk/pa/cm201213/cmpublic/enterprise/memo/err31.htm>.

The Competition Authority (2007), 'Public Consultation on the Operation and Implementation of the Competition Act 2002: Competition Authority Submission to the Department of Enterprise, Trade and Employment', S/07/008, December 2007.

The Competition Authority (2001), *Cartel Immunity Programme*, Dublin, 20 December 2001, <http://www.tca.ie/EN/Enforcing-Competition-Law/Cartel-Immunity-Programme.aspx>.

The Competition Bureau (2010), *Immunity Program under the Competition Act*, 7 June 2010, <http://www.competitionbureau.gc.ca/eic/site/cb-bc.nsf/eng/03248.html>.

Thépot, F. (2011), 'Leniency and Individual Liability: Opening the Black Box of the Cartel' (2011) 7(2) *Competition Law Review* 221.

Thomas, C. (2010), 'Are Juries Fair?', Ministry of Justice Research Series 1/10, February 2010, <http://www.justice.gov.uk/publications/are-juries-fair.htm>.

Thorelli, H.B. (1959), 'Antitrust in Europe: National Policies After 1945' (1959) 26(2) *University of Chicago Law Review* 222.

Thornton, D., Gunningham, N., and Kagan, R. (2005), 'General Deterrence and Corporate Environmental Behavior' (2005) 27 *Law and Policy* 262.

Tierno Centella, M.L. (2010), 'An Optimal Enforcement System against Cartels', in Lianos, I. and Kokorris, I. (eds), *The Reform of EC Competition Law: New Challenges*, Kluwer Law International, Amsterdam.

Tiersma, P.M. (1990), 'The Language of Perjury: "Literal Truth", Ambiguity and the False Statement Requirement' (1990) 63 *California Law Review* 373.

Toby, B., 'International Cartel Deterrence: A Selected Bibliography' (2011) 56(2) *Antitrust Bulletin* 501.

Torre, A. (2013), 'Evaluating Punishment Regimes for Competition Law Offences' (2013) 34(6) *European Competition Law Review* 309.

Townley, C. (2007), 'The Concept of an "Undertaking": The Boundaries of the Corporation—A Discussion of Agency, Employees and Subsidiaries', in Amato, G. and Ehlermann, C.D. (eds), *EC Competition Law: A Critical Assessment*, Hart Publishing, Oxford.

TPARC (2003), *Review of the Competition Provisions of the Trade Practices Act*, Trade Practice Act Review Committee, Australia, January.

Tridimas, T. (2006), *The General Principles of EU Law*, 2nd edn, Oxford University Press, Oxford.

Türk, A. (2006), 'Modernisation of EC Antitrust Enforcement', in Hofmann, H. and Türk, A. (eds), *EU Administrative Governance*, Edward Elgar Publishing, Cheltenham.

Twining, W. and Miers, D. (1991), *How To Do Things With Rules*, Weidenfeld and Nicholson, London.

Tyler, T. (2006), *Why People Obey the Law*, Princeton University Press, Princeton, NJ.

Tyler, T. and Darley, J. (2000), 'Building a Law-Abiding Society: Taking Public Views about Morality and the Legitimacy of Legal Authorities into Account When Formulating Substantive Law' (2000) 28 *Hofstra Law Review* 707.

US Attorney General (1955), *Report of the Attorney General's National Committee to Study the Antitrust Laws*, 31 March 1955.

US Sentencing Commission (2012), *Federal Sentencing Guidelines Manual*, Washington.

US Sentencing Commission (1999), *Federal Sentencing Guidelines Manual*, Washington.

Vamos, N. (2009), 'Please Don't Call It "Plea Bargaining"' [2009] *Criminal Law Review* 617.

van Bael, I. (1995), 'Fining à la Carte: The Lottery of EU Competition Law' (1995) 4 *European Competition Law Review* 237.

van den Bergh, R. and Camesasca, P. (2006), *European Competition Law and Economics: A Comparative Perspective*, 2nd edn, Sweet & Maxwell, London.

van den Broek, S., Kemp, R., Verschoor, W., and de Vries, A.C. (2012), 'Reputational Penalties to Firms Involved in Antitrust Investigations' (2012) 8(2) *Journal of Competition Law and Economics* 231.

van der Woude, M. (2004), 'Exchange of Information within the European Competition Network: Scope and Limits', in Ehlermann, C.D. and Atanasiu, I. (eds), *European Competition Law Annual 2002: Constructing the EU Network of Competition Authorities*, Hart Publishing, Oxford.

van Dijk, P. and van Hoof, F. (1998), *Theory and Practice of the European Convention on Human Rights*, 3rd edn, Kluwer International, The Hague.

van Zyl Smit, D. and Ashworth, A. (2004), 'Disproportionate Sentences as Human Rights Violations' (2004) 67 *Modern Law Review* 541.

Vaughan, D. (1998), 'Rational Choice, Situated Action, and the Social Control of Organizations' (1998) 32 *Law and Society Review* 23.

Veljanovski, C. (2011), 'Deterrence, Recidivism and European Cartel Fines' (2011) 7(4) *Journal of Competition Law and Economics* 871.

Veljanovski, C. (2009), 'European Cartel Prosecutions and Fines, 1998–2009—A Statistical Analysis of Fines under the 1998 Penalty Guidelines', 3 March 2009, <http://ssrn.com/abstract=1016014>.

Veljanovski, C. (2007), 'Cartel Fines in Europe: Law, Practice and Deterrence' (2007) 30(1) *World Competition* 65.

Veljanovski, C. (2006a), *The Economics of Law*, Institute of Economic Affairs, London.

Veljanovski, C. (2006b), 'Penalties for Price-Fixers: An Analysis of Fines Imposed on 39 Cartels by the EU Commission' (2006) 27(9) *European Competition Law Review* 510.

Venit, J. (2008), 'Criminalization and Civil Enforcement', The 10th Annual Sedona Conference, Florence, Italy, 17 September 2008.

Verma, P. and Billiet, P. (2009), 'Why Would Cartel Participants Still Refuse to Blow the Whistle under the Current EC Leniency Policy?' [2009] *Global Antitrust Review* 1.

Vervaele, J.A.E. (1994), 'Administrative Sanctioning Powers of and in the Community—Towards a System of European Administrative Sanctions?', in Vervaele, J.A.E. (ed.), *Administrative Law Application and Enforcement of Community Law in the Netherlands*, Kluwer Law and Taxation Publishers, Deventer.

Vesterdorf, B. (2011), 'Article 102 TFEU and Sanctions: Appropriate When?' (2011) 32(11) *European Competition Law Review* 573.

Vickers, J. (2003), 'Policy for Markets and Enterprise', British Chamber of Commerce, London, 31 March 2003.

Victor, A. (2004), 'US Antitrust Enforcement against International Cartels: Trends and Practical Considerations', in Hawk, B. (ed.), *International Antitrust Law & Policy: Fordham Corporate Law 2003*, Juris Publishing, New York.

Vogelaar, F. (2008), 'Are Criminal Sanctions the Ultimate Weapon against Cartels? Or Would There Be Any Alternatives?', Global Competition Law Centre, 4th Annual Conference, Brussels, 20 June 2008.

Vollmer, C. (2006), 'Experience with Criminal Law Sanctions for Competition Law Infringements in Germany', in Cseres, K., Schinkel, M. P., and Vogelaar, F. (eds), *Criminalization of Competition Law Enforcement: Economic and Legal Implications for the EU Member States*, Edward Elgar Publishing, Cheltenham.

von Hirsch, A. (2000), 'Proportionate Sentences: A Desert Perspective', in Ashworth, A. and von Hirsch, A. (eds), *Principled Sentencing: Readings on Theory and Policy*, Hart Publishing, Oxford.

von Hirsch, A. (1993), *Censure and Sanctions*, Clarendon Press, Oxford.

von Hirsch, A. (1990), 'Proportionality in the Philosophy of Punishment from "Why Punish?" to "How Much?"' (1990) 1 *Criminal Law Forum* 259.

von Hirsch, A. and Jareborg, N. (1991), 'Gauging Criminal Harm: A Living-Standard Analysis' (1991) 11(1) *Oxford Journal of Legal Studies* 1.

Waelbroeck, D. (2005), 'Twelve Feet All Dangling Down and Six Necks Exceeding Long. The EU Network of Competition Authorities and the European Convention on Fundamental Rights', in Ehlermann, C.D. and Atanasiu, I. (eds), *European Competition Law Annual 2002: The EU Network of Competition Authorities*, Hart Publishing, Oxford.

Waelbroeck, D. and Fosselard, D. (1994), 'Should the Decision-Making Power in EC Antitrust Procedures Be Left to an Independent Judge?—The Impact of the European Convention of Human Rights on EC Antitrust Procedures' (1994) 14 *Yearbook of European Law* 111.

Wagner-von Papp, F. (2011), 'What If All Bid Riggers Went to Prison and Nobody Noticed? Criminal Antitrust Law Enforcement in Germany', in Beaton-Wells, C. and Ezrachi, A. (eds), *Criminalising Cartels: A Critical Interdisciplinary Study of an International Regulatory Movement*, Hart Publishing, Oxford.

Walker, N. (1992a), 'Modern Retributivism', in Gross, H. and Harrison, R. (eds), *Jurisprudence: Cambridge Essays*, Oxford University Press, Oxford, 1992, reprinted in Ashworth, A. and von Hirsch, A. (eds), *Principled Sentencing: Readings on Theory and Policy*, Hart Publishing, Oxford, 2000.

Walker, N. (1992b), 'Legislating the Transcendental: Von Hirsch's Proportionality' (1992) 51(3) *Cambridge Law Journal* 530.

Walker, N. (1980), *Punishment, Danger and Stigma: The Morality of Criminal Justice*, Barnes & Noble, Totowa, NJ.

Walsh, D. (2009), 'Carrots and Sticks—Leniency and Fines in EC Cartel Cases' (2009) 30(1) *European Competition Law Review* 30.

Wardhaugh, B. (2014), *Cartels, Markets and Crime: A Normative Justification for the Criminalisation of Economic Collusion*, Cambridge University Press, Cambridge.

Wardhaugh, B. (2012a), 'The Cartel Offence within a "World Class" Competition Regime: An Assessment of the BIS Consultation Exercise and Its Results' (2012) 8(3) *European Competition Journal* 573.
Wardhaugh, B. (2012b), 'A Normative Approach to the Criminalisation of Cartel Activity' (2012) 32(3) *Legal Studies* 369.
Warin, F., Burns, D., and Chesley, J. (2006), 'To Plead or Not to Plead? Reviewing a Decade of Criminal Antitrust Trials', *Antitrust Source*, July 2006.
Warner, P. and Trebilcock, M. (1992–93), 'Rethinking Price-Fixing Law' (1992–93) 38 *McGill Law Journal* 680.
Warren-Boulton, F.R. (1990), 'Implications of US Experience with Horizontal Mergers and Takeovers for Canadian Competition Policy', in Mathewson, F., Trebilcock, M., and Walker, M. (eds), *The Law and Economics of Competition Policy*, Fraser Institute, Vancouver.
Wasmeier, M. and Thwaites, N. (2004), 'The "Battle of the Pillars": Does the European Community Have the Power to Approximate National Criminal Laws?' (2004) 29(5) *European Law Review* 613.
Wasserstrom, R. (1960), 'Strict Liability in the Criminal Law' (1960) 12 *Stanford Law Review* 731.
Watkins, M.W. (1961), 'Electrical Equipment Antitrust Cases: Their Implications for Government and for Business' (1961) 29(1) *University of Chicago Law Review* 97.
Wayland, J. (2012), 'International Cooperation at the Antitrust Division', International Bar Association's 16th Annual Competition Conference, Florence, 14 September 2012.
Wechsler, H. (1952), 'The Challenge of a Moral Penal Code' (1952) 65 *Harvard Law Review* 1097.
Wehmhörner, N. (2006), 'Optimal Pecuniary Sanctions and the US Sentencing and EU Fining Guidelines', in Cseres, K., Schinkel, M. P., and Vogelaar, F. (eds), *Criminalization of Competition Law Enforcement: Economic and Legal Implications for the EU Member States*, Edward Elgar Publishing, Cheltenham.
Wells, C. (2001), *Corporations and Criminal Responsibility*, 2nd edn, Oxford University Press, Oxford.
Werden, G. (2009), 'Sanctioning Cartel Activity: Let the Punishment Fit the Crime' (2009) 5(1) *European Competition Journal* 19.
Werden, G. (2007), 'Competition, Consumer Welfare, and the Sherman Act', Ninth Annual Sedona Conference on Antitrust Law & Litigation, Arizona, 25–6 October 2007.
Werden, G. (2003), 'The Effect of Antitrust Policy on Consumer Welfare: What Crandall and Winston Overlook', Economic Advisory Group Discussion Paper, EAG 03-2, January 2003.
Werden, G. (1998), 'Antitrust Analysis of Joint Ventures: An Overview' (1998) 66 *Antitrust Law Journal* 701.
Werden, G., Hammond, S., and Barnett, B. (2011), 'Deterrence and Detection of Cartels: Using All the Tools and Sanctions' (2011) 56(2) *Antitrust Bulletin* 207.
Werden, G. and Simon, M. (1987), 'Why Price Fixers Should Go to Prison' (1987) 32(4) *Antitrust Bulletin* 917.
Wesseling, R. and van der Woude, M. (2012), 'The Lawfulness and Acceptability of Enforcement of European Cartel Law' (2012) 35(4) *World Competition* 573.
Whalley, J. (1990–91), 'Crime and Punishment—Criminal Antitrust Enforcement in the 1990s' (1990–91) 59 *Antitrust Law Journal* 151.
Whalley, J. (1988), 'Priorities and Practices—the Antitrust Division's Criminal Enforcement Programme' (1988) 57 *Antitrust Law Journal* 569.
Whelan, P. (2013a), 'Cartel Criminalization and the Challenge of "Moral Wrongfulness"' (2013) 33(3) *Oxford Journal of Legal Studies* 535.
Whelan, P. (2013b), 'Cartel Criminalisation and Due Process: The Challenge of Imposing Criminal Sanctions alongside Administrative Sanctions within the EU' (2013) 64(2) *Northern Ireland Legal Quarterly* 143.

Whelan, P. (2013c), 'Book Review: M. Furse, *The Criminal Law of Competition in the UK and in the US: Failure and Success*' (2013) 9(2) *European Competition Journal* 497.

Whelan, P. (2013d), 'Strengthening Competition Law Enforcement in Ireland: The Competition (Amendment) Act 2012' (2013) 4(2) *Journal of European Competition Law & Practice* 175.

Whelan, P. (2013e), 'Does the UK's New Cartel Offence Contain a Devastating Flaw?', CCP Blog, ESRC Centre for Competition Policy, University of East Anglia, 21 May 2013, <http://competitionpolicy.wordpress.com/2013/05/21/does-the-uks-new-cartel-offence-contain-a-devastating-flaw/>.

Whelan, P. (2013f), 'Criminal Cartel Enforcement in the UK: Rectifying the Mistakes of the Past', Bergen Center for Competition Law and Economics (BECCLE), Bergen, Norway, 29 October 2013.

Whelan, P. (2012a), 'Legal Certainty and Cartel Criminalisation within the EU Member States' (2012) 71(3) *Cambridge Law Journal* 677.

Whelan, P. (2012b), 'Improving Criminal Cartel Enforcement in the UK: The Case for the Adoption of BIS's "Option 4"' (2012) 8(3) *European Competition Journal* 589.

Whelan, P. (2012c), 'Criminal Sanctions: An Overview of EU and National Case Law', e-Competitions, No. 41902, <http://www.concurrences.com>.

Whelan, P. (2012d), 'Submission to the Commerce Committee of the New Zealand Parliament on the Commerce (Cartels and Other Matters) Amendment Bill', 5 September 2005.

Whelan, P. (2011a), 'Criminal Cartel Enforcement in the European Union: Avoiding a Human Rights Trade-Off', in Beaton-Wells, C. and Ezrachi, A. (eds), *Criminalising Cartels: A Critical Interdisciplinary Study of an International Regulatory Movement*, Hart Publishing, Oxford.

Whelan, P. (2011b), 'Reforming the UK Cartel Offence: A Response to *A Competition Regime for Growth: A Consultation on Options for Reform*', Submitted to the Department for Business, Innovation and Skills, June 2011.

Whelan, P. (2010), 'Protecting Human Rights in the Context of European Antitrust Criminalisation', in Lianos, I. and Kokorris, I. (eds), *The Reform of EC Competition Law: New Challenges*, Kluwer Law International, Amsterdam.

Whelan, P. (2009a), 'Morality and Its Restraining Influence on European Antitrust Criminalisation' (2009) 12 *Trinity College Law Review* 40.

Whelan, P. (2009b), 'Resisting the Long Arm of Criminal Antitrust Laws: *Norris v. US*' (2009) 72(2) *Modern Law Review* 272.

Whelan, P. (2009c), 'The UK's Criminal Cartel Offence Survives Its First Major Legal Challenge', CCP Blog, ESRC Centre for Competition Policy, University of East Anglia, December 2009, <http://competitionpolicy.wordpress.com/2009/12/21/the-uks-criminal-cartel-offence-survives-its-first-major-legal-challenge/>.

Whelan, P. (2008), 'Contemplating the Future: Personal Criminal Sanctions for Infringement of EC Competition Law' (2008) 19(2) *King's Law Journal* 364.

Whelan, P. (2007), 'A Principled Argument for Personal Criminal Sanctions as Punishment under EC Cartel Law' (2007) 4(1) *Competition Law Review* 7.

Whelan, P. (2006), 'Book Review: *Criminalization of Competition Law Enforcement: Economic and Legal Implications for the EU Member States* (Cseres, Schinkel and Vogelaar (eds))' (2006) 2 *European Competition Journal* 451.

Whish, R. and Bailey, D. (2012), *Competition Law*, Oxford University Press, Oxford.

Whish, R. (2009), *Competition Law*, 6th edn, Oxford University Press, Oxford.

White, A. (1976), 'Intention, Purpose, Foresight and Desire' (1976) 92 *Law Quarterly Review* 569.

Wilks, S. (2011), 'Cartel Criminalisation as Juridification: Political and Regulatory Dangers', in Beaton-Wells, C. and Ezrachi, A. (eds), *Criminalising Cartels: A Critical Interdisciplinary Study of an International Regulatory Movement*, Hart Publishing, Oxford.

Williams, G. (1987), 'Oblique Intention' (1987) 46 *Cambridge Law Journal* 417.

Williams, G. (1955), 'The Definition of Crime' (1955) 8(1) *Current Legal Problems* 107.

Williams, R. (2011), 'Cartels in the Criminal Law Landscape', in Beaton-Wells, C. and Ezrachi, A. (eds), *Criminalising Cartels: A Critical Interdisciplinary Study of an International Regulatory Movement*, Hart Publishing, Oxford.

Willis, P. (2001), '"You Have the Right to Remain Silent...", Or Do You? The Privilege against Self-Incrimination Following *Mannesmannrohren-Werke* and Other Recent Decisions' (2001) 22(8) *European Competition Law Review* 313.

Wils, W. (2013), 'Ten Years of Regulation 1/2003—A Retrospective' (2013) 4(4) *Journal of European Competition Law & Practice* 293.

Wils, W. (2012), 'Recidivism in EU Antitrust Enforcement: A Legal and Economic Analysis' (2012) 35(1) *World Competition* 5.

Wils, W. (2011), 'Discretion and Prioritisation in the Public Antitrust Enforcement, in Particular EU Antitrust Enforcement' (2011) 34(3) *World Competition* 353.

Wils, W. (2010), 'The Increased Level of EU Antitrust Fines, Judicial Review, and the European Convention on Human Rights' (2010) 33(1) *World Competition* 5.

Wils, W. (2009), 'The Relationship between Public Antitrust Enforcement and Private Actions for Damages' (2009) 32(1) *World Competition* 3.

Wils, W. (2008a), *Efficiency and Justice in European Antitrust Enforcement*, Hart Publishing, Oxford.

Wils, W. (2008b), 'The Use of Settlements in Public Antitrust Enforcement: Objectives and Principles', 13th Annual EU Competition Law and Policy Workshop, European University Institute, Florence, 6–7 June 2008, <http://papers.ssrn.com/sol3/cf_dev/AbsByAuth.cfm?per_id=456087>.

Wils, W. (2007a), 'Leniency in Antitrust Enforcement: Theory and Practice' (2007) 30(1) *World Competition* 25.

Wils, W. (2007b), 'The European Commissions 2006 Guidelines on Antitrust Fines: A Legal and Economic Analysis' (2007) 30 *World Competition* 64.

Wils, W. (2006a), 'Optimal Antitrust Fines: Theory and Practice' (2006) 29(2) *World Competition* 183.

Wils, W. (2006b), 'Is Criminalization of EU Competition Law the Answer?', in Cseres, K., Schinkel, M. P., and Vogelaar, F. (eds), *Criminalization of Competition Law Enforcement: Economic and Legal Implications for the EU Member States*, Edward Elgar Publishing, Cheltenham.

Wils, W. (2005a), *Principles of European Antitrust Enforcement*, Hart Publishing, Oxford.

Wils, W. (2005b), 'Is Criminalization of EU Competition Law the Answer?' (2005) 28(2) *World Competition* 17.

Wils, W. (2004a), 'The Combination of the Investigative and Prosecutorial Function and the Adjudicative Function in EC Antitrust Enforcement: A Legal and Economic Analysis' (2004) 27(2) *World Competition* 201.

Wils, W. (2004b), 'Community Report', in Cahill, D. and Cooke, J.D. (eds) (2004), *The Modernisation of EU Competition Law Enforcement—FIDE 2004 National Reports*, Cambridge University Press, Cambridge.

Wils, W. (2003a), 'The EU Network of Competition Authorities, the European Convention on Human Rights and the Charter of Fundamental Rights of the EU', in Ehlermann, C.D. and Atanasiu, I. (eds), *European Competition Law Annual 2002: Constructing the EU Network of Competition Authorities*, Hart Publishing, Oxford.

Wils, W. (2003b), 'The Principle of *Ne Bis in Idem* in EC Antitrust Enforcement: A Legal and Economic Analysis' (2003) 26(2) *World Competition* 131.

Wils, W. (2003c), 'Should Private Antitrust Enforcement Be Encouraged in Europe?' (2003) 26(3) *World Competition* 473.

Wils, W. (2003d), 'Self-Incrimination in EC Antitrust Enforcement: A Legal and Economic Analysis' (2003) 26(4) *World Competition* 567.

Wils, W. (2002), *Optimal Enforcement of EC Antitrust Law: A Study in Law and Economics*, Kluwer Law International, London.

Wils, W. (1996), 'La Compatibilité des Procédures Communautaires en Matière de Concurrence avec la Convention Européenne des Droits de l'Homme' (1996) 32 *Cahiers de droit européen* 329.

Winter, S. and May, P. (2001), 'Motivation for Compliance with Environmental Regulations' (2001) 20 *Journal of Policy Analysis and Management* 675.

Yeung, K. (2006), 'Does the Australian Competition and Consumer Commission Engage in "Trial by Media"?' (2006) 27 *Law and Policy* 549.

Yeung, K. (2004), *Securing Compliance—A Principled Approach*, Hart Publishing, Oxford.

Yeung, K. (1999), 'Quantifying Regulatory Penalties: Australian Competition Law Penalties in Perspective' (1999) 23 *Melbourne University Law Review* 440.

Young, G., Willis, P., and Chisholm, J. (2009), 'New Understanding Will Uncover More Scottish Cartels', *Alert!*, June 2009.

Zedner, L. (1994), 'Reparation and Retribution: Are They Reconcilable?' (1994) 57(2) *Modern Law Review* 228.

Zilboorg, G. (1954), *The Psychology of the Criminal Act and Punishment*, Harcourt, Brace & Co., New York.

Zimbardo, P. (2008), *The Lucifer Effect: Understanding How Good People Turn Evil*, Random House, New York.

Zingales, N. (2008), 'European and American Leniency Programmes: Two Models Towards Convergence?' (2008) 5(1) *Competition Law Review* 5.

Zuleeg, M. (2002), 'Criminal Sanctions to be Imposed on Individuals as Enforcement Instruments in European Competition Law', in Ehlermann, C.D. and Atanasiu, I. (eds), *European Competition Law Annual 2001: Effective Private Enforcement of EC Antitrust Law*, Hart Publishing, Oxford.

Zweifach, L. and Creizman, E. (2008), 'The Sentencing of Individuals Convicted of Violating the United States Antitrust Laws: An Overview of Basic Principles under the Federal Sentencing Guidelines', The British Institute of International and Comparative Law International Cartels Conference 2008, BIICL, London, 26 February 2008.

Index

Printed and bound by CPI Group (UK) Ltd, Croydon, CR0 4YY